DESERT BIOLOGY

VOLUME II

Contributors

THOMAS C. BARGER

STANLEY N. DAVIS

JAMES E. DEACON

E. B. EDNEY

BERNARD L. FONTANA

E. IMRE FRIEDMANN

WALLACE H. FULLER

MARGALITH GALUN

CLAUDE J. GRENOT

PAUL F. HOYE

W. L. MINCKLEY

E. STADELMANN

H. WALTER

DESERT BIOLOGY

*SPECIAL TOPICS ON THE PHYSICAL AND
BIOLOGICAL ASPECTS OF ARID REGIONS*

Edited by

G. W. BROWN, JR.

COLLEGE OF FISHERIES
UNIVERSITY OF WASHINGTON
SEATTLE, WASHINGTON

VOLUME II

1974

ACADEMIC PRESS . NEW YORK and LONDON

A Subsidiary of Harcourt Brace Jovanovich, Publishers

ACADEMIC PRESS, INC.
111 Fifth Avenue, New York, New York 10003

United Kingdom Edition published by
ACADEMIC PRESS, INC. (LONDON) LTD.
24/28 Oval Road, London NW1

Library of Congress Cataloging in Publication Data

Brown, George Willard, Date
       Desert biology; special topics on the physical
and biological aspects of arid regions.

       Includes bibliographies.
       1.   Desert biology.   [DNLM: 1.   Biology.
2.   Desert climate. QH541.5 D4 B8d]
QH88.B7   574.909'5'4   68-23494
ISBN 0–12–135902–6 (v. 2)

PRINTED IN THE UNITED STATES OF AMERICA

"Desert Biology" is dedicated to the memory of Dr. John C. Sinclair, formerly Professor Emeritus of anatomy at the University of Texas Medical Branch, Galveston, Texas, where I taught biochemistry to medical students and where I met John. John Sinclair was an extraordinary individual—a truly "Renaissance Man." He was desert rat, porpoise and whale embryologist, weather physicist, human (humane) anatomist, and poet. A special reading of his poems, now published by the University of Texas Press, was held in our home here in Washington, and our guests attended every word. He lived as a man, scientist, and humanitarian.

CONTENTS

Chapter I. Hydrogeology of Arid Regions
Stanley N. Davis

Chapter II. Desert Soils
Wallace H. Fuller

Chapter III. **Physical and Vegetational Aspects of the Sahara Desert**

Claude J. Grenot

Chapter IV. **Desert Algae, Lichens, and Fungi**

E. Imre Friedmann and Margalith Galun

Chapter V. **A New Approach to the Water Relations of
Desert Plants**

H. Walter and E. Stadelmann

Chapter VI. **Desert Arthropods**
E. B. Edney

Chapter VII. **Desert Fishes**
James E. Deacon and W. L. Minckley

Chapter VIII. **Man in Arid Lands: The Piman Indians of the Sonoran Desert**
Bernard L. Fontana

Chapter IX. **Man in Arid Lands: North From Jiddah**
Paul F. Hoye

LIST OF CONTRIBUTORS

Numbers in parentheses indicate the pages on which the authors' contributions begin.

THOMAS C. BARGER* (547), Arabian American Oil Company, New York, New York

STANLEY N. DAVIS† (1), Department of Geology, University of Missouri-Columbia, Columbia, Missouri

JAMES E. DEACON (385), Department of Biological Sciences, University of Nevada, Las Vegas, Nevada

E. B. EDNEY‡ (311), Department of Biology, University of California, Riverside, California

BERNARD L. FONTANA (489), Arizona State Museum, The University of Arizona, Tucson, Arizona

E. IMRE FRIEDMANN (165), Department of Biological Science, Florida State University, Tallahassee, Florida

WALLACE H. FULLER (31), Department of Soils, Water and Engineering, College of Agriculture, Arizona Agricultural Experimental Station, The University of Arizona, Tucson, Arizona

MARGALITH GALUN (165), Department of Botany, Tel Aviv University, Tel Aviv, Israel

* Present address: 2685 Calle de Oro, La Jolla, California.
† Present address: Geology Department, Indiana University, Bloomington, Indiana.
‡ Present address: Laboratory for Nuclear Medicine and Radiation Biology, University of California, Los Angeles, California.

CLAUDE J. GRENOT (103), Centre de Recherches sur les Zones Arides (CNRS), and Laboratoire de Zoologie, Ecole Normale Superiéure, Paris, France

PAUL F. HOYE (529), Aramco World Magazine, Beirut, Lebanon

W. L. MINCKLEY (385), Department of Zoology, and Lower Colorado River Basin Research Laboratory, Arizona State University, Tempe, Arizona

E. STADELMANN (213), Department of Horticultural Science, University of Minnesota, St. Paul, Minnesota

H. WALTER (213), Botanisches Institut der Universität Hohenheim, Stuttgart, West Germany

PREFACE

The second volume of "Desert Biology" continues with a further documentation of conditions and of life in the arid regions of the world. It comes at a time when we are witnessing an accelerated interest in the hot, dry regions of our planet. Continued advances in functional architecture, in large-scale air-conditioning efforts, and in sanitary engineering practices have fostered comfortable desert living. New agricultural undertakings, improved business communications, creation of new sport and recreational facilities—coupled with decentralization of business, government, and organization offices—promise to bring about an increased immigration of people into the desert regions.

The desert looms important in man's concern for energy. Recent attention has been given to the high average solar radiation of desert areas, pointing toward possible development of solar energy farms using new solar–electronic power devices. And political and economic vicissitudes, especially in connection with oil, have focused attention anew on the arid regions of North Africa and the Middle-East with their petroleum reserves.

Persistent inquiry into the physical and biological aspects of desert structure and of man's relationship to it will provide foundations enabling society to deal intelligently with this oftentimes hostile, yet intriguing, frontier. Let us hope that the fragile and delicately poised arid regions are not subjected to the technological blunders made in other regions. I believe with many others that even slight ecological damage to arid regions may not be reparable for scores of years. Indeed, the damage may be irreversible. Let us act wisely.

Editing of this volume was carried out while I held a training grant from the U.S. Environmental Protection Agency or its predecessors. My wife Susan was always willing to help correct manuscripts, read proof, and give critical analysis of content, translations, and structure—thanks, Sue. Thanks, also, Eric, Jon, and Becky.

G. W. Brown, Jr.

CONTENTS OF VOLUME I

DESERT BIOLOGY

VOLUME II

CHAPTER I

HYDROGEOLOGY OF ARID REGIONS

Stanley N. Davis

It is a laid circle of stones large enough not to be disturbed by any ordinary hap, with an opening flanked by two parallel rows of similar stones, between which were an arrow placed, touching the opposite rim of the circle, thus it would point as the crow flies to the spring. It is the old, indubitable water mark of the Shoshones.

Mary Austin. The Land of Little Rain.

I. Introduction

From the standpoint of the total water present, most deserts are abundantly supplied. Unfortunately, the water is generally more than 100 meters below the surface, and even where it does reach the surface, it may have a high salinity. If the water quality is good, however, the influence on local plant and animal communities is profound. The understanding of groundwater systems is, therefore, important to the study of many aspects of desert biology.

Prehistoric man undoubtedly excavated his first wells in arid and semi-arid regions in an effort to survive in this harsh environment. These early wells were probably not much more than slightly deepened water holes. By the start of recorded history, however, wells were common throughout the Middle East. About 3000 years ago, both deep wells and extensive horizontal gallaries were in use in China, Iran, Egypt, Jordan, and adjacent countries (Davis and De Wiest, 1966; Tolman, 1937; Meinzer, 1942).

Despite an advanced technology of water recovery, theories concerning the origin and movement of groundwater were not developed until modern times. The brilliant writings of al-Bīrūnī (973–1048 AD) gave only a bare outline of the movement of groundwater in artesian systems. The hydrologic cycle of desert regions (Fig. 1) was not fully understood until the 18th century. Even today, the simple facts of the cycle are not commonly known by the public in general.

Popular literature dealing with deserts almost invariably mentions several misconceptions of physical geology, namely, stones exploding under solar heat, sand being blown to heights of several hundred feet, and the inevitable underground river. While it is true that recent basalt and some

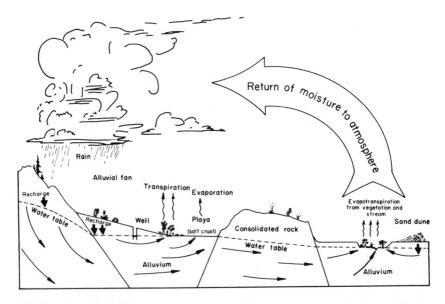

Fig. 1. Simplified hydrologic cycle for arid portions of the Basin and Range Physiographic Province, North America. Flow net is discussed in a later portion of Chapter I.

limestone may contain streams flowing in caverns, probably less than 1% of the springs and wells in deserts derive their water from such sources. Most underground water seeps slowly through small, interconnected openings in rocks and soil. Water-bearing materials may be confined locally to narrow valleys but more commonly are widespread tabular zones which underlie thousands of square kilometers of desert.

Modern research into the hydrogeology of arid regions is advancing rapidly along several lines such as hydrochemistry, exploration techniques, and economics of development. Despite the high level of activity, many questions remain. Our lack of knowledge stems in part from the difficulties of studying remote and inhospitable regions, but it stems mostly from the nature of the problems. Almost flat water tables and potentiometric gradients make determinations of directions of groundwater flow difficult. Lack of rain during long periods makes direct measurements of the hydrologic balance, including groundwater recharge, almost impossible. Excessive depths to reach water make the collection of hydrogeologic data difficult and expensive. Finally, in areas of artificial discharge of groundwater, levels in wells drop rapidly and do not lend themselves to steady-state analysis of groundwater movement.

II. Laws of Groundwater Motion

The laws of groundwater motion must be understood, at least in their rudimentary forms, before the general aspects of desert hydrogeology can be pieced together. Water in the subsurface will move in response to a number of energy sources. Differences in heat, surface tension, electrical potentials, pressure, gravity, and water chemistry will interact in a complicated manner to cause water to move. Normally, surface tension and gravity are most important where water and air occur together above the water table. Below the water table, and in other zones fully saturated with water, pressure and gravity are most important.

Movement of soil moisture owing to temperature gradients is a phenomenon observed commonly in desert regions. After a series of warm days, rapid, radiant cooling of thin, flat rocks, dark highway pavements, and other surficial objects will cause an accumulation of moisture on their undersides. Near bodies of desert brine, chemical osmosis may be effective through clays and silts. Theoretically, under special circumstances, chemical osmosis could be the dominant force causing water motion. Of the energy sources listed above, only natural electrical potentials are considered negligible within desert environments.

Forces which arise from the surface tension of water are called capillary forces if they are developed within small openings. If the surface tension is constant, as it would be at constant temperature and water chemistry, and if all the solid soil particles are assumed to be of the same composition, then capillary forces are inversely proportional to the diameters of the interconnected pores. As an example, if a glass tube could be constructed with an internal radius of exactly 1.0 μm, water would eventually rise in the tube to about 15 meters above the level to which it is emersed in water. An imaginary tube with an internal radius of only 0.1 μm would produce a water rise of about 150 meters. Natural deposits of clay size materials should have intergranular openings which range from 0.1 to 10 μm. One is tempted, therefore, to make a direct comparison between tubes and soil systems. This cannot be done for at least two reasons:

First, the irregular nature of the openings and the natural variations of bedded sedimentary materials means that the capillary effects are far from uniform and that a thin seam of sand or gravel could contain relatively large openings which are able to produce a capillary rise of only a few centimeters.

Second, the time required for the capillary rise of water increases as the grain diameter decreases.

For example, Terzaghi's equation (Terzaghi, 1942) can be used to calculate the time that it would take water to rise 135 meters in a very fine clay which has a potential ultimate rise of 150 meters. Making an assumption of a porosity of 45% and a hydraulic conductivity of 4.2×10^{-4} cm/day, the calculated time is 61,000 years (Fig. 2). Although the assumptions made are reasonable, the greatest value of the calculations is to emphasize the fact that a capillary rise of more than 100 meters is a very slow process, if it occurs at all. After reviewing all data available at his time, Tolman (1937) concluded that the natural capillary rise in fine material was less than about 3 meters. Although this is probably too conservative, assumptions of significant capillary rises of more than 20 meters are highly speculative.

From the standpoint of long-distance horizontal transfer of water below the surface, the only energy sources that normally are important are pressure and the force of gravity. Hubbert's (1940) force potential best describes the combined action of these two sources of energy. He stated that

$$\Phi = g \int_{z_0}^{z} dz + \int_{p_0}^{p} \frac{dp}{\rho}$$
$$\Phi = gz + p/\rho$$

or

$$\Phi = g(z + p/\gamma) = gh \tag{1}$$

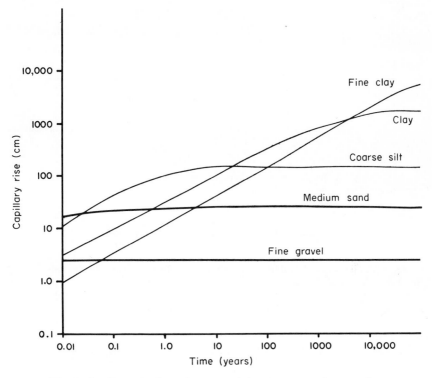

Fig. 2. Capillary rise in various materials using assumed properties.

in which Φ is the potential for producing water movement; g is the acceleration of gravity; p is pressure; ρ is fluid density; γ is the specific weight of the fluid, or $g\rho$; z is the elevation of a given fluid particle above a datum plane; and h is the elevation of the fluid surface in a manometer (Fig. 3).

As a first approximation, the fluid (water) can be considered constant in density and viscosity. Inasmuch as the gravitational field, for practical purposes, is also constant, the potential for water motion is measured directly by the water level in the manometer. Although some wells depart widely from the theoretical manometer, in general, water levels in wells give a reliable indication of potential provided only one water-bearing layer (aquifer) is tapped. Deep wells, which are common in deserts, may tap several aquifers each having distinct potentials. If so, water-level data from these wells may be of only limited use in determining direction of water motion, amount of pumping lift, and other items of hydrogeologic interest.

Equation (1) does not give the actual quantity of water flowing in the

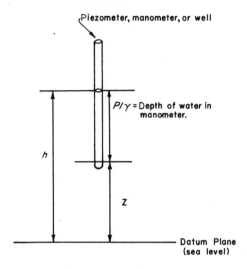

Fig. 3. Components of Hubbert's force potential. In most groundwater calculations, the hydraulic head is assumed to be equal to the elevation of the water in the well (manometer). p is the pressure at the bottom of the manometer, z the elevation of the manometer above the datum, and h is the hydraulic head.

subsurface. For this, Darcy's law must be used. One form of this law is

$$Q = -KA\frac{\partial h}{\partial s} \qquad (2)$$

in which Q is the volume of water flowing per unit time; K is a proportionality constant called hydraulic conductivity; A is the cross-sectional area normal to the direction of flow; and $\partial h/\partial s$ is the hydraulic gradient.

Equation (2) can be modified for flow in the horizontal direction x, by noting that for most natural flow systems

$$\Delta h/\Delta s \approx \Delta h/\Delta x$$

and

$$Q/A = q$$

so that

$$q = -K(\Delta h/\Delta x) \qquad (3)$$

This equation tells us that the amount of water flowing through a given cross section is directly proportional to both the hydraulic conductivity, K, and the hydraulic gradient, $\Delta h/\Delta x$.

A further modification of Darcy's law is useful for certain purposes. If a portion of a region of flow is subdivided as shown in Fig. 4, the follow-

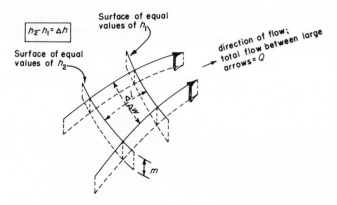

Fig. 4. Basic elements of flow-net construction. In practice the thickness of the aquifer, m, is commonly assumed to be constant, so the diagram is given in only two dimensions.

ing equation can be written

$$Q = Km(\Delta w)(\Delta h/\Delta l) \tag{4}$$

by construction, $\Delta w = \Delta l$, so

$$Q = Km\Delta h = T\Delta h \tag{5}$$

where T is a unit called transmissivity and is equal to the thickness of the water-bearing zone, m, multiplied by the hydraulic conductivity, K; m, the thickness of the water-bearing zone, is considered constant in Eq. (5); Δw is the incremental width of the flow tube; Δl is the length of the flow tube subdivision; and Δh is the hydraulic head drop along Δl.

If the entire flow field is subdivided into a flow net (Fig. 5), the following equation can be written:

$$Q_T = \Sigma Q_1 + Q_2 + Q_3 + \cdots + Q_n$$

in which Q_T is the total groundwater flow in the system composed of Q_1, Q_2, etc. If $\Delta h_1 = \Delta h_2 = \cdots \Delta h_n$, and T is a constant, then

$$Q_T = nT\Delta h \tag{6}$$

in which n is the total number of flow tubes.

III. Applications of Flow Equations

Flow equations are commonly used to determine well production capabilities and to outline regional patterns of water circulation. Problems of

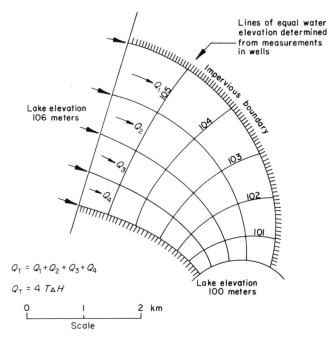

Fig. 5. Map of water levels in hypothetical valley connecting two lakes. If transmissivity, T, is known, then the total groundwater flow from one lake to the other is calculated by $Q = 4T\Delta h$. If $T = 10,000$ m^2/day, then $Q = 40,000$ m^3/day since $\Delta h = 1$ meter.

well production are quite involved and are not related directly to the hydrogeology of natural deserts. These problems are treated adequately elsewhere (Hantush, 1966; Walton, 1970). Regional patterns of water circulation are of utmost importance in understanding desert hydrogeology; therefore they will be treated in considerable detail in this chapter.

Three primary methods are used to obtain values necessary to solve Eq. (6). In all methods, the value $n\Delta h$ is determined by using water-level maps constructed from measurements of the elevations of water surfaces in wells and surface water, such as springs and rivers that are in direct contact with the groundwater. The most general method obtains a value of Q_T from a study of the hydrologic budget. For a groundwater basin which does not have subsurface inflow or outflow of groundwater, the hydrologic budget can be expressed as

precipitation = discharge of surface water from the basin
+ evapotranspiration ± changes in soil moisture
± changes in groundwater storage

All items except changes in groundwater storage can be measured or estimated. The difference between the two sides of the equation for a given budget period is, therefore, ascribed to changes in groundwater storage. If observation wells are available, changes in water levels in the wells can be related to changes in groundwater storage, and the accuracy of the hydrologic budget can be checked. Unfortunately, the groundwater increment of a given budget within a desert region is so small in comparison to other items that it is masked by errors of measurement of precipitation as well as the other budget items.

Another more direct hydrologic budget can commonly be used in local, well-defined groundwater basins where man has not upset the natural balance and where all groundwater eventually comes to the surface in springs or in areas of dense vegetation. Water discharge and evapotranspiration are estimated for these areas of groundwater discharge and are assumed to be equal to the long-term groundwater recharge. Such calculations must, of course, assume steady-state conditions for the basin.

In the budget methods, usually the only unknown value in Eq. (6) is T which can then be estimated by Eqs. (4) and (5).

A second method for solving Eq. (6) requires test drilling to measure m and laboratory measurements of K from samples of the aquifer recovered during drilling. Thus, Km (or T) is known and Q_T can be calculated. The number of laboratory determinations of K needed is excessive, so this method is expensive and tedious.

The third general method, that of aquifer tests, is most reliable. By injecting water into wells or by pumping water from the wells, artificial changes of hydraulic head are produced in the aquifer. These changes can be analyzed (Davis and De Wiest, 1966; Hantush, 1966; Walton, 1970) to determine values of T.

In practice, it is common to use both hydrologic budget studies and aquifer tests as independent methods to analyze desert basins.

Figure 6 presents a simple application of Eq. (6). An estimate of the total amount of water flowing in a desert valley is of interest. Aquifer tests indicate a value of T of 1200 m²/day. By construction of the flow net, $n = 3$ and $\Delta h = 0.4$ meter. The total flow Q_T is therefore

$$Q_T = nT\Delta h = (3)(1200)(0.4) \text{ m}^3/\text{day}$$
$$Q_T = 1440 \text{ m}^3/\text{day or } 381{,}000 \text{ gallons/day}$$

Although a scale showing horizontal distance is given in Fig. 6, it is important to note that this information is not needed for the calculation.

Flow nets can be used to assess the amount of recharge or discharge from a stream. The example in Fig. 7 shows two stream channels crossing

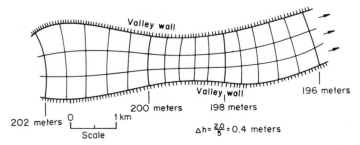

Fig. 6. A water-level map of a hypothetical desert valley bounded by impermeable mountains. Water-level contours were determined by measurements of water-level elevations in wells. See text for calculations of groundwater flow in the valley.

the lower slope of a bahada (coalescing alluvial fans). The northern ephemeral stream does not affect the direction of contours; hence it has no significant recharge or discharge. The southern stream, on the other hand, provides abundant groundwater recharge in the western part of the

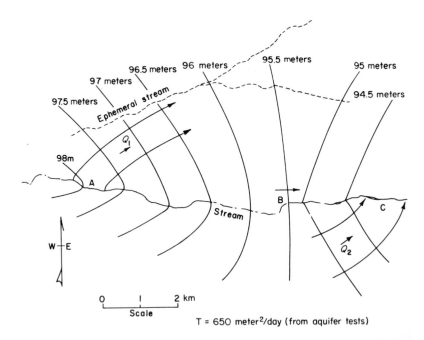

Fig. 7. Example of stream on large alluvial fan. Stream recharges groundwater on western part of map, but drains groundwater back into the stream in the eastern part of the map. The ephemeral stream channel in the northern part of the map does not affect the groundwater contours and is, therefore, a negligible source of groundwater recharge.

map and receives an inflow of water in the eastern edge. Using Eq. (5) and the flow net, together with the scale, the southern stream is calculated to be recharging the groundwater with 664 m^3/day/km at A, 0.0 m^3/day/km at B, and a discharge of 592 m^3/day/km to the stream at C.

These figures are calculated as follows:

$$Q_1 = Q_2$$

since both Δh and T are constant in the area of the map.

$$Q_1 = Q_2 = \Delta h(T) = (0.5) \text{ meters } (650) \text{ m}^2/\text{day} = 325 \text{ m}^3/\text{day}$$

the length of stream between flowlines at A = 0.98 km, and the length of stream between flowlines at C = 1.10 km, therefore the outflow at A = 325/0.98 = 332 m^3/day/km for one side of the stream, or a total outflow of 664 m^3/day/km; likewise at C the inflow is 592 m^3/day/km. Groundwater flow at B is parallel with the stream channel, hence water is neither entering or leaving the stream channel.

Flow nets can also be used to represent flow in a vertical plane. In fact, one of the most common applications of flow nets is in the analyses of seepage through dams within vertical sections (Davis and De Weist, 1966). The general water-table profile shown in Fig. 1 is commonly observed in desert mountains and valleys. Using flow-net sketching, one can demonstrate two reasonable configurations of flow that will explain the strong inflection in the water surface near the base of the mountains. One explanation assumes a change in Q owing to spring discharge. If large springs do not exist, then the other geologically reasonable assumption of a drastic change in hydraulic conductivity, K is favored. The vertical flow net also points out something of widespread importance concerning hydraulic heads, namely, wells will encounter decreasing heads with depth in areas of recharge and increasing heads with depth in areas of discharge.

IV. Groundwater Recharge

Recharge of groundwater is an extremely rare event in deserts except under very special hydrogeologic conditions (Dixey, 1962). Most precipitation, whether it totals 1 or 10 mm is returned to the atmosphere by evaporation within 2 or 3 days after the water reaches the desert surface. During periods of extremely heavy precipitation, soils may absorb a large fraction of the water. Capillary action will bring this water back to the soil surface where it is evaporated. Some of the soil water may also be taken up by xerophytic vegetation and be released more slowly by transpiration during succeeding weeks or months.

The minuscule quantity of water that becomes groundwater recharge enters the deep subsurface through beds of ephemeral streams, cracks in bare rock surfaces, talus at the bases of cliffs, and sand dunes. Soil-moisture deficiencies are normally so large that water from single rains of 20 to 40 mm can be stored easily in the upper meter of soil where it is eventually returned to the atmosphere by evapotranspiration. In contrast, rock rubble, as might be found in talus or stream beds, can only store a small amount of water (El Boushi and Davis, 1969), so a precipitation of 10 mm would commonly produce recharge. Furthermore, water tends to be concentrated along stream channels longer than the duration of the rainfall. This added time allows stream bed materials of low permeability to transmit significant amounts of water into the subsurface.

Sand dunes have long been recognized as important sites for groundwater recharge (Löwy, 1953; Moussu and Moussu, 1952; Ogilbee, 1964). The dune sand has a capacity to store between 1.5 and 8.0% water by volume after several months of gravity drainage. If the sand is dry, this volume of water must be absorbed before excess water drains downward to become recharge. As an example, if 3% water by volume is required in 1 meter of dry sand, then 30 mm of rain will be needed to initiate groundwater recharge through the thickness of 1 meter. Inasmuch as the permeability of dune sand is high enough to accept almost any intensity of rain, runoff of surface water from sand dunes will rarely, if ever, occur. Intense storms will, therefore, favor direct recharge into sand dunes.

In actively migrating dunes, dry sand accumulates on the leeward side at the expense of the windward side. Sand which is still moist from previous rains should be closest to the surface on the windard side which, therefore, should be the favored locality for recharge (Fig. 8).

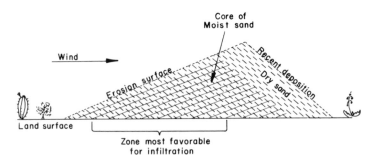

Fig. 8. Cross section of a simple sand dune showing core of moist sand preserved on windward side of dune.

Many aquifers in deserts receive their recharge from water not related to the hydrology of the desert itself. Examples are (1) aquifers near large rivers, such as the Nile, which are sustained by high precipitation outside of the desert; (2) aquifers recharged by surplus irrigation water such as those in the Imperial Valley, California; and (3) aquifers which have recharge areas outside of deserts such as extensive carbonate aquifers which crop out in the south flanks of the Atlas Mountains along the northwestern border of the Sahara Desert.

Few reliable data on recharge rates in deserts are available. Water-budget calculations for the semiarid portions of the Basin and Range region of North America suggest rates of 0.1–5 mm/year. These values are, of course, derived from averages of large areas. Actual maximum recharge rates in stream channels could exceed 3 meters/day for short periods (see data by Worts, 1951; Burkham, 1970). Minimum recharge rates through soil-covered surfaces in semiarid regions are close to zero unless annual precipitation exceeds at least 200 mm. If the period of rain coincides with the period of maximum plant growth, then the annual precipitation must exceed at least 400 mm before significant recharge takes place through normal soil cover. Exact local control on recharge depends, of course, on a complex set of variables such as antecedent soil moisture, intensity of precipitation, duration of precipitation, permeability characteristics of the soil, slope of the surface, temperature, etc.

V. Circulation of Groundwater

Water moves in the subsurface from higher areas of recharge to low areas of discharge. The path taken by the water will not be a straight line, but may be rather long and indirect (Fig. 9). The actual path taken by the groundwater is a function of the distribution of permeability and the boundary conditions in the saturated part of the medium. Some important aspects of the boundary conditions are the location and magnitude of water transfer into or out of the medium under consideration. The mistaken belief that topography necessarily influences the position of the water table is nowhere better refuted than in desert areas (see Fig. 9).

On a regional scale, nevertheless, topography influences the water table because low areas are commonly areas of groundwater discharge into rivers or lakes. Also, orographic precipitation may make more water available in highland areas. The water table is thus somewhat higher where recharge is more abundant.

Owing to the almost negligible recharge in vast parts of most deserts, groundwater gradients ($\Delta h/\Delta s$) need to be only from 0.001 to 0.0001 in

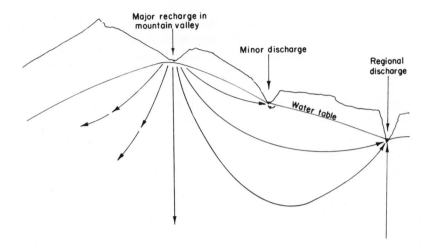

Fig. 9. Groundwater circulation in homogeneous rocks within desert mountains. Localized recharge causes groundwater mound under valley. Minor discharge produces small dimple in water surface.

order to transport the small amount of water available. The velocity of flow is, therefore, very small. Equation (3) can be rewritten as

$$q = \bar{v}\theta = -K(\Delta h/\Delta s) \tag{7}$$

where q, K, Δh, and Δs are as previously defined, $\bar{v}$ is the average velocity of groundwater, and θ is the effective pore space through which water will move.

Two examples below will serve as limiting values to be expected in desert regions.

EXAMPLE 1. Aquifer is fractured rock.

$K = 0.1$ meter/day (see Davis, 1969, for a representative range of values)
$\theta = 0.005$, $\Delta h/\Delta s = 0.001$

$$\bar{v} = (1/0.005)(0.1)(0.001) = 0.02 \text{ meter/day}$$

EXAMPLE 2. Aquifer is permeable alluvium.

$K = 100$ meters/day (see Davis, 1969, for a representative range of values)
$\theta = 0.3$, $\Delta h/\Delta s = 0.0001$

$$\bar{v} = (1/0.3)(100)(0.0001) = 0.033 \text{ meter/day}$$

Although the examples above are artificial, they are thought to represent realistic figures for aquifers containing desert-derived recharge. From calculations similar to those above, it can be assumed that most water in widespread desert aquifers is moving at rates of less than 0.1 meter/day.

Many desert aquifers extend for more than 200 km. If water is traveling at velocities of less than 0.1 meter/day, then water at a distance of 200 km from a recharge area is at least 5500 years old. This is the line of reasoning which suggested to early workers that water extracted from many desert aquifers was recharged thousands of years ago when climatic conditions were different than today. Recent studies of the ^{14}C content of desert groundwater (Tamers, 1967; Degens, 1961; Thatcher *et al.*, 1961) have supported this conclusion.

Some water buried within deep alluvial basins may have been part of the water that helped transport the sediments that fill the basin. If the basins have little or no hydraulic gradients in their central parts, the presently retained water in the basin could be very old indeed, perhaps with an age of more than one million years. Slow natural compaction of the sediments forces some of the old water to the surface where it may emerge in springs. In most places, this water probably mixes with younger water as it migrates to the surface.

Water that does not originate in a desert but still serves as recharge to desert aquifers may, after recharge because of copious quantities of water and steep hydraulic gradients, travel quite rapidly. For example, the Lambayeque Valley in the coastal desert of Peru receives recharge from the Rio Chancay which flows seaward from the Andes (Schoff and Sayan, 1969). Gradients are generally between 0.002 and 0.005. Hydraulic conductivites are estimated to be between 20 and 35 meters/day. If the effective porosity is assumed to be 0.3, then average water velocities are from 0.13 to 0.58 meter/day, or roughly an order of magnitude greater than velocities calculated above for average desert conditions.

VI. Groundwater Discharge

Discharge of groundwater in deserts will cause a striking change in the appearance of the desert. Large oasislike patches of vegetation and extensive salt crusts usually mark the presence of springs or groundwater at a shallow depth. Owing to the general scarcity of water, springs with large discharges are not common in deserts. Notable exceptions occur in regions of carbonate or volcanic rocks which can form extensive aquifers capable of collecting water from a large area and, because of the high permeabilities of these rocks, of discharging the water in local concentrated flows. Most commonly, however, water seeps to the surface over relatively large areas where it may be intercepted by vegetation before it reaches the surface.

The term *phreatophyte* was introduced by Meinzer (1927) to describe plant types that grow on dry land but habitually send their roots into the upper part of the zone which is saturated with water. Although the term has not gained wide acceptance among biologists, it is useful in considering problems of desert hydrology because it emphasizes the fact that some plants draw water directly from the groundwater reservoir while other types of plants, generally called xerophytes, utilize only water from infrequent precipitation.

Phreatophytes give some information concerning the general depth of the saturated zone, the quality of the water, and the total amount of groundwater which is lost by evapotranspiration. In general, grasses which are phreatophytes thrive where the water table is at a depth of less than 3 meters; shrubs thrive where it is at a depth of less than 10 meters; and trees grow where the depth is less than 30 meters. Exact depths are highly variable and depend on factors such as water salinity, plant species, and types of sediments or rocks penetrated by the plant roots.

Some plants are reliable indicators of water quality. Willows and cottonwood generally grow where potable groundwater is present. Pickleweed (*Allenrolfea occidentalis*) grows where the subsoil is saturated with saline water. Other plants such as palms and mesquite have a tolerance for a wide range of water quality.

The amount of water used by phreatophytes is a function of climate, species, general health of the plant, depth of the water, water quality, and density of growth. Estimates of water used by phreatophytes utilize direct measurements of evapotranspiration coupled with estimates of vegetation density (McDonald *et al.,* 1958). Plants such as saltcedar (*Tamarix gallica*) and cottonwood (*Populus*) will use between 2000 and 3000 mm of water per year for dense growths in a hot, dry climate (Robinson, 1958). Even though exact measurements of total water discharged by phreatophytes are difficult, rough estimates are easily made and are useful despite errors which may range up to 100% (Mann, 1958).

The quantity of water used by phreatophytes is truly spectacular. For example, a dense growth of saltcedar over an area of only 1 hectare (2.47 acres) will use at least 20,000 m^3 of water each year. This is 30 million liters, or 54,800 liters/day for an entire year, or enough to give a small village an abundant supply of water. In fact, as a general rule, people in cities use less water per unit area than dense growths of phreatophytes.

Groundwater is commonly evaporated directly from the soil surface. If the evaporation proceeds without rainfall, a salt crust will form. The salt concentration, in turn, will inhibit plant growth. If the salinity of the groundwater is known, then the rate of salt-crust accumulation can be related directly to the rate of groundwater evaporation (Feth and Brown, 1962). Under optimum conditions, the rate of evaporation from a moist soil surface will be about the same as from a free water surface. For hot dry deserts, this may be from 250 to 320 cm/year. As the salinity of the water increases, however, the rate of evaporation is reduced drastically (Fig. 10). Under certain conditions, moreover, condensation rather than evaporation can probably take place on the surface of the concentrated brine (Turk, 1970). Evaporation of groundwater from a playa surface with brine saturating a salt crust is therefore but a small fraction, perhaps less than one-tenth, of the rate of evaporation from a freshwater lake in the same region.

Considerable speculation exists in the literature concerning the loss of groundwater through capillary movement from great depths to the surface. Several lines of reasoning tend to argue against a large loss of water by this mechanism. First, larger pore spaces caused by strata of coarse-grained material can produce discontinuities in the capillary system. Second, only fine-grained material will have such a large capillary rise; however, the same material will be of such small grain size that the hydraulic conductivity will be exceedingly low (on the order of 10^{-5}–10^{-7} meters/day). Even with an unusually high hydraulic gradient of about 0.3 and an effective porosity of 0.3, only about 0.003–0.3 mm/year would be available for evaporation. Third, salinity of surface brines would slow the evaporation process.

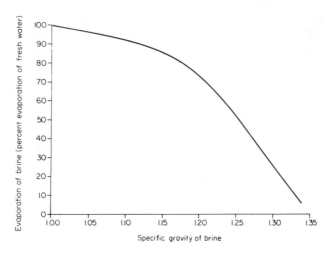

Fig. 10. Relation between density of brine and evaporation.

Even so, the total effect of upward capillary transport over large areas cannot be ignored, particularly if the depth to water is less than 5 meters. The presence of brine at the surface will also add an osmotic potential which could have an effect greater than the capillary potential in bringing water to the land surface where it will be evaporated.

VII. Water Quality

For human occupation of desert areas, water quality is probably a more severe limitation than the scarcity of water itself. Modern technology has overcome part of this difficulty by desalinization devices, but investment in equipment and cost of power still make most large-scale schemes to produce fresh water of questionable economic value.

Tolerance of organisms to salt varies widely according to the species, the health of the organism, its total water intake, and the specific constituents in the water. Most humans can tolerate up to 2.5 and 3.5 gm/liter of total dissolved solids provided specific constituents such as arsenic, selenium, and lead are virtually absent. Sheep and beef cattle can generally tolerate 4.0–10.0 gm/liter or even higher amounts under certain circumstances.

Most useful plants, on the other hand, have lower tolerances to salty water than do humans and stock animals. Citrus trees, peaches, pears, and most legumes are particularly sensitive. Date palms, suger beets, asparagus, and a few other plants, nevertheless, rival sheep and cattle in their tolerance of saline water.

An important key to irrigation is to supply excess water which is removed by drainage systems, thus preventing harmful salt accumulation through evapotranspiration. If copius amounts of water are used in well-drained sandy soils, some salt-tolerant crops can be grown with water containing more than 10 gm/liter of dissolved solids.

The bulk of all dissolved constituents in normal groundwater falls into seven main categories, namely, Na^+, Ca^{2+}, Mg^{2+}, HCO_3^-, Cl^-, SO_4^{2-}, and H_4SiO_4. Ions which may be of secondary importance are K^+, CO_3^{2-}, Fe^{2+}, and F^-. Under reducing conditions and a low pH, Fe^{2+} may become a dominant ion. Where contamination from ancient or modern animals persists, NO_3^- may become a dominant ion. Actual ionic species which are present in brines are not understood very well. As concentrations increase, dissolved constituents such as $Mg(OH)^+$, $CaSO_4$, and $MgCO_3$ undoubtedly become important. By convention, however, analyses of brines are given in the form of simple hypothetical ions found in waters of low concentration of dissolved solids. Analyses of some typical desert waters are shown in Table I.

TABLE I

SELECTED ANALYSES OF WATER FROM DESERT

Solute	Sample[a] (analysis in ppm)										
	1	2	3	4	5	6	7	8	9	10	11
SiO_2	36	4	27	21	30	16	6	—	—	—	30
Ca^{2+}	7	295	18	456	98	86	43	157	761	1,300	3
Mg^{2+}	0.5	58	4	113	15	44	26	128	83,400	1,000	3
Na^+	160	474	54	47	29	94	136	517	19,000	82,200	385
K^+	8	61	2.8	—	0.4	12	—	—	27,200	4,900	31
HCO_3^-	248	63	154	200	409	165	—	132	1,600	—	424
SO_4^{2-}	96	415	28	1460	16	112	38	748	34,000	3,500	0
Cl^-	53	1130	15	15	12	153	200	763	262,000	156,500	137
NO_3^-	4	0.3	1.2	0.2	0.0	—	—	—	—	—	—
B	—	18	—	—	0.16	—	—	—	—	5	—
Total dissolved solids	487	2469	224	—	402	712	1920	2,510	428,000	—	1010

[a] Sample 1 is from fresh well water from dry desert area of northern Chile (Castillo, 1960); 2, brackish well water from dry desert area of northern Chile (Castillo, 1960); 3, fresh water from spring in rhyolite, Socorro, New Mexico (Hall, 1963); 4, brackish water from spring in rocks with gypsum and calcite, near Socorro, New Mexico (Hall, 1963); 5, fresh water from well in coastal aquifer, northwestern Peru (Schoff and Sayan, 1969); 6, fresh water from shallow well in coastal sand dunes, Sitre, Libya (Ogilbee, 1964); 7, brackish water from well in Nubian sandstone of central Sudan (Rodis et al., 1968); 8, brackish groundwater from Tafilalt Region, Morocco (Margat, 1953); 9, brine from Saoura Wadi System, Morocco (Blanc and Conrad, 1968); 10, brine from Bonneville Salt, Flat, Utah (S. N. Davis, unpublished, 1966); 11, water from Great Artesian Basin of Australia, Corryaninna Bore (Ward, 1946).

As a general rule, groundwater is more saline in deserts than in other regions. This is true for the following reasons.

1. Evapotranspiration exceeds precipitation, so soluble salts originally in rain will tend to be concentrated by evaporation at the land surface. Occasional heavy rain will redissolve these salts, and runoff will carry the water and salts to points of groundwater recharge.

2. Dry fallout, which is almost ubiquitous in deserts, contains easily soluble salts. Precipitation which eventually becomes groundwater recharge will dissolve significant amounts of these salts.

3. Deserts favor the preservation of natural beds of gypsum, halite, and other evaporite deposits which will contribute dissolved material to water from infrequent storms.

4. Slow water movement in deserts will mean that flushing of connate saline water will also be very slow. Thus, some of the salinity in desert aquifers may be related to ancient saline water originally deposited with the sediments.

Brackish and saline groundwater from deserts generally have unusually large amounts of sodium, chloride, and, less commonly, sulfate (Table I, sample 8). If water is concentrated to a brine, calcium sulfate and some sodium chloride will be precipitated, leaving a brine enriched in potassium, magnesium, and chloride (Table I, sample 9).

Despite factors leading to high dissolved solids in deserts, fresh water can be found in some localities (Table I, samples 1, 3, 5, and 6; Feth, 1966). Conditions favorable for low dissolved solids in deserts are recharge water derived from outside the desert or aquifers that accept recharge from barren surfaces of dense rock which are generally devoid of dust and crusts of salt. Also, the origins of much of the fresh groundwater found in deserts of today probably antedates the formation of the deserts.

VIII. Large-Scale Groundwater Circulation

Many deserts have aquifers or groups of aquifers which allow a regional groundwater circulation to develop. Three of the largest and most important of these desert systems are discussed in this section. Other large regions, notably the southwestern Sahara, the northern Gobi, the western Australian, parts of the Kalahari, and the southwestern Arabian deserts, are underlain at a shallow depth by dense crystalline rocks which are capable of yielding only limited amounts of water except in the zone of weathering or in the basal parts of large accumulations of dune sand.

A. NUBIAN AQUIFER

The Nubian Aquifer underlies a large part of northeastern Africa (Fig. 11). Similar rocks are also important aquifers in part of the northeastern Arabian Peninsula (Naimi, 1965). In general, the aquifer contains potable water in the Sudan, the northeastern part of Chad, southeastern part of Libya, and the southern two-thirds of the United Arab Republic. The water grades from brackish to salty north of the Qattara Depression.

To date, little significant development has taken place in the aquifer except in the New Valley Project and near the various oases such as Dakhla, Farafra, and Bahariya in the United Arab Republic and near Khartoum in the Sudan. Natural discharge has been largely in the oases of the Western Desert and in the Qattara Depression. Nubian sandstone does not crop out in the Qattara Depression, but slow, upward leakage through overlying rocks probably takes place.

The Nubian Aquifer is designated as a sandstone in much of the geologic literature. Its lithology in detail, nevertheless, is quite varied. In the Sudan, conglomerate, coarse-grained sandstone and medium-grained sandstone are abundant in the Nubian Aquifer. Lesser amounts of mudstone, and hard ferruginous and siliceous layers are also present. Most of the coarser strata have abundant quantities of cement and clays. Lateral variations of lithology are abrupt (Rodis et al., 1968). To the north, in the United Arab Republic, the finer-grained units appear to dominate in the upper part of the unit. The maximum thickness of the Nubian Aquifer in the Sudan is about 500 meters (El Boushi and Whiteman, 1967) and roughly 700 meters in the west central part of the United Arab Republic (Said, 1962).

The exact age of the Nubian Aquifer is unknown. Most of the aquifer materials have a continental origin and lack fossils. Largely through dates on underlying and overlying beds, the Nubian Aquifer is assumed to be largely Lower and Middle Mesozoic. In other words, it was deposited during the period from roughly 200 to 100 million years ago. Owing to this great age and the fact that it is presently exposed at or near the surface, ample opportunity must have existed for flushing out the original pore water in all except the northernmost part of the aquifer. Water is, therefore, for the most part, probably less than a few hundred thousand years old.

One of the most interesting aspects of the Nubian Aquifer is the origin of the fresh to brackish water presently within the aquifer. Hydraulic gradients of today suggest that the water is flowing outward from the general region where the countries of Chad, Sudan, Libya, and the United Arab Republic join together (Jones, 1966). The climate in this region is, nevertheless, arid and could not produce much recharge under present condi-

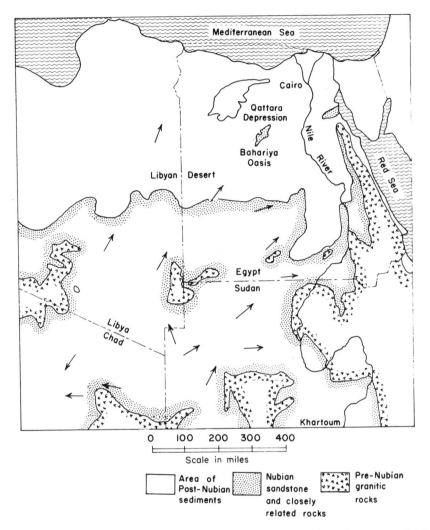

Fig. 11. Nubian sandstone in northeast Africa. Outcrop area includes some surficial sediments such as sand dunes and alluvium. Arrows show only approximate direction of regional migration of groundwater.

tions. Most workers have, therefore, postulated that water in the aquifer today had its origin during Late Pleistocene time when rainfall was probably much larger than present. Radiometric dates of the ^{14}C in the water tend to support this conclusion. Thatcher *et al.* (1961) report dates which suggest that much of the water may be from 20,000 to 30,000 years old.

The Nubian Aquifer has an almost limitless amount of water in storage.

Utilization of this water, however, is not a simple matter. A general restriction will always be the fact that water drawn from the aquifer will not be replenished by modern recharge. Replenishment must be through lateral migration of water from distant parts of the aquifer that are not developed as yet. A specific restriction in many areas is the fact that the aquifer is not very permeable. Yields of wells are sufficient only for small garden plots and a few homes but generally lower than desired for efficient irrigation. Initial yields of wells in the New Valley Project of the United Arab Republic were generally from 100 to 200 liters/second with pressures of more than 7 kg/cm^2 (Harshbarger, 1968). Like most deep artesian aquifers, pressures, and hence yields, have decreased rapidly after development of irrigation wells. In order to produce large quantities of water, either large numbers of wells must be drilled or the water levels in wells must be pumped down to a low level in order to create a steep hydraulic gradient toward the well. Both methods of obtaining large yields are costly. The quality of water also is a limiting factor, particularly in the northern half of the United Arab Republic. The accumulation of salt in irrigated regions must be prevented by using excessive amounts of water for leaching the salts into drainage systems. Again, this increases the cost of irrigation projects.

B. Great Artesian Basin of Australia

The Great Artesian Basin of Australia is probably the largest unified hydrogeologic system in the world. It covers a large part of the eastern half of Australia (Fig. 12). Much of the basin is arid and semiarid. The basin is also noted for its deep wells which are probably some of the deepest water wells in the world. A few exceed 2000 meters in depth. Water from some of the deepest wells reaches the surface with temperatures slightly greater than 100°C.

The primary use of deep artesian wells in eastcentral Australia has been to provide water for stock. Some wells supply domestic, municipal, and minor irrigation needs, although the chemical quality of the water is commonly marginal for these uses (see Table I, sample 11).

The deep artesian aquifers are Mesozoic continental sandstones, largely Jurassic, which are covered in much of the basin with thick Cretaceous clays. Two main water-bearing zones are generally present, the upper "Blythesdale Series" and the lower "Marburg and Bundamba Series." Each of the water-bearing "series" contains numerous individual aquifers that have only limited lateral continuity. Despite local facies changes, the water-bearing zones appear to behave in a regional sense as an integrated unit.

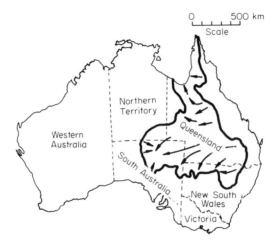

Fig. 12. Great Artesian Basin in eastern Australia. Arrows show only approximate direction of groundwater movement. Heavy lines show border of artesian basin.

Shallow, generally unconfined, aquifers are present along watercourses in the eastern part of the basin. Also, in the northeast, Permian sandstones below the primary artesian aquifers are probably water bearing. The cover of Cretaceous clay is absent along the southern margin of the basin where water is only semiconfined and has lacked a strong original artesian head (Ward, 1946).

Recharge to the artesian basin is thought to be through the sandstone outcrops along the eastern margin of the basin. The eastern margin is at a higher elevation and receives more precipitation than the rest of the basin, although under present climatic conditions little excess water is available for recharge. The main sandstone aquifers generally pinch out in the subsurface before reaching the western margin of the basin. Also, the western margin of the basin is arid, so little recharge from this direction is thought to have taken place during the past few thousand years.

Many questions exist concerning the natural discharge of the artesian system. The famous mound springs in the southern and northcentral parts of the basin may represent areas of upward leakage along fractures in the confining beds of the system. The mounds are generally 1–10 meters high and are made of travertine deposited by the artesian water. Discharge may also occur into the Gulf of Carpentaria in the northern extremity of the basin. The water in much of the Carpentaria Subbasin is brackish to saline (Whitehouse, 1945) suggesting that, if there is active discharge, it is sluggish. Natural discharge also occurs along the eastern margins of the basin where deeper valleys cut into the permeable intake beds.

The first deep wells were drilled in the basin during the late 19th century.

Initial water pressures encountered by wells were truly spectacular and stimulated a rapid development of groundwater. Unfortunately, despite high initial well yields, the sandstone has only a limited permeability, so that pressures have declined quite rapidly as water has been extracted. Today, most of the wells need pumps in order to produce significant quantities of water. Recent development of economic methods to deionize brackish water may place a greater demand on the artesian basin. As water levels decline, the cost of drilling new wells and the cost of lifting water to the surface will place economic restrictions on further development.

Oil discoveries in the southern and eastern margins of the basin during the late 1960's will undoubtedly stimulate the drilling of additional deep exploration holes in the remainder of the basin. The exploration activity, in turn, should contribute new hydrologic information to our knowledge of this vast region.

C. CARBONATE AQUIFERS OF EASTERN NEVADA

Paleozoic rocks of eastern and southern Nevada form one of the most interesting hydrologic systems to be found in arid and semiarid regions (Fig. 13). This system is in the northcentral part of the Basin and Range physiographic province which is characterized by rugged north–south trending mountain ranges with arid and semiarid valleys. Most of the valleys lack exterior surface drainage. It is commonly assumed that the basins which are closed topographically are also closed groundwater basins. Work in southern Nevada (Winograd, 1962) which was later extended to eastern Nevada (Eakin, 1966) suggests very strongly that Paleozoic carbonate rocks form an integrated subsurface drainage system for large parts of the entire region.

The best documented interbasin groundwater flow is from Nye County and adjacent parts of Lincoln and Clark Counties. Investigations in this area were stimulated by requirements for water for the Nevada Test Site of the U.S. Atomic Energy Commission. Hydrogeologists were surprised by the fact that water was not found directly under the playa surface. In fact, initial drilling in Frenchman Flat did not find water until almost 200 meters of valley fill had been penetrated. Later in Yucca Flat, water was found to be more than 300 meters below the surface. If Frenchman and Yucca Flats contained closed groundwater systems, they should eventually fill with water to near the surface. Also, the playas contained mainly dried mud flats and not extensive salt crusts, indicating that the playas were not the sump area for water evaporating from a local groundwater system.

Further hydrogeological studies which included deep drilling and extensive aquifer tests showed that fractured carbonate rock of Paleozoic age

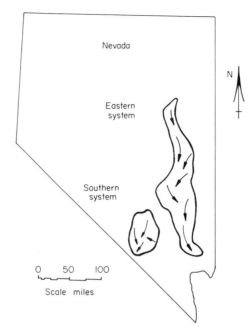

Fig. 13. Groundwater circulation in fractured carbonate rocks of eastern and southern Nevada.

underlay most of the valleys. The carbonate rock was found to be relatively permeable when compared to much of the pyroclastic material in the valley. Furthermore, the hydraulic heads in the valley fill were larger than the heads in the underlying carbonate rock. These facts suggested that the carbonate rocks formed an underdrain for the entire region. Extensive springs in Ash Meadows to the west of the Nevada Test Site were found to represent the natural discharge area of the underdrain system (Winograd, 1962).

Eakin (1966) has described a much larger area in eastern Nevada. Although not as thoroughly studied as the Nevada Test Site system, Eakin has assembled hydrologic geochemical and geologic data which suggest very strongly that a similar, but more complex, underdrainage system operates in a large region from southern Elko County southward to near the Arizona border. This is a total north–south distance of roughly 400 km. The groundwater system of eastern Nevada is in a region of thirteen distinct valleys of which seven are topographically closed and six are within the integrated drainage system of the "White River Wash."

Both the southern Nevada Test Site system and the eastern Nevada system are in areas of minor groundwater pumpage. The problems and economic implications of developing groundwater in these and similar systems have been discussed by Maxey (1968).

IX. Artificial Changes in the Hydrogeology of Deserts

Groundwater development in desert regions of the world will increase drastically in reponse to an increase in agricultural products (Simpson, 1968). Also, many of the coastal deserts of the world have mild climates well suited for recreational development (Meigs, 1966). Water-supply problems for this development will be even more severe than has been experienced in the semiarid part of southern Spain during the expansion of the tourist industry during the past two decades (1950–1970).

Inasmuch as water is such a critical factor in the biology of natural deserts, a summary of some of the potential changes caused by groundwater development might be a somber but useful conclusion to this chapter.

The most striking effect of groundwater development will be the eventual destruction of springs and areas of phreatophytic vegetation. All desert aquifers, except those near perennial sources of water, will be eventually depleted owing to the virtual lack of recharge. As water levels in the subsurface become lower, springs will tend to disappear (Fig. 14).

Another common effect where certain geologic conditions are present is the creation of perched bodies of water in zones which have been previously dry. Excess irrigation water may tend to pile up near the surface and in some places may produce new swampy areas.

If drainage is poor, the water added to the surface may evaporate to leave a salty residue which, in turn, may kill some types of vegetation.

Eventual depletion of groundwater reservoirs in desert regions will have the most drastic effects on irrigated agriculture. Maxey (1968), however, has pointed out that from a strictly economic standpoint, this need not be a disaster. In the first place, groundwater in an almost static condition represents a resource similar to oil and gas. Unless it is taken out of the ground, it has little economic value. Mining ground water can be a profitable enterprise, therefore, provided that proper plans are made for the entire life of the extraction process. Second, and perhaps most important, is the fact that groundwater extraction can help build a vigorous economy in a region which then, at a later date, can develop alternative sources of water when groundwater becomes depleted.

As new projects are planned, biologists should be fully aware of the numerous changes which may take place within the area of potential development as well as at distant points within the groundwater basin. These

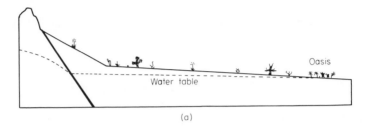

(a)

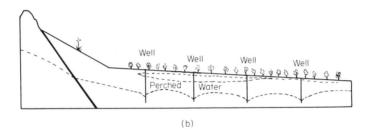

(b)

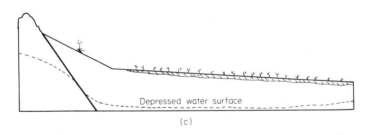

(c)

Fig. 14. Destruction of desert land through the development of irrigation using groundwater of marginal chemical quality. (a) Natural condition of the desert. (b) Irrigation with groundwater. Perched water develops owing to lack of drainage. (c) Perched water plus salinity kills orchards. Water supply is almost exhausted, and land is left almost sterile owing to high salinity of soil.

potential changes should then be called to the attention of all those involved with final decisions concerning the projects. It is possible that some small projects as well as a few large projects will actually produce aesthetic as well as economic damage which will exceed the expected benefits of the project.

REFERENCES

Blanc, P., and Conrad, G. (1968). Evolution géochimique des eaux de l'oued Saovra (Sahara nord-occidental). *Rev. Geogr. Phys.* **10**, 415–428.

Burkham, D. E. (1970). Depletion of streamflow by infiltration in the main channels of the Tucson Basin, Arizona. *U.S. Geol. Surv., Water-Supply Pap.* **1939-B**.

Castillo, O. (1960). El agua subterránea en el norte de la Pampa del Tamarugal (Chile). *Inst. Invest. Geol. Bol.* No. 5.

Davis, S. N. (1969). Porosity and permeability of natural materials. *In* "Flow Through Porous Media" (R. J. M. De Wiest, ed.), pp. 53–89. Academic Press, New York.

Davis, S. N., and De Wiest, R. J. M. (1966). "Hydrogeology." Wiley, New York.

Degens, E. T. (1961). Diagenesis of subsurface waters from the Libyan Desert. *Geol. Soc. Amer., Spec. Pap.* **68**, 160 (abstr.).

Dixey, F. (1962). Geology and geomorphology, and groundwater hydrology. *In* "The Problems of the Arid Zone," pp. 23–52. UNESCO, Paris.

Eakin, T. E. (1966). A regional interbasin ground-water system in the White River area, southeastern Nevada. *Water Resour. Res.* **2**, 251–271.

El Boushi, I. M., and Davis, S. N. (1969). Water-retention characteristics of coarse rock particles. *J. Hydrol.* **8**, 431–441.

El Boushi, I. M., and Whiteman, A. J. (1967). Ground water development, the Nubian Sandstone Formation, the major aquifer in Sudan Republic. *In* "Seminar on Community Water Supply 16-20 December 1967, Session II, pp. 1–36." Department of Geology, University of Khartoum, Sudan.

Feth, J. H. (1966). Reconnaissance survey of ground-water quality in the Great Basin. *U.S., Geol. Surv. Prof. Pap.* **550-D**, 237–241.

Feth, J. H., and Brown, R. J. (1962). Method for measuring upward leakage from artesian aquifers using rate of salt-crust accumulation. *U.S. Geol. Surv., Prof. Pap.* **450-B**, 100–101.

Hall, F. R. (1963). Springs in the vicinity of Socorro, New Mexico. *In* "New Mexico Geological Society, Guidebook for 14th Field Conference," pp. 160–179. New Mexico Geological Society, Socorro, New Mexico.

Hantush, M. S. (1966). Hydraulics of wells. *In* "Advances In Hydroscience" (V. T. Chow, ed.), Vol. 3, pp. 281–432. Academic Press, New York.

Harshbarger, J. W. (1968). Ground-water development in desert areas. *Ground Water* **6** (No. 5), 2–4.

Hubbert, M. K. (1940). The theory of ground-water motion. *J. Geol.* **48**, 785–944.

Jones, J. R. (1966). Ground-water exploration and development in Libya. *Water Well J.* **20**, 13–16 and 40.

Löwy, H. (1953). Senkwasser in Sandwüsten. *Neues Jahrb. Geol. Palaeontol., Monatsh.* No. 6, pp. 241–243.

McDonald, H. R., Horton, J. S., Thompson, C. B., Robinson, T. W., and Lowry, O. J. (1958). "A Guide to the Density Survey of Bottom Land and Streambank Vegetation," Open-File Report. Subcommittee on Phreatophytes, Pacific Southwest Inter-Agency Committee, U.S. Bureau Reclamation, Denver.

Mann, J. F. (1958). Estimating quantity and quality of ground water in dry regions using airphotographs. *Int. Ass. Sci. Hydrol., Gen. Assembly Toronto* **2**, 125–134.

Margat, J. F. (1953). La nappe phréatique du Tafilalt (Maroc), Bilan hydraulique, minéralisation des eaux et evaporation. *In* "L'Hydrogéologie des Régions Arides et Sub-Arides," pp. 169–185. 19th Sess., Sect. 8, Algiers. Intl. Geol. Congr.

Maxey, G. B. (1968). Hydrogeology of desert basins. *Ground Water* **6** (No. 5), 10–22.

Meigs, P. (1966). "Geography of Coastal Deserts." UNESCO, Paris.

Meinzer, O. E. (1927). Plants as indicators of ground water. *U.S., Geol. Surv., Water-Supply Pap.* **577.**

Meinzer, O. E., ed. (1942). "Hydrology." McGraw-Hill, New York.

Moussu, P., and Moussu, H. (1952). Etude hydrogéologique des dunes de Bone. *In* "La Géologie et les Problémes de l'eau en Algérie, Tome II, Données sur l'Hydrogéologie Algérienne," pp. 112–129. 19th Sess., Algiers. Int. Geol. Congress.

Naimi, A. I. (1965). The ground water of northeastern Saudi Arabia. *In* "Fifth Arab Petroleum Congress," 26 unnumbered pages in preprint. Cairo, United Arab Republic.

Ogilbee, W. (1964). Ground water in the Sirte Area, Tripolitania, United Kingdom of Libya. *U.S., Geol. Surv., Water-Supply Pap.* **1757-C.**

Robinson, T. W. (1958). Phreatophytes. *U.S., Geol. Surv., Water-Supply Pap.* **1423.**

Rodis, H. G., Hassan, A., and Wahadan, L. (1968). Ground-water geology of Kordofan Province, Sudan. *U.S., Geol. Surv., Water-Supply Pap.* **1757-J.**

Said, R. (1962). "The Geology of Egypt." Elsevier, Amsterdam.

Schoff, S. L., and Sayan, J. L. (1969). Ground-water resources of the Lambayeque Valley, Department of Lambayeque, northern Peru. *U.S., Geol. Surv., Water-Supply Pap.* **1663-F.**

Simpson, E. S. (1968). Ground-water hydrology of desert environments. *In* "Deserts of the World" (W. G. McGinnies, B. J. Goldman, and P. Paylore, eds.), pp. 723–744. Univ. of Arizona Press, Tucson.

Tamers, M. A. (1967). Surface-water infiltration and ground water movement in arid zones of Venezuela. *Isotop. Hydrol., Proc. Symp., 1966,* pp. 339–345.

Terzaghi, K. (1942). Soil moisture and capillary phenomena in soils. *In* "Hydrology" (O. E. Meinzer, ed.), pp. 331–363. McGraw-Hill, New York.

Thatcher, L., Rubin, M., and Brown, G. F. (1961). Dating desert ground water. *Science* **134,** 105–106.

Tolman, C. F. (1937). "Ground Water." McGraw-Hill, New York.

Turk, L. J. (1970). Evaporation of brine: A field study on the Bonneville Salt Flats, Utah. *Water Resour. Res.* **6,** 1209–1215.

Walton, W. C. (1970). "Groundwater Resource Evaluation." McGraw-Hill, New York.

Ward, L. K. (1946). The occurrence, composition, testing, and utilization of underground water in South Australia and the search for further supplies. *Geol. Surv. S. Aust., Bull.* **23.**

Whitehouse, F. W. (1945). Geological work on the Great Artesian Basin. *In* "First Interim Report of the Commission Appointed to Investigate Problems Relating to the Great Artesian Basin in Queensland, Australia," pp. 2–28. Queensland Parliament, Brisbane, Australia.

Winograd, I. J. (1962). Interbasin movement of ground water at the Nevada Test Site. Nevada. *U.S., Geol. Surv. Prof. Pap.* **450-C,** 108–111.

Worts, G. F., Jr. (1951). Geology and ground-water resources of the Santa Maria Valley area, California. *U.S., Geol. Surv., Water-Supply Pap.* **1000.**

CHAPTER II

DESERT SOILS

Wallace H. Fuller

> *In the desert path,*
> *Raising puffs of alkali dust—*
> *The roadrunner's bath.*
> W. H. Fuller, Roadrunner

I. Introduction

Through the action of physical, chemical, and biological agents of weathering, parent geological materials are synthesized into soils with time. Thus soils are a "genetic" product of their environment and represent a synthesizing living body as opposed to mere physical accumulation of degraded material. Not all of the thin veneer of unconsolidated earth crust, however, is considered to be soil, since some surface materials may not be developed significantly from what they were when originally exposed or subdivided in place or transported and deposited. Certain desert areas are characterized by surfaces on which well-developed soils have not formed. For example, some desert *Lithosols* occur as typical, shallow, broken-rock surfaces overlying bedrock and *Regosols* occur as shifting sand dunes. Other surfaces are encrusted with salt or constitute deep beds of lime or gypsum. Although deserts are noted for physical surfaces that do not represent mature soils in the classical sense, in this chapter the term "soil" will be used rather than "surface materials" (Dregne, 1967) since most surfaces of deserts will fit into the classification scheme as envisaged in the U.S. Department of Agriculture Seventh Approximation System (U.S. Soil Conservation Service, 1960, 1967).

Desert soils are found under extreme arid, arid, and semiarid climatic conditions of low rainfall. Arid soils receive less than 25 cm precipitation per year, although there are those in equatorial and other areas that may receive up to 50 cm. Certain coastal deserts may go rainless for several years. Precipitation in the desert is characterized most often as torrential although many exceptions can be cited. A year's supply can fall all at one time. Heaviest showers often occur during the summer months. Erosion, runoff, and evaporation seriously reduce the effectiveness of the rainfall for supporting plant life and leaching salts from the surface horizon. Some land forms typical of deserts are diagrammed in Fig. 1.

Temperature affects evaporation of moisture from soil more than any

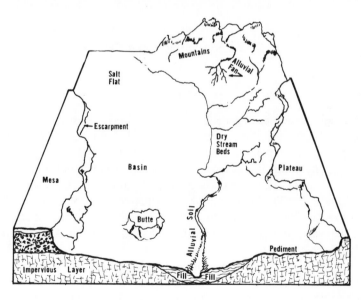

Fig. 1. Land forms under an arid climate. Pediment flank the upthrown mountains. Great basins were formed by dropping of local land areas in relation to the mountains. Erosion left plateaus, and buttes and stream–alluvium collected along gouged-out canyons and river beds.

other climatic factor. Thus, both temperature and precipitation have been combined in various indices to define aridity of an area (Thornthwaite, 1948; Trewartha, 1954). Some excellent reviews of desert climates are provided by Meigs (1953), McGinnies and Meadows (1968), Reitan and Green (1967), and Ramaley (1952). Seasonal as well as daily temperatures vary more in arid than humid climates. Monthly means will differ from $-12°C$ in coastal areas to over $15°C$ in interior basins. Diurnal temperatures range from $-1°$ to $10°C$, except in the seacoast deserts where ranges are much narrower. These temperature variations greatly affect evapotranspiration, plant cover, and soil microbial activity.

In general, desert vegetation is sparse, short, and develops as individual plants. Accumulation of soil organic matter is slow if at all. Ramaley (1952) attempted to prepare a composite map of world desert boundaries by surperimposing desert climate, desert vegetation, and desert soils maps on a common base. There is a wide variation among each of the authors as to the delineation of desert areas. The greatest differences occur in Asia and, to a lesser extent, in North America. In Asia all three values vary widely among authors whereas, in North America, climate and vegetation vary the most. Desert soils appear to have a wider distribution than the classificatory elements of climate and vegetation.

II. Desert Soil Surfaces and Classes

A. ARIDISOLS

Desert soils are classed "genetically" as *Aridisols,* i.e., soils of dry places. They are variously described as having an ochric epipedon that is normally soft when dry or that has a distinct structure. In addition they have one or more of the following diagnostic horizons: argillic, natric, or cambic horizons; calcic, gypsic, or salic horizons; or a duripan (U.S. Soil Conservation Service, 1967). An agricultural productive Aridisol is Mohave loam, seen in Fig. 2. Soil genetists do not include shifting desert sand, recent alluvial deposits, and shallow soils on bed rock with the Aridisols but as Entisols, described later.

Wind plays an important role in Aridisol genesis. Even though North American desert winds are less extreme than in other world deserts, dust storms are common, sand and dust are continually moving, leaving polished desert pavements of pebbles and stones and forming and reforming restless dunes or depositing loess (aeolian dust). Calcium carbonate and other salts accumulate in Aridisols by the downward penetration of salts

Fig. 2. Mohave soil is found well distributed in desert valleys of the Southwest United States. This is an excellent soil, fertile and highly productive when irrigated.

as a consequence of leachings from transient dust that settles during calms and are caught in a rainstorm. Carbonates concentrate in the soil horizons at depths depending on the mean extent of penetration of the precipitation. Because of shallow penetration of water, carbonates (lime) are common to all Aridisols. In desert soils they are distributed unevenly throughout the profile. Gypsum also is found variously distributed in desert soils. Differences in depth and thickness of lime and gypsum layers, salt deposits, mineral distribution, fossil bones, remnants of dry lake beds, and pollen (Wright, 1968) all indicate most deserts, at one time, were exposed to a more humid climate. Buried, truncated, and degraded remnants of well-developed soil profiles are not uncommon on broad desert surfaces. Such land surfaces appear to have been stabilized through glacial periods of humid and interglacial periods of dry climate. Relic characteristics of ancient soils are more prominent in desert than the more humid areas. The intensity of development of recent genetic horizons under humid conditions tends to "obscure" or "reduce" relic characteristics. Argillic (clayey) horizons, some with deep layers of lime, found on certain desert floors and buried in alluvial fans, also suggest that humid climates predominated at one time.

B. ENTISOLS

Genesis of desert soils is complicated further by recent deposits of alluvial debris from overflowing, raging streams during heavy rains in adjacent mountains and foothills. Alluvial fans in the deserts of the Southwestern United States, for example, are still being covered, uncovered, and dissected by arroyo floods from summer torrents. Soil patterns in desert valleys are diverse due to the cutting and filing action of streams flowing through the ages at different rates. Horizontal layerings of sand, silt and clay of varying thicknesses are interspersed by lenses or islands, also of different textures (see Fig. 3). Sparse vegetation invites shifting sand and

Fig. 3. Alluvial soil showing typical stratification of different textures of sand, silt, and clay.

dust; erosion and deposition. Desert lands thus present a high degree of variable soil patterns which make them most difficult to describe, define and classify. This makes it necessary to establish, in the classification scheme, a separate category of very young soils having little if any morphological differentiation into horizons.

Soils belonging to the order of *Entisols* appear universally under all climatic conditions and are prominent in deserts. Those that are found in arid and semiarid regions have been called Lithosols, Regosols, and alluvial soils and lack diagnostic horizons other than ochric epipedons. They occur on recent geomorphic surfaces, either on steep slopes that are undergoing active erosion or on fans and flood plains where recently eroded materials are deposited. The three suborders important to desert areas are *Fluvents* (recent alluvial stream deposition material), *Orthents* (Lithosols of thin, colluvial–alluvial or in-place material, with decreasing organic matter with depth), and *Psamments* (Regosols, Ergs, dunes, sand fields). Neither barren sand dunes nor salt flats of desert playas are considered to be soil unless they have some vegetation, even if it be ephemeral.

Since many of the characteristic desert surfaces are exposed subsurface horizons or derived from subsurface horizons or layers, their further discussion will be postponed until characteristic subsurfaces have been given attention. Excellent reviews of physical desert surfaces are given in publications of Clements *et al.* (1957), and the Office of Arid Lands Studies, University of Arizona (Dregne, 1967).

III. Characteristic Desert Subsurface Horizons

Subsurface horizons are those that form below the surface and are most often thought of as the B horizon, although some subsurface horizons are exceptions and may be considered as part of the upper A horizon.

A. ARGILLIC

An argillic horizon is a subsurface layer in which silica clay minerals have concentrated to a significant extent. In some instances erosive forces have left soils truncated and the clay layer exposed. The argillic layer forms in the B horizon below the upper A horizon as *in situ* clay, or it may occur as a "migrated" clay layer, a remnant or relic of a more humid climate. The amount of clay in the B horizon necessary for it to classify as an argillic horizon varies with the total clay content of the A horizon, but the B always will be appreciably higher.

B. Cambic

The cambic horizon is an altered layer that is light in color, low in organic matter, with fine textures and soil structure rather than rock structure. The tops of distinct prismatic structures may lie close to the surface. If the soil has no A1 horizon, the top of the cambic horizon lies at the surface. Carbonates usually are present.

C. Natric

The natric horizon is characterized as having sodium in the subsurface layer sufficient to cause particle dispersion with about 15% of the exchangeable cations replaced by sodium. It is a special kind of argillic horizon and more commonly known as Solonetz or solodized-Solonetz. The subsurface horizon has characteristic prismatic, columnar, or blocky structures.

D. Salic

The salic horizon is a subsurface layer which is 15 cm or more thick with secondary enrichments of salts more soluble in cold water than gypsum. It has 2% or more soluble salt by weight, and the product of the thickness in inches and percent salt by weight is 24% inches or more.

E. Calcic

Calcic horizons in desert regions develop readily since the very limited rainfall seems unable to remove lime even from the surface few centimeters. Where parent material is rich in carbonates or regular additions of carbonate accumulates from dust, the calcic horizon may become cemented into a hard, massive layer called a *petrocalcic* horizon. The calcic horizon is defined as having secondary carbonate enrichment that is more than 15 cm thick, a $CaCO_3$ equivalent content of more than 15%, and at least 5% more $CaCO_3$ equivalent than the C horizon.

F. Gypsic

The gypsic horizon is similar to the calcic horizon but is a secondary enrichment of the sulfate of calcium (gypsum) rather than the carbonate of calcium (lime). It is a layer more than 15 cm thick that has at least more than 5% more gypsum than the C or underlying stratum, and in which the product of the thickness in inches and the gypsum percent is equal to or greater than 60% inches.

G. Duripan

Silica cements the duripan subsurface horizon. Such layers will not slake in water or acid. Silica duripans often contain iron oxides and carbonates as accessory cementing agents. In arid soils, duripans are usually platy and often capped or coated with opal as well as a microcrystalline form of silica. Sand grains may appear in duripans cemented together by silica.

IV. Desert Soil Suborders and Great Groups

In the scheme of soil classification the desert order is called *Aridisols*. There are two suborders under Aridisols—*Argids* and *Orthids*.

A. Argids

Argids are Aridisols with an argillic or silica clay horizon. They characteristically have an illuvial horizon in which silicate clays have accumulated to a significant degree. Although the clay layer is formed below the surface of mineral soil, it later may be exposed by desert climatic erosion. Argillic layers do not form readily under arid climates. More often they are residual, presumably from glacial periods when rainfall was higher. However, during interglacial or more recent times petrocalcic layers (laminated, indurated limy layer) and duripans (hardpans, cemented with silica and/or aluminum silicate) may develop in the argillic horizons. Argids include five great groups: Durargids, Haplargids, Nadurargids, Natrargids, and Paleargids.

1. Durargids

Durargids are characterized by a platy or massive duripan or hardpan that is indurated in some subhorizon. These soils are rich in glass, which is the source of cementing silicate. The duripans thus may be cemented in part by silica, which exhibits solubility in concentrated alkali, as well as lime. In the United States deserts, duripans also may possess thin, alternate layers of iron and silica of high density in association with the upper surface of lime accumulation layer. In this case iron probably solubilized as a result of a "perched" water table on top of the lime accumulation layer as the downward penetration of water was impeded during periods when water was more plentiful.

2. Haplargids

Haplargids are Argids with an argillic horizon but not with a high solium content, such as natric horizons (Solonetz and solodized-Solonetz). They do not have a duripan or petrocalcic horizon within 1 meter of the surface. The clay gradually transists between the A and B horizons or the horizon has less than 35% clay.

3. Nadurargids

Nadurargids are Argids that have prominent structure and a natric (sodic) horizon above a duripan that appears within 1 meter of the surface. The hardpan is platy or massive and indurated.

4. Natrargids

Natrargids also have a natric horizon but not a duripan within 1 meter of the surface. Soil scientists recognize this group in more historic terms as Solonetz and solodized-Solonetz. Columnar structure is one of their widely recognized features. These soils are usually dry, pale in color at the surface and have more organic matter in the B than the A horizon. They are also known for their bare desert-pavement surfaces, soft vesicular crusts, and accumulation of lime and other soluble salts at moderate depths. They are like the soils with which they are associated in most of their properties. Sodium-affected horizons may develop in almost any soil. In general, these soils possess horizons having more than 15% of their cation-exchange capacity saturated with sodium. Magnesium in the exchange positions is quite common in sodic layers. If the exchangeable sodium plus magnesium exceeds that of calcium, the soil is placed in a natric group.

5. Paleargids

Paleargids are Argids that have either a petrocalcic horizon within 1 meter of the soil surface or that have an argillic horizon that has both 35% or more clay in some part and an abrupt increase in clay content at the upper boundary of the argillic horizon. These are dry soils that resemble the better known humid zone Planosols in some respects.

B. Orthids

The Orthids are Aridisols with no argillic or natric horizon (U.S. Soil Conservation Service, 1967). They are believed to have developed since late Pleistocene time (in the last 25×10^3 years) under an arid climate.

The subgroups have a cambic, calcic, petrocalcic, gypsic, or salic horizon, or duripan characteristics.

1. Calciorthids

Calciorthids have either a calcic or gypsic horizon that has its upper boundary within 1 meter of the surface. They have no duripan or petrocalcic horizon that has its upper boundary within 1 meter of the surface and no salic horizon above the calcic or gypsic horizon, although these soils are calcareous above the calcic or gypsic layer. Calciorthids are found commonly in North American deserts in various stages of formation. In early stages the lime is dispersed in the soil as a soft powder or appears as coatings or pendents on the lower sides of gravel and stones. As time progressed lime accumulated in and throughout the soil in pores until the calcic layer became packed with lime and cemented. In certain soils lime continued to be carried downward but because of inhibition of free movement of the water, it accumulated until it formed a continuous, smooth layer. This indurated lime layer then became a petrocalcic horizon and the soil is called petrocalcic Calciorthid. Certain of the Calciorthids may have very little if any lime in the upper few centimeters but a definite accumulation of lime at lower depths. Very sandy soils may be free of lime as deep as 10–12 cm but pass abruptly into heavy concentrations of lime. Gypsum often occurs with lime accumulations in desert soils of the Southwestern United States and Mexico in variable amounts. In general, however, the carbonates greatly exceed the sulfates. The calcium that accumulates is believed to come from relic deposits, parent material and/or transient dust, as explained earlier. Parent material *in situ* alone does not explain the large lime deposits often observed in calcic or gypsic soils.

2. Camborthids

Camborthids are Aridisols that have a changed or altered horizon (cambic horizon) or are young Aridisols that have received little carbonates. They have no duripan, salic, calcic, gypsic, or petrocalcic horizon that has its upper boundary within 1 meter of the surface. More recent soil-forming processes have altered the material such that structure may be observed if textures are suitable. Silica clays form with the loss of free iron oxides. The peds lack distinct coatings and, like argillic layers, have randomly oriented particles and little pore space in the matrix.

3. Durorthids

Durorthids are Orthids that have a duripan whose upper boundary is within 1 meter of the surface and are with or without a cambic horizon. They have no petrocalcic horizon whose upper boundary is within 1 meter of the surface. Like the Durargids they are relatively high in glass. The duripans are cemented with silica and usually contain some lime. With increasing depth, duripans often grade into petrocalcic horizons.

The Durorthids occur most frequently on fans or river terraces under sparse desert vegetation. All appear to have had volcanic ash or glass present at one time. There is evidence that the horizon has been influenced by a high water table at one time or another. Some are salty.

4. Salorthids

The Salorthids are the Orthids that have a salic (salty) horizon within 75 cm of the surface, or within 1 meter of the surface for 1 month or more if saturated with water. They have no calcic, gypsic horizon above the salic horizon or duripan within 1 meter of the surface. Salorthids may be known better as Solonchaks. Dry soils are encrusted with white salt in a thin or thick layer. The salts have come to the surface by capillary rise as well as deposit. Vegetation is sparse and salt tolerant. These soils occur most frequently in playas (intermittent lakes) but can be found on terraces, fans, and deltas.

5. Paleorthids

Paleorthids are Orthids with a petrocalcic horizon that has its upper boundary within 1 meter of the soil surface. They have no duripan within this limit nor do they have a salic horizon within 75 cm of the surface if saturated with water within 1 meter of the surface for 1 month or more.

V. Physical Desert Surfaces

A. Clay

Desert soils may, characteristically, have an argillic or clayey horizon formed or synthesized during one or more of the glacial periods when the climate was more humid. The silicate clays may have developed to a significant extent. During more recent times of drier climate, petrocalcic horizons and duripans may have formed and, in some instances, obscured the clayey characteristics.

The clay content of many desert Bt horizons is higher than in other horizons of the soil profile. In zonal desertic soils, the ratio of the clay in the B3 horizon to that in the A horizon ranges from 1.2 to 2.0 (Western Regional Soil Survey Work Group, 1964). Weathering processes in sierozems of Central Asia, for example, are suggested (Rozanov, 1951) as being sufficiently active to cause the accumulation of clay. In Arizona, Yesilsoy

(1962) reports a higher clay content in the Bt horizon of an old alluvial soil, than in the parent material or A horizon. This young soil profile developed in a well-drained valley from parent material composed of granite, rhyolite, and some gneiss, under arid climate, high temperatures, and sparse vegetation. The clay was formed *in situ*. Clays form more slowly in arid soils than in humid or wet soils.

Clay may be found deposited in depressed areas on valley floors, in playas, and bolsons ranging in thickness up to many meters (see Fig. 4). These clay depressions may be relics of accumulations under sea or lake conditions during more humid climates or alluvial "end" collections from flash floods. As the climate became more arid, the water evaporated, leaving basin soils of finely divided colloidal material. Because of slow permeability, water continued to collect in these enclosed drainage basins and evaporate into the air, leaving behind both clay and salts. Natric (sodium) and salic (salty) soils (Solonetz, solodized-Solonetz, and Solonchak) may develop under these conditions. The more soluble salt (sodium chloride) is located at the center where evaporation takes place last. Sulfates most often surround the chlorides and carbonates surround the sulfates where they have precipitated underneath the chlorides and sulfates.

Clay plains appear to have their origin as a result of lacustrine deposi-

Fig. 4. A flat clay basin, very slowly pervious to water (Willcox Playa, Arizona, U.S.A.). Ray Manley Photo.

tion. They are found extensively in Chad, Mauritania, Mali, Niger, and Sudan (Dieleman and de Ridder, 1964) as deep, clayey material, weakly developed on level topography. Where the clay is unusually fine and permeability is impaired, saline soils develop.

Alluvial deposits that form river valleys account for a large total area of desert soils (Denny, 1967). Sand, silt, and clay conspicuously stratify in horizontal directions as layers of graded particle sizes. Thin layers of clay, for example, will overlie silt which is over sand and finally gravel or coarse sand, just as one might find in miniature in a mud puddle in a rutty road. Particulate separations may occur in valley soils depending on the intensity of the water flows that deposited the material (see Fig. 5). Such stratifications lower water infiltration rate and often accumulate salts in the fine-textured layers.

B. SAND

1. Characteristics

To most people, the desert is sand and sun, and indeed these are most characteristic of some desert areas such as that depicted in Fig. 6. Although sand is a common property of deserts, the sand of wasteland, of shifting, moving "vagabond" dunes as seen in movies, is not as common in all deserts as in some, such as the Sahara. Other surfaces, just as spectacular, and productive soils with profile development inhabit large desert areas. Moving sands are not classified as soils unless they support vegeta-

Fig. 5. Eroded alluvial plains showing stratified materials.

Fig. 6. Sand dunes pictured along the west bank of the Colorado River (near Yuma, Arizona, U.S.A.). Manley Photo.

Fig. 7. Creeping sand dunes in Canyon de Chelly, Arizona, U.S.A. Manley Photo.

tion. If they have vegetation, even though only an ephemeral covering, they are classed as *Psamments* (G. D. Smith, 1965). Sand dunes and drifts are discussed by H. T. U. Smith (1968) in Volume I of this series. Therefore no attempt will be made to cover dune characteristics, but rather to supplement Smith's discussion by pointing out how sands form into soils and relate to agriculture.

Alluvial desert valleys may be stratified with layers of sand, silt and clay as well as gravel and stones as shown in Fig. 7. Sand as well as clay in horizontal layers and lenses play an important part in water-holding capacity, infiltration rate and root penetration. Surface sand can cause serious denuding of desert vegetation if it is blown across more stabilized soil surfaces. Economic damage to cultivated crops can occur by covering over of plants and shearing off young seedlings when it is blown through cultivated areas. Creeping sand dunes may bury well-developed soils and highly valuable cropland. Buried soil profiles are commonly found under deep sand overburdens. Wind control to reduce detrimental erosion of sand is a continuing subject of world study (Academia Sinica, Sand Control Team, 1962; Clements *et al.,* 1957; Food and Agriculture Organization, 1960; H. T. U. Smith, 1955; 1965; Yakubov, 1959; Kao Shang-tun, 1963).

2. Composition

Shifting sand can have a marked effect on soils even though it may only blow over the land and settle in a thin layer in a transitory fashion. Salts may be washed from the sand into the soil layers below as restless particles drop and again are moved across land by winds of varying velocities. The mineral composition of some North American sand dune material is reported to be primarily quartz, feldspar, and mica. Clay minerals and silt-sized quartz and mica make up clay-silt dunes. Gypsum dunes of sand-particle size are found in deserts (White Sands, New Mexico) as well as calcareous or lime dunes (Death Valley, California).

3. Vegetation Relationships

Certain desert plants (*Sporobolus airoides, Atriplex canescens,* and *Yucca elata*) appear to grow quite well in gypsum sand dunes where moisture is available. Dune sand and other sand surfaces either under native or irrigated vegetation, where recent erosion forces have been so active that morphological characteristics have not developed them into mature soils yet, are called *Regosols* or *Ergs*. These "squatter soils" occur on hummocky, duned, undulating, or rolling outwash plains, till plains, continental sediment plains, floodplains or aeolian deposits. When stabilized, sands can develop soil profile differentiations in a surprisingly short time under irrigated agriculture and urbanization.

C. GRAVEL, COBBLES, STONES

Gravel, cobbles, and *stones* appear on a variety of topographical positions such as stream outwash deposits, sediment plains, alluvial flood plains, volcanic plateaus, and alluvial fans and on consolidated upland such as foothills, denuded hills, lower mountains, steep upland, and residual upland mountains, most of which are highly dissected and subjected to erosion (see Fig. 8). Both arid and semiarid climates are represented in these topographical positions. Soil development is usually poor if at all, and the soils are immature and vegetation is sparse. These surfaces are characterized by pockets of unconnected soils and thin or shallow soils (see Fig. 9). They are predominantly Entisols occurring upon soil material of such recent age, or in areas where erosion and sedimentation are so active, that there has been little or no effect of climate and vegetation to produce morphologic character. None have a B horizon and the A horizon is usually thin.

Alluvial desert soils, as the name implies, appear on fans, low terraces and floodplains. The C horizon, parent material, is stratified alluvium, which often is stony or gravelly.

Lithosols occur on eroded and abraded ridges, hills, and plateaus as very thin soils with no B horizon. A weak horizon of lime enrichment may appear at or near the rock surface. These soils may be stony and rocky

Fig. 8. Rockland of the foot slopes above the desert floor. Heavy erosion washed away the finer particles of soil and alluvium material leaving exposed rock.

throughout. The A horizon may be absent due to erosion. For a more complete discussion of rock surfaces and rockland the reader is referred to H. T. U. Smith (1968) in this series. Areas within the miscellaneous rockland type have enough rock outcrops, rock rubble, or stones and boulders without or within very shallow soil material to dominate. Areas having varying degrees of depth and soil development may occupy only 10–15% of the type. Rock land usually is quite barren of vegetation.

D. PAVEMENT

1. Nature

Desert pavements (Fig. 10) form from gravels, cobbles, and stones accumulated on dry land as a result of wind or water carrying away the finer particles of sand, silt and clay. The stony residue material usually varies in size from 0.5 to 20 cm. These materials generally are cemented together or encrusted with various salts, gypsum, lime, and silicate, and often coated with dehydrated ferric hydroxide and manganese oxides that give them a "desert varnish," lacquered or polished appearance. Uplifted and dissected surfaces as well as desert flats, alluvial fans, bajadas, and regions

Fig. 9. Shallow pockets of entisols with sparse vegetation may be found among the rock outcroppings. These soils are poorly developed, shallow. They also are called Lithosols because of their A–C horizon characteristics, thinness, and poor development on original parent material.

bordering through flowing streams (Clements *et al.*, 1957; Denny, 1967) may be paved with stony accumulations.

2. Development

Springer (1958) found evidence that desert pavements may develop as a result of upward displacement of stones and gravel under the effect of soil shrinking as well as by removal of fine material through wind and water erosion. Jessup (1962) also believes upward movement of stones in the stony tableland of Australia takes place. He suggests the mechanism of alternate wetting and drying. Desert pavements are reported as a component of plant surface of regs and hamadas in North Africa and Central Asia (Dapples, 1941; Karschon, 1953; Durand, 1953); of Gobi in China (Chao, 1962); gibber in Australia (Teakle, 1950); and stone and gravel in Iran (Dewan and Famouri, 1964). In fact, desert pavements are common to all deserts of the world.

3. Composition

Desert pavement is highly siliceous in certain areas of Central Australia. Stones are not only cemented together and coated with silicates but frag-

Fig. 10. Desert pavement of pebbles. Note the uniformity and flatness of the land.

ments of cracked silicates form a part of the desert macropaving (Crocker, 1946). It is believed that this pavement is an erosion—exposed siliceous B horizon. The desert "varnish" is very glossy and smooth because of the glass. Arid zone soils of South Africa have desert pavements composed of a wide variety of stones from black igneous origin to white quartz (van der Merwe, 1954). Lime nodules form a carbonate pavement in the Caucasus (Kulik, 1959) and are observed on certain soils in Arizona in limited spots.

4. Distribution

In Sierozems of Central Asia's Turkestan desert, fairly large areas of pebble–gravel conglomerates are found on the wider depression (Rozanov, 1951). The hilly piedmont (proluvial) plains accumulate stony–pebbly sediments and loess which are either compact cemented masses (such as desert pavement) or consist of quaternary conglomerates with stratigraphically disturbed bedding. Flat summits of most of the Kyzyl Kum residual mountain formation are framed with narrow tracts of steeply sloping piedmont plains covered with stony–pebbly deposits. Stony and gravelly surfaces (dashts) are a characteristic of the Afghanistan deserts.

E. PIPINGS

Piping is mentioned here because it can become a serious economic problem when man settles on the land and accelerates gully formations in virgin or undisturbed soil. Piping is a "tunneling erosion" where the subsoil erodes out from under the surface (Fletcher and Carroll, 1948).

1. Types

In Arizona, some buildings and highways have been threatened with almost uncontrollable loss of foundations. Fletcher and Carroll (1948) report three main types of piping: (1) lateral flow of soil along a more stable subsoil into an open stream bank, (2) flow along cracks of surface water, and (3) flow taking place when dispersed surface soil is washed into pore spaces of coarse, poorly graded, upper subsoil. All cause sinking and caving of the soil in a "tubular" or "pipe-like" depression. Fletcher *et al.* (1954) describe five conditions necessary to initiate piping: (1) there must be a source of water, (2) the surface infiltration rate must exceed the permeability rate at some subsurface layer, (3) there must be an erodable layer immediately above the retarding layer, (4) the water above the retarding layer must be under a hydraulic gradient, and (5) there must be an outlet for the lateral flow. Piping is a serious problem to agricultural loess soils in Central Asia (Glukhov, 1956), in the Niger Valley of Mali, and parts of the Chad-Logone Valley. Saline and sodic soils in Australia (Downes, 1956), are frequently eroded by piping. Alluvium where differential particle-size distribution has taken place and where the subsoils are highly dispersed by soluble salts and exchangeable sodium are most susceptible to "piping erosion." Earth shrinking and cracking may initiate conditions for piping formations.

2. Methods of Controlling

Control of piping in building areas may be accomplished by deep plowing, ripping, or chiseling to mix the soil as much as possible to obtain a uniform texture and packing before construction gets underway. One of the suggested methods of control in agricultural land is to wet the soils thoroughly to compact them before cropping. Another is to obtain uniform soil mixing by use of deep farm tillage equipment.

F. SOIL STRUCTURE

Desert surfaces, as indicated in the earlier discussions, develop a wide variety of structures as shown Fig. 11. Desert soil surfaces are normally soft when dry. They may have a thin, platy structure which overlays a vesicular structure (Jackson, 1957; Lapham, 1932). The platy surface

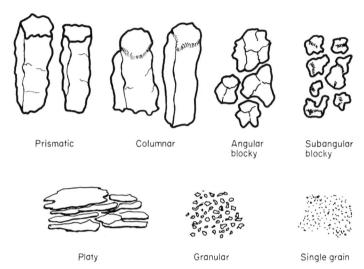

Prismatic   Columnar   Angular   Subangular
                                     blocky   blocky

Platy   Granular   Single grain

Fig. 11. Soil structures. Soil structure controls soil–water behavior, runoff, and soil moisture holding capacity.

forms from the beating of raindrops, whereas the vesicular structure forms as air escapes during wetting and drying. Soil crusts form on irrigated land in the arid climate of Southwestern United States after a rain. Crusts may become so hard upon drying that seeds, such as lettuce, carrots, tomato, alfalfa, and even cantaloupe, cannot emerge, requiring the land to be re-seeded. Carbonates are primarily responsible for the cementation.

Neither sand nor dust blown onto desert surfaces by winds remain long. Despite the cementing and aggregating action of carbonates and silica, most soil surfaces are readily eroded by wind action. Loose, fine particles may be blown away leaving gravel, pebbles, stones, and rock surfaces exposed as well as compact subsurfaces such as clay pans, duripans, and lime and gypsum layers. Salt accumulation and sodium dispersion tend to give surface soils a powdery, loose structure, except where they are in high excess and heavy crusting takes place.

Aggregation of arid soils of Israel has been studied in detail (Ravikovitch and Hagin, 1957) with the result that now there is good evidence of real differences in the intensity of aggregation and stability of aggregates in desert soils. Although loess and sand provide poor structures and exhibit poor aggregation, a high degree of aggregation appears with terra rossa and rendzina soils. Terra rossa colluvium, alluvial soils of Mediterranean red-earth origin, and gray calcareous soil, though not as strongly aggregated as the terra rossa and rendzina, still are well aggregated. Soil organic matter favors aggregation as does a high amount of lime (50–60%).

Removal of vegetation and farming to row—or grain—crops, results in a deterioration of aggregation and stable structure. Accumulation of sodium in cultivated soils as a result of irrigating with low-quality (sodic) water disperses soil and contributes to a less stable structure. The transitory nature of desert soil aggregation is readily demonstrated by saturating soil with water. Equipment and even animals have been known to sink to serious depths on flooded land.

G. Soil Temperature

Temperature is an important factor in the control of soil formation as well as the control of the biology of the desert. The rate of chemical reactions, for example, is known to increase about twofold for every 10°C rise in temperature. Within limits, biological activity in soils also is influenced by temperature in about the same magnitude. Physical changes of expansion, differential expansion and contraction, are controlled by temperature. The effect of temperature is seriously modified, however, by desiccation. In this respect desiccation under high temperatures and low rainfall has a similar effect on the soil-forming processes as does freezing. Thermal effects on soils are dependent upon the mineral composition, dry density, as well as moisture content (de Vries, 1958).

Diurnal air temperatures generally are greater in arid than in humid areas. Heat stored in the soil during the daytime, though, is lost to the atmosphere at night more rapidly in arid than in humid areas. Convection accounts for as much as half of the transfer from soil to air at night in Arizona (Guild, 1950). In California when the air temperature was 47°C at a level of 60 cm above the soil, the soil temperature was 62°C at 2.5 cm, 42°C at 7.5 cm, and 29°C at 60 cm below the surface (Smith, 1929). At an air temperature of 48°C, the range in soil temperature during this same year was 63°C at the 2.5 cm depth and 17°C at 80 cm. Variations of this magnitude are not unusual in other desert soils at other locations around the world. Soils have a great insulating effect against temperature changes.

VI. Accumulations in Desert Soils

A. Carbonates

1. Characteristics

Lime, calcium carbonate, is characteristically found in desert soils. It may be dispersed throughout the soil depth in powder dimension, in soft or hard nodules, in veinings along root or worm channels, or tongues, and in layers. Lime also is found coating soil particles, gravel, stones, and roots. Lime tends to accumulate in a layer in the soil at a place near or at the mean depth of moisture penetration. These carbonate layers vary considerably in concentration, depth, compaction, and density. In zonal and some intrazonal soils the carbonate-enriched layer generally develops at the bottom of the illuvial horizon from parent material. Lime also may accumulate as a result of the leaching of transient dust that blows onto the soil and is caught in a rainstorm. Some of the carbonates and more soluble salts are carried down into the soil and the dust moves on. This explains, in part at least, the observation that lime may be found in Aridisols even where the parent material is very low in calcium (Gile et al., 1966).

2. Origin

The origin of massive, thick lime or caliche and its genesis have been a matter of considerable speculation because of its varied nature even within short distances on the same terrain (Breazeale and Smith, 1930; Gile et al., 1966). Fossils of humid climates, lake beds, and solution cavities in thick, limy layers suggest that desert soil has not always been dry and that more than one pedogenic process has been involved. Massive, thick carbonate layers could form by means of deposition in bodies of water or translocation from the upper to the lower part of the profile. Some desert soils appear to have formed over lake bottom accumulations of lime. Others have formed over carbonate-rich layers not related to the present land surface. Yesilsoy (1962), for example, by using the carbon dating found that the age of deposit of the carbonate carbon increased considerably with depth in an old alluvium desert soil in Arizona. At about 1 meter the age of the $CaCO_3$ layer was found to be less than 2300 years before present, at 1.5 meter the age was about 9800 years, and at 2 meter over 32,000 years. It is believed that many of the present desert land surfaces appear to have been stable through one or more interglacial stages when the climate was dry. Soils on these surfaces may have had sufficient time to accumulate a thick lime layer. Evidences of solution cavities indicate alternate stages of wet and dry climates.

B. GYPSUM

1. Characteristics

Gypsum ($CaSO_4 \cdot 2H_2O$) accumulations are not uncommon in desert soils. They vary from salt-affected soils almost free of gypsum to large areas of gypsum sand dunes, such as those found near White Sands, New Mexico, the Great Salt Lake Desert, Utah, along the Pecos River, Texas, and as crusts in the Tunisia and other deserts. Deposition in confined desert valleys or playas may follow a definite order of solubility pattern. For example, in salt pans, chlorides are in the center of the pan or at the places on the surface where the ground water evaporates, sulfates surround the chloride accumulations and carbonates surround the sulfates and underlie them.

Gypsum, like any other salt, moves upward in solution by capillary action from gypsiferous deposits through unconsolidated materials and soils, evaporates, and accumulates as crystals on the soil surface. Gypsum may characteristically precipitate in root channels giving the soil the white-veined appearance seen in Fig. 12. Wind action drifts the gypsum sand crystals formed into dunes and the process continues, producing more crystals and more drifting gypsum sand. Marine sources of sand gypsum have been ruled out.

With certain slight changes in climate, gypsum may become covered with wind-deposited soil particles, forming a layer of loess. Soils formed

Fig. 12. Veinings of gypsum, deposited in soil root and worm channels. Commonly found under irrigated conditions where gypsum is a common salt constituent of the virgin soil.

this way may be quite productive, even when the loess deposit is as shallow as 15 cm. The maximum salinity of gypsum saturation water is about 30.5 mEq/liter at 24°C, well within the limit for growing many economic agricultural crops. A knowledge of the gypsum content of alkali soils (sodic) is important since gypsum is used as an inexpensive amendment to supply calcium for replacement of sodium in the improvement of the physical condition of soils.

Some gypsiferous soils have developed in sedimentary deposits containing gypsum. The Purgatory Series (Calciorthid) in the Southwest United States is such a soil. Gypsum is found throughout as crystals and as white patches on the surface. Although this is a productive agricultural soil, maximum productivity is not achieved, more because of the unusually high clay content in the B horizon than the gypsum.

2. Origin

The origin of gypsum accumulations in the eluvial horizon still is not settled, although many suggestions appear in the literature. According to Rozanov (1951), who has made an extensive study of the available data, gypsum formation depends on the sulfur content of the parent rock rather than on differences of hydrothermic regime in desert areas. Another widespread hypothesis assumes that gypsum is a relic and that it would have existed already in the parent rock, though in a diffuse form. During weathering processes, soils formed with gypsum stratified at certain depths, depending on the local conditions at the time of formation. Rozanov (1951) considers gypseous–eluvial accumulations resulting from primary calcium sulfate (parent rock), concentrated by weathering, to be merely a particular case. He suggests a general process consisting of gypsum formation by the oxidation of sulfurous compounds by sulfur bacteria.

The paucity of gypsum in the Gobi Desert is used to strengthen the suggestion that, gypsum accumulations in the weathering crust of deserts, are chiefly due to the petrographic composition of the weathered rock. The most abundant parent rocks in the Gobi and Eastern Betpak-Dala are igneous and metamorphic, which are notably poor in sulfur and sulfur compounds and thus are quite unable to give rise to appreciable accumulations of gypsum.

3. Distribution

It is further pointed out that gypsum accumulations and/or crusts are widespread in areas of the North African Desert, in the desert belt of Australia, and in the Egyptian Desert, where soils have developed over sulfur-containing material of sedimentary parent rock, limestone, and rocks of the Eocene age.

C. Silicates

1. Characteristics

Silica, that presumably has been solubilized by the alkaline reaction of desert soils, may be found associated with carbonates to form a cemented layer or with iron in alternating thin layers to form a duripan. Certain other desert duripans are cemented by an agent, suspected as being silica and/or aluminum silicate, that is soluble in concentrated alkali. Abu Fakhr (1961) describes a "gatch" hardpan in soils of Kuwait which is predominantly sand with a high carbonate content. The cementing agents are presumed to be, in order of concentration, silica, calcium, and magnesium carbonates, magnesium hydroxide, gypsum, alumina, and iron oxide. The last three are believed not to play as important a role in gatch pan formation as the other constituents but are mostly incidental inclusions. The saturation extract of gatch is higher in sodium than calcium, which is noted also by the pH of 8.5 and above.

2. Origin

Siliceous layers are found in some desert soils of the Kalahari Desert. These appear to be similar to those found in Australia where soils have developed on geologically old relics. Siliceous duripans (silcrete) are located below the indurated carbonate layer (calcrete) in Kalahari (Debenham, 1952).

Siliceous crusts have been described as appearing on soils of the Southern Sahara Desert. Silicates also have been claimed to be an important cementing agent of desert pavements. The stony Australian deserts are covered with broken silcrete which is described by Jackson (1957) as having a hard, intense varnish. The stony tablelands of Australia as well as North Africa and Southwest Asia are noted for their flat-topped mounds capped with silcrete. These tableland soils are usually calcareous, gypsiferous, or saline at some depth, as a probable result of earlier salt accumulations between the silcrete mounds.

3. Distribution

Chemical analyses of world desert materials indicate the widespread occurrence of precipitated silica in indurated "caliche" layers. The chemistry of weathering and soil formation of desert materials and accumulations of carbonate and sulfate under semiarid and arid alkaline conditions will allow for solubilization and precipitation of silica. The precipitation of silica or silicates in indurated lime layers under desert conditions may be responsible for imparting the hardness and impenetrable nature to these horizons. In places in North American deserts carbonate pans contain significant quantities of siliceous cements (Western Regional Soil Survey Work Group, 1964). Evaluation of data by Stuart *et al.* (1961) appears to support this hypothesis. They found the content of acid-extractable silica (SiO_2^{2-}) in the gray desert soils of northwestern United States (Idaho) to be highest in the hardest part of the indurated caliche layers.

D. IRON

1. Characteristics

Dark red, brown, and black stains ("desert varnish"), coating gravel, pebbles, and stones of desert pavements have been attributed to the presence of iron and manganese oxides. The most generally accepted hypothesis is that, under certain arid and semiarid climatic conditions, "desert varnish" results from alternate wetting and drying at relatively high temperatures. Biological conditions, such as the presence of iron oxidizing microorganisms and/or algae, may have played an important part in the formation of desert varnishes also. Certainly the common occurrence of algae living under the harsh desert conditions is well established (Fuller *et al.*, 1961). Their ability to survive long periods of desiccation and quickly recover and grow rapidly when it rains, as well as the ability of some to concentrate iron, makes them prime suspects as a factor in iron coatings of rocks.

2. Origin

The presence of duripans in deserts containing iron oxides are believed to be relics or partial relics formed under more humid conditions or under peculiar circumstances of a high, fluctuating water table. Thin, dehydrated, iron hydroxide stainings and layers have been observed capping indurated caliche in the Mohave Desert of the United States. These appear to have formed during periods of transitory perched water tables.

Desert soils of the U.S.S.R. exhibit little if any redistribution of sesquioxides (or iron oxides) in the profile (Shuvalov, 1949). In fact, Takyr-like desert soils (extremely arid) show little if any chemical differentiation. On the other hand, Lobova (1960) provides evidence that ferrugination occurs in desert soils subjected to periodic wetting. Intense heating dehydrates the iron hydroxides to red hematite or yellow-brown limonite. The yellow and red color of desert sands is due to the presence of these anhydrous forms of iron hydroxides. Iron comes from minerals that, under desert conditions, weather at a relatively rapid rate to form free hydroxides.

Iron leaves the crystal lattice of silicates readily under high-temperature conditions during the short periods of wetting. Dehydrated iron hydroxide formed upon drying at elevated temperatures appears as films or touches enveloping the soil minerals and sand as well as isolated scales on minerals. The amount of ferrugination depends on the iron content of the mineral from which the soils develop. Within a given area or zone the ferruginous coloration is more distinct in sandy or coarse-textured soils than in fine-textured soils.

3. Distribution

Rozanov (1951), who studied the chemical composition of desert soil colloids, found a high absolute as well as relative content of "free" Fe_2O_3. Iron oxides in the form of goethite were found in the colloidal fraction of a number of desert samples. X-ray lines for goethite appeared in upper as well as lower horizons of sierozem soils. Soils of arid Arizona also contain a higher absolute "free" Fe_2O_3 content than the parent materials from which they originated.

E. SOLUBLE SALTS

1. Characteristics

Aqueous extracts of desert soils generally contain more salt than extracts of soils of humid climates. Depressed alluvial soils are particularly abundant in soluble salts. Their presence as white powder or black crusts has been used to classify and identify the soils on which they lie. Highly soluble sodium and potassium salts also may be found buried and disguised beneath the soil surface in soils derived from saline shales and chloride-containing gypsiferous materials. Large gypsum mineral deposits are well distributed in arid lands, while salt beds of nitrate and borax are found particularly in extremely arid climates such as parts of the Atacama and Death Valley deserts. Desert basins, pans, and playas at one place or another, have supplied sodium chloride (salt) for human and farm animal consumption. Salt springs bring briny waters from ground waters to the surface where they either evaporate and salt accumulates or they join and pollute the more potable surface streams and rivers.

Lack of adequate drainage has resulted in movement of salts upward by capillary action to the surfaces of certain soils with consequential deterioration of desert land. Irrigation has accentuated this damaging effect on land productivity. Soluble salts represent an economic problem when they are allowed to accumulate on the surface and within the root zone of plants.

2. Origin

Salts that accumulate in solid form in desert soils may come from several sources: (1) weathered products of parent material, (2) marine deposits such as saline shales, (3) atmospheric transport of sea salt, (4) rainwater salts from certain terrestrial sources (dust) brought into the atmosphere by wind action, (5) fossil salt (marine inundations) which are of more local importance, and (6) transient dust that deposits during calms, are leached by rain, and are blown away again. Not all of these sources are expected to be operative in every desert and no single set of conditions is operative to satisfy the nature and extent of accumulations in all soils.

3. Distribution

Certain saline and sodic soils contain sufficient accumulations of salts to place them in special intrazonal great soil groups of the *Solonchak* and *Solonetz*. The soluble salts that accumulate in these soils come from a variety of sources. Solonchak soils have been referred to as "white" alkali soils and Solonetz as "black" alkali soils. Solubilization of soil organic matter by sodium gives the salt crust of Solonetz a dark color, thus the name, "black" alkali.

In Central Asia, Rozanov (1951) describes a network of migrations to account for both the nature and extent of accumulations of salts in desert soils depending on geomorphological conditions. Solution–deposition–resolution–redeposition takes place for each salt depending on its solubility constant and the geomorphical condition. Thus carbonates may precipitate out first, followed by gypsum and other sulfates, followed by chlorides. In the United States the cation solubilities of calcium, magnesium, sodium, and potassium salts are stressed the same way the anions are stressed in the Russian system.

An example of salt-deposition pattern is a more vertical distribution given by Hunt (1960) for salt pans in Death Valley, California. Chlorides appear in the center of the pan at the place where ground water evaporates: sulfates surround the chlorides and form beneath them; carbonates surround the sulfates and form below them. Salt surfaces appear most commonly in depressions on valley floors and playas with bolsons. They present variable surfaces described as white powdery, black crusty, smooth films, flaky, and rough and jagged (Hunt, 1966). Unfortunately for the taxonomist, salt patterns are not always this simple. Relic salt depositions; the changing topography, climate, and distribution; the amount and the composition of rivers and streams flowing through; and the periodic flooding will alter any natural and simplified salt accumulation trend. Polynov (1935) considered the flat desert regions of the sierozem zone as a vast area of chloride and sulfate accumulations. The foothills and low mountains would constitute the general areas of carbonate and silicate concentration. Although this may be a general concept for broad desert flats, narrow desert valleys may appear as exceptions and may or may not collect salts depending on local conditions. Much of the Chilean Atacama Desert, for example, is entirely barren of plants (Cameron *et al.,* 1965). Salts have accumulated in many places as borax "lakes," saline "dry lakes," and nitrate deposits which have provided exports.

Parent materials markedly influence the salt relationships in the arid soils of Western United States. In general, the parent materials contain moderate to high levels of alkaline-earth carbonates and soluble salts. Salts accumulate in these soils in or below the horizons of maximum carbonate accumulation. Carbonates, however, are found well distributed throughout the soil profile. The Gobi Desert is an example of a desert devoid of gypsum but fairly high in lime. At the other end of the central Asian Desert, Turkestan Desert soils accumulate gypsum. The difference is claimed to be due to differences in sulfate composition of parent materials. The broad processes affecting salt in desert soils are weathering and the transportation and accumulation of weathered products.

VII. Desert Soils as a Medium for Plants

A. MOISTURE

Moisture is the single most limiting factor for plant growth in desert soils. Water the soil and "the desert shall blossom as the rose" has been predicted many times in history (Thorne, 1951). Because water in arid climates is so limiting, an unusual amount of attention has been focused on soil–water–plant relationships.

Desert soils differ from most other soils with respect to their ability to take up or infiltrate rainwater. Many desert soils are dry and hard. Some are crusted. These characteristics markedly reduce the water infiltration rate. The beating action of raindrops on barren or near barren soils compacts the surface, reducing porosity. Raindrop action also keeps the surface layer dispersed. No matter how thin the dispersed layer is, it acts as a barrier to water infiltration. Certain salts, especially those containing sodium, cause soils to disperse, resulting in a low rate of water penetration and movement in the profile. As a consequence of many such factors, much of the rain that falls on sloping desert land runs off into low places and collects in basins where evaporation further concentrates salts in an already salty soil.

Clearing of the land of vegetation accelerates water runoff, reduces the

effectiveness of precipitation and contributes further to aridity and unde-
sirable salt collection in depressions. Overgrazing has an added deterioration effect on desert soils, since animal hooves break up desert pavement
that absorbs the fall of raindrops and destroys its protection against runoff
and compaction.

High evaporation and transpiration losses of moisture from arid soils
further reduce effectiveness of soil moisture. On the other hand, dry sand
has a low coefficient of conductivity and upward movement is slow. In
general, a greater loss of moisture occurs from salty than nonsalty soils.

B. Nitrogen

Of the required plant nutrients, nitrogen is the most limiting for maximum growth in desert soils. Nitrogen is particularly needed to maximize
crop plants when desert soils are irrigated (Fuller and Ray, 1965). Arid
and semiarid lands are characterized by low levels of organic matter and
consequently low nitrogen reserves since the soil organic matter is the
nitrogen carrier.

Nitrogen has been shown to increase the growth of native vegetation
in Arizona range soils (Stroehlein et al., 1968) under natural rainfall conditions. The effectiveness of nitrogen depends on the amount and distribution of rain at the time soil temperatures are most favorable for plant
growth. In an extension of this study the effect of nitrogen on desert grass
carried over for at least 2 years. Because of the sparse rainfall, downward
leaching of nitrogen is at a minimum compared with that of humid regions.
Arid grassland also produced higher yields and better quality forage in
California (Martin et al., 1957) when supplied nitrogen. The basic concepts of nitrogen reactions in calcareous soils under irrigated agriculture
are not the same as those for soils in humid climates (Fuller, 1963; Fuller
et al., 1950a,b).

Nitrogen relationships in desert soils, undisturbed by man, depend upon
a balance between gaseous loss of nitrogen due to chemical and bacterial
denitrification and N fixation by desert legumes, autotrophic algae, and
free-living soil bacteria. Some small quantities of nitrogen are added to
the soil through the sparse rainfall in deserts. The literature on quantitative
N fixation and loss in virgin desert soils is lacking.

C. Phosphorus

There is little indication that phosphorus is a limiting plant nutrient for
native vegetation in desert soils. On the other hand, certain crops grown
in desert soils under intensive irrigation agriculture are known to respond
to phosphorus (Fuller, 1953). Legumes, generally, have shown the greatest response. There is a remarkably high proportion of legumes present

in the deserts of North and South America (personal observations). Inorganic phosphorus moves downward in desert soils only very slowly but has been shown to move in organic form (Hannapel *et al.*, 1964). Organic phosphorus represents a significant proportion of total phosphorus of native desert soils even though organic matter is low (Fuller and McGeorge, 1950b) (see diagrams in Fig. 13).

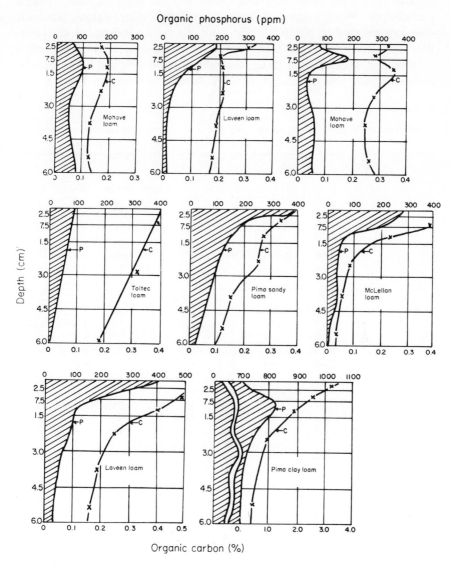

Fig. 13. Relationship between the soil organic phosphorus and organic carbon in some desert soils of the Southwest United States.

Phosphorus of desert soils in Arizona are primarily calcium phosphates which have a low degree of availability to plants (Fuller and McGeorge, 1950a). However compared with the predominantly aluminum and ferric phosphates in acid soils of humid regions, they are somewhat more available to plants. Desert soils contain an adequate supply of native phosphorus to produce crops for many centuries under present cropping systems, yet some soils show crop-yield response to phosphate fertilizer applications. Native vegetation under normal rainfall conditions, however, does not respond to phosphate additions. To better understand the phosphates in calcareous soils a study was undertaken on virgin soil profiles (Fuller and McGeorge, 1950c). The distribution of phosphorus in nine Arizona desert soils to a depth of the C horizon is shown in Table I.

TABLE I

RELATIONSHIP BETWEEN CARBON AND INORGANIC AND ORGANIC PHOSPHORUS AT VARIOUS DEPTHS IN SOME CALCAREOUS ARIZONA SOILS

Soil type	Soil depth (cm)	Total phosphorus (ppm)	Extractable phosphorus (ppm)	Organic P to total P (%)	Organic P to extractable P (%)	Ratio organic C to organic P	CO$_2$ Soluble organic P (ppm)	Total CO$_2$ soluble P (ppm)
Mohave loam	0–5	320	264	20	24	21	0.1	1.0
	5–15	450	400	22	25	19	0.4	1.0
	15–30	210	170	14	19	57	0.3	0.5
	30–45	270	228	13	16	42	0.3	0.6
	45–60	390	300	10	12	34	0.2	0.5
McClellan loam	0–3	1580	1208	34	45	76	1.0	6.0
	3–7	1100	980	37	42	41	1.1	5.5
	7–15	1020	890	31	36	29	0.9	2.2
	15–30	800	616	25	31	18	0.4	1.0
	30–45	680	520	9	11	15	0.6	1.0
	45–60	700	500	3	5	9	0.5	0.5
Laveen loam	0–3	890	704	29	37	17	0.3	3.3
	3–7	750	614	30	36	12	0.4	3.3
	7–15	560	440	16	21	24	0.3	1.1
	15–30	460	440	5	6	95	0.4	1.1
	30–45	420	380	4	4	118	0.4	0.8
	60–75	400	372	4	6	113	0.3	0.4

TABLE I (*Continued*)

Soil type	Soil depth (cm)	Total phosphorus (ppm)	Extractable phosphorus (ppm)	Organic P to total P (%)	Organic P to extractable P (%)	Ratio organic C to organic P	CO_2 Soluble organic P (ppm)	Total CO_2 soluble P (ppm)
Pima sandy	0–3	1183	1068	28	31	22	0.3	4.9
loam	3–7	1050	924	18	20	34	0.3	3.3
	7–15	822	780	18	19	38	0.1	2.4
	15–30	806	760	15	16	41	0	1.3
	30–45	800	736	11	11	36	0.2	0.9
	45–60	714	696	3	3	120	0.2	0.7
Pima clay	0–3	1720	1500	42	48	45	3.3	19.5
loam	3–7	1562	1408	52	57	31	3.0	23.1
	7–15	1611	1512	50	54	24	2.5	19.2
	15–30	1232	1165	60	64	12	0.3	3.7
	30–45	1125	1060	62	66	6	0.4	2.0
Sunrise loam	3–7	1320	1312	19	18	45	1.8	3.5
	7–15	1210	1160	8	8	85	0.8	1.3
	15–30	1010	944	6	6	84	0.2	0.5
	30–45	910	924	5	5	83	0	0.2
	45–60	600	568	8	9	70	0	Trace
Tolleson clay	0–3	790	668	40	47	65	0.4	0.6
loam	3–7	1100	1040	52	55	39	0.5	1.7
	7–15	900	832	43	47	35	0.1	1.2
	15–30	1100	1040	40	42	31	0.3	1.4
	30–45	1450	1412	29	30	37	0.3	1.1
	45–60	1370	1156	26	31	32	0.4	2.6
Tucson loam	0–2	480	334	19	27	34	1.7	3.3
	2–7	495	452	36	40	13	2.7	4.5
	7–15	300	244	15	13	67	0.5	1.6
	15–30	300	238	13	13	71	0.1	0.6
	30–45	310	236	18	24	43	0.4	0.7
	45–60	290	228	17	23	52	0.2	0.8
	60–75	270	192	18	27	52	0.1	0.5
Toltec loam	0–15	580	518	13	13	54	0.3	3.0
	15–41	510	416	13	16	54	0.4	2.8
	41–90	320	324	0	0	0	0	3.0

There appears to be a rather close relationship between phosphorus available to plants, as evaluated by the CO_2–H_2O extraction method, and "active" calcium in a single soil at different depths. "Available" P tended to decrease with depth. The finding that there was no correlation between "active" calcium and CO_2–H_2O extractable P for the same depth among different soils emphasizes that different soils possess inherently different characteristics, making it improbable that a single threshold value for calcium for all soils below which there will be sufficient P for maximum plant growth under irrigation can be established readily. The inorganic P content of calcareous soils, for example, has been shown to decrease in solubility in the presence of neutral salts as a result of the increasing soluble calcium (Olsen et al., 1961).

Organic P content of desert soils in Arizona is shown to decrease with an increase in soil depth (see Table I). Very little organic P is found below the root zone of plants.

The organic C to organic P ratio for the virgin desert soils is, for the most part, below that reported for soils of humid regions (Pearson and Simonson, 1940). Possibly the organic P is associated with a more highly decomposed organic residue in desert soils.

D. Potassium

Potassium is rarely deficient for plant growth in desert soils. Potassium is found abundantly in micaceous minerals. Desert soils of North and South American deserts contain micaceous minerals generally in good supply and seldom require additions of potassium (Fuller and Ray, 1965). Only total analyses figures for K in other world desert soils are readily available. Such data indicate that desert soils usually are well supplied with plant nutrients except nitrogen (Rozanov, 1951). Only in certain limited areas of Australia is K found to be deficient for cultivated crops (Stephens and Donald, 1958) and these do not include the extremely arid desert regions. They state, however, "that the marginal potassium status of great areas of Australian soils makes the increased use of potassium fertilizers inevitable." The literature on plant-available K in world deserts virtually is nonexistent.

E. Micronutrients

Of all the necessary trace or microelements for plant growth, iron and zinc are found to be the least available in desert soils, although plants in large areas of the Australian desert respond to copper, and molybdenum is deficient to plants on salodic soils. Copper deficiencies are reported to be severe for crops of the Coonamble Downs Desert region (Riceman, 1953). Molydenum deficiency appears to be associated with P deficiency in Australian soils. Manganese deficiencies are found in varying degrees in calcareous aeolian sand, Terra Rossas, solidized-Solonetz, and calcareous gray soils. Rozanov (1951) reports that soils of Central Asia are sufficiently supplied with "microelements."

Iron and zinc deficiencies are reported for scattered areas in Washington, Oregon, California, Arizona, New Mexico, and other western states. Iron deficiencies were observed by the author in some desert soils of South America.

F. ORGANIC MATTER

Organic matter content and composition in soils has received considerable attention because of its disproportionately favorable effect on chemical, physical, microbiological, and morphological properties of soil as compared with the mineral matter. Moreover soil organic matter is the nitrogen carrier. The rather narrow range of C to N ratios indicates the direct relationship of N with organic matter and the almost complete dependency of N fertility in virgin soils on organic matter. Soil organic matter consists of partially rotted residues of the plants that occupied the land and materials formed by soil organisms. Soil organic matter is not derived wholly from plants. Soil organisms make a substantial if not dominant contribution.

The accumulation of humus is low in desert soils compared with those of other climates, but the plant-ash residues, mainly carbonates, are higher. The organic matter of desert U.S.S.R. soils, for example, are reported (Ponomareva, 1956) to be intensely mineralized. She emphasizes the importance of the soil biology and humus on desert soil formation as exemplified by her statement: "The mineral forms of biogenic carbon and generally plant ash compounds shape the profile and properties of desert soils" (Ponomareva, 1956, p. 34).

The content of total humus in gray-brown desert soils of Central Asia ranges from 0.3 to 0.8% and seldom exceeds 1.0% (Lobova, 1960), whereas the total nitrogen varies from 0.03 to 0.3%. The Gray-brown desert soils have a low C to N ratio, 3–5, indicating extensive decomposition. Fulvic acids are proportionately higher, being two or three times as abundant in these highly mineralized soils as in other soils. Waxes and resins ("bitumens") are also proportionately high among arid soils. Desert plants, the source of organic residues, are abundantly supplied with waxes, resins, and essential oils. In the drier desert soils, the humus content is small and is distributed fairly uniformly throughout the soil profile

(Shuvalov, 1966). This is due to the roots of the shrublike desert plants not spreading out in the upper horizons which dry out rapidly but growing more uniformly deep.

The brown Sierozem soils have more organic matter than the Gray-browns and a C to N ratio in the order of 6–9.5 (Rozanov, 1951). Red desert soils of Arizona rarely accumulate more than 1.0% organic matter except in the thin surface (0–2.5-cm layer) near established vegetation. Winds redistribute fallen leaves, scale and plant parts which collect around stationary objects.

The conclusion (Rozanov, 1951) reached with respect to the quantitative nature of central Asian desert soils is that the relatively very low humus content is chiefly due to the activity of a highly biogenic soil process, and not, as previously supposed, to a low amount of vegetative remains entering the soil. In a virgin Sierozem of Central Asia the total reserve of root residues were found to be 2.13 kg/m^2 and the humus 4.9 kg/m^2. Most of the roots were concentrated in the 0–7-cm layer (Kononova, 1961). The amount of plant growth above the ground, and of root substance in certain desert soils are compared with the more humid soils (Rozanov, 1951) in Table II.

In the B horizon of desert soil profiles, iron-containing minerals may yield iron to soil-forming processes. The fixation of Fe_2O_3 and FeO *in situ* by repeated wetting and drying and microbial activity into molecules of soil organic acids is reported by Ponomareva (1956).

The presence of a significant amount of organic phosphorus compounds in desert soils has been established (Fuller and McGeorge, 1950b) (see Fig. 13). The organic ratio of P to C is lower in desert soils than in most soils of the humid climates.

TABLE II

A Comparison of the Plant Material above and Below Ground Level among Five Desert Soils and Four More Humid Soils of Central Asia[a]

Soil	Plant tops	Plant roots	Soil	Plant tops	Plant roots
	(metric tons/ha)			(metric tons/ha)	
Sandy sierozem	0.5	10.0	Light chestnut	0.8–1.5	—
Light-gray sierozem	1.0	15.0	Dark chestnut	5.2	13.2
Light-gray sierozem	0.5–1.5	21.4	Southern chernozem	7.0	25.0
Ordinary sierozem	2.1–4.5	—	Carbonate chernozem	—	25.8
Dark sierozem	4.5	30.0			

[a] Data obtained from Rozanov, 1951, Table 91, p. 342.

The mineral nitrogen in desert soils is almost exclusively in the form of nitrates. The amounts are low, however, and vary from season to season and with rainfall patterns. Very slowly hydrolizable or stable organic nitrogen compounds account for nearly 30% of total nitrogen in central Asian sierozem soils (Rozanov, 1951). About 55% of humus substances containing nitrogen are rather easily hydrolizable, whereas in the more humid northern prairie soils the amount of this form is much less.

The physicochemical properties of Sierozems do not favor the fixation of humus in the desert soils of the U.S.S.R. (Kononova, 1961). The rapid cycle of the formation–decomposition microbial process, in the short periods when soil moisture is available, accounts for the formation of substances of the fulvic acid type. The very rapid rate of decomposition of plant residues in desert soils of Arizona is also reported (Fuller, 1965) with C to N ratios ranging from 8–10 in the upper few centimeters as compared with ratios of 10–12 in the more humid soils of the Midwest Prairies.

G. SALT

1. Salt Accumulations

As a result of a combination of circumstances peculiar to arid and semiarid lands, salts may collect in desert soils in sufficient concentration to adversely affect vegetative growth. In fact, areas may be found in all the major deserts of the world where the land is barren and even microbial life retarded. Such harsh areas are avoided for irrigation projects or require reclamation management practices to make them agriculturally productive. The most widely distributed problems are associated with soils having excessive soluble salts, high exchangeable sodium, or both. These soils are called saline (salic), alkali (sodic), and saline-alkali, respectively.

2. Salt–Plant Relationship

Salts in desert soils influence plant growth in many ways (Bernstein, 1962). Moisture stress as a result of an increase in the osmotic pressure of the soil solution by the presence of salt can reduce the uptake of water by the plant. Thus less water may be available to the plant if the soil solution is saline than if it is not. Moisture stresses can be observed in a field of alfalfa or cotton in salty spots, for example, in the middle of a hot summer day when the surrounding nonsaline soil areas show no wilting. Vegetation in virgin soils may be seen to drop its leaves earlier in saline than nonsaline soils. Germinating seeds are sensitive to salinity and alkalinity of the soil solution. With certain plants this is the most critical or sensitive stage of their growth cycle and many kinds of plants are excluded from desert environments because of this.

3. Specific Effects of Salt

The distribution and concentration of native desert vegetation is markedly influenced by the kind and nature of the salts in soils. Chlorides in soils may be sufficiently high to accumulate in leaves and cause yellowing, tip and marginal burn, and finally leaf shedding. Certain plants will accumulate sodium in their leaves, whereas others will not. Sodium also may disperse the soil sufficiently to lower oxygen tension and reduce water uptake, particularly if the soils are fine textured (McGeorge and Breazeale, 1938; Hayward and Wadleigh, 1949; Richards, 1950). Salt and sodium in French Somaliland soils adversely affect vegetable crop production (Tkatchenko, 1951). The principal reasons are attributed to (1) deficient organic matter, (2) nonavailability of nutrients, (3) poor physical condition of the soil, (3) inadequate quantity of irrigation water, and (4) high osmotic pressure in the soil solution. In the Negev in Israel four kinds of native plants are classified according to their salt tolerance: (1) chloride-absorbing xerohalophytes having high osmotic potentials, (2) chloride-absorbing hydrohalophytes also having high osmotic potentials, (3) xerohalophytes absorbing salts other than chlorides having medium osmotic potentials, and (4) nonhalophytic xerophytes having low osmotic potentials (Tadmor et al., 1962). The chloride and sulfate content of native plants has been shown to be correlated with the chloride and sulfate content of the soil on which they grow (Akzhigitova, 1959). Excess lime in soils has been found to induce iron deficiency called, "iron-induced" chlorosis (McGeorge, 1949; Thorne, 1951; Thorne and Peterson, 1950) in soils of Western United States. The bicarbonate ion also produces a symptom in plants similar to "lime-induced" chlorosis (Wadleigh and Brown, 1952).

4. Salt-Injury Symptoms

In a review of vegetation of desert regions in the sierozem zone of Central Asia, Rozanov (1951) discusses the close relationships he observed between specific plant species and their presence on specific desert soil types. The occurrence of a specific plant species or dominance of certain colonies of species on a given desert soil type is related primarily to the moisture relationships in the root zone and the quantity and quality of soluble salts. The cation elements, usually in excess in desert soils are sodium, potassium, magnesium, and calcium, and the anions, Cl^-, SO_4^{2-} and HCO_3^-. Borates, nitrates, lithium, and selenium excesses have been reported also but are not as common. Bernstein (1964b) suggests that salt injury can be classified under three headings: (1) general osmotic effect in water competition not related to a specific ion, (2) specific ion effect on inhibition of nutrition, and (3) toxic effect, causing injury symptoms due to excess ion accumulation in the plant. Desert plants vary considerably in their reactions or susceptibility to the salt effects listed. Toxic effect of specific ions in excess in desert soils is an extensive topic all its own and cannot be discussed intelligently in the limited space here. The reader is referred to Bernstein (1962; 1964a,b), Hayward and Bernstein (1958), Bernstein and Hayward (1958), and others referenced earlier. Suffice it to point out that toxic concentrations of salts do appear in desert soils more commonly than in humid soils and these excesses influence the distribution and density of desert vegetation in one way or another.

H. Radioactive Debris

World-wide sampling of soil to evaluate radioactive fallout from nuclear testing activities has been underway since 1956 in an organized study that led to accurate quantitative data (Alexander, 1959). Concentration of fallout, ^{90}Sr, in soils was found to be directly related to precipitation (Meyer et al., 1968). This verifies the long recognition that precipitation scavenges tropospheric nuclear debris. Desert soils, therefore, are expected to have the least ^{90}Sr deposition, all other factors being equal. This is what generally is found (Meyer et al., 1968). For example, the lowest ^{90}Sr fallout on the continental United States has occurred in the arid Southwest (20–30 mCi/km^2).

VIII. Desert Soils and Microorganisms

A. Microbial Populations

1. Nature

The microbial population in desert soils may vary more widely than in any other climatic zone. Some harsh, barren deserts, such as the Atacama Desert of Chile, have low populations of microorganisms, particularly the more common grouping (Cameron et al., 1965). The low numbers are associated with the extremely low and irregular rainfall and absence of higher plant life. The microbial population in loose desert sands of the Sahara (Killian, 1940; Killian and Fehér, 1936) are minimal compared with most deserts. Cameron claims organisms can have little or no influence on the soil-forming process in extremely arid deserts, therefore little soil profile development may be observed.

2. Numbers

The numbers of microorganisms in desert soils appear to be closely associated with the abundance of carbonaceous food material available for degradation and synthesis. Although Killian (1940) suggests nitrogen also is an important factor in the abundance of soil microorganisms, Kononova (1961) presents data that may be interpreted as supporting the belief that soil nitrogen is not closely related to numbers. The number of microorganisms per unit weight of soil nitrogen is about 20 times higher in arid Central Asian soils than in humid podzol soils. In general, the numbers of microorganisms per unit of soil nitrogen increased markedly as the climate changed from the humid, cold soils to the arid, warm soils. The absolute counts, however, indicate that the microorganisms increase on passing from peat and forest soils to prairie or grassland soils and then decrease somewhat in desert soils. The greatest decrease in populations takes place between the desert soils and "soil-less", extremely arid deserts. Also in passing from the northern forest soils to the southern desert soils the population of microorganisms becomes more diverse and the mobilization of nitrogen reserves becomes more rapid, reaching a climax in irrigated desert soils (Kononova, 1961).

3. Activity

A review of the Russian literature (Rozanov, 1951) provides an overwhelming amount of evidence to the effect that the desert zone of Central Asia is rich in bacterial flora and microfauna. The high overall population of microorganisms in this desert area permits these soils to be classified as "rich" despite the low amount of humus. All of the usual physiological groups of microorganisms are present. Even the very dry and sandy *takyr* soils of this region are reported to be well supplied with microorganisms (Samsonov *et al.,* 1930). In a more recent study (Volobuev, 1963), however, desert soils of the central arid sierozem are depicted as having less active microbial populations and less nitrification activity than are reported by the earlier Russian studies.

4. Effect of Vegetation

The influence of plants on microbial populations is shown in soils of the Sahara by the discovery that greater numbers of bacteria are associated with the rhizosphere than in root-free soil (Vargues, 1963). In an Egyptian desert soil, *Azotobacter* and *Clostridium* (free-living nitrogen fixers) were isolated in soil near plant roots but not in soil away from the roots. Lobova (1960), Krasil'nikov (1958), Clark (1949), and others agree that intense microbiological activity is dependent upon the presence of vegetation of higher plants. In an Iraq desert soil, cultivated for many centuries and low in humus, the microbial activity was very low (Chandra et al., 1962). Additions of moisture and organic matter, however, raised the level of bacteria and fungi to an activity level comparable to a moderately fertile humid-region soil.

5. Groups

The abundancy ratios of microorganisms in six harsh California desert surface soils followed the order of: aerobes plus actinomycetes > anaerobes > facultative anaerobes > algae > fungi (Cameron and Blank, 1965). Microaerophilic bacteria were found to be abundant in all desert soils even when the more common species were impoverished.

B. Nitrogen Fixation and Transformation

Early workers in the central Asian area claim to have observed an abundance of nitrogen-fixing Azotobacter and nitrifying bacteria (Kostychev, 1930; Samsonov et al., 1930) in arid soils. A relationship between the abundance of Azotobacter and soil formation, plant cover, and moisture has been sugggested (Sushkina, 1949). In extremely arid soils of the Sahara (Pochon et al., 1957), certain central Asian takyr soils (Lobova, 1960), and the Chilean Desert of the Atacama (Cameron et al., 1965), neither Azotobacter, Clostridia, nor nitrifying bacteria were found. There was very little difference in the ammonia-oxidizing capacity of the desert and the more humid soils in Australia (Sims and Collins, 1960). Virgin red desert and range soils of Arizona contain Azotobacter only occasionally (Martin, 1940), whereas irrigated soils are well supplied. Martin further reported that Azotobacter were absent when the salt content of the soil solution exceeded about 3000 ppm of calcium or sodium. In contrast, Utah desert soils held dry at a level of 2% salt still had viable Azotobacter and ammonifiers after 20 years (Greaves and Jones, 1941). Nitrobacter and Nitrosococcus, nitrifying bacteria, did not survive. The abundance of Azotobacter in Egyptian soils along the Nile is claimed to be associated with the applications of irrigation water from the river (Abdel-Malek and Isham, 1963), which is well supplied with these organisms, although the soils of the Central Niger Delta are reputed to be very low in Azotobacter (Rubenchik, 1960).

C. Algae

The ability of algae to withstand adverse habitats of extreme moisture, temperature, and salt conditions, as well as their capacity to fix carbon and nitrogen, make them the primitive life that represents the forerunner of all organic life and therefore prominent dwellers in desert soils. (Fuller *et al.,* 1961). Many algae species are found in desert soils (Cameron, 1961). The greatest number belong to the blue-green and green groups. Coccoid green forms and filamentous blue-greens dominated the extremely dry desert soils examined in California. The green alga, most abundant, was *Protococcus grevillei* and the blue-greens were *Microcoleus vaginatus, M. chthonoplastes, Schizothrix calcicola, Plectonema nostocorum, Scytonema hofmannii,* or *Nostoc muscorum.* The latter are also the algae that are found associated with fungi to form lichens (Shields, 1957).

Algae are commonly identified with the crusts of takyrs, Solonetz, and other desert soils of Central Asia (Bolyshev, 1964). The algae may form crust on all the desert soils of the world, being most prominent wherever bare soil is exposed. These crusts or desert chips are high in nitrogen and other plant nutrients (Fuller *et al.,* 1961; Sims and Dregne, 1962; Mayland *et al.,* 1966). The nitrogen is primarily contained in the algal tissues in organic forms since ammonium and nitrite and nitrate nitrogen are rarely found in algal crusts (Mayland *et al.,* 1966; Shields *et al.,* 1957). Algae may adversely affect the moisture economy of irrigated crop land by inhibiting water penetration while favoring the nutritional economy by fixing atmospheric nitrogen and carbon as a source of organic matter and nitrogen. Algal crusts on virgin desert lands have been cited as improving water infiltration, reducing soil erosion, and aiding in plant seedling establishment. The intense wetting and drying of the native desert as compared with the necessity of more moist conditions for crop production explains the apparent discrepancy in the soil–algal–water relationships described.

Diatoms are found in soils of Central Asia (Lobova, 1960), the Great Salt Lake area of Utah and many other lake-bed areas. Their siliceous skeletons have accumulated in large quantities in old lake beds under many climatic conditions. However diatoms develop most rapidly under warm temperature conditions. As diatomaceous earth, these siliceous skeletal residues are now mined for numerous industrial and home uses.

Blue-green algae (Cyanophyta) are present universally in desert soils where water accumulates. They have the capacity of rapid development as warm rains wet them. The author has observed a doubling in the weight of algal crusts in the deserts of Arizona in as short a period as 2 hours after a warm rain. *Phormidium* is a common species (Lobova, 1960) to many deserts. Soil algae appear to be the most abundant microbial mass in harsh, barren deserts of North and South America, whereas microaerophillic bacteria are most prominent along the edge of the harshest deserts near the vegetation and in soils of greater development (Cameron, 1966).

D. PROTOZOA

Protozoa are well established in desert soils of the central Asian desert (Brodskii and Yankovskaya, 1930; Brodskii, 1935, 1937). In fact, all soils, even the sandy and takyr are purported to be rich in protozoa. They may be observed to be most prevalent in the humus layer or from 0–20 or 30 cm. Information on protozoa in desert soils is very limited.

Termites should be included here because cellulose-hydrolyzing protozoa are necessary for termite activity as flora of their digestive tracts. Very little is known about termites and soil development except they are found readily in deserts, transporting soil into mounds and digging channels to various depths in presumably bone-dry soil. Both termite and ant activity are prominent in desert soils.

E. ACTINOMYCETES

Actinomycetes and streptomycetes are abundantly present in desert soils (Lobova, 1960). In one of the harshest areas of the world, the Chilean Atacama Desert, A *Streptomyces* sp. appeared to be one of the dominant organisms in the soils sampled (Cameron et al., 1965). Actinomycetes are distributed widespread in soils, composts and on plant residues under natural environments. Ordinarily they grow on resistant carbonaceous material (Norman and Fuller, 1942) and soil organic matter at a low level of moisture. They are expected, therefore, to be well represented in arid soils and, indeed, they are. Observations in classroom exercises, including dilution-plate counting of microorganisms of desert soils, over the last 20 years, has convinced the author that actinomycetes and streptomycetes are as abundant in number, if not more abundant, than any other single group. Actinomycetes are unusually high in soil populations associated with alkaline conditions.

In localities such as the Bikini Atoll of the Pacific, actinomycetes accounted for 95% of the microorganisms reported (Johnstone, 1947). During periods of drought in Kenya, for example, actinomycetes became the dominant group of organisms remaining in the soil, replacing the dominance of the bacteria (Meiklejohn, 1957); algae and lichen presumably were not enumerated.

F. FUNGI

Numeration data of groups of organisms such as bacteria, fungi, algae, etc., are not easy to interpret. Studies of soil microbial populations and distributions (Cameron, 1966; Cameron et al., 1965; Cameron and Blank,

1965) indicate that soil fungi most often are the least abundant population group in desert soils. However, as pointed out so well by Alexander
(1961), methods of enumeration favor the small size of the bacterial cell,
which ranges from less than 0.2 μm to a maximum of about 5 μm, when in
effect in most well-aerated soils, the mass of total fungal protoplasm exceeds that of other microorganisms. Soil algae also suffer for the same reason in enumeration studies.

On the basis of enumeration data, nevertheless, the fungi in the harsh
deserts examined in North and South America are reported to be least
abundant of the microorganisms (Cameron, 1966). In the barren Atacama
Desert, only three species of fungi were found (Cameron et al., 1965).
Penicillium is most common to desert soils. There appears to be no simple
correlation between specific fungi and soil type or series or climate. In Central Iraq, a large number of fungal species were isolated with a decreasing
order of dominance of Hormodendrum, Aspergillus, Fusarium, Alternaria,
and Penicillium, but no correlations were evident (Al-Doory et al., 1959).
Large populations of diverse species are reported for North African deserts
(Nicot, 1955), Sudan (Nour, 1956), Nevada (Durrell and Shields, 1960),
Egypt (Sabet, 1939), and Mauritania (Audry and Rossetti, 1962). Over
102 species of fungi are reported from the Judean Desert and the Northern
Negev (Rayss and Borut, 1958). A great number of Aspergillus spp. and
Penicillium spp. occur in desert soils.

G. SPECIALIZED ORGANISMS

Specialized microorganisms often are the most conspicuous forms found
in deserts. For example, diatoms (Bacillariophyta) appear in salt crusts
and where rainwater accumulates and evaporates leaving salt deposits. Old
lake beds, relics of more humid climates, may be teeming with diatoms.
Algal crusts may dominate the surface of takyr soils. Sulfur-oxidizing bacteria are abundantly present where sulfides, sulfur and sulfur minerals are
present. Hot springs and sulfurous desert waters favor the presence of sulfur oxidizers. In the cold Valley of 10,000 Smokes Desert in Alaska, sulfur
as well as iron-oxidizing microorganisms concentrate where sulfur fumes
escape from the land and moisture is available (Cameron, 1966). Algae
and lichen form prominent crusts on bare desert soil surfaces and lichens
color bare rock surfaces. In desert soil ecosystems, slight changes in the
presence of certain chemical compounds, moisture, temperature and organic matter determine the presence or absence, abundance or poverty of
specialized organisms. Microenvironment is important in soil biology,
particularly in arid climates. For further discussion of desert cryptogams
(see Chapter V, Volume I and Chapter IV, this volume).

IX. Soils of Individual World Deserts

Soil science is still in its infancy relative to other associated sciences of physics, chemistry, botany, and bacteriology. Only recently has a universal nomenclature been proposed (U.S. Soil Conservation Service, 1960). Although the Russians have pioneered soil classification for some years and have contributed richly to the concepts embodied in the U.S. Department of Agriculture Seventh Approximation Soil Classification System (U.S. Soil Conservation Service, 1960), a great variety of terminology is still used throughout the world that has similar meanings. There may be a dozen different highly technical words that mean the same thing. This has led to some confusion. With the recent improvement in communications among scientists of different nations as initiated through U.S. programs of NSF, AID, UNESCO, Ford and Rockefeller Foundations, U.S. Army, O.N.R., (to mention only a few), differences are being ironed out. Much of the information available for this section was obtained through U.S. Government source materials.

The literature on soils of the deserts of the world is limited. Although volumes have been written, many more volumes remain to be written. Often soils information is confined to comments and notes of geologists and geographers who traveled through the harsh desert zones on missions not closely related to soil science. Results of these travels have frequently overemphasized the vast wilderness, harsh climate and unusual desert surfaces. Technical information is lacking and interpretation of such observational information and broad reconnaissance surveys difficult. Biology of desert soils is a science yet to be developed.

As a matter of convenience the world deserts to be further discussed will be divided into the following similar groups as suggested by Meigs (1953) and adopted by McGinnies and Meadows (1968) and Dregne (1967) in their excellent inventories of arid lands with only slight modifications in terminology of central Asian Deserts: Kalahari–Namib, Sahara, Somali–Chalbi, Arabian, Iranian, Thar, West Central Asia–Turkestan, Central Asia–Takla–Makan, East Central Asia–Gobi, Australian, Monte-Patagonia, Atacama–Peruvia, North American.

A. KALAHARI–NAMIB

The moisture in Kalahari–Namib Desert in Southern Africa is controlled on its equatorial side by tropical summer rains and on its pole side by winter cyclonic rainfall. Thus this desert is virtually a rainfall transition zone (Reitan and Green, 1967). The designated Kalahari–Namib Desert includes Angola, the Republic of South Africa, Southwest Africa, and Botswana. Desert land in Angola is small. The general soil patterns follow the rainfall distribution which increases from the Southwest to the Northeast (d'Hoore, 1964). The southwest African Desert may be roughly divided into three parts according to soil–climate interrelationships: (1) desert soils—south and west, (2) semidesert soils—south and middle, and (3) dry forest soils—north. In the Namib Desert three types of soil materials are delineated (Koch, 1962; Giess, 1962), (a) sands in a narrow strip along the coast, (b) sand dunes (Ergs) south of the Kuiseb River, and (c) stony and gravelly plains (Regs) north of the Kuiseb River on the Namib Flats (Dregne, 1967). Dregne points out that inland from the Namib Desert along the coast some weakly developed semiarid brown soil occur as small inclusions in the barren mountain ridge. The Kalahari Desert is east of these mountains and extends for great distances as a flat plain. Lime accumulations are common and exposed except where they are covered with thin layers of sand. The desert is divided into two general groups, brown to reddish brown desert soil over sand and ferruginous tropical soil also on sandy material where rainfall is higher.

Surface structures peculiar to the Kalahari Desert include indurated lime surfaces (calcrete), gypsum beds (gypcrete), siliceous layers (silcrete) from relic soils, ferrugenous desert pavements, loose sand and dune and clay pans (playas). Grasses at one time dominated the Kalahari Desert. Overgrazing has left much of the land barren and eroded (Debenham, 1952).

The Namib Desert has no vegetation except along its major river, the Kuiseb, flood plain.

Desert pebble and stone pavement are prominent in the South African Cape Province (van der Merwe, 1954). Lime-crusted and saline soils also occur. Most of the soils of the Kalahari–Namib Desert area are quite deep but the presence of indurated lime and silicate surfaces, stony pavements, shifting sand dunes, and saline spots breaks the continuity of the better soils.

B. Sahara

The Sahara Desert is one of the most barren and harshest of world deserts. Soil development in the large center area is weak where it exists, and consists mostly of structureless shifting dune sand. Other desert detritus and rock debris are little altered in the absence of rainfall and vegetation. This extremely arid part is represented by a strip approximately 1250 km wide and 4000 km long. Fortunately, not all of the Sahara is this dry and so little known. Desert soils have been described for the irrigated peripheral areas including oases and the Nile Valley in Egypt and Sudan.

Barren, exposed rock mountains, the Ahaggar and Tibesti, free of soils, extend through the middle section of the Sahara (Durand, 1953) with stony and gravelly residual debris concentrated mostly in the south. These rough surfaces are referred to as regs. They are relics of an earlier, humid climate, now exposed by wind action. Rocky plateaus, called hamadas, are distributed throughout the Sahara. When the gravelly and rocky plain surfaces occupy alluvial fan and floodplain positions, sometimes they are referred to as transported regs. Such surfaces occupy the talus positions along breaks of mountains.

Ergs (high, connected sand dunes) cover much of Southern Algeria and Tunisia, Northern Mali, Mauritania, and the Libyan Desert. Associated with the ergs are pebbly deserts and a few clay pans.

Compact calcium carbonate and indurated gypsum layers formed under another climate, are often exposed by erosion of wind. Some have been eroded by water at an earlier time. Limy accumulations are so compact and of such high quality in some places, they are mined for building material and ground for liming agricultural soils. They appear as exposed desert surfaces most conspicuously in Morocco, Northern Algeria, and Tunisia.

Prominent in Mauritania, Mali, Niger, Chad, and Sudan are the clay plains. These are broad, smooth plains of fine-textured lacustrine deposits which are so poorly weathered, soil development is very weak. Sand deposits and dunes cover a minor part of the clay plains and isolated saline depressions occur where water collects in depressions and penetration rate is slow. On the coastal plain, both north and south of Port Sudan, as well as the inland plains, Gray Desert soils are found. (Dixey and Aubert, 1962).

According to the map of d'Hoore (1964), soils are developed in Southern Tunisia and Mauritania where precipitation is higher. Oases soils show some soil development. In general, these Sierozems appear to be less well developed than the same type described in Central Asia.

The vegetation of the Sahara is described (McGinnies, 1967) as being very sparse with herbs and small shrubs except in limited areas where moisture is more abundant, larger shrubs and trees appear. Ephemerals grow widely scattered over the desert, but most abundantly in the north. Succulents are conspicuously absent and the large central desert is barren of vegetation.

C. SOMALI–CHALBI

The area designated as Somali–Chalbi Desert lies along the East African Coast extending both north and south of the equator, with almost all of it actually north of the equator. The countries of Somalia and Kenya are most involved. Soils maps with detail descriptions of the soils of this area are not available. The few broad reconnaissance-type maps give sketch information. As pointed out by Dregne (1967) the most detailed information about the soils is contained in the UNESCO "Arid Zone Research Series" (Pichi-Sermolli, 1955).

The Somali–Chalbi Desert soils, morphologically, are undeveloped. Some fine-textured, reddish-clay soils occur in plains of the Kenya–Somalia border region as well as in the upland associated with the Buiba and Scebeli Rivers.

Salt-affected soils occupy large areas of coarse and medium soils of French Somaliland as lime and gypsum accumulations. The coastal plains are well known for their saline characteristics. The Danakil pan is high in salts. Irrigation of certain soils has led to a salinization because of poor drainage conditions.

Stony and rock detritus are found in all parts of the Somali–Chalbi Desert but are concentrated most in French Somaliland. Sand dunes are confined mostly to the coastal plains. Soils formed on these materials are skeletal and poorly developed. The vegetation resembles that of the Sahara under comparable climatic conditions.

D. ARABIAN

Soils information on the area delineated as the Arabian Desert is extremely limited. Israel provides the best source material. Scant information is available on Iraq, Iran, and Saudi Arabian deserts (Dregne, 1967).

The broad expanse of Saudi Arabia of thin sandy soils and sand dunes and stony surfaces is better known for oil than agriculture. Irrigation quality water is lacking in most of Saudi Arabia, Kuwait, and Israel. The soils are in a very primitive state of development under the influence of prevailing arid conditions and scarcity or absence of natural vegetation. Outcroppings of partially weathered parent material, not yet soil, frequent this region (Abu Fakhr, 1961). Salt flats, "gatch pan" (lime–silica–sand indurated layers) and deep layers of gypsum and lime are common. Almost all plant vegetation is excluded although a native salt-tolerant plant, *Zygophyllum coccinium,* may grow in these extreme arid areas. Acacia trees have been planted on the irrigated periphery of the Saudi Arabian Desert but even these often die as a result of salt accumulation on top of "gatch." A typical profile described by Abu Fakhr (1961) in Kuwait is 0–5 cm of white sand over 5–30 cm of fine calcareous sand with some silt and clay, friable sand continues to the gatch hardpan at about 120–150 cm. Gatch pan is almost impervious to water and perches irrigation water sufficiently to cause upward movement of salts.

In the northern part, broad plains and tablelands and stony soil surfaces are found (regs, hamadas) even to the extent, in many places of having stony pavement characteristics. Calcium and gypsum layers accumulate in these soils.

The medium- to fine-textured soils follow the Tigris, Euphrates, and Jordan rivers. These old flood plain areas are used extensively for irrigated agriculture (Ravikovitch, 1960). Solonchak, Solonetz, and solodized-Solonetz are found in the alluvial irrigated plains of the Mesopotamian and other irrigated areas as well as depressions such as near the Dead Sea.

In the Central Negev of Israel the distribution of soils is said to be (1) rocky slopes 42% of the area; (2) dunes and plains, 22%; (3) loessial plains, 12%; (4) sandy plains, 10%; (5) gravelly (hamadas) plains, 8%; wadis, about 6%, etc. (Seligman et al., 1961).

On the less arid plains and plateau margins of the desert where rainfall ranges from 25 to 30 cm, Sierozem and isohumic brown soils have developed on loess and sand.

The Southern Arabian Desert is very similar to the Sahara. Most of the Arabian Peninsula is extremely arid, and soils develop poorly if at all.

The same type of vegetation as found in the Sahara extends across Central Asia and into India (McGinnies, 1967). Almost no true succulents occur. Perennials include halophytes. Ephemerals follow rains. The *Anabasis articulata/Retama raetam* plant communities dominate the sandy plains of Negrev. In lower Jordan *Anabasis articulata/Zilla spinosa* communities are common. The most common plants in Palestine are *Pistacia atlantica, Zizyphus lotus, Retama raetam* var. *raetam, Phlomis brachyodon, Rhus tripartita, Artemisia herba-alba, Noaea mucronata, Anabasis haussknechtii, Haloxylon articulatum,* and *Achillea santolina.*

E. IRANIAN

The Iranian Deserts are defined to include the arid areas of Iran, Afghanistan, and Pakistan which encompass (a) the Dasht-e-Kavir in the northwest, (b) Kavir-i-Namak in the north, (c) the Dasht-e-Lut in the southwest, (d) the Dasht-i-Naomid in the east, and (e) the Dasht-i-Margo in the southeast.

The Dasht-e-Kavir is known most widely for its extensive salt-crusted soils of solonchaks or halomorphics. Gypsum beds and saline marls underlie these soils. Salty soils also occur along the Persian Gulf, the Gulf of Oman, and the Arabian Sea.

Coarse-textured soils predominate in the Iranian Deserts. Fans of alluvial soils on upper slopes next to mountains and hills are coarse textured as are the Gray Desert soils lower down slope. Most are limy (Dewan and

Famouri, 1964). Gray Desert soils also appear on nearly level to slightly sloping land. They, too, are calcareous with a lime layer nearer the surface. Gravel and stone pavements form on some of the Gray Desert soils. The Iranian Sierozems resemble those of Turkestan (Rozanov, 1951). They are located on the plains between almost barren mountains and low hills that characterize the Iranian deserts. Sierozems appear mostly on loess of level to slightly undulating terrain. They are most prevalent in Afghanistan and least in Pakistan.

Almost any low level plain or basin will have some sand dunes. However, in the area south of Dasht-e-Lut and in Southern Afghanistan along the Pakistan border, they are most common. The dune sand in these two areas is constantly shifting over hard surfaces of finer-textured soil, some surfaces of which are cemented and others saline.

Agricultural land lies along rivers and streams where fine-textured alluvial soils have collected on low terraces and old bottom land. Irrigation has caused high water tables in some instances with resulting salinity problems.

The native vegetation of the southern part of the Iranian desert is scanty (McGinnies, 1967). Higher elevations support communities of *Artemisia herb-alba* and plants similar to those of the Great Basin Desert of the United States.

F. THAR

Desert soils of the Thar (known also as Rajasthan, Rajputana, and the Indian Desert) have received considerable study. Raheja (1966) describes Indian desert from a standpoint of their food-production capacity, but lightly treats the uncultivated soils. Wright (1964), on the other hand, treats all soils of the Southern Thar in detail, and Hunting Survey Corporation, Ltd. (1958) discusses soils of the Indus Plains of West Pakistan. The current status of soil classification in East Pakistan is reviewed by Islam (1966).

Undeveloped lithosols (thin soils), *brown* sandy soils, *desert* soils, sand, and gravelly footslopes constitute the major soil types. These have been grouped for convenience as (1) fine-textured, deep, saline alluvium on broad flooded flats of the Rann of Kutch; (2) sand dunes (ergs) of the Tharparkar north of the Rann; (3) sand dunes and sandy soils patched with saline alluvium northeast of Tharparkar area; and (4) medium-textured (silt and sand) of recent alluvium of the Indus Plain on the west. This is the area most extensively irrigated for agriculture. In Central Thar gray-brown soils appear on alluvium (Tamhane, 1952).

Moving sand and sand dunes restrict much of the Thar to wasteland.

The most productive land is in the Indus Plain where sand is not prevalent except in the Thal region. Salinity restricts crop production in much of the irrigated soils because of poor drainage and is dominant in the fine-textured uncultivated soils. Raheja (1966) describes the sand dunes area in the southeast and northwest directions of the Thar as having a high content of lime, low total nitrogen, mostly alkaline (pH of 7.9–8.6) and low organic matter. Boron is a problem in West and Central Thar, ranging from 2.6 to 12.2 ppm (Raheja, 1966) in many soils.

G. West Central Asia—Turkestan

The area delineated as the Turkestan Desert has a wealth of available information on soils, vegetation and climate. Two books (Lobova, 1960) (Rozanov, 1951) are particularly good. Because of the great complexity of the soils in the Turkestan Desert, it is not possible to cover the subject here in any detail. Unfortunately, only a brief insight can be gained.

Within the sierozem zone of the Turkestan Desert area Rozanov (1951) recognizes the following types.

a. Takyr Soils. These occur in the hottest part of the desert, on old alluvial valleys, lower proluvial slopes, at the foot of some hills and as troughs between mounds and ridges of Kara Kum (black sand) and Kyzyl Kum (red sand). They are very poorly formed, fine-textured soils often located in slight depressions. There is very little to no vegetation on Takyr soils. The fauna is composed mostly of desert wood lice and termites. Surfaces may be cracked, paved with cobblestones, crusted, or flat clay. Colors range from white to a reddish tinge. Salt and sodium accumulations are common.

b. Desert Serozom. These soils are better developed than the takyrs, have more vegetation and are extremely variable although they have common morphological features. Salty soils (Salorthids) and sodium soils (Haplargids), or in Russian terminology, the Solonchakus and Solonetsous soils, are prevalent. Gypsum-bearing soils (gypsozem) are common as are Kyr (structural) or "butte" soils.

c. Sierozems. These are typical desert soils and occur in the middle part. They are well developed, leached of salts in the surface, low in humus and lime at the surface. They are the more productive soils of the Turkestan Desert and lie on upper river terraces, piedmont plains and foothills wherever influence of ground water is excluded.

d. Sierozem-Meadow Soils. Where a shallow water table is of good quality and the land is more moist, grasses and shrubs grow well. Humus is abundant compared with other desert soils and the soil is limy with gli formations.

e. Marshy Soils. Marshy soils are located in low basins and accumulate peaty-marshy material, organic matter, and salt plus organic residues.

f. Anciently Irrigated Sierozem-Meadow Soils. They are as the name implies—irrigated ancient oases within the sierozem zone. They have formed from silt-suspended irrigation water and added organic fertilizers. The cultural deposition ranges from 1 to 2 meters. Soil profile differentiation is lacking and texture throughout is uniform. Carbonates have not accumulated appreciably.

g. Solonchaks. Solonchaks are salty soils. They appear in deep depressions, lowlands, on denuded plateaus, and on outcrops of salt-bearing rocks within the sierozem zone. Large areas stretch along the shores of the Caspian and Aral Seas.

h. Solonetses. The Solonetses can reach a maximum profile development and morphological structure in which sodium exercises its full effect. Some leached Solonchak soils are found interspersed in this class. They occupy only a small total acreage and occur in small, local spots only.

The Turkestan Desert has fairly deep soils compared with most deserts. Only a limited area is stony and gravelly. Salt-affected soils appear mostly in the Takyrs, Solonchaks, irrigated oases, river deltas, and Caspian coastal plains.

H. Central Asia—Takla–Makan

The Takla–Makan Desert lies between the Turkestan Desert on the west and the Gobi on the east. The Thar is to the south. Its elevation is between 700 and 1400 meters and is characterized by hot summers, cold winters, and extreme aridity. Several rivers flow into it from the Tien and Kunlan Mountains, which are important sources of water for irrigated agriculture concentrated along their flood plains. The Dzungaria Desert of North Sinkiang lies to the north of the Takla–Makan. Several smaller deserts occupy areas within the Takla–Makan but their soil characteristics are not sufficiently different to discuss them separately in this very limited review. Oases on the desert margins have produced grains for centuries but have been shrinking in size from the onslaught of sand invasion (Academia Sinica, Sand Control Team, 1962) as have the agronomic footslopes.

Thus the soil sequence seems to follow a pattern of sand and sand dunes in the largest portion of the desert, the center, expanding outwards and south, and saline soils in depressions on finer-textured material interspersed between high dunes. Near the base of mountains, coarse alluvial gravel, coarse sand, and stone (gobi) surfaces overlie limy skeletal soils. The texture of the soils becomes finer proceeding into the flatter and more arid central sand region of the Takla–Makan. Sierozem soils are widespread on the gently undulating plains in Eastern Takla–Makan (Kovda and Kondarskaya, 1957). Large saline flats are common, such as the famous Turfan and Lop Nor Depressions, which collect water that evaporates leaving salts. Soils in these flats are halomorphic.

The vegetation in the Takla-Makan is sparse (McGinnies, 1967). Along rivers, lush tugai communities grow. Halomorphic vegetation is found along old valleys, river deltas, and saline lake depressions.

I. East Central Asia—Gobi

The Gobi Desert is one of the most publicized deserts of the world, partly because of its harsh climate, its remoteness, and its historic isolation which give it an aura of mystery. Only recently, since World War II, has the soil surface been described in any detail and in scientific language (Bespalov, 1951; Academia Sinica, Sand Control Group, 1962). The Gobi Desert is the largest single desert in Asia. Associated with the Gobi Desert are four smaller deserts to the south and southwest, namely, Ordos, Ala Shan (Ala-Chan), Bei Shan (Peishan, Beichan), and Tsaidam (Petrov, 1966, Vol. 1). The Gobi Desert lives up to its name "gobi" which means "arid land of flat, stony surfaces." The Gobi is a monotony of repeating nearly barren mountains flanked by rough stony alluvium, colluvium, plains, depressions, and gentle slopes. Restless sand and sand dunes are scattered over about 20% of the desert. They are not as extensive as in the Sahara or the adjacent Takla–Makan. The Gobi appears on some of the highest desert elevations in the world with a range from 154 meters (the Turfan Depression) up to 2791 meters in the Bei Shan low mountain area (Petrov, 1966, Vol. 2). McGinnies (1967), in his review of major deserts, has estimated the mean elevations of some deserts to be as follows: Ordos, 1100–1400 meters; Ala Shan, 800–1600 meters; Bei Shan, 1000–2000 meters; and Tsaidam, 2700–3100 meters.

The principal developed soils of the Gobi Desert proper, belong to the *Brown Gobi* type. These are fairly deep well-drained soils. Lime is present throughout but accumulates in significant layers only in the subsoil. Unlike the Turkestan soils, gypsum is scarce. In some areas, crusted saline depressions are numerous. Solonchak and Solonetz soils occur mostly as a result of capillary rise of salts from areas of high water tables. Vegetation is sparse and has long been overgrazed. Short shrubs dot the plains; grasses appear on the sandy soils and stabilized dunes.

Soils of the Ordos are coarse textured. Along the Hsinchaoshan Range, gravels dominate. The lower piedmont plateau plain is covered with gravelly–sandy debris. Coarse-skeletal, gray-brown carbonated soils predominate. Meadow-Brown, meadow-Chestnut, and meadow-Solonchak occur in the wetter depressions. Shifting and overgrown sands, Brown and light-brown Chestnut, poorly developed soils are widely scattered over the eastern part of the desert.

The Ala Shan Desert soils are characterized by a paucity of vegetation, compact surface, very dry conditions, and low humus content. Lime and gypsum usually are present. A great portion of the land is covered with sand. The basic desert soils in the Ala Shan are the Gray-Brown. Solonchak (crusty and crusty-downy) are found in landlocked depressions. Gravel and rock debris surfaces are common.

Soils of the Bei Shan (Peishan) Desert are zonal gray-brown type, more or less salinized. Aeolian sands predominate in the northeastern portion, whereas coarse rock and gravel form the parent material in the other parts of the desert. Desert pavement of "varnished gravel" covers fine silty soils of the peripheral piedmont plains. Soils generally have pale colors of gray and tan. Meadow-Solonchak occur in the mountain depressions. Gypsum and lime accumulate in the lower soil horizons. Vegetation is sparsely present and it has a typical desert appearance. In dry river channels coragana, wolfberry, and calligonum are encountered.

In the Tsaidam Desert the climate is extremely arid and supports only immature soils. Desert Gray-brown, coarse-skeletal soils develop which are highly gypsiferous (Petrov, 1966, Vol. 2). They form on gravel, gravelly sand, and sand parent material. All soils contain some lime. Meadow-salt and Meadow and Meadow-Gray soils form in wet, saline depressions and lake bottoms. Much of this desert is saline. The total ground coverage with vegetation rarely exceeds 5–7% (Petrov, 1966, Vol. 2). Salt-tolerant plants predominate.

J. AUSTRALIAN

Over half of the land surface of the Australian continent is desert. However, land survey and soil classification has received unusually fine attention despite the vast, harsh wildernesses of stony and sandy surfaces. Agriculture is concentrated on the more humid soils at the periphery of the desert on bands of land nearest the oceans. The Australian deserts are located mostly at an elevation of 300–600 meters (Stephens, 1953; Fournier, 1963) on the Great Plateau.

Deep, partly mobile sand hills and partly stabilized dunes occupy extensive areas. The Simpson Desert and those south of the MacDonnell Ranges in Central Australia, and in the northern portion of Western Australia, are noted for red sandy soils with only slight evidence of profile development (Stephens, 1953, 1961). Smaller areas of sand are found along with desert loams and other arid soils. Dune sandhills are not grazed appreciably because the grass cover is thin and wind erode seriously when the native surface is disturbed.

Desert sand-plain soils of considerable acreage exist as relics of modified lateritic red earths. The brown to red, loose sandy surface is underlain by a more compact sand and finally at about 1 meter, lateritic gravel. Lime and lateritic gravel also may be found at varying depths to the surface. Red sand-plain soils are found in the arid regions of Western Australia, Queensland, and the Northern Territory. They are most extensive in the latter area. These soils are grazed sparingly because of the poor coverage of vegetation of spinifex and grasses.

Certain tablelands in Australia also may be extensively covered with stones which represent a former, more humid era. Their desert pavement surface is composed of broken and polished siliceous stones (Jessup, 1962). Brown-to-red loam to clay-loam textured A horizon lies below the pavement. In the B1, coarse-textured clay overlays a gypsiferous clay with some lime accumulated in the lighter colored B2. The stony desert tableland soils are found on the Gibson Desert in Western Australia, in South Australia, and the Stuart Desert extending into Queensland. They are poorly covered with sparse shrub-type steppe vegetation of low cattle and sheep carrying capacity (Jessup, 1951).

Gray-brown and red-calcareous desert soils occur extensively in the Nullarbor Plain of South and West Australia and to a certain extent in other arid regions (Jackson, 1957). Shrubs and grasses inhabit these soils sparsely but are little used.

Desert loams are fine-textured soils containing some lime and gypsum and frequently show signs of salt effects. They appear in the 12- to 25-cm rainfall areas of southern Australia and may be covered with thin layers of sand or stones. They are sparingly grazed. Vegetation consists of ephemeral natural herbage and perennial edible shrubs which resemble the shrub-type steppe vegetation.

Limy soils are concentrated more on the desert fringes than in the heart of the arid lands, whereas gypsiferous soils appear on the more arid lands. Solonchak (salty soils) and Solonetz (sodium-affected soils) are scattered in depressions and in soils with saline subsoils in all areas of Australia (Downes, 1954). Because of the extensive nature of the salt-affected land in Australia, Stephens (1961) suggests that the soil salinity is derived from wind-blown ocean spray. The parent materials on which salty soils occur cannot account for the salt accumulations observed.

A wide variety of desert soils are found in Australia. Sandy and stony soils are extensive and clay and loams are interspersed throughout the arid region as are salt-affected soils. Vegetation is sparse mostly because of

the aridity but also because of salinity, low fertility, and absence of certain
necessary trace elements for plant growth.

K. Monte–Patagonian

The Monte–Patagonian Deserts are located in Argentina east of the
Andes Mountain range running north and south almost from one end to
the other. Monte is the northern desert composed of mountains, narrow
valleys, and depressions. The Patagonian Desert is a high latitude east-coast
desert of low tablelands dissected by stream valleys. The high Andes
Mountains to the west are responsible for its dryness.

Soils in the Monte Desert valleys are not unlike those found in North
American deserts. They are gray in color, calcareous and composed of
variably textured materials (Dregne, 1967). Calcium carbonate is present
in accumulated amounts in the subsoil. The valley terraces and flood plains
grow fine crops. Local depressions accumulate salts in some places and
sodium affects productivity under irrigation in some depressions of the
flood plains. Sand does not dune as in the Arabian and Sahara. Certain
closed basins, such as the Salinas Grandes, are fine textured and sodic.
Vegetation is practically absent (Papadakis, 1963).

Foothills at the base of mountains belong to the red desert and desert
group (Vessel, 1946). Coarse and medium fine soils are found usually
with calcium carbonate in the subsoil. Grass appears in the low, wettest
soils and trees are absent except in scattered groves along river bottoms.
Much of the area is covered with resinous bushes such as the Zygo-
phyceae (McGinnies, 1967).

The Patagonian Plain soils develop on cemented gravel deposits as remnants of glacial river action. The surface textures of gravelly loams, sandy
loams and silt loams overlay B horizon of finer material which grades
abruptly into lime-cemented gravel. Along the rivers finer alluvial soils
occur. Saline soils appear in low spots. Isohumic Brown soils occur under
more moist conditions of the eastern side of the desert. Indurated calcium
carbonate called "tosca" is present in some of the brown soils just as
"caliche" is found in the Sonoran Desert soils of North America.

The vegetation is primarily widely spaced Exerophytic clumps of grass
and low, cushion-type shrubs. Low, wet spots support luxurious grass most
of the year.

L. Atacama–Peruvian

The Atacama–Peruvian Desert is extremely arid to arid. Portions of the
Atacama of Chile, particularly, are the harshest in the world (Cameron
et al., 1965). The Atacama–Peruvian strip of desert begins along the coast
of Central Chile and continues almost to the northern border of Peru. It

has very little soil. Most of the surfaces are barren, rough land of rocks and stony colluvial debris and outwash gravels. Even the more level terrain of the Meseta Central (20°–25°S latitude) is coarse material of geological erosion from the Andes. Agriculture is confined to the narrow river terraces and somewhat wider flood plains in the bottom of deep canyons and scattered oases. The rich nitrate beds west of Meseta Central are located on smooth, gently undulating slopes completely free of soil. Borax "lakes" and saline "dry lakes" also are common to the Atacama–Loma Desert region (Cameron *et al.,* 1965). Soils of this desert are limited to a few scattered Entisols or Aridisols.

North of Meseta Central the soils are salty and alkaline. South of this, however, they are less salty and appear as fine-textured marine terraces with some profile development. Scattered desert shrubs dot these terraces. In general, dunes so prevalent in the Peruvian Desert are not conspicuous in the Atacama Desert of Chile.

Vegetation in the Atacama Desert is confined to a few shrubs along the coast and rock lichens. The Peruvian Desert is a continuation of the coastal desert of Chile where it is somewhat broader (Meigs, 1953) in Peru. Only the soils of the northern part of the coastal plain are appreciably developed. As reported in the soils inventory by Dregne (1967), about 5% of the arid coastal region is alluvial soil, 65% are Lithosols, 25% are Regosols, and 5% are red desert and black clays. Agriculture is located on the alluvial soils of the transverse valleys along the coastal plains bordering the numerous rivers that flow into the Pacific. The red desert soils occur in the Northern Peruvial Desert where rainfall is slightly higher 2–25 cm/year. These are fine-textured, deep soils having lime concretions and lime horizons. Gray Desert soils of clay texture also are found here although they are deep, they are quite impermeable and alkaline.

Vegetation in the Atacama–Peruvian Desert is very scarce (McGinnies, 1967) except along streams and rivers. Sparse stands of *Tillandsia* may appear during the more moist winter months. Lichens occur on rocks (Cameron *et al.,* 1965). Some ephemeral vegetation is found on mist-covered (150–1500 meter) elevations. Vegetation is primitive and microbial populations favor the autotrophic rather than heterotrophic organisms such as the lichen and algae. Compared with other deserts of North and South America, Cameron *et al.* (1965) claim the soils contain a very low abundance of common groups of microorganisms.

M. NORTH AMERICAN

North American Desert soils are bordered by the Chihuahuan and Sonoran Deserts in Mexico on the south, and the Columbia Basin and the Upper Snake River Plains in the states of Washington and Idaho on the north. They extend through the Colorado Plateau of Northern Arizona, Utah and Colorado to the Wyoming Basin of the Rocky Mountains along the eastern border (Western Regional Soil Survey Work Group, 1964). The basin and range area, which occupies parts of Arizona, California, Nevada, and Utah, is the largest contiguous area. The Central and San Joaquin Valleys of California and Williamette Valley of Oregon roughly bound the desert region on the west.

A great variety of desert soils are mapped. They include the zonal *Red Desert, desert* (gray), and *Sierozem* soils and small acreages of *Brown* and *Chestnut* soils. Azonal *Regosols* (sandy outwashes and dunes) and *Lithosols* (shallow and rocky) are scattered throughout the zonal soils. Intrazonal *Calcisols* [lime accumulation (Cca layer)], *Solonetz* (sodic), and *Solonchak* (salic) also are scattered throughout the desert areas. They appear in low localities and represent only a small total area. The general topography of North American deserts changes abruptly from flat valleys to rugged mountains and from level plateaus to deep river canyons. Elevations range from below sea level to over 1800 meters and precipitation from 7.5 to 25 cm. In the southern deserts creosotebush (*Larrea divaricata*), mesquite (*Prosopis* spp.), Yucca (*Yucca* spp.), cactus (Cactaceae spp.), muhly grass (*Muhlenbergia* spp.), and annual grasses dominate. In the northern deserts sagebrush (*Artemisia* spp.), shadscale (*Atriplex confertifolia*), hopsage (*Grayia spinosa*), needlegrass (*Stipa* spp.), and Indian ricegrass (*Oryzopsis hymenoides*) dominate.

The chain of intermountain valleys and basins in the south that start in the Sonoran Desert of Mexico, have deep medium to coarse-textured red soils that extend north into the *Desert* soils of southern Nevada (Fuller, 1972). The Chihuahuan Desert of Mexico that crosses a part of Texas and extends into New Mexico also has *Red Desert* soils. They form in the hottest and most arid climate of the continent. The Red Desert soils are well drained, fertile, and very productive under irrigated agriculture. World record yields of crops have been grown on these soils under proper management (see Fig. 14). Water is an essential factor to this high productivity and often must be brought from great distances (see, for example, Fig. 15).

Salty soils (Solonchak and Solonetz) intersperse with the Red Desert soils in low-lying basin spots, flat bottoms and playas. Death Valley, for example, is a very hot interior basin with a high proportion of its soils as Calcisols, Solonetz, Solonchak, and Regosols. Calcisols and Regosols appear in localized areas of the red desert. The rough, rocky mountain slopes of thin soils support lithosols. Red Desert soils also develop in the Rio Grande and Pecos River Valleys on alluvial–colluvial fans and stream terraces.

Fig. 14. Rough tillage leaves the desert soil loose and amenable to good water penetration and development of good soil structure.

Narrow green strips of fertile irrigated land follow winding rivers, abundant with crops.

The *Desert* soils of Nevada merge into the Sierozems in the northern part of the state. *Desert* soils differ from the Red Desert and Sierozems in having more clay associated with the B horizon and a browner color.

Sierozems are prominent on the Colorado Plateau where they are associated with the Brown and Chestnut soils at the higher wooded elevations. Again lithosols occupy the rough canyon walls of the deeply stream-dissected plateau. Sierozems form in the more humid and cooler climate of the desert. They appear in desert basins, valleys, and mesas, as well as in plateaus. In higher elevations of the sierozem zone, big sagebrush, junipers, and piñon pine invade the grassland and shrubs.

The Wyoming Basin is similar to the Colorado Plateau in elevation and physical conditions. The climate of this high plain (2000–2600 meters) is warm and dry in the summer and cold and dry in the winter. It is vegetated primarily with sagebrush (*Artemisia* spp.), bluestem (*Andropogon* spp.), needle-grass (*Stipa* spp.), and wheatgrass (*Agropyron* spp.). The Sierozem and Desert soils predominate on the rolling plains of the Wyoming Basin. Only very limited patches of salt-affected soil and thin lithosols occur.

The mountain-isolated basin-like areas of the Upper Snake River area in Idaho and Washington are responsible for the arid climate of these narrower desert plains. *Sierozem* and *Desert* soils predominate. Basalt is very conspicuous in this as well as the neighboring Columbia Basin. Vegetation is similar in both desert areas. Sagebrush, wheatgrass, rabbit bush, Indian

ricegrass, and cheatgrass (*Bromus tactorum*) grow most abundantly. Large areas of the Gray Desert soils of the Columbia Basin support a luxurious irrigated agriculture. Wheat and other grain crops grow in alternate years of fallow without irrigation on the desert fringes of Brown, Chernozem, and Prairie soils. In the northern irrigated desert, winters are cold, allowing only one crop per season as compared with double season cropping in the southern irrigated red desert soils. The Columbia Basin soils are deep, well drained and medium to coarse textured. Desert soils form on loess (wind-blown deposits) that cover much of the Columbia Basin of basalt and coarse glacial outwash. Again, only limited acreage is occupied by sodic, salic, dune sand, or thin, rocky soils as compared with some of the harsher deserts of the world.

X. Concluding Statement

The desert brings out mixed emotions in people. To the contained eye it is desolate, romantic, or beautiful. And the "desert rat" finds it commandingly fascinating. More and more people are discovering a new life in an exciting environment, while the sick, with pain-wracked joints, end their wanderings and literally "take up their beds and walk" in the comforting radiations of the sun and dry air. Residents revel in the clarity of nature with its clean rock, clear air, colorful mountains, broad plains, deep gorges, and sand and soil—soil that blankets great distances in reds and grays or is encrusted in depressions with salts, lime, gypsum, or is paved with pebbles and varnished by nature's paint brush. Harsh physical geography is contrasted with bright green patchwork of lush crops under irrigation—heavily laden with fruit, nuts, vegetables, melons, grain, and hay, their roots nourished in rich soil. Gray, dry land and irrigated grass and legume pastures graze sheep and cattle, scattered as far as the eye can see where abundant sunlight, plants, good soil, temperature, and water are combined to feed a world still partly starving.

The desert charm is derived in part from its appearance of desolation—to the untrained eye—that acts to disguise a responsive biology that sleeps in the drought and heat of the sun only to awaken to seething activity of life with water. Desert soil is living, dynamic, and ever changing. Though it seems to be shrouded in lifelessness, water from rain or irrigation sets into motion the intense mechanisms of life, proliferating their basic unit—the cell. The center of this biological activity is the soil, which

Fig. 15. Water flows a long distance to wet the parched desert arid lands (Southwest United States). Manley Photo.

functions to shelter, feed, and store life—to cycle new life from old life—to integrate mineral and organic matter as a seat of the origin of life in a new and wonderful synthesis, much of which remains to be discovered.

REFERENCES

Abdel-Malek, Y., and Isham, Y. C. (1963). Abundance of *Azotobacter* in Egyptian soils. *Abstr., Int. Congr. Microbiol., 8th, 1962* No. B 14.6.
Abu Fahkr, M. S. S. (1961). Effect of saline waters on soil properties and plant nutrition in Kuwait. (University of Arizona, Tucson.) *Diss. Abstr.* **22** (2), 380–381; Univ. Microfilms, Ann Arbor, Michigan, Order No. 61-2916.
Academia Sinica, Sand Control Team (1962). "Research on Sand Control" (translated from the Chinese). JPRS No. 18, pp. 508–993. (Also available as OTS 63-31183.)
Akzhigitova, N. I. (1959). The relationship between chemical composition of plants and the salinization of soils. *Uzb. Biol. Zh.* **6**, 76–82.
Al-Doory, Y., Tolba, M. K., and Al-Ani, H. (1959). On the fungal flora of Iraqi soils. II. Central Iraq. *Mycologia* **51**, 429–439.
Alexander, L. T. (1959). "Strontium 90 Distribution as Determined by the Analysis of Soils." Soil Survey Laboratory, Soil Conservation Service, USDA. (Statement for Joint Committee on Atomic Energy, Congressional Hearings.)
Alexander, M. (1961). "Introduction to Soil Microbiology." Wiley, New York.
Audry, P., and Rossetti, C. (1962). Prospection écologique; études en Afrique occidentale. Observations sur les sols et la végétation en Mauritanie de sud-est sur la bordure adjacente du Mali, 1959 et 1961. FAO, Rome. UNSF/DL/ES/3.
Bernstein, L. (1962). Salt-affected soils and plants. UNESCO, Paris. *Arid Zone Res.* No. 18, pp. 139–174.
Bernstein, L. (1964a). Effects of salinity on mineral composition and growth of plants. *Plant Anal. Fert. Probl., Colloq., 4th, 1962* **IV**, 25–45.
Bernstein, L. (1964b). Salt tolerance of plants. *U.S., Dep. Agr., Agr. Inform. Bull.* **283**, 1–23.
Bernstein, L., and Hayward, H. E. (1958). Physiology of salt tolerance. *Annu. Rev. Plant Physiol.* **9**, 25–46.
Bespalov, N. D. (1951). "Soils of Outer Mongolia, Mongolian People's Republic," IPST Cat. No. 1147 (1964). Israel Program for Scientific Translation, Jerusalem. (Also available as OTS 64-11073.)
Bolyshev, N. N. (1964). Role of algae in soil formation. *Sov. Soil Sci.* No. 6, pp. 630–635.
Breazeale, J. F., and Smith, H. V. (1930). Caliche in Arizona. *Ariz., Agr. Exp. Sta., Bull.* **131**, 419–430.
Brodskii, A. L. (1935). Protozoa pochoy i ikh rol'n pochvennykh protsessakh. (Soil protozoa and their role in soil processes.) *Byull. Sredneaziat. Gos. Univ.* **3**, 99–182.
Brodskii, A. L. (1937). "Issledovaniya po faune pachv." (Studies of soil fauna.) Izel. Kometeta nau Uzhekskali. SSR (Published by the Comm. of the Uzbeb SSSR), Tashkent.
Brodskii, A. L., and Yankovskaya, A. (1930). Materialy k poznaniyu pochvennoi fauny Srednei Azii. (Data on the soil fauna of Central Asia.) *Pochvovedenie* [N.S.] **1/2.**

Cameron, R. E. (1961). Algae of the Sonoran Desert in Arizona. (University of Arizona, Tucson.) *Diss. Abstr.* **22** (3), 716; Univ. Microfilms, Ann Arbor, Michigan, Order No. Mic. 61-2992.

Cameron, R. E. (1966). Soil sampling parameters for extraterrestrial life detection. *J. Ariz. Acad. Sci.* **4**, 3–27.

Cameron, R. E., and Blank, G. B. (1965). A. Soil studies. Microflora of desert regions. VIII. Distribution and abundance of desert microflora. *Calif. Inst. Technol., Pasadena, Jet Propulsion Lab., Space Progr. Sum.* No. 37–34. **4**, pp. 193–202.

Cameron, R. E., Blank, G. B., Gensel, D. R., and Davies, R. W. (1965). C. Soil studies—desert microflora. X. Soil properties of samples from the Chile Atacama Desert. *Calif. Inst. Technol., Pasadena, Jet Propulsion Lab., Space Progr. Sum.* No. 37-35. **4**, pp. 214–223.

Chandra, P., Bollen, W. B., and Kadry, L. T. (1962). Microbial studies of two Iraqi soils representative of an ancient site. *Soil Sci.* **94**, 251–257.

Chao, Sung-ch'iao. (1962). A preliminary discussion of the types of Gobi in the northwestern part of ho-Hsi Tsou-Lang and its reclamation and utilization. *In* "Research on Sand Control" (Academia Sinica, Sand Control Team, ed.), JPRS No. 19,993, pp. 189–224.

Clark, F. E. (1949). Soil microorganisms and plant roots. *Advan. Agron.* **1**, 241–288.

Clements, T., Merriam, R. H., Stone, M. S., Eymann, B. S., and Reade, A. B. (1957). A study of desert surface conditions. *U.S. Army Quartermaster Res. Develop. Cent. Tech. Rep.* **EP-53**.

Crocker, R. L. (1946). The soils and vegetation of the Simpson Desert and its borders. *Trans. Roy. Soc. S. Aust.* **70**, 235–258.

Dapples, E. C. (1941). Surficial deposits of the desert of Syria, Trans-Jordan, Iraq, and Western Iran. *J. Sediment. Petrol.* **11**, 124–141.

Debenham, F. (1952). The Kalahari today. *Geogr. J.* **118**, 12–23.

Denny, C. S. (1967). Fans and pediments. *Amer. J. Sci.* **265**, 81–105.

de Vries, D. A. (1958). The thermal behaviors of soils. Proc. Canberra Symp. UNESCO, Paris. *Arid Zone Res.* **11**, 109–113.

Dewan, M. L., and Famouri, J. (1964). "The Soils of Iran." FAO, Rome.

d'Hoore, J. L. (1964). Soil map of Africa. *Comm. Tech. Coop. Afr., Lagos, Nigeria, Publ.* **93**.

Dieleman, P. J., and de Ridder, N. A. (1964). Studies on salt and water movement in the Bol Guini Polder, Chad Republic. *J. Hydrol.* **1**, 311–343.

Dixey, F., and Aubert, G. (1962). Arid zone research in the Sudan. *Arid Zone* [*Newsletter*] **16**, 5–16.

Downes, R. G. (1954). Cyclic salt as a dominant factor in the genesis of soils in Southeastern Australia. *Aust. J. Agr. Res.* **5**, 448–464.

Downes, R. G. (1956). Conservation problems on sodic soils in the state of Victoria (Australia). *J. Soil Water Conserv.* **11**, 228–232.

Dregne, H. E. (1967). Surface materials. *In* "An Inventory of Geographical Research on Desert Environments" (W. G. McGinnies, B. J. Goldman, and P. Paylore, eds.), Vol. V, pp. 1–3. Univ. of Arizona Press, Tucson.

Durand, J. H. (1953). Carte schématique des sols des environs de Beni Ounif. (Pedological investigation of the Beni-Ounif regions.) UNESCO and *Res. Councl. Israel. Spec. Pub. 2, Desert Res., Proc., Int. Symp., 1952* pp. 438–452.

Durrell, L. W., and Shields, L. M. (1960). Fungi isolated in culture from soils of the Nevada Test Site. *Mycologia* **52**, 636–641.

Fletcher, J. E., and Carroll, P. H. (1948). Some properties of soils associated with piping in Southern Arizona. *Soil Sci. Soc. Amer., Proc.* **13**, 545–547.

Fletcher, J. E., Harris, K., Peterson, H. B., and Chandler, V. N. (1954). Piping. *Trans. Amer. Geophys. Union* **35**, 258–263.

Food and Agriculture Organization. (1960). Soil erosion by wind and measures for its control on agricultural lands. (Agricultural Engineering Branch, Land and Water Development Division.) *FAO Agr. Develop. Pap.* **71**.

Fournier, F. (1963). The soils of Africa. *In* "A Review of the Natural Resources of the African Continent," pp. 221–248. Columbia Univ. Press, New York.

Fuller, W. H. (1953). Effect of kind of phosphate fertilizer and method of placement on phosphorus absorption by crops grown on Arizona calcarerous soil. *Ariz., Agr. Exp. Sta., Tech. Bull.* **128**, 235–255.

Fuller, W. H. (1963). Reactions of nitrogenous fertilizers in calcareous soils. *J. Agr. Food Chem.* **11**, 188–193.

Fuller W. H. (1965). Soil organic matter *Ariz., Agr. Exp. Sta., Bull.* **A-40**, 3–17.

Fuller, W. H. (1972). Soils. *In* "Arizona: Its People and Resources" 2nd Rev. ed. pp. 137–144. Univ. of Arizona Press, Tucson.

Fuller, W. H., and McGeorge, W. T. (1950a). Phosphates in calcareous Arizona soils. I. Solubilities of native phosphates and fixation of added phosphates. *Soil Sci.* **70**, 441–460.

Fuller, W. H., and McGeorge, W. T. (1950b). Phosphates in calcareous Arizona soils. II. Organic phosphorus. *Soil Sci.* **71**, 45–49.

Fuller, W. H., and McGeorge, W. T. (1950c). Phosphates in calcareous soils. III. Distribution in some representative profiles. *Soil Sci.* **71**, 315–323.

Fuller, W. H., and Ray, H. (1965). Basic concepts of nitrogen, phosphorus and potassium in calcareous soils. *Ariz., Agr. Exp. Sta., Bull.* **A-42**, 1–30.

Fuller, W. H., Caster, A. B., and McGeorge, W. T. (1950a). Behavior of nitrogenous fertilizers in alkaline calcareous soils. I. Nitrifying characteristics of some organic compounds under controlled conditions. *Ariz., Agr. Exp. Sta., Tech. Bull.* **120**, 451–467.

Fuller, W. H., Martin, W. P., and McGeorge, W. T. (1950b). Behavior of nitrogenous fertilizers in alkaline calcareous soils. II. Field experiments with organic and inorganic nitrogenous compounds. *Ariz., Agr. Exp. Sta., Tech. Bull.* **121**, 471–500.

Fuller, W. H., Cameron, R. E., and Raica, N., Jr. (1961). Fixation of nitrogen in desert soils by Algae. *Trans. Int. Congr. Soil Sci., 7th, 1960* Vol. **2**, pp. 617–624.

Giess, W. (1962). Some notes on the vegetation of Namib Desert with a list of plants collected in the area visited by Cape-Transvaal Museum Expedition during 1959. *Cimbabasia* **21**, 1–35.

Gile, L. H., Peterson, F. F., and Grossman, R. B. (1966). Morphological and genetic sequences of carbonate accumulation in desert soils. *Soil Sci.* **101**, 347–360.

Glukhov, I. G. (1956). Fil'tratsiya Vody iz Kanalov v Lessovykh Porodakhi Prosadochnyya Yavleniya na Droshayenykh Uchastkakh. (Seepage of water from canals in Loess formations and subsidence phenomena in irrigated areas.) *Gidrotekh. Melior.* **8**, 9–18. (Also cited as OTS 60-21152.)

Greaves, J. E., and Jones, L. W. (1941). The survival of microorganisms in alkali soils. *Soil Sci.* **52**, 359–364.

Guild, W. R. (1950). Note on heat transfer at the soil surface. *J. Meteorol.* **7**, 140–144.

Hannapel, R. J., Fuller, W. H., and Fox, R. H. (1964). Phosphorus movement in a calcareous soil. II. Soil microbial activity and organic phosphorus movement. *Soil Sci.* **97**, 421–427.

Hayward, H. E., and Bernstein, L. (1958). Plant-growth relationships on salt-affected soils. *Bot. Rev.* **24**, 584–635.

Hayward, H. E., and Wadleigh, C. H. (1949). Plant growth on saline and alkali soils. *Advan. Agron.* **1**, 1–38.

Hunt, C. B. (1960). The Death Valley salt pan; study of evaporites. *U.S., Geol. Surv., Prof. Pap.* **400-B**, 456–458.

Hunt, C. B. (1966). Patterned ground. *U.S., Geol. Surv., Prof. Pap.* **494-B**, 104–133.

Hunting Survey Corporation, Ltd. (1958). "Landforms, Soils and Land Use of the Indus Plains, West Pakistan," A Colombo Plan Coop. Proj. (a map). *Agri. Surv. Rep.,* Gov't. West Pakistan.

Islam, A. (1966). Current status of soil and land capability classification in East Pakistan. *CENTO (Cent. Treaty Organ.) Conf. on Land Classification for Non-Irrigated Lands, Ankara, Turkey, 1966* pp. 81–86. (CENTO Doc. EC/10/AG/D21.)

Jackson, E. A. (1957). Soil features in arid regions with particular reference to Australia. *J. Aust. Inst. Agr. Sci.* **23**, 196–208.

Jessup, R. W. (1951). The soils, geology, and vegetation of northwestern south Australia. *Trans. Roy. Soc. S. Aust.* **74**, 189–273.

Jessup, R. W. (1962). Stony tableland soils of inland Australia. *Aust. J. Sci.* **24**, 456–457.

Johnstone, D. B. (1947). Soil actinomycetes of Bikini Atoll with special reference to their antagonistic properties. *Soil Sci.* **64**, 453–458.

Kao Shang-tun (1963). Issledovania peschanoi pustyni i gobi v Sintszyana. (Investigation of the sand desert and Gobi in Sinkiang.) *Lin Yeh K'o Hsueh* **8**, 42–67 (in Chinese with Russian summary). (Also see, Dregne, 1967.)

Karschon, R. (1953). The hammada in Wadi Araba, its properties and possibilities of afforestation. *Ilanoth* **2**, 19–45.

Killian, C. (1940). Etudes comparatives de la biologie des sols du nord et du centre saharien. *Ann. Agron.* **10**, 56–100.

Killian, C., and Fehér, D. (1936). La fertilité des sols du Sahara. *Genie Civil* **108**, 114–124.

Koch, C. (1962). The Tenebrionidae of Southern Africa. XXXI. Comprehensive notes on the Tenebrionid fauna of the Namib Desert. *Namib Desert Res. Sta., Sci. Pap.* **No. 5** (X), p. 38.

Kononova, M. M. (1961). "Soil Organic Matter, its Nature, its Role in Soil Formation and in Soil Fertility" (translated from the Russian by T. Z. Nowakowski and G. A. Greenwood). Pergamon, Oxford.

Kostychev, S. P. (1930). Issledovaniĭa po biodinamike pochv. (Studies in soil biodynamics.) *Tr. Pochvennago Inst. Imeni V. V. Dokuchaeva* **3/4**, 149–160.

Kovda, V. A., and Kondorskaya, N. I. (1957). Novaya pochvennaya karta Kitaya. (A new soil map of China.) *Pochvovedenie* **12**, 45–51. [Translated into English by Israel Program for Scientific Translation, Jerusalem, PT-480 Cat. No. 39, 1961. (Also cited as OTS 60-21140.).]

Krasil'nikov, N. A. (1958). "Mikroorganizmy pochvy i vysshie rasteniya." (Microorganisms of soil and higher plants.) Izdatel. Akad. Nauk S.S.S.R., Moscow.

[Translated into English by Israel Program for Scientific Translation, Jerusalem, IPST Cat. No. 206, 1961. (Also cited as OTS 60-21126.).]

Kulik, N. (1959). Line concretions in semidesert soils. *Sov. Soil Sci.* **1**, 126.

Lapham, M. H. (1932). Genesis and morphology of desert soils. *Rep. 12th Annu. Meet. Amer. Soil Surv. Ass. Bull.* **13**, 34–52.

Lobova, E. V. (1960). "Pochvy pustynnoĭ zong SSSR." (Soils of the desert zone of the USSR.) Izdatel. Akad. Nauk S.S.S.R., Moscow [Translated into English by Israel Program for Scientific Translation, Jerusalem, IPST Cat. No. 1911, 1967. (Also cited as TT 67-51279.).]

McGeorge, W. T. (1949). Lime-induced chlorosis: Relation between active iron and citric and oxalic acids. *Soil Sci.* **68**, 381–390.

McGeorge, W. T., and Breazeale, J. F. (1938). Studies on soil structure: Effect of puddled soils on plant growth. *Ariz., Agr. Exp. Sta., Tech. Bull.* **72**, 413–447.

McGinnies, W. G. (1967). Inventory of research on vegetation of desert environments. *In* "An Inventory of Geographical Research on Desert Environments" (W. G. McGinnies, B. J. Goldman, and P. Paylore, eds.), Vol. VI, pp. 5–8. Univ. Arizona Press, Tucson.

McGinnies, W. G., and Meadows, J. W., Jr. (1968). Introduction. *In* "An Inventory of Geographical Research on Desert Environments" (W. G. McGinnies, B. J. Goldman, and P. Paylore, eds.), Vol. I, pp. 3–22. Univ. Arizona Press, Tucson.

Martin, W. E., Berry, L. J., and Williams, W. A. (1957). Range fertilization in a dry year. *Calif., Agr. Ext. Serv., Progr. Rep.* **4**, 1–39.

Martin, W. P. (1940). Distribution and activity of azotobacter in the range and cultivated soils of Arizona. *Ariz., Agr. Exp. Sta., Tech. Bull.* **83**, 332–369.

Mayland, H. F., McIntosh, T. H., and Fuller, W. H. (1966). Fixation of isotopic nitrogen on a semiarid soil by algal crust organisms. *Soil Sci. Soc. Amer., Proc.* **30**, 56–60.

Meigs, P. (1953). World distribution of arid and semiarid homo-climates. *Rev. Res. Arid Zone Hydrol.* UNESCO, Paris, *Arid Zone Programme* **1**, 203–209.

Meiklejohn, J. (1957). The number of bacteria and actinomycetes in Kenya soils. *J. Soil Sci.* **8**, 240–247.

Meyer, M. W., Allen, J. S., Alexander, L. T., and Hardy, E. (1968). Strontium-90 on the earth's surface. IV. Summary and interpretation of a world-wide soil sampling program: 1961–1967 results. *U.S. At. Energy Comm.* **TID-24341.**

Nicot, J. (1955). Remarques sur les peuplements de micromycetés des sables déserti-ques. *C. R. Acad. Sci.* **240**, 2082–2084.

Norman, A. G., and Fuller, W. H. (1942). Cellulose decomposition by microorga-nisms. *Advan. Enzymol.* **2**, 239–263.

Nour, M. A. (1956). A preliminary survey of fungi in some Sudan soils. *Trans. Brit. Mycol. Soc.* **39**, 357–360.

Olsen, S. R., Watanabe, F. S., and Cole, C. V. (1961). Phosphates in calcareous soil as affected by neutral salts. *Trans Int. Congr. Soil Sci., 7th, 1960* Vol. **2**, pp. 397–403.

Papadakis, J. (1963). Soils of Argentina. *Soil Sci.* **95**, 356–366.

Pearson, R. W., and Simonson, R. W. (1940). Organic phosphorus in seven Iowa soil profiles: Distribution and amount as compared to organic carbon and nitrogen. *Soil Sci. Soc. Amer., Proc.* **4**, 162–167.

Petrov, M. P. (1966). "Pustyni T'sentral'noĭ Azie," Vols. 1 and 2. (The deserts of Central Asia.) Science Publishing House, Moscow. [Translated into English by JPRS No. 39, 145 and No. 42, 772. (Also cited as TT 66-35568 and 67-33399.).]

Pichi-Sermolli, R. E. (1955). Tropical East Africa (Ethiopia, Somaliland, Kenya, Tanganyika). *Plant Ecol. Rev. Res.* UNESCO, Paris. *Arid Zone Res.* **6,** 302–360.

Pochon, J., de Barjar, H., and Lajudie, J. (1957). Recherches sur la microflore des sols Sahariens. *Ann. Inst. Pasteur, Paris* **92,** 833–836.

Polynov, B. B. (1935). Vynetuvania Sostev kontinental'nykh otlozhenii. (Weathering of rocks and composition of continental deposits.) *Akad. Nauk SSSR Geol. Assots, Tr.* **4.**

Ponomareva, V. V. (1956). Gumus takyrov. (Humus of takyrs.) *In* "Takyry Sapodnoi Turkneii i puti ikh sel'skokhozyaistvennogo osvaeniya," pp. 411–438. Izd. Akad. Nauk SSSR, Moscow (quoted from Lobova, 1960, p. 280).

Raheja, P. C. (1966). "Soil Productivity and Crop Growth." Asia Publishing House, New York.

Ramaley, F. (1952). World deserts: Limits and environmental characteristics. *U.S. Army Quartermaster Res. Develop. Cent., Tech. Rep.* **EP-57.**

Ravikovitch, S. (1960). "Soils of Israel; Classification of Soils of Israel." Faculty of Agriculture, Hebrew University, Jerusalem.

Ravikovitch, S., and Hagin, J. (1957). The state of aggregation in various soil types in Israel. *Ktavim* **7**(2/3), 107–122.

Rayss, T., and Borut, S. (1958). Contribution to the knowledge of soil fungi in Israel. *Mycopathol. Mycol. Appl.* **10,** 142–174.

Reitan, C. H., and Green, C. R. (1967). Inventory of research on weather and climate of desert environments. *In* "Inventory of Geographical Research on Desert Environments" (W. G. McGinnies, B. J. Goldman, and P. Paylore, eds.), Vol. II, pp. 1–72. Office of Arid Lands Studies, University of Arizona, Tucson.

Riceman, D. S. (1953). Minor element deficiencies and their correction. *Proc. Int. Grassland Congr., 6th,* 1952 Vol. **1,** pp. 710–717.

Richards, L. A. (1950). Chemical and physical characteristics of saline and alkali soils of Western United States. *Trans Int. Congr. Soil Sci., 4th,* 1950 Vol. **1,** pp. 378–382.

Rozanov, A. N. (1951). Serozemy Srednei Azii. (Serozems of Central Asia.) Izdatel'stvo Akademii Nauk SSSR, Moskva.) [Translated into English by Israel Program for Scientific Translation, Jerusalem, IPST Cat. No. 235, 1961 (Also cited as OTS 60-21834.).]

Rubenchik, L. I. (1960). *Azotobakter* i ego primenenie v sel'skom khozy-aistve. (*Azotobacter* and its uses in agriculture.) Izdatel. Akad. Nauk Ukr. S.S.R., Kiev. [Translated into English by Israel Program for Scientific Translation, Jerusalem, IPST Cat. No. PL 231), 1963. (Also cited as OTS 63-11076.).]

Sabet, Y. S. (1939). On some fungi isolated from soil in Egypt. *Cairo, Egypt. Fouad I. Univ., Fac. Sci. Bull.* **19,** 59–112.

Samsonov, P. F., Samsonov, M. F., and Chernova, T. A. (1930). Mikrobiologic-heskaya kharakteristika pochv Srednei Azii. (Microbiological characteristics of central Asia soils.) *Pochvovedenie* [N.S.] **1/2,** pp. 3–9.

Seligman, N. G., Tadmor, N. H., and Raz, Z. (1961). Range survey of the Central Negev. *Isr., Nat. Univ. Inst. Agr. Bull.* **67.**

Shields, L. M. (1957). Algal and lichen floras in relation to nitrogen content of certain volcanic and arid range soils. *Ecology* **38,** 661–663.

Shields, L. M., Mitchell, C., and Drouet, F. (1957). Alga- and lichen-stabilized surface crusts of soil nitrogen sources. *Amer. J. Bot.* **44,** 489–498.

Shuvalov, S. A. (1949). In regards to the complexness of the Ust Urt soil vegetation cover. (In Russian.) *Pochv. Inst. Imeni V. V. Dokuchaeva, Tr. Iubileninoi sessi* **28**, 166–182.

Shuvalov, S. A. (1966). Geographic-genetic patterns in the development of the desert-steppe and desert soils of the U.S.S.R. *Sov. Soil Sci.* **3**, 243–253.

Sims, C. M., and Collins, F. M. (1960). The numbers and distribution of ammonia-oxidizing bacteria in some Northern Territory and South Australian soils. *Aust. J. Agr. Res.* **2**, 505–512.

Sims, J. R., and Dregne, H. E. (1962). Fertilizer response on a sodium soil. *N. Mex., Agr. Exp. Sta., Res. Rep.* **63.**

Smith, A. (1929). Diurnal, average, and seasonal soil temperature changes at Davis, California. *Soil Sci.* **28**, 475–568.

Smith, G. D. (1965). Lectures on soil classification. *Pedologie (Moscow) Spec. Issue No.* **4**, 1–134.

Smith, H. T. U. (1955). Deflation basin in the Sechura Desert of Northern Peru. *Geol. Soc. Amer., Bull.* **66**, 1618.

Smith, H. T. U. (1965). Dune morphology and chronology in Central and Western Nebraska. *J. Geol.* **73**, 557–578.

Smith, H. T. U. (1968). Geologic and geomorphic aspects of deserts. *In* "Desert Biology" (G. W. Brown, Jr., ed.), Vol. 1, pp. 51–100. Academic Press, New York.

Springer, M. E. (1958). Desert pavement and vesicular layer of some soils of the desert and of the Lahontari Basin, Nevada. *Soil Sci. Soc. Amer., Proc.* **22**, 63–66.

Stephens, C. G. (1953). "A Manual of Australian Soils." CSIRO, Melbourne, Australia.

Stephens, C. G. (1961). The Australian soil landscape. *Trans. Int. Congr. Soil Sci., 7th, 1960* Vol. 3, pp. 20–26.

Stephens, C. G., and Donald, C. M. (1958). Australian soils and their responses to fertilizers. *Advan. Agron.* **10**, 167–256.

Stroehlein, J. L., Ogden, P. R., and Billy, B. (1968). Time of fertilizer application on desert grasslands. *J. Range. Manage.* **21**, 86–89.

Stuart, D. M., Fosberg, M. A., and Lewis, G. C. (1961). Caliche in southwestern Idaho. *Soil Sci. Soc. Amer., Proc.* **25**, 132–135.

Sushkina, N. N. (1949). Ekologo-geograficheskae respostranenie *Azotobaktera* v pochvakh SSR. (Ecological and geographical distribution of *Azotobacter* in the soils of the U.S.S.R.) Akad. Nauk S.S.S.R., Moskva.

Tadmor, N. H., Orshan, G., and Rawitz, E. (1962). Habitat analysis in the Negev Desert of Israel. *Bull. Res. Counc. Isr., Sect. D* **11**, 148–173.

Tamhane, R. V. (1952). Soils of the Rajputana and Sind Deserts. *Bull. Nat. Inst. Sci. India* **1**, 254–268.

Teakle, L. J. H. (1950). Red and brown hardpan soils of Western Australia. *J. Aust. Inst. Agr. Sci.* **16**, 15–17.

Thorne, D. W. (1951). The desert shall blossom as the rose. *Utah, Fac. Ass. Annu. Fac. Res. Lect.* No. 10.

Thorne, D. W., and Peterson, H. B. (1950). "Irrigated Soils, their Fertility and Management." McGraw-Hill (Blakiston), New York.

Thornthwaite, C. W. (1948). The desert vegetation of North America. *Bot. Rev.* **8**, 195–246.

Tkatchenko, B. (1951). Les sol solontchakoides de la Somalie francaise. (Solonchak-like soils of French Somaliland.) *Agron. Trop. (Paris)* **6**, 341–369.

Trewartha, G. T. (1954). "An Introduction to Climate," 3rd ed. McGraw-Hill, New York.

U.S. Soil Conservation Service. (1960). "Soil Classification, Comprehensive System," 7th approx. US Govt. Printing Office, Washington, D.C.

U.S. Soil Conservation Service. (1967). "Soil Classification, Comprehensive System," 7th approx., Suppl. US Govt. Printing Office, Washington, D.C.

van der Merwe, C. R. (1954). The soils of the desert and arid regions of South Africa. *Proc. Inter-Afr. Soils Conf.*, 2nd, 1954 Vol. 2, pp. 827–834.

Vargues, H. (1963). Etude microbiologique de quelques sols sahariens en relation avec la présence d'*Anabasis aretioides* Coss. et Moq. *Desert Res., Proc., Int. Symp., 1952, Res. Councl. Israel, Spec. Pub. 2*, pp. 318–324.

Vessel, A. J. (1946). Soil associations—areas of Argentine and Chile. *Soil Sci. Soc. Amer., Proc.* 11, 464–473.

Volobuev, V. R. (1963). Ekologiya pochv. (Ecology of soils.) Izdatel'stvo Akademii Nauk Azerbaidzhanskoi SSR, Baku. (Translated into English by the Israel Program for Scientific Translation, Jerusalem, IPST Cat. No. 2099, 1964.)

Wadleigh, C. H., and Brown, J. W. (1952). The chemical status of bean plants afflicted with bicarbonate-induced chlorosis. *Bot. Gaz.* 113, 373–392.

Western Regional Soil Survey Work Group. (1964). Soils of the Western United States. *Wash., Agr. Exp. Sta.* (A map.)

Wright, H. W. (1968). Natural environment of early food production North of Mesopotamia. *Science* 161, 334–339.

Wright, R. L. (1964). Land systems survey of the Nagarparkar peninsula, Pakistan. *Arid Zone (Newslett.)* 25, 5–13.

Yakubov, T. F. (1959). New contributions to the study and control of wind erosion of soils. I. Mechanisms and dynamics of wind erosion. *Sov. Soil Sci.* 7, 792–800.

Yesilsoy, M. (1962). Characterization and genesis of a Mohave sandy loam profile. M.S. Thesis, Arizona University, Tucson.

CHAPTER III

PHYSICAL AND VEGETATIONAL ASPECTS OF THE SAHARA DESERT*

Claude J. Grenot

> *Au chameau et au bouc, au*
> *véhicule et au récipient,*
> *aux deux seuls vainqueurs*
> *du Sahara.*
> Théodore Monod. Meharées (1937)

I. Introduction

The true desert is characterized by its typical climatic conditions. These conditions are the sparse and irregular local rainfalls, which can occur in the course of any season, and the extreme variations in temperature which can take place in a single day or from one season to another.

* Sections I and II translated by Nicole C. Lenfant; Section III translated by David R. Anderson.

Very few hot deserts are found in the world. The following are typical of the intrinsically hot deserts: central Sahara, Libya, southern Arabia, the desert of Lut in Iran, and also, perhaps, central Australia. However, we can also include here the littoral deserts of Chile and Peru, the southwest African Namib, the Atlantic Sahara, and Death Valley in North America. Thus, the warm deserts are mostly located inland and from 15° to 45° of latitude either north or south (Dubief, 1959, 1963; Cuny, 1961; MacGinnies et al., 1968; Planhol and Rognon, 1970; and see Logan, 1968).

Louis Emberger (1938, 1955a,b) applies the term "desertic" only to the central Sahara, as it certainly would not be suitable for most of the Asiatic deserts or even for the North American Great Basin Desert. As a matter of fact, the American deserts are more representative of desertic steppes than true deserts with the exception of Death Valley (California). The latter is a perfect desert in miniature. Figure 1 is a map of the Sahara.

From west to east the desertic regions of the Sahara are limited mostly by the Ghallaman-Karêt reg, the Hank, the Majâbat-al-Koubrâ, the Tanezrouft, the Erg Chech, the Tademait, the Aguemour, the Ténéré, and the Libyan Desert.*

The boundless space of the Sahara, devoid of a drop of water or a sprig of grass, is not indeed a picture of legend! One can sometimes travel for 400–500 km without seeing anything but sand, gravel, or slabs of rock.

In the Algerian Sahara, the Tanezrouft is a striking example of this "desert within the desert."†

II. Physical Environment of the Sahara Desert

A. BOUNDARIES OF THE SAHARA

The Sahara is the largest desert of the world not only because of its dimensions but also because of its degree of aridity (Nachtigal, 1879; Schirmer, 1893; Gautier, 1908, 1925, 1928; Capot-Rey, 1951, 1953; Verlet, 1962; Dubief, 1959, 1963). It represents almost one-quarter of the African continent. From the north to the south it covers a distance

---

*The principal geographic and hydrogeologic terms relative to the Sahara can be found in the glossary of Capot-Rey et al. (1963).

† A "Bibliographic Essay of the French Sahara and its Surroundings" by Blaudin de Thé, containing a great number of references, was published in 1960.

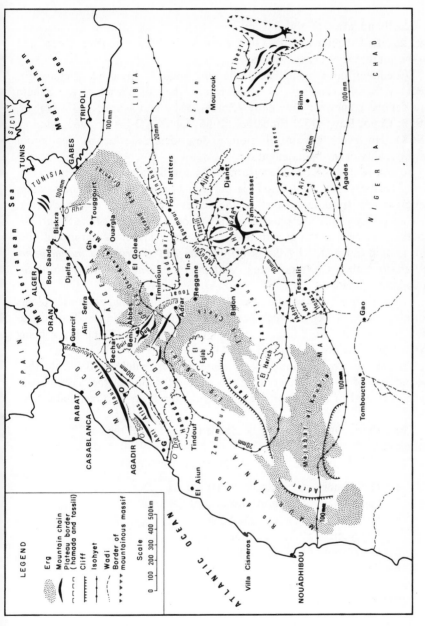

Fig. 1. General map of the Sahara.

of 1600 km, and from the Atlantic Ocean to the Red Sea roughly 4500 km.

The boundaries of the Sahara are essentially climatic. It lies between two zones of regular rainfalls: to the north, the Mediterranean Africa, and to the south, the Sudanese Africa.

Depending upon which scientific discipline is involved, meterology, geology, botany, zoology, or ethnography, the boundaries of the Sahara are defined somewhat differently (Zolotarevsky and Murat, 1938; Dubief, 1953; Capot-Rey, 1952; Emberger, 1955; UNESCO-FAO, 1963; Monod, 1968). However, they are all more or less identical which is clear proof of the reality of the Saharan entity.

To the north, the boundary formed by the Saharan Atlas is quite evident; to the south, however, it is only an approximation, as one passes progressively from the desert to the Sahel (the littoral of the desert).

Capot-Rey (1952) selected as a septentrional boundary of the Sahara the southern margin of the growth of Esparto grass, and as a meridional one, the margin delineated by the growth of the *had* (*Cornulaca monacantha,* a Saharo-sindian Chenopodiacea) and the *cram-cram* (*Cenchrus biflorus,* a Sudanese grass).

From the north to the south, we find a relatively humid zone with plants forming an open steppe which becomes progressively thinner. The vegetation passes from the "diffuse" type to the "constricted," the latter being typical of a true desert (Monod, 1954).

The 10-cm isohyet curve seems quite approximately to delineate the boundaries of the true desert (Fig. 1). The vegetation of the "constricted" type is typical of any region receiving less than 3 cm of precipitation per year.

The Sahara can, arbitrarily, be divided into several regions. The phytogeographic classification established by Monod (1957) and later used by Quézel (1965), divides it into seven principal domains:

1. The domain of the septentrional Sahara
2. The domain of the north occidental Sahara
3. The domain of the oceanic Sahara
4. The domain of the high mountains
5. The domain of the central Sahara
6. The domain of the occidental Sahara
7. The domain of the meridional Sahara, prolonged by the semiarid Sahelo–Sudanese region.

To the east, the Sahara stretches out into an extremely arid region, the Libyan Desert, which is separated from the Nubian Desert by the green valley of the Nile.

B. GEOLOGIC HISTORY

1. Geologic Boundaries

Geologically, the Sahara is bounded to the north by a large accidental tectonic feature, stretching out from Agadir to the Gulf of Gabès, and to the south by the valleys of the Senegal and of the Niger. A great number of works relative to the geological study of the Sahara has been published* (Kilian, 1922, 1925; Joléaud, 1938; Bernard, 1939; Monod, 1935, 1945; Hernandez-Pacheco and Hernandez-Pacheco, 1942; Hernandez-Pacheco et al., 1949; Lelubre, 1952; Menchikoff, 1930, 1957; Pareyn, 1962; Freulon, 1964; Rognon, 1967; Furon, 1964, 1968; Conrad, 1969; Caby, 1970).

2. Relief of the Sahara

According to Menchikoff (1957): "The Sahara is a typical example of a region of continental platform, composed of a Precambrian metamorphic subflooring, several, more or less folded, Paleozoic strata, and a subhorizontal substratum formed of secondary and tertiary deposits, themselves superimposed by several large quaternary zones and recent volcanic massifs."

The Paleozoic sea makes its appearance in the northwest of the platform as early as the Lower Cambrian stretching over the entire half of the western portion later on, and receding afterwards during the course of the midcarboniferous.† During the Mesozoic, the great mesocretaceous transgression spreads widely over the northern part of the central and eastern Sahara. Then, in the Tertiary the sea progressively recedes in the direction of the northeast.

Basically, the geological formation of the platform can be summarized as follows:

1. Precambrian metamorphic and granite subflooring, either flush with the sedimentary formations of the substratum or forming it
2. Paleozoic (hercynian) series, more or less folded
3. Mesozoic and Tertiary layers, more or less tabular in shape
4. With, in addition, some superimposed Quaternary layers, including a few recent volcanic series formations

---

* A geological bibliography of the north Africa and its surroundings, by Ph. Morin, containing a great number of references was published in 1965, 1970, and 1973.

† Carboniferous is used by European geologists to designate both the Pennsylvanian and Mississipian periods as a whole.

This diagram, which is mostly representative of the western portion of the platform, is often reduced to only three divisions as far as the eastern portion is concerned, either because of nonexistence of Paleozoic formations there or of their fusion with the base of the secondary series.

The subflooring—or ancient floor—of the Sahara is composed of Precambrian rock formations with local appearance of often important masses of granite. With the exception of a chain of small isolated Precambrian formations, located in the axial portion of the Anti-Atlas, one can say that the large flush formations of the ancient floor are found for the most part in the vicinity and along the Tropic, forming a protruding median hump, encroached with *ennoyages* (self-engorgements) which roughly divide the Sahara into a septentrional and a meridional zone.

This median hump is from west to east composed of

1. The Reguibat Shield (or crystalline region), large anticlinal loop, sort of dorsum stretching out over more than 1500 km, from the southwest to the northeast and splitting diagonally the entire western portion of the Sahara
2. The Tuareg Shield with its principal massif, Ahaggar (or Hoggar) and its two satellites, Adrar of Iforas in the southwest and Air in the southeast
3. The Tebbou Shield, smaller in size, which forms the subfloor of the volcanic massif of the Tibesti, and flush with it mostly in the northern part

Furthermore, one finds a series of small flush formations of the ancient floor arising from the Nubian sandstone cover, located in the Libyan Desert.

Finally, largest of them all is the Arabo–Nubian Shield, split in the middle by the Red Sea.

On top of the Precambrian flattened subflooring the Paleozoic formations appear irregular and erratic (tassilian unconformity). Although in certain areas they exhibit sharply pronounced folds, nevertheless we never find any metamorphism or even true granitic intrusions. In the northwest, and up until the Carboniferous, these formations are of a maritime origin; but, towards the south and the east, the importance of maritime facies progressively decreases, and the eastern Sahara, apart from a few exceptions, has remained wholly continental and this is true during the entire course of all the primary era.

In the western Sahara, the Paleozoic regions are composed of folded zones of various dimensions (Anti-Atlas, Ougarta chains, Zemmour) or of vast *syneclises* (shallow basins)—such as the Tindouf and Taoudenni—surrounding the Reguibat Shield.

In the Saharan Central Massif, the Paleozoic regions encircle the core of the Tuareg Shield with the "tassilian enclosure." The tassilis are essentially sandstone plateaus, slightly inclined in an outward direction. As outlined in the complete diagram established by Kilian (1925) they are composed of the following monoclinal elements: (1) internal tassilis (ordovician sandstone), (2) intratassilian depressions (gotlandian schists) (Upper Silurian, U.S.A.), (3) external tassilis (early Devonian sandstone), and (4) pretassilian zone (more recent Paleozoic). Very often the tassilis exhibit sharply curved folds and submeridian-oriented fractures.

Farther east, the folds are replaced by large undulations with a large curvature radius, and in the eastern Sahara, the primary formations (entirely continental) are often intermingled with the subhorizontal Mesozoic structural surface.

As a consequence of the hercynian movements, the Paleozoic sea withdraws completely from the Sahara leaving in its place a vast sedimentary lacune intercalated between the formations of the primary and secondary.

Following a few maritime encroachments in the northern part of the central Sahara during the Triassic and Jurassic periods, the great phase of the Mesozoic and Tertiary sedimentation then begins with the Cretaceous, spreading mostly over the northern part of the Sahara, with some extensions arising from the Sudanese regions infringing over the Nigerian Basin, in the meridional part of the Sahara.

These formations, generally almost completely devoid of any fault, constitute, in the north of the Sahara, a series of vast tabular regions called hamadas (the Tademait, the Tinghert Hamada, and the Mzab) (Bernard, 1939; Joly et al., 1954; Lavocat, 1955).

The alpine movements (Atlasic) causing the development of folded chains in Barbary, have only resulted, on the platform, in the formation of vast alterations with moderate degree of curvature.

3. Paleoclimate and Prehistory

The Quaternary is a particularly interesting period owing to the climatic variations sustained at that time by the Sahara (Balout, 1952; Chavaillon, 1964; Alimen, 1963).

According to Conrad (1971): "The evolution of the Sahara is governed by a succession of climatic pulsations which apparently occurred at a rather rapid rhythm, since, following the Neogene sedimentary formation of the hamadas, no less than five different climatosedimentary periods have been established over a 2–3 millions of years time."

"These climatic changes have affected regions located in the desertic belt centered on the Tropic of Cancer. The direction, duration and interactions of these variations which have determined the climate of the

Sahara, can be estimated only in the context of the general atmospheric circulation."

The Plioquaternary paleoclimatology of the Sahara seems to be dominated by a series of contractions and expansions of the desertic domain each of which are directly related to either a pluvial or an interpluvial phase.

The succession of climatosedimentary events occurring in the western part of the Algerian Sahara during that period is perfectly summarized in Table I established by Conrad (1969).

From these ancient and moister periods, we find (a) a vestigial remainder of a vast hydrographic network (Fig. 2) (b) skeletons of animals no longer existing in the Sahara today, but which are still found in Africa (giraffe, elephant, rhinoceros), as well as fossil wood (Lavauden, 1927; Boureau, 1958; Louvet, 1971); (c) presence of abundant material of stone implements (paleolithic and neolithic), rock paintings, and engravings which represent the animals mentioned above (Alimen, 1957; Huard, 1953a,b, 1957; Lhote, 1955, 1957, 1958); (d) discovery of pollens, in neolithic strata, pertaining to species of mediterranean trees that are now extinct in this region (Pons and Quézel, 1956; Van Campo et al., 1965); and (e) presence of relict species of trees such as the cypress of Duprez reported in Ajjer Tassili (Barry et al., 1970), as well as the *Myrtus nivellei,* the *Olea laperrini* and the *Pistacia atlantica* (Quézel, 1965).

C. Climatic Factors

The Sahara is of climatic origin. It is a desert because of its aridity and not because of the nature of its soil (Lasserre, 1930; Brooks, 1932; Perret, 1935; Emberger, 1938; Dubief, 1953, 1959, 1963; UNESCO, 1958; UNESCO-FAO, 1963; Monod, 1968, 1969; Planhol and Rognon, 1970). This aridity is due to an insufficient amount of atmospheric precipitation and also to an inadequate balance existing between the quantity of water provided by rainfalls and the quantity lost through evaporation. We will present here some unpublished meteorologic data obtained at Reggan, a hyperdesertic station of the central Sahara.

1. Rainfall

Because of the wind pattern and of its location far away from the sea, the true Sahara is characterized by the scarcity of its rainfalls and also by the irregularity of their yearly distribution, their volume and their intensity. There is less than 50 mm of precipitation per year. Rainfall in the Sahara is not seasonal, and it is therefore impossible to measure it on a

TABLE I

SUCCESSION OF CLIMATO-SEDIMENTARY EVENTS HAVING OCCURRED OVER THE
WESTERN ALGERIAN SAHARA DURING THE COURSE OF THE PLIO-QUATERNARY[a]

Geologic periods	Climatic manifestations	Sedimentary phenomena or morphologic evolution	Average climatic tendency
— 0 Year		Ergs	Hyperarid
	— — —1000 B. C. — — — — —		
Holocene	Neolithic humid	Low terraces Lacustrine erg formation, turfs	Arid to subarid
	— — — 4500 B. C. — — — — —		
8000 yrs B. C.		Great Western Erg formation	Hyperarid
	— — —12,000 B. C. — — — — —		
Upper Pleistocene	Upper Pleistocene Pluvial or Last Pluvial	Sandy terrace of the Saoura Small lacustrine cycle with *Cardium* and *Ostracod* vestiges (Ahnet, Chech erg)	Subarid
	— — >40,000 B. C. — — —		
— 65,000 —		Chech erg formation Fossil ergs (Great Eastern Erg)	Arid to hyperarid
	— — — — — ? — — — — — —		
Middle Pleistocene	Pluvial (S) of the Middle Pleistocene	Incrusted or armored intercalary glacis Conglomeritic terrace Regouging of the valleys	Subarid
	— — — — — — ? — — — — —		
— 250,000 —		Fossil ergs Late silicifications	Arid to hyperarid
	— — — — — — ? — — — — — —		
	Climatic revolution of the Upper Villafranchian	Incrusted or armored upper glacis High terraced wadis Great lacustrine cycle Great deepening of the valleys	Attenuated subarid
	— — — — — ? — — — — —	Small hamadas	
Villafranchian			Arid ?
	— — — — — ? — — — — —	Late silicifications	
— 2,000,000 —	Climatic revolution of the Pio-Villafranchian	Fluvio-lacustrine sedimentation of the Plio-Villafranchian (*Lates*, *Siluridae*, *Crocodiles*, *Ostracods*, *Characinidae*) Sketching of the hydrographic network Erosion of the Neogene hamadas	Attenuated subarid to semiarid
	— — — — — ? — — — —		
Pliocene			Arid ?
	— — — — — ? — — — —	Late silicifications	
— 8,000,000 —	Neogene climatic revolution	Hamadas lacustrine sedimentation (turfs, limestones, dolomites, sandstones)	Semiarid

[a] From Conrad (1969).

Fig. 2. Flush formations of the Lower Carboniferous, bordering a "fossil" wadi: the Chebbi. In the background: jebel's rim.

yearly basis. Calculations must be established for a period of 10 years or even over a century. One of the fundamental characteristics of this desert is that an absolute lack of precipitation can occur over periods of several consecutive years. For example, if we say that Reggan receives 1 cm of precipitation per year, this means, in fact, that during a period of 10 years there have been 2 or 3 rainfalls averaging 30 mm each (Table II). From an ecological point of view, it is literally impossible to speak of average precipitation, for under such circumstances it would be absolutely meaningless.

Rainfall in the Sahara occurs usually at random over no particular area and in one region or another. However, in 1951, at Béni-Abbès, the distribution of precipitation did occur entirely during the four winter months (Binet, 1955).

Mention is made in the literature of periods of extreme aridity without a drop of rain for several years in the Mzab, at In-Salah, in the Touat and in the Tanezrouft. In these regions, the annual mean of precipitation is less than 1 cm and might even be nil (Table II). For example, at Reggan the annual mean can vary from 0 to 10 mm from one year to the next.

However, the littoral deserts and the few Saharan mountain regions are an exception to this rule (the Hoggar, Ajjer Tassili, the Aïr, and the Tibesti). These regions receive a small but quite regular amount of summer and winter rainfall. This accumulated humidity makes possible the existence of woodlice and snails (Monod, 1931, 1969).

Rainfall in the Sahara occurs most of the time under the form of a sudden, heavy shower, streaming down over the surface of the ground with a relatively small amount of infiltration, launching the heavy growth of

TABLE II

PRECIPITATION AT REGGAN FROM FEBRUARY 1959 TO JANUARY 1965[a]

Year	Jan.	Feb.	March	April	May	June	July	Aug.	Sept.	Oct.	Nov.	Dec.	Total
1959		0.1	t	t	t	t			6.8	t	t		6.9
1960			0.1	t	t	2.7	0.2		t	t	t	t	3.0
1961				t	t	t				t			t
1962		5.1	t	t	t	0.6		t	t	t	6.9	t	12.6
1963	t	t	t			t	?	0.3			t		2.4
1964								t		2.1	t	28.4	28.4
1965	33.7												

[a] Rain in mm, t = traces.

ephemerals. Consequently, rainfalls providing only a small quantity of water ranging from 1 to 5 mm are totally ineffective, since the water evaporates before it can be accumulated. The hygrometric degree of the air remains low (Table III).

2. Temperature

Desert temperatures are characterized by high maxima and by great variations between winter and summer as well as between day and night (Fig. 3a,b and Tables IV and V) The dryness of the air is the factor which is responsible for causing these sudden variations of great amplitude (Schirmer, 1893).

At Reggan, in 1960–1961, the mean maximum air temperature was recorded as 45.5°C and the mean minimum as 31.0°C during the warmest month (July). During the coldest month (January), the mean maximum was 20.0°C, and the mean minimum 5.9°C (Table IV). That same year, the absolute temperature extremes were 48.1° and 1.2°C. An absolute temperature maximum of 59.1°C was recorded at Tindouf (Pierre, 1958) and 54.4°C at Timimoun (Planhol and Rognon, 1970).

Freezing temperatures in the northern and central Sahara are not exceptional; Béni-Abbès, Adrar, In Salah and Reggan, can get such temperatures for more than 1 week/year, but it rarely gets lower than −3°C. However, in other regions such as Tibesti, minimal temperatures might sometimes reach −22°C.

Grenot and Niaussat (1967) have observed in a reg near Reggan, temperatures below freezing on the ground surface during several nights in December, 1959 and January, 1960.

In the daytime, the soil warms up faster than the air, and as a consequence, the soil temperature is notably higher. However, at night, the sandy surface (erg) cools off faster than the air, while the rock surfaces (hamada) remain warmer (Fig. 3a,b and Table VI) (Grenot, 1968a).

The annual range of thermic variations can be greater than 60°C. The diurnal thermic amplitude, which is the difference between maximal temperature during the day and minimal temperature during the night, is quite often greater than 35°C. Temperature variations occur more abruptly in an erg than in any other type of surface formations. In the spring, the temperature of the sand surface in midday can be as high as 60°C, while the temperature of the air, directly adjacent to it, remains below 40°C. This temperature rise on the surface is not propagated deeply into the soil. At 20 cm, diurnal variations are quite diminished; this is true especially in rock formations, where temperature is seldom higher than 30°C, allowing the survival of various species of animals. During the summer, the sand

TABLE III

Monthly Average Relative Humidity (%) at Reggan from 1959 to 1962[a]

Year		Jan.	Feb.	March	April	May	June	Jul.	Aug.	Sept.	Oct.	Nov.	Dec.
1959	M	58	*62*		30	28	22	21	27	34	37	46	58
	m	27	25		13	11	10	9	11	14	16	21	23
	Hm	41	*42*	31	19	18	14	*13*	17	22	25	32	39
1960	M	47	36	39	43	28	30	26	17	25	30	40	*62*
	m	17	13	16	15	11	13	10	*9*	10	13	17	27
	Hm	31	23	26	27	19	20	17	*14*	16	20	27	*42*
1961	M	*57*	42	35	27	20	23	17	23	24	37	35	41
	m	22	14	12	11	*9*	10	*9*	10	11	16	15	19
	Hm	*37*	26	20	16	*13*	*10*	12	15	16	24	24	30
1962	M	46	48										
	m	16	18										
	Hm	30	31	22	16	13	*10*	*10*	13	17	23	25	*38*

[a] Maximum (M); minimum (m); humidity (mean) (Hm). Highest and lowest yearly values in italics.

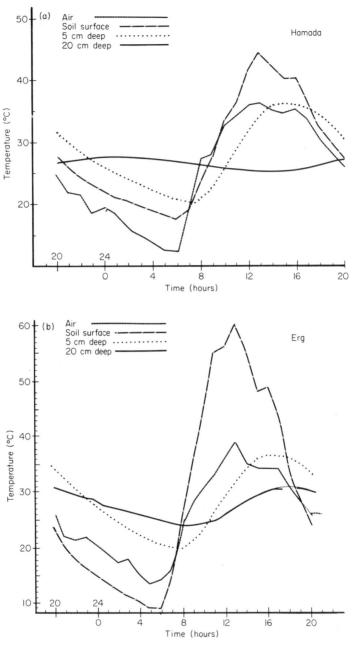

Fig. 3. (a) Temperature changes of the soil surface, underground layers (at depths of 5 and 20 cm) and of the air, during the day and night in a hamada (rocky substrata) *Uromastix* biotope. Data registered from May 7, 1967 at 8:00 PM to May 8, 1967 at 8:00 PM. (After C. Grenot, 1968a). (b) Temperature changes of the soil surface, underground layers (at depths of 5 and 20 cm) and of the air, during the day and night in an erg (sandy substrata); preferential biotope of *Varanus griseus*. Data registered at the same time as those of (a).

TABLE IV

Monthly Average Temperatures (°C) at Reggan from 1959 to 1965[a]

Year		Jan.	Feb.	March	April	May	June	Jul.	Aug.	Sept.	Oct.	Nov.	Dec.
1959	M	22.6	22.6	29.7	33.9	37.4	43.5	*44.6*	44.2	42.5	35.5	26.4	21.9
	m	*8.4*	10.0	14.9	18.0	22.9	28.1	29.5	30.1	28.4	21.6	13.3	8.5
1960	M	21.9	29.8	29.9	31.8	38.4	40.5	*45.5*	45.1	40.4	36.2	29.6	19.7
	m	*7.1*	13.5	14.7	17.1	24.0	27.2	31.0	30.7	26.1	22.1	15.2	7.3
1961	M	20.0	25.1	27.0	34.8	39.9	41.5	*44.2*	42.9	39.9	34.4	30.4	24.3
	m	*5.9*	9.4	12.4	19.3	24.7	27.7	30.9	29.6	25.8	20.7	17.5	10.1
1962	M	23.1	21.9	28.0	33.0	38.1	42.8	*44.8*	42.9	39.9	33.5	25.1	21.3
	m	9.2	9.2	14.8	18.4	23.4	28.4	30.5	29.3	27.2	21.0	13.3	*8.4*
1963	M	24.7	25.4	28.3	34.0	34.9	41.3	?	*44.5*	40.4	31.8	29.0	22.9
	m	11.9	11.4	13.2	19.3	20.5	28.1	?	31.4	27.1	18.5	14.8	*10.7*
1964	M	20.1	25.5	31.1	29.3	38.7	42.5	43.8	*44.5*	39.7	35.0	26.3	19.9
	m	*7.0*	10.3	16.0	16.4	24.4	27.6	30.1	30.8	26.0	20.6	12.3	9.2
1965	M	19.7	26.6	29.7									
	m	8.9	11.8	16.0									

[a] Maximum (M), minimum (m). Highest and lowest yearly values in italics.

TABLE V

Highest and Lowest Absolute Temperature Readings (°C) on the Plateau at Reggan from 1959 to 1965[a]

Year		Jan.	Feb.	March	April	May	June	July	Aug.	Sept.	Oct.	Nov.	Dec.
1959	M	27.3	28.8	35.7	40.6	42.2	*47.4*	47.0	46.9	46.4	39.1	31.2	25.8
	m	*2.2*	5.9	8.8	12.3	17.2	21.8	22.7	27.2	24.0	14.5	7.4	3.3
1960	M	27.7	38.3	33.0	37.8	43.5	46.2	47.2	*48.1*	44.2	40.1	34.9	23.7
	m	*1.2*	4.5	12.0	11.2	13.4	21.8	28.4	27.6	22.8	16.1	9.8	3.1
1961	M	24.4	29.0	34.5	42.4	*46.8*	45.8	45.4	45.3	42.3	39.1	36.7	28.9
	m	3.0	6.3	6.8	12.2	16.8	18.4	28.4	24.9	22.2	15.0	12.3	*2.8*
1962	M	28.2	28.2	33.4	38.0	42.3	46.3	*47.2*	45.2	39.9	39.4	30.1	28.5
	m	4.8	2.9	8.4	12.3	17.6	21.6	27.4	25.1	23.5	18.0	7.3	*1.9*
1963	M	29.8	29.3	34.5	41.5	40.5	46.3	?	*46.5*	44.4	39.0	33.8	28.
	m	7.0	5.9	6.3	14.2	17.7	18.0		28.5	21.7	14.8	7.7	4.
1964	M	25.1	34.3	35.8	38.3	41.4	47.2	*47.6*	46.4	42.5	39.8	32.8	25.0
	m	*2.9*	4.2	10.6	11.0	16.3	22.2	25.3	26.5	21.4	12.8	8.3	4.2
1965	M	30.5	31.9	36.4									
	m	4.1	5.0	11.2									

[a] Maximum (M), minimum (m). Highest and lowest yearly values given in italics.

TABLE VI

Maximum (T_M) and Minimum (T_m) Temperatures Recorded during
a Hot Day in Spring (May 7, 1967) at Béni-Abbès in the
Erg and on the Hamada

| | Temperature (°C) | | | |
| | Erg | | Hamada | |
Measurement taken	T_M	T_m	T_M	T_m
In air	39	13.5	36	12
At surface	60	9	44	18
At 5 cm depth	36	20	36	20.5
At 20 cm depth	31	24	27.5	25

temperature can rise above 70°C (Dubief, 1959, 1963; Planhol and Rognon, 1970).

3. Wind

In the Sahara, the wind is almost constant and quite turbulent. This has had a great impact on humans owing to its depressing effect on many individuals.

As a consequence of its location at the latitude of the Tropic of Cancer, the Sahara is subjected to very high temperatures and to a wind pattern characterized by the blowing of warm and dry currents. To the north, winds blowing from the Mediterranean Sea are hindered by the Atlas mountain chain. This results in a premature condensation of the atmospheric water vapor. To the east, the trade wind circulating along the Atlantic coast counteracts and detours the marine wind.

The general direction of the winds in the central Sahara, particularly at Reggan, is usually from the east or northeast. This is due both to the relatively low-pressure zone existing almost permanently over the intertropical zone, as well as to the high pressures present over the temperate zone of the north. However, a great number of other parameters are involved locally, such as thermic depressions of very low amplitude, or, on a wider scale, the Hoggar Massif, for instance, which through the action of northerly current succeeds in modifying the isobar curve.

One of the most important weathering agents responsible for the shaping of the desertic topography is the wind (Dubief, 1952). However, since its action is that of an extremely slow process, its importance might be underestimated (Meckelein, 1959; Dresch, 1966). The Sahara with its

Fig. 4. Typical evidence of the weathering effects: ruiniform rock formations sculptured by erosion (in one of the regs of the Tanezrouft).

relatively even relief is subjected to very high temperatures as well as to extreme variations between diurnal and nocturnal temperature ranges, resulting in the breaking, cracking, and progressive crumbling of the rock formations. The relief is also subjected to a nearly constant mechanical action of the wind which, by blowing particles of sand with great force, causes extensive erosion. The wind transforms granite and sandstone rock formations into tortuous-appearing features (Fig. 4). However, in certain protected areas (shallow basins), an important sedimentation process does occur, resulting in the formation of wind-blown sand dunes (Fig. 5).

The velocity of the wind may reach and even exceed 100 km/hour and its effects on the ground surface are of great amplitude. At Reggan, the wind mean monthly intensity is 14–28 km/hour. However, even more violent winds can occur each month reaching an intensity greater than 56 km/hour, and this is not uncommon. A maximal wind intensity of 104 km/hour was recorded in March, 1964.

Sandstone disaggregation owing to fluvial erosion is sufficient to account, not only, for the presence of large dune massifs, but also for less important sand formations scattered on the desert surface (Bellair, 1940, 1953). The old concept which claimed that the Sahara was a "dried out ocean floor" has long been rejected. Even the sand origin, just mentioned, is no

Fig. 5. Moving dunes and "ripple-marks" (Tanezrouft).

longer subject to discussion. As we discussed earlier, the constant agitation of the air in the Sahara would apparently be due to anticyclonic and low atmospheric pressure masses of a planetary origin, but it is, in fact, most of the time a direct result of the considerable daily thermic variations and of the repartition of the sand formations (ergs) and rock formations. The sandy surfaces warm up and cool off much more rapidly than the rock formations. The difference in thermal conduction of these two materials has a direct bearing upon the local distribution of the barometric pressures and thus create the formation of atmospheric currents (winds).

The "sand wind" is very turbulent and blows on the very dry sand surface, obstructing all visibility; the sand particles can be lifted up by tornadoes to an altitude of more than 1500 meters, and carried away at a distance of several hundred kilometers from their point of origin. This burning and dehydrating wind is locally known as sirocco, simoun, or harmattan. It originates in the high-pressure centers existing in the desertic continental zone and blows in the direction of low-pressure centers often observed in the occidental basin of the Mediterranean Sea. It has been quite vividly depicted by the painter and writer Fromentin (1856).

4. Evaporation

Evaporation is a physical phenomenon which increases with temperature, dryness, and air turbulence. The annual potential evaporation rate in the Algerian Sahara is extremely high, from 2.5 to 6 meters. It could reach 4.80 meters in Béni-Abbès, while in California or in the Australian desert, for example, it is generally less than 3 meters (Dubief, 1950).

Air hygrometric degree, or relative humidity, remains very low. "Nowhere else on the earth has air been found as dry as in the Sahara region" (Savornin, 1947). In the arid Sahara, delimited by the isohyet of 2 or 5 cm annually, the relative humidity varies between 4 and 20% (Table III). But in the septentrional Sahara it reaches 20 to 30% during the summer, and goes up to 50% during the winter.

Vegetation, a relay station between the water contents of the ground and of the atmosphere, plays an important role in contributing to humidity of the air. For example, in the same area and at the same moment, the relative humidity in a reg or hamada (bare ground) would be close to 10% as opposed to 90% in a palm grove (oasis). This fact already leads us to realize the importance of "microclimates."*

5. Luminosity

Because of the absence of nebulosity, the Sahara is one of the regions of the earth where direct solar insolation is the greatest, during 300–360 days/year. In 1964, at Reggan, the monthly mean cloud cover varied from 4% (July and September) to 31% (December). Such high luminosity is a dehydrating factor, since it increases the temperature effects. It could become a considerable source of energy. Each square meter of the Sahara receives from the sun an average of 1 kW of heat and luminous power. An area of 100×100 km receives approximately 25×10^{12} kWh annually, or the heat equivalent of roughly 2×10^9 metric tons of fuel, (derived from Chouard, 1957). Let us remember that the surface of the Sahara is 8×10^6 km^2.

6. Aridity Concepts

Aridity is closely related to rainfall and temperature. Thus, "water" and "temperature" counteract one another, particularly in regards to vegetation (Ozenda, 1958).

Aridity is defined by numerous formulas which vary according to their authors (de Martonne, 1926; Emberger, 1938; Bagnouls and Gaussen, 1953; Thornthwaite, 1948, 1958). We will only refer here to the definitions established by Capot-Rey (1951, 1953) and Dubief (1950, 1959,

---

* See also Volume I, pp. 6, 46, 364, and 399 for discussions dealing with microclimates—ED.

1963), as they seem to represent the biologic realities quite well. Aridity is represented by the ratio of rainfall to evaporation. The index chart drawn from it superimposes that of the pluviometry.

To sum up, the principal climatic characteristics of the Sahara are (a) low amount of precipitation received annually (mean annual rainfall is less than 10 cm) (see Fig. 1 and Table II), (b) extreme irregularity of rainfall frequency, (c) air dryness, and (d) wind amplitude. In the Sahara, seasons are not well delineated. It is generally possible, however, to distinguish a warm and a cold season.

D. Desert Relief

1. General Considerations

The Sahara is a peneplain with a few mountainous massifs jutting out, known as jebels, such as the mounts of Ougarta, the Adrar of Iforas, the Aïr, the Hoggar, and the Tibesti.

The relief of the Sahara has been greatly affected by the climatic variations of the Quaternary (rainfall, fluvial, and aeolian erosion), entirely reshaping the landscape and creating its distinctive features (Chavaillon, 1964; Planhol and Rognon, 1970). Only in a desert can one find this kind of erosion and transportation of the surface materials by the wind that reaches such an amplitude and violence (Figs. 4 and 5).

2 Rock Formations

When original rock formations are composed of large, homogeneous tabular beds, the effects of erosion result in the formation of rocky plateaus—the "hamada" or "tassili." These hamadas show traces of ancient fluvial erosion, as evidenced by remaining buttes capped most of the time with a hard, rock, tablelike feature, and known as "gour," (sing.: "gara") (Fig. 6) as well as by gorges dug into the plateaus (the Mouydir and the Ajjer Tassili). On the other hand, when the original rock formations are of the heterogeneous type, the wind disaggregates the less resistant components leaving only the hardest particles to form a gravelly surface, the "reg." If we consider the reg genesis, we can identify two major types of ergs: autochthonal, resulting from the dissociation of elements; and allochthonal, originating in the transport and accumulation of various elements, and which is also called alluvial reg. However, hard rock is often covered with some kind of a patina having the appearance of a varnished luster; this patina is, in fact, "a crust of chemicals which have been brought to the surface by capillarity and fixed by evaporation; it is of a dark red

Fig. 6. "Gour," tabular-topped butte, detached from the Tademaït plateau. In the foreground, the "reg," remaining glacis left from the erosion of the soft strata during the Lower Cretaceous.

or black coloring following the various oxidation processes involved; where the crust has burst open, the lighter colored core of the rock contrasts sharply with it" (Gautier, 1928).

3. Wind Action and Dune Formation

Wind-blown particles are deposited in sheltered areas and in shallow basins, where the wind velocity is lower, to form: (a) *nebka,* the small, arrow-shaped sand accumulations found under the wind and behind bushes and rock buttes (Fig. 7); (b) active dunes or *barkhanes,* crescent-shaped, and often isolated, whole convexity and concavity indicates the direction of the prevailing wind (Fig. 5); and (c) large dune massifs, or *ergs* (Brosset, 1939; Capot-Rey, 1943; Bellair, 1953; Monod, 1958; Conrad, 1969).

Dunes can reach a height of more than 100 meters and are composed of a yellow or orange, very fine sand, whose particle diameter varies between 54 and 480 μm (Alimen *et al.,* 1957, 1964). The nature of the sand is quite variable. In general, the erg dimensions are considerable; together the Great Occidental Erg (Capot-Rey, 1943) and the Great Oriental Erg, would equal the area of France.

The dune surface is constantly reshaped by the lightest wind. When a storm occurs, the dune "smokes" and the horizon disappears completely behind a sand haze; however, the dune itself, as a whole does not move. In fact, it is relatively fixed.

Fig. 7. "Nebka," at the foot of a Chenopodiaceae (*Traganum nudatum*) clump, in a reg near Reggan.

4. Individual Features

It is in the Sahara that the most typical desertic features are found.

a. Jebel. The jebel is a mountainous massif. Its slopes, where the vegetation is extremely scarce, are formed of huge blocks of rock generally covered with a shiny, black patina. Between jebels, we find dry stream channels or wadis, whose floors consist of broken rocks and gravels which fell from mountain slopes (Fig. 8). Vegetation density here is higher than on the surrounding jebels, consisting of a few plants and brushes.

b. The Hamada or Tassili. This is a desolate rocky plateau, usually formed of limestone or sandstone (Fig. 6); the vegetation is mostly that of scattered, scraggly shrubs, with hairy stems and leaves and often grayish in color (Joly *et al.*, 1954; Lavocat, 1955). The rocky plateaus of the septentrional Sahara, as well as the regs of the same region, are usually totally barren; however, one can find some enclosed depressions, i.e., *dayas,* where running water has accumulated. Such are the only areas where a diversified vegetation, often perennial, can grow (Conrad *et al.*, 1967).

c. The Reg. This is usually found on the location of an ancient alluvial plain, has a substratum composed of gravels, pebbles, and various dissociated materials (vast, Recent or Quaternary detrital sheets, fissile struc-

Fig. 8. Mounts of Ougarta (Rhenouma jebel). In the foreground, a wadi at intermittent flow allowing the growth of a permanent type of vegetation (*Acacia raddiana*).

tural layers, etc.). Here one finds the growth of a diffuse type of vegetation, with a preponderance of bushes of the Chenopodiaceae (Fig. 7). In the central Sahara, regs are generally barren and constitute the poorest environment of that region. In fact, in many large areas they can even be considered as abiotic (e.g., Tanezrouft) (Fig. 4).

d. *The Erg or Iguidi.* The dune massifs constitute an environment almost totally impenetrable to most human beings. Only nomads pass through it, following an itinerary outlined by wells where they graze their camels during the summer. The erg is the richest environment in water, after the wadi (see below) and oasis (Fig. 9). In hollows, evidence of moisture is found at a depth of only a few centimeters, and on the slopes at approximately 80 cm or so. The superficial stratum is always powdery. There are very few annual plants here, but there is a great number of perennials. Vegetation is characterized by a preponderance of drinn bushes (*Aristida pungens*). These are cespitose Gramineae whose rhizome resembles the rush of our moist grasslands, but which sometimes coexist with a vegetation composed of shrubby, leafless trees, such as the r'tem (*Retama retam*)

Fig. 9. Region of Béni-Abbès. The Saoura (wadi of permanent underflow) located at the intersection of the Guir hamada and the Great Occidental Erg.

and the *Calligonum* (*C. comosum*). Because of low but constant humidity, plants can remain green even in midsummer, while in the jebels and hamadas, the vegetation has months ago withered.

Nowhere else in the deserts of the New World, do we find the equivalent of the Saharan ergs. But the barkhanes, the small, walking dunes, can also be found in the Asiatic deserts and in Death Valley in North America.

e. The Wadi and Oasis. These are humid environments where the vegetation is relatively thick (Fig. 9). Wadi banks provide occasional pastures for the nomads, while the oases are representative of a sedentary form of habitat with gardens and agricultural developments (Chevalier, 1932, 1938; Chouard, 1957).

E. Water in the Sahara

1. Surface Water

In a true desert, such as the Sahara, the circulation of surface water is almost nonexistent. However, traces of a fossil hydrographic system have been found (Atlas, Tademaït, Hoggar). Most of the streambeds are dry except after sudden and extremely violent rainstorms (wadis with temporary flow) (Cornet, 1952, 1964) (Fig. 8).

The Saoura is one of the few wadis to have regular and annual rising flows (Fig. 9). The source of its water is melted snow which covers the summits of the Moroccan High Atlas chain. This wadi benefits from a permanent under-seepage (Dubief, 1953; Roche, 1968; Conrad, 1969). It can drain extra Saharan waters through the desert as far as the Touat with its meridional effluent, the Wadi Messaoud. In large wadis, there is, in fact, a seeping of the water, called "underflow," through the alluvia.

2. Subsurface Water

Underground hydrography maintains a ribbon of vegetation, discontinuous but persistent, at the surface of the ground. These valleys or shallow basins are mostly used as grazing areas. On the other hand, in regions where there is no underground water, only the scarce Saharan showers can initiate the growth of vegetation, which is then ephemeral and disappears rapidly and is known as *acheb* or *rbia*.

Under most of the great dune massifs exists an aquifer located at varied depths, whose waters for the most part originate out of heavy, local precipitations (soft waters without leaching of salts) but which had occurred during the course of the moister periods in the past. The aquifer of the Great Occidental Erg was replenished roughly 5000–7000 years ago during the neolithic humid era (Conrad and Fontes, 1970). It should be noted that the gradient of salinity of this aquifer runs from the north to the south which does correspond to the inclination of this water-bearing stratum (Roche, 1968). Cornet (1952) believes that the origin of such subsurface reservoir would be essentially from waters provided by the meridional slope of the Saharan Atlas. These waters would also supply, to the south, not only the erg but also the Gourara and Touat regions (Conrad and Roche, 1965). Away from the valleys, these phreatic reservoirs are accessible through some rare wells generally marking the crossings of various camel trails.

3. Salt Deposits

In certain porous formations where water is close to the surface, it evaporates after having carried with it to the surface various soluble salts from the soil. These are then deposited on the surface to form a compact crust of "évaporites," composed of gypsum, calcium, and chlorides (Conrad, 1969). Certain flat-floored depressions, perfect zones of evaporation for the running water, or underground waters, are characterized by the presence of saline deposits (gypsum) (Figs. 10 and 11). These have their origin in the "intercalary continental" beds, and are known under the name of *sebkha,* in which the flora is rather poor. Such flora is composed of well-adapted halophytic species such as the Chenopodiaceae.

Depending on the regions, the water can be quite pure (as in Béni-Abbès), or it may contain a great number of salts in solution, (Reggan)

Fig. 10. Evolution of the Sebkha-el-Melah. Intermittant lake collecting the high-rising waters of the Saoura wadi. Note the white salt deposits on the shore.

Fig. 11. Evolution of the Sebkha-el-Melah. Dried-out lakes "evaporites" or salt crusts, located at the surface of clayey deposits (polygonal network).

(Table VII) (Monod, 1958; Mission Berliet, 1962; Cornet, 1964; Conrad, 1963).

4. Permanent Pools

One also finds a few, rare, more or less permanent water pools called *guelta* in Arabic, and *aguelmane* in Tuareg. These are generally located in mountainous massifs. In the mountains of the central Sahara, these water holes are deep and large, located in the middle of rock formations,

TABLE VII

ANALYSES OF WATER AT REGGAN

(a) Bacteriological: Bacteriologically pure water no muddy sediment

(b) Chemical

Measurements	Wells of Reggan		Forage Plateau		Wells of "fifth company"
Degree of hardness	111°	104°	90°	95°	112°
pH	—	7.25	—	—	7.5
Dry residue (mg/liter)	3318	3446	2354	2228	—
Ca (mg/liter)	305	292	205	210	245
Mg (mg/liter)	85	75	94	103	123
Na (mg/liter)	727	699	475	388	754
Cl (mg/liter)	944	776	657	639	910
SO_4 (mg/liter)	1177	1216	782	757	1130
CO_3 (mg/liter)	81	59	64	65	82
Combined NO_3 (mg/liter)	—	—	66	—	—
Date and place of analysis	June 20, 1957 Paris	July 7, 1957 Paris	December 20, 1957 Algiers	December 27, 1957 Algiers	February 7, 1957 Reggan

and keep a constant water level for many years. Their supply is provided either by running water from the surface or from underground reserves collected in permeable or porous rock formations (sandstone or volcanic rocks.)

Life in the Saharan oases is based upon irrigation processes (Larnaude, 1937; Capot-Rey, 1953; Planhol and Rognon, 1970). Quite often, the water at an oasis is collected by various means, but there is always a prevailing utilization process characterizing a whole group of palm groves.

5. Artesian Wells

In the northern part of the Great Oriental Erg, water is supplied by springs or artesian wells. For example, the artesian system of the Wadi Rhir is formed by several phreatic underground reservoirs located at different depths; in ancient times, the superior ones are known to have been used by the natives. In the case of a true artesian water well, the captive water surges spontaneously out of the ground. Just as a spring can get dammed up with mud and obstructed, wells will dry out unless they are cleaned regularly; this is why the famous divers of Ouargla had to dive into wells as deep as 60 meters or even more in order to disengorge the springs.

In a semi-artesian well, the ascending movement is not sufficient to bring up the water to the surface and it has to be drawn out. In most of the Saharan oases (Souf and Mzab) there are no artesian wells, and these must be dug to reach the water reservoir. If the water is close enough to the surface, the well is equipped with a weight lever system (Fig. 12); if it is deeper a pulley mechanism is then used (Mzab and Fezzan).

Savornin (1927–1928, 1947) was the first to demonstrate the existence of a large fossil water basin, the Albian underground reservoir, stretching under the entire surface of the Sahara, from the Atlas to the Hoggar. Today this vast artesian system is exploited by means of mechanical boring devices, capable of drilling to great depths (Cornet, 1964; Furon, 1964).

6. Irrigation

The most original irrigation method in the Northern Sahara is still the foggara, typical of the Touat, Gourara, Tidikelt, and Fezzan regions.

In this irrigation process, the water is often collected at great distance by means of underground, slightly inclined tunnels with several shafts. The water seeping through the walls is collected and carried by gravity into the foggara (main tunnel), and from there into the seguia (aerial furrow), opening into the palm grove located downward.

Fig. 12. Well sweep in a palm grove of the Touat.

Each of the foggara owners, proportionally to his rights, then receives his portion of the water through the orifices cf a distributor shaped like a comb, from which it is stored in special basins (Fig. 13). This apparatus distributes the water in the irrigation system of pipes, or *seguia* (Fig. 14).

A foggara-irrigated region can easily be recognized at a distance by the lines of its water sumps. The inside of the foggara is high and wide enough to allow a man to walk through it for cleaning purposes and for getting rid of any debris which accumulate.

The actual hydrographic network of the Sahara is composed of super-

Fig. 13. Principal comb-shaped distributor dispensing the water surging out of the "foggara" (oasis of Timimoun).

ficial water streams running sporadically on its surface and which participate in replenishing the water-bearing strata linked to the *inferoflux* of the wadis (an example of this are the Saoura valley and the wadi's aquiferous stratum); these waters contain tritium of thermonuclear origin. Most of the ancient water-bearing strata are the suppliers of ancient waters which have been accumulated in aquiferous reservoirs thousands or even tens of thousands of years ago, such as, for example, the inferior continental Cretaceous one (Conrad and Fontes, 1970). The existence of such superficial and deep underground water-bearing strata, as well as the vast aquiferous system of the Sahara, are the determining factors of life in this boundless desert.

III. Vegetation in the Sahara Desert

A. GENERAL CONSIDERATIONS

1. Paucity

The phanerogamic flora of the Sahara is very poor if one compares the number of species of vascular plants (about 1200) in the desert to the

Fig. 14. Secondary distributor or "comb" situated in a *seguia* of the palm grove.

large number of vascular species of the Mediterranean or tropical regions which border the Sahara.

The Saharan cryptogamic flora is not well known, and a general survey of it is yet to be undertaken. Only certain zones, particularly the mountainous ones, have been worked on by researchers such as Maire (1933, 1940), who studied the Hoggar, Maire and Monod (1950), who dealt with Tibesti, and Quézel (1958), who also contributed to this field.

The algae of the Sahara have not been worked on since Gauthier-Lievre (1941, in Quézel, 1958) reported on the freshwater and salt marsh algae. An approximation of the number of the other cryptogams groups known is: 60 mushrooms, 90 lichens, and about 100 mosses (Faurel and Schotter, in Quézel, 1958). The number of known species of coprophilic, mycological vegetation in the Sahara is already more than 100 (Faurel and Schotter, 1965a,b, 1966). In spite of the rarity of the higher mushrooms in the open desert, often hypogenous mushrooms (closely related to truffles and known as *terfez*) develop after a spring rain as parasites on the roots of *Helianthemum*. These mushrooms are a delicacy for the nomads (Fig. 15).

Fig. 15. A mushroom, probably *Coprinus arenarius,* in an arenaceous zone of the Ougarta mountains.

2. Affinities

The Saharo-sindian zone, which extends over the central and septentrional Sahara, is linked by biogeographers to the "holarctic floral empire," while the Soudan-deccanian region, which corresponds to the meridional Sahara and the savanna, is linked to the "paleotropical floral empire" (Monod, 1931, 1957, 1968).

Thus there is a Saharo-sindian element in the Saharan flora near the north and center, and the Soudano-deccanian element becomes more and more important further south in the Sahara. However, in addition to these two elements, there is a penetration of Mediterranean influence in the septentrional Sahara and in the high mountainous regions, and a penetration of tropical influence in the meridional Sahara.

The Saharo-sindian element is characterized by its homogeneity. It is clearly predominant in the central Sahara where it is represented by a subgroup of endemic species which are not present in Asia.

The severity of the Saharan environment permits a high degree of endemism. At the species level, as many as 25% of the plants are endemic to the Saharan environment; the number of endemic varieties is even greater. Many species are of Mediterranean origin, especially in the mountainous regions of the central Sahara. Above 1800 meters there is a steppe, which is characterized by genera of Mediterranean origin not found elsewhere in the Sahara. Examples are *Myrtus,* with *M. nivellei* similar to *M. communis,* and *Olea,* with *O. laperrini* closely related to *O. europaea* (Monod, 1931, 1939; Ozenda, 1958). In Hoggar, Tibesti, and Ajjers Tassili, the degree of endemism is high, and it increases with altitude. The presence of these endemic species is proof of an ancient extension of the Mediterranean flora into these regions prior to the arrival of the desert climate during a later period.

However, there are other ecologically isolated regions where there is considerable endemism, such as at the great saharan ergs. The flora of the Great Oriental Erg is composed of only 100 species, of which several are endemic.

3. Systematic Composition

The phanerogamic flora is quite varied in its systematic and geographic composition. The three predominant families, Graminosae, Leguminosae (see *Acacia,* Fig. 16), and Compositae, represent more than one-third of the flora. The families with a holarctic distribution, such as Caryphyllaceae and Labiatae, are reduced. On the other hand, those with tropical affinities such as Convolvulaceae, Asclepiadaceae, and Capparidaceae are of more importance (Ozenda, 1958).

Saharan Chenopodiaceae of a true desert type are the result of a differentiation and of an impoverishment of the Mediterranean genera. *Anabasis* and *Nucularia* are two Saharan genera. The Crucifereae are very common

Fig. 16. A stand of *Acacia raddiana* or "talha" in a depression in the Igli region.

in the Sahara, but their number decreases as one gets closer to the tropical regions. The Zygophyllaceae are also represented by a large number of Saharan species; seven genera and about 30 species are present. Many of these play an important part in the physiognomy of the desert. Vegetation of the hamadas of the septentrional and central Sahara is characterized by *Fagonia glutinosa* (Grenot, 1968b).

The desertic environment has produced a general impoverishment of the vegetation which varies greatly from one family to another. This has not been compensated for by the development of typically Saharan families. In fact, no endemic families exist in the Sahara. Most of the families are represented by only one or two genera, and most of the genera by one or two species. These species are not necessarily the same from the central Sahara to the meridional Sahara. Few genera (*Euphorbia, Aristida, Fagonia*) occur with the same frequency from one end of the desert to another.

The generic coefficient, a ratio of the number of genera to the number of species, is very high, nearly 0.70. This high coefficient is characteristic of an impoverished flora (Corti, 1942; Guinet and Sauvage, in Joly *et al.*, 1954).

4. The Biology of Desert Plants

Are the effects of dryness leading directly to propitious "adaptations" permitting the survival of certain plants in an arid environment? This type of direct influence hypothesis follows the theories of Lamarck (Oppenheimer, 1961). But this hypothesis is not proved by actual facts. The facts can be more aptly explained by the Darwinistic theory that adaptations to the dryness are a result of natural selection on heterogeneous populations.

Tanezrouft and Ténéré are particularly abiotic regions of the Sahara. Aside from some special cases, vegetation does exist, but its density is directly related to the ambient humidity. Animal life depends largely on microclimates; these are often a function of the vegetation.

a. Adaptation to the Environment. In the desert, the cover of vegetation is discontinuous and very irregular. The plants occur in areas where there is adequate water and protection. Consequently, vegetation has a tendency to be concentrated in the more favorable areas which are often scarce and very localized and where the humidity factor is higher than in other areas (Killian, 1934; Boyko, 1951; Binet, 1955).

The quantity of water provided by rainfall is important for the onset of germination, but the prevailing atmospheric conditions are equally important for survival. Thus rainfall, temperature, and germination are closely related. In the Sahara, as in other desert regions, plant seeds germinate with considerable speed. Saturated with water after a rainshower, seeds of *Anabasis aretioides* unfold their embryos in 10 minutes. Ten hours later, their roots are anchored in the soil and the spread green cotyledons are capable of photosynthesis. But germination is equally a function of certain edaphic characters. Seeds of *Anabasis aretioides* germinate generally on the surface of permeable soil, soil free of chlorides and one which can retain a sufficient amount of water. The plants, widely scattered, are often spaced nearly 50 meters apart. They give no indication of being a cover of vegetation. This necessary spacing between each plant occurs by mutual elimination and progressively through competition. The more resistant vegetation exists as a consequence of minute adaptations which give the desert flora a unique physiognomy.

In spite of the plasticity of the Saharan plants, a "pasture" is composed of only a few species, and one of these predominates. It is the same for trees, in that, over vast stretches of land, one species of tree will dominate the landscape. It seems that climate, rather than the nature of the soil, dictates this localization. In this physical environment where the struggle for life is hard, the smallest accumulation of salt or chalk may render plant life impossible.

Natural selection and evolution have created the types of plants which are adapted to the rigors of an arid climate. Arid region plants—the xerophytes—can withstand the dryness, extreme heat, and intense sunlight. In the Sahara, soil surface temperatures sometimes exceed 70°C. Desert plants are also resistant to sand storms. However, not all of the plants of this region are necessarily adapted to eremic conditions. Some plants survive under a general scarcity of water, but these must, especially, be able to cope with the extreme irregularity of the hydrologic regime of the desert. There are often periods of several years without a drop of rain. Hence, the periods of plant activity are very short. Between such times of activity, the plants must remain in the dry air and soil, unable to benefit from heat and light which only aggravate the dryness.

Plants use various means to subsist during the long dry spells. Certain plants exhibit a shortened period of development, a stratagem ensuring maximum use of a minimum of water. Some desert plants may suppress all of the aerial parts during the dry period and remain as a seed or as a subterranean organ (for example, a bulb or a rhizome). Other plants, by contrast, maintain the aerial portion but expose anatomical and functional devices which assure them a better supply of water or a reduction of transpiration. The ephemeral and the permanent types of vegetation are distinguished below.

b. Ephemerals. These constitute a temporary vegetation consisting of annuals and geophytes. Annuals appear shortly after a rainfall and develop with surprising rapidity (see Fig. 17). The blanket of vegetation denoted

Fig. 17. A group of *Asphodelus* (Liliaceae) appeared following a short rain in a small wadi (north occidental Sahara).

as the *acheb,* on which domestic animals feed well, is thus formed. This is true of the small grass, *Aristida,* or *n'si,* which in places constitutes the true ephemeral prairies as found in Adrar of Iforas (Hardy, 1930). The ephemerals remain dwarfed. They bloom even though they may have only two leaves, and they bring their seeds to maturity in a few weeks or sometimes a few days before the soil dries out. They thus escape the long periods of drought (several years by Tanezrouft) which occur in "true" deserts.

Geophytes are long-lived plants which survive not by seeds but by subterranean organs operating at a reduced metabolic rate. Examples are provided by the bulbous Liliaceae: *Urginea noctiflora, Androcymbium saharae,* and *A. punctatum* (the latter shown in Fig. 18). Included in this category also would be *Ferula* (Apiaceae) with its fleshy rhizomes. The aerial portions of these plants follow an annual cycle.

The adaptations of the temporary vegetation are essentially a reduction of the length of the vegetative cycle (Lemée, 1953, 1954). Certain long-lived plants in the Mediterranean or Sudanese zones become annuals in the Sahara and follow a regime of intermittent activity.

c. Perennials. Among the perennials, there are a number of anatomical adaptations, aside from a variety of physiological adaptations, which are as yet poorly understood. The morphological adaptations consist of a particularly large growth of the root system (hence increasing absorptive surface)

Fig. 18. *Androcymbium punctatum,* a Liliaceae with a bulb deeply anchored in the soil.

and a reduction in the leaf surface area (hence, decreasing transpiration). Other devices exist such as villosity, fleshy or thick leaves, and the adaptations of cutinization, reduction and protection of stoma, tissue aquifers, increased palisade and sclerenchyma tissues, and others. Some typical plants are shown in Figs. 19 and 20.

The plants which best resist desiccation are those in which vital functions continue in spite of the scarcity of water. This group is composed of Euphorbiaceae and other succulents such as the Chenopodiaceae; non-succulents like desert shrubs that are devoid of leaves; and certain Papilionaceae and Gramineae which pass the dry season in more or less a state of dormancy. It is among these plants that the ability to store water and use it sparingly is shown most clearly by adaptive characters. The Genista of the desert, *Retama retam,* (see Fig. 21) is characteristic of dunes and is an extremely valuable shrub for the nomad. It is his firewood and is the major source of wood for his work. Tent posts, stakes, and other items are made from the yellow, fibrous, and most resistant portion of the wood. Cinders of the firewood are even mixed with tobacco for chewing.*

    d. The Problem of Absorption. Desert plants as a whole have a hypertrophied root system. The volume of the root system is much greater than

---

* The latter practice must have predated charcoal-containing chewing gum—ED.

Fig. 19. A tuft of *Perralderia coronopifolia* in the shelter of a rock. The finely divided leaves are very toxic.

Fig. 20. *Lotus roudairei,* a silky plant with leaves which appear gray because of the presence of numerous small fibers or down.

the aerial portion of the plant. The length of the roots can be astonishing (Kachkarov and Korovine, 1942). Small grass that are a few centimeters high can have a root that is more than 1 meter long.

Fig. 21. Shrubs of the sand, *Retama retam* (mounts of Ougarta).

It is principally because of the density of the root system of the colo-cynth (*Colocynthis vulgaris*), seen in Fig. 22, and other Cucurbitaceae that they are able to resist drought. These roots are characterized by long slender "rain roots," which form rapidly after a rain. They increase the surface area for absorption and permit the plant to profit from very short periods of hydration.

The underground apparatus of desert vegetation is frequently specialized for a particular mode of absorption. Thus in sand plants, the roots form a horizontal net which can utilize rainwater as well as moisture conden-sates. When rainwater is not available, the phreatic nappe and roots can penetrate several meters below ground in search of water.

The majority of species living in the desert have a layer of sand aggluti-nated to the roots which aids in protection against desiccation. A similar phenomenon owing to the presence of glandular pockets occurs on the leafy portion of several desert plants, such as *Cleome, Matthiola, Hyo-scyamus,* and *Fagonia.* Thus the seedlings of *Fagonia glutinosa* are flat-tened on the ground with the leaves completely impregnated with sand. Numerous examples can be cited of roots extending to great depths in the wadis. Roots of the *Acacia* have been found to extend to a depth of 30 meters. The well-known *Arbre du Ténéré* (*Acacia*) found totally isolated in the desert is a good example of the effectiveness of this stratagem. The degree of resistance of plants to a lack of water often depends upon the depth to which the roots penetrate.

Fig. 22. *Colocynthis vulgaris* on the dry ground—only the yellow fruits persist.

e. The Problem of Retention. In general, transpiration in plants occurs by the diffusion of water vapor through the epidermis of the leaves. The external wall of the epidermis is thickened by a cuticle of impermeable waxy substances. In contrast, a large amount of water vapor can escape through the stomata. These stomata, usually on the under side of the leaves, are bordered by specialized cells which bulge, enabling a regulation of the size of the opening to correspond to the amount of water in the cells. The rate of transpiration is high in plants with a large number of stomata and thin cuticles. Transpiration increases the rate of drying as does high temperature and the movement of air.

The reduced leaf surface area and decreased rate of transpiration in desert plants aid in conserving water reserves of the internal tissues. The reduction in surface area is achieved by reduction of both size and number of leaves. The shape of a leaf is also important. A leaf with a spherical shape has a minimum surface area for the maximum volume. The normal leaf shape for the Saharan plants is an exception. In effect, many Saharan species have small leaves (examples, *Genista,* Chenopodiaceae). Often leaves are reduced to small scales as in *Tamarix* shown in Fig. 23.

Sometimes the leaves even disappear; in this case the branches replace the leaves as the site of photosynthesis (for example, *Pituranthos*). Certain plants, veritable underground trees, have nothing exposed above ground except thin, leafed stems which are relatively short. Others, without modifying their structure, produce leaves during favorable periods, and the leaves

Fig. 23. An old *Tamarix* or "Tlaia" resistant to salts and the lack of water in the desert.

drop off during dry periods (for example, desert *Acacia, Zilla*). Often, leaves are replaced by spines, a stratagem to reduce water loss. These spinous plants are characteristic of the desert and also of the high mountains.

In some species of plants there seem to be two types of branches. In a cluster of *Launea arborescens* (Fig. 24), Binet (1955) noted that the periphery of the bushes had "sun branches," tough, spiny, and leafless, and that the interior had "shade branches," dark green, flexible, and with leaves and tender spines. This distinction is simply the result of adverse climatic conditions: wind, desiccation, or freezing of the leaf buds.

However, some species have two types of morphology, e.g., *Zilla macroptera*. Those that develop in the sun are short, squat, hemispherical bushes, very spiny and devoid of leaves. Those that develop in the shade of rocks or bushes are thinner and have well-developed leaves that last for a long period. These morphological differences are due to the extreme conditions of light and heat that the plant encounters.

The economy that is afforded by the reduction of the leaf surface is improved by mechanisms that check transpiration through the epidermis. These modifications consist of a thickening of the leaves or branches to reduce the surface/volume ratio (sclerophyta) or a covering of down. Among a large number of Gramineae, leaves persist but the stoma are tak-

Fig. 24. The spiny bush of *Launea arborescens,* a Compositae without leaves.

en care of in a unique manner. The leaves curl along their axis and form a hollow cylinder with the stomata now on the inside curled surface.*

The general form of the plant can be modified to reduce overheating. The leaves extend parallel not perpendicular to the rays of the sun, as is the case in other areas of the world. The plant can take on the aspect of a ball or a small cushion; this is a defense against the high intensity of the solar radiation and the violence of the wind. One of the most characteristic of such plants, *Anabasis aretioides,* has a dense distribution of branches (see Fig. 25). This Chenopodiaceae, commonly called cauliflower of Bou-Hammama or desert cauliflower, is ideally adapted to life in the desert. Its area of distribution is limited to a restricted zone of the north occidental Sahara. The more or less hemispherical shape resembles a mossy boulder. The trunk and the principal branches are stunted; distally they trap sand between them, and as the branches atrophy, the spiny leaves form a peripheral crust. The dried trunk is excellent firewood. The external crust, carefully cut, is given to sheep and camels to eat. In areas devoid

---

* This configuration of the leaf, as well as the presence of bulbiferous cells above the stomata and stomatiferous furrows with sunken stoma protected by bristles and a chamber or well, serves to reduce the movement of air and the loss of water by evaporation.

Fig. 25. The desert cauliflower, *Anabasis aretioides,* on hamada of Guir.

of rocks, the cauliflower of Bou-Hammama can be formed into a low wall by nomads for protection from the wind and sand.

Other plants, such as *Gymnarrhena micrantha* and *Bubonium graveolens,* have branches which are sensitive to variations in the moisture content of the air. A typical example is a crucifer, the rose of Jericho (genus *Anastatica*). In dry air the plant folds up into a ball; in moist air, the plant extends to form a star.

f. Accumulation of Water in the Tissues. Succulents characterize the American deserts, but they are rare in the Sahara. Contrary to popular ideas, no Cactaceae originated in the Old World (with the possible exception of *Rhipsalis*). But certain *Euphorbia* and the African Asclepiadaceae (examples, *Euphorbia echinus* and *Caralluma* sp.) resemble them closely—they are convergent forms. It is probable that the metabolic work needed to give rise to the larger desert plants, for example, the American and Mexican *Cereus* spp., is impossible under the extremely arid conditions of the Sahara.

The fleshy plants have reserves of water located in the leaves and in the stems. They grow slowly, respire and transpire little, and have long life spans. There are also plants having subterranean stems or relatively thick succulent roots in which the plant stores water and nutrients. The stems are at a sufficient depth to protect them from the heat of the sun or from fire. A good example of a plant of this type is *Erodium guttatum* which has partially tuberous roots.

Mechanisms used by desert vegetation to survive the dry season are very similar to those used by high mountain plants in the temperate regions to survive the winter (Binet, 1955).

Fig. 26. Halophilic vegetation in the Zousfana Wadi. Tufts of Chenopodiaceae and knolls of *Tamarix*. The knolls are purely local accumulations around the trunks.

g. Resistance to Heat and to Salt. Elevated temperatures are beneficial when water is present, but in a dry environment high temperatures are detrimental because they augment the rate of evaporation. Like dryness, the salinity of certain soils draws a lot of water from the plant (high osmotic pressure). The salinity of the soil itself permits water vapor to be drawn from the air. Such water then becomes available to the plant from the soil.

Halophytes sometimes succeed because of the accumulation of an excess of salts through a salt secretion. In *Tamarix* (see Fig. 26) and in *Limonium,* the salts absorbed by the roots are, in part, excreted by salt glands on the reduced surface of the leaves. When placed in saline soil, the secretion of calcium carbonate is greater than that of sodium chloride. Parasitism, possibly for the purpose of securing water, occurs in the Sahara: *Cistanche tinctoria* (Fig. 27), is parasitic upon roots of *Tamarix.*

Most halophytic vegetation does not have this adaptive apparatus, and for them the accumulation of salts acts as a favorable influence on the water balance (Al-Ani *et al.,* 1971). Thus when the salinity is high only a small minority of the succulent plants can survive, in particular the Chenopodiaceae. *Halocnemum strobilaceum* is a plant that has a strong resistance to salt. This African and Asian plant is found even in soils where the tension exceeds 20 gm of chlorides per kilogram (of soil). However, *Halopeplis amplexicaulis* probably has the highest salt tolerance in the

Fig. 27. *Cistanche tinctoria,* a parasitic plant attached to the root of a *Tamarix* (nebka of Kheneg Tlaia).

north Sahara (Killian and Faurel, 1936). The Chenopodiaceae of the Sahara and the salt marshes of the temperate regions are biologically alike.

The establishment of high osmotic gradients in the tissues of certain plants (*had, guetaf,* and *zeita*), is probably one of the factors responsible for the construction of voluminous organs rich in secondary formations and strong and resistant to low temperatures. However, the rain decreases the osmotic pressure on the scleromorphs (Killian, 1935).

Salt tolerance appears to be an efficient means of resistance for desert plants. Many plants have a high salt concentration in their sap; this is an excellent means of reducing the vapor tension of tissue water and enables the accumulation of the water vapor during low atmospheric humidity, thus protecting them against the arid environment.

h. Dissemination. In an arid environment, the natural propagation of plants by seed has certain problems: irregularity of rains and drought, destruction by mechanical action and by animals, and very strong concentrations of soluble salts in the soil. Moreover, the intensity of the heat and of the sun's direct rays are much more harmful for the germinating young plants than for the better protected adults.

The dissemination of plants is often facilitated by wind and animals. Anemochores (composed of Gramineae, Compositae, Asclepiadaceae, and Cruciferae) have fruits with hooks or equipped with tufts. Other complex types of fruits are those of *Aristida* and of *Erodium,* which, after being transported by the wind, fall and literally screw themselves into the soil as a consequence of their configuration and their particular pilosity. The *Schouwia purpurea,* once dry, is frequently blown off the plant and is rolled great distances by the wind.

The zoochores are represented by a certain number of Gramineae, Compositae, and Boraginaceae, which have fruits with hooked denticles, which cling to animals' fur. The seed of *Neurada procumbens* (Rosaceae) becomes attached to the feet of animals. The fruit, in the shape of a button, has spines on the superior surface which attach to the animals' feet and thus assure dispersion of the seed (Van der Pijl, 1972).

B. VEGETATION GROUPS

1. Generalities

a. Objectives. The first botanical objective is a thorough knowledge of the flora. However, systematic lists are soon covered with notations about the vegetation and the grouping of species. The major important points are found in a number of major works (Maire, 1931, 1933, 1940, 1952–1968; Corti, 1942; Hernandez-Pacheco *et al.,* 1949; Sauvage, 1949; Guinochet, 1951; Guinet and Sauvage, in Joly *et al.,* 1954; Guinochet and Quézel, 1954; Quézel, 1954a,b; Leredde, 1957; Ozenda, 1958).

Another botanical objective is phytogeographic understanding— domaines and sectors—fixed by the origin of the flora, its life cycle, the climate, and the soil (Eig, 1931; Monod, 1939, 1945, 1957; Murat, 1944; Ozenda, 1954; Quézel and Santa, 1962; Quézel, 1965).

b. Bioclimatic Stages. This concept is similar to the phytogeographic subdivisions, but it uses mainly climate as a factor. Le Houérou (1962) found two bioclimatic stages in south Tunisia, the upper and the lower Sahara. Quézel (1965) found three principal stages in the Sahara: (1) the upper stage of Saharan vegetation, the superior desert stage, composed of the hyperarid zones practically devoid of vegetation; it represents only one quarter of the surface of the Sahara; (2) a middle stage of Saharan vegetation, the middle desert stage, where the annual precipitation is between 20 and 50 mm; it is characterized by diffuse vegetation; and finally

(3) the lower Saharan vegetation, the inferior desert stage, where the annual precipitation is in excess of 50 mm. Here there is contracted vegetation.

At the level of the lower desert stage, it is difficult to determine associations because the vegetation is diffuse. Higher levels of classification associations can be determined.

c. *Cartography.* Cartographic representations of the vegetation of the vast area have just begun to be formulated. There are already several sketches, made on a large scale, but with much approximation: Béni-Abbès (South Oranais) at 1 to 2×10^6, Guinet (1954); Gabes-sidi Chammakh (South Tunesia) at 1 to 2×10^5, Le Houérou (1955); Ghardaia (South Algeria-Constantine) at 1 to 5×10^5, Barry and Faurel (1963); Largeau (Mid Sahara) at 1 to 1×10^6, Quézel and Gillet (1964); Alger-Laghouat at 1 to 1×10^6, Barry *et al.* (1970); El Golea at 1 to 1×10^6, Barry *et al.* (1970); In Salah at 1 to 1×10^6, Barry *et al.* (1970).

It is premature to give a presentation of the groups of vegetation of the Sahara. An attempt to synthesize all that is known about these groups was made by Quézel (1965). Certain types of vegetation common to parts or all of the Sahara were studied.

2. Groups of Edaphic Origin

The whole of the Sahara is well represented by groups of hydrophiles and psammophiles.

a. *Hydrophil Groups.* Sources of nonsaline water are rare in the Sahara. These few sources, trickling water or ponds, have a poor flora, consisting of tempered elements or cosmopolitans, such as the associations of a marsh in the heart of the Sahara (see Fig. 28) with reeds and rushes of more temperate lands (Corti, 1942; Leredde, 1954; Bruneau de Miré and Quézel, 1957). Thus the hydrophilic vegetation is composed of ubiquitous species, such as *Samolus valerandi, Juncus maritimus, Scirpus holoschoenus,* and *Tamarix gallica.*

b. *Psammophile Groups.* The works of botanical geography concerning the vegetation of the Sahara sands are numerous (Zolotarevsky and Murat, 1938; Maire, 1933, 1940; Braun-Blanquet, 1939; Guinochet, 1951; Quézel, 1956; Leredde, 1957; Le Houérou, 1962; J. Killian, 1960). The vegetation of living dunes and ergs is characterized by the association of *Calligonum comosum* and *Aristida pungens.* It is composed of few nearly identical species throughout the Sahara. There is, however, a preponderance of hemicryptophytes. The most characteristic plants for the Saharan sands are *Aristida pungens, Cyperus conglomeratus, Malcolmia aegyptiaca,* and *Cornulaca monacantha,* but some bushy vegetation,

Fig. 28. Hydrophilic groups in the Saoura Wadi.

such as *Ephedra alata, Retama retam, Genista saharae,* and *Calligonum azel,* can be included (see Fig. 29).

The vegetation of the sandy regs (association of *Danthonia forskalii* and *Plantago ciliata*) is composed especially of the ephemerophytes; in particular, the strictly psammophilic annuals with a short vegetative cycle following a rain. This group of *Danthonia forskalii* and *Plantago ciliata* characterizes the sandy regs of the whole Sahara. They are in the most arid zones such as Tanzrouft and Ténéré. Although the association *Calligonum comosum—Aristida pungens* and that of *Danthonia forskalii—Plantago ciliata* are quite close, they are two entities that are phytosociologically distinct. (J. Killian, 1961; Quézel and Simonneau, 1960). The analysis of ethological and biogeographical spectra between the two associations of psammophils is very dissimilar. They represent the type of vegetation best adapted to the Saharan climate; in fact, the percentage of the species of Saharo-sindian stump is greater than 90% (Quézel, 1965).

3. Groups of Mixed Origin, Edaphoclimatic

These are represented essentially by localized halogypsophile vegetation localized to saline or gypsosaline terrain which are rather rare in the Sahara (Killian and Lemée, 1948, 1949; Guinochet, 1951; Guinochet and Quézel, 1954; Quézel and Simonneau, 1960; Le Houérou, 1962).

Already at this level, it is necessary to make a regional separation: The principal halophilic and halogypsophilic groups of the northern Sahara

Fig. 29. Bushy vegetation characteristic of the Great Erg; on the right, *Ephedra alata* spp. *alenda* (gymnosperm); on the left, *Calligonum* sp. (Polygonaceae). Note the wind-blown detritus around the base of the bushes.

and of the Saoura valley integrate in the same relationship. The following individual relationships can be distinguished.

1. A hyperhalophilic association of *Halocnemum strobilaceum* localized the dried sebkhas in the summer
2. Two hyperhalophilic associations (the association of *Arthocnemum indicum* and the association of *Salicornia arabica–Phragmites communis*) linked to consistently damp soils
3. Two halogypsophilic associations (the association of *Salsola sieberi* var. *zygophylla–Zygophyllum cornutum* and the association *Zygophyllum geslini–Tragnum nudatum*)
4. The association *Suaeda vermiculata–Salsola foetida* linked to sand with lime and gypsum

On the other hand, the halophilic and halogypsophilic groups of the oceanic and occidental Sahara are not very well known. We note, however, the presence of a group of *Limoniastrum ifniense* and *Nitraria retusa* in the beds of the wadis.

The halophilic vegetation of the littoral oceanic and of the sebkhas of the occidental Sahara are characterized by the presence of succulent Salsolaceae or Zygophyllacea, in particular, by a steppe of *Zygophyllum*.

The halophilic vegetation is rare in the central Sahara and the meridional Sahara where the rigorous climate excludes all vegetable life on the salty or gypseous surface.

The halophilic and halogypsophilic groups are especially localized in the northern and occidental regions of the Sahara. They are strangely influenced by Mediterranean progeny. The hyperhalophilic groups are even considered veritable infiltrations from the Mediterranean region.

4. Groups of Climatic Origin

It is necessary to characterize the large phytogeographic sectors of the Sahara for these groups.

a. The Oceanic and Western Sahara. (1) The oceanic Sahara is characterized by an original, not very Saharan, vegetation because of the humidity and the high altitude there. The vegetation is constituted especially by a steppe of mixed shrubs and succulent plants; among them the genus *Euphorbia* is well represented. The Mediterranean infiltrations are again numerous in the sector. Nevertheless, one must note a large number of Macronesian species and a high degree of endemism (Murat, 1944; Monod, 1938, 1952; Sauvage, 1946; Hernando-Pacheco *et al.*, 1949). (2) The western Sahara has a very heterogenous flora, essentially composed of elements from the Saharan zones which border it. The desert savannah frequently has *Acacia–Panicum*. Not many studies of the flora have been carried out (Maire, 1938; Sauvage, 1949; Quézel and Simonneau, 1960).

b. The Northern Sahara. The northern Sahara is characterized by a relatively dense vegetation where annual plants are well represented whereas trees are absent.

From a biogeographic viewpoint, the Sahara-sindian lines dominate, but the influence of the mediterranean world is very important. On the other hand, the tropical lines are absent. Outside of the halophilic and psammophilic groups, the individualized associations are related to the saxicole group. The northern Sahara can be divided into two parts:

(1) The northeastern Sahara: The northern region is characterized by two groups of rockwork and hamada in the northern portion of Mzab (the association of *Moricandia arvensis* sp. *spinosa–Cymbopogon schoenanthus* and the association of *Anthyllis sericea* var. *hennonia–Fagonia microphylla* var. *fruticans*), and by two groups of special vegetation of the south-constantinous Sahara: one is tied to the regs of encrusted gypsum, the association of *Stephanochilus omphalodes–Arthrophytum schmittianum;* the other to lime sands, the association of *Brocchia cinerea* and *Heliotropium bacciferum*. The meridional region is only represented by very diffuse

populations of *Arthrophytum*. However, after a rain one can see in the rocky debris a group characterized by annual species; the group of *Ammosperma cinereum* and *Volutaria saharae*. (2) In the northwestern Sahara, two parts are equally distinct: in the northern region a new type of vegetation that develops in the beds of the sandy or non-salt-type rock wadis and where the tropical infiltrations are already apparent (important populations of *Acacia raddiana*) (see Fig. 16). Several associations can be distinguished: *Acacia raddiana–Ziziphus lotus, Acacia raddiana–Rhus tripartitum,* and *Acacia raddiana–Panicum turgidum–Foleyola billotii.* However, on the hamadas and rock work, other types of vegetable groups, remarkable for their richness in endemics, form a uniform phytosociologic complex (Lemée, 1953; Guinet and Sauvage, in Joly *et al.,* 1954; Guinet, 1958; Quézel and Simonneau, 1960). One can distinguish an association of *Anabasis aretioides,* where the pseudosteppe of *Anabasis aretioides* develops so well on the surface of the hamadas, and an association of *Whitania adpressa–Linaria sagittata* var. *heterophylla.* A meridional region: the increasing of the aridity of the climate toward the south causes a considerable decrease in the flora and new types of vegetation appear. The association *Plantago ciliata–Ormeonis lonadioides* (characteristic of the dayas and hamadas of the Saoura, Guir, South-marocan, and Tademait) represent an aspect of the increasing poverty of the groups of the beds of the wadis of *Acacia.* The associations of *Enartrophyton chevallieri–Tourneuxia variifolia* colonize the inclined rock work of the hamadas. The steppes of Salsolaceae live parallel to those which are individualized in the northeastern region of the northern Sahara.

c. The Central Sahara. This region is provided with vegetation that is well known, thanks to the works of Gram (1935) on Mouydir, of Maire (1933, 1940) on the Saharan central massif, of Maire and Monod (1950) on Tibesti, of Leredde (1957) on Tassili, and of Quézel (1954a,b, 1956, 1958) on the Hoggar, the Tefedest, and the Tibesti.

This sector (the high mountains excluded) is characterized by the development of a flora of sahelian origin, of which *Acacia–Panicum* of the desert savannah colonizes the wadis of the massifs. On the contrary, a vegetation of Saharo-sindian predominates on the sandy and rocky substrates outside the beds of the wadis.

d. High Mountain. A high mountain Saharan vegetation particularly rich in endemic elements extends up about 1800 meters. The vegetation then becomes diffuse. The characteristic trees of the lower regions disappear and are replaced by other types of trees: *Olea laperrini, Myrtus nivellei,* and *Erhetia obtusifolia.* A steppe of chamephytes (sage brush and *Ephedra*) appears most often at the higher summits. Also present are *Acacia seyal* and *A. laeta.*

The high mountain is characterized on the biogeographic plan as an interaction of the Saharo-sindian, Mediterranean, and African lines. Those species of Saharo-sindian stock, not numerous, live only in the groups of small pools located outside the wadi beds. At Hoggar, the Mediterranean influences predominate as well as at Tibesti. Between 1800 and 2400 meters are found the species of tropical stock which dominate, and on the summits are found the mediterranean species.

e. The Meridional Sahara. This region constitutes the most arid part of the Sahara. The hyperarid zones are composed of, from east to west, Djourab, Ténéré, Tanezrouft, Azaouad, and Majâbat. They are characterized by the uniformity and the extreme poverty of their flora. Two groups of psammophiles, however, can appear: the association of *Aristida acutiflora–Indigofera semitrijuga* and the association of *Danthonia forskalii–Plantago ciliata.*

Monod (1958), over a surface nearly 200,000 km^2 in Majâbat-al-Koubrâ, counted seven species of Phanerogams, viz., *Aristida pungens, A. acutiflora, Cornulaca monacantha, Cistanche phelypaea, Danthonia fragilis, Neurada procumbens,* and *Malcolmia aegyptiaca.* In this region, this single flora constitutes a locally diffuse vegetation, an aspect of a steppe.

On the other hand, in Tanezrouft, in Ténéré (Mission Berliet, 1962) and in Borkou, Quézel (1965) observed only very loose populations in examining 50 to 100 km^2 for *Aristida plumosa, A. acutiflora, Boerhavia repens, Neurada procumbens.*

5. Conclusions

The Saharan is first fixed by the general climate and arbitrarily by the localized edaphic factors in the particular zones: sources of water, borders of wadis, terrain, salt beds, ergs.

The historical interpretation takes into consideration the floristic parentage. Thus the mesogeean Sahara comes from the holarctic domain as well as do the meridional and tropical Sahara come from the palearctic domain. It is shown even in the vegetation of the high mountains: in the central Sahara and in particular in Hoggar, the Mediterranean elements predominate, and the endemism is composed essentially of Mediterranean types. As in Aïr and Tibesti, the tropical influences are important.

C. THE SOILS—ECOLOGICAL CHARACTERS

The Saharan soils have variable physicochemical conditions from one type to another (Ozenda, 1958). In general, they have sufficient amounts of nutrients indispensable for plants. Because of the absence of infiltration and leaching, the mineral elements remain near the surface of the ground. These soils have a good fertility potential when the water problem is solved.

The desert soils have a certain microorganismic activity that includes members of bacteria (especially those intervening in the nitrogen cycle), microscopic algae, and fungi (Nègre, 1918; Killan and Feher, 1935, 1938; Killian, 1944; Nicot, 1955, 1956; Rougieux, 1966). Where dead and decaying plants and animals are found, putrifying bacteria proliferate and fertilize the soils. Biological phenomena such as nitrification occur here in the same manner, but at a lesser intensity than in more favorable climates.

The primordial factor for plants is the quantity of water available, and this depends on the ability of the soil to store water and to make it available to the plant (involving porosity, imbibition, etc.). The dunes represent a relatively humid environment—at least for the Sahara. Here evaporation is important; water stays in the sand, in part, and does not leave as rapidly as from other soil types. Thus water can be obtained by plants that are adapted to dune life, especially those with long, deep roots. The water is easily given up to the plants because it is not tied to the sand by imbibition as is the case with the clay soils.

The soil and the vegetation can offer shelter for the fauna, not because of the shade and protection from the sun, but largely because of the microclimates created. During the day, no animal can exist around these tufts of vegetation. However, in the morning, one can see numerous tracks in the sand about them. F. Bernard (1953) has commented: "The least plant concentrates around it a faunistic ensemble more abundant than any analogous plant in the humid regions."

D. The Microclimates

The ecological importance of microclimates in the Sahara is considerable. For many animals the microclimate in which they live is more important than the climate of the region (UNESCO, 1958). The propagation of a species depends only indirectly on the general climate; it is tied to the variable conditions of the substrata. Each animal lives in a microenvironment, of which the climate may be said to be a microclimate.

The microreliefs (sand under rocks, the rugged terraine, and the overhangs), the bushes, and the burrows, all minimize the physical factors of temperature, aridity, light, and wind, yielding special microclimates (Kachkarov and Korovine, 1942). The stones on the regs can be a refuge for arthropods such as scorpions, lepismantids, tenebrionid beetles, and mantids, the so-called *Eremiaphila*.

The shadows produced by stones and bushes often modify the temperature of the surface of the soil; thus there can be a temperature difference of greater than 15°C between the shade and the sun. The temperature of the surface of the sand is not as high in a tuft of vegetation as beyond it. Also, the relative humidity of the air in the soil is higher in the tuft.

The burrows of rodents and reptiles and the nests of insects—the ants and the termites—are microclimates analogous to those of the mass of sand or rocks (Kachkarov and Korovine, 1942; Pierre, 1958; Petter, 1961; Grenot, 1967, 1968a). The relative humidity in the tunnels and deep chambers is a function of the proximity to the zones imbibed with water and isolated from external conditions. Thanks to the microclimatic conditions in the refuges where they stay during the hottest hours of the day, numerous small animals can escape the noxious effects of the desert climate.

ACKNOWLEDGMENT

I am greatly indebted to Professor Théodore Monod, Member of the Institute of France, for having read the manuscript and for providing helpful criticisms. Also, I wish to thank Mr. Louis Faurel, Joint Director of the Laboratory of Mycology and Tropical Phytopathology of l'Ecole Pratique des Hautes Etudes de Paris for his invaluable counseling in the preparation of Section III of this chapter. Animal life on the Sahara, the author's field, will be discussed in a separate publication.

REFERENCES

Al-Ani, T. A., Habib, I. M., Abdulaziz, A. I. and Ouda, N. A. (1971). Plant indicators. II. Mineral composition of native plants in relation to soils and selective absorption. *Plant Soil* **35**, 29–36.
Alimen, H. (1957). "The Prehistory of Africa" Hurchinson and Technical, London (translated by A. H. Brodrik).
Alimen, H. (1963). Considérations sur la chronologie du Quaternaire saharien. *Bull. Soc. Géol. Fr.* [7] **5**, 627–634.
Alimen, H., Doudoux-Fenet, D., Ferrère, J., and Palau-Caddoux, M. (1957). Sables quaternaires du Sahara nord-occidental (Saoura-Ougarta). *Publ. Serv. Géol. Alger., Bull.* [N.S.] **15**, 1–219.
Alimen, H., Chavaillon, J., and Duplaix, S. (1964). Minéraux lourds des sédiments quaternaires du Sahara nord-occidental. *Publ. Cent. Rech. Zones Arides, Cent. Nat. Rech. Sci., Sér. Géol.* **4**, 1–73.
Bagnouls, F., and Gaussen, H. (1953). Saison sèche et indice xérothermique. *Doc. Carte Prod. Vég. (Toulouse)* **1**, Art. 8, 1–47.
Balout, L. (1952). Pluviaux interglaciaires et préhistoire saharienne. *Trav. Inst. Rech. Sahar.* **8**, 9–21.
Barry, J. P., and Faurel, L. (1963). "Carte de la végétation de l'Algérie, Ghardaïa au 1/500,000." Institut Cartographie de la Végétation de l'Université d'Alger.
Barry, J. P., Celles, J. C., and Faurel, L. (1970). Carte de la végétation de l'Algérie au 1/1 000.000°. 1. Alger-Laghouat, 2. El Goléa. 3. In Salah.

Bellair, P. (1940). Les sables de la dorsale saharienne et du bassin de l'Oued Rhir. *Bull. Serv. Carte Géol. Alger., Sér.* 5 **5,** 1–80.

Bellair, P. (1953). Sables désertiques et morphologie éolienne. *Congr. Geol. Int., C.R., 19th, 1952* Vol. 8, pp. 113–118.

Bernard, A. (1939). Afrique septentrionale et occidentale. 2° partie: Sahara-Afrique occidentale. *In* "Géographie Universelle de Vidal de la Blache et Gallois," Vol. 11, pp. 285–529.

Bernard, F. (1953). Introduction générale Itinéraires et stations étudiées. I: Recherches zoologiques et médicales. *Mission Scientifique au Tassili des Ajjer Trav., Inst. Rech. Sahara, Alger* pp. 7–48.

Binet, P. (1955). Action du climat désertique sur *Zilla macroptera* Coss. *Trav. Cent. Rech. Sahar.* **1,** 1–177.

Blaudin de Thé, B. (1960). "Essai de Bibliographie du Sahara Français et des Régions Avoisinantes" (édité avec le concours de l'Organisation Commune des Régions Sahariennes). Arts et Métiers Graphiques, Paris.

Boureau, E. (1958). Paléobotanique africaine. Evolution des flores disparues de l'Afrique nord-équatoriale. *Bull. Sci. Com. Trav. Hist.* **2,** 1–64.

Boyko, H. (1951). On regeneration problems of the vegetation in arid zones. *Int. Union Biol. Sci., Sér. B: Colloq.* 962–980.

Braun-Blanquet, J. (1939). Premier aperçu phytosociologique du Sahara tunisien. *Mém. Soc. Hist. Natur. Afr. Nord* pp. 1–39.

Brooks, C. E. P. (1932). Le climat du Sahara et de l'Arabie. *In* "Le Sahara," Vol. 1, pp. 25–105. Soc. Editions Géographiques, Maritimes et Coloniales, Paris.

Brosset, D. (1939). Essai sur les ergs du Sahara occidental. *Bull. Inst. Fr. Afr. Noire* **1,** 657–690.

Bruneau de Miré, P., and Quézel, P. (1957). La végétation des points d'eau permanents de la portion orientale du Sahara méridional. *J. Agr. Trop. Bot. App.* **12,** 632–644.

Caby, R. (1970). La chaine Pharusienne dans le Nord-ouest de l'Ahaggar (Sahara central, Algérie); sa place dans l'orogenèse du Précambrien supérieur en Afrique. Thesis, Montpellier.

Capot-Rey, R. (1943). La morphologie de l'Erg occidental. *Trav. Inst. Rech. Sahar.* **2,** 69–104.

Capot-Rey, R. (1951). Une carte de l'indice d'aridité au Sahara français. *Bull. Ass. Géogr. Fr.* **216,** 73–76.

Capot-Rey, R. (1952). Les limites du Sahara français. *Trav. Inst. Rech. Sahar.* **8,** 23–48.

Capot-Rey, R. (1953). "Le Sahara Français." Presses Univ. de France, Paris.

Capot-Rey, R., Cornet, A., and Blaudin de Thé, B. (1963). "Glossaire des Principaux Termes Géographiques et Hydrogéologiques Sahariens." Inst. Rech. Sahar., Univ. Alger.

Chavaillon, J. (1964). Les formations quaternaires du Sahara nord-occidental. *Mém. Cent. Rech. Zone Arides, Cent. Nat. Rech. Sci.* **5,** 1–394.

Chevalier, A. (1932). Ressources végétales du Sahara et de ses confins nord et sud. Passé, present et avenir. *Rev. Bot. Appl.* **12,** 132–134 and 669–919.

Chevalier, A. (1938). Le Sahara, centre d'origine de plantes cultivées. *Mém. Soc. Biogéogr.* **6,** 307–322.

Chouard, P. (1957). Le centre de recherches sahariennes de Béni-Abbès et les recherches biologiques et agronomiques au Sahara. *C. R. Acad. Agr. Fr.* **43,** 477–488.

Conrad, G. (1969). L'évolution continentale post-hercynienne du Sahara algérien (Saoura, Erg Chech, Tanezrouft, Ahnet-Mouydir). *Publ. Cent. Rech. Zones Arides, Cent. Nat. Rech. Sci., Ser. Géol.* **10,** 1–530.

Conrad, G. (1971). Synthèse de l'évolution continentale post-hercynienne du Sahara algérien. *Bull. Serv. Carte Géol. Alger.* **41,** 143–159.

Conrad, G., and Fontes, J.-C. (1970). Hydrologie isotopique du Sahara nord-occidental. *In* "Isotope Hydrology 1970," pp. 405–419. IAEA, Vienna.

Conrad, G., and Roche, M.-A. (1965). Etude stratigraphique et hydrogéologique de l'extrémité méridionale de la Hamada du Guir. *Bull. Soc. Géol. Fr.* **7,** 695–712.

Conrad, G., Gèze, B., and Paloc, H. (1967). Phénomenes karstiques et pseudo-karstiques du Sahara. *Rev. Géogr. Phys.* **9,** 357–370.

Cornet, A. (1952). Essai sur l'hydrogéologie du Grand Erg Occidental et des régions limitrophes. *Trav. Inst. Rech. Sahar.* **8,** 71–122.

Cornet, A. (1964). Introduction à l'hydrogéologie saharienne. *Rev. Géogr. Phys.* **6,** 5–72.

Corti, R. (1942). "Flora e Vegetazione del Fezzan e della Regione di Gat." Florence.

Cuny, H. (1961). "Les Déserts dans le Monde." Payot, Paris.

De Martonne, E. (1926). Une nouvelle fonction climatologique: L'indice d'aridité. *Météorologie* **2,** 449–458.

Dresch, J. (1966). La zone aride. *In* "Géographie Générale," pp. 712–766. Encyclopédie de la Pléiade, Paris.

Dubief, J. (1950). Evaporation et coefficients climatiques au Sahara. *Trav. Inst. Rech. Sahar.* **6,** 13–44.

Dubief, J. (1952). Le vent et le déplacement du sable au Sahara. *Trav. Inst. Rech. Sahar.* **8,** 123–164.

Dubief, J. (1953). "Essai sur L'Hydrographie superficielle au Sahara." Direction du Service de la Colonisation et de l'Hydraulique, Birmandreis, Alger.

Dubief, J. (1959). "Le Climat du Sahara," Vol. 1. Mém. Inst. Rech. Sahar.

Dubief, J. (1963). "Le Climat du Sahara," Vol. 2. Mém. Inst. Rech. Sahar.

Eig, A. (1931). Les éléments et les groupes phytogéographiques auxiliaires dans la flore palestinienne. *Feddes Repert., Beih.* **63,** 1–201.

Emberger, L. (1938). La définition phytogéographique du climat désertique. *Mém, Soc. Biogéogr.* **6,** 9–14.

Emberger, L. (1955a). Afrique du Nord-Ouest. *In* "Recherches sur la Zone Aride," Vol. 6, pp. 219–249. UNESCO.

Emberger, L. (1955b). Projet d'une classification biogéographique des climats. *Année Biol.* [3] **31,** 249–255.

Faurel, L., and Schotter, G. (1965a). Note mycologique. III. Quelques champignons coprophiles au sud algérois. *Rev. Mycol.* **29,** 284–295.

Faurel, L., and Schotter, G. (1965b). Note mycologique. IV. Champignons coprophiles du Sahara central et notamment de la Tefedest. *Rev. Mycol.* **30,** 141–164.

Faurel, L., and Schotter, G. (1966). Note mycologique. V. Champignons coprophiles du Tibesti. *Rev. Mycol.* **30,** 330–351.

Faurel, L., Ozenda, P., and Schotter, G. (1953). Les lichens du Sahara algérien. *Desert Res., Proc., Int. Symp., 1952* pp. 310–317.

Freulon, J. M. (1964). "Etude géologique des séries Primaires du Sahara Central." *Publ. Cent. Rech. Zones Arides, Cent. Nat. Rech. Sci., Ser. Géol.* **3,** 1–198.

Fromentin, E. (1856). "Un Eté dans le Sahara." Sudel, Paris.

Furon, R. (1964). "Le Sahara. Géologie. Ressources Minérales. Mise en Valeur." Payot, Paris.

Furon, R. (1968). "Géologie de l'Afrique." Payot. Paris.

Gauthier-Lievre, L. (1941). Algues du Sahara Septentrional et Central. *Bull. Soc. Hist. Natur. Afr. Nord* **32,** 79–125.

Gautier, E. F. (1908). "Le Sahara Algérien." Colin, Paris.

Gautier, E. F. (1925). Déserts comparés: Amérique et Afrique. *Ann. Géogr.* **34,** 146–162.

Gautier, E. F. (1928). "Le Sahara." Payot, Paris.

Gram, L. (1935). "Karplantenvegetationen i Mouydir (Emmidir) i Central Sahara." Copenhagen.

Grenot, C. (1967). Observations physio-écologiques sur la régulation thermique chez le Lézard *Uromastix acanthinurus* Bell. *Bull. Soc. Zool. Fr.* **92,** 51–66.

Grenot, C. (1968a). Etude comparative de la résistance à la chaleur d'*Uromastix acanthinurus* et de *Varanus griseus. Terre Vie* **4,** 390–409.

Grenot, C. (1968b). Adaptation des plantes au climat désertique chaud. *Sci. Nature* **87,** 18–28.

Grenot, C., and Niaussat, P. (1967). Aperçu écologique sur une région hyper-désertique du Sahara central (Reggan). *Sci. Nature* **81,** 12–26.

Guinet, P. (1953). "Carte de la végétation de l'Algérie au 1/200.000°: Feuille de Béni-Abbès" (publiée sous la direction de M. H. Gaussen, par le Gourvernement général de l'Algérie).

Guinet, P. (1958). Notice détaillée de la feuille Béni-Abbès. *Extr. Bull. Serv. Carte Phytogéogr., Sér. A* **3,** 1–96.

Guinochet, M. (1951). Contribution à l'étude phytosociologique du Sud tunisien. *Bull. Soc. Hist. Natur. Afr. Nord* **42,** 131–153.

Guinochet, M., and Quézel, P. (1954). Reconnaissances phytosociologiques autour du Grand Erg Occidental. *Trav. Inst. Rech. Sahar.* **12,** 11–27.

Hardy, G. (1930). "Le Sahara." Alph. Lemaire (Collect. Monde et Science), Paris.

Hernandez-Pacheco, E., and Hernandez-Pacheco, F. (1942). "Sahara Español. Espedición Cientifica de 1941." Universidád de Madrid, Madrid.

Hernandez-Pacheco, E., Alia Medina, F., Vidal-Box, O., and Guinea-Lopez, E. (1949). "El Sahara Español. Estudio Geológico y Botánico." Cons. Super. Invest. Cient. Inst. Estud. Afr., Madrid.

Huard, P. (1953a). Répertoire des stations rupestres du Sahara oriental français (confins nigero-tchadiens, Tibesti, Borkou, Ennedi). *J. S. Afr.* **23.**

Huard, P. (1953b). Gravures et peintures rupestres du Borkou. *Trav. Inst. Etude. Centrafr. (Brazzaville)* **6,** 149–161.

Huard, P. (1957). Nouvelles gravures rupestres du Djado, de l'Afafi et du Tibesti. *Bull. Inst. Fr. Afr. Noire, Sér. B* **19,** 184–223.

Joleaud, L. (1938). Paléogéographie du Sahara: Histoire de la formation d'un désert. *Mém. Soc. Biogéogr.* **6,** 21–48.

Joly, F., Poueyto, A., Guinet, P., Sauvage, C., Panouse, J. B., Vachon, M., Kocher, L., and Reymond, A. (1954). Les Hamada sud marocaines. *Trav. Inst. Sci. Chérifien, Sér. Gén.* **2,** 1–190.

Kachkarov, P. N., and Korovine, E. P. (1942). "La Vie dans les Déserts." Edition française par Monod, Paris.

Kilian, C. (1922). Aperçu général de la structure des Tassilis des Ajjer. *C. R. Acad. Sci.* **175,** 875.

Kilian, C. (1925). "Au Hoggar," Vol. 1. Soc. d'Editions Géographiques, Maritimes et Coloniales, Paris.

Killian, Ch. (1934). Conditions édaphiques et ravitaillement en eau chez les plantes du désert. *Rev. Sci.* **72,** 477–482.

Killian, Ch. (1935). Etudes écologiques sur les fluctuations de la pression osmotique chez les psammophytes et quelques halophytes sahariens. *Ann. Physiol. Physicochim. Biol.* **2,** 70.

Killian, Ch. (1939). *Anabasis aretioïdes* Coss et Moq., endémique du Sud oranais; sa biologie. *Bull. Soc. Hist. Natur. Afr. Nord* **30,** 422–436.

Killian, Ch. (1944). "Un cas très particulier d'humidification au désert due à l'activité des micro-organismes dans le sol des Nebka'." Publ. Cent. Nat. Rech. Sci., Alger.

Killian, Ch. (1956). Les Xérophytes; leur économie d'eau. *In* "Handbuch der Pflanzenphysiologie" (W. Ruhland, ed.), Vol. 3, pp. 787–824. Springer-Verlag, Berlin and New York.

Killian, Ch., and Faurel, L. (1936). La pression osmotique des végétaux du Sud algérien: ses rapports avec les facteurs édaphiques et climatiques. *Ann. Physiol. Physicochim. Biol.* **12,** 859–908.

Killian, Ch., and Feher, D. (1935). Recherches sur les phénomènes microbiologiques des sols sahariens. *Ann. Inst. Pasteur, Paris* **55,** 573–622.

Killian, Ch., and Feher, D. (1938). Le rôle et l'importance de l'exploration microbiologique des sols sahariens. *Mém. Soc. Biogéogr.* **6,** 81–106.

Killian, Ch., and Lemée, G. (1948). Etude sociologique, morphologique et écologique de quelques halophytes sahariens. *Rev. Gen. Bot.* **55,** 376–402.

Killian, Ch., and Lemée, G. (1949). *Rev. Gen. Bot.* **56,** 28–48.

Killian, J. (1960). Contribution à l'étude phytosociologique de Grand Erg Oriental. *Terres Eaux* **37.**

Larnaude, M. (1937). L'eau dans le Sahara algérien. *Grands Lacs* **5–6,** 285–291.

Lasserre, M. (1930). Aperçu météorologique. *In* "Les Territoires du Sud." Alger Vol. 1, pp. 175–262.

Lavauden, L. (1927). Les forêts du Sahara. *Rev. Eaux For.,* Juin 1927.

Lavocat, R. (1955). Reconnaissance géologique dans les Hamadas des confines algéro-marocains du Sud. *Notes Mém. Serv. Géol. Maroc.* **116,** 1–122.

Le Houérou, H. (1955). Contribution à l'étude de la végétation de la région de Gabès. Notice détaillée de la carte au 1/200.000° des groupements végétaux de Gabès-Sidi Chemmakh. *Ann. Sér. Bot. Tunis.* **28.**

Le Houérou, H. (1962). Recherches écologiques et floristiques sur la végétation de la Tunisie méridionale. Les milieux naturels, la végétation, 1–323. *Mém. Inst. Rech. Sahar., Alger.* **6,** 1–281.

Lelubre, M. (1952). Recherches sur la géologie de l'Ahaggar central et occidental (Sahara central). Thesis, Paris, 1951. *Bull. Serv. Carte Géol. Alger., Sér. 2,* 22.

Lemée, G. (1953). Contribution à la connaissance phytosociologique des confins saharo-marocains: Les associations à thérophytes des dépressions sableuses et limoneuses non salées. *Vegetatio, Haag* **4,** 137–154.

Lemée, G. (1954). L'économie de l'eau chez quelques Graminées vivaces du Sahara septentrional. *Vegetatio, Haag* **5,** 534–541.

Leredde, C. (1954). Note préliminaire sur les formations hygrophiles au Tassili des Ajjer. *Bull. Soc. Hist. Natur. Toulouse* **89,** 1–8.

Leredde, C. (1957). Etude écologique et phytogéographique du Tassili n'Ajjer. *Trav. Inst. Rech. Sahar.* (*Mém. Miss. Sci. Tassili n'Ajjer*) pp. 1–454.

Lhote, H. (1955). Préhistoire et art rupestre au Sahara. *Cah. Ch. Foucault* **38**, 57–72.

Lhote, H. (1957). "Peintures Préhistoriques du Sahara. Mission H. Lhote au Tassili. Preface de l'Abbé Breuil." Les Presses Artistiques (Musée des Arts Décoratifs), Paris.

Lhote, H. (1958). "A la découverte des Fresques du Tassili." Arthaud, Paris and Grenoble.

Logan, R. F. (1968). Causes, climates, and distribution of deserts. *In* "Desert Biology" (G. W. Brown, Jr., ed.), Vol. 1, pp. 21–50. Academic Press, New York.

Louvet, P. (1971). Sur l'évolution des flores tertiaires de l'Afrique nord-équatoriale. Thesis, 2 vols., Paris. (Arch. Orig., Cent. Nat. Rech. Sci. **5613.**)

MacGinnies, W. G., Goldman, B. J., and Paylore, P. (1968). "Deserts of the World: An Appraisal of Research into Physical and Biological Environments." Univ. of Arizona Press, Tucson.

Maire, R. (1926). "Notice Phytogéographique de l'Algérie et de la Tunisie." Carte, Alger.

Maire, R. (1931). "Les Progrès des Connaissances Botaniques en Algérie depuis 1830." Masson, Paris.

Maire, R. (1933). Etudes sur la flore et la végétation du Sahara central. *Mém. Soc. Hist. Natur. Afr. Nord* pp. 1–272.

Maire, R. (1938). La flore et la végétation du Sahara occidental. *Mém. Soc. Biogéogr.* **6**, 325–333.

Maire, R. (1940). *Mém. Soc. Hist. Natur. Afr. Nord* pp. 273–433.

Maire, R. (1952–1968). "Flore de l'Afrique du Nord." Vols. 1–13. Lechevalier, Paris.

Maire, R., and Monod, Th. (1950). Etudes sur la flore et la végétation au Tibesti. *Mem. Inst. Fr. Afr. Noire* **8**, 1–140.

Meckelein, W. (1959). "Forschungen in der Zentralen Sahara." Braunschweig (see Capot-Rey, 1900).

Menchikoff, N. (1930). Esquisse géologique du Nord du Sahara occidental (fond topographique dressé par le lieutenant Pigeot, échelle: 1/1 000 000°). Thesis, Serv. Géogr. de l'Armée.

Menchikoff, N. (1957). Les grandes lignes de la géologie saharienne. *Rev. Géogr. Phys.* **2**, 37–45.

Mission Berliet. (1962). "Ténéré-Tchad, 1959–1960," Doc. Sci. H. Hugot, Arts et Métiers Graphiques, Paris.

Monod, Th. (1931). Remarques biologiques sur le Sahara. *Rev. Gén. Sci. Pures Appl.* **42**, 609–616.

Monod, Th. (1935). Remarques sur la structure du Sahara sud-occidental. *Bull. Soc. Géol. Fr.* **5**, 513–518.

Monod, Th. (1937). "Méharées." Je Sers, Paris.

Monod, Th. (1938). Notes botaniques sur le Sahara occidental et ses confins sahéliens. *Mém. Soc. Biogéogr.* **6**, 351–374.

Monod, Th. (1939). Phanérogames. *Publ. Com. Etude. Hist. Sci. Afr. Occ. Fr.* **12**, 35–152.

Monod, Th. (1945). La structure du Sahara atlantique. *Trav. Inst. Rech. Sahar.* **3**, 27–55.

Monod, Th. (1952). Contribution à l'étude du peuplement de la Mauritanie. Notes botaniques sur l'Adrar (Saharien occidental). *Bull. Inst. Fr. Afr. Noire* **14**, 405–449.

Monod, Th. (1954). Modes "contracté" et "diffus" de la végétation saharienne. *In* "Biology of Deserts". *Proc. Symp. Biol. Hot Cold Deserts, Inst. Biol., London,* pp. 35–44.

Monod, Th. (1957). Les grandes divisions chorologiques de l'Afrique. *C. S. A.* **24.**

Monod, Th. (1958). Majâbat-al-Koubrâ, Contribution a l'étude de l' "Empty-quarter" Ouest-saharien. *Mém. Inst. Fr. Afr. Noire* **52,** 1–400.

Monod, Th. (1968). Les bases d'une division géographique du domaine saharien. *Bull. Inst. Fr. Afr. Noire* **30,** 269–288.

Monod, Th. (1969). Sahara d'hier et d'aujourd'hui. *Atlas* **34,** 12–49.

Morin, Ph. (1965). Bibliographie analytique des sciences de la Terre: Maroc et régions limitrophes (depuis le début des recherches géologiques à 1964). *Notes Mém. Serv. Géol. Maroc* No. 182, 1–1724.

Morin, Ph. (1970). Bibliographie analytique des sciences de la Terre: Maroc et régions limitrophes (1965–1969). *Notes Mém. Serv. Géol.* Maroc, No. 212, 1–407.

Morin, Ph. (1973). Bibliographie analytique des sciences de la Terre: Tunisie et régions limitrophes (depuis le début des recherches géologiques à 1971). *Publ. Cent. Rech. Zones Arides, Cent. Nat. Rech. Sci., Sér. Géol.* **13,** 1–646.

Murat, M. (1944). Esquisse phytogéographique du Sahara occidental. *Trav. Com. Etude. Biol. Acrid.* **1,** ser. B, n °5.

Nachtigal, G. (1879). "Sahara und Sudan," Vol. I, p. 22. Leipzig.

Nègre, L. (1918). Contribution à l'étude des bactéries thermophiles. Etude biologique de la flore bactérienne du Sahara. Thesis, Paris.

Nicot, J. (1955). Remarques sur les peuplements de Micromycètes des sables désertiques. *C. R. Acad. Sci.* **240,** 2082–2084.

Nicot, J. (1956). Répartition verticale des champignons microscopiques dans un sol de daya. *C. R. Acad. Sci.* **242,** 1067–1069.

Oppenheimer, H. R. (1961). L'adaptation à la sécheresse: Le xérophytisme. *In* "Recherches sur les Zones Arides," Vol. 15, pp. 115–153. UNESCO.

Ozenda, P. (1954). Observations sur la végétation d'une région semi-aride: Les Hauts-Plateaux du Sud algérois. *Bull. Soc. Hist. Natur. Afr. Nord* **45,** 189–224.

Ozenda, P. (1958). "Flore du Sahara Septentrional et Central," pp. 1–489. CNRS, Paris.

Pareyn, C. (1962). "Les Massifs Carbonifères du Sahara Sud-oranais," 2 vols. CNRS, Paris.

Perret, R. (1935). Le climat du Sahara. *Ann. Géogr.* **44,** 162–186.

Petter, F. (1961). Répartition géographique et écologie des Rongeurs désertiques (du Sahara occidental a l'Iran oriental). *Mammalia* **25,** 1–222.

Pierre, F. (1958). Ecologie et peuplement entomologique des sables vifs du Sahara Nord-occidental. *Publ. Cent. Rech. Sahar., Cent. Nat. Rech. Sci., Ser. Biol.* **1,** 1–332.

Planhol, de X., and Rognon, P. (1970). "Les zones tropicales arides et subtropicales," Collection U, Ser. "Géographie." Colin, Paris.

Pons, A., and Quézel, P. (1956). Premiers résultats de l'analyses palynologique de quelques paléosols sahariens. *C. R. Acad. Sci.* **243,** 1656–1658.

Quézel, P. (1954a). Contribution à la flore de l'Afrique du nord. IV. Contribution à la flore du Hoggar. *Bull. Soc. Hist. Natur. Afr. Nord* **44,** 55–67.

Quézel, P. (1954b). Contribution à l'étude de la flore et de la végétation du Hoggar. *Trav. Inst. Rech. Sahar., Monogr. Rég.* **2,** 1–164.

Quézel, P. (1956). Contribution à la flore de l'Afrique du nord. VI. Contribution à l'étude de la flore de Tefedest (Hoggar). *Bull. Soc. Hist. Natur. Afr. Nord* **47**, 131–136.

Quézel, P. (1958). Mission Bontanique au Tibesti. *Mém. Inst. Rech. Sahar.* **4**, 1–357.

Quézel, P. (1964). "Carte international du tapis végétal au 1/1 000.000: Feuille de Largeau." I.G.N., Paris.

Quézel, P. (1965). "La Végétation du Sahara, du Tchad à la Mauritanie." Fischer, Stuttgart.

Quézel, P., and Santa, S. (1962). "Nouvelle flore de l'Algérie et des régions désertiques méridionales," pp. 1–565. CNRS, Paris.

Quézel, P., and Simonneau, P. (1960). Note sur la végétation halophile du Sahara Occidental. *Bull. Res. Counc. Isr., Sect. D* **8**, 253–262.

Quézel, P., and Simonneau, P. (1962). Contribution a l'étude phytosociologique du Sahara Occidental. L'action des irrigations sur la végétation spontanée. *Ann. Agron.* **13**, 221–253.

Roche, M.-A. (1968). L'eau dans la haute Saoura (Sahara Nord-occidental). Thesis, 3rd cycle, Paris.

Rognon, P. (1967). "Le Massif de l'Atakor et ses Bordures (Sahara Central): Etude Géomorphologique." *Publ. Cent. Rech. Zones Arides, Cent. Nat. Rech. Sci., Sér. Géol.* **9**, 1–559.

Rougieux, R. (1966). Contribution à l'étude de l'activité microbienne en sol désertique (Sahara). Thesis, Bordeaux.

Sauvage, C. (1946). Notes botaniques sur le Zemmour oriental (Mauritanie septentrionale). *Mém. Off. Nat. Anti-Acrid., Alger* **2**.

Sauvage, C. (1949). Nouvelles notes botaniques sur le Zemmour oriental (Mauritanie septentrionale). *Mém. Soc. Hist. Natur. Afr. Nord* **2**, 279–289.

Savornin, J. (1927–1928). Les Eaux artésiennes du Sahara. *C. R. Acad. Sci. Col.* **10**, 337–353.

Savornin, J. (1947). Le plus grand appareil hydraulique du Sahara (nappe artésienne dite de l'Albien). *Trav. Inst. Rech. Sahar.* **4**, 25–66.

Schirmer, H. (1893). "Le Sahara." Paris.

Thornthwaite, C. W. (1948). An approach toward a rational classification of climate. *Géogr. Rev.* **38**, 55–94.

Thornthwaite, C. W. (1958). The water balance in arid and semiarid climates. *Res. Counc. Isr., Desert Res., Proc., Int. Symp. Spec. Publ.*, **2**, pp. 112–135.

UNESCO (1958). Climatology and microclimatology. *Arid Zone Res.* **11**.

UNESCO-FAO (1963). Bioclimatic map of the Mediterranean zone—explanatory notes. *Arid Zone Res.* **21**.

Van Campo, M., Cohen, J., Guinet, P., and Rognon, P. (1965). Contribution à l'étude du peuplement végétal quaternaire des montagnes sahariennes. II. Flore contemporaine d'un gisement de Mammifères tropicaux dans l'Atakor. *Pollen Spores* **7**, 361–371.

Van der Pijl, L. (1972). "Principles of Dispersal in Higher Plants." Springer-Verlag, Berlin.

Verlet, B. (1962). "Le Sahara." Que sais-je, No. 766. Presses Univ. de France, Paris.

Zolotarevsky, B., and Murat, M. (1938). Divisions naturelles du Sahara et sa limite méridionale, *Mém. Soc. Biogéogr.* **6**, 335–350.

CHAPTER IV

DESERT ALGAE, LICHENS, AND FUNGI

E. Imre Friedmann and Margalith Galun

והיה כערער בערבה ולא יראה כי יבוא טוב,
ושכן חררים במדבר, ארץ מלחה ולא תשב.
ירמיהו י"ז פסוק 6

For he shall be like the heath in the desert, and shall not see when good cometh; but shall inhabit the parched places in the wilderness in a salt land and not inhabited.
Jeremiah, Chapter 17:6 (King James Version)

I. Desert Algae

A. INTRODUCTION

In deserts, algae occur in both aquatic and nonaquatic localities. The nonaquatic (xeric) algal habitats are characteristic of deserts, and their inhabitants may properly be considered "desert algae." Some of these are free-living (i.e., nonlichenized) forms, while others occur as lichen phycobionts. This chapter deals with the nonaquatic, free-living, desert algae, and the lichenized forms are only occasionally mentioned.

Any attempt to compile a general account of desert algal flora runs into difficulties because, at the present time, no consensus exists regarding the basic principles of taxonomy of green and blue-green microalgae. A short explanation of these circumstances may be helpful in understanding the often confusing discrepancies in published data.

In Myxophyceae, species descriptions were brought into synthesis in the monumental book of Geitler (1932). This was followed by several comprehensive works, the latest of which is Starmach's (1966) flora. In recent years, efforts have been made to improve the purely morphological approach of the "classical" system by searching for species characteristics based on numerical taxonomy, microbiological methods, and on pure cultures of the organisms. An entirely different approach was suggested by Drouet and Daily (1956) and Drouet (1968). By reducing the number of specific and generic taxa, they relegated literally hundreds of "classical" species to synonyms. Whitton (1969), writing about the "present chaotic stage of blue-green algal classification" recommends that, until a new Myxophycean taxonomy can be established, the classical nomenclature should be used for practical purposes as a workable though admittedly artificial system.

As for green microalgae, taxonomic identifications in earlier floristic works are more often than not unreliable. Starr (1955) and Bold (1970) and his followers, working with pure cultures, established a number of new genera and species based on biochemical and sophisticated morphological characteristics. In contrast, Drouet and Daily (1956), stressed the importance of herbarium material and united a number of coccoid green microalgal species in taxa which are not used by the followers of Bold: *Protococcus grevillei* (Ag.) Crouan, *Palmogloea protuberans* (Sm. et Sow.) Kütz, *Phytoconis botryoides* (L.) Bory, and *Protosiphon cinnamomeus* (Menegh.) Drouet.

As a result of these differences, floristic data of authors using different and conflicting nomenclatures are often not comparable. It may be noted that among students of desert algae referred to in this paper, Cameron and Forest usually employ the taxonomy proposed by Drouet, while Bold and collaborators, Schwabe, the Soviet authors, and the writer of this survey generally adhere to the "classical" nomenclature.

B. DISTRIBUTION

As with most microalgae, the distribution of desert algae is not limited by geographic barriers. Information recently summarized by Schlichting (1969) indicates that viable cells of microalgae are present in the atmosphere and are probably carried throughout the world by the wind. To name one relevant example, Brown, et al. (1964) found viable cells of the green alga *Friedmannia* in a Texas air sample. This organism is known from several desert localities in the Negev Desert of Israel (Chantanachat and Bold, 1962; R. Ocampo-Paus, unpublished) and in Arizona (R. Ocampo-Paus, unpublished). It would seem, therefore, that the occurrence and distribution of desert microalgae depends largely on whether prevailing ecological conditions are conducive to the growth of the organisms in question. However, conclusions based on the "ecological" distribution of desert microalgae are somewhat contradictory. Comprehensive floristic works are few: Fehér's studies (1936, 1945, 1948), impressive as they are through the multitude of data and their worldwide scope, are based on uncertain identifications. Cameron (1960) concludes that filamentous blue-green and coccoid green algae are predominant in most xeric environments, while coccoid blue-green algae appear with increasing humidity. But in the arid Negev Desert, Friedmann et al. (1967) found a somewhat different situation: Unicellular or few-celled green algae (mainly Chlorosphaerales) and filamentous blue-green algae occur in endedaphic, epedaphic, and hypolithic habitats and also in chasmolithic habitats in calcareous and dolomitic rocks. Coccoid blue-green algae are dominant in hypolithic growths on flint stones, in chasmolithic habitats in plutonic rocks, and they seem to inhabit exclusively all endolithic habitats.

According to Cameron (1966, 1969) and Cameron et al. (1970a), the algal floras of hot deserts and Antarctic xeric, mesophilic, and perhaps hydrophilic habitats are composed of the same species. The following taxa (usually used in the sense of the taxonomic principles of Drouet) are listed:

Green algae: *Protoccoccus grevillei* (Ag.) Crouan, *Protosiphon cinnamomeus* (Menegh.) Drouet et Daily, *Palmogloea protuberans* (Sm. et Sow.) Kütz., *Chlorella vulgaris* Beij., *Stichococcus subtilis* (Kütz.) Klerck.

Blue-green algae: *Schizothrix calcicola* (Ag.) Gom., *Microcoleus chtonoplastes* (Mert.) Zanard., and *Microcoleus vaginatus* (Vauch.) Gom.; also *Nostoc muscorum* Ag., *Scytonema hofmannii* Ag., *Porphyrosiphon fuscus* Gom., *Microcoleus paludosus* (Kütz.) Crouan; and in less xeric environments *Nostoc ellipsosporum* Rabenh., *Symploca kieneri* Drouet, *Symploca muscorum* (Ag.) Gom., *Oscillatoria brevis* Kütz., *Microcoleus lyngbyaceus* (Kütz.) Crouan, *Schizothrix macbridei* Drouet, *Calothrix parietina* (Näg.) Thur., *Anacystis montana* (Lightf.) Drouet et Daily, *Anacystis thermalis* (Menegh.) Drouet et Daily, *Anacystis marina* (Hansg.) Drouet et Daily, *Coccochloris peniocystis* (Kütz.) Drouet et Daily, and *Coccochloris stagnina* Spreng.

Cameron's results are based on a rather broad view of the species concept and followers of a more differentiating taxonomy may arrive at a dissimilar conclusion. Data presented in the following survey of desert algal habitats seem to indicate that the floristic composition of each is distinctive and characteristic. If the taxonomic principles on which their descriptions have been based prove valid, species such as *Calothrix desertica* Schwabe, *Schizothrix atacamensis* Schwabe, *Friedmannia israeliensis* Chantanchat et Bold, and the yet incompletely studied endolithic *Gloeocapsa* spp. may be restricted in their occurrence to certain well-defined desert habitats.

C. Desert Algal Habitats

The following scheme of desert algal habitats proposed by Friedmann *et al.* (1967) and based on conditions in the Negev Desert can be conveniently used for a general survey (Fig. 1):

1. Edaphic (soil) algae
   a. Endedaphic algae
   b. Epedaphic algae
   c. Hypolithic algae
2. Lithophytic (rock) algae
   a. Chasmolithic algae
   b. Endolithic algae

1. Edaphic (Soil) Algae

Edaphic (soil) algae live in or in direct contact with the soil.

a. Endedaphic Algae. These live in soil. They have been reported in desert and semidesert areas in many parts of the world (Bolyshev, 1968; Bolyshev and Manucharova, 1947; But, 1967; Cameron, 1963, 1964a,b, 1969; Cameron and Blank, 1965, 1966; Cameron *et al.,* 1970a; Chantana-

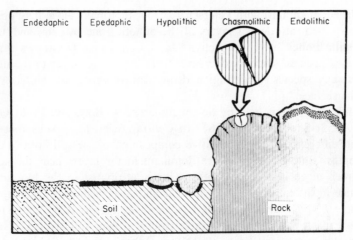

Fig. 1. Diagrammatic representation of desert algal habitats: Endedaphic (algae in soil); epedaphic (algae on the surface of soil); hypolithic (algae on the lower surface of stones partially buried in soil); chasmolithic (algae in fissures of rocks); endolithic (algae in the rock fabric).

chat and Bold, 1962; Durrell, 1962; Fehér, 1936, 1945, 1948; Forest and Weston, 1966; Gromov, 1957; Hunt and Durrell, 1966; Killian and Fehér, 1939; Melnikova, 1955; Moewus, 1953; Schwabe, 1960a,b, 1963; Sdobnikova, 1956, 1959, 1967; Shields and Drouet, 1962; Shtina and Bolyshev, 1963; Troitskaya, 1965).

At first sight, the abundance of microscopic algae in desert soils may seem surprising. Yet Schwabe (1963) [citing Geiger (1950)] points out that soils which are without a vegetation of higher plants retain more moisture than those covered by plants. Thus, it is precisely the scarcity of higher vegetation in deserts which might account for a relatively more favorable water balance, which, in turn, sustains a comparatively rich growth of soil algae.

As a rule, the number of algae decreases with depth. In the North American deserts, Cameron and Blank (1965) found viable algae up to about 60 cm in depth below the surface. Bolyshev (1968) reports that in Central Asian deserts soils under the takyr crust algae live in 200 cm depth; about 50 cm under the surface or below, algae may be completely absent, but they reappear again between 100–200 cm. Although several (particularly microscopic green) algae are known to be able to exist heterotrophically without light (Parker, 1961), Schwabe (1963) regards data concerning the occurrence of soil algae in the aphotic zone as doubtful and believes that light is an essential factor for their active growth. He maintains, with Petersen (1935), that living algae may possibly be transported into deeper layers of the aphotic zone by rain, and subsist there with limited metabolic activity for long periods. He argues that the number of species generally decreases from the surface layer to the depths, without any species appearing in deeper layers which was not observed near the surface.

A different view is held by Soviet researchers (Bolyshev, 1968; Goller-bakh, 1953; Sdobnikova, 1956). In Central Asian takyr soils there is a marked difference in the qualitative composition of the soil flora in different depths. Blue-green algae are dominant in the layers near the surface and green algae in greater depths. This is attributed to the low level of tolerance in the latter group to drought and to insolation. Certain species, such as *Chlorella terricola* Hollerb., *Chlorella vulgaris* Beij., and *Muriella magna* Fritsch et John, are characteristic of deeper soil layers. In species such as *Chlorococcum humicola* (Näg.) Rabenh. and *Phormidium autumnale* (Ag.) Trevis., which inhabit a wide range of depths, morphological differences such as cell size exist between forms living near the surface and those living at greater depths, and these characteristics were found to be hereditary (Gollerbakh, 1953).

Despite numerous papers on endedaphic algae in deserts, it is difficult to draw the general characteristics of their floristic composition, mainly because reports are based on often conflicting nomenclatures. It can only be stated that coccoid green and filamentous blue-green algae are dominant, and coccoid blue-green algae, Chrysophyceae, and diatoms are present in lesser numbers. (This, however, is not necessarily a characteristic of deserts, since similar situations also exist in other soil types.) A few examples from published data may be cited here. Chantanachat and Bold (1962) isolated from desert soil samples in Arizona, Utah, Chihuahua (Mexico), Saudi Arabia, and the Negev Desert (Israel) the following genera: green algae—*Bracteacoccus, Chlamydomonas, Chlorococcum, Chlorosarcina, Chlorosarcinopsis, Neochloris, Protosiphon, Radiosphaera, Scenedesmus, Spongiochloris,* and *Tetraspora;* blue-green algae—*Anabaena, Lyngbya, Nostoc, Oscillatoria,* and *Scytonema;* Xanthophycean algae and diatoms. Sdobnikova (1959) and Shtina and Bolyshev (1963) report the following algal genera from Central Asian desert soils: blue-green algae—*Synechococcus, Synechocystis, Microcystis, Gloeocapsa, Amorphonostoc, Sphaeronostoc, Stratonostoc, Anabaena, Scytonema, Calothrix, Tolypothrix, Oscillatoria, Borzia, Phormidium, Lyngbya, Schizothrix, Microcoleus,* and *Plectonema;* green algae—*Chlamydomonas, Coccomyxa, Chlorosphaera, Actinochloris, Chlorococcum, Dictyococcus, Chlorochytrium, Macrochloris, Trochiscia, Fernandinella, Chloroplana, Trebouxia, Chlorella, Pleurococcus, Borodinella, Gloeotila, Ulothrix, Hormidium,*

Stichococcus, Gongrosira, Cylindrocystis, and *Cosmarium;* Xantho-phyceae—*Pleurochloris, Chloridella, Botrydiopsis, Polyedrella, Gloeobo-trys, Bumilleriopsis, Heterothrix, Tribonema,* and *Heterococcus;* diatoms—*Stauroneis, Navicula, Pinnularia,* and *Hantzschia.*

But (1967) describes several soil algal associations from the high deserts of Western Pamir. The dominant species are blue-green algae (*Plectonema, Phormidium, Amorphonostoc,* and *Microcoleus*), Xantho-phyceae (*Pleurochloris* and *Heterothrix*), and diatoms (*Navicula*). Besides these, species of *Botrydiopsis, Hantzschia, Tolypothrix,* and *Chlorella* may be subdominant.

Peculiar conditions seem to prevail in the extremely dry Atacama Desert. Forest and Weston (1966) report *Anacystis montana* (Lightf.) Drouet et Daily, *Coccochloris peniocystis* (Kütz.) Drouet et Daily, and *Schizothrix calcicola* (Ag.) Gom. (uncertain). Schwabe (1963) obtained from laboratory cultures of Atacama soils four unusual blue-green algae: *Calothrix desertica* Schwabe, *Plectonema polymorphum* Schwabe var. *viridis* Schwabe, *Schizothrix adunca* Schwabe, and *Schizothrix atacamensis* Schwabe. These organisms are said to represent the total algal flora. They are slow both in germination and in growth and are resistant to high levels of irradiation and to desiccation. In sterile sand cultures, the algae pene-trate the surface and grow into small cushion-like pellets (Fig. 2a) formed by the gelatinous sheaths of the filaments which glue the sand grains into a compact mass. In nature, the algal pellets presumably shade the underly-ing soil portion from evaporation and thus each pellet creates in effect a tiny water reservoir. A peculiar association exists between *Calothrix desertica* Schwabe and *Schizothrix atacamensis* Schwabe. These two spe-cies form joint colonies in which the upper part is formed by a cushion-like mat of *Calothrix* with an underlying layer of *Schizothrix* (Fig. 2b). These structures may represent one of the peculiar ecological adaptations in algae to extreme xeric desert conditions.

Cameron (1964b, 1969) found that in desert soil algae, spore-producing forms are notably rare. However, Bolyshev (1968) reports that spore-forming algae such as *Anabaena variablis* Kütz. f. *rotundispora* Hollerb., *Nodularia harveyana* (Thwaites) Thuret, and *Anabaena salicola* Kondra-tieva are characteristic of salt-desert solonchak soils in Central Asia, and he considers spore formation as an adaptive phenomenon which enables these forms to survive prolonged periods of high salt concentration.

b. Epedaphic Algae. These algae live on the surface of the soil and usu-ally form visible growths there. They are widely distributed in deserts and semideserts and may form, as in the Central Asian takyr, a very conspicu-ous crust. In extremely dry deserts, however, they seem to be absent or infrequent. The literature on epedaphic algae is extensive (Bolyshev, 1952,

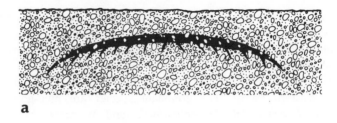

a

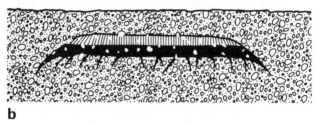

b

Fig. 2. Diagrammatic representation of the growth pattern of certain endedaphic blue-green algae in the Atacama Desert, cross sections. (a) Cushion-like microscopic colonies of filamentous algae cementing sand grains into a compact pellet. (b) Joint colonies of *Calothrix desertica* Schwabe (hatched) and *Schizothrix atacamensis* Schwabe (black). Redrawn after Schwabe (1960a).

1955, 1968; Bolyshev and Evdokimova, 1944; Cameron, 1960, 1963, 1964a,b; Cameron and Blank, 1966; Cameron and Fuller, 1960; Cameron *et al.,* 1970a; Durrell, 1962; Durrell and Shields, 1961; Fletcher and Martin, 1948; Forest, 1965; Friedmann, *et al.,* 1967; Fuller *et al.,* 1961; Hunt and Durrell, 1966; Mayland *et al.,* 1966; Shields, 1957; Shields and Drouet, 1962; Shields *et al.,* 1957; Shtina and Bolyshev, 1963; Vogel, 1955).

Epedaphic algae may be free-living or they are accompanied by fungal hyphae forming a lichen association. Despite the great number of papers dealing with surface growths of algae, the nature and degree of lichenization of these forms has not been sufficiently investigated.

Cameron and Blank (1966) summarized available information based mainly on deserts of the Southwestern United States and distinguish three types of growth: (1) *Raincrusts* appear in slight depressions in the soil micro-relief where water stands for a short period after rains. This is a smooth thin stratum of algae which characteristically warps upon drying, curves upwards and breaks into polygonal fragments. (2) *Algal soil crusts* probably represent a more stabilized formation. The color is soil-like or darker, reddish, blackish, or brownish. Some algal crusts show a fuzzy growth due to the presence of filamentous blue-green algae. (3) *Lichen soil crusts* are usually more conspicuous than raincrusts or algal soil crust, their structure is dense and they may attain 2–5 cm thickness. Their color is dark brownish, blackish, or, after rains, greenish, retaining moisture for a longer period than algal soil crusts. Lichen soil crusts often become folded and reticulate, extending above the soil surface and separating from the substrate. According to Cameron and Blank (1966), the algal components are most frequently *Schizothrix calcicola* (Ag.) Gom., *Microcoleus chtonoplastes* (Mert.) Zanard., and *Microcoleus vaginatus* (Vauch.) Gom. They also point out that "most of the algae in Southwestern United States desert soil crusts tend to become parasitized, eventually developing into distinctive crustose soil lichens." This however does not seem to be the case in more arid deserts, such as the Sahara (Killian, 1953) or in the Negev. In the Negev, Friedmann *et al.* (1967), Friedmann and Ocampo-Paus (1965, 1966), Ocampo-Paus and Friedmann (1966), and R. Ocampo (unpublished) found the following species in thin evanescent nonlichenized algal crusts: *Bracteacoccus minor* (Chodat) Petrová var. *desertorum* Friedmann et Ocampo-Paus, *Chlorosarcinopsis eremi* Chantanachat et Bold, *Chlorosarcinopsis negevensis* fa. *negevensis* Friedmann et Ocampo-Paus, *Chlorosarcinopsis negevensis* fa. *ferruguinea* Friedmann et Ocampo-Paus, *Protosiphon botryiodes,* (Kütz.) Klebs, *Radiosphaera negevensis* fa. *negevensis* Ocampo-Paus et Friedmann, *Radiosphaera negevensis* fa. *minor* Ocampo-Paus et Friedmann, *Oscillatoria* sp., and *Botrydium granulatum* (L.) Grev.

In the South African desert, Vogel (1955) describes two distinctive types of epedaphic algal growth. In the Knervslakte (Fig. 3), the algal crust is covered by a dust layer less than 1 mm thick. Below this a *Schizothrix* species forms a zone about 1–1.5 mm thick, followed by a 1.5–5.0 mm thick layer of fungus hyphae. In the Little Karroo (Fig. 4), an epedaphic growth of blue-green algae is formed on the soil surface by *Chrococcus westii* Boye Petersen, *Gloeocapsa dermochroa* Näg., and *Tolypothrix byssoidea* (Berkeley) Kirchner (the latter associated with a fungus).

Takyrs (in Turkic languages, "place without plants") cover large areas of the desert and semidesert regions of Central Asia. Bolyshev (1955) describes takyr as a flat area characteristically devoid of higher vegetation and covered by a thin, brownish, elastic, somewhat lustrous, and velvety algal crust. The surface of the crust is fragmented into polygonal areoles of approximately uniform size (5–25 cm). Takyr crusts are formed primarily by filamentous blue-green algae of the family Oscillatoriaceae which cement the soil particles into a firm layer. The most common species is

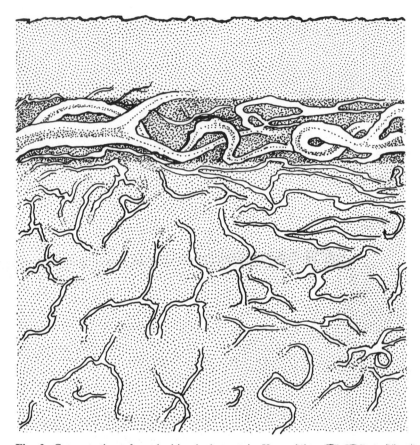

Fig. 3. Cross section of epedaphic algal crust in Knervslakte (S. Africa). Upper layer is dust, followed by a darker zone of *Schizothrix* sp. and below, a zone of fungus hyphae. Redrawn after Vogel (1955).

Microcoleus vaginatus (Vauch.) Gom. which, due to its adaptability, inhabits a wide range of substrates of different salt and moisture contents. Bolyshev lists from two localities (Kazakhskaya S.S.R. and Turkmenskaya S.S.R.) 31 species of blue-green algae (10 *Phormidum*, 9 *Lyngba*, 4 *Nostoc*, 2 *Oscillatoria*, 2 *Microcoleus*, and 1 each of *Aphanothece, Nodularia, Schizothrix*, and *Calothrix*), 3 diatoms (*Hantzschia, Navicula*), 12 green algae (*Chlamydomonas, Chlorococcum, Chlorella, Cystococcus, Palmella, Protococcus, Scenedesmus*), and a moss protonema. Takyr crusts may become lichenized, and the lichens [most frequently *Collema minor* (Pach.) Tomin] appear first in the cracks which border the polygonal crust fragment. From here, they progressively advance, partly by the fungus

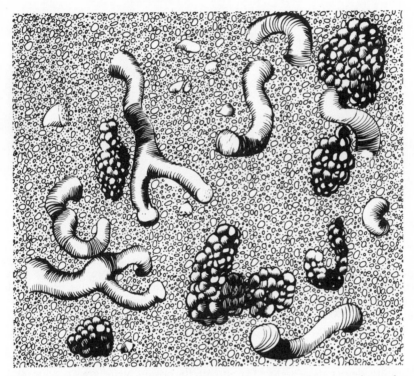

Fig. 4. Soil surface with epedaphic algal growth formed by *Gloeocapsa dermochroa* Näg. (cell clusters) and *Tolypothrix byssoidea* (Berkeley) Kirchner (filaments) in Little Karroo (S. Africa). Redrawn after Vogel (1955).

hyphae entering into a lichen association with the algae of the crust and partly by the algicidal effect of the lichen substances produced. The fragments of the algal crust diminish in size until they completely disappear and are replaced by lichens.

Forest (1965) found in two takyr crust samples *Symploca atlantica* Gom., *Schizothrix calcicola* (Ag.,) Gom., and *Microcoleus chtonoplastes* (Mert.) Zanard.

c. Hypolithic Algae. These algae grow on the lower surface of stones or other solid objects lying on or partially buried in the soil (Figs. 5 and 6). They are characteristic of deserts and semideserts including those of the Southwestern United States, the Middle East, South Africa, Australia, and Antarctica (Cameron, 1963, 1964a,b; Cameron and Blank, 1966; Durrell, 1962; Friedmann, 1964; Friedmann *et al.*, 1967; Fukushima, 1959; Hunt and Durrell, 1966; Shields and Drouet, 1962; Tchan and Beadle, 1955; Vogel, 1955). Hypolithic algae are frequent under stones

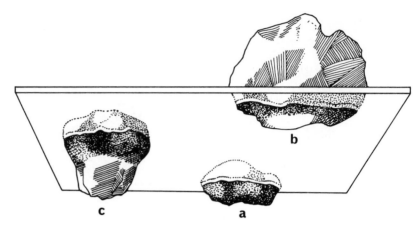

Fig. 5. Diagrammatic illustration of hypolithic algal growth on semitransluscent stones showing the effect of light intensity on algal growth. The upper soil crust is shown as a glass plate. (a) The light passes through a short path in the stone, the entire lower surface is covered by algae. (b) and (c) The light passes through a longer path. Only the flanks are covered by algae, the depth of the algal zone depends on the thickness of the stone above the soil surface. Redrawn after Vogel (1955).

forming desert pavements. The stones harboring algae are translucent to varying degrees and usually light-colored, e.g., white or milky quartz, chalcedony, gypsum, agate, calcite, limestone, or dolomite. A variety of calcareous objects of animal origin such as bones, teeth, fossil bivalve shells, snail shells, etc., are also suitable substrates. The labyrinth of dead snails lying on the soil may be coated by a green layer of algal growth (Friedmann *et al.* 1967). Although in some desert areas dark stones and pebbles do not carry hypolithic growth, the most frequent hypolithic substrate in the Negev is dark brown (although somewhat translucent) flint stone.

The ecological aspects of the hypolithic habitat were thoroughly studied by Vogel (1955) in the Southwestern African desert. The translucent stones create a favorable microenvironment by reducing the intensity of light to a suitable level and by collecting and conserving moisture. The algae occupy, on the lower surface of the stone, a usually well-defined horizontal zone and the depth of this depends upon the thickness of stone layer which the light traverses (Fig. 5). Within the amplitude of this algal zone, light is reduced to about 30.0–0.06% of the ambient intensity by reflection, dispersion, and absorption. Model experiments showed that rainwater penetrates along the stone–soil interphase more deeply than at other places and that a small water reservoir persists under the stone after the water has evaporated from the surrounding area.

In the South African desert, a remarkable ecological convergence exists between algae, higher plants and lichens. Certain higher plants—succulent Aizoaceae and Liliaceae appropriately called in German *Fensterpflanzen*—are reduced to a few cylindrical, truncate, fleshy leaves, which are buried in the soil with their flattened upper side at surface level. Through this "window" light penetrates the colorless, fleshy parenchymatous tissue of the plant where it is scattered and partly absorbed. The assimilating cells line the inner surface of the fleshy tissue. This tissue functionally corresponds to the translucent stone, and the position of the chlorophyll-carrying cells is similar to that of the algal growth under the stone.

In lichens (*Lecidea, Toninia, Endocarpon, Eremastrella*) which also grow buried in the soil with their upper side at surface level, the translucent, colorless, light-absorbing substance is represented by a mass of fungal hyphae. The position of the phycobionts corresponds to the photosynthesizing tissue in the higher window plants or to the hypolithic algal layer under the quartz stones.

The flora of hypolithic habitats is usually varied and comprises filamentous and coccoid blue-green and green algae. In the Negev Desert, Friedmann *et al.* (1967) and R. Ocampo (unpublished) found the following species: green algae—*Bracteacoccus* sp., *Chlorosarcinopsis negevensis* Friedmann et Ocampo-Paus, *Chlorosarcinopsis* sp., *Friedmannia israeliensis* Chatanachat et Bold, *Hormidium sterile* Deason et Bold, *Hormidium subtilissimum* (Rabenh.) Mattox et Bold, *Radiosphaera negevensis* Ocampo-Paus et Friedmann, *Stichococcus* sp., *Trebouxia* sp., (probably lichen phycobiont), *Trochiscia* sp., and *Ulothrix minuta* Mattox et Bold; blue-green algae—*Paracapsa* sp., (perhaps a growth form of *Gloeocapsa*) seems to be the most characteristic organism on flint stones, also *Aphanocapsa* sp., *Aphanothece* sp., *Gloeocapsa* spp., *Lyngbya* spp., *Microcoleus chtonoplastes* Thur., *Myxosarcina* sp., *Nostoc* spp., *Plectonoma* sp., *Schizothrix calcicola* (Ag.) Gom., *Schizothrix* spp., *Scytonema* sp., and *Tolypothrix byssoidea* (Berkeley) Kirchner. *Scytonema ocellatum* Lyngbye is reported from Heliopolis, Egypt. Durrell (1962) lists from Death Valley *Tolypothrix distorta* Kütz., *Nostoc muscorum* Ag., *Microcoleus vaginatus* (Vauch.) Gom., *Anacystis montana* (Lightf.) Drouet et Daily, *Phormidium tenue* (Menegh.) Gom., *Phormidium retzii* (Ag.) Kütz., *Phormidium subcapitatum* Boye Peters, and *Chorella vulgaris* Beij. *Phormidium tenue* (Menegh.) Gom., which occurs under crusts of salt in Death Valley, perhaps represents a peculiar form of hypolithic growth.

2. Lithophytic (Rock) Algae

Lithophytic (rock) algae live in rocks below the surface. As a rule, they are either in the fissures (chasmolithic forms), or in the internal air spaces of the rock fabric (endolithic forms), though intermediary forms also occur.

a. Chasmolithic Algae. These are known from the deserts of Central Asia and the Arctic (Odintsova, 1941; Glazovskaya, 1950; Gromov, 1957; Royzin, 1960), the Negev (Friedmann, 1964; Friedmann *et al.,* 1967), and the Southwestern United States and Mexico (Friedmann 1972, and unpublished). They occur in a variety of rocks in spaces which range from coarse cracks to microscopic fissures (Fig. 7). In perpendicular fissures the algae may appear on the exposed surface of the split as a thin horizontal belt running a few millimeters under the surface.

In certain other cases, as in heavily weathered and crumbling granites, the algae grow, in a rather irregular fashion, between disintegrated particles of the rock. Under weathered and flaking crusts of limestone, dolomite, granite, or quartz, chasmolithic algae may form extended horizontal growths. It is characteristic of chasmolithic growths that the space occupied by algae is open onto the rock surface. Thus, especially in coarser fissures, a soil-like debris may accumulate and ecological conditions may become somewhat similar to hypolithic habitats. This situation is then reflected in the composition of the flora as in coarse cracks in limestone rocks of the Negev Desert. In these localities the flora is similar to hypolithic habitats, while in weathered granites (Western Pamir, Israel, and North American deserts) it is formed by species of *Gloeocapsa.*

b. Endolithic Algae. In contrast to chasmolithophytes, endolithic algae occupy a space in the rock fabric with no apparent connection to the outer rock surface; they have been found in the Negev Desert of Israel and in Death Valley in sandstone, crystalline limestone (Fig. 8) and amorphous limestone (Fig. 9) rocks (Friedmann, 1964; Friedmann *et al.,* 1967; Friedmann, 1971). The rocks colonized by endolithic algae, though both chemically and petrologically of different types, share certain common characteristics: They are light colored and their physical structure is porous and sponge-like. The algae occupy a horizontally extended zone in the rock and colonize the spaces between the particles. As a rule, the algal zone runs under the surface in a remarkably uniform depth and follows its contours.

Above the algal zone, the spaces between the particles of the porous rock are filled with mineral substance. This results in a dense surface crust which seals the internal air space system from the outside environment. The crust is normally about 0.1–3.0 mm thick and the algal zone itself

Fig. 6. Examples of hypolithic algal growth, all viewed from the lower surface which was in contact with the soil. *a:* Quartz from desert pavement, Mojave Desert, California Route 58. Algal growth is restricted to a translucent-white zone of the opaque-violet stone; *b:* Calcite from desert pavement, Nevada, US Road 95 at junction to Cold Creek; *c:* Limestone from desert pavement, Negev Desert, near Sde Boqer; *d:* Flint from desert pavement, Negev Desert, km 56 on the road Beer-Sheva - Sodom; *e:* Quartz pebble, Egypt, E of Heliopolis; *f:* Fossil *Tridacna* shell fragment, Negev Desert, near Eilat. Scale in cm. Original.

Fig. 7. Chasmolithic algal growth in granite, surface of a vertical crack in the rock, Sonoran Desert, Mexico Route 8, 70 km from Puerto Penasco. Scale in mm. Original.

Fig. 8. Endolithic algal growth in crystalline limestone. Cross section-like portion of the vertically fractured rock. Negev Desert, Makhtesh Gadol, x38. Original.

Fig. 9. Endolithic algal growth in amorphous fossiliferous limestone. Cross section-like portion of the vertically fractured rock. Negev Desert, km 76 on the road Sodom-Eilat (cf. Fig. 13). x38. Original.

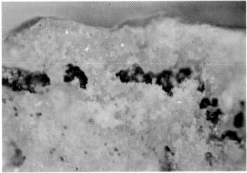

measures about 0.1–2.5 mm. As far as known to date, these algae are members of the blue-green order Chroocaccales, and probably belong to the genus *Gloeocapsa*. They seem to form monospecific populations in the rock although they may be accompanied by bacteria. Scanning electron microscopic studies have shown that the algal cells adhere to the surfaces of calcite (Fig. 10) or quartz crystals (Figs. 11 and 12) of which the rock is composed, or they fill the microscopic cavities of the amorphous limestone (Fig. 13).

Since the light-colored rocks are translucent to some extent, it is obvious that a steep and decreasing gradient of light intensity exists in the upper layer of the rock. Light intensity is an important factor in the vertical distribution of algae in the rock, and the upper and generally sharp borderline of the endolithic algal zone may be determined by the maximum tolerable level of irradiation, while the lower level probably indicates the minimum threshold of useful light. Indeed, in the upper level of the algal zone, cells show morphological characteristics of adaptation to high light intensities (thick, layered, dark-pigmented sheaths, brownish cell contents) while cells in the lower levels are typical shadow forms with thin, unpigmented sheaths and vivid green cell contents.

The porous rock with its imperforate surface layer represents a system eminently suitable to trap and to retain moisture and to ensure balanced temperature conditions in a hot desert macroclimate. Available water, be it from dew or rain, is imbibed in the porous rock by capillary force. The dense surface crust is pervious to water, yet as air temperature rises during daytime, it retards evaporation. Thus a slowly evaporating water reservoir is retained in the porous rock, maintaining a comparatively high level of moisture during the daytime.

The low heat conductivity of the porous rock, together with high reflectance owing to its light color, prevents a sudden temperature rise which might result from high insolation. The cooling effect of the protracted daytime evaporation from the rock further reduces wide temperature fluctuation.

D. WATER SOURCE

Water is obviously a pivotal problem for all desert cryptogams. Rain is scarce, and its uneven distribution further reduces its usefulness and availability to organisms. However, macrometeorological data such as rainfall do not necessarily give a correct picture of the situation prevailing in the microscopic ecological niches where microorganisms live. Vogel (1955), Schwabe (1960a), Friedmann *et al.* (1967), and Friedmann (1971) point out that the main water source of desert algae is probably

Fig. 10. Scanning electron micrograph of endolithic algae in crystalline limestone. Negev Desert, 100 km on the road Beer-Sheva–Eilat. Due to the activity of the

the nightly dew condensation. Under arid conditions the daily temperature fluctuation of soil or rock surface layers is much higher than macroclimatic conditions would indicate, and this is why nightly water condensation frequently occurs in deserts. Unfortunately, very few data are available on dew fall in desert areas. But Table I, based on the work of Evenari *et al.* (1963–1968) at the Avdat Experimental Farm in Israel provides some pertinent information. It shows that while rainfall was variable in quantity, limited to a few winter days, and unevenly distributed, the amount of dew was remarkably constant over 5 years of measurement. It was also evenly distributed throughout the year.

In practically all desert algal habitats water is conserved by the physical microstructure of the environment, such as the capillaries of soil, fissures or pores of rocks, etc. In these spaces, however, the water does not necessarily stay in liquid form but is perhaps present only as a higher vapor pressure. Lange (1969b) and Lange *et al.* (1968, 1970a,b) have shown that desert lichens are capable of using atmospheric vapor as a water source, and it is quite probable that algae can do the same.

None of the water-conserving devices will, however, prevent occasional desiccation which occurs, for instance, during extended dry spells. Draught resistance in some algae is considerable. Since Bristol's report (1919), it is well known that soil algae (green and blue-green algae and diatoms) may retain their viability in dry conditions for surprisingly long periods. Bristol was able to culture algae from dry samples preserved in the laboratory for up to 70 years and Parker *et al.* (1969) after 60 years.

Trainor (1962) obtained both green and blue-green algal growth from soil samples which were oven dried at 100°C for 1 hour, and one green alga (*Chlorella*) even survived desiccation for 1 hour at 130°C. Cameron *et al.* (1970b) reported that different desert soil microorganisms such as coccoid green algae, filamentous and coccoid blue-green algae, and the mold *Alternaria* sp. survived after 5 years of exposure to continuous high vacuum. However, the recent work of Trainor (1970) demonstrated that only a few of the "typical" soil algal species possess the capacity to survive in desiccated condition for prolonged periods, and it is obvious that only those forms which are able to do so can survive in desert environments.

---

endolithic alga (a small-celled *Gloeocapsa* sp.), the coherence of the crystal components of the rock is reduced and thus the rock splits easily along the algal zone, separating the surface crust from the rest of the substrate. The micrograph shows a portion of the lower surface of such a separated surface crust. Between the rhombic calcite crystals, the air spaces result in a porous rock structure. The colonies of algae adhere to the crystal surfaces. ×1000. After Friedmann (1971).

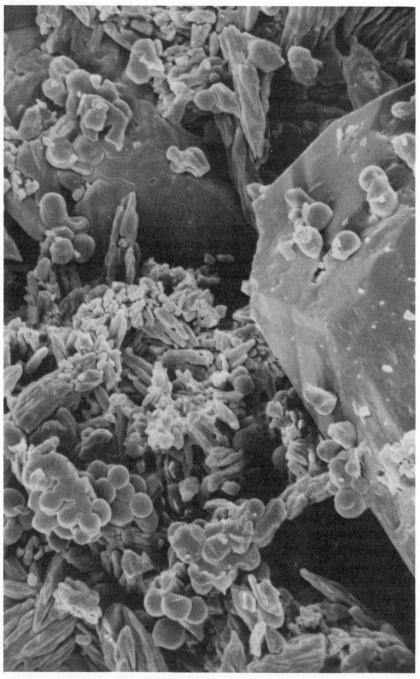

Fig. 11. Endolithic algal growth in sandstone, Negev Desert, near Nahal Timna. The scanning electron micrograph shows a fractured portion of the porous rock

E. Insolation: Temperature and Light

Although desert algal habitats are often exposed to extreme fluctuations of temperature, it is clear from the preceding discussion that, due to insulation and the slow evaporation of their water reservoirs, their microenvironment is often cooler and more balanced in temperature than the surrounding macroclimate. Vogel (1955) points out that heat resistance is less of a problem for these organisms, since desiccation generally occurs before temperature rises to extreme values, and heat resistance in dry and inactive cells is much higher than it would be in a liquid medium (see Section I,D above).

In most desert algal habitats mechanisms exist which prevent exposure to excessive illumination. The limitation of algal growth to certain horizontal zones with well-defined vertical boundaries (see Sections I,C,1, d, I,C,2,a, and I,C,2,b above) indicates that algae exist within the confines of tolerable light limits. The dark pigmentation of sheaths such as it occurs in the upper levels of endolithic growth (see Section I,C,2,b) is obviously a light-filtering device.

F. Nitrogen Fixation

Numerous reports exist about the nitrogen-fixing activity of desert algae, and their role in the biology of nitrogen-deficient desert soils is considerable. The nitrogen-fixing activity of endedaphic and epedaphic blue-green algae (the latter both in algal crusts and lichen crusts) has been reported by Fletcher and Martin (1948), Shields et al. (1957), Cameron and Fuller (1960), Fuller et al. (1961), Shields and Drouet (1962), Mayland and McIntosh (1966a,b), and Mayland et al. (1966). Fuller et al. (1961) and Mayland and McIntosh (1966a) presented experimental evidence that the nitrogen fixed by algae is available to higher plants. Tchan and Beadle (1955) described nitrogen-fixing blue-green algae from endadaphic and hypolithic habitats in Australia. Soviet research on N-fixing soil algae is summarized by Bolyshev (1968) and by Gollerbakh and Shtina (1969).

Odintsova (1941) reports on the nitrogen-fixing activity of chasmolithic algae in the cold desert of Western Pamir. In a zone which stretches from about the margin of the permanent snow to 4000 meters above sea level, several rock types contain considerable amounts of nitrates. The rocks

---

composed of large hexagonal quartz crystals and small plates of a carbonate matrix. Single cells and colonies of a large-celled endolithic *Gloeocapsa* sp. are attached to the surface of the quartz crystals. A grape-like cell group on the left side became separated from the substrate and the flat base adhering to the crystal surface is exposed. ×2000. After Friedmann (1971).

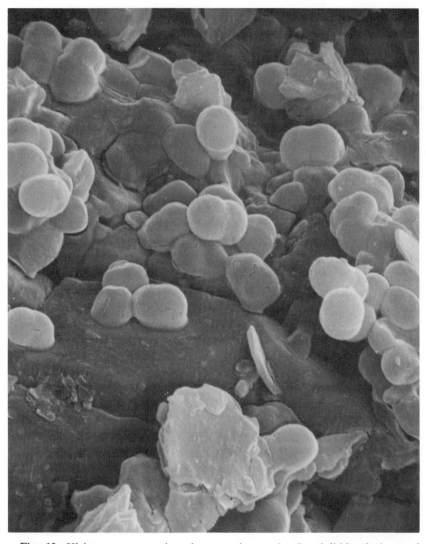

Fig. 12. Higher-power scanning electron micrograph of endolithic algal growth in sandstone from the Negev Desert, near Nahal Timna. Specimen similar to Fig. 11, showing relation of quartz crystals, plate-like matrix crystals and cells of endolithic algae. ×3500. After Friedmann (1971).

within the nitrate zone are friable and traversed by numerous cracks harboring a small-celled blue-green alga, *Gloeocapsa minor* (Kütz.) Hollerb. This organism was shown to fix atmospheric nitrogen under laboratory conditions. As no nitrogen-fixing bacteria of the *Azotobacter* type were

Fig. 13. Endolithic algal growth in the amorphous fossiliferous limestone shown in Fig. 9. Negev Desert, 76 km on the road Sodom–Eilat. Scanning electron micrograph of the algal zone in a fractured rock. Gelatinous masses of the small-celled endolithic *Gloeocapsa* sp. (arrows) fill microscopic cavities in the porous rock. ×400. After Friedmann (1971).

TABLE I

RAIN AND DEW MEASUREMENTS AT AVDAT IN THE NEGEV DESERT, ISRAEL[a]

Total rainfall and number of rainy days during seven winter seasons

	1962–1963	1963–1964	1964–1965	1965–1966	1966–1967
Rain (cm)	2.56	15.27	14.07	8.43	6.93
Days	10	29	28	17	24

Total amount of dew on the upper side of the Duvdevani dew gauge at soil level (0) and 1 meter (1) above soil level and number of nights with dew

	1962		1963		1964		1965		1966		Average	
Height (meters)	0	1	0	1	0	1	0	1	0	1	0	1
Dew (cm)	b	2.3	3.2	2.9	3.7	3.1	3.5	3.3	2.6	2.6	3.3	2.8
Nights	b	146	176	162	216	198	198	189	190	166	195	172

[a] After Evenari et al. (1963–1968).
[b] No measurements.

found in the rock samples, Odintsova attributes the total amount of nitrates present in the rocks to the N-fixing activity of algae. Yet, blue-green algae may not always be the principal agents of biological N fixation in desert rocks. A recent study of granitic rocks in the Sonoran Desert of Mexico which harbor abundant growths of chasmolithic unicellular blue-green algae revealed the consistent presence of aerobic N-fixing bacteria of the *Azotobacter* type (E. I. Friedmann and R. C. Ocampo, unpublished).

G. ROCK WEATHERING, DESERT VARNISH, AND ALGAE

The weathering of rocks in deserts has often been attributed to the activity of microorganisms, and specifically algae (Glazovskaya, 1950; Gromov, 1957; Royzin, 1960; Krumbein, 1968, 1969). These reports are based on microbial counts in surface layer samples of weathered rocks, and Friedmann (1971) points out the desirability of *in situ* microscopic demonstration of cells in the upper rock layers. In fact, the scanning electron microscope demonstrated the presence of blue-green algae under a weathered crust of crystalline limestone (Fig. 10). However, the laboratory demonstration of mineral solubilizing effect of an alga isolated from weathering desert rocks is still outstanding.

It has also been claimed that algae, as well as fungi and bacteria, contribute to the formation of desert varnish. Desert varnish is a dark brown or blackish, up to 1 mm thick, layer of iron and manganese oxide and hydroxide. It appears on a variety of rocks in deserts such as sandstones, limestones, silicified limestones, etc. (Scheffer *et al.*, 1963; Krumbein, 1969). These authors point out that the chelating activity of the metabolic products of algae may have a role in the deposition of manganese and iron.

II. Desert Lichens

A. Introduction

Lichens can exist under the most stringent conditions in terrestrial desert regions; their ability to adapt to xeric environments has enabled some types of lichens to dominate in habitats where competition from other plants is very slight. In such areas, they may be among the pioneers and at the same time form the last stage in plant succession. Hale (1967) assumes that " . . . at some early stage in evolution, both the lichenized fungi and *Trebouxia* [which is the most common alga of lichens] may have been faced with near extinction in competition with nonlichenized fungi and algae. Through lichenization they have passed from a very precarious existence to their present numerical superiority over other plants in pioneer habitats."

B. Floristic Accounts

An early impression that extremely arid desert areas are poor in lichens (Von Humboldt, 1826; Zukal, 1896) has been refuted by later investigators. Herre (1911), although he believed that desert conditions are in the main unfavorable to the growth of lichens as evidenced by the limited number of genera and species represented, has nevertheless observed ". . . almost everywhere (in the desert) the rocks are just as thickly covered with lichens as in other regions of greater humidity and less sunshine. The desert does not lack in number of individuals, but in number of species of lichens able to adapt themselves to its conditions."

More recent surveys, however, apparently based on more detailed observations which permitted the identification of barely distinguishable species, indicate that a relatively great number of genera and species of lichens exist in desert regions. Follmann (1965a) reported on 153 lichen species in the Atacama Desert, as compared with 49 phanerogams in the same area.

Clumps of *Teloschistes peruensis* (Ach.) Thoms., sometimes intermingled with *Anaptychia neoleucomelaena* f. *squarrosa* (Vain.) Kurok. have been found by Iltis (Thomson and Iltis, 1968) on a small strip of land in the coastal desert of southern Peru, which is one of the world's most arid regions. This region is completely lacking in phanerogamic plants and is designated by the authors as a fog-induced "lichen oasis," the only source of moisture apparently being clouds or fog moving over the area. On open clay–soil depressions, the same authors also found *Buellia auriculata* Malme, *Solenopsora requienii* Mass., *Acarospora chilensis* Magn., *Caloplaca cirrochroa* (Ach.) Th. Fr., and fragments of *Collema* and *Ramalina* species.

Weber (1962) claims that despite the slow growth of the crustose lichens, the dominating growth form in arid regions, the lichen floras encountered in arid sites are unusually rich in species belonging to the desert–steppe, circumboreal, and subtropical elements. In his opinion, this phenomenon arises from local peculiarities in topography and exposure, which result in the coexistence of arid and mesic elements in relatively small areas.

Faurel *et al.* (1953) made a data compilation (Bouly de Lesdain, 1911; Flagey, 1896; Hue, 1921; Maire, 1933; Nylander, 1878; Steiner, 1902*; Tits, 1925; Werner, 1950) on lichens of the Sahara. Taking also into account their own collections, they recorded 114 lichen species, as compared with 1000 phanerogams, in the Algerian Sahara and Tibesti region. None of the 114 species belong to the fruticose growth form, and only three are foliose; all the rest are crustose types. Of the latter, 20% are Pyrenolichenes, 28% belong to the Cyanophilia and 13% to the Acarosporaceae. Similar proportions are apparent in the composition of other desert lichen floras: *Dermatocarpon* and *Heppia* are represented by 23 species, 20% of the components of the Sahara lichens so far reported. This is a surprisingly large amount considering that these two genera are less than 1% of the total global lichen flora.

In a more recent publication, Faurel and Schotter (1958) added 17 species to the list of lichens identified in Tibesti. An abundance of *Acarospora* species (*A. bella, A. sulphurata, A. pitardi, A. strigata, A.* cf. *versicolor, A.* cf. *intermixta, A.* cf. *veronensis*) as well as of individuals of these species in Tibesti has been reported by Quézel. Many of these *Acarosporas* are deteriorated by the blue-green alga *Stigonema minutissimum* f. *lichenicolum,* which settles in the thallus and fruiting-body depressions.

A rather rich lichen flora, both as regards the number of species and the abundance of individuals has been found in the Negev Desert of Israel, a region 9000 km² in area (Galun and Reichert, 1960; Galun, 1966, 1967). Of the 44 species reported, *Ramalina maciformis* (Del.) Bory and *Teloschistes lacunosa* (Rupr.) Sav. [= *T. brevior* (Nyl.) Wain. f. *halophilus* (Elenk.) Oxn.] are the only fruticose lichens in this area. The

* There was also an earlier report on Sahara lichens by Steiner (1895).

few foliose types are mainly epigean species, such as *Squamarina crassa* (Huds.) Poelt and *S. lentigera* (Web.) Poelt. The only foliose saxicolous species is *Xanthoria aureola* (Ach.) Erichs. var. *isidioidea* Beltr. All the others belong to the crustose growth form. Endolithic species and several *Aspicilias,* which are rather common in the Negev, are not included in the numbers reported. They may be assumed to comprise about 15 species.

Most lichens reported by Müller Argovensis (1880) in Egypt are typical of the desert environment. In common with the Negev lichen flora are *R. maciformis, R. lacunosa, Caloplaca ehrenbergii* (Müll. Arg.) Zahlbr., *C. aurantia* (Pers.) Hellb., *C. erythrina* (Müll. Arg.) Zahlbr. var. *pulvinata* (Müll. Arg.) Zahlbr., *C. aegyptiaca* (Müll. Arg.) Stein., *Fulgensia fulgens* (Sw.) Elenk., *Squamarina lentigera* (Web.) Poelt, *Acarospora reagens* Zahlbr. f. *radicans* (Nyl.) Magn., *Lecidea decipiens* (Ehrh.) Ach., *Buellia canescens* (Dicks.) DeNot., *B. epipolia* (Ach.) Mong., *B. venusta* (Korb.) Lett., *Lecanora crenulata* Nyl., *L.* (*Aspicilia*) *hoffmannii* Müll. Arg., *Lecania subcaesia* (Nyl.) Szat., *Rinodina bischoffii* (Hepp) Mass. var. *aegyptica* Müll. Arg. *Dermatocarpon hepaticum* (Ach.) Th. Fr., and *Blastenia rejecta* Th. Fr. var. *bicolor* (Müll. Arg.) Zahlbr.

Steiner (1916) mentions the presence of two interesting lichens, *Roccella fucoides* (Dicks.) Wain. and *Parmelia tinctorum* Despr. in the Arabian Dahna Desert; they are used by oriental women as a hair dye.

Among the 248 lichens known in Iran (Szatala, 1957) those found in the desert and steppe areas are mainly species of the Verrucariaceae, Dermatocarpaceae, Pyrenopsidaeae, Heppiaceae, Lecideaceae, Lecanoraceae, Acarosporaceae, Teloschistaceae, *Rinodina,* and *Buellia.*

The genera dominating in the "steppe and desert-like" areas of Central Asia (Magnusson, 1940–1944) are *Lecanora, Acarospora, Caloplaca, Lecidea, Buellia, Rinodina, Heppia, Dermatocarpon,* and species of the Pyrenopsidaceae. The only fruticose lichen mentioned by Magnusson is *Teloschistes brevior*; the few foliose species reported are mainly terricolous species.

The terricolous species *Dermatocarpon hepaticum, Collema tenax, Toninia coeruleonigricans, Fulgensia fulgens, Lecidea decipiens, Squamarina crassa,* and *S. lentigera* are very often mentioned among the components of lichen vegetation in steppe and desert regions. These species are not particularly restricted to arid and semiarid areas. Ditches at the base of boulders, rock crevices and fissures, stone pits, and depressions provide them with a suitable microenvironment, presumably similar to the conditions of their natural, more moderate habitat. As will be mentioned later, these species do, however, undergo morphological modifications in arid areas. *Cladonia folicacea* var. *convoluta, C. pyxidata,* and *C. rangiformis* were recorded by Keller (1926) and Tomin (1926) in West Asian steppes, semideserts, and deserts. These species, too, represent penetrations from more moderate environments. It is doubtful if the identifications of some of the other soil lichens mentioned by Tomin, such as *Biatorella fossarum, Candelariella cerinella* var. *unilocularis, Kelleria polyspora, Placodium* (= *Caloplaca*) *desertorum, Rinodina nimbosa* f. *sareptana,* and *Squamarina muralis* f. *argilicola,* are correct.

An abundance of *Lecanora esculenta* (Pall.) Eversm., a loose, subfoliose lichen (*Wanderflechte*) in North African and West Asian steppe regions, has been reported by Elenkin (1901), Eversmann (1831), Keller (1926), Tomin (1926), and more recently by Klement (1966) in Mongolia. *Lecanora esculenta* has become legendary by the suggestion that it is the manna which was eaten by the ancient Israelites during the Exodus from Egypt. In recent surveys in the Sinai Peninsula, *L. esculenta* could not be found (Galun and Garty, 1972; Garty, 1972). Sheep in the Libyan Desert are reported to graze on *L. esculenta* (Hale, 1967).

Roccella cervicornis Follm., *Parmelia vagans* (Nyl.) Nyl., *Dermatocarpon vagans* Imsh., *Tornabenia ephebaea* (Ach.) Kur., *T. intricata* Trevis., and *Teloschistes brevior* f. *halophilus* (Elenk.) Oxn. [= *T. lacunosa* (Rupr.) Sav.] (Elenkin, 1901; Follmann, 1966; Imshaug, 1950; Klement, 1966), and perhaps *Ramalina maciformis* (Del.) Bory, belong to the same ecotype of loose *Wanderflechten,* in steppe and desert terrain.

Zukal (1896) and Fink (1909) believed that lichen formations of horizontally exposed rocks in regions of average rainfall, as well as those of perpendicular or inclined southward facing rocks are similar to the lichen formations of desert rocks.

C. PHYTOGEOGRAPHY

Reichert (1936, 1937a–d, 1940, 1953) studied the lichen vegetation in steppes and deserts of the Eastern Holarctis in relation to phanerogams and suggested that the xerofrigid plant formations of Arctic tundras are characterized by the genus *Cladonia* (section *Cladina*); the xerothermic steppes of the Mediterranean and Irano–Turanian regions are characterized by *Artemisia* and species of the genus *Diploschistes. Diploschistes steppicus* Reich., in particular, represents a very sensitive indicator of this region. In the xerothermic deserts the Zygophyllaceae predominate, accompanied by *Ramalina maciformis.*

Reichert argues, on the basis of the continental drift theory, that the *Lecanora* (*Aspicilia*) *esculenta* group originated in the high mountains of the Irano-Turanian region during the Miocene period, when the eastern part of the Thetis Sea dried up. During this period the *esculenta* group, together with *Astragalus tragacantha* spp., underwent an extreme xerophytic transformation. The *esculenta* and *tragacantha* vegetation migrated from Central Asia to the west and to the south; while the *tragacantha* group stopped at the Balkans, the *esculenta* group further migrated to North Africa through the ancient Italic Bridge. The "desert forms" of the *esculenta* group are according to Elenkin (1901), *desertoides* Elenk., *foliacea* Elenk., and *esculenta–tesquina* (Pall.) Elenk.

It seems that within a particular area the substrate has a crucial influence on lichen settlement. According to Galun (1963), the lichen population of the Irano–Turanian and the Saharo–Sindian region in the Negev Desert can be subdivided according to the substrate on which they grow. The lichen population of the Irano-Turanian region is composed of

1. Terrestial species
   a. species characteristic of this region
   b. species not characteristic of this region
2. Saxicole species, all of them not characteristic of this region
   a. growing on flint
   b. growing on calcareous stones

The lichen population of the Saharo-Sindian region in the Negev Desert is composed of

1. Terrestrial species, all of them not characteristic of this region
2. Saxicole species
   a. growing on flint
      i. characteristic
      ii. not characteristic
   b. growing on calcareous stones
      i. characteristic
      ii. not characteristic

According to Faurel *et al.* (1953) 30% of the 114 lichen species found in the Algerian Sahara are endemic to North Africa, while 21% are restricted to the Algerian Sahara only. Weber (1962) is of the opinion that a misunderstanding of environmental modificants has led to a belief in a great amount of local endemisms. He points out the high correlation between the lichens of the Southwestern American desert and the deserts of Central Asia (as reported by Magnusson, 1944) and states that ". . . the correlations may be extended in part to include the deserts of North Africa, South America and Australia." Follmann (1965a) indicates that the lichens of the Atacama Desert belong to the same families as those mentioned by Doidge (1950) and Vogel (1955) in the South African Little Karroo Desert and Namaqualand, namely, Buelliaceae, Dermatocarpaceae, and Lecideaceae, but not Acarosporaceae. The spectrum of the species is, however, a different one.

Weber (1962) in discussing the flora of the Southwestern United States says that this flora ". . . consists of widespread circumpolar species particularly localized in the Rocky Mountains; a significant number belong to a desert–steppe element disjunctly distributed in the isolated semiarid regions of both hemispheres; and a small percentage are pan-subtropical in distribution."

It should be pointed out that the information on lichens in arid zones and desert regions is scarce and scattered. Furthermore, a great number of inadequately researched taxa have received recognition, causing chaos in the nomenclature. Therefore, it is difficult to be conclusive in regard to the distribution patterns, and it is premature to expect appropriate comparison to be made with the distributional pattern of the higher plants.

D. MORPHOLOGY

Morphological adaptation to xeric conditions protects lichens from desiccation and against the excessive radiation of direct sunlight. One relevant example is the reduction of the evaporating surface. Most of the heteromerous desert lichens belong to the crustose type, which have the ventral side of the thallus closely attached to the substrate and only the upper surface exposed to atmospheric factors. Another common feature in desert lichens is a thickened cortex (Vogel, 1955) and various amorphous exterior layers, such as a powdery cover (the pruina), thick necrotic or gelatinous layers covering the living tissue underneath (Galun, 1963). For example, the reddish squamules of *Lecidea decipiens* are heavily pruinose in the deserts, but naked in moderate regions. *Buellia canescens*, which grows in Sweden, has no amorphous upper layer, whereas the same species growing in the Negev Desert is covered by a thick superficial amorphous layer. Although this sort of protection is only of limited duration, it does prolong the daytime photosynthetic activity by slowing down the decrease in water content.

Also considered a xeromorphic character is the bright or pale color of the thalli of many desert lichens, which presumably reduces heat ray absorption. Even if the basic color of the cortex is dark, it is in many cases concealed by a flowery or powdery whitish cover (Galun, 1963). The members of the Northern Chilean *Buellietum albulae* lichen association are covered by a fine layer of sand and dust, which according to Follmann (1965b) reduces the amount of light transmitted to the algal layer.

Vogel (1955) describes the inverted structure of the thallus of a *Buellia* species, which frequently settles on quartz in the South African desert.

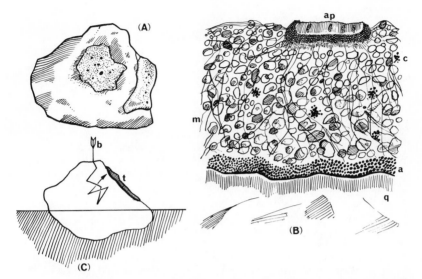

Fig. 14. *Buellia* sp., a desert lichen on quartz in Knervslakte (South-Africa) with "inverted" thallus. (A) Habitus (natural size). (B) Section through the thallus. (C) Sunlight reaching algal layer indirectly through dispersion in the quartz substrate. Mycelium interwoven among soil particles (m), apothecium (ap), groups of algal cells (c), basal algal layer (a), quartz substrate (q), light beam (b), thallus (t). Redrawn after Vogel (1955).

He assumes that the algal layer receives light through the quartz on which it is directly deposited and is protected from above by a "pseudomedulla" rendered less transparent by embedded soil and dust particles (see Fig. 14).

It is relevant also to mention the relative abundance of endolithic lichens in deserts, mainly species of the Verrucariaceae, which have their thallus partly or entirely sunk in the substrate and protected by it.

The great flexibility of lichens, in general, in response to environmental factors was mentioned first by Herre (1942). Weber (1962) finds environmental influences especially significant in rigorous climates, such as the Arctic, Antarctic, and the major desert areas of the world. He illustrates as an example the curious alteration in lichen thalli caused by erosive forces of strong winds in arid regions. *Acarospora bullata* Anzi, which has an effigurate thallus when growing in protected areas, is composed of individual scattered areoles when subjected to erosion. The effuse thallus of *A. fuscata* (Schrad.) Arn., when exposed to the severe desert climate, also assumes the form of scattered areoles.

Weber (1962) regards *A. tucsonensis* Zahlbr., *A. carnegiei* Zahlbr., and *A. gallica* Magn. as altered forms of *A. fuscata* which have been misinter-

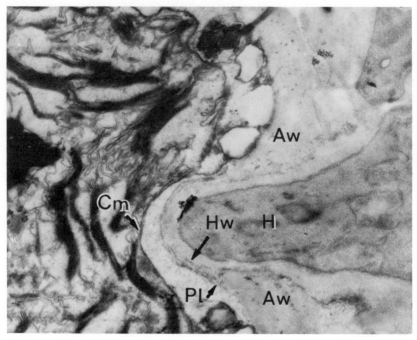

Fig. 15. Section through an intracellular haustorium in *Caloplaca aurantia* var. *aurantia*. Haustorial wall (Hw), algal wall (Aw), plasmalemma (Pl), hypha (H), chloroplast membrane (Cm). ×20,000. After Ben-Shaul *et al.* (1969).

preted. He also mentions modifications due to erosion in other genera of crustose lichens such as *Caloplaca, Lecidea, Staurothele,* and *Rhizocarpon.*

Lately Weber (1968) came to the surprising conclusion that the subgenus *Xanthothallia* (*Acarospora*) includes only two variable species, *A. schleicheri* and *A. chlorophana,* and that all the 80 species known mainly from Magnusson (the monographer of the genus) are merely modifications of these two species. Although the majority of *Xanthothallia* species—the yellow *Acarosporas*—are members of the lichen vegetation in xeric climates, and thus exposed to rigorous environmental influences, such an extreme restriction of the subgenus is beyond expectation.

Submicroscopical adjustment to xeric conditions has been observed in *Caloplaca aurantia* var. *aurantia* by Ben-Shaul *et al.* (1969) and in *Lecanora radiosa* by Galun *et al.* (1970b). The phycobiont in both of these lichens is the green alga *Trebouxia. Caloplaca aurantia* (Pers.) Hellb. var. *aurantia* Poelt is a widespread species, common both in mesic and in arid climates. A comparative study of the phycobiont-mycobiont interrelation in specimens from desert and from moderate environmental

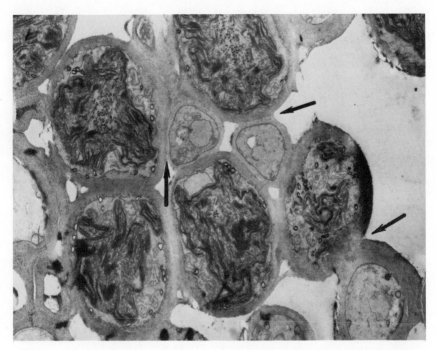

Fig. 16. Section through a region with the symbionts' walls in close contact (arrows) in *Caloplaca aurantia* var. *aurantia.* ×9000.

conditions revealed the following. In the desert specimens, the fungus in-
trudes into 12–15% of the algal cells. Some of the penetrations are intracellular (Fig. 15), while others are enveloped by a thinned algal cell wall,
supposedly an intermediate stage. The association between the two components in specimens from localities in the Mediterranean area consists only
of a close attachment of their cell walls (Fig. 16).

An essentially similar situation was found in *Lecanora radiosa* (Hoffm.)
Schaer. when specimens from desert locations in the Sinai Peninsula and
from a mountainous *Quercus* forest in the Upper Galilee were compared.
Though these conditions may represent a widespread phenomenon, the
physiological significance of the more intimate contact between the symbionts in response to xeric conditions is still puzzling. A similar relation
has been found only in more primitive growth forms. In these cases, however, it was independent of extreme environmental influences (Plessl,
1963; Galun *et al.,* 1970a).

A somewhat different situation may exist in two *Gonohymenia* species
which contain the blue-green alga *Gloeocapsa* as phycobiont (Paran *et
al.,* 1971). Both in *G. sinaica* Galun et Marton (Galun and Marton, 1970)

a lichen from xeric environment in the Sinai Desert, and in *G. meso-potamica* Stein, a species growing under moderate climatic conditions in the Golan Heights, the fungus–alga relationship was found to be similar and thus apparently unaffected by environmental factors.

E. LICHEN–SUBSTRATE RELATIONSHIP

There has been a general belief that lichens play a significant role in rock weathering and breakdown. Thus, Krumbein (1969) claims that in humid climates the lichens usually protect rocks from weathering, whereas in arid climates they are one of the most effective agents in rock decay and deterioration. He finds a correlation between the quantity of microbial population, including fruticose, crustose, and endolithic lichens, algae, fungi, and bacteria, and the rate of the weathering process. Placodial soil lichens of arid regions, subjected to high winds and extreme temperature fluctuations, develop extraordinarily strong and relatively long strands of rhizines or rhizoidal hyphae (Vogel, 1955; Poelt and Baumgärtner, 1964) for a better and more stable attachment. Although penetrating deeply into the substrate, these rhizines have apparently no role in the water relation of the lichens (Poelt and Baumgärtner, 1964).

F. PHYSIOLOGY

Water absorption and water loss are both entirely physical processes in lichens. Furthermore, lichens possess no mechanism for water conservation. Their water content is, therefore, subject to fluctuations governed by environmental conditions. In conditions of severe drought the water content may be as low as 5% of the dry weight of the lichen (Lange *et al.,* 1968), while after water is supplied for even short periods, either as vapor or in liquid form, their water content may rise considerably, often to above 100% of the dry weight.

Some understanding of the water-dependent metabolic processes, such as photosynthesis and respiration, which they can maintain in barren habitats unsuitable for most other kinds of plants, may be gained from the investigations of Lange and his collaborators (Lange and Bertsch, 1965; Lange *et al.,* 1968, 1970a,b; Lange, 1969a,b). Lange, using elaborate techniques, measured CO_2 gas exchange simulating the natural conditions of a "true" desert—the Israeli Negev Desert. The small amount of annual rainfall (less than 100 mm) in this region is restricted to a few days during the short winter season. Throughout the rest of the year, dew is the main source of moisture for a positive balance of carbon dioxide assimilation, as shown in Fig. 17 for *Ramalina maciformis.* When there is no dew, the

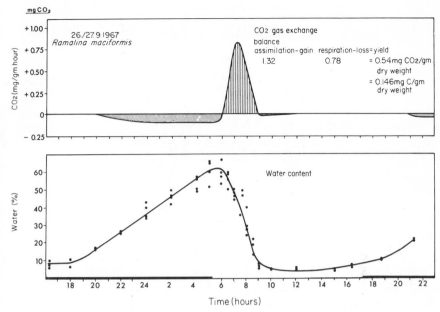

Fig. 17. Carbon dioxide gas exchange (above) and water content (below) in *Ramalina maciformis,* during a day and night with dew of average intensity (after Lange, 1969a).

supply of water required for survival is obtained from the atmospheric humidity (Fig. 18). The amount of water absorbed from the air allows about $\frac{1}{6}$ of the maximal CO_2 uptake, which can be achieved under optimal conditions.

Values of CO_2 gas exchange in epilithic and endolithic crustose lichens from the same area were similar to those obtained for the fruticose species *R. maciformis.* With the gradually increasing temperature and insolation following the early morning hours—when there is a peak in CO_2 uptake—the water content of the lichen declines (Fig. 17) to an extent where CO_2 gas exchange is too low to be recorded. Lange refers to this as the "latent stage" which is reactivated again after sunset (Fig. 17), when respiration starts.

Lichens can even tolerate longer periods of drought and higher temperatures than actually occur in nature. *Ramalina maciformis* was able to resume normal physiological activity after being subjected to a 1 year period of drought. However, their heat-resistance is drought-dependent. The optimal temperature for photosynthesis in the moist thallus of *R. maciformis* is 10°–20°C, which is the actual temperature prevailing in the Negev during the early morning hours. Exposing the wet thallus to higher tempera-

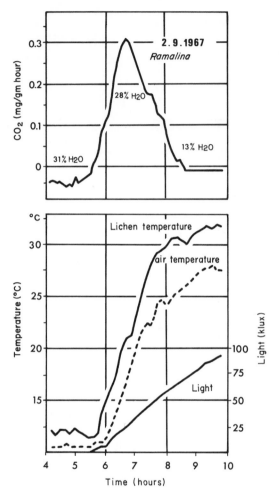

Fig. 18. CO₂ gas exchange in *Ramalina maciformis* (above), lichen temperature air temperature and light (below) during 4 to 10 A.M. after water vapor uptake (after Lange, 1969a).

tures (36°–40°C) brings about a rapid rise in respiration, which leads to a net loss of carbon dioxide. The critical temperature values differ among the species indigenous to different areas and show a remarkable adaptation to the habitat. This may be exemplified by comparing the optimal temperature (10°–20°C) for photosynthesis in the moist thallus of *R. maciformis* and other species growing in the Negev, with the optimal temperature for a similar metabolic activity in a *Neuropogon* species from the "cold desert" of the Antarctic, 0°–5°C (Lange, 1969a).

The cultured phycobiont is less resistant to high temperatures than the algae in the thallus. However, a correlation between the habitat and the degree of resistance exists in cultivated algae similar to that found for the intact thallus (Lange, 1953). There are no data on the degree of resistance of the cultured mycobiont.

The studies of Lange and collaborators have shed much light on the problem of water relations and their consequences in lichens and have resolved some conflicting views concerning this subject in the earlier literature. Jumelle (1892) could not observe differences in the behavior of the free-living algae and the phycobiont of the lichen thallus. He, therefore, refuted a previous assumption by van Tieghem (1874) that the algal component of the thallus is protected by the surrounding hyphae. The report by Thomas (1921) on the survival of a crustose lichen from Libya after a 5-year period of drought is based on visual observation and is therefore rather doubtful. Follmann (1965b) assumes that the relatively large amount of lichenin and protein, which he found in the Atacama Desert lichens, slows down the rate of dehydration.

Blyum (1964, 1965) studied the rate of water reserve consumption in several foliose, fruticose, and crustose lichens from "meso- and xerotic habitats." He concluded that the rate of water reserve consumption is not always correlated with the nature of the habitat and that xeromorphic adaptations do not always function as a protection against evaporation.

III. Desert Fungi

A. Introduction

Most of the information available on desert fungi concerns soil micromycetes although higher fungi also occur in deserts. Micromycetes may also be present on desert rock substrates, but at this time nearly nothing is known about these organisms. The micromycete parasites of desert plants are not considered in this review.

B. Soil Micromycetes: Flora

Killian and Fehér (1939) listed 38 species of fungi in their pioneering work on the Sahara soil microflora and described *Aspergillus*, *Penicillium*, *Syncephalastrum*, and *Trichoderma* as the most characteristic genera. Unfortunately, the usefulness of their data is rather limited, due to inexact taxonomy. In later studies on Sahara soils, Nicot (1955, 1960) found that the mycoflora of the pure sands of the Grand Erg dunes is very sparse and is composed mainly of species of *Penicillium*. In the soil of the *dayas* (shallow sand basins with phanerogamic hamada vegetation), there is a comparatively rich mycoflora composed mainly of Dematiaceae (*Helminthosporium, Curvularia, Alternaria,* and *Stemphylium*), as well as ascomycetes, Mucorineae, and some *Fusarium* spp. concentrated mainly in the upper 5-cm-thick soil layer. Below this, the number of fungi sharply decreases and under 10 cm *Aspergillus fumigatus* Fres. (accompanied only by a few other *Aspergillus* and *Penicillium* spp.) is almost absolutely dominant.

In the northern Negev Desert, Rayss and Borut (1958) and Borut (1960) found a varied soil mycoflora. Borut listed 4 phycomycetes, 43 ascomycetes (3 Gymnoascaceae, 21 *Penicillium* spp., 14 *Aspergillus* spp.), and 35 deuteromycetes (4 Sphaeropsidaceae, 6 Mucedinaceae, 18 Dematiaceae, 2 Stilbaceae, 3 Tuberculariaceae, 3 Mycelia sterilia). Nour (1956) found in virgin soils near Khartoum, Sudan species of *Rhizopus, Aspergillus, Alternaria, Curvularia,* and *Cladosporium*.

Durrell and Shields (1960) isolated 41 micromycetes from soils of the Neveda Test Site. The prevalent organisms were *Stemphylium ilicis* Tengwall, *Fusarium* sp., *Phoma* sp., and *Penicillium oxalicum* Currie et Thom. Hunt and Durrell (1966) listed 48 species from the Death Valley, among these were 10 species of *Aspergillus,* 2 of *Curvularia,* and 3 of *Stemphylium*.

Khudairi (1969) described mycorrhizae from desert soils in Iraq, associated with roots of *Phoenix dactylifera* L., *Ziziphus spina-christi* Willd., and *Peganum harmala* L.

Fletcher and Martin (1948) found *Rhizopus, Mucor,* and possibly *Botrytis* in desert raincrusts in Arizona, but no actinomycetes. In the Atacama Desert, Cameron *et al.* (1965, 1966) and Opfell and Zeball (1967) found a sparse mycoflora, consisting of *Penicillium* sp. and actinomycetes.

Myxomycetes also occur in deserts (Evenson, 1961). In southern Arizona, myxomycetes were "extremely common" in moist chamber cultures of desert plant material, though the number of species was limited [*Badhamia macrocarpa* (Ces.) Rost. *Perichaena depressa* Libert, *P. vermicularis* (Schw.) Rost.].

C. SOIL MICROMYCETES: ECOLOGY AND PHYSIOLOGY

Borut (1960), in agreement with other authors, points out that desert soil micromycetes, though their number in the soil is generally less than in nondesert regions, are generally species of world-wide distribution. However, the species composition of desert soil mycofloras is characteristic. Nicot (1960) summarized their general features and points out the two prevalent biological types of adaptation to desert conditions:

The first type is characterized by brown-pigmented mycelia and/or spores or conida, such as Dematiaceae, also Sphaeropsidales with carbonaceous linings, and Mycelia sterilia with chlamydospores and bulbils. It is believed that the pigments act as a light filter. Also, the thick cell walls in many forms may be considered as a light reducing device. The second type shows an extraordinarily rapid development which may exploit short periods of favorable growth conditions. This, together with multicellular spores ("multiplication of reproductive structures") results in a "vast reproductive capacity" of the organisms.

Durrell and Shields (1960) showed in illumination experiments that not all dark melanin pigments in fungal spores or conidia act as an effective light filter against excessive solar irradiation. When irradiated with UV light of 253.7 nm wavelength, the survival time of *Stemphylium ilicis* Tengwall (a typical desert form) was 60 minutes as against 2 minutes for the equally dark conidia of *Aspergillus niger* Van Tiegh. They also found that the pigment produced by *Stemphylium* absorbs light between 200 and 2000 nm and is insoluble in organic solvents, while the pigment of *Aspergillus* has a wide transmission band and is soluble in methyl alcohol.

Borut (1960) tested some of the fungi isolated from Negev soils for their temperature tolerance. Most species had a growth optimum at about 26°C, some species around 30°C, and *Aspergillus fumigatus* Fres. and *A. niveus* Blochw. at 36°C. With some exceptions, the majority of species does not grow at 40°C. Borut points out, however, that soil temperatures, with the obvious exception of surface layers, do not generally reach this value.

Mahmoud *et al.* (1964) studied the effect of the rhizosphere on the microflora of desert soils in Egypt and found a significantly higher density of microbial population (fungi and actinomycetes) in the rhizosphere than in the soil apart. While *Penicillium* sp. was dominant in the soil, *Alternaria* sp., *Fusarium* sp., and *Aspergillus* sp. were characteristic of the rhizosphere. These effects are attributed partly to the organic matter and root secretion furnished by the growing roots of desert plants, and partly to the higher moisture contents.

Microscopic soil fungi have a significant biological role in deserts. As these soils are generally of low organic content, the decomposing activity of fungi is especially important (Borut, 1960; Khudairi, 1969). Fungal hyphae (together with filaments of blue-green algae) also play a basic role in the stabilization of desert soils and soil crusts. The stabilized soil crusts reduce erosion (Fletcher and Martin, 1948) and also affect the biology of certain desert animals.

Went and Stark (1968) studied the microfungi of sandy soils in the Southwestern United States *in situ*. They found that there is no bonding whatsoever between soil particles in active sand dunes. But in other desert soils, where mycorrhizae associated with higher plants or other fungal hyphae are present: "It is possible to dig the sand away from underneath the surface without its caving in. This is what many burrowing animals, from ants to rats to foxes, do especially in dry sandy areas, and their burrows do not collapse." In an experiment in the Nevada Desert, 2-mm-thick wooden pegs were inserted in the soil during late fall or winter. Provided that there were one or two rains while the pegs were in place, it took 3–4 months for a mycelium layer 1 mm thick to form that would hold sand particles to the peg. After 1 year, the pegs were so strongly anchored in the soil that often a 1 cm³ mass of soil was removed with the peg. After 2–3 years, the peg was usually sufficiently decomposed so that it could not be pulled out, but broke off near the soil surface.

D. MACROMYCETES IN DESERTS

Long and Miller (1945) describe a "desert *Coprinus*" from the Southwestern United States. Davidson and Mielke (1947) report from the same area a heart-rot fungus, *Fomes robustus,* which is parasitic on cacti (saguaro and several chollas) and on other desert plants.

An interesting ecological adaptation is the presence of hypogaeic fungi in desert soils, e.g., truffles (*Tuber* sp.) in Iraq (Khudairi, 1954) and *Terfezia leonis* Tul. and *Tirmania africana* Chat. in the Negev Desert (Rayss, 1959).

IV. Addendum

A. PROBLEMS OF ALGAL TAXONOMY

In the controversy on blue-green algal taxonomy, the recent work of Stanier, Kunisawa, Mandel, and Cohen-Bazire (1971) presents a novel approach. The taxonomic status of *Palmogloea protuberans* is discussed by Fott and Nováková (1971).

Ocampo (1973) studied unicellular blue-green algae which constitute the flora of chasmolithic and endolithic rocks in North American and Middle Eastern deserts. Among 110 strains isolated in culture, 2 were identified as *Chloroococcus turgidus* (Kütz.)Näg. while 108 strains, showing close affinities to the genus *Gloeocapsa,* were found to form a cluster of morphological types connected by gradients of intermediary types. There seemed to be no distinct differences between floras of different rock types or geographic areas.

B. Ecology of Desert Algae

Friedmann (1972) discussed the ecology of endolithic and chasmolithic algal habitats. Field measurements in the Sonoran Desert of Mexico demonstrated the extreme microclimate of the rock surface. In granite with chasmolithic algal growth, the temperature of the rock at the surface and at a depth of 2 cm below the surface and the temperature and relative humidity of the air close to the surface and 1 meter above the rock were monitored over a period of 24 hours.

Cameron (1971) and Horowitz, Cameron, and Hubbard (1972) discuss the microbial ecology of Antarctic deserts and offer data relevant to soil algae, fungi, and lichens in cold deserts.

Novichkova-Ivanova (1972) gives interesting data about soil algae in Central Asian deserts. The number of taxa (species and forms) of soil algae in the arid regions of the U.S.S.R. is more than 400. There are 147 algal taxa known from the takyrs and only 30 from sand deserts. In the Kakakum sand desert, the number of algal cells in soil was found to be correlated with soil moisture content. According to earlier measurements quoted by Novichkova-Ivanova, the dry organic matter formed by algae in Southwestern Turkmenian takyrs amounts from 0.5 t to 1.4 t/ha (50 gm — 140 gm/m^2) or more.

The biomass of endolithic and chasmolithic algae in Middle Eastern and North American desert rocks was estimated from chlorophyll fluorescence as between 2.1 gm and 62.0 gm dry weight/m^2 rock surface while total organic matter, based on N analysis, ranged from 20.5 to 207.4 gm dry weight/m^2 (E. I. Friedmann and R. C. Ocampo, unpublished).

C. Floristics and Ecology of Desert Lichens

Garty (1972) and Galun and Garty (1972) report 51 lichen species from the North and Central Sinai Desert. The species composition of the main habitats are described and the ecology of the lichen–substrate relationship is discussed.

Lange and Evenari (1971) found that the annual growth rate of *Caloplaca aurantia*(Pers.)Hellb. in the Negev Desert was within the range of other crustose lichens living in nondesert climates.

Acknowledgment

This work was supported, in part, by Grant No. GB-27521 from the National Science Foundation to E. I. Friedmann.

References

Ben-Shaul, Y., Paran, N., and Galun, M. (1969). The ultrastructure of the association between phycobiont and mycobiont in three ecotypes of the lichen *Caloplaca aurantia* var. *aurantia. J. Microsc. (Paris)* **8,** 415–422.

Blyum, O. B. (1964). Pohlynannya kraplynno-ridkoi volohy kushchystymy ta lystuvatymy lyshainykamy mezo-ta kserotychnykh mischevyrostan'. (Absorption of liquid-drop water by fruticose and foliose lichens of meso- and xerotic habitats.) *Ukr. Bot. Zh.* **21,** 32–41.

Blyum, O. B. (1965). Shvydkist' vytrachannya vodnoho zapasu v kushchystykh ta lystuvatykh lyshainykiv mezo-ta kserotychnykh mischevyrostan'. (Rates of water reserve consumption in fruticose and foliose lichens of meso-and xerotic habitats.) *Ukr. Bot. Zh.* **22,** 26–34.

Bold, H. C. (1970). Some aspects of the taxonomy of soil algae. *Ann. N.Y. Acad. Sci.* **175,** 601–616.

Bolyshev, N. N. (1952). Proiskhozhdenie i evolyutsiya pochv takyrov. (The origin and evolution of takyr soils.) *Pochvovedenie* [N.S.] **5,** 403–417.

Bolyshev, N. N. (1955). "Proiskhozhdenie i evolyutsia pochv takyrov." (The origin and evolution of takyr soils.) Moscow Univ. Press, Moscow.

Bolyshev, N. N. (1968). "Vodorosli i ikh rol v obrazovanii pochv." (Algae and their role in the formation of soils.) Moscow Univ. Press, Moscow.

Bolyshev, N. N., and Evdokimova, T. I. O. (1944). O prirode korochek takyrov. (The nature of takyr crusts.) *Pochvovedenie* [N.S.] **7–8,** 345–352.

Bolyshev, N. N., and Manucharova, E. A. (1947). Raspredelenie vodoroslei v profile nekotorykh pochv pustynnoi zony. (The distribution of algae in the profile of some desert soils.) *Vestn. Mosk. Univ.* **8,** 115–130.

Borut, S. (1960). An ecological and physiological study of soil fungi of the northern Negev (Israel). *Bull. Res. Counc. Isr., Sect. D* **8,** 65–80.

Bouly de Lesdain, M. (1911). Lichens du Sud Algerie recueillis par M. Seurat. *Bull. Soc. Hist. Natur. Afr. Nord* **3,** 95–98.

Bristol, B. M. (1919). On the retention of viability by algae from old stored soils. *New Phytol.* **18,** 92–107.

Brown, R. M., Jr., Larson, D. A., and Bold, H. C. (1964). Airborne algae: Their abundance and heterogeneity. *Science* **143,** 583–585.

But, V. P. (1967). Pochvennye vodorosli rastitel'nykh assotsiatsii zapadnogo Pamira. (Soil algae of the vegetation associations in Western Pamir.) In "Sovremennoe sostoyanie i perspektivy izucheniya pochvennykh vodorslei v SSSR" (The present state and prospects of the study of soil algae in the U.S.S.R.) Trudy Mezhvuzovskoi Konferentsii (E. A. Shtina, ed.), pp. 113–118. Trudy Kirovskogo Sel'skokhozyaistvennogo Instituta Vol 20, No. 20.

Cameron, R. E. (1960). Communities of soil algae occurring in the Sonoran Desert in Arizona. *J. Ariz. Acad. Sci.* **1,** 85–88.

Cameron, R. E. (1963). Algae of Southern Arizona. Part I. Introduction—blue-green algae. *Rev. Alg.* pp. 282–318.

Cameron, R. E. (1964a). Algae of Southern Arizona. Part II. Algal flora (exclusive of blue-green algae). *Rev. Alg.* pp. 151–177.

Cameron, R. E. (1964b). Terrestial algae of Southern Arizona. *Trans Amer. Microsc. Soc.* **83,** 212–218.

Cameron, R. E. (1966). Soil studies—desert microflora. XIII. Identification of some algae from Antarctica, *JPL Space Programs Summ.* **37–40,** Vol. IV, 123–133.

Cameron, R. E. (1969). Abundance of microflora in soils of desert regions. *JPL Tech. Rep.* **32–1378**, 1–16. Jet Propulsion Lab., California Inst. Techn., Pasadena.

Cameron, R. E. (1971). Antarctic soil microbial and ecological investigations. *In* "Research in the Antarctic" (Louis O. Quam, ed.) pp. 137–189. Amer. Assoc. Advance. Sci. Washington, D.C.

Cameron, R. E., and Blank, G. B. (1965). Soil studies—microflora of desert regions. VIII. Distribution and abundance of desert microflora. *JPL Space Programs Summ.* **37–34**, Vol. IV, 193–202. Jet Propulsion Lab., California Inst. Techn., Pasadena.

Cameron, R. E., and Blank, G. B. (1966). Desert algae: Soil crusts and diaphonous substrata as algal habitats. *JPL Tech. Rep.* **32–971**, 1–41. Jet Propulsion Lab., California Inst. Techn., Pasadena.

Cameron, R. E., and Conrow, H. P. (1969). Soil moisture, relative humidity and microbial abundance in dry valleys of Southern Victoria Land. *Antarct. J. U.S.* **4**, 23–28.

Cameron, R. E., and Fuller, W. H. (1960). Nitrogen fixation by some algae in Arizona soils. *Soil Sci. Soc. Amer., Proc.* **24**, 353–356.

Cameron, R. E., Blank, G. B., Gensel, D. R., and Davies, R. W. (1965). C. Soil properties of samples from the Chile Atacama Desert. *JPL Space Programs Summ.* **37–35**, Vol. IV, 214–223. Jet Propulsion Lab., California Inst. Techn., Pasadena.

Cameron, R. E., Gensel, D. R., Blank, G. B. (1966). Soil studies—desert microflora. XII. Abundance of microflora in soil samples from the Chile Atacama Desert. *JPL Space Programs Summ.* **37–38**, Vol. IV, 140–147. Jet Propulsion Lab., California Inst. Techn., Pasadena.

Cameron, R. E., King, J., and David, C. N. (1970a). Soil microbial ecology of Wheller Valley, Antarctica. *Soil. Sci.* **109**, 110–120.

Cameron, R. E., Morelli, F. A., and Conrow, H. P. (1970b). Survival of microorganisms in desert soil exposed to five years of continuous very high vacuum. *JPL Tech. Rep.* **32–1454**, 1–11. Jet Propulsion Lab., California Inst. Techn., Pasadena.

Chantanachat, S., and Bold, H. C. (1962). Phycological studies. II. Some algae from arid soils. *Tex., Univ., Publ.* **6218**, 1–75.

Davidson, R. W. and Mielke, J. L. (1947). *Fomes robustus,* a heart-rot fungus on cacti and other desert plants. *Mycologia* **39**, 210–217.

Doidge, E. M. (1950). The South-African fungi and lichens to the end of 1945. *Bothalia* **5**, 1–1094.

Drouet, F. (1968). Revision of the classification of the Oscillatoriaceae. 370 p. The Academy of Natural Sciences of Philadelphia (Pennsylvania).

Drouet, F., and Daily, W. A. (1956). Revision of the coccoid Myxophyceae. *Butler Univ. Bot. Stud.* **12**, 1–218.

Durrell, L. W. (1962). Algae of Death Valley. *Trans. Amer. Microsc. Soc.* **81**, 267–273.

Durrell, L. W., and Shields, L. M. (1960). Fungi isolated in culture from soils of the Nevada test site. *Mycologia* **52**, 636–641.

Durrell, L. W., and Shields, L. M. (1961). Characteristics of soil algae relating to crust formation. *Trans. Amer. Microsc. Soc.* **80**, 73–79.

Elenkin, A. (1901). Kochuyushchie lishainiki pustyn i stepei. (Wanderflechten der Steppen und Wüsten.) *Izv. Imp. Sankt-Peterburgskago Bot. Sada* **18**, 1–17.

Evenari, M., Shanan, L., and Tadmor, N. H. (1963–1968). "Run-off Farming in the Negev Desert of Israel," Vols I-IV. Progress reports on the Avdat and Shivta farm projects. National and University Institute of Agriculture, Rehovot, and Dept. of Botany, Hebrew University, Jerusalem.

Evenson, A. E. (1961). A preliminary report of the Myxomycetes of Southern Arizona. *Mycologia* **13**, 137–144.

Eversmann, E. (1831). In Lichenem esculentam Pallasii et species consimilis adversaria. *Nova Acta Leopold.* **15**, 349–358.

Faurel, L., and Schotter, G. (1958). Lichens. *In* "Mission Botanique au Tibesti" (P. Quézel, ed.), pp. 67–79. Institut de Recherches Sahariennes, Université d'Alger, Alger.

Faurel, L., Ozenda, P., and Schotter, G. (1953). Les lichens du Sahara Algérien. *Desert Research. Proc. Internat. Symp. Res. Counc. Isr., Spec. Pub.* **2**, 310–317.

Fehér, D. (1936). Untersuchungen über die regionale Verbreitung der Bodenalgen. *Arch. Mikrobiol.* **7**, 439–476.

Fehér, D. (1945). Der Wüstenboden als Lebensraum. *Erdeszeti Kiserl.* **45**, 213–340.

Fehér, D. (1948). Researches on the geographical distribution of soil microflora. Part II. The geographical distribution of soil algae. *Commun. Bot. Inst. Hung. Univ. Tech. Econ. Sci., Sopron (Hungary)*. **21**, 1–37.

Fink, B. (1909). The composition of a desert lichen flora. *Mycologia* **1**, 87–103.

Flagey, C. (1896). "Catalogue des Lichens de l'Algérie." Tyopgraphie Adolphe Jourdan, Alger.

Fletcher, J. E., and Martin, W. P. (1948). Some effects of algae and molds in the rain-crust of desert soils. *Ecology* **29**, 95–100.

Follmann, G. (1965a). Fensterflechten in der Atacamawüste. *Naturwissenschaften* **14**, 434–435.

Follmann, G. (1965b). Eine gesteinsbewohnende Flechtengesellschaft der nordchilenischen Wüstenformationen mit kennzeichnender *Buellia albula* (Nyl.) Mull. Agr. *Nova Hedwigia* **10**, 243–256.

Follmann, G. (1966). Chilenische Wanderflechten. *Ber. Deut. Bot. Ges.* **79**, 453–462.

Forest, H. S. (1965). The soil algal community. II. Soviet soil studies. *J. Phycol.* **1**, 164–171.

Forest, H. S., and Weston, C. R. (1966). Blue-green algae from the Atacama desert of Northern Chile. *J. Phycol.* **2**, 163–164.

Fott, B. and Nováková, M. (1971). Taxonomy of the palmelloid genera *Gloeocystis* Nägeli and *Palmogloea* Kützing (Chlorophyceae). *Arch. Protistenk.* **113**, 322–333.

Friedmann, I. (1964). Xerophytic algae in the Negev Desert. *Abstr. Int. Bot. Congr., 10th, 1964* 290–291.

Friedmann, E. I. (1968). Endolithic algae in calcareous desert rocks. *Amer. Zool.* **8**, 79A.

Friedmann, E. I. (1971). Reflected light and scanning electron microscopy of endolithic desert algae. *Phycologia* **10**, 411–428.

Friedmann, E. I. (1972). Ecology of lithophytic algal habitats in Middle Eastern and North American deserts. *In*: "Eco-Physiological Foundation of Ecosystems Productivity in Arid Zone" (L. E. Rodin, ed.) pp. 182–185. U.S.S.R. Academy of Sciences, Publishing House Nauka, Leningrad.

Friedmann, I., and Ocampo-Paus, R. (1965). A new *Chlorosarcinopsis* from the Negev Desert. *J. Phycol.* **1**, 185–191.

Friedmann, I., and Ocampo-Paus, R. (1966). *Bracteacoccus minor* (Chodat) Petrová var. *desertorum* n. var., a remarkable alga from the Negev. *Nova Hedwigia* **10**, 481–494.

Friedmann, I., Lipkin, Y., and Ocampo-Paus, R. (1967). Desert algae of the Negev (Israel). *Phycologia* **6**, 185–196.

Fukushima, H. (1959). General report on fauna and flora of the Ongul Island, Antarctica, especially of freshwater algae. *Yokohama Shiritsu Daigaku Kiyo C: Shizen Kaigaku (Yokohama Nat. Univ. J., Ser. C, Natur. Sci.)* **31** (112), 1–10.

Fuller, W. H., Cameron, R. E., and Raica, N. (1961). Fixation of nitrogen in desert soils by algae. *Proc. Int. Congr. Soil Sci., 7th, 1960* pp. 617–624.

Galun, M. (1963). Autecological and synecological observations on lichens of the Negev, Israel. *Isr. J. Bot.* **12**, 179–187.

Galun, M. (1966). Additions to the lichen flora of the Negev, Israel. *Isr. J. Bot.* **15**, 144–149.

Galun, M. (1967). A new species of *Catillaria* from Israel. *Lichenologist* **3**, 423–424.

Galun, M. and Garty, Y. (1972). Lichens of North and Central Sinai. *Isr. J. Bot.* **21**, 243–254.

Galun, M., and Marton, K. (1970). A new species of *Gonhymenia* from the Sinai Peninsula and its position in the genus. *Bryologist* **73**, 378–380.

Galun, M., and Reichert, I. (1960). A study of lichens of the Negev. *Bull. Res. Counc. Isr., Sect. D* **9**, 127–148.

Galun, M., Paran, N., and Ben-Shaul, Y. (1970a). The fungus-alga association in Lecanoraceae. An ultrastructural study. *New Phytol.* **69**, 599–603.

Galun, M., Paran, N., and Ben-Shaul, Y. (1970b). An ultrastructural study of the fungus-alga association in *Lecanora radiosa* growing under different environmental conditions. *J. Microsc. (Paris)* **9**, 801–806.

Garty, Y. (1972). Seker floristi vehakarat ha'ekologiyah shel hahazaziyot bitsfon ubemerkaz hatzi ha'i Sinai (Floristic and ecological research on lichens of North and Central Sinai). In Hebrew, with English summary. Thesis. Tel-Aviv University.

Geiger, R. (1950). "The Climate Near the Ground" (transl. of the 2nd German ed., "Das Klima der bodennahen Luftschicht"). Harvard Univ. Press, Cambridge, Massachusetts.

Geitler, L. (1932). Cyanophyceae. *In* "Dr. L. Rabenhorst's Kryptogamen-Flora von Deutschland, Österreich und der Schweiz," Vol. 14, pp. 1–1196. Akad. Verlagsges., Leipzig.

Glazovskaya, M. A. (1950). Vyvetrivanie gornykh porod v nival'nom poyase tsentral'nogo Tyan-Shanya. (Rock weathering in the arable belt of Central Tyan-Shan.) *Tr. Pochv. Inst., Akad. Nauk SSSR* **34**, 28–48.

Gollerbakh, M. M. (1953). Rol vodoroslei v pochvennykh protsessakh. (The role of algae in soil processes.) *Tr. Konf. Vop. Pochv. Mikrobiol., 1951* pp. 98–108 and 221–222.

Gollerbakh, M. M., and Shtina, E. A. (1969). "Pochvennye vodorosli" (Soil algae). Izdatelystovo "Nauka," Leningrad.

Gromov, B. V. (1957). Mikroflora skal'nykh porod i primitivnykh pochv nekotorykh severnykh raionov SSSR. (The microflora of rock layers and primitive soils of some northern districts of the U.S.S.R.) *Mikrobiologya* **26**, 52–59.

Hale, M. E. (1967). "The Biology of Lichens." Arnold, London.

Herre, A. W. (1911). The desert lichens of Reno, Nevada. *Bot. Gaz. (Chicago)* **51**, 286–297.

Herre, A. W. (1942). Additions to and comments upon the lichen flora of the Santa Cruz Peninsula, California. *Amer. Midl. Natur.* **28**, 752–755.

Horowitz, N. H., Cameron, R. E., and Hubbard, J. S. (1972). Microbiology of the Dry Valleys of Antarctica. *Science* **176**, 242–245.

Hue, A. (1921). Lichenes in Africa tropica occidentali et praecipue in Mauritania a Cl. Chudeau, annis 1908–1912 lectos. *Mem. Soc. Bot. Fr.* **30**, 1–17.

Hunt, C. B., and Durrell, L. W. (1966). Distribution of fungi and algae. *U.S., Geol. Surv., Prof. Pap.* **509**, 55–66.

Imshaug, H. A. (1950). A new species of *Dermatocarpon*. *Mycologia* **42**, 753–757.

Jumelle, H. (1892). Recherches physiologiques sur les Lichens. *Rev. Gen. Bot.* **4**, 49–64, 103–121, 159–175, 220–231, 259–272, and 305–320.

Keller, B. A. (1926). Nizshie rasteniya na zonal'nykh pochvakh i stolbchatykh solontsakh polupustyni. (Niedere Pflanzen auf den charakteristischen Halb-wüstenböden.) *In* "Rastitel'nyi mir russkikh stepei, polupustyn i pustyn" (Die Pflanzenwelt der Russischen Steppen, Halbwüsten und Wüsten) (B. A. Keller, ed.), Vol. 2, pp. 1–16. Gosudarstvennyi Institut po Izucheniyu Zasushlivykh Oblastei (GIZO), Voronezh.

Khudairi, A. K. (1954). Desert truffles. *Mag. Iraqi Agr.* **9**, 252–254. (Cited in Khudairi, 1969).

Khudairi, A. K. (1969). Mycorrhiza in desert soils. *BioScience* **19**, 598–599.

Killian, C. (1953). Symposium discussion in: Desert Research. *Proc. Int. Symp. Res. Counc. Isr., Spec. Publ.* **2**, 301.

Killian, C., and Fehér, D. (1939). Recherches sur la microbiologie des sols désertiques. *Encycl. Biol.* **21**, 1–127.

Klement, O. (1966). Flechten aus der Mongolischen Volksrepublik. *Feddes Reportorium* **72**, 98–123.

Krumbein, W. E. (1968). Geomicrobiology and geochemistry of the "Nari-Lime-Crust" (Israel). *In* "Recent Developments in Carbonate Sedimentology in Central Europe" (G. Müller and G. M. Friedman, eds.), pp. 138–147. Springer-Verlag, Berlin and New York.

Krumbein, W. E. (1969). Über den Einfluss der Mikroflora auf die exogene Dynamik (Verwitterung und Krustenbildung). *Geol. Rundsch.* **58**, 333–365.

Lange, O. L. (1953). Hitze- und Trockenresistenz der Flechten in Beziehung zu ihrer Verbreitung. *Flora (Jena) Abt. B.* **140**, 39–97.

Lange, O. L. (1969a). Die funktionellen Anpassungen der Flechten an die ökologischen Bedingungen arider Gebiete. *Ber. Deut. Bot. Ges.* **82**, 3–22.

Lange, O. L. (1969b). Experimentell–ökologische Untersuchungen an Flechten der Negev-Wüste. I. CO$_2$-Gaswechsel von *Ramalina maciformis* (Del.) Bory unter kontrollierten Bedingungen im Laboratorium. *Flora (Jena), Abt. B.* **158**, 324–359.

Lange, O. L., and Bertsch, A. (1965). Photosynthese der Wüstenflechte *Ramalina maciformis* nach Wasserdampfaufnahme aus dem Luftraum. *Naturwissenschaften* **52**, 215–216.

Lange, O. L., Schulze, E. D., and Koch, W. (1968). Photosynthese von Wüsten-flechten am natürlichen Standort nach Wasserdampfaufnahme aus dem Luftraum. *Naturwissenschaften* **55**, 658–659.

Lange, O. L., Schulze, E. D., and Koch, W. (1970a). Experimentell-ökologische Untersuchungen an Flechten der Negev-Wüste. II. CO$_2$-Gaswechsel und Wasserhaushalt von *Ramalina maciformis* (Del.) Bory am natürlichen Standort während der sommerlichen Trockenperiode. *Flora (Jena), Abt. B* **159**, 38–62.

Lange, O. L., Schulze, E. D., and Koch, W. (1970b). Experimentell-ökologische Untersuchungen an den Flechten der Negev-Wüste. III. CO$_2$-Gaswechsel und

Wasserhaushalt von Krusten-und Blattflechten am natürlichen Standort während der sommerlichen Trockenperiode. Ecophysiological investigations on lichens of the Negev Desert. III. CO_2 gas exchange and water relations of crustose and foliose lichens in their natural habitat during the summer dry period. *Flora (Jena), Abt. B* **159**, 525–528.

Lange, O. L. and Evenari, M. (1971). Experimentell-ökologische Untersuchungen an den Flechten der Negev-Wüste. IV. Wachstumsmessungen an *Caloplaca aurantiaca*(Pers.)Hellb. Ecophysiological investigations on the lichens of the Negev Desert. IV. Growth measurements with *Caloplaca aurantiaca* (Pers.)Hellb. *Flora (Jena), Abt. B* **160**, 100–104.

Long, H. and Miller, V. M. (1945). A new desert *Corprinus. Mycologia* **37**, 120–123.

Magnusson, A. H. (1940–1944). "Lichens from Central Asia." Reports from the scientific expedition to the north-western provinces of China under the leadership of Dr. Sven Hedin, Sino-Swedish Expedition. Publ. 13, XI. Botany, 1. and Publ. 22. XI. Botany, **2**. Stockholm.

Mahmoud, S. A., El-Fadl, M. Abu, and El-Mofty, M. K. (1964). Studies on the rhizosphere microflora of desert plants. *Folia Microbiol. (Prague)* **9**, 1–8.

Maire, R. (1933). Etudes sur la flore et la végétation du Sahara central. *Mem. Soc. Hist. Natur. Afr. Nord* **3**, Mission du Hoggar, No. II.

Mayland, H. F., and McIntosh, T. H. (1966a). Availability of biologically fixed atmospheric nitrogen-15 to higher plants. *Nature (London)* **209**, 421–422.

Mayland, H. F., and McIntosh, T. H. (1966b). Distribution of nitrogen fixed in desert algal-crust. *Soil Sci. Soc. Amer., Proc.* **30**, 606–609.

Mayland, H. F., McIntosh, T. H., and Fuller, W. H. (1966). Fixation of isotopic nitrogen on a semi-arid soil by algal crust organisms. *Soil Sci. Soc. Amer., Proc.* **30**, 56–60.

Melnikova, V. V. (1955). O flore vodoroslei serozemnykh pochv Yuzhnogo Tadzhikistana. (Algal flora of serozem soils of Southern Tadzhikistan.) *Izv. Otd. Estestv. Nauk, Akad. Nauk Tadzh. SSR* **9**, 131–141.

Moewus, L. (1953). About the occurrence of freshwater algae in the semi-desert Round Broken Hill (New South Wales, Australia). *Bot. Notis.* pp. 399–416.

Müller Argovensis, J. (1880). Les lichens d'Egypte. *Rev. Mycol.* **2**, 6–21.

Nicot, J. (1955). Remarques sur les peuplements de micromycètes des sables désertiques. *C.R. Acad. Sci.* **240**, 2082–2084.

Nicot, J. (1960). Some characteristics of the microflora of desert soils. *In* "International Symposium on the Ecology of Soil Fungi" (D. Parkinson and J. S. Ward, eds.), pp. 94–97. Liverpool Univ. Press, Liverpool.

Nour, U. A. (1956). A preliminary survey of fungi in some Sudan soils. *Trans. Brit. Mycol. Soc.* **39**, 357–360.

Novichkova-Ivanova, L. N. (1972). Soil algae of Middle Asia deserts. *In* "Eco-Physiological Foundation of Ecosystems Productivity in Arid Zone" (L. E. Rodin, ed.). pp. 180–182. U.S.S.R. Academy of Sciences, Publishing House Nauka, Leningrad.

Nylander W. (1878). Symbolae quaedam ad lichenographiam Sahariensem. *Flora (Jena)* **61**, 337–345.

Ocampo, R. C. (1973). Contributions towards an experimental taxonomy of unicellular blue-green algae (Chroococcales). Ph.D. Dissertation. Florida State University, Tallahassee.

Ocampo-Paus, R., and Friedmann, I. (1966). *Radiosphaera negevensis* sp. n., a new chlorococcalean desert alga. *Amer. J. Bot.* **53**, 663–671.

Odintsova, S. V. (1941). Obrazovanie selitry v pustyne. (Niter formation in deserts.) *Dokl. Akad. Nauk SSSR* **32**, 578–580.

Opfell, J. B., and Zebal, G. P. (1967). Ecological patterns of microorganisms in desert soils. *In* "Life Sciences and Space Research" (A. H. Brown and F. G. Favorite, eds.) Vol. V, pp. 187–203. North-Holland Publ., Amsterdam.

Paran, N., Ben-Shaul, Y., and Galun, M. (1971). Fine structure of the blue-green phycobiont and its relation to the mycobiont in two *Gonhymenia* lichens. *Arch. Mikrobiol.* **76**, 103–113.

Parker, B. C. (1961). Facultative hetertrophy in certain soil algae from the ecological vewpoint. *Ecology* **42**, 381–386.

Parker, B. C., Schanen, N., and Renner, R. (1969). Viable soil algae from the herbarium of the Missouri Botanical Gardens. *Ann. Mo. Bot. Gard.* **56**, 113–119.

Petersen, J. B. (1935). Studies on the biology and taxonomy of soil algae. *Dan. Bot. Ark.* **8** (9), 1–183.

Plessl, A. (1963). Über die Beziehungen von Pilz und Alge im Flechtenthallus. *Oesterr. Bot. Z.* **110**, 194–269.

Poelt, M. J., and Baumgärtner, H. (1964). Über Rhizinenstränge bei placodialen Flechten. *Oesterr. Bot. Z.* **111**, 1–18.

Rayss, T. (1959). Champignons hypogés dans les régions désertiques d'Israel. "Omagiu lui Traian Săvulescu," pp. 655–659. Acad. Repub. Pop. Rom., Bucureşti.

Rayss, T., and Borut, S. (1958). Contributions to the knowledge of soil fungi in Israel. *Mycopathol. Mycol. Appl.* **10**, 142–174.

Reichert, I. (1936). L'Afrique du Nord et sa position phytogéographique au point de vue lichenologique. *Bull. Soc. Bot. Fr.* **83**, 836–841.

Reichert, I. (1937a). Eine lichenogeographische Skizze Palästinas. *Verh. Zool.-Bot. Ges. Wien* **86–87**, 288–296.

Reichert, I. (1937b). La Libia e la sua posizione fitogeografica dal punto di vista lichenologica. *Nuovo G. Bot. Ital.* **44**, 188–196.

Reichert, I. (1937c). La position phyto-géographique de l'Afrique du Nord au point de vue lichenologique. *Rev. Mycol.* **10**, 37–46.

Reichert, I. (1937d). Steppe and desert in the light of lichen vegetation. *Proc. Linn. Soc. London* **199**, 19–23.

Reichert, I. (1940). A new species of *Diploschistes* from oriental steppes and its phytogeographical significance. *Palestine J. Bot., Rehovot Ser.* **3**, 162–182.

Reichert, I. (1953). Steppes and deserts in the Eastern Holarctic in relation to lichens. *Proc. Int. Bot. Congr., 7th, 1950* p. 676.

Royzin, M. B. (1960). Mikroflora skal i primitivnykh pochv vysokogornoi arkticheskoi pustyni. (The microflora of rocks and primitive soils of the high altitude arctic desert.) *Bot. Zh.* (*Leningrad*) **45**, 997–1008.

Scheffer, F., Meyer, B., and Kalk, E. (1963). Biologische Ursachen der Wüstenlackbildung. Zur Frage der chemischen Verwitterung in ariden Gebieten. *Z. Geomorphol.* [N. S.] **7**, 112–119.

Schlichting, H. E. (1969). The importance of airborne algae and protozoa. *J. Air Pollut. Contr. Ass.* **19**, 946–951.

Schwabe, G. H. (1960a). Blaualgen aus ariden Böden. *Forsch. Fortschr.* **34**, 194–197.

Schwabe, G. H. (1960b). Zur autotrophen Vegetation in ariden Böden. Blaualgen und Lebensraum. IV. *Oesterr. Bot. Z.* **107**, 281–309.

Schwabe, G. H. (1963). Blaualgen der phototrophen Grenzschicht. Blaualgen und Lebensraum. VII. *Pedobiologia* 2, 132–152.

Sdobnikova, N. V. (1956). Pochvennye vodorosli takyrov severnoi chasti Turanskoi nizmennosti. (Soil algae of the takyrs in the northern part of the Turanian Lowland.) Candidate's Thesis, Akad. Nauk S.S.S.R., V. L. Komarov Bot. Inst., Leningrad. (Cited in Bolyshev, 1968.)

Sdobnikova, N. V. (1959). Nekotorye dannye o vodoroslyakh, obitayushchikh v peskakh srednei Azii. (Nonnulla facta de algis in arenosis Asiae Mediae habitantibus.) *Akad. Nauk SSSR Leningrad, Bot. Inst. Otd. Sporovykh Rast., Bot. Mater.* 12, 143–148.

Sdobnikova, N. V. (1967). Pochvenno-al'gologicheskie issledovaniya v stepnykh, pustynno-stepnykh i pustynnykh raionakh Kazakhstana. (Invesigations on soil algae of the steppe, desert-steppe, and desert regions of Kazakhstan.) *In* "Sovremennoe sostoyanie i perspektivy izucheniya pochvennykh vodoroslei v SSSR" (The present state and prospects of the study of the soil algae in the U.S.S.R.) Trudy Mezhvuzovskoi Konferentsii (E. A. Shtina, ed.), pp. 103–108. Trudy Kirovskogo Sel'skokhozyaistvennogo Instituta Vol. 20, No. 20.

Shields, L. M. (1957). Algal and lichen floras in relation to nitrogen content of certain volcanic and arid range soils. *Ecology* 38, 661–663.

Shields, L. M., and Drouet, F. (1962). Distribution of terrestrial algae within the Nevada test site. *Amer. J. Bot.* 48, 547–554.

Shields, L. M., Mitchell, C., and Drouet, F. (1957). Alga- and lichen-stabilized surface crusts as soil nitrogen sources. *Amer. J. Bot.* 44, 489–498.

Shtina, E. A., and Bolyshev, N. N. (1963). Soobshchestva vodoroslei v pochvakh sukhikh i pustynnykh stepei. (Algal communities in the soils of arid steppes and desert steppes.) *Bot. Zh.* (*Leningrad*) 48, 670–680.

Stanier, R. Y., Kunisawa, R., Mandel, M. and Cohen-Bazire, G. (1971). Purification and properties of unicellular blue-green algae (order Chroococcales). *Bacteriol. Rev.* 35, 171–205.

Starmach, K. (1966). Cyanophyta-Sinice, Glaucophyta-Glaukofity. *In* "Flora Slodkowodna Polski" (K. Starmach, ed.), Vol. 2, pp. 1–808. Polska Akademia Nauk, Państwowe Wydawnictwo Naukowe, Warszawa.

Starr, R. C. (1955). A comparative study of *Chlorococcum* Meneghini and other spherical, zoospore-producing genera of the Chlorococcales. *Indiana Univ. Publ., Sci. Ser.* 20, 1–111.

Steiner, J. (1895). Ein Beitrag zur Flechtenflora der Sahara. *Sitzungsber. Kaiserl. Akad. Wiss. Wien, Math.-Naturwiss. Kl., Abt. 1* 104, 384–393.

Steiner, J. (1902). Zweiter Beitrag zur Flechtenflora Algiers. *Verh. Zool.-Bot. Ges. Wien* 52, 469–487.

Steiner, J. (1916). Aufzählung der von J. Bornmüller im Oriente gesammelten Flechten. *Ann. Naturhist. Mus. Wien* 30, 24–39.

Szatala, Ö. (1957). Prodromus einer Flechtenflora des Irans. *Ann. Hist.-Natur. Mus Nat. Hung.* 8, 101–154.

Tchan, Y. T. and Beadle, N. C. W. (1955). Nitrogen economy in semi-arid plant communities. Part II. The non-symbiotic nitrogen-fixing organisms. *Proc. Linn Soc. N. S. W.* 80, 97–104.

Thomas, H. H. (1921). Some observations on plants in the Libyan Desert. *J. Ecol.* 9, 75–88.

Thomson, J. W., and Iltis, H. H. (1968). A fog-induced lichen community in the coastal desert of Southern Peru. *Bryologist* **71**, 31–34.

Tits, D. (1925). Le Sahara occidental, contribution phytogéographique. *Bull. Soc. Roy. Bot. Belg.* **58**, 39–91.

Tomin, M. P. (1926). Lishainiki, vstrechayushchiesya na solontsevatykh pochvakh v polupustynnoi oblasti Yugo-vostoka. (Über die Bodenflechten aus den Halbwüsten von Süd-Ost-Russland). *In* "Rastitel'nyi mir russkikh stepei, polupustyn i pustyn" (Die Pflanzenwelt der Russischen Steppen, Halbwüsten und Wüsten) (B. A. Keller, ed.), Vol. 2, pp. 17–32. Gosudarstvennyi Institut po Izucheniyi Zasushlivykh Oblastei (GIZO), Voronezh.

Trainor, F. R. (1962). Temperature tolerance of algae in dry soil. *Phycol. Soc. Amer., News Bull.* **15**, 3–4.

Trainor, F. R. (1970). Survival of algae in a desiccated soil. *Phycologia* **9**, 111–113.

Troitskaya, E. N. (1965). Sezonnye izmeneniya v razvitii vodoroslei nekotorykh pustynnikh pochv. (Seasonal changes in the development of algae of some desert vegetational formations.) *In* "Sporovye rasteniya Srednei Azii i Kazakhstana" (Spore plants of Central Asia and Kazakhstan). Izdatelystvo "Nauka" Uzb. S.S.S.R., Tashkent. (Cited in Gollerbakh and Shtina, 1969.)

van Tieghem, P. (1874). Discussion remark. *Bull. Soc. Bot. Fr.* **21**, 348–350.

von Humboldt, A. (1826). "Ansichten der Natur mit wissenschaftlichen Erläuterungen," 2nd ed., 2 vols. Cotta, Stuttgart and Tübingen.

Vogel, S. (1955). Niedere "Fensterpflanzen" in der südafrikanischen Wüste. *Beitr. Biol. Pflanz.* **31**, 45–135.

Weber, W. A. (1962). Environmental modification and the taxonomy of the crustose lichens. *Sv. Bot. Tidskr.* **56**, 293–333.

Weber, W. A. (1968). A taxonomic revision of *Acarospora,* Subgenus *Xanthothallia. Lichenologist* **4**, 16–31.

Went, F. W., and Stark, N. (1968). The biological and mechanical role of soil fungi. *Proc. Nat. Acad. Sci. U.S.* **60**, 497–509.

Werner, R. G. (1950). Lichenes. *In* R. Maire and T. Monod: "Etudes sur la flore et la végétation du Tibesti." Larose, Paris.

Whitton, B. A. (1969). The taxonomy of blue-green algae. *Brit. Phycol. J.* **4**, 121–123.

Zukal, H. (1896). Morphologische und biologische Untersuchungen über die Flechten. *Sitzungsber. Kaiserl. Akad. Wiss. Wien, Math.-Naturwiss. Kl., Abt. 1* **105**, 197–264.

CHAPTER V

A NEW APPROACH TO THE WATER RELATIONS
OF DESERT PLANTS

H. Walter and E. Stadelmann

Frankincense, for which of old they went
Through plain and desert waterless, and faced
The Lion-haunted woods that edged the waste.
William Morris. The Earthly Paradise III

I. Introduction

The results of Walter's early work formed the basis for the book "Die Hydratur der Pflanze und ihre physiologischökologische Bedeutung (Untersuchungen über den osmotischen Wert; 1931)." The main conclusion drawn from the experimental observations was that the fundamental problem for plants in arid zones is the maintenance of a sufficiently high degree of hydration of the living protoplasm during periods of drought so that the level of metabolism necessary to sustain life can be maintained. To quantitate the degree of hydration Walter introduced a new term, the "hydrature," which is now defined thermodynamically as the "relative water activity" in the cell (see Section VI). Meanwhile further investigations on plant water relations in almost all of the deserts of the earth were made by Walter (1936, 1939, 1960, p. 7, 1946, p. 8, 1968, p. 6). These investigations were based on concepts advanced in 1931.

This chapter will give a brief survey of Walter's results from four decades of investigations on desert plant ecology. Data from less accessible publications will often be mentioned, but it is not intended to include all of the literature in this field. Parts of Sections X–XXI are taken from Walter and Kreeb (1970).

Since this chapter was written further contributions containing additional material on water relations and ecophysiology of desert plants were published by Walter (1971, 1972, 1973a).

II. Rainfall and Water Supply of Desert Plants

The usual measurement of rainfall is given in millimeters and indicates the amount of water in liters falling per square meter of ground surface. Such measurement is by no means an indicator of the water supply of the plants in arid regions. Rather it is necessary to consider also the density of the plant cover and to know its transpiring surface also measured per square meter of ground surface.

A very striking feature of all deserts is the low density of vegetation which they support. Because of the low density of plant cover in deserts, the bare ground or rock is widely exposed. This exposure becomes more pronounced with decreasing rainfall and increasing dryness.

The quantitative relationship between the amount of yearly rainfall and the density of plant cover can be investigated meaningfully only where there is a gradual increase in rainfall from one part of a region to another and where additional factors which influence plant cover remain constant throughout the region. Such additional factors are (1) the distribution of rainfall throughout the year, (2) the more or less constant temperature throughout the entire region, (3) the uniformity of soil composition and life forms of plants, and (4) the lack of interference by human activity.

A region where these conditions are fulfilled was found in Southwest Africa. Here, the cold oceanic Benguela stream comes close to the seashore. Just inland along the coast is the Namib Desert, which receives no rainfall. Further inland the amount of annual rainfall increases gradually and reaches 500 mm/year at the border of the Kalahari (see Fig. 1). Rain-

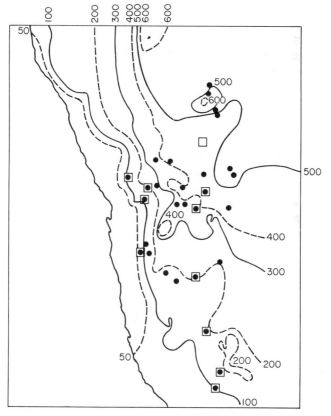

Fig. 1. Distribution of rainfall in Southwest Africa (in mm/year): Test plots for determination of productivity of the grassland (□); locations of samplings for the analysis of forage plants (●) (from Walter and Volk, 1954, p. 97).

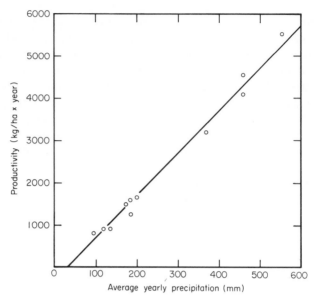

Fig. 2. Productivity of grassland in Southwest Africa in relation to annual rainfall. Ordinate: production of dry matter in kg/ha year; abscissa: average yearly rainfall in mm (after Walter, 1939, p. 855).

fall over the whole region occurs only during the summer (December–March). Seasonal temperature changes also are more or less uniform over the region. Only the coastal area which has heavy fogs is cooler, but since this area is nearly without vegetation it is excluded from the present discussion. The soil of the test plots is deep and composed uniformly of loamy sand.

A very light grass cover is found only in areas where the rainfall is about 100 mm/year. Less than this amount does not support permanent vegetation in the region. With an increase in annual rainfall, the grass grows taller and density of plant cover is increased. Gradually, the vegetation becomes a savanna with widely scattered woody plants in a closed grass cover. It is always possible to find test plots as large as 25 m² with pure grass cover. At the end of the rainy season the grass gets dry. Therefore, it is easy to determine dry matter production of the above-ground plant organs. The effects of increasing rainfall on productivity are shown in Fig. 2. The productivity of the grass cover, expressed as dry weight, is a linear function of rainfall; an increase of rainfall of about 100 mm/year increases dry matter production by approximately 1000 kg/ha. Productivity among years varies much less than does rainfall. Only natural areas which have not been grazed by cattle or sheep for many years were chosen as plots for taking the samples for this calculation. Even light grazing causes a marked reduction in productivity. Naturally, the species composition of the grassland changes with increasing rainfall. For more humid climates, larger and more productive grass species (e.g., *Aristida* spp., *Eragrostis* spp.) are found compared with those growing in less humid climates.

Calculations based on the values obtained by Loneragan (Walter, 1964, p. 312) show that the linear relationship between annual rainfall (in the range of 500–1500 mm) and production is also true for the *Eucalyptus* forest area in Southwest Australia. The annual production of dry matter in the leaf litter per square meter of soil surface is directly proportional to yearly rainfall. This relationship was also found for the total leaf litter surface.

For grasses of Southwest Africa it may also be assumed that the transpiring plant surface is proportional to the dry matter produced above ground and therefore is also proportional to annual rainfall.* Plant density of *Larrea divaricata* was found to increase directly with annual rainfall in the Sonora and Mojave desert (Woodell *et al.*, 1969, p. 40).

From these considerations the following important conclusion can be drawn: The unit of the transpiring plant surface receives about the same amount of rainfall in arid and in humid regions. In other words, the water supply of an individual plant per unit of its transpiring surface is not significantly less in arid climates than it is in humid regions.

The chief response of vegetation of arid regions against water loss is reduction of the transpiring plant surface per unit of land area. Of course, other adaptations are required to endure a long drought season. They are mostly of a morphological and anatomical nature.

With decreasing density of the plant cover, the plants are farther apart. Each plant has more soil area available and the plant has a larger root system which can develop more extensively horizontally. This indicates another significant feature: Root systems become larger as the climate becomes increasingly more arid, when comparing plants of similar life forms of arid and humid areas, and the ratio of shoot mass to root mass decreases (see Table I).

In deserts with a large proportion of succulents and hygrohalophytes, the contribution of the underground parts to the whole phytomass is low (62% for deserts with hygrohalophytes). The ratio is very high in the tun-

---

* This rule also holds true for plantations in arid zones, e.g., olive trees are cultivated in Tunisia in regions with 200–800 mm annual rainfall. Correspondingly, the tree density increases from about 20 trees per hectare to about 80 trees per hectare. Since the olive harvest per tree (about 20 kg) is about the same in arid regions as in humid, proportionality exists between olive yield and amount of annual rainfall (Le Houérou, 1959, p. 32, Table III).

TABLE I

Portion of Underground Plant Parts to the Total Phytomass
for Various Vegetation Zones[a]

Vegetation zone	Contribution to the phytomass (%)
Moist tropical forest	18
Subtropical evergreen forests	20
Boreal coniferous forests	22
Temperate oak forests	24
Temperate beech forests	26
Savannas	42
Steppes	82
Dry steppes	85
Deserts	84–87
Haloxylon aphyllum desert	90

[a] From Rodin and Bazilevič (1965, p. 216, Table 35) and Rodin and Bazilevič (1966, pp. 370–371, Table 1).

dra (70–80%), where plants have rhizomes or portions of underground woody shoots protected during the long cold season.

III. "Diffuse" and "Contracted" Vegetation

The vegetation of an arid region which is distributed more or less evenly over the surface of an almost flat area will be called "diffuse" vegetation. In extreme deserts, however, with an average rainfall less than 100 mm/year, the vegetation pattern changes. In such deserts the soil surface is usually crusted. The infrequent rainfall normally does not penetrate into the soil, but runs off in scarcely noticeable, gently sloping sand-filled runnels or gulleys into valleys, where the soil is moistened to a considerable depth. The distribution of vegetation over the surface is altered under such conditions with "diffuse" vegetation changing to a "contracted" one (*végétation contractée,* Monod, 1954, p. 35). In such extreme deserts most of the area is without vegetation and plants are more and more confined to gulleys, valleys, and depressions (see Fig. 3). The soil in these places is moist to a relatively deep level, so that available water for these plants in extreme deserts is not necessarily less than in more humid regions.

In the desert near Cairo, for example, the average yearly rainfall totals approximately 25 mm, and may range between 0 and 90 mm in some years. Assuming that 40% of the 25 mm of rain runs off into the valleys, which constitute only 2% of the total surface, the plants in the valleys

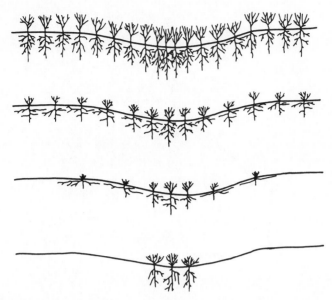

Fig. 3. Transition from "diffuse" to "contracted" vegetation, with decreasing average rainfall in extremely arid areas (from Walter, 1964, 1st ed., p. 313).

would have an available water supply equivalent to a yearly rainfall of about 500 mm. This calculation is not a theoretical one; it was confirmed by the results of Batanouny (1963, p. 254ff). He found that plant cover on the first terrace in Wadi Hoff (south of Cairo) transpired 400 mm of water per year (Abd El Rahman and Batanouny, 1965, p. 145). As the plants showed no increase in cell sap concentration during summer drought, availability of water was high. The sandy soils in the desert east of Cairo contain throughout the year at least 2.4% (oven dry weight) of water (wilting point 0.8%) at a depth greater than 75 cm, and therefore the soil never dries out completely (Migahid and Abd El Rahman, 1953b, p. 26ff; cf. also 1953a,c). Roots of some of these plants can grow to a depth of more than 5 meters (Kausch, 1960, p. 13; see Fig. 4). This soil water content and the deep rooting of some plants results in a flora of as many as over 200 native species of flowering plants near Cairo despite the prevailing aridity.

IV. The Significance of Soil Texture for the Water Supply of Desert Plants

The amount of water accumulated in the soil determines the availability of water to plants. The quantity of accumulated water depends not only

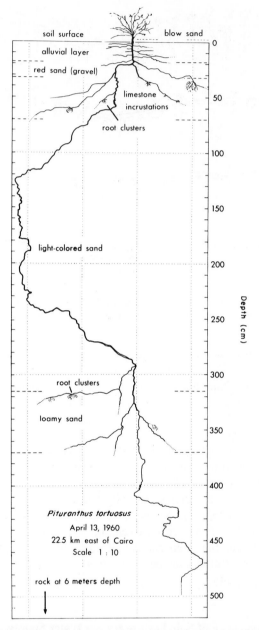

soil surface   blow sand

alluvial layer

red sand (gravel)

limestone
incrustations

root clusters

light-colored sand

root clusters

loamy sand

Pituranthus tortuosus
April 13, 1960
22.5 km east of Cairo
Scale 1 : 10

rock at 6 meters depth

Depth (cm)

0

50

100

150

200

250

300

350

400

450

500

Fig. 4. Depth of rooting of a *Pituranthos tortuosus* plant growing 22.5 km east of Cairo (after Kausch, first published in Walter, 1964, p. 480).

on the amount of water percolating into the soil after rain, but also on the amount evaporated from the soil surface. Only the upper soil layers are moistened in plain habitats of arid regions, and the maximum depth of the penetrating water depends on the texture and the field capacity of the soil. This can be explained in the following example: Assuming that 50 mm of rain falls and penetrates a dry desert soil completely, the approximate maximum depth of penetration will be through the upper 50 cm in sandy soil (sufficient to bring the soil to field capacity). In clay soils penetration may occur to only about 10 cm (since the field capacity is about five times as high as that of sandy soil). In rocky soils having only cracks the penetration is much deeper than in sandy soil, sometimes to 100 cm or more.

After the rain ends, evaporation begins. If in clays the uppermost 5 cm of soil dries out, 50% of the penetrated rain water is lost for plant use. The sandy soil does not dry out as easily as the clay soil. When the sandy soil dries by evaporation to a 5 cm depth, however, the amount of water lost would be only 10% of the total water accumulated. With rocky soil, in general, almost no water is lost by evaporation and all precipitation remains available to plant roots (see Fig. 5).

These considerations show that, in contrast to conditions in humid climates, a clay soil is the driest habitat for plants in arid regions, and that sandy soils guarantee a better water supply for desert plants than clay. Soils of cleft rock are the most moisture-containing soils when rain can penetrate easily into them and enough fine soil is present in the clefts to

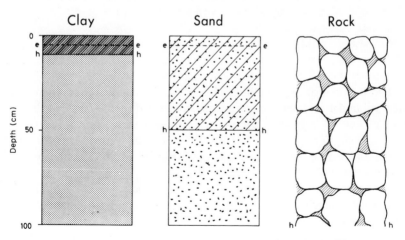

Fig. 5. Penetration depth of a given amount of rain in soils of different texture. h–h, lower limit of the soil layer moistened after the rain; e–e, lower limit of the soil layer dried out by evaporation (from Walter, 1932, p. 499).

retain the water (Walter, 1932, p. 498ff). These conclusions were verified by measurements in the Negev Desert (Hillel and Tadmor, 1962, p. 41). With the same annual rainfall the amount of water available for plants was 35 mm in loess soil, 90 mm in sandy soils, 50 mm in rocky soils with appreciable runoff, and 250–500 mm in dry valleys with high water inflow.

When sandy or rocky soils become moistened down to the water table roots of plants can grow deep enough to reach the ground water.* The water supply of the plant is then assured. An example of this was found north of Basrah (Iraq). The water table in this region is 15 meters deep and supplied with water from the Euphrates and Tigris rivers through layers of gravel. An annual rainfall of 120 mm moistens only the uppermost layers of the soil and hence the roots of plants cannot reach the ground water. Only a scanty ephemeral vegetation covers the soil after the light winter rains. The natives dig wells and use the water to grow vegetables. The plants are planted in furrows and watered 5 times a day in hot summers. Maximum air temperatures in summer may reach 50°C. Because the high evaporation causes salt accumulation on the soil surface vegetables can only be cultivated for 1 year. However, *Tamarix articulata* cuttings which root readily are already planted between the vegetables in the first year.

The irrigated soil is moistened down to the level of the ground water, and it remains moist during the following year, although it is no longer irrigated. Hence, *Tamarix* roots grow deeper during the following years and finally reach the ground water level and form larger trees. These trees are cut every 25 years for fuel and suckers form again from the stump. In this way all previously irrigated vegetable land of the desert is converted to *Tamarix* forest.

All deserts of this type with deep ground water can be reforested if the planted young trees are irrigated during the first year intensively enough to moisten the soil down to the water table.

The better growing conditions for plants in sandy soil compared with clay soil under arid climate are also demonstrated by the fact that the same type of natural vegetation grows on sandy soil with less rainfall than on clayish soil. For example, Smith (1949, p. 10ff) found *Acacia tortilis* in the Sudan in a semidesert area with a rainfall of 50–250 mm on sandy soil; on clay soil this vegetation grew only in areas with a rainfall of at least 400 mm/year. Correspondingly, the *Acacia mellifera* short grass savanna developed on sandy soils with a rainfall of 250–400 mm/year and on clay soils only when rainfall reached 400–600 mm/year.

---

* Roots of desert plants grow deep only in sandy or rocky soils. Normally, the roots grow near the soil surface because only the upper layers of the soil are moistened after rainfall.

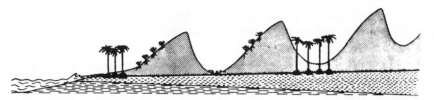

Fig. 6. Schematic drawing of groundwater table in the dunes at the seashore near El Arish (Sinai peninsula) and distribution of date palms and *Ricinus* cultivation. Dotted area, sand dunes; short dashes, fresh groundwater zone; long dashes, salt groundwater advancing from the seashore. Halophyte vegetation shown in the first dune valley due to salt accumulation by evaporation (after Walter, 1964, p. 537).

Where moving dunes in deserts support no vegetation at all, the scanty rain water is stored in the sand and sinks slowly down until a ground water table is formed. Every year brings an additional quantity of water which collects under the dunes (even at such low rainfalls as 100 mm) over an impermeable layer or over saline water with a higher specific weight, and it thereby builds up a ground water table. Such ground water may make cultivation possible, e.g., of date palms, as in the northern part of the Sinai Desert (Walter, 1964, p. 536ff; Fig. 6).

The favorable water storage qualities of rocky soil in arid regions can be demonstrated in locations where trees grow amid a low vegetation typical of a fine granular soil (e.g., on bluffs in the Great Plains).

Salt-containing soils with a halophytic vegetation are also characteristic of arid regions. However, the salt problem is only indirectly related to the water problem and therefore will be considered separately.

V. Distinctive Features of Deserts

Characterization of a region as a desert is always a relative one. The North American who lives in the humid eastern part of the continent considers the Southwest as the Sonora Desert, although the average yearly rainfall in Tucson amounts to 293 mm. In contrast, when someone coming from Cairo visits the Mediterranean coast of Egypt he believes himself to be no longer in the desert, although only a little over 100 mm of rain falls annually on the Mediterranean coast. Thus, arid regions have to include semideserts as well as deserts. Only a few deserts have no rainfall at all.

The climatically arid regions are characterized by a very high potential evaporation compared with rainfall and sparse vegetation with a ground cover of less than 25%. Neither the Kalahari nor the Gibson and Simpson deserts in Central Australia can be considered as real deserts with regard to the climate. Rather, these areas are difficult to cross unpopulated sandy regions without open water places, yet they have considerable vegetation.

The climate of the arid regions on the various continents is not at all similar. These regions may be classified at first with regard to their temperature ranges:

1. *Arid regions of the tropics* with very little differences in the average monthly temperature include the islands of the South Caribbean Sea and on the north coast of Venezuela; northern part of Somalia; Island of Sokotra (off the east coast of Africa).

2. *Subtropical arid regions* with considerable temperature fluctuation during the year and occasional frost include the Sonora Desert (Northern Mexico and Southern Arizona); the Mojave Deserts of Southern California; the Sahara–Arabian Desert region, the South Iranian Desert and the Thar Desert (India), including part of the Sind region (West Pakistan). In the Southern Hemisphere are the Southern Peruvian–Northern Chilean region, the Namib Desert (Southwest Africa), Karroo region (South Africa), and the driest regions of Australia.

3. *Arid regions of temperate zones* which often have very cold winters include the Great Basin west of the Rocky Mountains (North America), the transitional regions between the Syrian–Mesopotamian and the Iranian–Turkmenian Desert north of the border line for date palm cultivation, the Kazakhstanian–Dzungarian (Sinkiang) Desert, the Tarim basin with the Takla Makan Desert (Sinkiang), Bei-shan (Sinkiang/Inner Mongolia), the Alay Shan Desert (Inner Mongolia), Ordos Desert (Inner Mongolia) and the Gobi Desert (Mongolian Republic/Inner Mongolia). In the temperate zone of the Southern Hemisphere the only arid region of this kind is Patagonia (Argentina).

4. *Cold highland deserts* are the Puna in the Andes Mountains (South America), Pamir (Central Asia), and Tibet.

For the vegetation of arid regions, however, the absolute amount of the monthly rainfall, and especially the seasonal distribution of rainfall, is more important than the temperature of these areas. Thus, these arid regions can be classified on the basis of rainfall into the following groups (1) *arid areas with two rainy seasons:* North Venezuela (A), Southwestern Somalia (B), Sonora Desert (C), Karroo region (South Africa, D); (the letters here and below refer to the climate diagrams of Figs. 7 and 8, given as examples for these regions.); (2) *arid regions with winter rains:* Mojave desert (E), Northern Libya (F), Mesopotamia (G), Northern Chile (H), Northern Sahara; (3) *arid regions with summer rains:* Nubian Desert (I),

Ordos Desert (Inner Mongolia) (J), Central Australia (K), Southern Peruvian region (L), Southern Sahara; (4) *arid regions seldom having rain,* which may fall at any time during the year: Lake Eyre basin (South Australia, Fig. 9); (5) *fog deserts almost without measurable rainfall:* Southern Peruvian–Northern Chilean region (M), Namib Desert [Southwest Africa (N)]; and (6) *deserts almost without rain and vegetation:* Central Sahara (O), Southern Egyptian Desert (P).

The floristic kingdom to which the vegetation of an arid region belongs also has some influence on the type of vegetation. Often particular families with characteristic life forms strongly predominate. In those American deserts which belong to the Neotropics, the Cactaceae, in South America, a few Bromeliaceae are prevalent in addition. In South Africa (Capensis), Mesembrianthemaceae and also some succulent Euphorbiaceae are characteristic. In the arid regions of the Holarctic, numerous species of halophytic Chenopodiaceae are found. Australia has no true succulents and in the driest parts the halophytic saltbush (*Atriplex vesicaria*) and the bluebush (*Kochia sedoides*) are the most important species.

The climatic differences and edaphic factors together with the floristic composition of each arid region give every desert its uniqueness and make it difficult to compare one desert with another. Much misunderstanding in the ecological evaluation of the desert plants has been caused during the past few decades by overgeneralization. A single investigator usually knows only one type of desert region or type of desert well and believes his findings to be applicable to all desert plants. Because of the individual peculiarities of various deserts, each was dealt with separately by Walter (1964, 1968); this is not possible in this chapter. Therefore, the similarities will be emphasized more and the differences will be mentioned less.

VI. Hydration of Protoplasm and Osmotic Potential

The thermodynamic activity of water inside the living protoplasm plays a special role in the life of plants.

The relative thermodynamic activity (*a*) of water can be defined as

$$a = \frac{p}{p_0} = \frac{\text{vapor pressure over a solution (or an imbibant)}}{\text{saturation water pressure over pure water}} \quad (1)$$

where p and p_0 are both to be measured under the same temperature and pressure conditions (Kreeb and Borchard, 1967, p. 200). Walter (1931, p. 6) introduced the term *hydrature* (hy) for the product $(p/p_0) \times 100$.

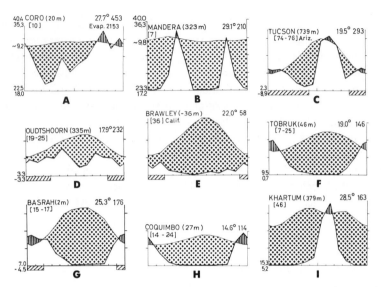

Fig. 7. Representative climate diagrams for the different types of arid regions; for explanation of the diagram see caption to Fig. 8. (A) Coro (North Venezuela), (B) Mandera (Northeast Kenya), (C) Tucson (Arizona), (D) Outshoorn (South Africa, Cape Province), (E) Brawley (Southeast California), (F) Tobruk (Libya), (G) Basrah (Iraq), (H) Coquimbo (South of Atacama Desert, Chile), (I) Khartum (South of Nubian Desert, Sudan). (From Walter and Lieth, 1967.)

Hydrature is quite a general term. It can be applied to indicate (1) air humidity, (2) relative water vapor pressure over a solution or an imbibant in percent, and (3) thermodynamic relative water activity in percent.

Temperature is a measure of molecular kinetic activity; hydrature is a measure of the relative water activity.

The term "hydrature of a plant" refers to the average hydrature of the most important part of the plant, to the *hydrature of the protoplasm*. It differs in its value from the hydrature of air in the intercellular spaces or from hydrature of the outer plant surfaces.

The hydrature of protoplasm of a vacuolated cell is in equilibrium with the hydrature of the cell sap. [See the schematic presentation of the interrelationships between protoplasmic swelling, external concentration and cell sap in Walter and Stadelmann (1968, p. 696, Fig. 2).] The cell sap hydrature is measured by the osmotic potential ψ_s by the following equation:

$$\psi_s = \frac{R \times T}{V_w} \times \ln \frac{p}{p_0} = \frac{R \times T}{V_w} \times \ln (a) = \frac{R \times T}{V_w} \times \ln \frac{hy}{100}$$

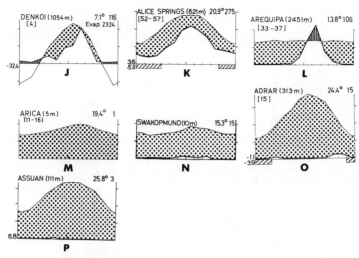

Fig. 8. Representative climate diagrams for the different types of arid regions (continued). (J) Denkoi (Inner Mongolia), (K) Alice Springs (Central Australia), (L) Arequipa (Peru), (M) Arica (Northern Chile), (N) Swakopmund (Southwest Africa), (O) Adrar (Algeria), (P) Assuan (Egypt). The climate diagrams (Figs. 7 and 8) are graphical representations for the climate for a given location. The x axis is divided into 12 equal sections corresponding to the month of the year and beginning with January for stations on the Northern Hemisphere and with July for locations on the Southern Hemisphere. On the y axis the monthly means of temperature (in °C, thin line) and of precipitation (in mm, thick line) are plotted, beginning with 0°C and 0 mm precipitation at $y = 0$. One division corresponds to 10°C and 20 mm. In this presentation a dry season is indicated when the temperature curve is above the curve for precipitation, while a humid period exists during times when the temperature curve is below the curve for precipitation. The respective areas are dotted or hatched. The name of the location and its elevation are indicated inside the upper left corner of the climate diagram. The figures in brackets below this name indicate the number of years of observations (when two numbers, the first indicates the length for the temperature record and the second one the number of years for the records of the precipitation). The first number in the right upper corner indicates annual mean temperature in °C and the second, the annual precipitation in mm. The upper number outside the diagram in the upper left-hand corner gives absolute maximum temperature for the hottest month and the lower number the average daily maximum for the hottest month. The number at the lower left corner indicates the mean of the daily minima of the coldest month and the figure below it gives the lowest recorded temperature. Locations in tropic regions have a monthly mean temperature which fluctuates very little, although the daily variations may be considerable. To indicate their amplitude the mean daily temperature variation of the warmest month is given at the left side of the diagram at the level of the temperature line (e.g., for diagram B, Fig. 7, the mean daily temperature variation is 9.8°C). The hatched blocks below the x axis indicate months with frost, where an absolute minimum below 0°C was observed at least on one day. (From Walter and Lieth, 1967.)

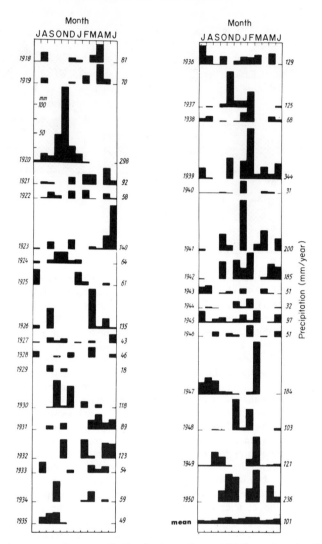

Fig. 9. Amount and seasonal distribution of precipitations for the Lake Eyre Basin (Mulka, South Australia) for the years 1918–1950. (From Walter, 1964, p. 449, Fig. 348.)

For $T = 293°K$ (20°C) the results are

$$\psi_s = 3067 \times \log (a) = 3067 \times \log \frac{hy}{100} \qquad (2)$$

where ψ_s is the osmotic potential of the solution; R is the gas constant (82 cm^3 atm mole^{-1} grad K^{-1}); T is the absolute temperature (grad K);

V_w is the mole volume of water (18 cm^3 mole^{-1}); p is the vapor pressure over the solution; p_0 is the vapor pressure over pure water; hy is the hydrature of solution; and a is the relative water activity.

The hydrature of protoplasm is not identical with its hydration. The former indicates the relative thermodynamic activity of water in protoplasm. Hydration measures the imbibition (swelling) as water content per gram dry weight. However, there is a linear relationship between both functions in the physiological range (96–100% hydrature, cf. imbibition curve of protoplasm, Walter, 1923, p. 176; Walter and Stadelmann, 1968, p. 697, Fig. 4).

The frequently expressed opinion that hydration of protoplasm depends upon the water potential (suction potential, DPD) and that the protoplasm shows maximum swelling in a water-saturated cell can be negated by thermodynamic considerations. The relative activity of water (hydrature) of the cell sap and, therefore, also of protoplasm is always smaller than that of pure water; therefore maximum swelling of protoplasm is not reached (Walter and Stadelmann, 1968, p. 696).

When the osmotic potential of the cell sap ψ_s is known, Eq. (1) can be used to calculate the hydrature of living protoplasm (see Walter, 1931, p. 159, Tables I and II), which otherwise cannot be measured directly. (It should be remembered that ψ_s is temperature dependent while hy is not.) The osmotic potential is of special importance for ecological aspects of the water relations of desert plants.

The many thousands of determinations of potential osmotic pressure carried out on hundreds of plant species in all climatic regions and under very different ecological conditions have been used to develop osmotic spectra (Fig. 10 shows one of these spectra for the Arizona desert). An osmotic spectrum characterizes the plant life form of a vegetation (e.g., grass, leaf succulents, and deciduous trees) by the maxima and minima values for π^* of each constituent plant species (see Walter, 1960, p. 239). [The potential osmotic pressure π^* is the negative value of the osmotic potential ψ_s and was used to indicate the hydrature before the thermodynamic terminology was established (see Walter, 1960)].

VII. Plant Hydrature and Environmental Water Conditions

Changes in hydrature in the plant with the variations of the available water from the environment indicate that two different types of plants exist.

a. Poikilohydric Plants. The protoplasmic hydrature of poikilohydric plants changes with and is directly related to hydrature of the environment (air humidity). Among the land plants the algae, fungi, lichens, and bryo-

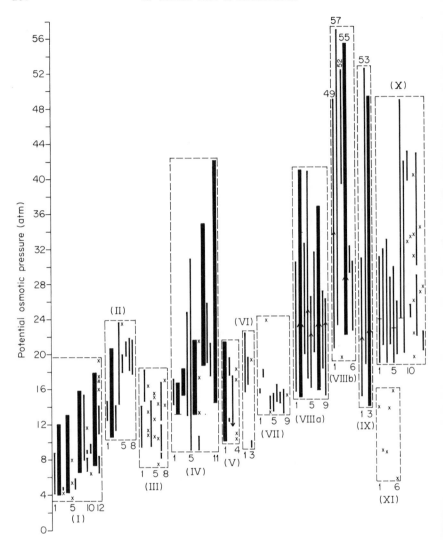

Fig. 10. Osmotic spectra of the different life forms from the cactus desert and the lower forest level from Arizona (about 900 individual measurements) Ordinate: Potential osmotic pressure π^*. Heavy lines indicate species for which a higher number of determinations of π^* were available for plotting of the spectrum; x = single measurements; the arabic numbers indicate the plant species in the different ecological groups indicated by roman numerals; species in each group are arranged in the order from low potential osmotic pressure (mean value) to high osmotic pressure (after Walter 1960, p. 250).

(I) Cactaceae: 1 *Pachycereus pringlei;* 2 *Carnegiea gigantea* (66 determinations); 3 *Lemaireocereus thurberi* and *Lophocereus schottii;* 4 *Ferocactus wislizenii* (75 determinations); 5 *Echinocereus polyacanthus* (lowest value), *E. rigidissimus* (middle value and *E. fendleri* highest value for each species only one value was determined);

6 *Mammilaria grahami;* 7 *Opuntia phaeacantha-toumeyi* (45 determinations); 8 *O. phaeacantha-blakeana;* 9 *O. castillae, O. santa-rita* and *O. discata;* 10 *O. laevis* and *O. chlorotica;* 11 *O. versicolor;* 12 *O. fulgida, O. lepticaulis, O. spinosior, O. basilaris, O. polyacantha* and *O. arbuscula.* (The potential osmotic pressures are low: the more water stored by the plant species, the lower the potential osmotic pressures.)

(II) Leaf succulents: 1 *Agave americana;* 2 *A. palmeri;* 3 *A. schottii;* 4 *Yucca schottii;* 5 *Y. elata* and *Y. baccata;* 6 *Y.* sp. (Mexico); 7 *Dasylirion wheeleri;* 8 *Nolina microcarpa.* (The potential osmotic pressure increases in these leaf succulents, as in other plants, with decreasing degree of succulence.)

(III) Winter ephemeral plants: 1 *Parietaria obtusa;* 2 *Streptanthus arizonicus;* 3 *Senecio douglasii, Plantago ignota, Erodium texanum* and *Phacelia tanacetifolia;* 4 *Erodium cicutarium;* 5 *Sonchus asper, Hordeum murinum, Malva silvestris, Marrubium vulgare* (all ruderal); 6 *Brodiaea* sp., *Delphinium scaposum, Verbena ciliata;* 7 *Sicyos* sp., *Rumex hymenosepala, Penstemon wrightii;* 8 *Anemone sphenophylla, Sphaeralcea pedata.* [The growth period is completely restricted to the winter rainy season. These species survive the drought season and the summer as seeds (few species with underground organs) and germinate (or bud) after the first winter rain. The winter climate is similar to the summer climate in Central Europe, except that night temperatures are lower in this desert. Therefore, the potential osmotic pressures of these species are of the same magnitude as those of the summer ephemeral plants of Central Europe.]

(IV) Summer ephemeral plants: 1 *Amaranthus palmeri;* 2 *Euphorbia heterophylla;* 3 *Kallstroemia grandiflora;* 4 *Allionia incarnata;* 5 *Trianthema portulacastrum;* 6 *Tribulus terrestris;* 7 *Martynia louisiana, Cucurbita digitata, Maurandia antirrhinoides,* and *Menodora scabra;* 8 *Cladothrix lanuginosa;* 9 *Ambrosia psilostachya* (in shade); 10 *Euphorbia glyptosperma;* 11 *Solanum elaeagnifolium* (15 determinations). (Most of these plants are annual therophytes, which germinate after the first summer rain and dry out during the fall drought period.)

(V) Rain phanerophytes: 1 *Fouquieria splendens* (28 determinations, maximum 21.4 atm, yellowing leaves 11.7 atm); 2 *Idria columnaris* (lower values from the succulent stem); 3 *Jatropha cardiophylla* (yellowing); 4 *Jatropha cinerea* (leafless stem), *Elaphrium macdougali* (leafless stem), *Jatropha spathulifolia* (young leaves), *Elaphrium microphyllum* (old leaves). (The leaves of these plants are photosynthetic active as long as there is enough water supply from the soil to cover transpiration loss. When water deficits occur, the leaves do not dry but yellow and abscise. New leaves grow after each substantial rainfall. The potential osmotic pressure remains constant or may even decrease.)

(VI) Deciduous trees and shrubs: 1 *Populus macdougali;* 2 *Fraxinus toumeyi;* 3 *Vitis arizonica* (budding) and *Celtis reticulata* (leaves just reached full size). (These species depend upon ground water and therefore have no water shortage during the drought period. Leaves are dropped at the beginning of the low temperature season. The potential osmotic pressure is similar to that of the corresponding species in Central Europe.)

(VII) Poikilohydric ferns: 1 *Cheilanthes wrightii* (with very tender leaves, hygromorphic); 2 *C. fendleri* (abaxial leaf surface with dense hair cover); 3 *C. lindheimeri* (both leaf surfaces with dense hair cover); 4 *Gymnopteris hispida* and *Pellaea mucronata* (sclerophyllous); 5 *Selaginella arizonica* (green variety); 6 *S. arizonica* (gray variety); 7 *Notholaena hookeri;* 8 *N. aschenborniana* (with scales as on *Ceterach);* 9 *N. sinuata* var. *integerrima* (leaves xeromorphous). (These phytes belong to this group as well as some pteridophytes of arid regions which withstand complete desiccation without damage. Only very few angiosperms (e.g., *Myrothamnus*) are in this group.

b. Homoiohydric Plants. The protoplasmic hydrature of homoiohydric plants is (within certain limits) independent of hydrature (air humidity) of the atmosphere because the vacuome (a term which refers to all of the vacuoles in a plant collectively) is an internal aqueous medium for the protoplasm. In this way the hydrature of protoplasm becomes essentially independent of the external conditions. Most land plants are homoio-

---

plants survive complete desiccation. The leaves are rolled during drought and less conspicuous. After rain the leaves spread out. During this period of active life, the potential osmotic pressure is relatively low.)

(VIIIa) Perennial shrubs, slightly xeromorphic: 1 *Clematis ligusticifolia;* 2 *Prosopis velutina* (26 determinations); 3 *Olneya tesota;* 4 *Acacia paucispina;* 5 *Acacia greggii;* 6 *Cassia covesii;* 7 *Cercidium (Parkinsonia) microphylla* (23 determinations); 8 *C. torreyana;* 9 *C. aculeata.* (These species favor more humid habitats between rocks or in river valleys. Under extreme drought the leguminosae drop their leaflets.) (VIIIb) Heavily xeromorphic perennial desert shrubs: 1 *Simmondsia californica;* 2 *Mortonia scabrella;* 3 *Lycium californicum* (with succulent leaves) and *Frankenia palmeri;* 4 *Larrea divaricata* (= *L. tridentata* = *Covillea glutinosa;* 68 values); 5 *Celtis pallida;* 6 *Ephedra trifurca.* (The optimal potential osmotic pressure of these plants is relatively high. Increase of π^* occurs only after prolonged drought, since these plants have the ability to maintain their osmotic potential under unfavorable conditions for a considerable length of time, probably by reduction of transpiration.)

(IX) Perennial malacophyllous xerophytes: 1 *Lippia wrightii;* 2 *Gaertneria deltoidea;* 3 *Encelia farinosa* (over 100 determinations). (The potential osmotic pressure increases considerably under water shortage. When the maximum value is reached, the leaves dry out and are dropped. The shrubs survive the drought period in the leafless stage.)

(X) Sclerophyllous woody species from the lower forest level: 1 *Quercus oblongifolia* (30 determinations); 2 *Q. emoryi* (23 determinations); 3 *Q. arizonica;* 4 *Q. reticulata;* 5 *Q. hypoleuca;* 6 *Arbutus arizonica;* 7 *Arctostaphylos pungens;* 8 *Garrya wrightii;* 9 *Cercocarpus ledifolius* and *Vauquelinia californica;* 10 *Dodonaea angustifolia* and *Lepargyrea* (= *Shephardia) rotundifolia;* 11 *Rhamnus* sp., *Berberis haematocarpa, Mahonia wilcoxii, Rhus ovata, R. coriophylla* and *Garrya veatchii;* 12 *Juniperus pachyphloeus* and *J. utahensis;* 13 *J. scopulorum,* and *Cupressus arizonica;* 14 *Pinus chihuahuensis* and *P. monophylla.* (These truly sclerophyllous species do not occur in the desert itself, but in the next higher level of vegetation, the evergreen oak forests. The measurements of potential osmotic pressure are incomplete since they were made only during the winter season. The sclerophyllous plants correspond to the Mediterranean species in Europe.)

(XI) Herbaceous plants from the lower forest level (humid locations): 1 *Aquilegia chrysantha;* 2 *Nasturtium officinale;* 3 *Rumex* sp., 4 *Adiantum capillus veneris;* 5 *Epicampes rigens* (xeromorphic grass); 6 *Dudleya* sp. (Sedum-like succulent). (These samples show low values for the potential osmotic pressure of herbaceous species in favorable habitats during the winter season.)

hydric, including all gymnosperms, almost all angiosperms, and most of pteridophytes. In homoiohydric plants the hydrature of the protoplasm depends on the hydrature of the vacuome, i.e., the cell sap concentration (for further discussion, see Walter and Stadelmann, 1968).

With optimum water supply, the cells of a particular tissue or organ have an osmotic potential (ψ_s) which may be called optimal ($\psi_{s\ opt}$). This value is characteristic of a certain tissue of a species. It has been shown that the same species in America and in Europe has the same $\psi_{s\ opt}$ for cells of the same organ (Walter, 1960, p. 225).

Normally, leaf samples collected in the field will not show the optimum value, but a somewhat lower one, since an optimal water supply is relatively seldom realized in nature. Values higher than $\psi_{s\ opt}$ can be found only in immature organs or in plants in deep shade where the CO_2 balance is temporarily negative. Under high water stress ψ_s can be very much lower than the optimal value. The lowest value of ψ_s at which the first visible tissue damage from drying may be directly seen is called the minimum osmotic potential ($\psi_{s\ min}$). An example of the range of the variation of the osmotic potential is given in Fig. 11 for leaves of *Artemisia tridentata* calculated from the results of Harris (1934). Unfortunately, the author did not specify the growth stage of the plant and the actual environmental conditions. Therefore only statistical evaluation is possible. There are 208 individual determinations of ψ_s. The values range from −13.8 to −72.9 atm.

The histogram is asymmetric, and most values of ψ_s are in the range of −25 to −29.9 atm. Values over −15 atm and under −40 atm are few. Since the optimum value is only seldom reached under natural conditions, it must be sought near −14 to −15 atm. The highest ψ_s values recorded

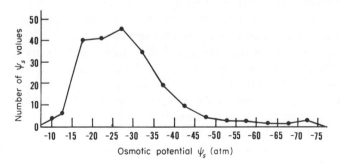

Fig. 11. Osmotic potential of leaves of *Artemisia tridentata* calculated from 208 samples. Abscissa: ranges of osmotic potential ψ_s in atm. Ordinate: number of values of ψ_s found in the particular range. (Width of the range 5 atm. First range from −7.5 to −14.9 atm.) (After Walter, 1936, p. 196, 1960, p. 238.)

were probably found in immature shoots. Frequently, samples might have been taken during suboptimal water conditions. The extremely low values may result from samples taken from plants under high water stress.

The difference $\psi_s - \psi_{s\ opt}$ indicates the condition of the actual water supply of a plant. It measures the deviation of the actual value of the relative activity of water in the living protoplasm from its optimum value.

Usually the physical aspects of plant water relations, the water absorption, water movement, and the transpiration, have been emphasized, and studies of water activity of protoplasm have been neglected (cf. Gates, 1964, p. 4ff; Stadelmann, 1971, p. 341); however, the protoplasm is the site of all metabolic activity on which growth and development of the plant depend, and protoplasmic hydration controls to a great extent metabolic activity and therefore plant growth and production. This ecophysiological aspect of plant–water relations has been almost totally neglected and is hence especially emphasized here.

The osmotic potential of the cell sap is a measure for the hydrature of protoplasm and, therefore, the osmotic potential (ψ_s) and its variations will indicate the changes occurring in the protoplasmic hydration.

VIII. Diurnal Fluctuation of the Osmotic Potential (ψ_s)

The osmotic potential reaches the value which is characteristic for a particular plant species only under optimum environmental conditions. Sometimes considerable differences also exist in the ψ_s value of the different plant organs and between different parts of the plant organs (Table II).

As soon as leaf transpiration exceeds water replacement from the roots, the plant dehydrates. Concurrently, the concentration of the cell sap increases with resulting decreasing osmotic potential and hydrature of protoplasm. Since transpiration increases faster than water uptake and conduction during the first part of each day, the osmotic potential exhibits diurnal fluctuations. On sunny days the ψ_s values of leaves are maximal at sunrise and minimal during the afternoon. The amplitude depends upon the water supply and the intensity of transpiration (see example in Table III). The diurnal fluctuations in leaves are primarily caused by the midday decrease of the water content and subsequent increased cell sap concentration; hence the product (osmotic potential $\times$ water content) does not change significantly. Only during the afternoon a small accumulation of sugar may temporarily cause a very slight increase of cell sap concentration (Pisek and Cartillieri, 1932, p. 225; Biebl, 1962, p. 128ff). The amplitude of the diurnal change of ψ_s varies even among species in the same habitat, since plants differ in root formation, water-conducting system, transpiring sur-

TABLE II

A. EXAMPLE FOR DIFFERENT ψ_s VALUES (MEASURED IN ATM) IN THE SAME PLANT DEPENDING ON AGE

Species	Conifer needles[a]	
	1-year-old needles	2-year-old needles
Pinus flexilis	−17.7	−19.6
Pinus aristata	−15.0	−21.7
Abies concolor	−19.0	−22.1

B. EXAMPLE FOR DIFFERENT ψ_s VALUES (MEASURED IN ATM) IN THE SAME PLANT DEPENDING ON TISSUES OR ORGANS

1. Meristematic tissue and stem water storage tissues in Cactaceae[b]

Species	Apical meristem	Stem water storage tissue
Carnegiea gigantea	−10.0	−5.6 to −6.4
Ferocactus wislizenii	− 6.9	−4.2 to −5.3

2. In herbaceous winter annuals from Arizona[c]

Species	Stem	Leaves
Sphaerostigma chamaenerioides	−11.3	−11.5
Calycoseris wrightii	−11.8	−11.6
Streptanthus arizonicus	−16.9	−14.7
Eulobus californicus	− 8.7	−10.7
Nemoseris neo-mexicana	−15.0	−14.1

3. In plants of the western part of the U.S.A.[d]

Allium cernuum	inflorescences	−11.4
	leaves	− 7.8
	bulbs	− 8.4
	roots	− 6.7
Mentzelia multiflora	leaves	−10.9
	tap root	− 4.7
Iris missouriensis	leaves	−11.4
	rhizome	−10.5

4. Organ section: Gradients of ψ_s in a leaf of *Yucca glauca*[e]

	leaf tip	−14.9
	middle part	−14.2
	leaf base	−12.6

[a] From Walter (1931, p. 44, Table 35).
[b] From Walter (1931, pp. 104–105).
[c] From Harris and Lawrence (1916, pp. 40, 38, 41, 39, and 34).
[d] From Walter (1931, p. 41, Table 26).
[e] From Walter (1931, p. 42, Table 32).

TABLE III

DIURNAL VARIATIONS FOR THE OSMOTIC POTENTIAL ψ_s

Shade plants
Fluctuations are scarcely detectable, measurements made in a small forest bordering a Nebraska prairie[a]

Species	ψ_s (atm)	% of morning value of ψ_s
Ampelopsis quinquefolia	not detectable	
Vitis vulpina	not detectable	
Galium aparine	0.1	1.2
Smilax hispida	0.2	1.7
Polygonatum commutatum	0.4	3.8
Acalypha virginica	0.5	4.4

Swamp plants
Diurnal variations of ψ_s under conditions of good water supply and bright sunlight are only significant for plants protruding above the water surface; a change in resistance of the water conducting system might be involved; measurements made on plants in Hungary[b]

Species	ψ_s (atm)	% of morning value of ψ_s
Iris pseudacorus	not detectable	
Epilobium hirsutum	0.3	3
Lysimachia vulgaris	0.4	4
Lythrum salicaria	0.7	6
Scirpus lacustris	1.7	17
Carex acutiformis	2.3	18
Phragmites communis	2.5	17

Sun plants
Diurnal variations are great with relatively good water supply, plants are from a Nebraska prairie in the early summer[c]

Species	ψ_s (atm)	% of morning value of ψ_s
Sporobolus heterolepis	1.1	11
Tragopogon pratensis (flowering)	1.2	12
Amorpha fruticosa (flowering)	2.1	17
Astragalus crassipes (fruiting)	2.6	19
Erigeron ramosus (flowering)	2.9	23
Psoralea floribunda (flowering)	2.6	27
Stipa spartea (fruiting)	3.2	26

Woody plants
Most of these plants have a very good control of their water balance and diurnal variations of ψ_s are in general low even under conditions of high potential evaporation[d]

Species	ψ_s (atm)	% of morning value of ψ_s
Pinus nigra (Hungary, in shade)	0.3	2
Pinus nigra (Hungary, in sun)	1.1	7
Robinia pseudacacia (Hungary, in shade)	0.4	3.4
Quercus ilex (South France)	2.3	12.0
Pistacia lentiscus (South France)	2.7	11.0

Succulents
No diurnal fluctuations of ψ_s were found

[a] From Walter (1936, p. 51, Table 43).
[b] From Walter (1931, p. 51, Table 44).
[c] From Walter (1931, p. 52).
[d] From Walter (1931, p. 52).

TABLE IV

CHANGES IN THE DIURNAL VARIATIONS OF ψ_s IN *Pirus elaeagrifolia*
(CENTRAL ANATOLIA, TURKEY) DURING SUMMER DROUGHT[a]

	Month					
Parameter	April	May	June	July	August	September
ψ_s in atm (measured in the morning)	−17.6	−19.9	−24.2	−29.9	−34.0	−34.9
Diurnal variations (%)	8.4	10.0	8.1	2.7	0.1	0.0

[a] After Birand (1938, p. 139).

face area, and stomatal control. These differences are particularly striking in desert plants where the water content of the soil also varies over short distances.

When water supply to plants is initially high, e.g., before the beginning of a long drought period, and then decreases gradually during drought, the diurnal variations of ψ_s at first are small but increase gradually. Later in the drought period, however, the diurnal variations decrease in amplitude and finally disappear because the stomata close earlier and earlier in the morning, until they finally may not open at all. The morning ψ_s values decrease continuously during the drought period since the leaves no longer become water saturated during the night (Table IV).

IX. Annual Variations of the Osmotic Potential (ψ_s)

The annual variations of ψ_s are more pronounced than diurnal fluctuations especially in areas where rain and drought periods alternate during the year as in Arizona (see Fig. 12). The annual fluctuations are smaller on habitats with a good water supply. Succulents with their large water storage tissue have a very constant osmotic potential ψ_s.

Annual variations of ψ_s were often investigated in species of the Mediterranean region which have a winter rainy period and a summer drought (see Fig. 13). Deep-rooting, sclerophyllous plants show very little annual fluctuations (e.g., *Quercus ilex, Q. coccifera,* and *Pistacia lentiscus*). On the other hand, shallow rooting species with soft leaves (malacophyllous plants) show pronounced fluctuations (e.g., *Viburnum tinus, Cistus albida,* and *Thymus vulgaris*). Great variations are also observed in herbaceous

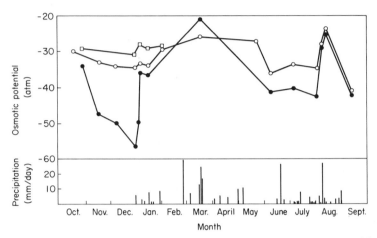

Fig. 12. Annual variation of the osmotic potential in leaves of *Larrea tridentata* (= *L. divaricata*) near the desert laboratory in Tucson, Arizona. (○———○) favorable habitat (*Carnegiea–Encelia* association), (●———●) very dry habitat; (□———□) irrigated plants. Histogram (below): daily rainfalls (after Walter, 1960, p. 236).

species (Fig. 14). In these plants the leaves may dry out completely and abscise during a drought. Only *Sedum* and *Euphorbia* show almost no variation of ψ_s. The annual variations of ψ_s and the water content of *Elegia stipularis* (Restionaceae, Cape region, South Africa; see Fig. 15) are quite high. This shrub has a shallow root system which makes the plant quite sensitive to dryness of the upper soil layer. The osmotic potential ψ_s and the water content change inversely; the product ($\psi_s \times$ water content) is always around 2800 which indicates that the changes in the osmotic potential are primarily caused by changes in the water content.

X. The Ecological Types of Desert Plants

The reaction of a plant to a drought condition depends on its morphological and physiological features, e.g., the intensity of transpiration (or the degree of transpiration resistance by morphological factors), sensitivity of stomatal control, water conductivity of the vascular system, and size of the root system. Since these factors are very different from one species to another, desert plants may be typed ecologically according to their response during droughts.

One grouping uses the range of osmotic potentials as a criterion. Here *stenohydric* and *euryhydric* species are distinguished. In the first group the difference $\psi_{s\ opt} - \psi_{s\ min}$ is relatively small. Thus these plants are easily

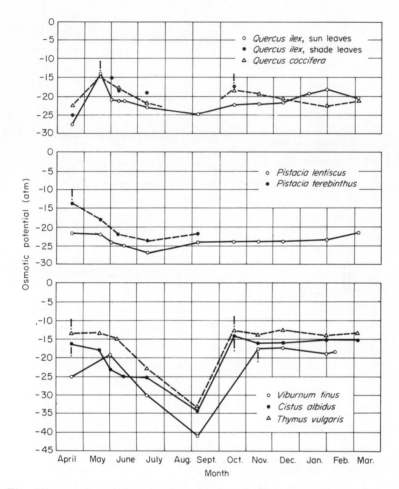

Fig. 13. Annual variations of the osmotic potential ψ_s of sclerophyllous and malacophyllous species. Abscissa: April to March of next year (redrawn after Braun-Blanquet and Walter, 1931, pp. 716, 717, and 720). !, young leaves.

damaged by water deficits. In contrast, euryhydric species can withstand large water deficits and a great decrease of ψ_s (i.e., decrease in hydrature of the protoplasm). The difference $\psi_{s\ opt} - \psi_{s\ min}$ is relatively great.

Another grouping distinguishes between *hydrolabile* and *hydrostabile* species. Hydrolabile species respond to droughts very rapidly with a decrease of ψ_s. Hydrostabile species exhibit a highly stable osmotic potential which results in a relatively constant hydrature of protoplasm. Faster closure of stomata to reduce water loss under drought conditions or

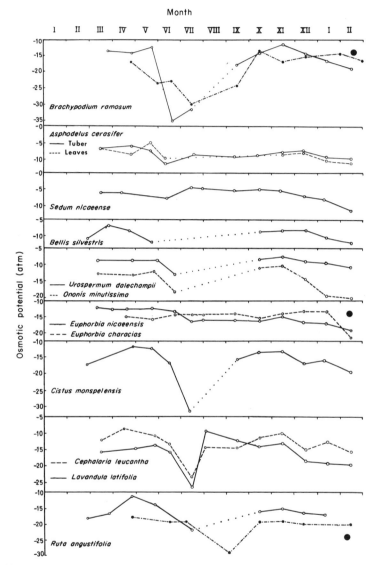

Fig. 14. Annual variations of the osmotic potential ψ_s for some semishrubs and herbaceous species: stenohydrous xerophytes (*Euphorbia* species), succulents (*Sedum*), geophytes (*Asphodelus*), grasses (*Brachypodium*) and others. Dotted line: months of 1931, when no material (fresh leaves) was available. (After Bharucha, 1932, pp. 345, 354, 353, 350, 347, and 348; ● after Braun-Blanquet and Walter, 1931, pp. 721 and 726.)

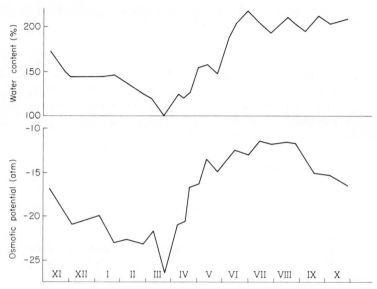

Fig. 15. Annual variation of the osmotic potential ψ_s (lower graph) and the water content (upper graph) of *Elegia stipularis* (Restionaceae) (after Walter and van Staden, 1965, p. 230).

a deep and efficient root system, which compensates by increasing water uptake for the higher transpiration losses, may explain their osmotic potential stability. Only prolonged drought conditions lead to a decrease of ψ_s also in hydrostabile plants.

Photosynthetic activity is always closely related to water conditions. The open stomata simultaneously release water vapor from the intercellular spaces to the exterior and allow uptake of CO_2. A limitation of transpiration by stomatal closure at the same time checks photosynthesis. Transpiration may be considered to be to some extent an "inevitable evil" for plants in order to be able to assimilate CO_2. Insufficient water supply leads to stress conditions, a decrease of ψ_s, and of protoplasmic hydrature. Thus, in desert plants a dilemma often exists between (1) maintenance of photosynthetic activity at the expense of hydrature decrease or (2) maintenance of the hydrature of the protoplasm through stomatal closure but inhibition of photosynthesis resulting in low growth rate or even starvation of the plant. Various ecological groups of plants handle this dilemma quite differently. How this is done will be discussed later after analyzing osmotic features of plant cells and the terminology involved.

XI. Osmotic Quantities and Importance of Hydrature for Growth and Xeromorphism

The different terminologies used in the designation of the osmotic parameters of the plant cell have caused considerable confusion and their definition is still not yet precisely settled (cf. Stadelmann, 1966, p. 146; Taylor, 1968). Ursprung and Blum (1916, p. 530) were the first to clearly point out the meaning of the different osmotic quantities by establishing the relation

$$\frac{\text{Suction force}}{\text{of the cell}} = \frac{\text{suction force}}{\text{of the cell content}} - \text{wall pressure}$$

(all indicated in atm)

Since then, osmotic quantities have been named differently. Instead of "suction force," suction tension was introduced because a "force" cannot be given in atmospheres. To avoid confusing suction tension of the cell with the suction tension of the cell content, the latter was designated as the osmotic value (Walter, 1931, p. 11ff). Previously the term "osmotic value" had been introduced to indicate the cell sap concentration (Ursprung and Blum, 1916, p. 88) and was measured by an isotonic concentration of a standard solute, e.g., glucose or saccharose (Höfler, 1920, p. 288). Wall pressure was replaced by turgor pressure (P) which is equal in magnitude and opposite in direction. When the absolute value for the turgor pressure (P) is used the above equation reads (Walter, 1962, p. 61):

$$\text{Suction tension } (S) = \text{osmotic value } (W) - \text{turgor pressure } (P) \quad (3)$$

Instead of "osmotic value" also the term "potential osmotic pressure (π^*)" was introduced (Kreeb and Borchard, 1967, p. 189).

Meyer (1938, p. 535) developed the concept of a physically not measurable "diffusion pressure" and the equation

$$\text{DPD} = \text{OP} - \text{TP} \quad (4)$$

where DPD is the diffusion pressure deficit, OP is the osmotic pressure, and TP is the turgor pressure.

Taylor and Slatyer (1961, p. 344) emphasized a need for a thermodynamic terminology in plant water relations. When the matric potential, which is generally zero for plant cells, is omitted and the new symbols (Slatyer, 1967, p. 82) are applied, the following equation results:

$$\psi = \psi_s + \psi_p \quad (5)$$

where ψ is the water potential, ψ_s is the osmotic potential, and ψ_p is the pressure potential (cf. Knipling, 1969).

The term water potential was first introduced by Stocker (1947, p. 363). The water potential is highest with pure water and this value is arbitrarily set at zero. Therefore, the values for the water potential of the cell as well as those for the osmotic potential are always negative. Thus, when the absolute value of ψ_s increases (this absolute value is identical with the potential osmotic pressure π^*) the real value of ψ_s decreases, i.e., becomes more negative, and vice versa.

The pressure potential for cells with positive turgor is positive.

Since

$$\text{Pressure} = \frac{\text{energy}}{\text{volume}} = \frac{\text{force}}{\text{area}} \tag{6}$$

potential values measured in erg/cm³ are equal to dyn/cm² and therefore can be expressed as pressure in atm or bar (1 atm = 1.013 bar).

From the above the following identities result:

$$\text{Water potential} = -\text{DPD} = -\text{suction tension} \tag{7}$$

Osmotic potential $= -\text{OP} = -$ osmotic value

$$= -\text{potential osmotic pressure } (\pi^*) \tag{8}$$

Pressure potential $= \text{TP} =$ wall pressure or turgor pressure

$$\text{(absolute value)} \tag{9}$$

This thermodynamic terminology will be followed here. Occasionally osmotic value or potential osmotic pressure will be used instead of the osmotic potential.

The three potentials describe quite different features of the cell water relations and should not be confused:

1. The water potential ($-\text{DPD}$) is the decisive factor for water movement in the plant.

2. The osmotic potential [$-\text{OP} = -$ osmotic value $= -$ potential osmotic pressure (π^*)] is an indicator of hydrature of the protoplasm.

3. The pressure potential [$\text{TP} =$ (absolute value of) turgor pressure] causes stretching of the cell wall and therefore gives the cells of nonlignified tissues and herbaceous organs mechanical strength and turgor.

Routine determination of the water potential frequently is difficult and time consuming (cf. Ursprung, 1939; Barrs, 1968, p. 263ff), while the osmotic potential ψ_s can be measured more easily. The pressure potential, in general, can only be calculated from the difference $\psi_s - \psi$, but under rare circumstances direct measurement is possible (Barrs, 1968, p. 336ff).

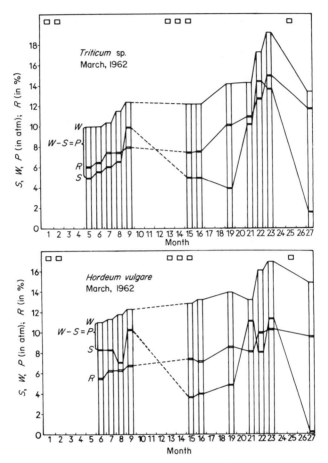

Fig. 16. Suction tension (S), osmotic value (W), and turgor pressure (P) in *Triticum* sp. and *Hordeum vulgare* plants cultivated in pots during drought and watering ($\square$) periods. R is the refractometric value of the expressed sap indicated as percent sugar content; S is the suction potential ($-$ water potential ψ); W is the potential osmotic pressure ($-$osmotic potential ψ_s). The values of R parallel approximately the osmotic values (after Kreeb, 1964, p. 79).

Simultaneous determinations of water potential and osmotic potential in the same experiment have been made occasionally (e.g., Boyer, 1965, p. 231; Weatherley, 1965, p. 165). Kreeb (1964, p. 79) measured both osmotic quantities for *Triticum* sp. and *Hordeum vulgare* plants cultivated in pots subjected to periods of drought and watering (Fig. 16). The change in water balance affects strongly the suction tension S ($-$water potential ψ). The potential osmotic pressure π^* ($-$osmotic potential ψ_s)

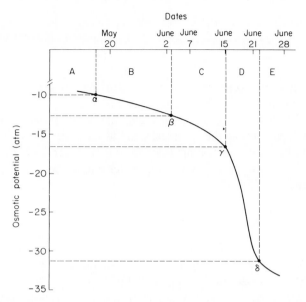

Fig. 17. Hydrature of nonirrigated *Medicago sativa* from May 20 to June 28. Abscissa: dates (May/June). Ordinate: osmotic potential in atm. A to E: phases of hydrature. The Greek letters indicate the beginning of these phases: α, beginning of low water stress conditions; β, starting point for a fast decrease in hydrature; γ, beginning of drought damage, any growth stops; and δ, starting of the final phase, dry weight decreases. (After Bauman, 1957, p. 77.)

changes in the same direction as S but to a much lesser degree. After heavy watering on March 25, the suction tension dropped on March 27 almost to zero; the cells were then water saturated and very turgid. The potential osmotic pressure, π^*, decreased also, but it did not again reach the original value from March 6 and remained at a higher level. This higher π^* indicates that a greater amount of osmotically active substance was present in the vacuole at the end of the experiment when the cells were fully water saturated than at partial water saturation at the beginning of the experiment ($S = 5$ atm for *Triticum;* $S = 8$ atm for *Hordeum*).

The 3 weeks of water shortage had led to an active adaptation of the potential osmotic pressure to the water stress conditions by passage of additional osmotic material (in most cases sugars) into the vacuole. Such release of solutes from the protoplasm into the vacuole during longer periods of low water stress conditions indicates an irreversible change in the protoplasm. The resulting limited drought-hardening of the protoplasm parallels the concentration increase of sugar in the vacuole and is an important ecological factor.

The molecular basis of these protoplasmic changes is not yet known. It is thought to involve such factors as water binding and SH groups of proteins (cf. Parker, 1968, p. 223ff; Levitt, 1962; Parichia and Levitt, 1967). Recently, Tumanow (1967, p. 523/442) emphasized the transition of protoplasmic colloids from the gel to the sol state during frost hardening, with accumulation of sugars in the water of the intermicellar spaces (p. 529/446). However, this hypothesis does not account for transport of sugar through the tonoplast into the vacuole.

Several phases can be distinguished during the decrease of osmotic potential ψ_s (increase of π^*) when the water supply becomes more and more deficient (see Fig. 17):

Phase A: (good water supply) optimal value of the osmotic potential ψ_s

Phase B: small decrease of ψ_s, unimportant retardation of growth

Phase C: the osmotic potential decreases more rapidly; only small increases in dry weight of the plant

Phase D: rapid decrease of ψ_s, a critical stage is reached and no further increase in dry weight occurs

Phase E: final phase before death of plant, the dry weight decreases

Bauman (1957, p. 76ff) established this classification from experiments with alfalfa (*Medicago sativa* var. *Ladak*) in the Canadian prairie region of Alberta (Table V; Fig. 17). No rainfall occurred in the later part of the spring (after May 24) and the soil water content decreased rapidly.

When fields are irrigated, the water stress of phase B should not be exceeded to provide maximum yield. Without artificial irrigation the right

TABLE V

Osmotic Potential, ψ_s, Fresh Weight, and Dry Weight of *Medicago sativa* Plants during a Drought Period[a]

Parameter	Samples taken			
	6/7	6/15	6/21	6/28
ψ_s (atm)	−13.6	−17.0	−29.8	−33.6
Fresh weight (gm)	504	442	321	212
Dry weight (gm)	84.6	87.5	87.5	81.8
Relative content of dry material (in % of fresh weight)	16.8	19.8	27.2	38.6

[a] From Bauman (1957, p. 75).

TABLE VI

DIURNAL VARIATIONS OF OSMOTIC POTENTIAL ψ_s IN LEAVES
OF *Robinia pseudacacia*[a]

Time of day	ψ_s (atm)		
	Sun leaves I	Shade leaves II	Difference I–II
Morning	−17.3	−12.2	−5.1
Noon	−18.1	−12.6	−5.5
Evening	−17.6	−12.5	−5.1

[a] From Walter (1962, p. 337).

date for harvesting would have been about June 15, since harvesting later does not further increase dry weight and soil water is used up without resulting in higher yield.

A striking example for the adjustment of ψ_s to water supply conditions is demonstrated by shade leaves and the sun leaves of a tree. Both types of leaves are supplied with water from the same root system, but they are exposed to different transpiration conditions. During water saturation ($\psi = 0$) the osmotic potential ψ_s of sun leaves is always a few atmospheres lower than for the shade leaves. The higher transpiration of the sun leaves is visible in the daily variations of ψ_s which is twice as high (0.8 atm) as that of shade leaves (0.4 atm; Table VI). In the morning when water saturation of all leaves can be assumed ψ_s of the sun leaves is 5.1 atm lower than for the shade leaves, which might indicate a certain drought hardening of the protoplasm of the sun leaves.

The higher drought hardiness of sun leaves is also suggested by their xeromorphism: smaller leaf surface and cell size, higher density of vascular bundles, more stomata and hairs per square millimeter of the leaf surface than for the shade leaves (Table VII). The development of sun leaves and of their osmotic potential ψ_s is a special case of drought adaptation, since the buds of these leaves are formed in the preceding year. The meristematic cells of buds from twigs exposed to sunlight have a lower hydrature of their protoplasm than the shade twigs. The leaf initials of buds on sun twigs therefore will develop into leaves with a more xeromorphic structure. The lower hydrature of meristematic cells on sun twigs results from the relation between their hydrature and the average water potential (= −cohesion tension) in the closest vessel element (Walter, 1965, p. 106; Walter and Stadelmann, 1968, p. 698). This water potential is lower

TABLE VII

Differences in Anatomical Features of Sun Leaves and Shade Leaves of *Robinia pseudacacia*[a]

Leaf	Leaf area (cm²)	Leaf thickness (μm)	Venation density (mm/cm²)	Stomatal frequency (per mm²)	Guard cell length (μm)	Diameter of epidermal cells (μm)	Number of hairs	
							Upper side (per mm²)	Lower side (per mm²)
Sun leaf	40.8	154	1420	495	17	315	74	119
Shade leaf	351.8	126	1000	352	22	626	49	63

[a] From Walter (1965, p. 107).

than in shade leaves due to a higher transpiration of sun leaves. This example illustrates the very close relationship between osmotic potential of the leaves and the hydrature of the protoplasm in the meristematic cells and thus between ψ_s and xeromorphism of the leaf.

XII. Osmotic Potential (ψ_s), Growth, and Production of Organic Matter

The water balance of a plant is determined by the water content and water retention of soil and by potential evaporation. The measurement of environmental conditions, however, indicates little about their actual effects on plants. For homoiohydric plants, the effect of external conditions on hydrature is the most important factor for growth. This can be demonstrated for plants of the same species which are growing under different environmental conditions when the osmotic potential of their vacuome is determined.

Such a test was made for *Solanum elaeagnifolium* growing on river terraces of the Santa Cruz River in Arizona. Following a rain in that area, water is retained in small, inconspicuous depressions of soil. While the level ground quickly dries out again, the areas in the depressions are more intensively moistened the deeper they are located. Thorough moistening of soil at the bottom of the depression is shown by the presence of *Prosopis* shrubs. After a rain, summer ephemeral plants grow. *Solanum elaeagnifolium* is found in the center as well as at the edges of a depression. The size of these plants decreases from approximately 60 cm to only 1 cm in height as their position is closer to the edge of the depression. The osmotic potential of tall plants is about -15 atm; of the dwarf plants about -30 atm. Plant height and osmotic potential are parallel to each other (see Fig. 18).

Dwarf plants of ephemeral species are seen in a desert after an occasionally heavy rainfall. Their shoot growth is always considerably less than is their root growth. This shift in growth rate may be a valuable adaptation to the arid environment.

An experiment with seedlings of *Pisum sativum* clearly shows the different effects of a decrease in hydrature for shoots and roots (Walter, 1962, p. 344ff). At first, *Pisum* seeds were germinated in wet saw dust. In a series of sealed vessels sugar solutions of stepwise increased concentration were prepared. In each of these vessels the germinated seeds were placed over the sugar solution so that only the roots were immersed in the solution. In this way the germinating seeds were exposed to air humidity corresponding to relative vapor pressure over the solution, and the same hy-

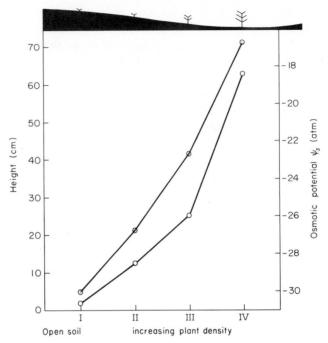

Fig. 18. Relation between osmotic potential (ψ_s) (left curve) and height of plants (right curve) of *Solanum elaeagnifolium* (after Walter, 1931, p. 123).

dratures of shoots and root meristems developed in response to prevailing relative humidity of the air. Shoot growth was very sensitive to decrease in hydrature and stopped at about 98.5% hydrature. However, with decreasing hydrature, root growth first increased to a maximum at 99.5% hydrature. Eventually root growth was stopped at a low hydrature of 97.5% hydrature (Fig. 19).

To simulate the conditions of a desert, Kiecksee (1964) grew *Brassica napus* seeds in vessels with sand. He supplied the water by spraying. The percent water content of the soil (calculated for the total amount of soil in the vessel) by this method was for vessel A, 15.9%; for B, 9.4%; for C, 5.2%; for D, 4.3%; and for E, 1.7%. The soil was not uniformly moistened since the water reached the following depths: A, 19 cm; B, 18 cm; C, 15 cm; D, 12 cm; and E, 4 cm. The *Brassica* seeds were laid out on the sand surface and germinated. After 11 days the lengths of the hypocotyl and roots were measured. Hypocotyl length decreased throughout from vessels A to E. The length of the main root increased from vessels A to C but decreased from C to E. This decrease in root length is caused by lower penetration depth of water into the soil. Sap could be pressed

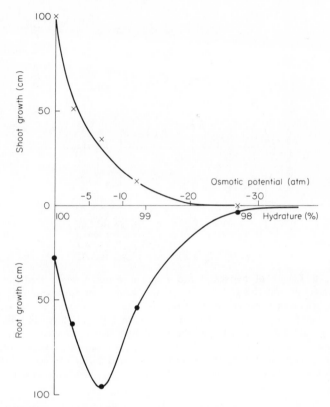

Fig. 19. Relation between osmotic potential (hydrature) and root and shoot growth of *Pisum sativum* seedlings (after Walter, 1924, p. 409, Fig. 10, 1962, p. 345. Fig. 231).

from plants of the first three vessels only. The osmotic potential decreased from —3 atm (vessel A) to —11 atm for vessel C (see Fig. 20).

In a similar experiment the soil was moistened uniformly throughout the vessels to A, 15.5%; B, 6.7%; C, 4.3%; D, 2.5%; E, 1.3%. The presoaked *Brassica* seeds were put on the soil surface and the root and shoot length of the seedlings measured after 5 days. The height of the above-ground parts of the plants decreased from 19 mm (A) to 7 mm (E). Although the length of the main root increased from 21 mm (A) to 38 mm (E), the root was less branched and thinner. At high soil moisture contents, the main root was shorter than at low moisture content but formed numerous lateral roots (Fig. 21).

The relation between osmotic potential ψ_s, root and shoot growth, and the importance of ψ_s as an ecophysiological indicator was also shown in

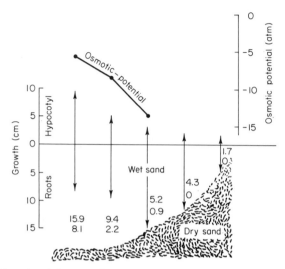

Fig. 20. Length of hypocotyl and roots of *Brassica napus* seedlings related to the degree of watering (left scale). Water content of the sand (in percent dry weight) as mean value calculated from the total sand volume in the vessel. Upper figure immediately after watering, lower figure after 11 days. The limit between dry sand and wet sand indicates the penetration depth of water immediately after watering. Right scale: osmotic potential of the press sap of the seedlings at termination of experiment. For water regimes of 4.3 and 1.7 initial water content plants were too small to obtain press sap (after Kiecksee, 1964, Figs. 20a and 20b).

Fig. 21. *Brassica* seedlings growing in sand at different water content, 5 days after germination. a, 15.5%; b, 6.7%; c, 4.3%; d, 2.5%; e, 1.3% of water content (a group of three plants is shown for each sample) (after a photograph from Kiecksee, 1964).

TABLE VIII

GROWTH AND WATER SUPPLY OF *Hordeum*[a]

Water supply (mm)	Osmotic potential[b] ψ_s (atm)	Fraction contributed to NaCl[c] (atm)	Root length (cm)	Plant height (cm)
157	−30.0	−8.1	35	20
257	−29.1	−7.3	33	27
307	−26.5	−7.1	30	29
357	−25.7	−6.7	25	34

[a] After Abd El Rahman *et al.* (1966, pp. 265–266).

[b] At the end of the vegetation period.

[c] Indicates that fraction of the osmotic potential which can be attributed to the osmotic activity of NaCl found in the press sap and determined quantitatively.

field experiments with *Hordeum vulgare* var. *mariutis* (Abd El Rahman, *et al.*, 1966, p. 264ff; Table VIII). The nonirrigated control plot had a total rainfall of 157 mm; the total water supply to the three irrigated experimental plots corresponded to 257, 307, and 357 mm, respectively. With decreasing water supply the length of the shoots decreased from 34 to 20 cm, and that of the roots increased from 25 to 35 cm. With an increase in available water the number of branch roots increased.

A decrease of 40% in dry matter production was found in *Trifolium incarnatum* when grown for 25 days at soil moisture of 30% field capacity and compared with plants cultivated at 80% field capacity (Simonis, 1948, p. 212). The relative contribution of the stem material to total dry matter produced was about the same under both conditions. Root growth was enhanced and leaf growth decreased under dry conditions.

The relation between osmotic potenital ψ_s and plant yield was first investigated on *Triticum vulgare* (winter wheat, var. *Trubilo*) by Stieglitz (1936). The ψ_s values for the main part of the growth period (middle of May to July) were considerably lower for 1934 (which had a dry period during the summer) than for 1933, a year with normal precipitation (Fig. 22). Grain yield in 1934 was only 56% of that in 1933, and production of straw decreased even more drastically.

Irrigation tests in the Canadian Prairie (Alberta) proved that yield of various agricultural crops decreased with lowering of mean osmotic potential ψ_s of the vegetation period (Table IX).

The work of Lobov (1951, p. 27) (see Walter, 1955) on irrigated plots in the Don region (Russia) and the results of Kreeb (1957) also confirm the close relation between ψ_s and yield.

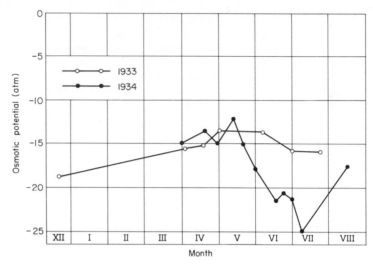

Fig. 22. Osmotic potential for leaves of *Triticum vulgare* (winter wheat, var. *Trubilo*) in 1933 (normal precipitation) and 1934 (dry year). Plot was fertilized (after Stieglitz, 1936, pp. 161 and 165).

TABLE IX

OSMOTIC POTENTIAL ψ_s (IN ATM) AND YIELD [MEASURED IN (I) t/ha OR (II) hl/ha] OF CROP PLANTS IN THE CANADIAN PRAIRIE[a]

Medicago sativa (Alfalfa)	ψ_s	−10.6	−11.5	−11.9	−14.7	−17.2	−19.9
first cutting fresh weight	(I)	24.4	19.2	21.8	16.6	11.7	8.1
Medicago sativa (Alfalfa)	ψ_s	−10.3	−10.4	−10.9	−13.1	−14.1	−30.3
second cutting fresh weight	(I)	21.8	20.6	17.0	13.9	12.8	0.7
Triticum vulgare	ψ_s	−10.5	−10.7	−11.7	−11.9	−12.3	−12.8
var. "Thatcher" yield	(II)	33.3	32.7	31.4	28.1	25.1	24.4
Triticum vulgare	ψ_s	−10.4	−11.0	−11.1	−11.3	−11.4	−21.2
var. "Lemhi" yield	(II)	43.0	40.8	30.0	28.0	32.2	28.0
Hordeum sativum	ψ_s	−10.3	−10.7	−11.8	−12.0	−12.6	−14.6
var. "Montcalm" yield	(II)	43.4	41.5	36.2	36.6	32.3	27.6
Avena sativa	ψ_s	−9.4	−10.1	−10.4	−10.6	−11.0	−14.4
var. "Eagle" yield	(II)	85.5	70.0	60.7	64.3	59.7	56.5
Beta vulgaris ssp. *vulgaris* var. *altissima*	ψ_s	−12.1	−12.6	−13.2	−13.6	−13.6	−22.4
(sugar beet) yield	(I)	35.6	33.6	28.4	30.0	28.7	11.9
Solanum tuberosum	ψ_s	−8.6	−8.7	−9.4	−9.4	−9.4	−10.5
(potato) yield	(II)	326	248	264	214	182	62.9

[a] After Bauman (1957, p. 72ff).

Yield is always influenced by balances among physiological processes such as photosynthesis and respiration. Equally important is the conversion of photosynthetic products into plant tissues. Organic matter may be used in a productive way for increase in leaf size or number, or, nonproductively, for formation of mechanical tissues in the stem only (Walter, 1960, p. 399). Different patterns in the utilization of assimilate cause, for example, differences in dry matter production between a *Helianthus annuus* plant and a 1-year-old *Fagus* seedling under the same environmental conditions: whereas intensity of photosynthesis of the unit of leaf surface area in *Helianthus* is only four to five times higher than in leaves of *Fagus,* the annual production of dry matter is about forty times higher in *Helianthus* than in *Fagus.* The latter plant develops already in the first year a woody stem and only two or three leaves.

In the final analysis, all the physiological factors in the plant depend upon the living protoplasm and its activity, which in turn depends upon protoplasmic hydrature. Secondary control mechanisms may also cooperate, for instance, in photosynthesis, the regulation of stomatal opening which influences rates of photosynthesis. An analysis of all the factors which affect yield and utilization of assimilates is not yet available (Walter nd Kreeb, 1970, p. 191).

The discussion above dealt with quantitative changes caused by drought. However, these changes are always accompanied by qualitative alterations of structure and the development of plant organs. These differences in structure are especially evident in desert plants, and for their development water stress generally is the controlling factor.

XIII. The Relation between the Osmotic Potential (ψ_s) and the Anatomical and Morphological Characteristics of Plants

A. *Encelia farinosa*

Interactions often exist between osmotic potential and the anatomical and morphological features of plants. The case of the shade leaves and sun leaves was mentioned previously. An even more striking example involves the composite *Encelia farinosa,* a semishrub characteristic of the Sonora Desert of Arizona (Walter, 1931, p. 134ff). The plant (Fig. 23) has soft and hairy leaves which vary considerably in form (Fig. 24). The close correlation between leaf form and ψ_s indicates a dependence of leaf form on osmotic potential.

After a rainy period the leaves of *Encelia* are large, greenish, and hygromorphic with few hairs; their osmotic potential is about -22 to

Fig. 23. *Encelia farinosa,* semishrub, from the Tumamoc Hill near Tucson, Arizona (from Walter, 1931, p. 135, Fig. 56; photograph by E. Walter).

Fig. 24. Hygromorphic, mesomorphic, and xeromorphic leaves from *Encelia farinosa.* The twigs in the center of the photograph bear leaf primordia densely covered with white hairs (from Walter, 1931, p. 135, Fig. 57; photograph by E. Walter).

—23 atm. During drought ψ_s decreases to —28 atm and the new leaves are smaller, mesomorphic, and more pubescent than those formed after rains. At ψ_s = —32 atm, only small, white, fleshy, and very pubescent xeromorphic leaves develop. The hygromorphic leaves desiccate and abscise at ψ_s = —36 atm. Soon the mesomorphic leaves also abscise. When ψ_s reaches —40 atm, the xeromorphic leaves abscise and only the terminal buds with the leaf initials (protected by a dense hair cover) which can withstand osmotic potentials as low as —49 atm remain on the twigs.

When *Encelia* grows in stony soil between rocks on a north slope with sufficient water supply during the drought season ψ_s values do not decrease as mentioned before. Only hygromorphic leaves develop and flowers are few.

B. Other Heterophyllic Plants

Ecologically caused heterophylly as in *Encelia* is found quite often. *Poterium spinosum, Artemisia monosperma,* and *Helianthemum ellipticum* growing in Palestine develop summer leaves with a transpiring mass about three–six times smaller than in winter leaves (Orshan, 1954, pp. 442 and 443). Both leaf types have similar transpiration rates per gram of leaf fresh weight in *Poterium spinosum, Ononis natrix,* and *Artemisia monosperma;* hence, there is much less water loss during the summer. This smaller size of the summer leaves is probably caused by a lowering of ψ_s; however, these values were not measured.

C. Cactaceae

Another example of the relation between ψ_s and plant anatomical structure is found in *Ferocactus* (*Echinocactus*) *wislizenii* in Arizona (Walter, 1931, p. 141ff). Growth of this plant is reduced most on its southwest side, which is exposed to the hottest afternoon sun. The unequal growth causes the tip of the plant to bend toward the southwest (Fig. 25). The cross section of the stem is asymmetric since the ribs are closer together at the southwest side and further apart on the northeast side (Fig. 26). The effect becomes more pronounced as the plant ages. The vessels and sclerenchyma of the centrally located xylem are developed more on the southwest side than on the northeast side. Therefore, the plant has only a single northeast to southwest plane of symmetry. Samples of similar tissues taken from different places of the cross section indicate that the structural differences are reflected in changes of the osmotic potential, as can be seen from the isosmotic curves (Fig. 26). Lowest ψ_s values (highest potential osmotic pressures) are found in the southwest side of the stem and highest ψ_s in the northeast.

Fig. 25. Small specimen of *Ferocactus wislizenii* (from Walter, 1931, p. 141, Fig. 61; photograph by E. Walter).

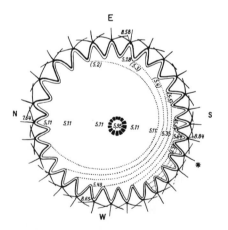

Fig. 26. Stem cross section of *Ferocactus wislizenii*. N, north; S, south; W, west; E, east. The dotted lines connect points with the same osmotic potential. The numerical value (in atm) is indicated for each line in parenthesis. The results of individual measurements are given without parenthesis. Note the proximity of the ribs in the southwest-exposed region (from Walter, 1931, p. 142).

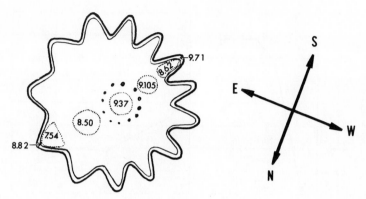

Fig. 27. Distribution of the potential osmotic pressure π^* (— osmotic potential) in the cross section of *Carnegiea gigantea* 25 cm below the growing point (π^* indicated in atm; cross section reduced 1:3; the thorns are omitted in the drawing (after Walter, 1931, p. 144).

These differences in potential osmotic pressure are caused by the water balance. The suction tension (—water potential) is highest at the southwest side; therefore, the ψ_s values there are the lowest and the decreased hydrature in the protoplasm of the meristematic cells results in slower growth rate.

A similar symmetry pattern of rib distribution and osmotic potential is found in cross sections of other columnar cacti of Arizona, such as *Carnegiea gigantea* (Fig. 27). However, growth rates do not vary among different sections of the periphery of the stem and the columnar stem grows perfectly vertically.

Water loss during the dry season causes reduction in volume of storage parenchyma, which in turn leads to shrinkage and decrease of stem volume. The diameter of the stem becomes smaller and the ribs move closer together. After rainfall the water storage tissue again fills with water, the stem swells quickly, and the ribs are drawn further apart. The water uptake proceeds rapidly and with great intensity at the south side of the stem, probably because the water potential is lower (more negative) there and the water-conducting tissue more extensive than in other sections of the stem. Swelling of the north side of the stem, which begins only after a few days, is slower and proceeds for a longer time than swelling at the south side, so that it may even continue into the beginning of the next drought period when the south side of the stem already shows shrinkage. Correspondingly, the distance between the ribs of the column increases after rainfall more rapidly at the south side than on the north side of the stem (Fig. 28).

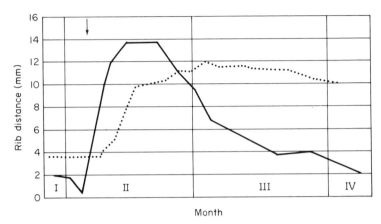

Month

Fig. 28. Change of the rib distance on the south side (———) and north side (·······) of *Carnegiea gigantea* after rainfall on February 6 (arrow). The expansion of the stem begins at the south side immediately after rainfall, at the north side, it is delayed for several days. After data from E. Spalding (Walter, 1931, p. 145).

The water uptake in the cells of the water storage tissue at the south side causes an increase of the osmotic potential which may become temporarily higher than that of storage tissue of the north side of the stem (Fig. 29). These water relations were determined for the water-storage parenchyma tissue only, and it is not established if such a temporary reversal in the ψ_s values of the north and south side of the stem occurs in the assimilatory parenchyma also. Data of only one observation are available (Table X). The ψ_s values on the north and south sides of the stem show reversal for the water-storage tissue only.

The asymmetry of the isosmotic curves in the stem sections of *Carnegiea gigantea* is caused only by the differences in the environmental conditions between the north and south sides. The vertically growing branches show the same characteristic rib distribution and ψ_s values as the main stem when they are equally exposed in all directions to light and atmosphere. Branches shadowed on their south side by the main stem or other branches, however, develop equidistant ribs and have uniform ψ_s values throughout the water-storage tissue. Also the columnar cacti in Venezuela, where the sun shines from the south during the winter and from the north in the summer, show equal distribution of ribs.

The difference in hydrature between the southwest and the northeast sides of the columnar cacti from Arizona also leads to differences in distribution of flowers on the apical parts of their stems. Flower buds develop first, and they open first on the ribs of the southwest side of the plant. Blooming progresses from the southwest side of the stem in both direc-

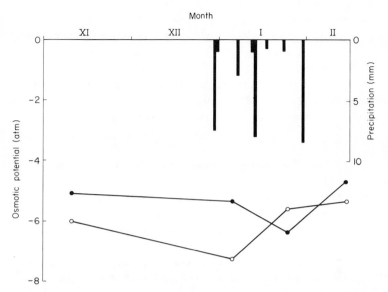

Fig. 29. Osmotic potential ψ_s in the water-storage parenchyma cells of the ribs of *Carnegiea gigantea* on the north side (●) and the south side (○) of the stem. Abscissa: Month, November (XI) to February (II), before, during, and after the rainy period. Left ordinate: ψ_s; right ordinate: precipitation in mm. The samples were taken from different plants (after Walter, 1931, p. 145).

tions, toward west and northwest, and south and southeast. Flower buds do not develop on the northeast side of the stem. The sequence in the development of flower buds corresponds in this instance to a gradient of increasing (i.e., less negative) ψ_s values. It has been frequently found that a decrease in hydrature favors formation of flower buds. In dwarf forms of ephemeral plants early flowering coincides with decreasing (more negative) osmotic potential. These findings agree with the general observation that plants growing continuously under favorable water supply have luxuri-

TABLE X

Osmotic Potential ψ_s of the Assimilatory and Water Storage Tissue of *Carnegiea gigantea* Three Days after a Heavy Rainfall of 56 mm[a]

Tissue	North side of stem (atm)	South side of stem (atm)
Assimilatory tissue	−7.7	−8.1
Water storage tissue (rib)	−5.8	−5.2

[a] After Walter (1931, p. 146).

ous vegetative growth, but little floral development. Marginal water supply reduces vegetative growth, but enhances reproductive development. This relationship may indicate that decreased protoplasmic hydrature is important for flower bud formation. Hydrature changes might possibly act indirectly on flower bud formation by changing the intensity of hormone synthesis, but no investigations on the relation of hydration of protoplasm to reproductive development are known to the authors.

XIV. The Ecological Plant Types in Arid Regions

Protoplasmic hydrature becomes less important for plant growth and development as the climate becomes increasingly humid. This explains why the concept of hydrature was derived from observations made in an arid region (Arizona; Walter, 1931, p. 6). It may also be difficult to recognize the importance of hydrature without field experience in arid regions, since most laboratory experiments are performed with plants grown with an abundant water supply.

Classification of plants into ecological types based upon their hydrature is important mainly for plants in arid regions. Previously, when knowledge about these plants was restricted, all plants growing in arid regions were called xerophytes.* At that time the differences among arid regions were often overlooked (see p. 223ff). Arid regions can be defined as those areas with low annual precipitation, while potential evaporation is relatively high. Many of the arid regions so defined have regular rainfall during certain seasons of the year so that there is a shorter or longer period each year when water availability is relatively high. It would be inappropriate to consider as xerophytes those plants which restrict their development to a period of sufficient water supply. Such drought-avoiding plants are the summer- and winter-ephemeral species; they are either annuals or geophytes. The dormant organs of the latter survive the drought period beneath the soil surface.

Erodium cicutarium, an adventive weed plant in Central Europe, belongs to the winter ephemeral plants of arid regions. In Arizona this species has an osmotic potential between -8.8 and -14 atm and should never be called a xerophyte. The range of hydrature of the winter annuals corresponds throughout to the hydrature of the herbaceous plants of Central

---

* The term "xerophyte" is generally thought to have been introduced by Schouw (1822). However this author has not yet used this word, which seems to be first mentioned by Drude (1890, p. 81). "Xerophyte" originally designated plants which occurred in dry habitats. Later, and incorrectly, the meaning of this term was extended to include all plants growing in arid regions.

Europe or the eastern part of North America: The osmotic potentials of those plants in Arizona are, for instance, for *Parietaria debilis* —9.5 atm; *Delphinium scaposum,* near —18.9 atm; and *Galium asperrimum,* —9.6 atm. These plants grow in shade (Harris and Lawrence, 1916, pp. 15, 23, and 25), although the ψ_s values are not much higher even when such species grow in more sunny places: *Lepidium medium,* —13.5 to —14.6 atm; *Sophia pinnata,* —17.7 atm. (Harris and Lawrence, 1916, pp. 39 and 40).

Small moist niches can be found in all arid regions. These niches at first glance may appear to be quite dry, e.g., north slopes in cleft rocks, on the lower end of talus, or areas in dry river beds with a relatively high water table of fresh water. In those habitats plants may have access to an ample water supply throughout the whole year. Species growing in such places often have their main distribution area in more humid tropic regions with summer rains, e.g., various species of *Acacia,* and other trees and shrubs, *Citrullus,* etc. It would certainly be misleading to call these plants xerophytes.

The other plant species of arid regions, which do not belong to the annuals or geophytes, have above-ground organs which stay alive all year, even during the dry season. These plants must survive with whatever rainfall reaches their habitat. One group of these plants, the leaf and stem succulents and the less known root succulents, accumulate large amounts of water and can survive droughts without significant water uptake from the soil. The other group includes, apart from the halophytes, plants growing on saline soil, the *true xerophytes.* The latter can be subdivided with regard to their features of hydrature into several subgroups.

XV. Hydrature in True Xerophytes

True xerophytes are those nonsucculent and nonhalophytic plants of arid regions which maintain living, above-ground organs throughout the year, including drought periods, and obtain their water supply from local precipitation or atmospheric moisture only.

Four subdivisions of the true xerophytes can be made:

1. Poikilohydrous xerophtes
2. Malacophyllous xerophytes
3. Sclerophyllous or aphyllous xerophytes
4. Stenohydrous xerophytes

Plant types with an intermediary position between these subdivisions can also be found.

A. Poikilohydric Xerophytes

Poikilohydric cryptogams are the only vegetation (500–600 kg dry weight per ha) of the Takyr plains in Central Asia. In that area clay soils are inundated for a short period during the spring. A variety of 43 species of Cyanophyceae (mostly *Phormidium, Microcoleus,* and others), 49 Chlorophyceae, Flagellatae, Diatoms, and Xanthophyta were found in a takyr in the northern part of the Kara kum Desert (Turkmenistan). For a takyr at the foothills of the Kopet-Dag 95 Cyanophyceae, 54 Chlorophyceae, two Xanthophyceae, 33 Diatoms and two Euglenaceae (total 186 algal species) are reported (Rodin, 1963, p. 255). Higher plains which are never inundated have lichens (*Diploschistes albissimus, Squamarna lentigera,* and others). These lichens absorb water from the exceedingly humid air during the night. Their CO_2 assimilation is positive during the morning hours (cf. also *Ramalina maciforma* in the Negev Desert, Lange, 1969, p. 6).

Desert plants called window algae grow on the lower side of transparent quartz stones (Tchan and Beadle, 1955, p. 101; Vogel, 1955, p. 52ff). Light rains occur frequently and dew runs along the surface of the stones to provide the underlaying algae with moisture and to protect them against evaporation. Earth lichens with thalli a few millimeters long are able to utilize dew (Vogel, 1955, p. 115). Window algae and lichens were recorded in the foggy Namib Desert but are not found further inland where no fog develops, although summer rains may occur there. Window algae also occur in other arid regions (Walter, 1964, p. 387).

Xeromorphic mosses (e.g., certain Ricciaceae) with partly subterranean thalli, which are found in many arid regions, have not been as yet studied ecologically. Lower plants of the desert, in general, have hardly been investigated in this regard.

Poikilohydric pteridophyta have air-dry leaves during drought periods, but they regain turgidity and green color within only 15–30 minutes after the first rain. These ferns are widely distributed through the arid regions of South Africa and America but do not grow in extreme deserts. The ψ_s values of their leaves during the rainy period are high (Table XI), but still lower than for most winter annuals. This difference is generally found and is characteristic for the pteridophytes, which do not have a very efficient water-conducting system.

The leaves of most of these fern species roll and dry when the dry season begins and the available soil moisture supply decreases. Loss of turgidity occurs rapidly and half-dried and incompletely rolled fern leaves rarely are seen. The rolling mechanism of these leaves (Walter and Bauer, 1937) and the photosynthesis and respiration of the poikilohydric ferns before

TABLE XI

ψ_s VALUES OF POIKILOHYDRIC PTERIDOPHYTES DURING THE RAINY PERIOD
IN THE SONORAN DESERT[a]

Plant	Osmotic potential (atm)
Notholaena hockeri	-14.6 to -15.8
Notholaena sinuata	-15.4
Notholaena aschenborniana	-13.4 to -16.1
Pellaea mucronata	-14.1 to -14.6
Gymnopteris hispida	-13.4
Cheilanthes wrightii	-15.9 to -16.0
Cheilanthes fendleri	-17.7 to -18.3
Cheilanthes lindheimeri	-24.1 (on dry habitat)
Selaginella arizonica	-14.8 to -15.6 (on drier habitats -16.7)

[a] After Walter (1931, p. 21).

and after desiccation (Ziegler and Vieweg, 1970, p. 90ff; Stuart, 1968) have been investigated. Application of liquid water to the dried leaves is necessary to reactivate them. *Polypodium polypodioides,* an epiphytic poikilohydric fern growing on *Quercus virginiana* in Florida, was studied by Stuart (1968, pp. 191 and 200). In moisture-saturated air the water content of the leaves is about 90% of their maximum water content. At 98% relative air humidity, the leaves are about half-rolled, and at 96% relative air humidity, completely rolled. The anatomical leaf structure of this poikilohydric fern is the same as of leaves of homoiohydric species; there is also no difference in the internal cell structure except the vacuolar content of the cells is more viscous and solidifies when the leaf dries.

An example of a poikilohydric angiosperm is *Myrothamnus flabellifolia* (Myrothamnaceae, Rosales), which is very abundant in the inner border regions of the Namib Desert in Southwest Africa. The leaves of this plant can withstand several years of dryness, during which time they develop measurable amounts of CO_2. Dried leaves are not damaged by transfer into liquid nitrogen ($-195°C$) for 30 minutes or by heating to $+80°C$ for 4 hours. The plasma in the cells of the dried leaves is extremely dense and the organelles contrast only slightly from the ground plasma in the electron microscopic picture. Transfer of twigs with dried leaves into water-saturated air increases release of CO_2 but does not induce photosynthesis. Wetting the leaves with water immediately increases respiration by an order of 100, with a significant increase in aldolase activity; photosynthesis begins after a certain delay depending on the temperature (Vieweg and Ziegler, 1969, p. 34). There are no differences in submicroscopic cell morphology or plastid and mitochondria structure between the cells of fresh leaves and those of homoiohydric angiosperms. The fresh leaves become damaged after prolonged exposure to a temperature of 50°C (Ziegler and Vieweg, 1970, p. 106).

B. Malacophyllous Xerophytes

Species belonging to this group are highly characteristic of steppes and prairies with relatively short drought periods and extended periods of readily available water during spring and early summer. Maximov (1923) mistakenly attempted to extend the result of his studies of this subgroup to all xerophytes.

The malacophyllous xerophytes restrict their transpiration only very slightly at the beginning of a drought period; hence large water deficits result. The leaves are able to withstand this water deficit to a certain degree. The rapid decrease of the ψ_s values indicates that these species are hydrolabile. The great difference between $\psi_{s\ opt}$ and $\psi_{s\ min}$ characterizes these species as euryhydric plants. Species of *Cistus; Phlomis, Lavendula, Thymus, Rosmarinus,* and other genera of the Mediterranean region belong to the malacophyllous xerophytes. From Arizona, *Encelia farinosa, Artemisia tridentata,* and *Gaertneria (Franseria) deltoides* (a composite with $\psi_{s\ opt}$ around —20 atm and $\psi_{s\ min}$ below —52.5 atm) are malacophyllous species. Many genera from Labiatae, Compositae, and Cistaceae found in arid regions belong to this subgroup of xerophytes.

The reaction of a typical malacophyllous xerophyte to an extended drought period was discussed for *Encelia farinosa* (see Section XIII,A). In the Mediterranean region, these plants drop almost all their leaves during the summer drought and retain only the small terminal buds. Transpiration of these buds is very small, so that a minimal water uptake from the soil is sufficient to keep the water balance at the level adequate for survival. The leaves of the malacophyllous xerophytes of the steppes usually remain exceedingly wilted but recover after rain. The ability to withstand large water deficits was considered by Maximov (1923) as the most significant feature of xerophytes. This is true for the malacophyllous xerophytes but is incorrect for the next subgroup.

C. Sclerophyllous and Aphyllous Xerophytes

Sclerophyllous shrubs are found in all arid areas with a Mediterranean climate, as in the Mediterranean region, Southern California, in Central Chile, in the Cape region, and Southwestern and Southern Australia, where Proteaceae are the most frequent representatives of this group. *Eucalyptus* may also be classified within this subgroup. However, its leaves are rather coriaceous and not strengthened with sclerenchyma. Aphyllous species are *Spartium junceum* and many *Genista* species of the Mediterranean region. Other aphyllous rod shrubs often have leaves reduced to very small scales, or stems transformed into thorny phylloclades (e.g., species of *Colletia* in Argentina). Rod shrubs belonging to different families are very frequently found in North Patagonia.

The evergreen oaks of the Mediterranean region, especially *Quercus ilex,* are the ecologically most studied sclerophyllous species (cf. Walter, 1968, p. 44ff; Breckle, 1966).

In contrast to malacophyllous plants, the sclerophyllous xerophytes are able to retain a favorable internal water balance by restricting transpiration during drought periods ("xerophytes," after Schimper, 1898, p. 4). The ψ_s values hardly decrease at all during the summer drought period. These plants enter a kind of resting period during the summer only when the habitat is exceptionally dry. This means that they reduce their gas exchange (and therefore also their photosynthesis). A limited amount of moisture seems to be available over the whole year for the root system which penetrates deep into the soil. Plants which grow on locations so dry that their stomata remain closed during the summer drought appear to lack vigor.

In most species, the small sclerophyllous and evergreen leaves remain on the plant for 2 or more years. Hence, the transpiring surface of the plant is not reduced during the drought season. The species are hydrostable and have a position midway between the stenohydric and euryhydric groups. Little information is available on $\psi_{s\ min}$ values, since drought-injured plants are rarely found in their natural habitats.

In Arizona, *Cercidium microphyllum* (its name palo verde refers to the stem, which remains green even in very old trees), a 5–6-meters (maximum, 8–10-meters) tall tree, which may be considered as an aphyllous plant, and the evergreen *Quercus* species of the encinal vegetation in Arizona belong to this subgroup.

The stem and twigs are the main assimilating organs of *Cercidium microphyllum,* since the paired pinnately compound leaf with three–five pairs of leaflets (smaller than 1 mm) are ephemeral. The leaves grow only after longer winter and summer rains and seldom survive more than 6–10 weeks. At first the leaflets are dropped, later also the rachis. With all leaves on the plant, their total surface area is still smaller than that of the stems and twigs. The ψ_s values of the leaves are quite constant between −26.6 and −31.5 atm, for dry locations −34.7 to −36.8 atm. Leaves from young plants have surface areas about four times as great as the leaves from older plants.

Larrea divaricata (= *L. tridentata,* Creosote bush) is intermediary between the malacophyllous and sclerophyllous subgroups. This plant is characteristic of the driest habitats in Arizona. In Argentina, it occurs at the foot of the eastern slope of the Andes in a narrow desert region 2000 km long. The leaves of this plant are small, hard, but without sclerenchymatous tissue and very drought resistant. They have a low degree of hydrostability but mostly remain on the branches during drought.

Sclerophyllous species of this subgroup are also found in extreme deserts, but with increasing drought their habitats are restricted to gulleys and valleys (contracted vegetation, see Section III), i.e., habitats which provide limited water supply from the soil even during extended drought periods. Ground water is not required; a certain amount of soil moisture is sufficient for survival of these species in such valleys.

In the xeromorphic leaves of sclerophyllous shrubs water stress conditions may cause a water potential ψ which is considerably lower than the osmotic potential ψ_s (Kreeb, 1960, p. 278; 1961, p. 484; Önal, 1962, p. 42ff). Such low ψ develops when twigs of these plants were left in the laboratory for about 8 days (e.g., *Buxus sempervirens* leaves exhibit $\psi_s = -65$ atm, and $\psi = -110$ atm). The viability of the twigs was proven by photosynthesis and testing for the light compensation point. *Buxus sempervirens* twigs, after being subjected to such water stress, reached the light compensation point at several hundred lux indicating that the water stress had not yet caused a permanent damage to the cells.

The excess of ψ over ψ_s results in a negative turgor pressure which is caused by the thickened and relatively rigid cell walls when higher water deficits develop. In contrast to sclerophyllous xerophytes, mesophytes do not develop a negative wall pressure (Önal, 1962, p. 52).

The ecophysiological importance of a negative wall pressure has been discussed for some time, since it was thought possibly to contribute considerably to the water potential of the cell during drought periods and to promote a better water supply. However, under natural conditions during drought periods negative wall pressure of leaf cells was never found to be higher than 5–10 atm in plants of the arid zones of Egypt and Spain. Therefore negative wall pressure does not contribute a significant portion of the total water potential (Kreeb, 1961, p. 486; 1963, p. 456) and does not appear to be of ecological importance.

D. Stenohydric Xerophytes

Plants belonging to this scarcely studied subgroup completely close their stomata when the water balance is only slightly disturbed, so that almost no decrease of ψ_s is observed. These species therefore are hydrostable. However, stomatal closure leads to cessation of gas exchange and therefore of photosynthesis, which in turn causes a starvation condition in

TABLE XII

ψ_s Values in atm of Leaves of Stenohydric Xerophytes during a Drought Period at Different Degrees of Yellowing

Plant	State of leaves	
	Green	Yellowing
Euphorbia heterophylla	-16.9	-16.1 to -15.8
Jatropha cardiophylla	-17.6	-12.6 to -11.8
Fouquieria splendens	-10.4 to 14.4^a	
Fouquieria splendens	-14.4	-11.7
Fouquieria splendens	-17.2 to -19.6^b	
Fouquieria splendens	-21.4^c	

^{a} Young not yet fully developed green leaves.
^{b} Fully grown leaves intensively transpiring.
^{c} Transitory decrease of ψ_s under water stress.

which the sugar of the cell sap is depleted in respiration. An increase (less negative value) rather than a decrease of ψ_s results, caused by the decrease in sugar content. The leaves do not dry, but may yellow and abscise later. It may be assumed that during yellowing important nutritional materials are translocated into the stem before the leaves die.

Representatives of this group in the Mediterranean region are *Euphorbia characias* and the plants with tubers or bulbs which retain their leaves during drought periods. Stenohydric xerophytes of Arizona include *Euphorbia heterophylla, Jatropha cardiophylla,* and *Fouquieria splendens* (see Table XII). The latter species develops up to 25 unbranched slender twigs 3 to 4 meters (to 10 meters) high which emerge from the roots near ground level at an angle of 30° to the vertical, in all directions. These long shoots have delicate leaves. The blades soon die and the petiole develops into a thorn. Their axillary buds form short shoots with 1.5–4 cm long and 0.5–1.5 cm wide hygromorphic leaves, arranged in a rosette (as in *Berberis vulgaris*). The leaves grow at any season after heavy rain, yellow when the soil becomes dry again, and abscise. In this way new leaves can develop up to five to six times a year. On the day after a rain the buds are clearly swollen; 1 day later the leaves are 7–8 mm long, and the next day the leaf length may be 15 mm. Such leaf development can be initiated also by irrigation during the drought. Within 5 days after the beginning of irrigation the shrub is covered with green leaves. Translocation of essential nutrients from the yellowing leaf into the stem may be especially important for this type of plant, which has frequent flushes of new leaves.

The stenohydric xerophytes for which $\psi_{s\ opt}$ is almost identical with $\psi_{s\ min}$ exhibit a high degree of stability for the ψ_s value and are in this respect similar to the succulents. However, the stenohydric plants do not develop a water storage organ and the yellowing of their assimilatory organs often begins already after a relatively short dry period, whereas succulents yellow rarely, in extreme cases only, after months or even 1 year of drought. Plants with latex ducts (Euphorbia, Apocynaceae), thick tap root (Umbelliferae), bulbs, or tubers are stenohydric.

XVI. The Hydrature of Succulents

Plants with water storage tissues differ so significantly from the types described above that they should not be considered to be true xerophytes, although they could be included in Section XV as a fifth subgroup, "succulent xerophytes."

Water storage, the most characteristic feature of succulents, makes them independent for periods of varying length of water uptake from the soil. Of other plant groups, only the poikilohydric plants are able to survive temporarily without requiring external water supply. However, the poikilohydric plants lapse during the drought into a dormant state, whereas the succulents do not.

The water-storage tissues of succulents are filled when rain falls and the uppermost layers of the soil become moistened. The succulents do not need deep roots. The tender, absorbing, lateral roots die when the upper soil layers become dry during a drought, but new lateral roots are formed very fast when the soil is remoistened by rainfall. New lateral root formation was tested in the laboratory after a 6-month drought period. Such formation began in *Opuntia puberula* after 8 hours, for the other cacti tested 50% of the plants had clearly visible roots after 24 hours, and 80% after 72 hours. *Pseudolobivia kermesina,* however, needed 8 days to form new roots (Kausch, 1965, p. 231). The ability of succulents to live without water uptake from the soil for an extended period makes it possible for them to grow in humid areas on shallow soil, where species with higher water requirements cannot survive, for instance, on almost bare rocks, or as epiphytes on trees. In other locations in humid areas the succulents cannot survive competition with nonsucculents, since their production of dry matter, and therefore their growth, is slow. The stored water is used economically, the intensity of transpiration is low for all succulents (especially low transpiration values result when calculated on a fresh weight basis) and therefore gas exchange with the atmosphere is also limited, with consequently low photosynthetic activity. The assimilating surface of the plant is small, further lowering dry matter increment. Little organic material, however, is needed for building the internal structures in the cactus plant since over 90% of the fresh weight of the stem is water.

Succulents grow best in regions with two rainy periods yearly so they can refill the depleted storage tissue twice a year. But these regions have to be so dry that fast-growing species cannot compete. Regions with two seasonal rains (the Karoo in South Africa and the Sonora Desert in Arizona and Northern Mexico) are geographically located between the Mediterranean-like regions with winter rains and areas with summer rains. In Australia, where the climate is similar, true succulents are absent, and all species with succulent leaves belong to the halophytes (Chenopodiaceae), which are a different ecological group (see Section XVIII). Arid regions with two regular rain periods are absent in Australia.

Water-storage organs in succulent plants may be leaves or above-ground stems or subterranean parts (morphologically not limited to roots). Most "root succulents" are not found in deserts but in areas of dry sands such as the Kalahari region, which should not be considered a climatic desert. *Pachypodium succulentum* is an example of a "root succulent." For an old plant the weight of the subterranean tuber was 7 kg, whereas that of the shoot was only 68 gm (Marloth, 1908, p. 237). The tuber of another specimen of this plant had accumulated 266 gm of water (950% of its dry weight) and the osmotic potential of the cell sap was quite high ($\psi_s = -4.2$ atm; Walter, 1964, p. 439).

A special feature of some succulents is the growth of the entire plant below the soil surface with only the flattened leaf tips at the level of the soil surface; for example, *Lithops, Nananthus,* (Fig. 30), *Conophytum,* etc. (Mesembryanthemoideae). Similar "soil cacti" are mentioned for the North Chilian Desert (Weisser, 1967; Walter, 1973b, pp. 551, 726).

In general the stem succulents seem to be of the most drought-resistant type. However, *Aloë dichotoma,* a leaf succulent with a stem attaining a

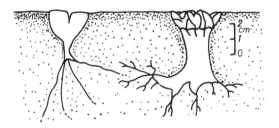

Fig. 30. Diagrammatic presentation of plants of *Lithops salicola* (left) and *Nananthus vittatus* (right) with root system. Both plants are entirely within the soil and only the leaf tips are at the level of the soil surface (after Walter, 1939, p. 762).

considerable thickness, also has its area of growth extended into the extreme desert. The ψ_s values of the leaf succulents are high (-4 to -10 atm). The Mesembryanthemoideae are exceptions. Their ψ_s values are always below -16 atm, even in areas where they grow together with other succulents. As the cell sap of the Mesembryanthemoideae contains appreciable chlorides (more than 40% of the osmotically active substance) the group is intermediate to the halophytes. Some Mesembryanthemoideae grow also on saline soils where ψ_s decreases to -50 atm and the chloride fraction of the cell sap may reach 80%.

The true succulents are very sensitive to salt. Cacti are occasionally found in locations with saline soils (North Venezuela, Argentina). However, they grow on small sand mounds which do not contain salts. The roots of these cacti do not reach the saline soil and can get fresh water during rainy periods. The cell sap of these plants contains only traces of salt.

The succulents lose a large quantity of their water during a drought period without a significant change in relative water content. For instance, *Opuntia phaeacantha-toumeyi* lost 60% of its original weight during a drought period of 189 days, but the water content on dry weight basis decreased from 84.75 to 72.68% only (Walter, 1964, p. 366), since during this long drought not only dehydration occurred but also dry weight decreased because of respiration. If the rate of both processes (dehydration and respiratory losses) is equal, the relative water content remains unchanged. Correspondingly ψ_s changes only little and may even increase when the plant is kept in the dark (Table XIII; Walter, 1931, p. 101).

Many succulents exhibit the "de Saussure effect." Their stomata open during the night and the absorbed CO_2 is fixed as organic acids and photosynthetically used during the day when the stomata are closed. Coutinho (1964, p. 106ff; 1965, p. 402; 1969, pp. 79–87) discovered this "diurnal organic acid cycle" also in some succulent epiphytes (Orchidaceae and Bromeliaceae) of the Tropical Rain Forest. Thus, this cycle is not at all

TABLE XIII

Changes in the Osmotic Potential ψ_s in an Uprooted Specimen
of *Opuntia phaeacantha-toumey* after a Drought Period of 1 Month

Condition	Osmotic potential (atm)
Before the beginning of the experiment	-7.64
Uprooted specimen placed on the ground in the natural habitat	-11.27
Kept in the dark in the laboratory	-7.23

limited to the Crassulaceae and therefore should not be called Crassulacean acid metabolism.

Experiments for simultaneous measurement of CO_2 absorption and transpiration of *Bryophyllum daigremontianum* (grown in pots, with the above-ground part of the plant in a cuvette, and in a 12-hour dark–light cycle, with 7000-lux light intensity) showed a very close parallelism between CO_2 absorption and transpiration in well-watered plants (Kluge and Fischer, 1967). As earlier reported, changes in stomatal aperture corresponded with gas exchange. At the beginning of the light period, as stomata open, a temporary increase in CO_2 absorption and transpiration occurred. One hour later, transpiration and CO_2 absorption dropped sharply with closure of the stomata, and there was even a slight release of CO_2. Whether the temporary increase of CO_2 uptake and transpiration at the beginning of the light period is caused by the sudden exposure to illumination, which does not occur in nature, was not checked.

Toward the end of the light period, transpiration and CO_2 absorption increased slightly and, after the beginning of the dark period, a transient, sudden drop in CO_2 absorption and transpiration was again shown. However, 30 minutes after the beginning of the dark period, this transient reaction was overcome and transpiration and CO_2 absorption increased constantly toward a maximum value, parallel with the opening of the stomata.

Bryophyllum plants having leaves without epidermis (the epidermis can be easily stripped off without damaging the tissue underneath) showed with the same light–dark cycle a similar trend of increase and decrease in CO_2 absorption as did plants having intact leaves (Fig. 31). This indicates that stomatal absorption of CO_2 is controlled by the leaf mesophyll rather than by stomatal aperture, which in turn is synchronized by the concentration of CO_2 in the intercellular spaces. Transpiration, however, depends on stomatal aperture, and shows no cyclic changes in plants with leaves without epidermis (Fig. 31B). In this case transpiration becomes a passive process and approaches evaporation.

When irrigation of the *Bryophyllum* plant is discontinued and water stress develops gradually, the curve for CO_2 absorption during the light period becomes lower, and finally goes below the zero line. The peak at the beginning of the light period becomes lower, whereas the one at the end disappears completely. Finally, CO_2 uptake occurs only during the dark period and to a lesser degree. At high water stress, CO_2 uptake may be limited by hydroactive stomatal closure. Transpiration parallels CO_2 uptake indicating stomatal control of gas exchange. The original cycle is reestablished almost immediately after rewatering (Fig. 32).

The change of CO_2 absorption and transpiration in *Bryophyllum* under water stress condition is a good example of a biologically controlled pro-

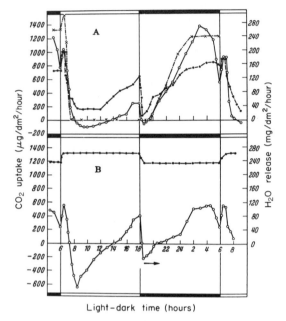

Fig. 31. CO_2 absorption and transpiration of *Bryophyllum daigremontianum* in a 12 hours light–dark cycle. (A) intact plant; (B) plant with leaves from which the epidermis was stripped off (16 hours after the stripping). ○——○, CO_2 (left scale); ●——●, transpiration (right scale). (From Kluge and Fischer, 1967, p. 216.)

cess: CO_2 absorption takes place while maintaining the maximum possible hydrature of the protoplasm by keeping water loss to a minimum.

XVII. Saline Soils in Arid Regions

Salinity, as well as water supply, is an important determining factor in plant growth in arid regions. Areas without adequate drainage are frequent since the potential evaporation is always greater than the precipitation. For this reason, highly soluble salts often accumulate in arid regions, in contrast to humid regions, where rivers drain these materials into the sea.

Textbooks frequently state that highly soluble salts originate from the weathering of crystalline rocks. However, the origin of these salts is more complex (see p. 279; Walter 1964, pp. 332–335). Although the majority of salts of arid regions are chlorides ($NaCl$, $MgCl_2$), the element chlorine is found in only a few rare minerals. Hence, chlorides cannot come from weathering of crystalline rocks. In fact, saline soils are not found where these rocks are exposed at the surface. The brackishness of the soils, however, becomes significant in those arid areas where marine sedimentary rocks (Jurassic, Cretaceous, or Tertiary) are exposed, e.g., in the northern part of the Sahara Desert. Often efflorescence of salt is seen at the limits of certain layers in these rocks. This salt originated from the seawater and became included into the rocks during sedimentation of the sea bed. During weathering these salts are exposed at the soil surface and the small amounts of precipitation wash the salt into undrained depressions. There, evaporation over an extended period of time causes a considerable accumulation of salt and thus salt pans are formed. The more elevated parts of the landscape of those regions, therefore, are seldom brackish, whereas salt pans are frequently found in the lower parts. In the Central Sahara, which has no rainfall, displacement of salts does not occur and therefore salt soils are not found. When the water moves underground, salt is deposited where the water comes to the surface and evaporates, then a salt crust is formed (Fig. 33).

Saline soils can also develop from a previous sea bed or big lake, when the basin dries out slowly, so that finally only one large or several small salt lakes remain. Examples of this type of formation of salt soils are the Caspian depression, the Great Basin with the Great Salt Lake in Utah and the area around the salt lake, Tuz Gölü, in central Anatolia (Turkey).

Even when the salt content of the ground water is low, a brackish soil can develop in arid areas with time, if the ground water level is high enough to moisten the soil surface by capillarity and if water evaporates continuously. This kind of capillarity-caused brackishness is often climate-dependent. Good examples of this correlation are found in Eastern European lowlands, where the temperature increases and the precipitation decreases from NNW to SSE. Thus, the climate changes from a humid one to a subhumid, semiarid, and arid climate. Correspondingly the composition of the ground water changes also gradually and the following types can be distinguished:

1. In extremely humid regions the groundwater is acid and free of salts. Humus colloids give the groundwater a brown color. On wet soils oligotrophic bogs develop. In less humid areas, the ground water is less acid, since small amounts of $Ca(HCO_3)_2$ are dissolved in it and in wet locations eutrophic bogs usually occur. No brackishness develops from this type of ground water.

2. In subhumid areas the content of limestone in ground water is considerable, but no highly soluble sodium salts are present. On places where the ground water level is high, $CaCO_3$ accumulates at the soil surface. Alkalitrophic bogs, which are characteristic for the transition zone between forest and forest steppe, develop there.

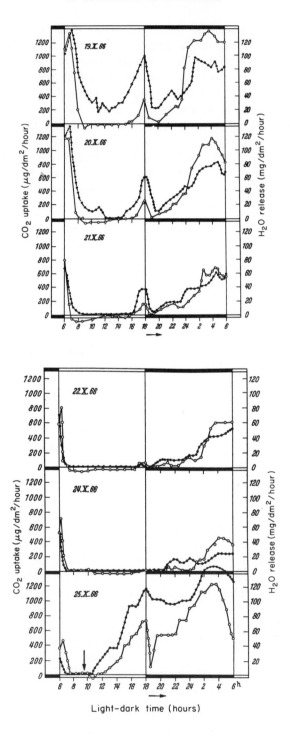

Light-dark time (hours)

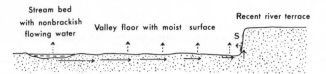

Fig. 33. Salt accumulation in the Swakop Valley (Namib Desert, Southwest Africa). The solid-line arrows indicate the direction and intensity of the underground water flow. Arrows with dotted lines indicate evaporation. The salt concentration increases towards the edge of the valley. The salt efflorescence forms at the base of the terraces, where the subterranean water flow is used up completely by evaporation (from Walter, 1936, p. 167; 1964, p. 333).

3. In the semiarid zone undrained depressions develop temporarily, so that not all the sodium salts produced by weathering are washed out. In wet soils the Ca ions in the sorption complex of the humus horizon are replaced by Na^+ to form Na humates. During the wet season the water in the humus horizon is rich in CO_2 so that hydrolysis takes place, and the sodium ion is exchanged for hydrogen ions and soda ($NaHCO_3$) is formed. Another mode for soda formation is the reaction between sodium silicate and $Ca(HCO_3)_2$. Soda together with humus sols accumulate at the soil surface where the ground water level is high during the dry season. This development of brackishness by soda is characteristic for the forest steppe zone of East Europe, or Manchuria, and other semiarid regions. The humus particles give the salt crust a black appearance. Such soils are called black alkali soils (soda–Solontchak soils).

4. Finally, in the arid steppes and semideserts where sedimentary rocks occur, highly soluble chlorides and sulfates accumulate in the groundwater of the undrained area. In all depressions where the ground water reaches the soil surface by capillarity, a white salt crust develops. This process is called chloride-sulfate brackening (white alkali soils, true Solontchak soils).

Significant differences in species composition are found between soda-containing soils and chloride-sulfate soils. In general, the former have a

---

Fig. 32. CO_2 absorption and transpiration of a *Bryophyllum daigremontianum* plant in a 12 hours light–dark cycle during a drought period. Plants were watered for the last time on Oct. 17 (17.X.66) and again on Oct. 25 (25.X.66). CO_2 absorption (left scale), ○——○; Transpiration (right scale), ●——● (from Kluge and Fischer, 1967, pp. 218–219). The diagrams indicate different values at the break line (6 hours) for each of two subsequent sections. This inconsistency is apparent only: The first value (for 6 hours at the right margin of a section) was determined immediately before illumination; the second value (for 6 hours at the left margin in the following section) gives the measurement about 5–10 minutes after beginning of the light period. This time difference was not considered in the drawing of the graph.

TABLE XIV

Climate, Composition of the Groundwater, and Type of Vegetation
on Soils Having a High Ground Water Level

Climate	Composition of the groundwater	Vegetation on soils with high ground water level or type of the brackening process
Extremely humid	Electrolyte free, very acid, colored brown by humus colloids	Oligotrophic bogs
Humid	Generally neutral or slightly alkaline	Eutrophic bogs
Subhumid	High content of $Ca(HCO_3)_2$	Alkalitrophic bogs
Semiarid	Low content of $NaHCO_3$	Soda brackening (black alkali soils)
Arid	Low amount of sodium chloride or sodium sulfate	Chloride or sulfate brackening (white alkali soils)

low salt concentration and a high pH around or over 9; the latter have high salt concentration and a pH slightly over 7.

Table XIV summarizes the relation between climate, groundwater composition, and vegetation.

Saline soils may also develop by aeolian processes when salt dust, originating from finely dispersed water droplets from breakers, develops at the seashore and is blown into the interior of the land. The outer region of the Namib Desert in Southwest Africa is an example of development of brackishness by wind action. There the brackish soils reach from the seashore to about 50 km inland, as far as the sea fog reaches. The water from this fog contains 244 mg salts per liter. The total amount of salt deposited by the fog in this area annually is estimated at 20 gm NaCl per square meter (Walter, 1964, p. 395).

The salt pans in the arid part of Western Australia also are of aeolian origin. Salt dust comes from a heavy surf along the west shore. Therefore the rain in West Australia always contains salt which is deposited on the soil surface. In the humid regions this salt is washed by rainwater into rivers and transported to the sea (cyclic salt). In undrained arid areas, however, salt is washed into the depressions and accumulates there. When the salt pans dry out, wind may blow the fine, crystalline salt further into the interior of the continent and causes development of brackishness there, too. Such "salt dusting" is also important for formation of Solonetz soils north of the Crimean Peninsula in Southern East Europe. The salt dust originates there from the "foul seas" (Siwash), which dry out during the summers.

The examples given above show that the chlorides of saline soils directly or indirectly are always of marine origin. Sea salts have accumulated gradually over the periods of earth history. Most probably the chlorine originates from the volcanic emissions which contain HCl as well as SO_2 (Dauvillier, 1965, p. 86).

XVIII. Halophytes and Salt Uptake

Halophytes are plants which are able to grow on salt soils. In reviews of desert plants the halophytes were frequently discussed together with xerophytes and succulents of nonsaline soils (Ruhland, "Encyclopedia of Plant Physiology," Volume III, 1956). Such a grouping, however, does not seem to be adequate from a physiological or ecological point of view and goes back to Schimper's theory of "physiological dryness" of saline soils. This hypothesis assumes that the osmotic concentration in saline soils makes water uptake by the plants more difficult, in a way similar to that of physical dryness of soil in arid regions. Such an assumption would be correct only when the plants do not absorb salts. However, all halophytes accumulate salts in the cell sap (Steiner, 1934, p. 152), and especially in cells of transpiring tissues (Walter and Steiner, 1936, p. 163ff). Glycophytes which grow on saline soils also accumulate salts. The concentration of salt in the cell sap of leaf cells is mostly as high as that of the soil solution or even higher. Thus, the osmotic effect of the soil solution is compensated for and absorption of water is not impeded.

There are basic differences in response to salt of the protoplasm of halophytes and glycophytes. The protoplasm of the glycophytes is sensitive to toxic effects of the salts and the salts soon reach a lethal concentration. The protoplasm of the halophytes is very salt tolerant. True halophytes show a furthering of growth in salt solutions (Mozafar et al., 1970, p. 478 for *Atriplex halimus*) whereas glycophytes or salt-tolerant plants always grow best on nonsaline soils.

The different effects of electrolytes (NaCl, KNO_3) and nonelectrolytes (saccharose, mannitol) in hydroponic culture is shown clearly in experiments with *Solanum lycopersicum* (Slatyer, 1961). These plants were grown first in normal nutrient ($\psi_s = -0.7$ atm) and later transferred to NaCl solutions (with ^{36}Cl) or mannitol solutions (with ^{14}C). Each solution had an osmotic potential $\psi_s = -10$ atm. In both solutions, the plants after the transfer became strongly wilted, but after 28 hours those in the NaCl solution were turgid again whereas those in the mannitol solution were not.

The recovery of plants in the NaCl solution was caused by salt uptake.

The osmotic potential decreased from −10.7 to −21.6 atm. For the controls in the standard nutrient solution (−0.7 atm), the osmotic potential remained at −10.9 atm. The rate of photosynthesis was not altered. Plants transferred into the mannitol solution remained wilted. Their ψ_s values, however, also decreased to −21.0 atm, but this decrease was caused by water loss. No increase in dry weight (indicative of photosynthetic activity) occurred.

Effects similar to those obtained with NaCl solutions were found also with plants grown in KNO_3 solutions, although the increase in dry weight was higher than in the controls, since KNO_3 may act as a nutrient. In sucrose solutions, the uptake of sucrose was slower than that of the electrolytes (Slatyer, 1961, pp. 524 and 525, Figs. 1 and 2).

Salt tolerance of the protoplasm of glycophytes used in this type of experiment is an important factor in survival. When *Vicia faba* plants were transferred from a pure Knop solution to a Knop solution containing NaCl (in a concentration corresponding to a decrease of osmotic potential of −7.5 atm of the solution), the osmotic potential of the leaves reached its final value twice as fast as in those plants transferred to Knop solutions plus dextrans with the same osmotic potential. However, when the adapted plants are transferred again into pure Knop solution, the plants of the dextran experiment showed no damage, whereas plants of the NaCl experiment were damaged. This indicated that protoplasm of *Vicia faba* was not salt tolerant and NaCl at the concentration applied caused disturbances of protein synthesis (Lapina, 1967, p. 321/273; 326/276).

After transfer of *Phaseolus vulgaris* plants from a nutrient solution into a nutrient solution with added salt, the water stress triggered an osmoregulatory mechanism of additional ion uptake (initially K ions) into the vacuole which adjusted the cell sap relatively quickly to the increased concentration of the external solution [within 1 day for an increment of ψ_s = −1 atm (Bernstein, 1963); for effects of the magnitude of the daily concentration increase on *Hedysarum carnosum,* see Hamza, 1969].

A similar reaction is found for seed germination in salt solutions. The sum of the matric potential (capillarity, imbibition, hygroscopicity) and of the osmotic potential resulting from salt content of the soil solution gives total soil moisture stress. For the rate of germination of seeds only the matric potential of the soil is of importance, while the osmotic potential is compensated by salt uptake of the seeds. This was demonstrated in germination experiments with seeds of *Medicago sativa* and caryopses from *Avena sativa* and *Lolium perenne* placed on sintered-glass plates which were in contact with water (Collis-George and Sands, 1962, p. 581ff). By increasing the water level difference in the experiment, the matric potential component of the water stress was increased and seed germination was considerably slower. On the other hand, when osmotic potential (NaCl solution with a much lower osmotic potential) was applied, the seeds most probably compensated the increase in water stress by uptake of salts and germination was not impeded. Sodium chloride (0.5 osmolal) was also found to have toxic effects on germination of *Phaseolus vulgaris* (Prisco and O'Leary, 1970, p. 182). Thus, with regard to seed germination there is no summation of the effect of matric and osmotic potentials. Correspondingly, seeds of *Suaeda depressa, S. linearis, Salicornia europaea,* and *Spergularia marina* showed relatively high germination percentage up to a salt content of 1–2% of the germination medium. At higher salt percentage germination decreased sharply, caused by osmotic action (Ungar, 1962, p. 764).

The problem of halophytes is primarily one of salt balance and not water balance, since the salts which are absorbed by plants have specific effects on protoplasm and may cause damage when the protoplasm is not salt-resistant (Repp, 1958, p. 556.)

Therefore, not only the external conditions of the plants have to be considered for the halophyte problem but especially the conditions inside the cells which are decisive for normal functioning of living protoplasm. It is not sufficient to know the salt concentration in the soil or the nutrient solution; rather the salt concentration in the cell sap should be determined. However, salts in the soil may have indirect effects on the water balance of plants by changing soil structure. For instance, the heavily soluble sodium salts caused a considerable decrease in porosity of soil and an unfavorable change of its structure. These effects of salts on soils are of great importance for agricultural use but are beyond the scope of this chapter.

XIX. The Effects of Ions on Protoplasm

The salts which are absorbed by halophytes accumulate particularly in transpiring organs. The presence of salt in cell vacuoles of these organs causes a decrease of osmotic potential. It can be assumed that some kind of equilibrium will be established between ion concentration in the vacuole and in the cytoplasm. Therefore, the decrease in the osmotic potential of the vacuoles in those cells will not affect the hydration of the protoplasm in the same way as will a decrease of osmotic potential from water stress. Such conditions cause a decrease in hydrature and dehydration of protoplasm.

The ions have to pass through the plasmalemma, mesoplasm, and tonoplast in order to accumulate in the vacuole. The passive permeability of the plasmalemma and tonoplast for ions is very low (Stadelmann, 1969,

p. 592) It is also low in cells of halophytes (Repp, 1958, p. 472), and passive permeation could not account for the degree of accumulation found in living cells. Rather, some species of ions are taken up actively and transported into the vacuole by (probably immobile) carriers of the plasmalemma and/or the tonoplast (cf. Sitte, 1969, p. 341; Hill, 1969). Other ion species (of opposite charge) move along passively to maintain electroneutrality. Many species of ions are present in the vacuole in a higher concentration than in the external solution. While there is certainly a relationship between ion concentration in the protoplasm and in the cell sap, little is known about the absolute concentration values (cf. MacRobbie, 1962, p. 867, Table III; Gutknecht, 1966, p. 34). Salts seem to enter the protoplasm much easier than they can penetrate into the vacuole (Repp, 1958, p. 483). It may be thought that ions which enhance imbibition of protoplasm will be at a higher concentration there than in the vacuole (positive absorption into the cytoplasm). Such an assumption is in agreement with the findings of MacRobbie (1962) that potassium and sodium ion concentrations in the cytoplasm are higher than in the vacuole. On the other hand, exclusion (negative absorption) may occur for ions which decrease protoplasmic hydration.

The presence of ions in protoplasm will modify the capacity of the protoplasm for hydration. For higher ionic concentrations the action depends on the kind of ions (*lyotropic* or *Hofmeister* series, see Bull, 1964, p. 79ff). Swelling is increased more by univalent ions (cations or anions) than by bivalent or trivalent ions. If an intermediate degree of protoplasmic imbibition is already present, addition of monovalent ions will further hydration, while bivalent ions will decrease it. Ion effects on protoplasm can be most easily demonstrated by microscopical observation of plasmolysis forms of cells after addition of ions to the plasmolyticum or after plasmolyzing directly in salt solutions. Alkali salts (e.g., KNO_3) increase water absorption by the protoplasm and cause cap plasmolysis, convex plasmolysis, or vacuolar contraction (tonoplast plasmolysis, see Stadelmann, 1956, p. 89ff), while alkaline-earth salts (e.g., $CaCl_2$) increase viscosity and cause concave plasmolysis forms.

Pure salt solutions often are poisonous for protoplasm of many species (cf. Kaho, 1923, p. 140ff; De Haan, 1933, p. 254ff; Iliin, 1935; Stadelmann, 1956, p. 192) while in mixtures of solutions of alkali and alkaline earth salts (cf. LaHaye and Epstein, 1969, 1970; Bernstein, 1970) or more complex salt mixtures, the damaging effect of the single salt is reduced or nullified (ion antagonism). The compensating effect by a low concentration of an added ion is shown in the equilibrated salt solutions where the addition of a relatively small amount of other ions is sufficient to neutralize the damaging effect of an excessively high concentration of a particular ion species [e.g., cap plasmolysis no longer develops when the plasmolyzing solution is made up of 1 part of an 0.39 M $CaCl_2$ solution and 8 parts of an 0.6 M KNO_3 solution (Höfler, 1928, p. 80)]. An equilibrated salt solution with a minimum of harmful effects for plant cells is the Brenner mixture (Brenner, 1920, p. 284): 100 gm H_2O, 1.82 gm NaCl, 0.06 gm KCl, 0.47 gm $MgCl_2 \cdot 6H_2O$, 0.28 gm $MgSO_4 \cdot 7H_2O$, 1.6 gm $CaCl_2 \cdot 6H_2O$.

Except for saline soils, the salt concentration in the soil of natural habitats of higher plants is always very low and other than the essential ions taken up for incorporation into membranes, enzymes, and other macromolecules, only small amounts of nonessential salts are usually taken up as ballast elements (see Levitt, 1969, p. 132). Therefore, salt concentration of such soils cannot significantly affect colloidal qualities and metabolic activity of protoplasm. The hydrature and the water balance remain the major factors determining protoplasmic imbibition.

However, when saline soils are considered, the effect of the ions absorbed by the protoplasm must be considered, since the salts (primarily NaCl) will be taken up in considerable amounts as ballast materials. Since NaCl is highly soluble, it cannot be precipitated inside the cell. It accumulates in many cell elements and in the vacuome of the transpiring organs especially (see Ziegler and Lüttge, 1967, p. 14). Only a few plant species have developed salt glands, which excrete (recrete) the unused salts.

The most frequently found salt in arid zones is NaCl. However, Na_2SO_4 and $MgSO_4$ are very common and sometimes may predominate (e.g., in soils around the lake of Neusiedel, Austria; Walter, 1936, p. 185). To decide whether the effect of NaCl on protoplasm is caused mainly by the Na ion or the Cl ion, their specific effects have to be considered. A high degree of absorption of NaCl may disturb the cation equilibrium in the cell. The plant does not take up Na ions and Cl ions in equivalent amounts, but frequently replaces the Na ion partially with potassium ions. In contrast to animals, plants have a high requirement for the potassium ion whereas sodium is generally not essential (p. 281). However, under certain conditions some glycophytes may be able to replace potassium partially by sodium (see Stiles, 1958, p. 600).

The Na ion concentration in the cell sap of halophytes usually is considerably higher than of glycophytes (see the analysis of salt marsh plants, Steiner, 1934, p. 152). However, in even low concentrations, other cations (K^+, Ca^{2+}, Mg^{2+}) can nullify possible damaging effects of an excess Na ion content by their antagonistic action on the protoplasm. Such action of the K^+ ion is considered by Joshi (1973, p. 139; 1971, p. 25) for the protoplasmic salt resistance of halophytes. *Atriplex halimus* plants synthesize considerably more dry matter in a one to one mixture of KCl and NaCl than plants grown in KCl or NaCl of the same concentration (Mozafar *et al.*, 1970, p. 479). Contrary to Heimann (1966), sodium ions cannot be considered to be particularly deleterious to plants and the effect of high soil salt contents on plants certainly is not merely caused by the Na ion. For effect of the salts on the soil and its structure see also Section XVIII.

The effect of the Cl ion can only be counterbalanced by the SO_4^{2-} anion (cf. Walter, 1960, p. 487; Karmarkar and Joshi, 1969, p. 46), since the sulfate ion has a dehydrating effect on colloids (Walter, 1936, p. 186; Strogonov, 1964, pp. 253 and 254). Unfortunately the sulfate ions are taken up by plants mostly in very small amounts, and are used as a supply of sulfur for synthesis of amino acids for proteins and enzymes containing sulfo or sulfhydryl groups.

The Cl ion cannot be considered to be highly toxic to protoplasm since Cl^- is found in all plants and accumulates to very high concentrations in the cell sap of salt resistant plants. However, the Cl ion has a specific (not only osmotic) effect on the protoplasm. A visible manifestation of this effect is the increase of succulence of leaves (see Biebl and Kinzel, 1965, p. 77ff). Experiments in which $CaCl_2$ or $MgCl_2$ was substituted for NaCl resulted in the same increase in succulence as with NaCl. However, when Na_2SO_4 or $NaNO_3$ was used, no increase in succulence was observed (see Table XV). These observations clearly indicate that succulence is caused by the Cl ion (see also Kramer, 1969, p. 314). However, a high chloride concentration seems to be essential in causing succulence. Therefore the transpiring organs, in particular, where high concentrations of chlorides accumulate, will become succulent. The effectiveness of a particular anion to cause succulence depends mainly upon its location in the lyotropic anion

TABLE XV

Degrees of Succulence (Water Content/Surface Area)
in *Salicornia herbacea* Leaves in Relation to the Salts
and Their Concentration in the Nutrient Solution[a]

Concentration (Molar)	Degree of succulence					
	NaCl	KCl	Na_2SO_4	$NaNO_3$	$MgCl_2$	$CaCl_2$
0	33 ± 1	33 ± 1	33 ± 1	33 ± 1	33 ± 1	33 ± 1
1/12	36 ± 1.5	39 ± 1.2	36 ± 0.9	36 ± 1.8	41 ± 1.4	40 ± 1
2/12	39 ± 2.1	39 ± 1.2	—	37 ± 1.7	42 ± 1.4	47 ± 3
4/12	45 ± 1.2	42 ± 1	36 ± 0.3	34 ± 1.2	45 ± 2	—
6/12	43 ± 1.5	43 ± 1.1	—	—	—	—
8/12	51 ± 4	42 ± 1	—	—	—	—

[a] After van Eijk (1939, p. 584, Table 1).

series (Walter, 1936, p. 186). The objection of van Eijk (1939, p. 587) against the importance of the lyotropic series is based on the absence of succulence when Cl⁻ in the nutrient solution is replaced by NO_3^-, while nitrate is even more effective than Cl⁻ in the lyotropic series. However, van Eijk did not determine the actual concentration of the cell sap and did not account for the metabolic utilization of the nitrate ion.

It should be emphasized that the chloride content of the soil is of little importance for estimating the chloride present in the leaf since the different plant species and varieties absorb chloride ions to different degrees. Also the chloride content of the leaf ash gives no indication of chloride concentration inside leaf cells.

Aside from the usual uptake through roots, plants growing on the seashore are able to take up chloride through leaves when moistened by seawater spray. Leaves exposed to the wind have a Cl⁻ content about three–six times higher than leaves on the lee side (Boyce, 1954, p. 54). The succulence observed in these experiments resulted from an increase in size of the chlorophyll-free mesophyll cells and was especially pronounced in salt-tolerant species. Here, too, development of succulence was found to be a specific effect of the chloride ion independent of the cation applied. Sulfate ions do not cause such succulence.

XX. Chloride Accumulation in Halophytes

Since there are no basic differences between halophytes of arid lands and of the seashore, the latter will also be included in this discussion. Most experiments of salt effects were performed with more or less salt-tolerant species or varieties of economically important agricultural plants, although these plants are glycophytes and therefore grow best on salt-free soils. In contrast, true halophytes grow better in soils with limited salt content. When these plants are cultivated in salt-free soil, they take up traces of chlorides, which are found in every soil, and accumulate them in leaves, so that the chloride content of the leaf cell sap is relatively high (see p. 287).* Also in natural habitat the chloride uptake is relatively higher at low soil chloride content than at high salt content (Önal, 1966, pp. 225–226). However, with increasing soil salt concentration, most halophytic plants take up only enough salt to compensate the osmotic potential of the soil solution.

* Such chloride accumulation may be found already in varieties close to halophytes as in the sugar beet (*Beta vulgaris* spp. *vulgaris* var. *altissima*), which developed from the coastal *Beta vulgaris* spp. *maritima*. Leaves of the sugar beet have an ash content of about 15.5% chlorides (*Trifolium pratense* has only 3.8%).

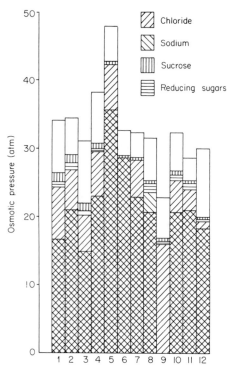

Fig. 34. The contribution of the individual ion species concentration for the osmotic pressure of the press sap of leaves from salt marsh plants. 1, *Spartina glabra;* 2, *Spartina patens;* 3, *Distichlis spicata;* 4, *Juncus gerardi;* 5, *Salicornia mucronata;* 6, *Salicornia europea;* 7, *Plantago decipiens;* 8, *Atriplex hastata;* 9, *Aster subulatus;* 10, *Limonium carolinianum;* 11, *Suaeda linearis;* and 12, *Iva ovaria.* The concentration of Na⁺ and Cl⁻ were determined separately by chemical analysis of the press sap. From the (always higher) value of Cl⁻ the osmotic pressure was calculated for the corresponding concentration of NaCl. (After Steiner, 1934, p. 152, Fig. 27; Walter, 1960, p. 481.)

The salt concentration of expressed leaf sap was determined by a few investigators only. Steiner (1934) investigated the marsh plants on the Atlantic coast of Connecticut and measured the total osmotic potential of expressed sap as well as the contribution of chloride, sodium, and sugars to this potential (see Fig. 34). Almost all saps of these plants showed an osmotic potential of about −30 to −35 atm. Only the ψ_s values of *Salicornia mucronata,* which grows in small salt pans with temporarily very high soil salt concentrations, are considerably lower. Higher (less negative) ψ_s values were measured in *Aster subulatus* growing in locations with low salt content. The contribution of chloride salts to the total osmotic potential (−30 to −35 atm) is on the average about 75–80% (i.e., −24 to −25 atm). The remaining portion of all the osmotically active material of the cell sap only contributes −5 to −10 atm to the total osmotic potential of the cell sap. The concentration of the sodium ion in expressed sap was always less than that of the chloride ion, with the exception of *Atriplex hastata*. Most likely, the excess chloride ions are neutralized by potassium ions. The expressed sap of *Atriplex hastata* has a higher concentration of sodium ions than of chloride ions. The excess sodium in this case probably is neutralized by sufate ions or organic anions.

A similar composition of expressed sap was found in leaves of East African mangrove vegetation (Walter and Steiner, 1936, p. 122ff). The osmotic potential of the sap of all investigated plant species is around −35 atm (see Fig. 35), of which the chlorides of the cell sap contribute an average of about −25 atm. The osmotic potential of the sea water (primarily caused by the NaCl content) is around −25.5 atm. In an inland

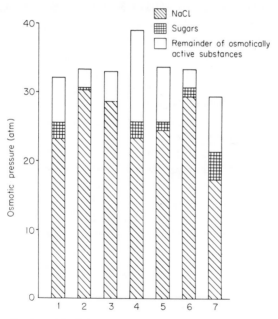

Fig. 35. Contribution of individual cell sap components to the total osmotic pressure of the press sap in east Africa mangrove plants (Walter, 1960, p. 481; Fig. 250). Height of column: Total potential osmotic pressure. ▨ NaCl, ▦ sugars, ☐ remainder of osmotically active substances. 1, *Sonneratia alba;* 2, *Rhizophora mucronata;* 3, *Ceriops tagal* (= *candolliana*); 4, *Avicennia marina;* 5, *Bruguiera gymnorrhiza;* 6, *Lumnitzera racemosa;* 7, *Xylocarpus obovatus* (from Walter 1960, p. 481, Fig. 250).

TABLE XVI

RELATIONSHIP BETWEEN NaCl CONTENT OF NUTRIENT SOLUTION
AND SALT CONTENT IN *Salicornia* PLANTS[a]

	NaCl content of nutrient solution				
	Trace	0.23%	0.47%	0.70%	0.94%
NaCl content of *Salicornia* (in % of water content)	0.33	1.41	1.74	1.63	2.30

[a] From Schratz (1936, p. 181, Table 12).

direction where the chloride content of the soil solution increases, the cell sap of the plants growing there exhibits an almost proportional increase in chlorides. Biebl and Kinzel (1965, p. 80) investigated the mangrove vegetation of Puerto Rico and found high chloride and high sodium concentrations in the leaves of *Laguncularia racemosa*.

Schratz (1936) and Pompe (1941) confirmed that most halophytes on the shores of Borkum and Wangenrooge (East Fresian Islands) and of the island Hiddensee (Baltic Sea) accumulate salt to such an extent that the cell sap concentration always remains above the soil salt concentration (Schratz, 1936, p. 175; Pompe, 1941, p. 304). *Salicornia* grown in nutrient solution ($\psi_s = -4$ atm) containing different amounts of NaCl accumulates proportionally more NaCl when grown in nutrient solutions having only traces of NaCl, than in solutions with a higher salt concentration (Table XVI, Schratz, 1936, p. 186).

A similar relationship is found for other halophytes grown in pots. However, it is difficult to determine the salt concentrations of soil accurately (Table XVII).

One group of halophytes excludes NaCl when it is present above a certain concentration in the soil, so that their cell sap salt concentration is lower than that of the soil. However, when the salt content of the soil

TABLE XVII

NaCl CONTENT OF *Plantago maritima* PLANTS (GROWN IN POTS)
AT DIFFERENT SOIL SALT LEVELS[a]

	NaCl in soil (% of soil solution at field capacity)		
	Traces	0.9	1.6
NaCl in plants (% of water content)	1.33	1.69	1.96

[a] From Schratz (1936, p. 183, Table 13).

TABLE XVIII

NaCl Content of Some Plant Species at Different NaCl Concentrations of the Soil Solution[a,b]

Plant species	NaCl in soil (%)[c]	NaCl in plant (%)[d]
Pucciniella maritima	0.32	0.79
	1.06	1.15
	1.45	1.46
	1.75	1.52
Aster tripolium	0.07	0.45
	0.60	1.19
	2.18	1.38
	2.48	1.89
Malcolmia maritima	0.20	0.37
	0.67	0.63
	1.61	0.76
	2.65	1.26
Lepidium sativum (Glycophyte)	0.07	traces
	1.20	0.90
	1.47	1.02
	2.85	1.65

[a] Plants grown in pots.
[b] After Schratz (1936, p. 183, Table 14).
[c] In % of the soil solution at field capacity.
[d] In % of water content.

is low, these plants also accumulate NaCl (Table XVIII). *Lepidium sativum,* a glycophyte, does not follow this pattern and does not accumulate any NaCl at low sodium chloride concentrations in the soil. This species takes up salt only at higher soil salt levels; however, the concentration always remains below the one from the soil salt solution (Table XVIII).

Increase in leaf NaCl concentration results in an increase in succulence (Table XIX). At the end of the growth period, when NaCl can no longer be translocated to any growing plant part, salt concentration is mainly controlled by the plant by a change in water uptake. In *Alyssum maritimum,* increased salt content leads to smaller and thicker leaves. Also the form of the plant changes from upright growth to a compressed one with the lateral branches oppressed on the soil surface. This results from the obtuse angle of insertion of lateral branches at the axis (Schratz, 1936, p. 183). *Plantago coronopus* also accumulates salts in leaves and older leaves have a higher salt content than young ones.

TABLE XIX

Degree of Succulence (in Water Content per Unit Area Leaf Surface), Salt Content (in Percent of Water Content) and Water Content (in Percent of Dry Weight) of *Alyssum maritimum* during the Main Flowering Time (A) and 4 Weeks Later at the End of the Main Flowering Time (B) in Relation to the Addition of NaCl Solutions to the Soil[a]

	Amount of NaCl added to the soil (ml)[b]			
	0	100	250	300
(A)				
Degree of succulence	1.6	1.7	2.8	3.2
Water content	856	913	966	1022
Salt content	0.37	2.00	2.01	3.00
(B)				
Degree of succulence	2.7	2.8	4.1	4.9
Water content	1360	1100	1515	1508
Salt content	0.31	1.86	2.18	2.50

[a] After Schratz (1936, p. 184, Table 15).
[b] Probably a 1 M NaCl solution was used (see Schratz 1935 p. 69).

The seasonal changes of the osmotic potential of soil and leaf press sap and the contribution of NaCl were investigated for some halophytes and glycophytes at natural habitats on the sea shore near Naples (Italy). In all species tested NaCl contributed about 50–90% of the total osmotic potential of the cell sap (Table XX). The salt concentration in the soil and in the cell sap changes seasonally. The highest uptake of NaCl into the plants occurs in spring when plants grow fastest (Önal, 1966, p. 226).

A close relationship between the degree of succulence and the chloride fraction of the osmotic potential of the leaf press sap was found in mangrove plants (Table XXI; see also Mishra 1967, p. 100; Mishra and Joshi 1966, pp. 27, 28). The degree of succulence for halophytes grown in nutrient solutions with added NaCl parallels the NaCl concentration. When KCl is added to the nutrient solution the degree of succulence is less than with NaCl. Therefore, a specific action of the cations on succulence may also be assumed (Önal, 1969b, p. 328).

Optimal NaCl concentration in the nutrient solution is for *Salicornia herbacea* 1.0%, for *Spergularia salina* 0–0.5%, and for *Suaeda maritima* and *Salsola kali* 0.5%. With higher NaCl concentrations fresh weight and dry weight decrease. Depending upon the species the shoot growth is more inhibited (*Spergularia*) or less inhibited (*Suaeda, Salsola*) than the root

TABLE XX

Osmotic Potential and NaCl Content of Cell Sap and Soil
and Their Seasonal Changes[a]

| Species | Date of test | Osmotic potential (atm) | | | | NaCl fractions: cell sap soil $= \dfrac{B}{D}$ |
| | | Cell sap | | Soil | | |
		Total (A)	NaCl fraction (B)	Total (C)	NaCl fraction (D)	
Halophytes						
Atriplex	Feb. 12	−31.9	−25.7	−13.6	−12.7	2.1
portulacoides	Apr. 19	−37.1	−29.0	−23.8	−19.0	1.5
	May 22	−41.0	−36.4	−31.4	−27.7	1.3
	Aug. 1	−69.1	−55.3	−48.8	−40.0	1.3
	Sep. 12	−66.9	−49.6	−46.2	−41.8	1.1
Salicornia	Apr. 19	−34.8	−29.4	−23.4	−17.8	1.6
fruticosa	May 22	−41.3	−31.7	−21.5	−20.6	1.5
	Aug. 1	−59.5	−49.7	−48.0	−38.0	1.3
	Sep. 12	−52.9	−49.8	−54.7	−49.2	1.0
Statice	Feb. 12	−20.8	−9.8	−4.6	−4.0	2.4
limonium	May 22	−23.4	−18.5	−12.8	−10.5	1.7
	Aug. 1	−40.1	−31.9	−40.7	−30.2	1.0
	Sep. 12	−44.4	−31.0	−41.2	−30.9	1.0
Juncus acutus	Feb. 12	−18.5	−8.7	−5.9	−4.5	1.9
	Apr. 19	−18.9	−7.9	−7.5	−5.1	1.4
	May 22	−19.4	−11.9	−11.0	−9.3	1.3
	Aug. 1	−25.4	−10.8	−22.3	−20.2	0.53
	Sep. 12	−24.7	−11.3	−19.5	−17.5	0.65
Salt tolerant glycophytes						
Inula viscosa	May 22	−12.9	−4.9	−3.2	−1.8	2.7
	Aug. 1	−18.2	−10.7	−9.4	−8.7	1.2
Plantago	Feb. 12	−13.5	−8.1	−2.1	−1.8	4.5
coronopus	Aug. 1	−19.4	−14.8	−10.1	−8.9	1.6

[a] After Önal (1966, p. 226, Table 4).

growth. Optimal NaCl concentration for root growth is also optimal for shoot growth (Önal, 1969a, p. 323).

The relationship between soil salt concentration, salt concentration of the leaf press sap, and the degree of succulence obtained from plants grown

TABLE XXI

LEAF PRESS SAP OSMOTIC POTENTIAL, ψ_s, CHLORIDE FRACTION OF ψ_s
AND LEAF THICKNESS FOR TWO MANGROVE SPECIES[a]

Species	Osmotic potential (atm)	Chloride fraction of osmotic potential		Leaf thickness (mm)
		(atm)	(% of total)	
Sonneratia				
alba	−32.6	−23.0	70	0.44
	−33.6	−29.8	89	1.10
	−35.1	−33.8	96	2.46
Rhizophora	−32.8	−22.4	68	normal
mucronata	−33.9	−31.3	92	abnormal thick

[a] After Walter and Steiner (1936, pp. 127 and 134).

experimentally was further confirmed by results with plants in natural habitats (see Önal, 1964, p. 97, 1965, p. 69; 1966, p. 227ff). For plants growing in soil the salt concentration of the soil solution in the rhizosphere is important for salt uptake of the plant (Pompe, 1941, p. 305ff). The salt content of the different soil layers often varies considerably. Often, salt accumulation occurs at the soil surface. When the surface layer is wet, water evaporates continuously and salt solution from deeper soil layers ascends. Rainfall washes the salt from the upper soil layers again downward so that the salt concentration of the lower layers increases.

In sandy soil with low field capacity, the upper layers dry out rapidly and their salt concentration increases considerably. This creates a deleterious environment for shallow rooting plant species (such as *Salicornia*, which has roots about 4–6 cm below soil surface) and probably is the reason why these plants prefer clay soil and only grow poorly or not at all on sandy soils. Species growing on sandy soil always have deep roots.

XXI. Types of Halophytes

All halophytes mentioned thus far are *hygro-halophytes*. They grow in areas with more or less (but continuously) wet salt soil with a very high water table, such as in depressions without drainage, in salt pans, and around salt lakes. Those soils are heavy, highly impermeable clay soils, often with a salt crust at the surface. When the salt concentration reaches very high values, the upper tolerance limit for salt accumulation in the cell sap may be surpassed, even in the most extreme halophytes, and the plants die. Even below this tolerance limit the plants grow poorly and exhibit a heavy red coloring, which is quite common in Chenopodiaceae.

Plants in salty soil often exhibit a yellowing of normally green parts (chlorosis) or just a lower chlorophyll content (see Shetty, 1971, p. 106 for *Acrostichum aureum*). *Clerodendrum inerme* (Verbenaceae, a shrub growing on salt soil on the edge of the mangrove vegetation at the coast of Bombay, India, and also grown as hedge plant in salt-free soils) growing in a natural habitat has succulent and chlorotic leaves which absorbed more $^{14}CO_2$ during the daytime than did the green leaves of the cultivated *Clerodendrum* plants, although the chlorophyll content of the former plants was lower. Chlorosis seems not to change the light compensation point, an index for the ability for CO_2 assimilation. The leaves of the wild *Clerodendrum* plants had a lower concentration of sugar and organic acids, but a higher concentration of amino acids than the leaves from cultivated plants from salt-free soil (Mishra, 1967, p. 143). Amino acid synthesis increases in the dark at the expense of the organic acids. For different species of marine plants the amino acid synthesis is directly related to the chloride content of the plant tissue (Joshi, 1965, p. 260). Such enhanced amino acid synthesis was also observed in the mesophytic *Bryophyllum pinnatum* grown in nutrient media containing 0.04 M NaCl (Karmarkar and Joshi, 1968, p. 43). These observations may indicate the involvement of an alternate pathway of carbohydrate metabolism in halophytes (C_4-dicarboxylic acid pathway; see Hatch, 1969).

Opposite to the hygro-halophytes are the xerohalophytes, growing on elevated locations in soils which are not continuously wet. The salt content of these soils, relative to the dry weight, may be very low, often only 0.1% or less. This low salt content causes doubt as to whether plants growing on these soils are truly halophytic plants. However, the water content in the soil often is very low also (a few percent), and this results in a rather high salt concentration of the soil solution. For instance, the *Atriplex* species in the Australian "salt bush" region have low osmotic potentials and a high chloride fraction of the leaf press sap (Walter, 1964, p. 462). Like all true halophytes, *Atriplex nummularia* and *A. vesicaria* grow better in nutrient solutions with NaCl added than in solutions without NaCl. It was also proven by Brownell and Wood (1957) that Na is an essential element for *A. vesicaria*.

Other xerohalophytes are the *Atriplex* species of the western arid regions of North America, the various Chenopodiacean shrubs and semishrubs of the Middle Asian and Central Asian deserts, the *Zygophyllum* species in these latter deserts, and in the North African and South African deserts, most of the *Mesembryanthemum* species, and others.

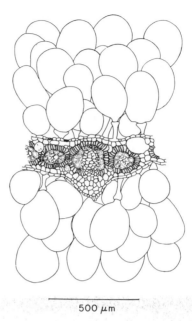

500 μm

Fig. 36. Cross section of the leaf of *Atriplex mollis* with the vesicular hairs (from Berger-Landefeldt, 1959, p. 12, Fig. 9).

Xerohalophytes have been as yet little investigated. Very low values for the osmotic potential of the leaf press sap were reported for *Atriplex* (below —100 atm, as low as —200 atm) (Walter, 1964, p. 465). However, these results are questionable. The leaf surfaces of the *Atriplex* species are densely covered with vesicular hairs having a high chloride-containing cell sap (see also Mozafar and Goodin, 1970). These hairs soon dry up and are replaced by younger hairs (Fig. 36). The salts originating from the dry dead hairs are not washed off in these dry regions and remain on the leaf surface. This salt tends to contaminate the press sap prepared from these leaves and the values obtained are consequently too high (see Berger-Landefeldt, 1959, p. 36).

Some of the xerohalophytes show little succulence. Strikingly, the expressed sap of these plants contains sulfate ions in addition to chlorides (Table XXII). Presence of sulfate ions in the cell sap distinctly decreases the degree of succulence or prevents development of succulence (see Walter, 1936, p. 182). Highly succulent halophytes have cell saps containing (aside from the considerable quantities of chlorides) only 0.3% of the cell sap salts as sulfates. Less succulent species have 3–9% sulfate and nonsucculent halophytes may have about 15–62% of their salts as sulfates. Thus, distinction has to be made between chloride halophytes and sulfate halophytes.

TABLE XXII

CHLORIDE AND SULFATE FRACTION IN THE CELL SAP (PRESS SAP) OF SOME
XERO-HALOPHYTES[a]

Plants (from the Karroo, South Africa)	Osmotic potential (atm)	Contributions to the osmotic potential	
		Chlorides (%)	Sulfates (%)
Salsola sp.	-51 to -65	23	17
Atriplex nummularia (cultivated)	-52 to -57	29	16

[a] After Walter (1939, p. 803).

The importance of concentration and composition of salts in soil in growth and structure of plants was recently emphasized by Strogonov (1964). He also mentioned the different effects of SO_4 and Cl ions. In his experiments with halophytes and crop plants Strogonov controlled the soil salt content by addition of chlorides and/or sulfates but did not determine these ions in the plant leaves. Changes in physiological and morphological parameters of the plants were determined (Table XXIII). However, there is no simple correlation between ion composition of the soil solution and ion uptake. Chloride and sulfate halophytes may grow beside

TABLE XXIII

PLANT DEVELOPMENT AND TRANSPIRATION OF *Gossypium herbaceum* IN RELATION
TO SOIL SALINITY[a,b]

Parameter	Control	Sulfate salinity	Chloride salinity
Water content (in % of fresh weight)	78.16	78.48	83.34
Fresh weight of 100 cm² leaf area (in gm)	2.08	2.53	4.00
Amount of water in 100 cm² leaf area (in gm)	1.60	1.98	3.40
Amount of dry matter in 100 cm² leaf area (in gm)	0.48	0.55	0.60
Transpiration (in gm/m²/ hour)	188.4	243.6	109.8
Transpiration (in % of water content)	120.6	135.0	35.4
Leaf area per plant in cm²	3628	2505	685
Dry matter of roots per plant (in gm)	4.34	3.22	1.46

[a] From Strogonov (1964, p. 105, Tables 40, 43, 45).
[b] The water content of the soil is 70% of field capacity; the salt content of the soil was brought to 1% of the soil dry weight.

TABLE XXIV

GROWTH OF *Salicornia herbacea* IN SALINE SOILS[a]

Parameter	Control	Sulfate salinity	Chloride salinity
Number of nodes on main stem	18.7	17.0	21.8
Fresh weight of plant (in gm)	1.33	3.19	6.36
Dry weight of plant (in gm)[b]	0.33	0.60	0.82

[a] From Strogonov (1964, p. 57, Table 23).
[b] Most probably including the salts accumulated in the plant.

each other on the same soil, since certain species take up chlorides almost exclusively, while others also absorb relatively great amounts of sulfates in addition to the chlorides. The former species are succulent, the latter xeromorphic (Walter, 1936, p. 186ff).

The increase in dry weight for 100 cm² leaf surface found in Table XXIII for plants grown in the salt-containing soil may be largely caused by salt accumulation in the leaves. Transpiration (which also decreases with higher NaCl concentrations; see Önal, 1971, p. 2) is highly reduced in the chloride soil compared to the sulfate containing soil, while the degree of succulence increases in the chloride soil. The increased succulence results in a water content per unit surface area which is greater than twice the control value, whereas in sulfate-containing soil the water content per surface unit of the (less succulent) leaf is only 24% higher than the control.

When salt mixtures (natural soils always contain mixtures of salts) with a preponderance of the sulfate ion over the chloride ion are added to the soil, the osmotic potential of the expressed leaf sap does not differ from the control ($\psi_s = -9.6$ atm), while ψ_s considerably decreases (to -13.3 atm) for plants grown in soils with preponderately chloride ions. Protoplasmic viscosity (determined as plasmolysis time) for the epidermal cells of leaves of *Gossypium herbaceum* grown in the chloride-rich soil is about nine times as high as that of the control, but in sulfate-rich soils only about four times the value of the control (Strogonov, 1964, p. 110). This viscosity change clearly indicates the impact of the Cl⁻ ion on the protoplasmic qualities: A lower degree of protoplasmic hydration results than with sulfate-rich soil. Chloride salinity of soils causes halo-succulence, sulfate salinity causes haloxeromorphism.

While growth of crop plants is greatly inhibited by soil salinity (and with chloride salinity much more than with sulfate salinity), chloride salinity of soil causes enhanced growth in *Salicornia herbacea* (Table XXIV).

TABLE XXV

GROWTH OF *Suaeda glauca* IN SALINE SOILS[a]

	Control	Sulfate salinity	Chloride salinity
Height of plant (in cm)	39.8	51.2	30.6
Number of branches	20.6	33.3	15.6
Fresh weight of plant (in gm)	8.5	22.6	10.7

[a] From Strogonov (1964, p. 59, Table 24).

In contrast to *Salicornia*, *Suaeda glauca* exhibits enhanced growth in sulfate soils, while chloride soils lead to some growth inhibition (Table XXV).

Changes in anatomy of plants (above all the increase in succulence when growing in chloride-containing soils) have been discussed frequently since the first description of Batalin (1876) and Lesage (1889) on halophyte culture. However, the reaction of the various plant species to soil salinity is not always the same. The degree of succulence in Gramineae, for instance, does not increase, and the number of stomates per square millimeter leaf surface may either decrease or increase. However, the specific effects of sulfate and chloride ions were not always considered in the earlier literature.

Leaves of *Gossypium herbaceum* have a greater surface area when grown in sulfate soil than in chloride soil, but leaf thickness is greater for plants grown in chloride soil (506 μm vs. 251 μm; control, 189 μm) (Strogonov, 1964, p. 84, Table 30, p. 252). *Hordeum vulgare* leaves from plants in sulfate soil have almost the same thickness and width as controls, whereas chloride soils produce plants with thinner leaves of reduced width. Enhancement of leaf succulence and reduction of xylem in chloride soils and xeromorphism in sulfate soil were also found in *Solanum lycopersicum* and *Vicia faba* (Strogonov, 1964, pp. 86 and 89).

Since no easy microchemical method has been hitherto available for routine determination of SO_4 ions in the leaf press sap, data are insufficient for further conclusions about sulfate concentration in the vacuole.

Strogonov's (1964, p. 57) results on growth of *Salicornia* in sulfate- and chloride-containing soils confirm the data of van Eijk (1939, see also Table 15). Analysis of cell sap of a few marsh and dune plants near Naples, Italy (Önal, 1965, p. 71) showed low sulfate content. All these plants were succulents. The degree of succulence of the mangrove *Laguncularia racemosa* is closely correlated to the Cl- content of the leaf when calculated per leaf surface unit (Biebl and Kinzel, 1965, p. 77).

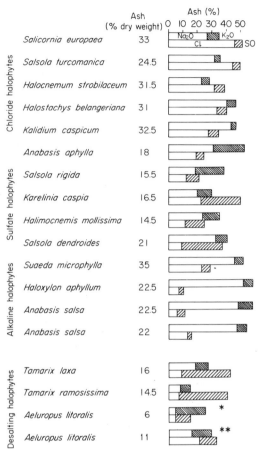

Fig. 37. Diagrammatic presentation of the salt composition in the ash of halophytes. (*) Percentage indicated based on the non-SiO₂ portion of the ash. The ash contained 65% SiO₂. (**) Percentage indicated based on the non-SiO₂ portion of the ash. The ash contained 36% SiO₂ (from Walter, 1968, p. 785; calculated, with data from Rodin, 1963, pp. 96–98, 105, 112 and 131).

Chloride and sulfate halophytes can be clearly distinguished by ash analysis as shown for species of the Central Asian Desert (see Figs. 37 and 38). Generally, ash content in halophytes is extremely high (15–30% of dry matter). Most of the salts found in the ash are present in the plant in solution. It is essential that the high ash content of dry matter be considered when quantities based on dry weight (e.g., water content) are calculated. Such figures must be based on ashfree dry matter (i.e., total dry matter minus ash), otherwise erroneous data result. For example, in a

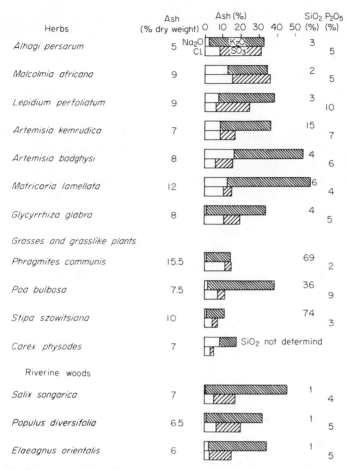

Fig. 38. Salt composition in the ash of nonhalophytic plants (glycophytes) of the Central Asian Desert (from Walter, 1968, p. 785; calculated with data from Rodin, 1963, p. 105ff).

species growing on salt-free and salt-containing soil the water content of a plant, based on total dry matter may be the same, e.g., 400% of total dry weight. When soluble salts in the plants growing on salt-free soil are assumed to be 5% of the total dry matter and in plants grown on saline soil 30%, the water content based on ash-free dry matter will be 420% (400% for 95% of total dry matter) and 570% (400% for 70% of total dry matter), respectively. Such difference in water content would indicate a strong increase in succulence for plants grown on the saline soil. If calculated on the basis of total dry matter, such difference in succulence would not be apparent (for both plant types 400% water content was assumed).

Two different types of halophytes can be clearly distinguished from Fig. 37:

1. The chloride halophytes having ash with low sulfate content which may in part originate from organic compounds.

2. The sulfate halophytes, characterized by a sulfate content which in most cases exceeds the chloride content of the ash.

The salt content is given in Figs. 37 and 38 in percent of the ash. An indication in equivalents would be more accurate; however, such recalculation would not significantly change the graphic presentation in Figs. 37 and 38. The SO_4^{2-} bars would become shorter relative to the Cl^- bars, and the K_2O bars would be shorter with regard to the Na_2O bars. The Na_2O bars remain about the same.

The graph indicates in addition a third type of halophyte: one which contains much higher equivalents of cations (Na^+ and K^+) than of inorganic anions (Cl^- and SO_4^{2-}). This group consists of plants which may be called alkaline halophytes. *Anabasis aphylla,* a chloride halophyte, could also be classified as an alkaline halophyte (Fig. 37). During ashing (but also in the normal decomposition of these halophytes in their habitat) the sodium ion combines with CO_3^{2-} (formed in the burning process of organic material) to form soda. These species, therefore, cause soda enrichment of soil. In the intact plants, the Na^+ ions are neutralized by the organic anions (often oxalic) of the cell sap. Since the content of organic anions is greater than the Na^+ content, the cell sap has a low pH.

A fourth group consists of *desalting halophytes.* These plants excrete salts (mainly NaCl) through special organs, the salt glands. Desalting halophytes contain considerably less Na^+ and Cl^- in their total dry matter than nondesalting halophytes, and are nonsucculent (Fig. 37). The only exception is *Avicennia* which has a Cl^- content of over 50% in the ash and hence some degree of leaf succulence. In the cell sap about 87% of the Cl^- ions are neutralized by Na^+ and only 5.8% by K^+ (Scholander et al., 1962, p. 723).

The expressed sap of glycophytes (nonhalophytes) has an ash content of less than 10% of the total dry matter (for grasses, the SiO_2 content is not considered here) and the ash contains much more potassium than Na^+ and Cl^- (Fig. 38).

The regulation of salt concentration of leaves of halophytes is still little understood. For halophytic land plants this concentration is related to salt concentration of soil (see p. 288ff). Some details about regulation of leaf salt concentration are known for mangrove plants. Their xylem sap was found to have a rather low salt concentration. Even in the desalting species, *Avicennia,* the NaCl concentration of xylem sap is only 0.2–0.5% and in nondesalting mangroves it is even ten times smaller (Scholander *et al.*, 1962, p. 728). This indicates that some tissue of the root acts as a semipermeable membrane which excludes most of the salt and gives passage to a very dilute salt solution only. Upward water movement in the xylem is still possible since water potential in the leaves is lower than that of seawater (Scholander, 1968, p. 260). This situation leads to high tension of the water columns in the xylem vessels. The low water potential of leaves is the result of salt accumulation in the vacuoles of mesophyll cells.

The high salt concentration in the leaves develops soon after seeds germinate. The viviparous seedlings germinating on the mother plant have a very high osmotic potential (e.g., − 13 to − 18 atm for *Rhizophora mucronata*) (Walter and Steiner, 1936, p. 168) and a low NaCl concentration. The mother plant supplies the seedlings with water by the glandular action of the cotyledonar body. As soon as the seedlings separate from the mother plant and root in the seawater-saturated mud, they accumulate salt very fast. This accumulation indicates an appreciable salt permeability of the root at this stage of development. Soon the leaves of seedlings reach the same low osmotic potential and the high chloride fraction of expressed leaf sap as the mother plants. When this stage is reached the root system becomes highly impermeable for salts, since only small quantities of salts are taken up to supplement the amount of salt needed to maintain a constant salt concentration while the total volume of the vacuome increases in the growing plant.

The nondesalting mangrove regulates the salt concentration of cell sap of leaf cells by (1) salt translocation from senescing leaves into young leaf primordia, (2) increase of leaf succulence with age of the leaf (which counteracts to some extent a too high salt concentration, since succulence involves water uptake), and (3) removal of excess salt from the plant by abscission of senescent salt-containing leaves.

The regulation of salt content in desalting halophytes can be visualized to be less complicated than in nondesalting species. The roots of desalting halophytes generally absorb more salts than the roots of the nondesalting species.

Mechanisms similar to those of the mangrove for regulation of the salt content in the plant seem to operate in the halophytes of arid zones, where desalting and nondesalting species also are found. The seeds of halophytes of different species have a low salt content (Schratz, 1936, p. 186; Joshi, 1971, p. 8) and the seedling roots take up salts for a limited time period after germination only. Later only small amounts of salts are taken up and the xylem sap has a relatively low salt concentration.

Steiner (1934, p. 185ff) distinguishes three types of halophytes with regard to regulation of their salt concentration: (1) regulation by increase of succulence and hence dilution of the salt concentration in the cell sap, (2) regulation by salt excretion in the desalting halophytes with salt glands, and (3) absence of regulation, leading to a constant but slow increase in the salt concentration during the vegetative period as in some halophytic *Juncus* species.

The preceding sections on halophytes indicate that these plants are considerably different from xerophytes in their salt relations. The xerohalophytes, which are characteristic of certain arid zones, have been little investigated. For this group the water relations as well as the salt relations are important. Little is known also about the ecophysiology of the sulfate halophytes and the alkali halophytes. Intensive research is needed in the natural habitat as well as in the laboratory to advance our very fragmentary knowledge of the relation of the halophytes to their environment and of the physiological mechanisms which regulate the increased internal salt concentration. Here also the protoplasmic basis of halophytism is eminent as a possible clue for better general understanding of salt actions on the individual cell.

ACKNOWLEDGMENTS

This work was supported by the Minnesota Agricultural Experiment Station. Scientific Journal Series, Paper No. 7332. The authors wish to thank Professor T. T. Kozlowski, University of Wisconsin, Madison, Wisconsin, for his help for review of the manuscript. For revision of English and style, thanks is given to Virginia Pedeliski, University of Minnesota.

REFERENCES

Abd El Rahman, A. A., and Batanouny, K. H. (1965). The water output of the desert vegetation in the different microhabitats of Wadi Hoff. *J. Ecol.* **53,** 139–145.

Abd El Rahman, A. A., Batanouny, K. H., and Ezzat, N. H. (1966). Water economy of barley under desert conditions. *Flora (Jena), Abt.* B **156,** 252–270.

Barrs, H. D. (1968). Determination of water deficits in plant tissues. *In* "Water Deficits and Plant Growth" (T. T. Kozlowski, ed.), Vol. 1. pp. 235–368. Academic Press, New York.

Batalin, A. (1876). Cultur der Salzpflanzen. *Gartenflora* **25,** 136–138.

Batanouny, K. H. (1963). Water economy of desert plants in Wadi Hoff. Ph.D. Thesis, Cairo University.

Bauman, L. (1957). Über die Beziehung zwischen Hydratur und Ertrag. *Ber. Deut. Bot. Ges.* **70,** 67–78.

Berger-Landefeldt, U. (1959). Beiträge zur Ökologie der Pflanzen nordafrikanischer Salzpfannen. IV. Vegetation. *Vegetatio (Haag),* **9,** 1–47.

Bernstein, L. (1963). Osmotic adjustment of plants to saline media. II. Dynamic phase. *Amer. J. Bot.* **50,** 360–370.

Bernstein, L. (1970). Calcium and salt tolerance of plants. *Science* **167**, 1387.

Bharucha, F. R. (1932). Etude écologique et phytosociologique de l'association à *Brachypodium ramosum* et *Phlomis lychnitis* des Garigues Languedociennes. *Commun. Sta. Int. Geobot. Medit. Alp.* (Montpellier) No. 18, pp. 247–379.

Biebl, R. (1962). Protoplasmatische Ökologie der Pflanzen. Wasser und Temperatur. *In* "Protoplasmatologia" (L. V. Heilbrunn and F. Weber, eds.), Vol. XII, Part 1. Springer-Verlag, Wien and New York.

Biebl, R., and Kinzel, H. (1965). Blattbau und Salzhaushalt von *Laguncularia racemosa* (L) Gaertn. f. und anderer Mangrovebäume auf Puerto Rico. *Österr. Bot. Z.* **112**, 56–93.

Birand, H. A. (1938). Untersuchungen zur Wasserökologie der Steppenpflanzen bei Ankara. *Jahrb. Wiss. Bot.* **87**, 93–172.

Boyce, S. G. (1954). The salt spray community. *Ecol. Monogr.* **24**, 29–67.

Boyer, J. S. (1965). Effects of osmotic water stress on metabolic rates of cotton plants with open stomata. *Plant Physiol.* **40**, 229–234.

Braun-Blanquet, J., and Walter, H. (1931). Zur Ökologie der Medittrranpflanzen. (Untersuchungen über den osmotischen Wert). *Jahrb. Wiss. Bot.* **74**, 697–748.

Breckle, S. W. (1966). Ökologische Untersuchungen im Korkeichenwald Kataloniens (Nordspanien). Ph.D. Thesis, University of Hohenheim, Hohenheim, Stuttgart, Germany.

Brenner, W. (1920). Über die Wirkung von Neutralsalzen auf die Säureresistenz, Permeabilität und Lebensdauer der Protoplasten. *Ber. Deut. Bot. Ges.* **38**, 277–285.

Brownell, P. F., and Wood, J. G. (1957). Sodium as an essential micronutrient element for *Atriplex vesicaria* Herward. *Nature* **179**, 635–636.

Bull, H. R. (1964). "An Introduction to Physical Biochemistry." Davis, Philadelphia, Pennsylvania.

Collis-George, W., and Sands, J. E. (1962). Comparison of the effects of physical and chemical components of soil water energy on seed germination. *Austral. J. Agr. Res.* **13**, 575–584.

Coutinho, L. M. (1964). Untersuchungen über die Lage des Lichtkompensationspunktes einiger Pflanzen zu verschiedenen Zeiten mit besonderer Berücksichtigung des "de Saussure-Effektes" bei Sukkulenten. *In* "Beiträge zur Phytologie" (K. Kreeb, ed.), pp. 101–108. Ulmer, Stuttgart.

Coutinho, L. M. (1965). Algumas informações sôbre a capacidade rítmica diária da fixacão e acumulacão de CO2 no escuro em epífitas a erbáceas terrestres de mata pluvial. *Univ. São Paulo, Fac. Fil., Ciênc. Letras, Bol. 294, Bot.* **21**, 397–408.

Coutinho, L. M. (1969). Novas observações sôbre a ocuurrência de "Efeito de de Saussure" e suas relações com a suculência, a temperatura folhear e os movimentos estomáticos. *Univ. São Paulo, Fac. Fil., Ciênc. Letras, Bol. 331, Bot.* **24**, 79–102.

Dauvillier, A. (1965). "The Photochemical Origin of Life." Academic Press, New York.

De Haan, I. (1933). Protoplasmaquellung und Wasserpermeabilität. *Rec. Trav. Bot. Néerl.* **30**, 234–335.

Drude, O. (1890). "Handbuch der Pflanzengeographie." J. Engelhorn, Stuttgart.

Gates, G. T. (1964). The effect of water stress on plant growth. *J. Austral. Inst. Agr. Sci.* **30**, 3–22.

Gutknecht, J. (1966). Sodium, potassium, and chloride transport and membrane potentials in *Valonia ventricosa*. *Biol. Bull.* **130**, 331–344.

Hamza, M. (1969). Effet d'augmentations fractionnées de la concentration du chlorure de sodium dans le milieu sur la pression osmotique interne d'une plante tolérante au sel. *C. R. Acad. Sci.* **268**, 1925–1927.

Harris, J. A. (1934). "The Physico-chemical Properties of Plant Sap in Relation to Phytogeography." Univ. of Minnesota Press, Minneapolis.

Harris, J. A., and Lawrence, J. V. (1916). The cryoscopic constants of expressed vegetable saps as related to local environmental conditions in the Arizona deserts. *Physiol. Res.* **2**, 1–49.

Hatch, M. D. (1969). Comparative energy costs in terms of ATP and NADPH$_2$ for CO_2-fixation by plants with different photosynthetic pathways. *In* "Productivity of Photosynthetic Systems, Models and Methods" (I. Šetlik, ed.), pp. 77–82. Czech. Acad. Sci., Prague.

Heimann, H. (1966). Plant growth under saline conditions and the balance of the ionic environment. *In* "Salinity and Aridity. New Approaches to Old Problems" (H. Boyko, ed.), pp. 201–213. Junk, The Hague.

Hill, T. L. (1969). A proposed common allosteric mechanism for active transport, muscle contraction, and ribosomal translocation. *Proc. Nat. Acad. Sci. U.S.* **64**, 268–274.

Hillel, D., and Tadmor, N. (1962). Water regime and vegetation in the Central Negev Highlands of Israel. *Ecology* **43**, 33–41.

Höfler, K. (1920). Ein Schema für die osmotische Leistung der Pflanzenzelle. *Ber. Deut. Bot. Ges.* **38**, 288–298.

Höfler, K. (1928). Über Kappenplasmolyse. *Ber. Deut. Bot. Ges.* **46**, (73)–(82).

Iljin, W. S. (1935). Das Absterben der Pflanzenzellen in reinen und balancierten Salzlösungen. *Protoplasma* **24**, 409–430.

Joshi, G. V. (1965). Studies in photosynthesis in marine plants of Bombay. *In* "Proceedings of the Seminar on Sea, Salt, and Plants" (V. Krishnamurthy, ed.) pp. 256–264. Central Salt and Marine Chemicals Research Institute Bhavnagar, India.

Joshi, G. V. (1971). Physiological studies in mangroves. Proceedings of the International Symposium on Physiology of Differentiation in Plants. Organized by the Indian Society for Plant Physiology (in press).

Joshi, G. V. (1973). Soil plant relationship in the plants of the saline soils of the Deccan. *In* "Symposium on Deccan Trap Country," held at the University of Poona (India), Oct. 1968.

Kaho (Kahho), H. (1923). Über die physiologische Wirkung der Neutralsalze auf das Pflanzenplasma. *Acta Univ. Dorpat. (Tartu), Ser. A.* **5**, 1–167 (= Universitatis Dorpatensis instituti botanici opera No. 18).

Karmarkar, S. M., and Joshi, G. V. (1968). Effect of sodium chloride on $^{14}CO_2$ dark fixation in *Bryophyllum pinnatum*. *Indian J. Exp. Biol.* **6**, 42–44.

Karmarkar, S. M., and Joshi, G. V. (1969). Effect of Sand Culture and Sodium Chloride on growth physical structure and organic acid metabolism in *Bryophyllum pinnatum*. *Plant Soil* **30**, 41–48.

Kausch, W. (1960). Bericht über die ökologischen Untersuchungen der Wüstenvegetation in der ägyptisch-arabischen Wüste (UNESCO document NS/914/58). 1. Fortsetzung. English translation (incomplete): Report on Ecological Studies of Egyptian Desert Plants. UNESCO/NS/AZ/565 (Paris, 9 November 1960).

Kausch, W. (1965). Beziehungen zwischen Wurzelwachstum, Transpiration und CO_2-Gaswechsel bei einigen Kakteen. *Planta* **66**, 229–238.

Kiecksee, U. (1964). "Die Eigenschaften des Lutrol als Osmotikum und das Spross-und Wurzelwachstum unter verschiedenen Hydraturverhältnissen." Exam. Paper, Universität Stuttgart-Hohenheim (unpublished).

Kluge, M., and Fischer, K. (1967). Über Zusammenhänge zwischen dem CO_2-Austausch und der Abgabe von Wasserdampf durch *Bryophyllum daigremontianum* Berg. Planta **77**, 212–223.

Knipling, E. B. (1969). The concept of water potential. *What's New in Plant Physiol.* July 1969 (G. J. Fritz, Univ. of Florida, Gainesville, ed.).

Kramer, P. J. (1969). "Plant and Soil Water Relationships. A Modern Synthesis." McGraw-Hill, New York.

Kreeb, K. (1957). Hydratur und Ertrag. *Ber. Deut. Bot. Ges.* **70**, 121–136.

Kreeb, K. (1960). Über die gravimetrische Methode zur Bestimmung der Saugspannung und das Problem des negativen Turgors. I. Mitteilung. *Planta* **55**, 274–282.

Kreeb, K. (1961). Zur Frage des negativen Turgors bei mediterranen Hartlaubpflanzen unter natürlichen Bedingungen. *Planta* **56**, 479–489.

Kreeb, K. (1963). Untersuchungen zum Wasserhaushalt der Pflanzen unter extrem ariden Bedingungen. *Planta* **59**, 442–458.

Kreeb, K. (1964). "Ökologische Grundlagen der Bewässerungskulturen in den Subtropen." Fischer, Stuttgart.

Kreeb, K., and Borchard, W. (1967). Thermodynamische Betrachtungen zum Wasserhaushalt der Pflanze. *Z. Pflanzenphysiol.* **56**, 186–202.

LaHaye, P. A., and Epstein, E. (1969). Salt toleration by plants: Enhancement with calcium. *Science* **166**, 395–396.

LaHaye, P. A., and Epstein, E. (1970). Calcium and salt tolerance of plants. *Science* **167**, 1388.

Lange, O. L., (1969). Die funktionellen Anpassungen der Flechten an die ökologischen Bedingungen arider Gebiete. *Ber. Deut. Bot. Ges.* **82**, 3–22.

Lapina, L. P. (1967). O dejstvii i posledejstvii vysokih izoosmotičeskih koncentracij NaCl i dekstrana na rastenija konskih bobov. (Effect and aftereffect of high isosomotic concentrations of NaCl and dextran on horse bean plants.) *Fiziol. Rast.* **14**, 319–327; *Sov. Plant Physiol.* **14**, 271–277.

Le Houérou, H.-N. (1959). Ecologie, phytosociologie et productivité de l'olivier en Tunisie méridionale. *Bull. Serv. Carte Phytogeogr., Sér. B.* **4**(1), 7–72.

Lesage, P. (1889). Influence du bord da la mer sur la structure des feuilles. *C. R. Acad. Sci.* **109**, 204–206.

Levitt, J. (1962). A sulfurhydryl-disulfide hypothesis for frost injury and resistance in plants. *J. Theor. Biol.* **3**, 355–391.

Levitt, J. (1969). "Introduction to Plant Physiology." Mosby. St. Louis, Missouri.

Lobov, M. F. (1951). Sootnošenija meždu rostom i koncentraciej kletočnogo soka u rastenij. (The relation between growth and cellsap concentration in plants) *Bot. Zh. (Leningrad)* **36**, 21–28.

MacRobbie, E. A. C. (1962). Ionic relations of *Nitella translucens. J. Gen. Physiol.* **45**, 861–878.

Marloth, R. (1908). Das Kapland, insonderheit das Reich der Kapflora, das Waldgebiet und die Karroo, pflanzengeographisch dargestellt. *In* "Wissenschaftliche Ergebnisse der deutschen Tiefsee-Expedition auf dem Dampfer 'Valdivia' 1898–1899" (C. Chun, ed.), Vol. 2, Part 3, pp. 1–436. Fischer, Jena.

Maximov, N. A. (1923). Physiologisch-ökologische Untersuchungen über die Dürreresistenz der Xerophyten. *Jahrb. Wiss. Bot.* **62**, 128–143.

Meyer, B. S. (1938). The water relations of plant cells. *Bot. Rev.* **4,** 531–547.

Migahid, A. M., and Abd El Rahman, A. A. (1953a). Studies in the water economy of Egyptian desert plants. I. Desert climate and its relation to vegetation. *Bull. Inst Désert d'Egypte* [=Bull. Ma'had Al-sahara Al-misriyah, Le Caire (Cairo)] **3,** 5–24.

Migahid, A. M., and Abd El Rahman, A. A. (1953b). Studies in the water economy of Egyptian desert plants. II. Soil water conditions and their relations. *Bull. Inst. Désert d'Egypte* [=Bull. Ma'had Al-sahara Al-misriyah, Le Caire (Cairo)] **3,** 25–57.

Migahid, A. M., and Abd El Rahman, A. A. (1953c). Studies in the water economy of Egyptian desert plants. III. Observation on the drought resistance of desert plants. *Bull. Inst. Désert d'Egypte* [= Bull. Ma'had Al-sahara Al-misriyah, Le Caire (Cairo)] **3,** 59–83.

Mishra, S. D. (1967). Physiological studies in Mangrove of Bombay (Studies in *Clerodendron innerme* Gaertn.) Ph.D. Thesis, Bombay University.

Mishra, S. D., and Joshi (1966). Studies in inorganic nutrition in *Clerodendron innerme* Gaertn. *Proc. 53rd Indian Sci Congress, Chandigarh 1966* Pt. IV, pp. 27–28.

Monod, T. (1954). Modes 'contracté' et 'diffus' de la végétation Saharienne. *In* "Biology of Deserts" (J. L. Cloudsley-Thompson, ed.), pp. 35–44. Institute of Biology, London.

Mozafar, A., and Goodin, J. R. (1970). Vesiculated hairs: A mechanism for salt tolerance in *Atriplex halimus* L. *Plant Physiol.* **45,** 62–65.

Mozafar, A., Goodin, J. R., and Oertli, J. J. (1970). Na and K interactions in increasing the salt tolerance of *Atriplex halimus* L. I. Yield characteristics and osmotic potential. *Agron. J.* **62,** 478–481.

Önal, M. (1962). Untersuchungen über den Wasserhaushalt einiger Kultur- und Holzpflanzen. Ph.D. Thesis, Landwirtschaftliche Hochschule (Agric. University), Hohenheim, Stuttgart, Germany.

Önal, M. (1964). Zusammensetzung des Zellsaftes einiger Salzmarschen- und Dünenpflanzen in der Umgebung Neapels. *In* "Beiträge zur Phytologie" (K. Kreeb, ed.), pp. 89–100. Ulmer, Stuttgart.

Önal, M. (1965). Beiträge zum Halophytenproblem. *Ber. Deut. Bot. Ges.* **78,** 68–72.

Önal, M. (1966). Vergleichende ökologische Untersuchungen bei Halophyten und Glycophyten in der Nähe von Neapel. *Istanbul Üniv. Fen Fak. Mecm., Ser. B* **31,** 209–248.

Önal, M. (1969a). Der Einfluss des Natriumchlorids auf das Wachstum einiger Halophyten. *Istanbul Üniv. Fen Fak. Mecm., Ser. B* **34,** 313–326.

Önal, M. (1969b). Der Einfluss steigender Natrium- und Kaliumchloridkonzentrationen auf den Sukkulenzgrad bei einigen Halophyten. *Istanbul Üniv. Fen Fak. Mecm., Ser. B* **34,** 327–337.

Önal, M. (1971). Der Einfluss steigender Natriumchlorid-Konzentrationen auf den Transpirationskoeffizient einiger Halophyten. *Istanbul Üniv. Fen Fak. Mecm., Ser. B* **36,** 1–8.

Orshan, G. (1954). Surface reduction and its significance as a hydroecological factor, *J. Ecol.* **42,** 442–444.

Parichia, P. E., and Levitt, J. (1967). Enhancement of drought tolerance by applied thiols. *Physiol. Plant* **20,** 83–89.

Parker, J. (1968). Drought-resistance mechanisms. *In* "Water Deficits and Plant Growth" (T. T. Kozlowski, ed.), Vol. 1, pp. 195–234. Academic Press, New York.

Pisek, A., and Cartillieri, E. (1932). Zur Kenntnis des Wasserhaushaltes der Pflanzen. I. Sonnenpflanzen. *Jahrb. Wiss. Bot.* **75**, 195–251.

Pompe, E. (1941). Beiträge zur Ökologie der Hiddensee Halophyten. *Beih. Bot. Zentralbl.* **60** (A), 223–326.

Prisco, J. T., and O'Leary, J. W. (1970). Osmotic and "toxic" effects of salinity on germination of *Phaseolus vulgaris* L. seeds. *Turrialba* **20**, 177–184.

Repp, G. (1958). Die Salztoleranz der Pflanzen. I. Salzhaushalt und Salzresistenz von Marschpflanzen der Nordseeküste Dänemarks in Beziehung zum Standort. *Österr. Bot. Z.* **104**, 454–490.

Rodin, L. E. (1963). "Rastitel'nost' pustyn' sapadnoi Turkmenii." Akad. Nauk SSSR, Moskva-Leningrad.

Rodin, L. E., and Bazilevič, N. I. (1965). "Dinamika organicheskogo veščhestva i biologicheskij krugovorot zol'nyh ělmentov i azota v osnovijh tipah rastitel'nosti zemnogo šara. (Dynamics of the organic matter and biological turnover of ash elements and nitrogen in the main types of the world vegetation). Izd. Nauka, Moskva-Leningrad.

Rodin, L. E., and Bazilevič, N. I. (1966). The biological productivity of the main vegetation types in the northern hemisphere of the old world. *Forest. Abstr.* **27**, 369–372 (Forestry Abstracts leading articles series No. 38).

Schimper, A. F. W. (1898). "Pflanzengeographie auf physiologischer Grundlage." Fischer, Jena.

Scholander, P. F. (1968). How mangroves desalinate sea water. *Physiol. Plant.* **21**, 251–261.

Scholander, P. F., Hammel, H. T., Hemmingsen, E., and Garey, W. (1962). Salt-balance in mangroves. *Plant Physiol.* **37**, 722–729.

Schouw, J. F. (1822). "Grundtäk til en Almindelig Plantgeografi." Paa den Gyldendalske Boghandlings Forlag, Kjöbenhaven.

Schratz, E. (1934). Beiträge zur Biologie der Halophyten. I. Zur Keimungsphysiologie. *Jahrb. Wiss. Bot.* **80**, 112–142.

Schratz, E. (1935). Beiträge zur Biologie der Halophyten. II. Untersuchungen über den Wasserhaushalt. *Jahrb. Wiss. Bot.* **81**, 59–93.

Schratz, E. (1936). Beiträge zur Biologie der Halophyten. III. Über Verteilung, Ausbildung und NaCl-Gehalt der Strandpflanzen in ihrer Abhängigkeit vom Salzgehalt des Standorts. *Jahrb. Wiss. Bot.* **83**, 133–189.

Shetty, G. P. (1971). Physiology of growth and salt tolerance of plants. Shivaji University (Kolhapur, Mharashtra, India), PhD thesis.

Simonis, W. (1948). CO_2-Assimilation und Stoffproduktion trocken gezogener Pflanzen. *Planta* **35**, 188–224.

Sitte, P. (1969). Biomembranen: Struktur und Funktion. *Ber. Deut. Bot. Ges.* **82**, 407–413.

Slatyer, R. O. (1961). Effects of several osmotic substrates on the water relationships of tomato. *Austral. J. Biol. Sci.* **14**, 519–540.

Slatyer, R. O. (1967). "Plant-Water Relationships." Academic Press, New York.

Smith, J. (1949). "Distribution of Tree Species in the Sudan in Relation to Rainfall and Soil Texture." Ministry of Agriculture, Khartoum, Sudan.

Stadelmann, Ed. (1956). Plasmolyse und Deplasmolyse. *In* "Handbuch der Pflanzenphysiologie" (W. Ruhland, ed.), Vol. 2, pp. 71–115. Springer-Verlag, Berlin.

Stadelmann, Ed. (1966). Evaluation of turgidity, plasmolysis, and deplasmolysis of plant cells. *In* "Methods in cell physiology" (D. M. Prescott, ed.), Vol. 2 pp. 143–216. Academic Press, New York.

Stadelmann, Ed. (1969). Permeability of the plant cell. *Annu. Rev. Plant Physiol.* **20,** 585–606.

Stadelmann, Ed. (1971). The protoplasmic basis for drought-resistance. *In* "Food, Fiber, and the Arid lands" (W. G. McGinnies, B. J. Goldman, and P. Paylore, eds.), pp. 337–352. Univ. of Arizona Press, Tucson.

Steiner, M. (1934). Zur Ökologie der Salzmarschen der nordöstl. Vereinigten Staaten von Nordamerika. *Jahrb. Wiss. Bot.* **81,** 94–202.

Stieglitz, H. (1936). Beiträge zur Zellsaftchemie des Winterweizens. *Z. Pflanzenernäh. Düng. Bodenk.* **43,** 152–170.

Stiles, W. (1958). Other elements. *In* "Handbuch der Pflanzenphysiologie" (W. Ruhland, ed.), Vol. 4, pp. 599–614. Springer-Verlag, Berlin and New York.

Stocker, O. (1947). Probleme der pflanzlichen Dürreresistenz. *Naturwissenschaften* **34,** 362–371.

Strogonov, B. P. (1964). "Physiological Basis of Salt Tolerance of Plants (As Affected by Various Types of Salinity)" Israel Program for Scientific Translations, Jerusalem. [Translation from B. P. Strogonov, "Fiziologicheskie osnovy soleustoichivosti rastenii (Pri raznokachestvennom zasolenii pochvy)." Iz. Akad. Nauk SSR, Moskva, 1962.]

Stuart, T. S. (1968). Revival of respiration and photosynthesis in dried leaves of *Polypodium polypodioides. Planta* **83,** 185–206.

Taylor, S. A. (1968). Terminology in plant and soil water relations. *In* "Water Deficits and Plant Growth" (T. T. Kozlowski, ed.), Vol. I, pp. 49–72. Academic Press, New York.

Taylor, S. A., and Slatyer, R. O. (1961). Proposals for a unified terminology in studies of plant-soil-water relationships. *Arid Zone Res.* **16,** 339–349.

Tchan, Y. T., and Beadle, N. C. W. (1955). Nitrogen economy in semi-arid plant communities. *Proc. Linn. Soc. N. S. W.* **80,** 97–104.

Tumanow, I. I. (1967). O Fiziologičeskom mehanizme morozostojkosti rastenij. (Physiological mechanism of frost resistance in plants.) *Fiziol. Rast.* **14,** 520–539; *Sov. Plant Physiol.* **14,** 440–445.

Ungar, I. A. (1962). Influence of salinity on seed germination in succulent halophytes. *Ecology* **43,** 763–764.

Ursprung, A. (1939). Die Messung der osmotischen Zustandsgrössen pflanzlicher Zellen und Gewebe. Die Messung des Widerstandes, den das Substrat (Boden, Lösung, Luft) dem Wasserentzug durch die Pflanze entgegensetzt. *In* "Handbuch der biologischen Arbeitsmethoden" (E. Abderhalden, ed.), Sect. XI, Vol. 4, Part 2, pp. 1109–1572. Urban & Schwarzenberg, Berlin.

Ursprung, A., and Blum, G. (1916). Zur Methode der Saugkraftmessung. *Ber. Deut. Bot. Ges.* **34,** 525–539.

van Eijk, M. (1939). Analyse der Wirkung des NaCl auf die Entwicklung, Sukkulenz und Transpiration bei *Salicornia herbacea,* sowie Untersuchungen über den Einfluss der Salzaufnahme auf die Wurzelatmung bei *Aster tripolium. Rec. Trav. Bot. Néer.* **36,** 559–657.

Vieweg, G. H., and Ziegler, H. (1969). Zur Physiologie von *Myrothamnus flabellifolia. Ber. Deut. Bot. Ges.* **82,** 29–36.

Vogel, S. (1955). Niedere Fensterpflanzen in der südafrikanischen Wüste. *Beitr. Biol. Pflanz.* **31,** 45–135.

Walter, H. (1923). Protoplasma- und Membranquellung bei Plasmolyse. Untersuchungen an *Bangia fusco-purpurea* und anderen Algen. *Jahrb. Wiss. Bot.* **62,** 145–213.

Walter, H. (1924). Plasmaquellung und Wachstum. *Z. Bot.* **16,** 353–417.

Walter, H. (1931). "Die Hydratur der Pflanze und ihre physiologisch-ökologische Bedeutung (Untersuchungen über den osmotischen Wert)." Fischer, Jena.

Walter, H. (1932). Die Wasserverhältnisse an verschiedenen Standorten in humiden und ariden Gebieten. *Beih. Bot. Zentralbl.* **49,** (Erg.-Bd) 495–514.

Walter, H. (1936). Die ökologischen Verhältnisse in der Namib-Nebelwüste (Südwestafrika). *Jahrb. Wiss. Bot.* **84,** 58–222.

Walter, H. (1939). Grasland, Savanne und Busch der ariden Teile Afrikas in ihrer ökologischen Bedingtheit. *Jahrb. Wiss. Bot.* **87,** 750–860.

Walter, H. (1955). The water economy and the hydrature of plants. *Annu. Rev. Plant Physiol.* **6,** 239–252.

* Walter, H. (1960). "Einführung in die Phytologie," Vol. III: "Grundlagen der Pflanzenverbreitung"; Part 1: "Standortslehre (analytisch-ökologische Geobotanik)." 2nd ed. Ulmer, Stuttgart.

* Walter, H. (1962). "Einführung in die Phytologie," Vol. I: "Grundlagen des Pflanzenlebens." 4th ed. Ulmer Stuttgart.

*Walter, H. (1964). "Die Vegetation der Erde in öko-physiologischer Betrachtung, 2nd ed., Vol. 1. Fischer, Jena (see English Translations Walter, 1971 and 1973).

Walter, H. (1965). Zur Klärung des spezifischen Wasserzustandes im Plasma. Teil III. Öko-physiologische Betrachtungen. *Ber. Deut. Bot. Ges.* **78,** 104–114.

Walter, H. (1968). "Die Vegetation der Erde in öko-physiologischer Betrachtung," Vol. 2. Fischer, Jena.

Walter, H. (1971). "Ecology of Tropical and Subtropical Vegetation." Oliver & Boyd, Edinburgh.

Walter, H. (1972). "Der Wasserhaushalt der Pflanzen in kausaler und kybernetischer Betrachtung. Festschr. Hundertjahrfeier Hochsch. Bodenkultur Wien, Vol. II, pp. 315–331. Cf. *Ber. Deut. Bot. Ges.* **85,** 301–313.

Walter, H. (1973a). "Vegetation of the Earth in Relation to Climate and the Eco-physiological Conditions." Springer-Verlag, New York. Science Library vol. 15.

*Walter, H. (1973b). See Walter (1964), 3rd ed.

Walter, H., and Bauer, G. (1937). Über das Einrollen der Blätter bei Farnen und Blütenpflanzen. *Flora (Jena)* **131,** 387–399.

Walter, H., and Kreeb, K. (1970). Die Hydratation und Hydratur des Protoplasmas von Pflanzen in ihrer öko-physiologischen Bedeutung. *In* "Protoplasmatologia" (L. V. Heilbrunn and F. Weber, eds.), Vol. II, Part C, No. 6. Springer-Verlag, Berlin and New York.

Walter, H., and Lieth, H. (1967). "Klimadiagramm-Weltatlas." Fischer, Jena.

Walter, H., and Stadelmann, Ed. (1968). The physiological prerequisites for the transition of autotrophic plants from water to terrestrial life. *Bioscience* **18,** 694–701.

Walter, H., and van Staden, J. (1965). Über die Jahreskurven des osmotischen Wertes bei einigen Hartlaubarten des Kaplandes. *J. South Afr. Bot.* **31,** 225–236.

Walter, H., and Steiner, M. (1936). Die Ökologie der ostafrikanischen Mangroven. *Z. Bot.* **30,** 65–193

---

* Most of the cited information was already given in the first edition or even in earlier publications of the senior author (H. W.). Because of easier bibliographic accesibility, latest edition only is here indicated.

Walter, H., and Volk, O. H. (1954). "Grundlagen der Weidewirtschaft in Südwest-afrika." Ulmer, Stuttgart.

Weatherly, P. E. (1965). The state and movement of water in the leaf. *Symp. Soc. Exp. Biol.* **19,** 157–184.

Weisser, P. (1967). Zur Kenntnis der Erdkakteen in Chile. *Ber. Deut. Bot. Ges.* **80,** 331–338.

Woodell, S. J. R., Mooney, H. A., and Hill, A. J. (1969). The behavior of *Larrea divaricata* (Creosote bush) in response to rainfall in California. *J. Ecol.* **57,** 37–44.

Ziegler, H., and Lüttge, V. (1967). Die Salzdrüsen von *Limonium vulgare.* II. Mitteilung: Die Lokalisierung des Chlorids. *Planta* **74,** 1–17.

Ziegler, H., and Viewig, G. H. (1970). Poikilohydre Pteridophyta (Farngewächse). Poikilohydre Spermatophyta (Samenpflanzen). In Walter and Kreeb (1970, pp. 88–108).

Das Laboratorium des Ökologen
ist Gottes Natur
Und sein Arbeitsfeld
die ganze Welt.

CHAPTER VI

DESERT ARTHROPODS

E. B. Edney

> *Go to the ant, thou sluggard;*
> *Consider her ways, and be wise.*
> Proverbs 7:6

I. Introduction

Most reviews of desert biology deplore the lack of knowledge about animals that live there, and the point has recently been reemphasised by Lowe (1968) in "Deserts of the World." Owing to this state of affairs, it is impossible at present to make firm statements regarding the comparative importance of different groups of animals insofar as biomass or anything else is concerned. Hopefully this situation will be relieved as a result of the current work being done by the Desert Biome Section of the International Biological Program in the United States.

Arthropods certainly figure highly in regard to the number of species concerned, and one might hazard the guess that they also contribute importantly to the total biomass. Insects, as usual, are the most conspicuous arthropods present; mites, collembolans, beetles, ants, and grasshoppers being particularly abundant, but wasps, dipterous flies, and lepidopterans may also prove to be populous once they are looked for.

Schlinger and his colleagues at Riverside have been collecting information about the occurrence of arthropods at the Deep Canyon Desert Research Center near Palm Springs in California, and this information has been stored in computer form for easy access. Examination of their records shows an impressive variety of species (1160 to May, 1970) for a region in which the annual rainfall is less than 75 mm (see Table I). Counts of species numbers for other deserts are not common, but Pierre (1958) estimates that there are 800 species of insects in the northern Sahara Desert, as many as 200 of which occur in sandy areas, and the long term intensive work of Schleeper (of Long Beach State University) and his colleagues, on invertebrates of the Nevada Test Site, will add greatly to our information about the numbers, distribution, and phenology of the arthropods of that area.

Arachnids are common enough in most deserts. The large camel spider, *Galeodes* (a solpugid) reported on by Cloudsley-Thompson (1961b) is numerous in some areas, as are several species of tarantulas and scorpions. One of the most conspicuous arachnids when it appears above ground is the giant red velvet mite, *Dinothrombium,* of which there are several species in the Old and New Worlds (Tevis and Newell, 1962). The adult mites emerge in large numbers after rain and feed voraciously on alate termites with whose emergence their own is beautifully coordinated.

Centipedes are not uncommon; even a julid millipede occurs in large numbers in the sand dunes of southern California. Most unexpected of all, perhaps, is the presence of isopod crustaceans (woodlice or sowbugs) in deserts. Several species occur in the North African, Asiatic, and New

TABLE I

DESERT ARTHROPODS[a]

Order	Families	Genera	Species
Araneae	16	25	25
Opiliones	1	1	1
Scorpiones	1	1	1
Solifugae	1	2	3
Isopoda	1	1	1
Thysanura	1	3	3
Ephemeroptera	1	1	1
Dermaptera	3	3	3
Orthoptera	7	18	18
Odonata	6	6	6
Plecoptera	2	2	2
Hemiptera	24	27	31
Homoptera	10	43	48
Thysanoptera	4	21	27
Neuroptera	7	13	32
Megaloptera	1	2	2
Trichoptera	3	4	4
Lepidoptera	22	96	118
Coleoptera	54	169	213
Hymenoptera	28	132	267
Diptera	52	226	354
Total	245	796	1160

[a] Arthropods collected by Dr. Evert Schlinger, Saul Frommer, Michael Irwin, and others in the Deep Canyon Desert Research Area, near Palm Springs, California. Only those which have been identified at least to genus are included. The information has been extracted from a computer program prepared by Peter Rauch.

World deserts (Cloudsley-Thompson, 1956, 1969; Warburg, 1965a,b,c); one of them digs vertical holes in the soil for shelter.

In view of the ubiquity of arthropods as constituents of the desert fauna, it is surprising that they have not received more attention by ecologists and physiologists. On the other hand, we do have a great deal of information concerning the physiology of arthropods in general (particularly insects), much of which is relevant to water and heat relationships. It will be the purpose of this chapter to use such knowledge in an attempt to define some of the problems which confront desert species, and to see how, given their particular organization, these animals cope with the rigorous conditions of their environment.

II. The Insect Organization

The great importance of size in matters of heat and water balance is well known. If certain assumptions are made, it can be shown that the rate at which a mammal must lose water in order to remain in thermal equilibrium is proportional to its surface area, and that the absolute amounts involved become prohibitively large in relation to the total water reserves in small animals such as kangaroo rats (Schmidt-Nielson, 1954).

For an insect to cool itself by transpiration, the penalty in terms of water loss would be even greater. The extent of this penalty can be seen in Fig. 1, where the curve shown in Schmidt-Nielsen's paper (1954) has been drawn on a logarithmic scale and extended by values calculated for large and small arthropods. It turns out that an insect such as a tsetse fly weighing 0.02 gm would have to lose more than twice its total body weight of water each hour in order to keep cool.

Calculations such as this, rough approximations as they are, serve to show that for animals the size of insects this way of coping with the high temperatures of deserts is ruled out as a long-term solution. There is an important exception, however, for although it is clearly impossible to lose

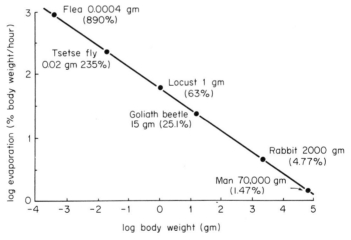

Fig. 1. To maintain a given body temperature depression below ambient, water must evaporate from an animal at a particular rate per unit surface area. In desert conditions, such a rate is tolerable for some hours by a large animal because it represents only a small percentage of total weight, but a small animal would have to lose several times its own weight of water per hour. Figures in parentheses show the amount of water, expressed as a percentage of total weight, to be evaporated each hour by animals whose weights are also shown. From Edney (1960); data in part from Schmidt-Nielsen (1954).

water at this rate for an hour, the same rate for a minute or so in emergencies is not out of the question, and as we shall see, there are several cases where evaporative cooling in arthropods has been demonstrated.

In general, however, even apart from desert environments, any small animal with pretensions to full terrestrialness must have a relatively waterproof integument, for even at low temperatures their surface-to-volume ratio is so high that evaporation of water would soon lead to desiccation.

Size, then, is one important aspect of insect organization, and this in turn implies an impermeable integument. The properties of the integument are very relevant to our present purpose and may be considered briefly before proceeding further. Information about the physical and chemical properties of arthropod cuticles in relation to function has been reviewed by Hackman (1971).

Impermeability is to a large extent conferred by a layer of orientated lipid molecules near the outer surface, as demonstrated by Beament (1945, 1958, 1961, although theoretical considerations suggest that the apical membranes of the underlying epithelial cells may be of more importance in this respect than has been recognized hitherto (Berridge, 1970). Figure 2 represents a generalized insect integument and emphasizes the superficial position and the thinness of the impermeable, waxlike lipid layer. Mechanical properties are conferred by lamellae of a chitin–protein complex in the inner or procuticle representing daily cycles of deposition, fibrils lying in one preferred position (those laid down by day) alternating with fibrils forming a helicoidal arrangement (those laid down by night) (Neville *et al.,* 1969; Neville and Luke, 1969a,b; Neville, 1970). The protein components of this complex may be tanned to produce the hard, dark material known as sclerotin. Pliability at the joints is associated with local reductions in thickness of the cuticle, leaving not much more than the epicuticle. Movement is thus permitted without sacrificing impermeability—a very good reason for having the impermeable layer near the surface.

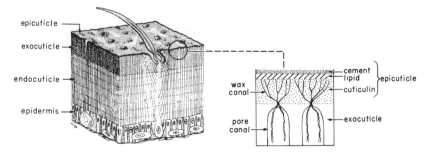

Fig. 2. A diagram of a generalized insect integument. After Wigglesworth (1965) with additions. Inset partly after Locke (1961).

Growth in insects entails periodic shedding of the integument and the development of a new one by a highly complex series of events controlled by the underlying epidermal cells. Finally, the greater part of the cuticle is in a real sense "living," since it is traversed by fine pore canals which at times, at least, contain cytoplasmic extensions of the epidermal cells, and since it forms part of the general metabolic pool, as Locke (1961, 1964) has pointed out.

The existence of an impermeable lipid layer has been demonstrated or inferred in spiders, solpugids, ticks, scorpions, and even in certain isopods.

Two other aspects of the general organization of insects concern us here: the respiratory system, because respiratory membranes are necessarily sites of water loss, and the "excretory" system insofar as this is significant in osmotic and ionic regulation. The respiratory system consists of ramifying tubules, the tracheae, which are morphologically invaginations of the integument, and like it, lined with a lipid layer. Tracheae terminate internally in still finer tubules, the tracheoles, which are morphologically intracellular. The main tracheal trunks open at the surface by segmentally arranged spiracles.

The fact that the tracheal system is internal rather than superficial is by itself of no advantage to an animal insofar as water conservation is concerned, because a reduction in the rate of diffusion of water outward occasioned by the long diffusion paths from the moist surfaces to the dry outside air involves an even greater reduction in the rate of O_2 diffusion inward. What does matter is that it is possible, with an internal system, to reduce ventilation to the necessary minimum by closing the spiracles (for further treatment, see Bursell, 1970). The extent to which loss of water from the respiratory membranes is so controlled will be considered below.

The excretory system consists of a number of blind Malpighian tubules opening proximately directly into the hindgut. Waste nitrogen is excreted mainly as uric acid which is nearly insoluble in water and therefore exerts very little osmotic pressure; it can be eliminated as a semisolid mass. Glandular areas in the rectal walls function in cooperation with the Malpighian tubules as osmotic and ionic regulators. These matters also will be considered further in the context of particular cases.

III. Water Balance

A. WATER IN THE ENVIRONMENT

Humidity may be expressed either on a relative or an absolute scale, and each form has its appropriate applications. The relationship between

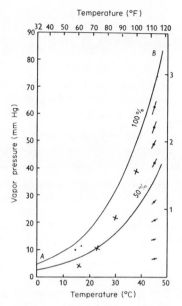

Fig. 3. The curve A–B shows the saturation vapor pressure of water in air at various temperatures. The curve for 50% relative humidity is also drawn and other relative humidities are indicated. The crosses all indicate a vapor pressure deficit of 10 mm Hg at different temperatures. From Buxton (1931). Relative humidities from 0–100% are equivalent to water activities (a_w) from 0–1.

the two may be seen from Fig. 3. Relative humidity says nothing about the amount of water vapor present—it is a ratio, expressed as a percentage, between the amount of water present and the amount that would be present if the air were saturated at the same temperature. Water vapor pressure however, is an absolute measure of the amount present, expressed as weight per unit volume or, more frequently, as the partial pressure (in mm Hg) of water vapor in air. The vapor pressure deficit measures the difference in absolute terms between the water vapor present and the amount necessary to saturate air at the same temperature. Since air may contain much more water vapor at high temperatures than at low ones, a given vapor pressure will produce different values for relative humidity as the air sample is cooled or heated.

Wharton and Devine (1968) make a plea for all parameters concerned with water concentration, such as relative humidity, vapor pressure, osmotic pressure, and other colligative properties, to be related to one, namely, water activity (a_w), and they provide a convenient table for doing so. On this notation, relative humidities of 100 to 0% would correspond

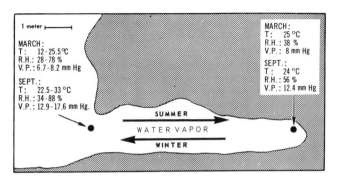

Fig. 4. Diagram of an imaginary cave to illustrate real measurements made by Williams (1954) in a cave near Cairo, Egypt. Water vapor moves into the cave during the summer and out during the winter, although the relative humidity in the cave is higher in summer than in winter. T is temperature, RH is relative humidity, and VP is vapor pressure.

with water activities of 1 to 0. The attractiveness of such a change is clear, and the present writer, as one who has been guilty of using a multiplicity of terms, commends the proposal.

Water vapor moves from a region of higher partial pressure to one of lower partial pressure (higher to lower activity), unless it is prevented from doing so, and this has some important ecological consequences. For example, if the air some distance above a lake is at 25°C and the relative humidity is 75%, it has a vapor pressure deficit of 5.9 mm Hg. But if the lake surface itself is at a temperature of 20°C or lower, then water vapor will leave the air above and condense on the lake, where the vapor pressure deficit is virtually zero, because the absolute vapor pressure at the surface is less.

In desert environments the phenomenon may be of great significance, as Williams (1924, 1954) found many years ago in the Egyptian Desert. More than 10 meters or so inside a cave, the temperature is nearly constant throughout the year, whereas the temperature outside is, of course, warmer in summer than in winter. However, the absolute water vapor pressure outside is higher in summer than it is in winter (although the relative humidity is much lower). Consequently, water vapor moves *into* the cave in summer and *out* in winter, in a direction opposite to the relative humidity fluctuations (see Fig. 4). The same thing probably applies to crevices inhabited by insects and to rodents' burrows. It helps to explain how, even when no liquid water is about, microclimates in deserts may be less harsh than would at first appear.

B. Loss of Water through the Cuticle

We have seen that the impermeability to water of an arthropod's cuticle is largely due to a layer of lipid in the epicuticle. The evidence for this is compelling and need not be restated here (Beament, 1945; Lees, 1947; Wigglesworth, 1945, 1965) (see, however p. 315 above). But the effect of temperature on transpiration must now be considered. In dry air the effect of raising the temperature is to increase the rate of transpiration, and this is due in part to the fact that the vapor pressure deficit increases at higher temperatures, so that the activity gradient across the cuticle and adjacent air is greater. However, if differences in the vapor pressure deficit are allowed for in calculating the results, transpiration still rises with temperature, showing that the cuticle does indeed become more permeable as the temperature rises. In some insects cuticle permeability appears to increase rather suddenly at a particular temperature and to go on increasing as the temperature rises further (see Fig. 5). It has been proposed that the existence of such a "transition temperature" indicates a reorientation of the lipid molecules which are responsible for the impermeability of the cuticle

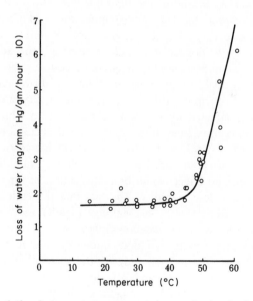

Fig. 5. The relation between temperature and transpiration in the migratory locust. Since increased vapor pressure deficits at higher temperatures have been allowed for, the curve shows the permeability of the cuticle, and this increases in the region of 48°C and continues to increase at higher temperatures. From Loveridge (1968a).

at lower temperatures (Beament, 1964 and other papers); however, the precise nature of the change in the lipid layer is by no means clear (Bursell, 1970) and the matter deserves further consideration (Hackman, 1971; Gilby, 1965 and quoted by Hackman, 1971; Edney and McFarlane, 1973).

The temperature above which permeability increases rather rapidly varies among species. In many, such as the blood-sucking bug *Rhodnius,* the mealworm *Tenebrio,* or the pupa of *Pieris,* this is well above the lethal temperature of the insect concerned (from 50° to 60°C) (Wigglesworth, 1945). In others the transition temperature is a good deal lower, about 30°C in cockroaches (Beament, 1958; Ramsay, 1935). Often the transition temperature is higher in insects with generally lower cuticular permeabilities; for example, Ahearn (1970a) found transition temperatures of 40°, 47.5°, and 50°C for the three desert tenebrionid beetles, *Eleodes armata, Cryptoglossa verrucosa,* and *Centrioptera muricata,* respectively, and the beetles stood in that order of decreasing cuticle permeability (see Table II). Again, three Saharan desert arthropods studied by Délye (1969) (*Eremiaphila,* a cockroach; *Prionotheca,* a tenebrionid beetle; and *Othoes,* a solfugid) all have low transpiration rates, and high transition temperatures insofar as the latter are determinable. But even in the very xeric firebrat *Thermobia,* the transition temperature, 28°C, is apparently below that of the insect's preference temperature (Beament *et al.,* 1964). Thus the ecological significance is not clear, although the adaptive value of the lipid-mediated impermeability itself is of course very evident.

The situation is probably more complex than the above statement suggests. For example, Loveridge (1968a) believes that in *Locusta,* permeability of the cuticle is affected by the relative humidity to which the insect is exposed. His measurements show that in dead locusts with blocked spiracles the rate of water loss through the cuticle increases from about 0.080 to 0.097 mg/gm/hour/mm Hg as the relative humidity increases from 0 to 25%. Such an effect would be highly adaptive for an arthropod exposed periodically to low humidity. The fact that the cuticle is differentially permeable in different areas, as Makings (1968) showed for Slifer's patches in the desert locust, is an added complication.

There is, in addition, great variation among species in what may be called the "basal" transpiration rate, that is the rate below the transition temperature, at about 20°–30°C, and it is clearly of importance to know whether these values are related to conditions to which the species are normally exposed. As Table II shows, in general, they are so related. Furthermore, large differences in basal rate of transpiration are often observed between different developmental stages of the same species—eggs and pupae, for example, are often much less permeable than larvae or adults, as indeed they may well be, for these inactive stages cannot replenish lost water by feeding.

The cuticle of tsetse fly pupae (*Glossina morsitans*) is 630 times less permeable to water than that of caterpillars of the swift moth *Hepialus;* the desert isopod *Hemilepistus* loses water at only one-fifth the rate of *Porcellio,* a mesic species; the cuticle of the blowfly *Calliphora* is about 10 times more permeable than that of the mealworm *Tenebrio;* and the tropical forest scorpion *Pandinus* is about 100 times more permeable than the desert form, *Androctonus.* The overall picture is clear enough. We should beware, however, of applying the relationship universally, for it does not hold at all levels. Desert scorpions, for example, lose water at something like one-quarter to one-tenth the rate for desert beetles when both are expressed as percentages of total weight per unit time (Hadley, 1970a), and when Bursell (1959b) made comparisons among species within the genus *Glossina,* no correlation appeared between resistance to desiccation and habitat in adult flies, although such correlation was strong in the case of pupae (Bursell, 1958).

It is often difficult to make valid comparisons between different arthropods in regard to water loss because workers have expressed their results in different, perhaps nonconvertible, terms. Ahearn (1970a) for example, expressed his results as percentages of original weight lost per unit time. This is certainly an ecologically significant measure, but because of the differences in size (about which no information was provided), the measure says nothing about cuticle permeability. For example, a scorpion may weigh 100 times as much as a thysanuran, and if both lose an equal percentage of their weight in unit time, the rate of loss per unit area will be five times greater in the scorpion than in the thysanuran (for further discussion, see Edney, 1971a).

Comparative rates of weight loss—largely water—by a number of species of beetles all living in the same general habitat, the Namib Desert, are shown in Table III. Here differences in rates of transpiration are adapted to the habits of the organisms, since, in general, those species which show low transpiration rates, such as *Omymacris plana,* are active by day while those showing high rates of loss, such as *Lepidochora porti,* are active by night. For comparison, two other tenebrionid species from a more mesic environment (Grahamstown in the Eastern Cape Province) are included, and they clearly lose water much more rapidly. Finally, with respect to its size, the thysanuran *Ctenolepisma pauliana* seems to be remarkably well waterproofed, and it lives in one of the driest and hottest habitats—under granite rocks in the stony desert.

It seems, then, that the arthropod integument is organized in such a way as to permit a high degree of waterproofing if necessary, and that by and

TABLE II
Arthropod Transpiration[a]

Species	Habitat	$\mu g/cm^2/$ hour/mm Hg	cm/second $\times 10^b$	Authority
Isopod crustaceans				
Porcellio scaber	hygric	110	323	Edney (1951)
Venezillio arizonicus	xeric	32	94	Warburg (1965c)
Hemilepistus reaumuri	xeric	23	68	Cloudsley-Thompson (1956)
Insects				
Agriotes larvae	hygric	600[c]	1760	Wigglesworth (1931)
Agriotes pupae	hygric	23	94	Wigglesworth (1931)
Calliphora erythrocephala	mesic	51	149	Mead-Briggs (1956)
Blatta orientalis	mesic	48	141	Mead-Briggs (1956)
Glossina palpalis adults	mesic	12	35	Mead-Briggs (1956)
Glossina morsitans adults	mesic–xeric	8	23.5	Bursell (1957a)
Glossina morsitans pupae	xeric	0.3	0.9	Bursell (1958)
Tenebrio molitor larvae	xeric	5	14.7	Mead-Briggs (1956)
Tenebrio molitor pupae	xeric	1	2.9	Holdgate and Seal (1956)
Thermobia domestica adults	xeric	15	44	Beament (1964)
Locusta adults	xeric	22	65	Loveridge (1968a)
Eleodes armata adults[d]	xeric	17.2	50.4	Ahearn and Hadley (1969)
Cryptoglossa verrucosa adults[d]	xeric	8.4	24.6	Ahearn and Hadley (1969)
Centrioptera muricata adults[d]	xeric	6.3	18.5	Ahearn (1970b)
Eremiaphila monodi	xeric	8.0	24.0	Delye (1969)
Arenivaga investigata	xeric	12.1	36.3	Edney and McFarlane (1973)

Myriapods				
Lithobius sp.	hygric	270	792	Mead-Briggs (1956)
Glomeris marginata	hygric	200	588	Edney (1951)
Arachnids				
Pandinus imperator (scorpion)	mesic	82	212	Cloudsley-Thompson (1959)
Androctonus australis (scorpion)	xeric	0.8	2.4	Cloudsley-Thompson (1956)
Leirurus quinquestriatus (scorpion)	xeric	2.1	6.2	Cloudsley-Thompson (1961a)
Hadrurus arizonensis[d] (scorpion)	xeric	2.0	5.9	Hadley (1970a)
Hadrurus hirsutus (scorpion)	xeric	25.0	74.0	Cloudsley-Thompson (1967)
Galeodes arabs (solfugid)	xeric	6.6	19.4	Cloudsley-Thompson (1961b)
Eurypelma sp. (tarantula)	xeric	10.3	31.2	Cloudsley-Thompson (1967)
Izodes ricinus (tick)	mesic	60	176	Lees (1947)
Ornithodorus moubata (tick)	xeric	4.0	12	Lees (1947)
Mastigoproctus (Uropygi)[d] (whip scorpion)	mesic	21.0	62.0	Ahearn (1970c)

[a] Transpiration in arthropods from various habitats measured in dry air at temperatures between 2° and 30°C.

[b] If the vapor pressure deficit is expressed in terms of mg/cm^3 instead of mm Hg, all units cancel out except cm/second. The reciprocal, seconds/cm, is a measure of r, the resistance of the system.

[c] This is for larvae whose integuments have been abraded by movement through soil. It is not, therefore, a measure of the permeability of the intact cuticle.

[d] Derived from figures given in terms of percentages of total weight lost, and therefore very approximate.

TABLE III

WEIGHT LOSS OF DESERT BEETLES[a]

Species	Loss of weight (as % original wet weight) in 5 days	Original weight range (gm)	Habitat	Active period (in summer months)
Onymacris plana	6.4	1.2 −0.6	Sandy plains between dunes	Day (full sun)
Onymacris rugatipennis	7.3	0.7 −0.3	Dry river bed	Morning and afternoon
Calosis amabilis	8.5	0.05 −0.02	Stony desert	Day
Ctenolepisma pauliana	10.0	0.021−0.004	Stony desert	Night
O. laeviceps	10.6	0.6 −0.3	Dunes	Morning and evening
Gyrosis moralesi	11.6	0.15 −0.06	Sandy plains between dunes	Morning and evening
Lepidochora porti	14.0	0.22 −0.12	Dune heights	Night
L. argentogrisea	15.9	0.12 −0.06	Dune heights	Night
Trigonopus capicola	21.6	0.45 −0.30	Mesic woodland (Grahamstown)	
Trigonopus sp.	25.7	0.18 −0.10	Mesic woodland (Grahamstown)	

[a] Loss of weight (largely water) by species of tenebrionid beetles (and *Ctenolepisma*, a thysanuran) from the Namib Desert and from Grahamstown, South Africa. Species active by day lose water more slowly than those active by night. Mesic species of tenebrionids lose water much more rapidly.

large this has occurred during the evolution of the most xeric groups. The converse question, why are not all arthropods' cuticles strongly water-proofed, has not so far been considered.

C. LOSS OF WATER THROUGH THE SPIRACLES

Loss of water through the cuticle can be drastically reduced, as we have seen. Loss from the respiratory membranes, however, is probably inevitable, because the surface must be kept moist to permit a sufficiently rapid diffusion inwards of O_2. Land arthropods without occlusible tracheal or similar systems would seem to be at a grave disadvantage. Isopods, for example, absorb O_2 through gill-like pleopods, and many of them use the general integument for absorption too (Edney and Spencer, 1955). Isopods from more terrestrial habitats have indeed developed tuftlike invaginations of the pleopods, the pseudotracheae, although it is difficult to see the advantage of these unless the openings are occlusible, and spiracles seem to be absent. Perhaps these crustaceans do not have a morphological or physiological basis appropriate to really dry environments, although some of them do show some degree of adaptation and a few species inhabit deserts. *Hemilepistus* has already been mentioned above; *Venezillo arizonicus* is another from Arizona in which Warburg (1965a) has found evidence suggesting a cuticular-lipid waterproofing layer. It would be interesting to know about the water loss from the respiratory system of this species.

In those arthropods with tracheal systems, stringent control over water loss by closing the spiracles has been demonstrated. It seems that the degree of control so exercised by an insect such as the tsetse fly depends upon the humidity of the surrounding air and the state of the water reserves of the insect (Bursell, 1957a, 1959a). Evidence for this is that transpiration does not increase linearly with increasing vapor pressure deficit but falls off in drier air, presumably when the spiracles begin to close. The rate also falls off with decreasing body water content even though the humidity is kept constant (Fig. 6a,b). Finally, the greater the loss of water sustained during the larval stage of the tsetse fly, the lower is the rate of loss when it becomes a pupa. Similar observations have been made by Baker and Lloyd (1970) on the boll weevil, *Anthonomus grandis*.

Locusts, too, show an ability to regulate respiratory water loss according to need. Loveridge (1968b) observed that in air containing up to 30% CO_2, the spiracles of *Locusta* opened and strong ventilatory movements of the body occurred, while in 80% CO_2, although the spiracles remained open, ventilatory movement ceased. In the latter case, the rate of water

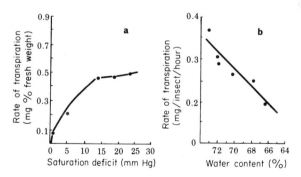

Fig. 6. (a) The rate of transpiration from tsetse flies (*Glossina morsitans*) does not increase linearly with increasing vapor pressure deficit but falls off at higher deficits. After Bursell (1964a). (b) At lower body water contents the rate of transpiration decreases, even though temperature (25°C) and humidity (dry air) are constant. After Bursell (1964a).

loss was little more than in normal air, whereas when ventilation occurred, the rate more than doubled. Furthermore, locusts preconditioned to dry air, lost far less water through the spiracles than locusts preconditioned to 96% relative humidity, when both were exposed to the same conditions—3.2 and 5.3 mg/gm/hours, respectively. At the same time the "dry" locusts ventilated less frequently, and this suggest that reduction of the extent of ventilatory movements may conserve water.

In this case and perhaps in others as well, it may be worth wondering whether the regulatory system works both ways. Perhaps the onset of vigorous respiratory movements is triggered not by the need for oxygen —indeed this seems very unlikely since the "dry" locusts did not show such movements—but rather by the need to eliminate water.

Be that as it may, some very effective mechanisms for regulating water loss are at work in insects such as tsetse flies and locusts, whose habitats are fairly xeric. On the other hand, the mealworm larva, *Tenebrio,* is said to lose water at a rate independent of its own water content (Mellanby, 1958) so that conservation mechanisms are not invariably found where they might be expected. Further information about other insects is given by Bursell (1964a, 1970).

Evidence has been obtained in recent years that some insects (usually in the pupal or other inactive stage) do not release CO_2 continuously but release it in widely separated bursts (Buck and Keister, 1955; Buck, 1958, 1962; Schneiderman and Williams, 1955). The subject has been reviewed by Miller (1964). During such cyclical CO_2 release, oxygen uptake is continuous, and it seems that during interburst periods the spiracles are left very narrowly open. This permits an inward movement of air to compensate for the reduced internal pressure which itself results from uptake of O_2 from the tracheoles. Such inward movement reduces the outward diffusion of CO_2 and forces the latter temporarily into solution in the tissues.

The importance of this phenomenon from out point of view is that outward diffusion of water vapor is also reduced, and Buck believes that the process is indeed an adaptation which enhances water conservation. The fact that it has been observed mostly in inactive insects, and that it does not occur in pupae kept in high humidity, are consistent with this interpretation, but further experimental evidence is very desirable. Perhaps Loveridge's locusts reduce water loss in a somewhat similar way. Certainly the incidence of pauses between breathing movements increased when his insects were exposed to dry air. Ahearn (1970a) believes that unidirectional airflow and discontinuous ventilation may decrease water loss in the desert beetle, *Eleodes armata,* but as he implies, the evidence is inconclusive.

No general statement can be made regarding the relative amounts of water lost from respiratory and integumental surfaces, because spiracular loss increases greatly when the animal is active and because the cuticles of different species vary greatly in permeability. In tsetse flies the total loss by transpiration rises from 0.12 mg/hour for a resting fly to 0.21 mg/hour if the fly is active for only 30% of the time, and this reflects the need to open the spiracles in order to obtain more O_2 for activity (Bursell, 1957a). Flies with blocked spiracles lose only 0.09 mg/hour; thus in this insect about 75% of water loss occurs through the cuticle, but the proportion drops to 40% as a result of partial activity. In the desert locust, *Schistocerca gregaria,* about 65% of the water loss takes place through the spiracles during flight, while in the resting insect very little indeed is so lost (Church, 1960). In flying *Locusta,* Loveridge (1968b) found that tracheal water loss was about four times greater than loss through the cuticle.

Ahearn (1969, 1970b) has made a useful analysis of the situation in three desert tenebrionids. He found that at all temperatures up to 40°C loss from the respiratory surfaces was very low, but above this temperature spiracular loss rose rapidly and reached about ⅓ of total loss, probably as a result of greater O_2 need causing the spiracles to open.

In the scorpion, *Hadrurus arizonensis,* overall water loss is low (0.028% of weight per hour at 30°C), and, as in Ahearn's beetles referred to above, Hadley (1970a) found respiratory water loss to be negligible up to 35°C and to rise steeply at higher temperatures, until at 45°C it was about five times as great as cuticular loss. Once again the great increase probably results from ventilation necessary to cope with the high O_2 needs.

Recently, in an interesting study on the whip scorpion, *Mastigoproctus giganteus,* Ahearn (1970c) found a large increase in rate of water loss at temperatures above 37.5°C, an increase which seems to result from a change in cuticle permeability, since O_2 uptake increased more regularly with temperature. *Mastigoproctus* is not a desert arthropod, but it is interesting to compare its water balance mechanisms with others that are. In fact, its water loss rate is some ten times greater than in some similarly sized desert scorpions (see Table II).

The relation between spiracular water loss and O_2 uptake is not necessarily a simple one. In tsetse flies, for example, the metabolic rate is increased 22 times during flight, but the water loss increases only six times (Bursell, 1959b). In any case, the extent of water loss incurred as a result of O_2 absorption depends upon the relative humidity of the inspired air. Furthermore, some such device as the intermittent CO_2 release described above could permit greater O_2 uptake without a concomitant increase in water loss. We shall return to this discussion in the context of metabolic water.

D. WATER LOSS IN EXCRETION AND DEFECATION

We turn now to the last of the main sources of water loss—the elimination of waste material. The products of nitrogen metabolism are eliminated mainly as uric acid by insects, as in birds and saurian reptiles, so that little or no liquid water need be involved. Arachnids mostly use the related compound guanine, with the same effect. The disadvantage of excreting nitrogen as ammonia (NH_3) is that the latter is highly toxic and usually needs much water for its elimination. Furthermore it is more wasteful of unoxidized H so that less oxidation water results. However, isopods, in spite of their terrestrial habit, eliminate much of their nitrogen as NH_3, not in solution in water, but directly as ammonia gas (W. C. Sloan, personal communication; Wieser and Schweizer, 1970), as do certain terrestrial snails (Speeg and Campbell, 1968).

The classical picture of excretion in insects was obtained by Wigglesworth (1931) for *Rhodnius* and is briefly as follows. Uric acid enters the distal part of the Malpighian tubules as the soluble potassium salt. As it moves down the tubule, CO_2 is added, the pH goes down from 7.2 to 6.3, and uric acid is precipitated out while $KHCO_3$ and H_2O are reabsorbed, either in the proximal tubule or, more usually, later in the rectum. More recent work of Berridge (1968, 1969) has shown that urine formation depends upon the active transport of potassium and an anion (phosphate or chloride), and Berridge (1967) and Berridge and Oschman (1969) have provided an attractive model for the mechanism, based on information concerning the microstructure of the tubules (see below). The Malpighian tubule–rectal gland system in insects (see Fig. 7) functions in a manner analogous to that of the vertebrate kidney nephron, achieving both osmotic and ionic regulation by selective absorption of water and of ions. Good evidence of this was found by Phillips (1964) who gave desert locusts either tap water or strong saline to drink and observed the effects on their hemolymph and rectal fluid. Ionic concentration of the hemolymph rose in the saline-fed locusts, but did not nearly reach the concentration in the water they drank. Rectal fluid showed very high concentrations in the saline-fed locusts and very low concentrations in the controls (see Table IV). Work in this field has been reviewed by Stobbart and Shaw (1964), by Phillips (1970), and by Riegel (1971). An admirably full account of the mechanisms involved, including hormonal control, is provided by Maddrell (1971).

The rate at which urine is formed in the Malpighian tubule is strongly affected by ionic concentration in the hemolymph, in particular K^+, and

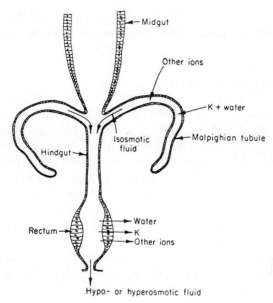

Fig. 7. Diagram of the water and salt circulation in the excretory system of an insect. From Stobbart and Shaw (1964).

by the overall osmotic concentration, at least in isolated preparations. But the tubule itself has never been shown to act as an ionic regulator (Maddrell, 1969), neither does it form hypertonic urine [except, perhaps, in the cryptonephric system of the mealworm described by Ramsay (1964),

TABLE IV

IONIC CONCENTRATIONS OF LOCUST FLUIDS[a]

	Ionic concentration (mean values in mEq/liter)		
Fluid	Na	K	Cl
Saline for drinking	300	150	450
Hemolymph			
With water to drink	108	11	115
With saline to drink	158	19	163
Rectal fluid			
With water to drink	1	22	5
With saline to drink	405	241	569

[a] If desert locusts are given strong saline to drink, ionic concentrations in their hemolymph rise, but not to the level of the saline. Ionic concentrations in their rectal fluid become higher than those in the saline. From Phillips (1964).

and referred to on p. 334]. This function is reserved for the rectum, where selective absorption, regulatory in effect, occurs. However, the tubule plays a part in overall osmotic regulation by affecting the rate of secretion, and the balance between this and the rate of reabsorption in the rectum determines the final rate of elimination.

The tsetse fly provides a good example of an insect's ability to regulate its excretory loss of water when short of this material. Flies usually feed on blood at intervals of 3 or 4 days, and since blood contains much water there is a temporary excess after feeding and this has to be voided. Bursell (1960) found that this primary excretion, which takes place during the first few hours after feeding, is adjusted in amount to the water needs of the insect. In flies whose water content is low when they feed (about 66% of the body weight) only 30% of the blood meal is excreted as water, but this increases to 50% if the fly's body water is at the satisfactory level of 73% or so (see Fig. 8).

Once the primary excretion is over, fecal material of tsetse flies is paste-like and its water content depends upon the humidity to which the fly is exposed—some 80% in high humidities, 40% in dry air. As Bursell points out, in connection with tsetse flies, the facts now available make nonsense of the naive belief that water loss is proportional to vapor pressure deficit. In tsetse flies, at least, and probably in other insects as well, the relationship between fecal water and humidity almost cancels out the effect of humidity on transpiration, and makes the whole insect virtually independent of vapor pressure deficit so far as water loss is concerned.

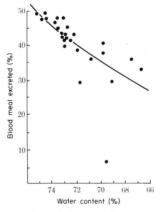

Fig. 8. Tsetse flies which already have a high body water content when they feed excrete a greater proportion of the water content of their blood meal than flies with a low initial body water content. From Bursell (1964a).

In many vertebrates the water content and volume of urine is under endocrine control, particularly by the antidiuretic hormone from the neurohypophysis of the pituitary gland. In insects too there is growing evidence of hormonal control of urine production. One of the earliest demonstrations was that of Nunez (1956) who found neuro-endocrinal control in *Anisotarsus;* but recently, particularly following the work of Maddrell (1962) and Berridge (1965, 1966), the field has been very active and, as an almost inevitable consequence, conclusions have been tentative and sometimes conflicting. Good reviews by Maddrell (1967, 1970, 1971) exist, and I shall do no more than draw attention to certain aspects of the work which are of interest in the present context.

It seems that both diuretic and antidiuretic factors exist. The former are more commonly observed, but the latter have been demonstrated in *Periplaneta* (Wall and Ralph, 1964; Wall, 1967; de Bessé and Cazal, 1968; Mills, 1967), in *Locusta* and *Gryllus* (de Bessé and Cazal, 1968), and perhaps in others. The sites of production and release of the factors are various: the protocerebrum and corpora cardiaca of the stick insect, *Carausius* (Pilcher, 1970a,b), the corpora allata in *Periplaneta* (Mills, 1967; Wall and Ralph, 1964), the mesothoracic ganglia of *Rhodnius* (Maddrell, 1964), and the terminal abdominal ganglion of *Periplaneta* (Mills and Whitehead, 1970).

Pilcher (1970a) points to a number of interesting adaptive differences between the systems in *Rhodnius* and *Carausius*. The former feeds infrequently on blood, while the stick insect feeds continually on green plant material. In *Rhodnius,* diuretic hormone is released only after a meal, and the Malpighian tubules respond fully even to a low concentration, while in *Carausius,* hormone is produced continuously in small quantities, and the tubules respond only to rather high concentrations. Rapid onset of diuresis is ensured in *Rhodnius* by release of the hormone close to the site of action by peripheral abdominal nerves (Maddrell, 1966), but in *Carausius,* where disturbance of water balance is less sudden or large, the hormone is released anteriorly, perhaps by the corpora cardiaca, and is conveyed to the tubules by hemolymph.

Mordue (1969) has used the desert locust (*Schistocerca gregaria*) to demonstrate the interesting fact that, in this insect at least, a diuretic factor from the corpora cardiaca exerts its effect in two different ways on two separate target organs: urine production by the tubules is increased, while resorption from the rectum is inhibited.

Exploration of this fast growing and fascinating field of hormonal control of water balance in arthropods is only just beginning. The processes are of the greatest significance in the lives of desert forms, and there can be little doubt that the use of desert species in further elucidation of the problems would be desirable and probably very profitable.

E. Reabsorption of Water from the Rectal Lumen

We must now consider in greater detail what is known of the mechanisms of reabsorption of water from the rectal lumen, as illustrated by work on the desert locust and other insects.

Reabsorption of water by the rectum has been elegantly demonstrated in the locust by Phillips (1964). He ligated the rectum from the more anterior hindgut and injected various solutions into it. Then by taking samples at intervals afterwards he could obtain information about the action of the rectal walls (see Fig. 9).

When he injected a solution of the sugar xylose at an osmotic concentration 40% greater than that of the hemolymph, he found that in a few hours the volume injected had been reduced by 70% and, most significantly, its osmotic pressure had risen to a value 2.3 times that of the hemolymph. Absorption of water continued against the gradient until a

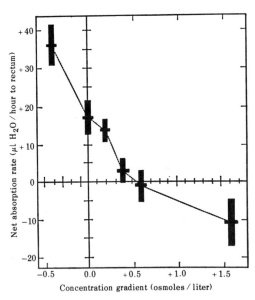

Fig. 9. The relationship between the initial osmotic pressure gradient and net rate of water movement across the rectal wall in the desert locust, *Schistocerca*. A positive sign indicates movement from the lumen outwards (ordinate), or that the rectal fluid is more concentrated than the hemolymph (abscissa). From Phillips (1964).

critical osmotic pressure difference was established. If the difference was larger still, water then moved in the opposite direction (i.e., into the lumen of the rectum). The critical difference was not constant, however, but depended upon the water reserves of the locust. Under water stress, imposed by keeping the insects at 60% relative humidity with saline water to drink, the critical osmotic pressure difference was about twice that for insects with access to tap water. Clearly, the excretory system of the desert locust is physiologically well adapted to regulate the insect's water content. We cannot legitimately claim this as an adaptation found only in desert insects, however, since Phillips found similar properties in the blowfly, *Calliphora*.

As regards the actual mechanism of water uptake, Phillips found that although a small amount of xylose was also taken up, he obtained similar results with trehalose, which is a nonpenetrating solute, so that it is not the case that water simply followed an active absorption of solute. Neither can the slight increase in hydrostatic pressure following injection account for the movement of water, for this was negligible (about 12 cm of water) compared with the large osmotic pressure difference in the opposite direction. Finally, the possibility of electro-osmosis as an explanation was ruled out since the establishment of contrary potential differences across the wall did not prevent uptake. He was left, then, with the firm impression that water itself is moved by an active process against a strong osmotic gradient.

However, recent work on the blowfly, *Calliphora* (Gupta and Berridge, 1966; Berridge and Gupta, 1967, 1968), and on the cockroach, *Periplaneta* (Oschman and Wall, 1969), suggests another mechanism which does not involve active transport of water, but only of K^+ or other ions. By means of electron microscopy, Gupta and Berridge found that within each rectal papilla in the blowfly there is a complex system of intercellular spaces and sinuses which are in connection, by means of a one-way valve, with the hemocoel, and that the walls of the cells lining this system are themselves complexly infolded to provide innumerable stacks of plasma membranes. The authors believe that the plasma membrane stacks are sites of active transport of KCl into the morphologically intercellular spaces, thus raising the osmotic pressure there and causing the withdrawal of water from the cytoplasm and ultimately from the rectal lumen. The resultant increase in volume causes a mass flow of water and solutes through the valve into the hemocoele. Energy-releasing enzyme systems exist on the intracellular surfaces of the plasma membranes, where they could well supply energy for the active transport of ions (Berridge and Gupta, 1968).

A similar mechanism, also based on the more general model proposed by Diamond and Tormey (1966), has been suggested for the transport of water and ions across the tubule wall in isosmotic proportions during the formation of urine (Berridge and Oschman, 1969).

Possibly rectal water absorption by locusts may work in a similar way, as Stobbart (1968) suggests, and Irvine and Phillips (1971) agree. Certainly the cockroach rectal pads have a microstructure that strongly suggests a function analogous to that in the blowfly, and Sauer et al. (1970), using dinitrophenol to inhibit active transport, have shown that the extent of resorption of water in vitro, at least, from the cockroach lumen is adapted to the state of the insect's water reserves. These authors also propose a mechanism for the control of water and solute transport across the wall, also based essentially on the model of Diamond and Tormey (1966).

Finally, some interesting information has recently been obtained from the adult mealworm beetle, Tenebrio molitor, bearing on the same problem. This insect and several others, notably those where water may be in short supply (Wigglesworth, 1965), possess a so-called cryptonephridial system in which the distal ends of the Malpighian tubules are closely applied to the rectal wall and held there by a firm perirectal membrane (Fig. 10). It has been thought for some time that this system might help in some way to extract water from the rectal contents, and some very illuminating work by Ramsay (1964) and by Grimstone et al. (1968) goes a long way toward explaining just how this may occur.

The rectum of Tenebrio is covered by the convoluted ends of six Malpighian tubules bound down by a double membrane which is impermeable except at a number of thin windows or leptophragmata. When the insect is in water shortage (but not otherwise) the rectal complex is set in action, perhaps by the relatively high osmotic pressure of the hemolymph (Δ 1.4°C compared with the normal Δ 0.7°C).

The tubules then actively absorb ions, but not water, from the hemolymph through the leptophragmata, thus raising the osmotic concentration in their lumina. Sodium and potassium are also taken up from the perirectal fluid. Water then moves passively from the perirectal fluid inwards to the tubules, and the osmolarity of the former rises, not as a result of an increase in electrolytes, but rather by the concentration of large molecules and of nonelectrolytes. Such a high osmolarity on the inner side of the rectal cells reduces the gradient against which they have to work in absorbing water from the rectal contents. Finally the tubular fluid which consists of water and electrolytes, and possibly the perirectal fluid, passes out of the rectal complex and becomes generally available.

The osmotic pressure in the posterior region of the tubules (where it is greatest) is as high as Δ 8°C (which is equivalent to about 2 M KCl, or a theoretical 90 atm). The efficiency of the system can be judged by the fact that the fecal pellets of Tenebrio may be produced with a water content which is in equilibrium with air at 90% relative humidity or lower;

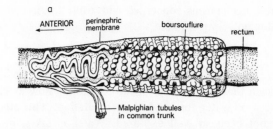

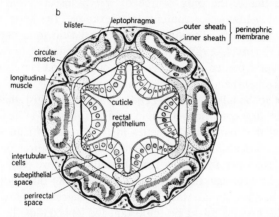

Fig. 10. (a) Diagram showing the cryptonephric system of adult *Tenebrio molitor*, the mealworm beetle. Three of the six Malpighian tubules are shown, enclosed in the perinephric membrane. The number of convolutions of the tubules and of the boursoflures has been reduced. (b) Diagram of the rectal complex as seen in a transverse section through the posterior region. From Grimstone *et al.* (1968).

indeed Grimstone *et al.* (1968) believe that the posterior part of the rectum contains air from which water vapor is absorbed by the rectal cells as water is evaporated into it from the fecal pellets. A relative humidity of 90% is theoretically equivalent to an osmotic pressure of 140 atm, so that the osmotic work of the rectal cells is indeed reduced by the presence of a perirectal fluid with an osmotic pressure of something like Δ 8°C. We shall refer to these matters again below under "water vapor absorption."

Most of the information so far available about water balance in relation to excretion has been derived from nondesert insects (*Calliphora* and *Periplaneta*) but it is very relevant to the present enquiry. Investigation of the organs and mechanisms concerned with excretion in true desert species would probably be very profitable.

F. Gain of Water by Eating and by Drinking

We have seen that a good deal of information is now available concerning the sources of water loss and their regulation. The other side of the balance has not been so well explored. Water is taken in with food by all insects, whether they feed on blood, plant juices, or "dry" material. Dry grain, for instance, usually contains about 15% water, and in some cases, where this is the only source of water, insects seem to make do with remarkably low water contents. For example, the flour moth, *Ephestia,* and the mealworm, *Tenebrio,* can both exist on food containing only 1% water (Fraenkel, 1929). The question is whether or not an insect controls its water content by eating more or less food simply for the sake of the water content, and evidence on this point is scarce.

According to Schultz (1930) *Tenebrio* larvae do just this, consuming more food in dry conditions than in moist. Buxton (1922) many years ago suggested that tenebrionid beetles in the North African Desert might feed at night on dead plant material which had a moisture content of 60% owing to hygroscopic absorption from humidities above 80%, but he does not say that he ever saw this happen. Pierre (1958) does not believe that tenebrionid beetles obtain water in this way since they are mostly carnivorous. The process might be important for lepismatids, he suggests, although the water content of the dry plant material available was only 2% after a night in summer. Taylor (1968), on the other hand, found that leaves of a desert shrub, *Disperma* sp., have a water content as high as 40% after about 8 hours in air at 85% relative humidity, and form an important source of water for oryx and Grant's gazelle in Kenya. Further observation on these points is most desirable.

Intake of liquid water directly by drinking is widespread among insects when such water is available, and here there is little doubt that the amount drunk is related to need at the time. Bees consume more water at lower humidity than at higher humidity (Altmann, 1956), and the amount they consume can be increased by exposing them to CO_2, which causes the spiracles to open and thus leads to greater water loss. It seems that blood volume is important in determining how much the blowfly, *Calliphora,* drinks (Dethier and Evans, 1961), and injection of strong (0.4 M) solutions of NaCl into the hemocoel of *Lucilia* also stimulates the drinking response (Barton-Browne, 1964).

The desert cockroach, *Arenivaga,* when in water shortage, seeks out and drinks water when this is available (Hawke and Farley, 1973).

Drinking from moist surfaces has also been observed in several arthropods. Spiders may drink against a suction pressure of as much as 600 mm Hg (Parry, 1954), and both oral and anal drinking from moist surfaces (although at very much lower suction pressures) occurs in isopods (Spencer and Edney, 1954). These animals were, in fact, able to replace all the water they lost through transpiration (and their integuments are rather permeable) by such drinking, provided that the relative humidity was at least 80%. Drinking from moist surfaces may prove to be of considerable significance, particularly for desert forms, where water in bulk is rare, and moist soil is more often available.

G. Oxidation Water

It is important to distinguish clearly between water taken in with the food and oxidation water. Oxidation of hydrogen-containing food materials necessarily leads to the production of water, and indeed this is a valuable, sometimes a sole, source of water supply. But it is not the case, as is sometimes implied, that some animals "use" oxidation water while others do not. Oxidation water simply enters the balance on the input side—whether or not this results in an overall positive or negative balance depends upon the size of all other constituents of the balance, such as loss by transpiration and excretion, which are themselves dependent to a greater or less extent on environmental conditions. The subject has been reviewed by Edney (1957).

Information concerning the amounts of oxidation water derivable from various classes of substrate is readily available (Schmidt-Nielsen, 1964), and need not be repeated here, but brief reference to two further points may be useful. First, we want to know whether insects metabolize more food material in conditions of water stress and thus derive more oxidation water than they otherwise would. The early work in this field (Buxton, 1930; Fraenkel and Blewett, 1944; Mellanby, 1932a) was held to demonstrate that this did occur. In *Tenebrio* larvae the metabolic rate was indeed higher in dry than in moist air, although such an effect was not apparent in other insects such as *Cimex* (Mellanby, 1932b, 1934).

In tsetse flies, Buxton and Lewis (1934) found an increase in metabolic rate in dry air. But as Bursell (1957b) pointed out, tsetse flies are more active in dry air than in moist air, and this, rather than an attempt to regulate the water balance, would account for the increased metabolism. In any case (and perhaps this is the main point) an increase in metabolic rate can by no means be relied upon to increase the water reserves, since more O_2 is needed and this could result in a greater loss of water from the respiratory surfaces if the spiracles have to be kept open, as Mellanby (1942) pointed out.

H. Oxidation Water and the Migration of Locusts

There is no doubt that oxidation water forms an important component of the water balance of desert arthropods as it does of desert mammals, and this has important ecological consequences. The point is well illustrated by the work of Weis-Fogh (1967) on the desert locust, *Schistocerca,* and we shall now consider this.

The ventilation rate of a resting locust is about 30 ml of air/gm/hour, but this increases to about 320 ml/gm/hour through the thorax alone when the insect flies. Most of this ventilation results from the thoracic deformation caused by flight movements.

Such a high level of ventilation leads to a high rate of water loss, and the question arises as to how a locust can remain in water balance during long migratory flights. The rate of metabolism during level flight is known. It is about 65 cal/gm/hour, and since fat is the fuel, this results in the liberation about 8.1 mg of water/gm/hour. In level flight, at an ambient temperature of 30°C in air at a relative humidity of 60%, a locust's thoracic temperature in the absence of radiation is about 36°C and it loses water at the rate of 8.0 mg/gm/hour so that it is in positive water balance.

In direct sunshine under a radiation load of 1.25 cal/cm²/minute, the insect's temperature is about 4.0°C higher than ambient, so that evaporation of water would be more rapid, and we see that whether or not it remains in water balance depends upon (1) the radiation intensity, (2) the relative humidity, and (3) the ambient temperature. Weis-Fogh (1967) has calculated a series of curves which show these relationships conveniently (see Fig. 11), and which lead to the following conclusions, among others.

Unless the relative humidity is above 90% or so, continuous flight at 30°C ambient temperature in sunlight will lead to negative water balance. On the other hand, in the absence of solar radiation, and in air at 25°C, a relative humidity of only 35% is sufficient to maintain water balance. Under true desert conditions it is, therefore, advantageous for locusts to fly high where it is cooler. After allowing for the decrease in air density and of barometric pressure at higher altitudes, Weis-Fogh (1967) concludes: "A decrease in temperature from 35°C at ground level to 23°C at 3 km altitude should permit sustained flight at 35% relative humidity even in sunshine. At ground level this amount of water corresponds to only 18% relative humidity as in a true desert. Provided that a swarm of locusts is lifted to a height of 2–3 km by means of thermal upcurrents

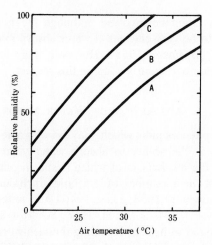

Fig. 11. The relationship between the relative humidity and air temperature at which flying desert locusts lose water by evaporation and through the spiracles at the same rate as water is produced by the combustion of fat. (A) No net radiative heating; (B) thoracic temperature increased by 2°C relative to A by net absorption of radiation; (C) increased by 4°C. For points above the curves locusts gain water, while they lose water at points below the curves. From Weis-Fogh (1967).

it should be able to cross a large desert without suffering from water shortage when on the wing."

We may end this subsection by reverting to the question as to whether insects can improve their water balance by metabolizing faster. Such a process is not impossible, for an increase in oxygen uptake need not result in a proportionate increase in water loss (see above, p. 327), but there is no general answer, and the outcome will depend upon the interaction of several factors in each case.

I. GAIN OF WATER BY CUTANEOUS ABSORPTION

The eggs of many insects, including desert and migratory locusts, are known to absorb liquid water directly from moist substrates (Popov, 1958; Shulov, 1956; Shulov and Pener, 1963), sometimes against an osmotic gradient (Matthée, 1951), perhaps mediated by specialized structures known as hydropyles (Slifer, 1938). The mechanisms associated with absorption are still being actively discussed (McFarlane, 1970; Moriarty, 1969; Browning, 1969a,b), and will not be considered further here. Quite possibly water absorption by insects' eggs will prove to be of great significance in the lives of desert species, but so far there is no information directly on this point. Post-embryonic stages are also known to absorb water cutaneously, and special structures such as the ventral tube of certain collembolans may again be involved, although the normal cuticle of the cockroach seems to be very efficient at water absorption even against steep osmotic gradients (Beament, 1965). However, there is no suggestion that desert arthropods are particularly adept in this respect.

J. Absorption of Water Vapor

An interesting phenomenon which may be of great adaptive value for desert arthropods is the ability to absorb water vapor from unsaturated air. This process, the mechanism of which is still incompletely understood, is known to occur in a number of arachnids including both ixodid and argassid ticks (Browning, 1954; Lees, 1946) and mites (Kanungo, 1965; Knulle and Wharton, 1964; Solomon, 1966; Wharton and Devine, 1968). It has also been found in insects, including the mealworm *Tenebrio molitor* (Mellanby, 1932a), fleas (Edney, 1947; Knulle, 1967), firebrats (*Thermobia*) (Beament *et al.*, 1964; Noble-Nesbitt, 1969), the related thysanuram *Ctenolepisma* (Heeg, 1967; Edney, 1971a) and the psocid *Liposcelis* (Knulle and Spadafora, 1969). In most cases the limiting humidity lies between 80 and 90%, but it may be as low as 50% in fleas and firebrats and 58% in psocids. More complete lists are given by Noble-Nesbitt (1969) and by Berridge (1970) who included equilibrium humidities.

The habitat of most of these arthropods is on the whole xeric, with little free water available, so that the process could be a useful one. It is therefore interesting to find a further insectan example from the sand dunes of a typical desert. The insect is a species of polyphagid cockroach, *Arenivaga investigata* (Friauf and Edney, 1969). It has never been found apart from sand dunes, where it seems to be associated with such plants as the creosote bush (*Larrea divaricata*) a salt bush (*Atriplex canescens*) and *Dalea fremonti*. The adult females are neotenic and wingless (Fig. 12), while the adult males are fully winged and look much like an ordinary cockroach. Very little is known about their natural history, although some aspects of their behavior have been reported by Edney *et al.* (1973). Males, females, and nymphs all live below the surface of sand, although the alate males often emerge and may be taken at lights by night. Nymphs and females wander about just below the surface at night leaving telltale ridges on the sand as they go. Occasionally a female may emerge above the surface, and Fig. 12b shows evidence of this in the form of her tracks. These insects feed on a variety of plant and animal remains which are fairly abundant in the dunes—we have never found them feeding on living plants. Scorpions have been seen feeding on them. Temperatures and humidities in the habitat of these sand roaches have now been adequately

Fig. 12. (a) Adult males (winged) and females of the desert cockroach *Arenivaga investigata,* from sand dunes in the Colorado Desert near Palm Springs, California. (b) At night adult females and nymphs wander just below the surface, leaving ridges. Occasionally they emerge and leave the tracks shown in the center of the photograph. The smaller sinusoidal ridge below is made by the larva of a therevid fly.

measured and we refer to this aspect of their ecology on p. 365, where it will be shown that even on the hottest and dryest days, equable temperatures and humidities above 80% are always available.

If partially dehydrated sand roaches are put into air with a relative humidity of 82.5% or above, nymphs and adult females but not adult males

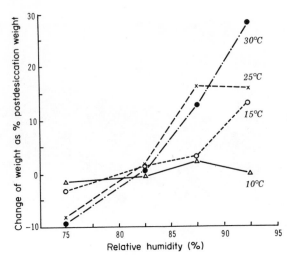

Fig. 13. At or above 82.5% relative humidity, desert cockroaches (*Arenivaga investigata*) increase in weight as a result of water vapor absorption. The rate at which this occurs is higher at higher temperatures. Below 82.5% relative humidity, weight is lost, again at a rate dependent on temperature. Each point represents the mean weight change of five or more nymphs after 7 days in the condition shown. From Edney (1966a).

increase in weight even though they are fasted, owing to absorption of water vapor which becomes part of the general metabolic pool (Edney, 1966a). Absorption continues for several days until the insects are fully hydrated and then ceases, so that it is truly regulatory in effect.

In all arthropods, in which the process has so far been studied, whether or not water uptake occurs depends upon a particular relative humidity— not upon vapor pressure, and this is also true of *Arenivaga* (see Fig. 13). Above the critical equilibrium humidity, absorption occurs faster at higher humidities, and it is also accelerated by high temperatures. Molting temporarily inhibits the process, as does even slight abrasion of the cuticle. Blocking the spiracles effectively also kills the insects, therefore we do not know for certain whether absorption occurs through the cuticle, the tracheal system, both, or elsewhere. In some ticks, Lees (1946) and Browning (1954) have evidence that the cuticle is involved. In others, as in *Dermacentor variabilis*, studied by Knulle and Devine (1972), and in most mites, such as *Acarus siro* (Knulle, 1965), tracheae are absent, so that the integument is strongly indicated as the site of water vapor uptake.

Another alternative site for uptake, the rectum, was recently suggested by Noble-Nesbitt (1970a,b), on the grounds that in the firebrat *Thermobia*, at least, uptake was inhibited by blocking the anus. This is particularly intriguing in view of the suggestion of Grimstone *et al.* (see above, p. 335) showing that in *Tenebrio* larvae the posterior part of the rectum contains feces from which water is absorbed by the rectal cells until their water activity is the same as that of air at 90% RH. However, Okasha (1971, 1972), continuing the work on *Thermobia,* believes that rehydration is a response to decreased volume of the insect, rather than to decreased proportional water content, and that anal blockage may act indirectly by interfering with the sensory nervous pathways involved rather than directly by preventing the entrance of water vapor into the rectum.

Maddrell (1971), basing his calculations on the measured rate of vapor uptake in *Thermobia* of 5 μg min^{-1}, found that the rectum of that insect would have to fill with air and empty 80 times a second—a highly unlikely process. However, he also showed that since the rectum is short and near the surface, water vapor could enter by diffusion alone at the required rate. In some preliminary experiments in my laboratory with *Arenivaga,* rectal blockage prevented uptake, but so did blockage of the mouth. The theoretical possibility of rectal uptake exists, but further experimental inquiry is needed.

Okasha's work also showed that *Thermobia* continued to take water up beyond the amount necessary to restore the normal proportion of water to dry matter, until its original wet weight was reached, and this may well be true of most arthropods that show the property of water vapor uptake.

Whether or not the mechanism that mediates sorption above a critical relative humidity also helps to reduce the rate of loss when the external humidity is below that level is an interesting question. Noble-Nesbitt (1969) has evidence suggesting that in *Thermobia* the mechanism does not restrict water loss in these conditions, since rates of transpiration indicate that the cuticle has a water activity similar to that of the hemolymph rather than one equivalent to the critical relative humidity (about 50%). The problem has also been approached by Knulle and Devine (1972) who used tritiated water to measure net exchange of water in the tick, *Dermacentor variabilis,* which takes up water from air down to an activity of 0.85 (85% relative humidity). Their results point to a net active absorption rate of 0.044 μg/hour at 92.5% RH and 25°C, and further, that active absorption occurs only at or above the equilibrium humidity—it is not a component of total water exchange below this humidity.

In *Arenivaga* almost certainly the process is adaptive. If the sand roaches are exposed to dry sand at high temperatures while feeding and this results in their losing water, they have only to move downwards to a region where the relative humidity is above 80% or so to become rehydrated.

It would be interesting to know whether other desert arthropods possess this facility. We have information about a few: *Arenivaga floridensis* behaves in a similar way, and the giant red velvet mite, *Dinothrombium*, also absorbs water vapor although extremely slowly [our results differed from those of Cloudsley-Thompson (1962b) in this respect]. The cockroaches, *Periplaneta* and *Blatta*, with which we experimented at the same time as the sand roach, do not; neither do the desert tenebrionid, *Eleodes armata*, the cricket, *Macrobaenetes* sp., nor the noctuid larva, *Copablepharon* (E. B. Edney, unpublished).

K. Osmoregulation in the Sand Roach *Arenivaga*

Having found that the sand roach gains weight in high humidities, I wanted to make sure that this was due to the absorption of water, and to find what effect, if any, it had on the hemolymph concentration. Fortunately *Arenivaga* is a fairly large insect—adult females weigh up to 800 mg—so that sampling and analyzing the blood of single individuals is possible. Most of the other arthropods which are known to absorb water vapor are so small that experimentation on individual animals is technically unattractive.

A population of nymphs was divided into three similar groups, so that total water content, dry matter, and hemolymph concentrations could be measured at three points in a dehydration–rehydration cycle. The overall picture is shown in Fig. 14. Before dehydration the "normal" insects had a mean water content of 67.2% of their total wet weight and a hemolymph osmotic pressure of 433 milliosmoles/liter (which is equivalent to a sodium chloride solution of about 1.3%). Four days later, after dehydration in dry air at 25°C, the second group had lost 26.2% of their original weight, of which 4.5% was accounted for by fecal pellets (the third group behaved very similarly). Their absolute water content had fallen to 48.2% of the original wet weight but, since the dry weight had also decreased, their water content worked out at 65.1% of their own wet weight.

At this stage hemolymph osmotic pressure was 452 milliosmoles/liter—a rise, but nothing like the rise (to 616 milliosmoles/liter) which would be expected from the amount of water lost, so that regulation was evident, perhaps by the removal of solutes from the hemolymph or by the addition of water to it from the tissues. The third group of nymphs, after precisely similar dehydration, was transferred to 95% relative humidity for an additional 7 days, during which time they increased in weight from 73.8% of original to 91.9%, while their dry material had decreased by an additional 2.3%. The difference was accounted for by an absolute increase in water content of 15.7%. The mean hemolymph concentration had fallen

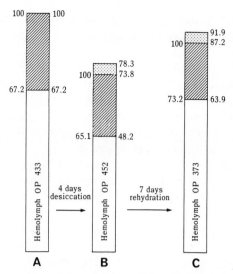

Fig. 14. Analysis of the water content (blank areas) and hemolymph osmotic pressure (OP) in *Arenivaga* nymphs (A) before dehydration, (B) after dehydration, and (C) after rehydration. Numbers to the right of each column are arbitrary weight units, those to the left are percentages of total wet weight at the times concerned. During rehydration there is a net movement of water from the air into the insects. From Edney (1966a).

to 373 milliosmoles—a large drop in concentration, but again not as far as the expected 342 millliosmoles/liter, so that regulation was again evident.

How much of the additional water found was the result of oxidation of food materials? The respiratory quotient (RQ) proved to be fairly constant among individuals at about 0.92, so that mostly carbohydrates were being used. A loss of 2.3 mg of dry weight would provide perhaps as much as 2.0 mg of water by oxidation, so that the remaining 13.7 mg of water gained must have come from the atmosphere.

More recently the effects of dehydration on hemolymph volume have been measured (Edney, 1968). This work showed that dehydration leading to a total water loss of 15.1% (from 68.3 to 53.2%) of the original total weight also produced a drop in the hemolymph volume from 18.7 to 15.2 μl per 100 mg of the original weight, so that water was lost from the hemolymph and tissues to about the same proportional extent. However, the osmotic pressure of the hemolymph, at least, is regulated against water loss as we have seen, and this seems to suggest a removal of osmotically active substances from the hemolymph. In the desert locust, *Schistocerca,* Lee (1961) observed a net movement of water from the hemolymph to the tissues as dehydration proceeded, but I was not able to see this in *Arenivaga* until dehydration was far advanced.

Djajakusumah and Miles (1966) found a similar effect to that in *Arenivaga* in the Australian locust, *Chortoicetes terminifera,* where the hemolymph osmotic pressure (OP) remained nearly constant in the face of volume changes of 25% or more after dehydration and rehydration. In these insects there were concomitant changes of amino acids into soluble proteins and vice versa; changes which would contribute to, but not account fully for, the osmoregulation observed.

Earlier work on *Periplaneta* by Munson and Yeager (1949), by Wharton *et al.* (1965), and by Yeager and Muson (1950) suggests that both water and ions may be moved between tissues and hemolymph under water stress, and Wall (1970) not only confirmed and extended my own observations on *Periplaneta,* finding a similar osmoregulatory ability, but also calculated the extent of solute movement between hemolymph and tissues. However, the mechanism of this process, and indeed the advantage of maintaining the hemolymph OP constant at the expense of transferring salts to the tissues (if this is what happens) are still somewhat obscure.

L. THE ENERGETICS OF WATER VAPOR ABSORPTION

The ability to absorb water vapor is indeed remarkable, particularly in view of the steep osmotic gradient against which it occurs. If we express the concentrations concerned in terms of osmotic pressures, the difference between the water activity of the sand roach hemolymph and that of air at 82.5% relative humidity is 258 atm. We can calculate the amount of energy involved in moving water against this gradient from the relation $\Delta G = -nRT \ln (a_2/a_1)$, where ΔG is the Gibbs' free energy change, n the moles of water involved, R the gas constant, T the absolute temperature, and a_1 and a_2 the activities in the initial and final states, respectively. The most rapid rate of absorption thus far found in a sand roach was 6 mg in a day from air at 90.0% relative humidity by a nymph weighing 100 mg. Concentration of water through the required gradient takes about 3.10 cal/gm, so the insect expended 0.0186 cal in a day in absorbing 6 mg of water. Now such an insect's O_2 uptake is about 22 μl/hour, which is equivalent to 2.6 cal/day, so that even if we allow for thermodynamic inefficiency in the system, the extra energy involved in the absorption of water vapor is very small compared with the energy resources of the insect. Lees (1948), Kanungo (1965), and Ramsay (1964) came to essentially similar conclusions for the ticks, mites, and mealworm beetles, respectively, with which they worked.

Wharton and Devine (1968), using tritiated water, measured the rate of exchange of water between a mite and the surrounding air, and calculated rate constants for transpiration and absorption. They conclude that a hypothetical cyclical pump moving water against the known gradient, would have to pump only 0.0001 μg of water once a second. Maddrell, (1971), using Noble-Nesbitt's (1969) data for *Thermobia,* concluded that even if the process were only 10% efficient the energy involved would be much less (per unit body weight) than that used by a flying insect; although, if all the energy were used in the rectum, that tissue would have to be one of the most active known in any animal.

To show that little energy is involved by no means explains the mechanism of course, and this is still essentially a mystery. Up to this point there have been two main suggestions regarding mechanisms, one by Beament (1964, 1965), the other by Locke (1964, 1965). Beament's proposal involves the cyclical exposure of polar groups on protein molecules which would strongly attract water, coupled with a rectifying mechanism provided by the epicuticular lipid molecules. Locke's involves the depolymerization of glycoprotein molecules to produce locally low water activities (high osmotic pressure). Both proposals have in common the generation of water activity in the cuticle that is low enough to produce an inward movement of water from the outside air. This is not the place to consider what is essentially a biophysical problem in further detail. The mechanisms are well discussed by Berridge (1970) and by Maddrell (1970).

IV. Tolerance of Water Depletion and of High Temperatures

For all arthropods, and for desert ones particularly, it would clearly be advantageous to be able to withstand considerable loss of water and to tolerate high temperatures. So far as water is concerned, the "normal" content varies greatly among species, from over 90% of the total body weight in soft-bodied caterpillars to less than 50% in highly sclerotized beetles. Such figures are often imprecise since the amount of fat present, and the gut contents, may seriously affect the measurements. A figure generally acceptable for the majority of insects would be about 75% (Bursell, 1964a) and this may be reduced by transpiration to about 60% without lethal effects. Values in this vicinity, based on fat-free weights, have been found for tsetse flies (Bursell, 1959a).

In the desert sand roach, *Arenivaga,* the normal water content is about 67%, and the insects can generally survive a loss of water by transpiration equal to 30% of their wet weight during 1 week. Allowing for oxidation water produced during this time, the final water content would be about 60%. It has been reported that the desert grasshopper, *Poecilocerus hiero-*

glyphicus, not only lives longer in dry air, but tolerates a greater degree of dehydration than does the more mesic grasshopper, *Anacridium melano-rhodon*. The former withstood dehydration for 18 days and lost 35% of its original weight, while the latter died after losing 26% in 11 days (Abushama, 1968, 1970). But this is an isolated instance, and there is, in fact, insufficient evidence to say whether or not desert species are able to tolerate greater water loss or lower water contents than others. However, the known tolerances are much greater than that of man, where a loss of 10–12% renders subsequent recovery doubtful, and at least equal to that of the renowned camel (Schmidt-Nielsen, 1964). But the reason why some arthropods survive in dry conditions longer than others is much more likely to be found in their greater efficiency with respect to water conservation.

Turning now to temperature tolerances, we find an almost equally unsatisfactory situation; not on account of a lack of statements about lethal temperatures, but because the information has been obtained in so many different ways as to make comparisons almost pointless. Duration of exposure obviously affects the lethal level, so does the rate at which the rise in temperature is imposed. Humidity affects the lethal temperature (although probably only if this is measured as an ambient temperature), so does previous acclimation (for a review of these matters, see Bursell, 1964b, 1970).

It may very well be true that by and large arthropods subject to high temperatures in their natural habitats have higher lethal temperatures than others. Examples can be chosen to illustrate this point—thus the mole cricket, *Gryllotalpa*, is normally active between $-2.5°$ and $+11.5°C$ and is killed if the temperature is raised to $20.5°C$, while the firebrat, *Thermobia*, a favorite habitat of which is bakers' hobs, is active between $12°$ and $50°C$ and dies at $51.3°C$ (Edwards and Nutting, 1950). It would be rash to say, however, that the relationship has been generally established. In most insects the upper limit lies somewhere between $40°$ and $50°C$. Cloudsley-Thompson (1962a) found some desert arthropods to have the following lethal temperatures for 24 hours exposures at 10% relative humidity: the scorpion, *Leiurus,* at $47°C$; the camel spider, *Galeodes* at $50°C$; and the beetles, *Pimelia grandis* and *Ocnera hispida,* at $43°$ and $45°C$, respectively. Hafez and Makky (1959) found the tenebriond beetle, *Adesmia,* to be able to withstand slowly rising soil temperatures up to $53°C$, and Berry and Cloudsley-Thompson (1960) recorded the presence of one grasshopper while the surface temperature in the Red Sea Hills was $83.5°C$, (but we do not know the temperature of the insects themselves). The desert beetle, *Centrioptera muricata,* lives for nearly 30 minutes at $50°C$ in nearly dry air (Ahearn, 1970a).

Desert sand roaches, *Arenivaga investigata,* have an upper lethal temperature of about 48.5°C in dry air and about 46.5°C in moist air (for 30 minutes exposures), unless they have been acclimated to lower temperatures, when the figures are 47.5° and 45.5°C, respectively (E. B. Edney, unpublished). These figures are slightly higher than those for the domestic cockroach, *Periplaneta americana.* At the lower end of the range, cold-acclimated *arenivage* can withstand 1°C for 5 minutes, while warm-acclimated ones go into a cold coma even at 4°C. Once again *Periplaneta* is rather less hardy, so that it looks as if *Arenivaga* has both a higher and a lower temperature tolerance than *Periplaneta.*

I have recently measured the upper lethal temperatures of some tenebrionid beetles that live in the Namib Desert of southwest Africa and of others that live in the moister surroundings of the Eastern Cape Province (Edney, 1971b). The highest temperature tolerable for 30 minutes in saturated air was 51°C for *Onymacris plana,* a large beetle of the sand dunes which is active by day. Other species, such as *O. rugatipennis* and *O. laeviceps,* which seek cover earlier in the forenoon and emerge later in the afternoon, were not quite so hardy, surviving at 49°–50°C, while the more mesic species, *Trigonopus capicola* and another *Trigonopus* species, died at 45°C.

There has been some useful recent work on the determination of body temperatures in the field, and this is discussed in Section V. Here we note the general point that even for small animals, body temperature may be significantly different from either air or soil temperature in the vicinity, and a better understanding of the heat relationships of desert arthropods will be achieved only when we know a good deal more about actual body temperatures in relation to desert conditions.

A few examples of extremely high temperature tolerances during cryptobiosis have been established. Larvae of the chironomid midge, *Polypedilum vanderplanki,* live in rock pools which periodically dry up. The larvae then suffer almost complete dehydration, and in this condition can withstand 102°C for 1 minute or so, after which, upon rehydration, they pupate successfully (Hinton, 1960). This is certainly an outstanding example of adaptation to a desert environment, even though the animal can hardly be said to be alive at the time of maximum stress.

V. Body Temperature in the Field

A. GENERAL CONSIDERATIONS

The manner in which body temperature is determined by environmental factors is very complex. The factors involved, including solar radiation (direct and reflected), long-wave radiation, reflectivity of the animal's surface, temperature, humidity and velocity of the air, and size and configuration of the animal's surface, to mention the most important ones, are sometimes extremely difficult to measure accurately, and in any case may vary from one minute to the next. It would therefore seem to be a waste of time to try to deduce an animal's temperature from a knowledge of the value of each of the parameters concerned, even though usable equations are now available (Gates, 1962; Porter and Gates, 1969). On the other hand, as Stower and Griffiths (1966) point out, it is desirable to construct thermal balance sheets if only as a check to one's hypotheses. For example, if we wish to know whether or not evaporation of water from a particular arthropod is of significance in determining its body temperature, we can get a lead by checking the relative importance of evaporation in a heat balance sheet. For a review of the earlier work in this field, see Gunn (1942) and Edney (1957).

In fact, the relative significance of each component varies greatly in different circumstances. The contribution of metabolic heat in arthropods is often negligible. However, if all other sources of energy flow are small, as in an insect resting in the shade, or if the insect has a well-insulated integument such as the furry covering of some moths and bees (Adams and Heath, 1964a; Church, 1960), metabolic heat production may be very significant. In a large hawk moth during flight, a thoracic temperature excess (above ambient) of 8°C has been measured and ascribed to metabolic heat (see also below p. 352 for further measurements in *Manduca*), and even in locusts the temperature excess during flight may amount to 7.1°C or more (Church, 1960; Weis-Fogh, 1967).

In direct solar radiation, metabolism and evaporation are, in insects, relatively unimportant (Parry, 1951) and most of the heat loss occurs by convection. Another factor of importance in direct sunlight is size. Larger insects attain a higher temperature than smaller ones, and Digby (1955) found experimentally that the temperature excess of locust-shaped insects varies with the 0.4 power of the linear size, while for insects shaped like bees or flies, the excess varies directly with linear size. Orientation to the sun's rays may also affect temperature, as Fraenkel (1929), Kennedy (1939), and more recently Stower and Griffiths (1966) have found for locusts, and as I have observed in the tenebrionids, *Onymacris rugatipennis* and *O. brinki* (Edney, 1971b). Air movement, by affecting the convection component, is usually of major importance.

B. BODY TEMPERATURE AND THERMAL BALANCE

A good example of the modern approach is to be found in Stower and Griffiths' (1966) work with the desert locust, *Schistocerca*. Using thermocouples inserted directly into the thoracic musculature, they measured body temperatures in a variety of situations. In an environment where air movement and direct solar radiation were both very low they found that large hoppers (nymphs) had temperatures up to 3°C higher than ambient if the latter was about 22°C, but the excess decreased with rising ambient temperature to 31°C, above which there was actually a body temperature depression of a few degrees. The reason for these differences is not clear— perhaps metabolism is involved, but the temperature depression effect suggests evaporative cooling. However, in direct sunlight there was no difference between temperature excess in different humidities.

When exposed to solar radiation, temperature excesses were larger (up to 8°C) in large hoppers than in small ones (2.5°C), and the latter were established more quickly (1 minute compared with 15 minutes), as would be expected on physical grounds. Stower and Griffiths found ambient air temperature to be the most important of all factors in determining a resting locust's temperature. Attitude to the sun's rays was very important, and produced temperature differences up to 6°C in hoppers. The question of surface color will be considered below.

These conclusions were, in general, borne out by thermal energy balance sheets based on measurement of radiation and other factors, and not involving too many assumptions. For example, for a particular set of circumstances: air temperature 24°C, relative humidity 65%, orientation at right angles to the sun's rays, net radiation load 0.7 cal/cm²/minute, air movement parallel to the insect's long axis 50 cm/second, the thermal balance of a hopper was calculated to be as follows (in summary form).

	(cal/hopper/minute)
Net radiation load	+0.9874
Metabolism	+0.0900
Total input	+1.0774
Convection (external)	−1.0206
Convection (internal through tracheae)	−0.0004
Evaporation (cuticular)	−0.0484
Evaporation (tracheal)	−0.0030
Total output	−1.0724

To achieve this balance, a temperature excess of 5.0°C is theoretically necessary, and the mean of several observed temperature excesses was within 0.2°C of this figure.

Hadley (1970b) has recently made a useful enquiry into the temperature relationships of a beetle, *Eleodes armata,* and a scorpion, *Hadrurus arizonensis,* in the Sonoran Desert of Arizona. By attaching thermocouples to scorpions, and thus having the sensors carried down burrows, he obtained information about the temperatures experienced by the scorpions. During the day, when soil surface temperatures were as high as 65°C, a scorpion at −20 cm below the soil was at 34°C, and conversely, during the night, subterranean burrows provided a warm shelter. One scorpion, coming to the surface from −20 cm below, at 2 P.M., experienced a drop in body temperature from 33° to 21°C.

On one day, *Eleodes* beetles had a body temperatue of 42°C while the air was at 32°C and the ground was 42°C. Assuming a value of 63% for surface reflectivity of the beetle, Hadley calculated a heat balance which read as follows, in cal cm^{-2} min^{-1}: radiation (0.141) + metabolism (0.003) + conduction (?) = convection (0.134) + evaporation (0.008).

Clearly the roles of evaporative heat loss and of metabolism were minor in these circumstances, and this seems to be the general rule for many insects and other arthropods. In flying locusts, for example, the thoracic temperature in dry air is but 1°C below that in moist air where transpiration is prevented (Church, 1960), and a further instance is supplied by my own measurements on *Onymacris* spp. in the Namib Desert (Edney, 1971b) referred to below in connection with the effects of surface color. On the other hand, not all arthropods have highly impermeable integuments, and in these evaporative cooling may be of importance.

It has been known for a long time that many insects go through a period of warming up by shivering before flight, and hawk moths provide good examples. Heinrich and Bartholomew (1971) showed that in *Manduca sexta,* which lives in the Mojave Desert of California and feeds on *Datura stramonium* (Jimson weed), the thorax is warmed to 37°–39°C before flight by muscular activity, the rate of increase being linear but depending on ambient temperature. Interestingly enough, the temperature of the abdomen during this warm-up period remains near the ambient temperature, probably as a result of the cessation of blood flow from the thorax. During free flight, *Manduca* maintains its thoracic temperature within 1° of 42°C in ambient temperatures from 17°–32°C (Heinrich, 1970, 1971). Metabolic heat generated by the flight muscles tends to overheat the thorax, but the excess is carried away by circulating blood which is pumped rather vigorously by the dorsal tubular heart into the hemocoele of the thorax from where it flows back to the cooler abdomen.

C. EVAPORATIVE COOLING IN ISOPODS

Some years ago, I investigated the situation in isopods and the sea slater *Ligia,* a littoral isopod about the size of *Blatta orientalis.* (These are by no means desert animals, but the information about them may serve to

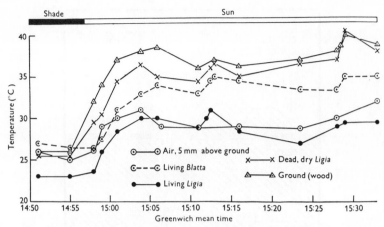

Fig. 15. Internal body temperatures of a living cockroach (*Blatta*), a living sea slater (*Ligia*) and a dead, dry sea slater, exposed to direct sunlight. Evaporation of water from their surfaces helps to cool the living animals. Relative humidity 39–45%, wind speed about 50 cm/second. From Edney (1953).

illustrate a relevant point.) One way of finding the effect of evaporation, if any, is to compare the body temperature of a living specimen with that of a dead, dry one in the same situation. When this was done, a living *Ligia* exposed to direct sunlight attained an equilibrium temperature about 5.3°C lower than that of the dry control (Fig. 15). Other species of isopods showed smaller temperature depressions, according to their cuticle permeability (Edney, 1953). In these conditions the main components of the heat balance in *Ligia* were radiation, convection and evaporation as follows (all values being expressed in cal/cm²/minute):

radiation (0.287) + metabolism (0.0014) $\simeq$ convection (0.140) + evaporation (0.142)

There was a good correspondence between theory and experimental result, and evaporation in this case was important.

A cockroach, *Blatta,* was exposed side by side with *Ligia* to the same conditions, and its temperature was a degree or so below that of the dead, dry *Ligia,* so that even in this insect some effect of evaporative cooling was apparent.

The relevance of the above illustration to desert conditions can be demonstrated by reference to another species of terrestrial isopod, *Hemilepistus reaumuri*, in the Algerian Sahara. In the spring of 1955 near Biskra, these animals were living in a claylike alluvial deposit alongside a large wadi. At that time of the year soil and air temperatures were by no means ex-

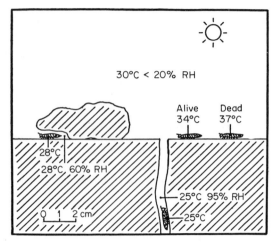

Fig. 16. A set of observations in the habitat of *Hemilepistus reaumuri* (Isopoda) in the Algerian Desert near Biskra. Transpiration is sufficiently rapid to reduce the body temperature of a living animal by 3°C, compared with a dead, dry control specimen. RH is relative humidity. These animals dig vertical holes in which conditions are relatively equable. From Edney (1960).

treme, indeed they would often be exceeded in summer in a temperate climate—but the humidity was always very low. During the hottest part of the day, between 11 A.M. and 3 P.M., no animals were to be seen on the desert surface. Before and after this time, however, they emerged from holes in very large numbers, wandered over the surface and fed upon a scrubby desert plant. Air movement seemed not to inhibit emergence; but during periods of alternating sunshine and shade, the former caused the animals rapidly to retreat to their holes. Measurements were made to find out, among other things, whether transpiration is of any advantage to these animals as it is in other land isopods.

One set of such measurements is shown in Fig. 16. The temperature of a living *Hemilepistus,* exposed to insolation, was 3°C lower than that of a dead, dry control specimen—a depression which could well be of value in an ecological crisis (Edney, 1958). The figure also illustrates how the environment contains niches such as the holes dug by the animals, and crevices under stones, which provide shelter from the high temperatures and low humidities outside.

D. EVAPORATIVE COOLING IN INSECTS

Control of temperature by evaporative cooling in small animals can be only a very temporary measure. But even among insects the phenomenon is not unknown. An example is that of the sphingid moth, *Pholus achemon* (Adams and Heath, 1964b), which extrudes a drop of water from the proboscis if its body temperature rises above 40°C. The water is cooled by evaporation and the insect then sucks it in again. Temperature control by heat distribution around the body in another sphinged is referred to above on p. 352.

Generally there is a good deal of evidence that the highest temperatures which insects can withstand are higher in dry than in humid air (Bursell, 1964b), but this can hardly be termed regulation—it is an inevitable result of high vapor pressure deficit raising the rate of transpiration. In tsetse flies, *Glossina morsitans,* however, which are likewise known to resist higher temperatures in dry air, Edney and Barrass (1962) found a truly regulatory process.

Flies were mounted in such a way that their thoracic spiracles could be observed while the temperature of the ambient air and of the flies themselves was accurately monitored. Slowly rising air temperatures were closely followed by the fly's body temperature, until the former reeached about 39°C. At this temperature the spiracles (hitherto closed) were seen to flutter, and then to open widely, while at the same time the fly's body temperature remained constant even though the air temperature continued to rise, until a temperature depression of nearly 2°C was achieved (Fig. 17). The phenomenon was reversible, and also repeatable in one fly. No such effect was found, however, if the air was saturated with water vapor, or if the fly's spiracles had been blocked.

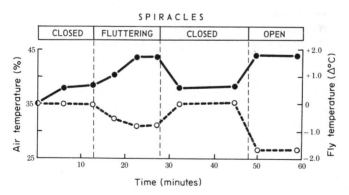

Fig. 17. The effect of spiracular opening on the internal temperature of a tsetse fly. Air temperatures: ●——●, difference between air and fly temperature: ○– – –○. At about 39°C the spiracles flutter or open, and at the same time the body temperature is depressed. Not shown in this figure is the fact that temperature depression is inhibited either by saturated air or by blocked spiracles. After Edney and Barrass (1962).

Thus we have good evidence that in tsetse flies evaporative cooling does regulate body temperature, but the question remains as to whether such a comparatively small temperature depression is of survival value. At first sight this would certainly seem to be unlikely, since the normal response of an insect to high sublethal temperatures is to move away rather than to lose precious water by regulating against them. However, some observations that I made in the field, with the help of J. Ford, suggest that in certain circumstances the process might be of value. Measurements were made in a tsetse fly area in Rhodesia at the hottest time of the year. Flies observed to feed at a bait ox were marked, released, and subsequently found in the vicinity resting on branches of trees and bushes, where, at the hottest time of the day, they were exposed to air temperatures (measured precisely where the flies were sitting) of 38°C and above, the relative humidity lying between 25 and 35%. Temperatures on the surface of the bait animal at this time varied between 36°–37.5°C, in the shade and 40°–41.5°C when exposed to the sun. One reading of 47°C was obtained on the animal's flank in the sun.

Tsetse flies are bound to feed (and during the process they inbibe warm blood) so that they may occasionally be exposed for short periods to conditions in which an ability to drop the body temperature is critical for survival.

VI. Morphological Adaptations, Including Surface Color

A very useful and beautifully illustrated discussion of the interaction of evolutionary history and present habits and habitats in psammophilous tenebrionid beetles is given by Koch (1961).

Some of the morphological modifications described as being adaptive for desert life are, in fact, adaptive to a psammophilous existence. One has only to compare the flat, plate-like structure of *Arenivaga* (Fig. 12) or the tenebrionid beetle, *Lepidochora porti,* with the long spindly-legged *Onymacris plana* to recognize that the former is highly adaptive to swimming through sand, the latter to running rapidly over the hot surface (Koch, 1961). The legs of endopsammophilous forms are usually modified by the development of flat oarlike surfaces or large clawlike spines (Fig. 18), associated with digging in sand or swimming through it. Tinkham (1965, 1968, and earlier papers) has described several such adaptations in crickets and other sand dune insects.

An even closer approximation to swimming is shown by a therevid fly larva from the dunes of southern California which moves below the surface with a typical undulatory swimming action. It leaves the track shown in the bottom of Fig. 12b.

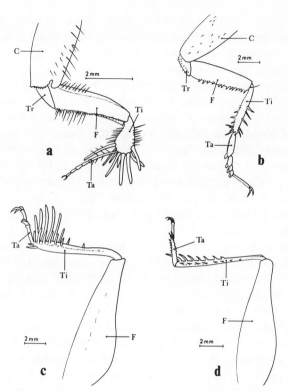

Fig. 18. Legs of the cockroaches (a) *Arenivaga investigata* and (b) *Periplaneta americana,* and of the crickets (c) *Macrobaenetes* sp. and (d) *Gryllus assimilis.* (a) and (c) are psammophilous forms, and their tibiae are provided with large spines which assist in burrowing through sand. C, coxa; Tr, trochanter; F, femur; Ti, tibia; Ta, tarsus.

The surface of the sand roach, *Arenivaga,* is covered with a thin pile of fine hairs—unusual for a cockroach—which may prevent abrasion of the cuticular surface by the sand, for even slight abrasion, by destroying the continuity of the impermeable lipid layer, leads to an enormous increase in the rate of transpiration.

Pierre (1958) in the course of a monograph on the insect fauna of shifting sands in the northwest Sahara Desert lists a number of morphological features which are found predominantly in such insects. Thus, compared with their less specialized relatives, sand-living insects all have a greater development of trichoid and other forms of sensillae; their legs are highly modified, usually abbreviated; the claws are hypertrophied; and the tarsi are strongly ciliated. Apterism is also very frequent. The relevance of these adaptations (save perhaps of the sensillae) is not difficult to appreciate. Pierre recognizes two groups of sand insects: those living near the surface, which are xerophilic and highly specialized; and those living deeper, which are hygrophilic and less specialized.

Less clear in their adaptiveness are some features of the larvae of desert tenebrionid beetles described by Schulze (1969). The structure of the ninth abdominal segment of these insects is often used as an important indicator of phylogenetic affinity. Yet Schulze shows very clearly that certain pronounced abnormalities including strong modifications of the shape of the notum and the replacement of normal setae by knoblike spherical ones, among other changes, are characteristic of psammophilous species, no matter what their phyletic associations may be. The function of these modifications in unknown, but it is a good guess that they are adaptive in some way.

There has been a good deal of discussion about the significance of surface coloration in desert arthropods, but thus far there is little agreement on this very interesting topic. Many of the diurnal species—particularly grasshoppers—are cryptically marked and colored (there is no controversy here), but so are nondeserticolous forms. Others, as Buxton (1923) pointed out, are often strikingly black or white, while nocturnal species are generally pale-colored. Attempts have been made to account for this pattern of coloration, in terms of radiation load. Black, it has been suggested, prevents the penetration of ultraviolet light to the deeper tissues; but most insects' cuticles are opaque to ultraviolet whether or not they are black. The surfaces of some insects have been shown to reflect strongly, though differentially, in the infrared region,* but infrared radiation can hardly be responsible for the visible color differences.

Digby (1955) carried out a useful analysis of the effects of visible surface colors on body temperatures of insects. He found an effect, but concluded that since much of the energy of solar radiation is in the infrared region, and since most insects are differently colored in different parts of the body, "temperature differences due to color will be of minor importance." Buxton (1922) reported that a dark-colored form of the grasshopper, *Calyptamus,* was 4.5°C warmer than a light-colored form when both were exposed to solar radiation, and the same was true of black and green locust hoppers. But no such differences could be found between dark and light forms of the grasshopper, *Melanoplus,* by Pepper and Hastings (1952). It seems that there is no easy explanation of the black and white

* Rucker (1939) found that carabid beetle elytra reflected 39% of the energy at 1100 nm, 17% at 2150 nm, and 46% at 3000 nm, while *Pieris* wings reflected 69, 59, and 35%, respectively. Most of the infrared solar energy that reaches the earth's surface lies in wavelengths between 800 and 2000 nm.

colors of many desert beetles in terms of heat load, and in a long series of comparative measurements under a variety of conditions, Stower and Griffiths (1966) found no significant difference ($P > 0.2$) between the body temperatures of the extreme green (light) and red (dark) forms of desert locust hoppers (*Schistocerca*). W. J. Hamilton (personal communication) believes that the black coloration of so many desert beetles serves to raise their temperature early in the morning by absorbing most of the incident radiation. Cloudsley-Thompson (1964a,b) believes that while pale colors in desert insects are probably cryptic, the very common black color is an example of Müllerian mimicry: black beetles taste unpleasant and it is an advantage to all such bad-tasting species if this fact can be learned quickly by potential predators.

In some earlier work, Bolwig (1957) found somewhat higher temperatures in the subelytral space of the black beetle, *Onymacris multistriata,* than in the white, *O. bicolor,* except above 38°C when the black beetle was cooler, perhaps because of ventilation. Hadley (1970b) examined the problem indirectly in *Eleodes armata* by painting the black elytral surface white and measuring the resulting subelytral and body temperatures. He found a fairly consistent depression of subelytral cavity temperature in the "white" beetle (about 4°C) but the "white" beetle's body temperature was not consistently lower than that of the normal black beetle, at least during 15 minutes exposures.

Two species of tenebrionids in the Namib Desert provide a good opportunity for looking at this question: One, *Onymacris rugatipennis,* is black all over, while another, *O. brincki,* which is fairly similar in size, has white elytra, (Fig. 19). In an extended series of measurements of temperatures in the thorax and on the surface of the abdomen below the elytra of these beetles, I reached the conclusion that in sunshine (about 0.9 cal cm^{-2} min^{-1}) a white surface may depress the temperature of the abdomen by some 4°–5°C compared with that of the abdomen of a beetle with black elytra (Edney, 1971b).

The abdominal temperature of living *O. brincki* was lower than that of its own thorax (which is black) and also lower than the abdominal temperature of *O. rugatipennis* (Fig. 20). The same was true of dead insects, so that the higher thoracic temperature of *O. rugatipennis* was not ascribable to muscular activity, and the effect was abolished by painting the white elytra with carbon black.

Attitude to the sun's rays affects the temperature of different parts of a beetle very significantly, and it is not always easy to be sure in field experiments that this variable is controlled. However, in laboratory experiments where the beetles were exposed to the sun so that the angle of incidence of solar radiation could be varied from directly in front to directly

Fig. 19. (a) *Onymacris rugatipennis,* the most common beetle in the dry Kuiseb riverbed at Gobabeb in southwest Africa, mounted on a wooden base with a thermocouple inserted. This species is more plentiful in the summer (when it has a bimodal daily activity distribution) than in the winter (when its activity is unimodal). Weight about 600 mg. (b) *Onymacris brincki,* a diurnal, coastal species, with white elytra, the rest of the body being black. Weight about 500 mg.

behind the beetles, the effects both of incident angle and of surface color remained very clear (Fig. 21).

When the two species concerned were exposed to insolation in natural conditions, we can assume from the work of Parry (1951) that the contribution of metabolism to the total heat budget was negligible. Evaporation was measured (Edney, 1971a), and again its contribution to the heat budget was found to be negligible, so that heat balance at equilibrium was struck when net radiation was equal to convection. If we assume a beetle to be a cylinder, convective heat loss can be estimated (Gates, 1962; Porter and Gates, 1969), and thus values for net radiation obtained. A little further calculation enables one to estimate the reflectances of the

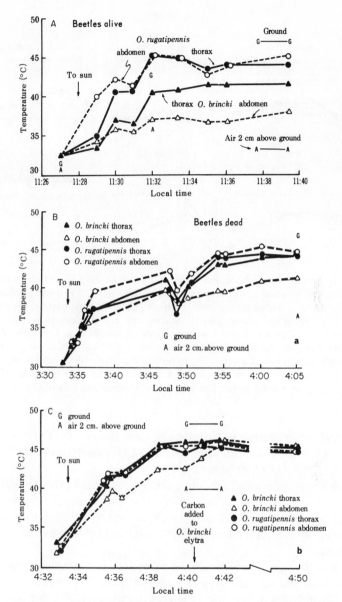

Fig. 20. Body temperatures of *Onymacris brincki* (with white elytra) and *O. rugatipennis* (entirely black). (A) When living insects were transferred from shade to sunshine the abdomen of *O. brincki* was cooler than its thorax, while the abdomen and thorax of *O. rugatipennis* were at about the same temperature. (B) A similar effect was obtained when dead insects were used, showing that temperature differences were not due to differences in muscular activity. (C) When the white elytra of *brincki* were covered with carbon black, the abdominal temperature rose to equal that of the black abdomen of *O. rugatipennis*. From Edney (1971b).

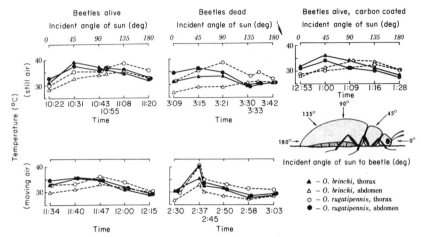

Fig. 21. Thoracic and abdominal temperatures of *O. brincki* and *O. rugatipennis* when subjected to solar radiation from different directions. When the incident angle was varied from 0° (head on) to 180° (sun directly behind the beetle), the abdomen of *O. brincki* remained cooler than its thorax until the incident angle was 135° to 180°C, and even then was scarcely warmer. In *O. rugatipennis,* however, the abdomen became warmer than the thorax at 45°–90°C, and at 135° and 180°C was considerably warmer. The effects are clearest in the upper middle graph (dead beetles in still air). In the upper right-hand graph, carbon black painted on the white elytra of *O. brincki* eliminated most of the difference between its temperature and that of *O. rugatipennis.*

black and white surfaces (for details, see Edney, 1971b), and these worked out at 38% for the black surface of *O rugatipennis* and 79% for the white surface of *O. brincki.*

It should be understood, however, that calculations of this kind are subject to considerable error. Their chief value lies in directing attention to the need for certain kinds of data (such as surface reflectivity) which are necessary if we want to understand the components of heat balance in desert arthropods.

So far as the significance of surface color itself is concerned, experiments such as those just referred to may show that there is a temperature effect, but this is not to say that the ecological significance of color lies in this direction. Desert arthropods probably control their temperature simply and adequately by behavioral means, and Cloudsley-Thompson's suggestion that the colors of many desert beetles are aposematic and in some cases represent Müllerian mimicry (see above) deserves attention.

It has also been suggested that the subelytral air space is adaptive in restricting water loss. Bolwig (1957) suggests that at high sublethal temperatures *Onymacris bicolor* actively ventilates the air space by abdominal and head movements, but his evidence needs confirmation. Cloudsley-Thompson (1964a) was unable to measure any differences in temperature or humidity between the air inside and outside the subelytral cavity of *Pimelia grandis,* although he found that removal of the elytra, thus exposing the tergites of the abdomen, led to an increase in transpiration which he ascribed to air movement in the vicinity of the spiracles. However, it would seem that if air movement lowers the water activity outside an open spiracle it would also raise the oxygen activity, so that the spiracles could be more nearly closed.

There is no correlation between strongly convex elytral surfaces and diurnally active species, both flat and curved elytra being found in these as well as in nocturnally active beetles (Koch, 1961). Furthermore the extent of the underlying cavity varies greatly with the degree of nourishment and particularly with the state of hydration of individual insects.

The question is not whether the elytra by their presence reduce water loss. The work of Dizer (1955), Cloudsley-Thompson (1964a), Ahearn and Hadley (1969), and Hadley (1970b) shows clearly that this is so. The question is whether an air cavity between the elytra and the cuticle of the abdominal tergites reduces water loss—and this is not proven. For the present, the conclusion, as Cloudsley-Thompson suggests, must be that the size of subelytral cavities of desert tenebrionids has not been shown to be adaptive for heat or water balance.

VII. Phenology and Behavior

In this final section we come to a consideration of the parts played by phenology and behavioral mechanisms in adapting arthropods to deserts, and there is good evidence that they are of the greatest significance. Timing of life cycles, leading to appearance and feeding at the right time, is very general. The cricket, *Macrobaenetes,* occurs in very large numbers on a few nights in spring in the sand dunes of the Coachella Valley in southern California. Lawrence (1959) refers to the sand dunes of the Namib Desert in southwest Africa as being "virtually covered" with a flat, ivory-colored beetle, *Lepidochora,* at certain seasons. These sudden flushes of very large numbers of individuals of a species have often been reported (Edney, 1966b).

There is reason to believe that many desert forms are slow developers (Bodenheimer, 1953; Hafez and Makky, 1959; Tinkham, 1965), and I suspect that *Arenivaga* takes at least 1 year to reach maturity in the field. In the laboratory it takes up to 18 months. This is all the more striking in view of the high temperatures encountered. Linked with slow development, perhaps, is the remarkable ability of desert species to undergo long periods of starvation. Dinothrombid mites feed only once a year, scorpions can exist for months without food, and the beetle, *Blaps requieni,* lived for 5 years without food according to Cloudsley-Thompson and Chadwick (1964). In addition, many species enter diapause during difficult periods: the red locust, *Nomadacris,* for example, diapauses as an adult in the dry season. The desert locust, *Schistocerca,* is delayed in reaching sexual maturity if it feeds on senescent vegetation (Ellis and Carlisle, 1965), a striking adaptation which has the effect of coordinating oviposition and the appearance of young hoppers with the onset of rains and the growth of green vegetation.

A. PHENOLOGY OF LOCUSTS

Locust eggs require water to develop, nymphs require plentiful green vegetation to feed on, and adults need fresh food to develop sexual maturity and moist ground in which to lay eggs (Woodrow, 1965a,b). Yet these insects live in deserts. This underlines several important points about the relationship of arthropods and deserts: (1) that deserts are not always dry, (2) that in areas which are by and large very dry, humid niches exist, (3) that physiological mechanisms which combine to time the occurrence of the various stages of development are important, and (4) that behavioral mechanisms (including the formation of swarms) may permit survival in an otherwise impossible environment.

The story of locust migrations has been well told by Rainey and others (Rainey, 1951; Rainey *et al.,* 1957). The direction in which flying swarms move is determined by the prevailing wind, and since these winds usually blow into areas of convergence of air masses where rain falls, locust swarms by and large are also conveyed to places where conditions are admirably suited for egg laying and hopper development.

The changes in behavior, physiology, and morphology which occur as locusts pass from the "solitary" phase, where they are no more than grasshoppers, to the "gregarious" phase, when they swarm and inflict so much damage, are fascinating examples of adaptations to desert conditions. The buildup, from September through November, 1967 of an outbreak of the desert locust in the Tamesna area of Mali and Niger Republics has been vividly described by Roffey and Popov (1968). These authors recognize three stages in the process—concentration, multiplication, and gregarization—and they stress that by observing different groups of insects in different localities, examples of all three stages in the process could be found at any one time, although concentratioon was more frequent early on and gregarization later.

Concentration occurred as solitary locusts flew into the region by night, and settled in areas of green vegetation. Such flights were usually upwind, and may have been initiated by chemical substances released by the vegetation. During the daytime, however, visual clues seemed to keep the locusts in their habitats. Once within the habitat, conditions were very favorable for sexual maturation, and further concentration occurred as a result of small daytime flights and ground movements associated with roosting, basking, and the search for egg laying and mating sites.

Multiplication occurred as a result of reproduction—each female producing on average 3 egg pods, totaling 400 eggs. There was high hopper mortality, the causes of which were unknown, but even so the population of nymphs increased by several times.

The third component, gregarization, resulted in changes in behavior, and ultimately in physiology and morphology. At low population levels hoppers tended to avoid contact with each other, at higher concentrations they became indifferent, and finally at the highest concentration they exhibited mutual attraction and formed large, compact marching bands. Such behavioral changes did take place during the ontogeny of an individual, but their onset was related rather to population density than to ontogenetic stage. Thus the hoppers of partially gregarized adults themselves showed incipient gregarization both in behavior and in color, and adults behaved differently according to their history as hoppers. Gregarization continued during the early adult stage as roosting and basking groups were formed, and finally there occurred small swarmlets of adults. Unlike the night-flying solitary adults, these locusts flew and migrated by day. They would have merged to form large swarms, had not control measures prevented this consummation.

B. ACTIVITY CYCLES

A somewhat different aspect of behavior, daily cycles of activity, which may or may not be "circadian rhythms" according to whether or not they continue in constant conditions, have been reviewed in relation to desert animals by Cloudsley-Thompson and Chadwick (1964; see also Cloudsley-Thompson, 1970). Such rhythms of activity, correlated with one or another of the main physical parameters of the environment, provide another mechanism ensuring that the animals are out and about at the right time.

A good example of daily activity is provided by the desert cockroach, *Arenivaga investigata*. We have already seen that the upper lethal temperature of this insect is quite high ($45.5°$–$48.5°$C according to conditions, see p. 349), but this level is often exceeded in the insects' environment,

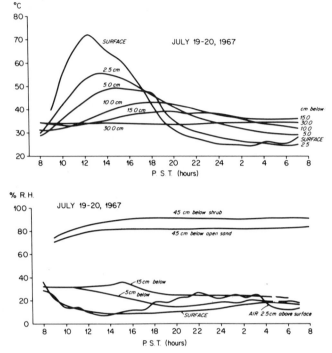

Fig. 22. Temperatures and humidities in the sand in which the desert cockroach, *Arenivaga investigata,* lives, measured during one of the hottest days in the summer. Equable temperatures and humidities at which water vapor uptake is possible were available not far below the hot, dry surface.

at least at the sand surface. Figure 22 shows the temperatures and humidities at various levels below the sand on the hottest day in the summer of 1967. The measurements show that, even when the surface temperature was 72°C (just after noon), temperatures well below 40°C were available only 10 cm below, and although the surface humidity was 10% RH, humidities above 82% were available less than 45 cm below the surface. At this humidity, as we have seen, *Arenivaga* is capable of taking up water vapor.

The insects' behavior is well adapted to this problem—they remain below the sand all day. Samples have shown that all stages from very young nymphs to adult males (which are winged) and adult females (which are apterous and larviform) are present down to at least 12 inches, and they probably go deeper. In the evening, however, some of them come up and move about just below the surface. Our observations showed that they first became active in this way somewhat later in the summer months than in the spring and fall, but what triggers this daily rhythm of activity is not clear. Certainly the actual surface temperatures at the time of activity vary widely from month to month so that this by itself can hardly provide an explanation.

However, the level of the temperature inversion (i.e., that level above which the temperature becomes cooler as the surface is approached) moves downwards during the afternoon and evening (Fig. 23), and it seems possible that this may play a part in determining the onset of daily subsurface activity, by acting as a *zeitgeber* and keeping the circadian mechanism in phase with the daily march of events. Such a relationship has not been demonstrated, however, and the problem will be solved only by further experimental work.

Hawke and Farley (1973), working with a different species of *Arenivaga* in a different locality, found that the humidity in the environment of their insects did not appear to rise above 54%, and they consider

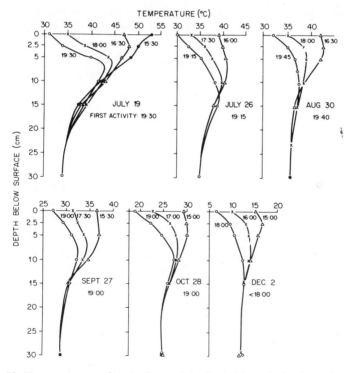

Fig. 23. Temperature profiles in the sand in the habitat of *Arenivaga investigata*. Subsurface activity begins at different times of the day at different seasons of the year and may be triggered by the downward movement of the temperature inversion point.

that the insects obtained water from plant food. Their insects, like ours, showed a daily subsurface activity pattern, commencing after dark, but Hawke and Farley were unable to come to a firm conclusion as to the controlling mechanisms involved.

During a recent visit to the Namib Desert, I was able to collaborate with Erik Holm in obtaining some information about the daily cycles of activity in relation to microclimatic conditions (Holm and Edney, 1973). For example, in the dry Kuiseb River bed *Onymacris rugatipennis* and *Physosterna cribripes* were both very plentiful in summer and winter. Figures 24 and 25 show the activity distribution and microclimatic data for *O. rugatipennis*. In the summer, maximum beetle activity occurred between 9 and 10 A.M. when the sand surface temperature was 50°C in the sun and 37°C in the shade. Activity was very low between noon and 3 P.M. during which time the surface temperature rose to 66°C. A second lesser peak of activity occurred from 4 to 6 P.M., when the surface was 43°C in sunlight and 34°C in the shade (Fig. 24). At night, and in the heat of the day, the insects retired into *Eragrostis* bushes or into the sand. In the winter, however, beetle activity was unimodal, with a broad activity peak centered at 1 P.M. when the surface temperature in the sun varied between 39° and 51°C on different days (Fig. 25).

In the sand dune areas, species of beetles tend to replace one another in activity cycles throughout the day and night. For example, during the summer, *O. laeviceps* was most active from 7 to 8 A.M. and again from 6 to 8 P.M., while *O. plana* was active from 9 A.M. to noon and from 4 to 6 P.M. Both species were bimodal in activity but the modes occurred at different times.

Ahearn and Hadley (1969) similarly found that of the two tenebrionids, *Eleodes armata* and *Cryptoglossa verrucosa,* both from the Sonoran Desert in Arizona, the latter lost water less rapidly than the former, and they were able to correlate this with the phenology of the species—thus *C. verrucosa* alone was active during the hottest summer months, while *E. armata* became more abundant on the surface in late summer and fall.

Scorpions also exhibit daily activity cycles, as Hadley and Williams (1968) observed in the Sonoran Desert of Mexico. By using ultraviolet light and counting the numbers of scorpions seen in standard rounds, they found that two species, *Vejovis confusus* and *V. mesaensis,* were active early in the night and became progressively less active later, while *Centruroides sculpturatus* was equally active throughout the night. The activity pattern of any one individual was apparently very variable (e.g., they did not all come out every night), and the authors were unable to identify any one environmental factor as being responsible for determining the times of activity, although activity did not occur in two winter months, so that

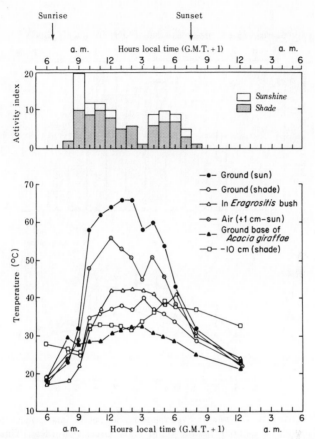

Fig. 24. Activity of *Onymacris rugatipennis* and microclimatic measurements in its habitat during a 24-hour period in the summer (G.M.T. is Greenwich Mean Time). Activity was bimodal with a major peak during the morning. (From Holm and Edney, 1973).

temperature was probably involved. Feeding and courtship seemed to be the most commonly observed activity during emergence.

Finally a good example of a daily activity cycle, probably related to temperature, is provided by the desert cicada, *Diceroprocta apache*. Heath and Wilkin (1970) found that these insects never flew when their body temperature was below 22°C. Above this, the insects remained exposed to direct sunshine until their body temperature rose to 39°C, when they moved into shade. However, they maintained full motor control up to 46.6°C. By sitting on the north (shaded) side of mesquite tree branches, they utilize a microclimate where the air is a little cooler than on the south

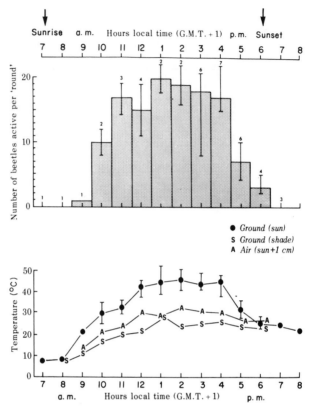

Fig. 25. Activity of *Onymacris rugatipennis* and microclimatic measurements in its habitat during a 24-hour period (G.M.T. is Greenwich Mean Time) in the winter. In the histogram (above) the number of observations at each hour is shown in brackets. Extremes are shown by vertical lines. (From Holm and Edney, 1973).

side (42.5°C instead of 44.5°C), and in these circumstances they sing during the hottest part of the day, thus avoiding many of their predators, including birds and cicada wasps, which are inactivated by the high temperature. Continued flight raises the insects' temperature by as much as 8°C, so that during the hottest part of the day flights are restricted to less than 3-seconds duration, to avoid loss of motor control.

Behavior, then, leading to the choice of a suitable habitat, and of movement within the habitat, is clearly of major importance. A good deal is known about the various ways in which arthropods respond to light, temperature, and humidity (Markl and Lindauer, 1965), but there are very few systematic investigations on the application of such mechanisms to desert arthropods. What, for example, triggers the sudden nightly onset of activity in the desert cockroach? Does their response to a humidity gradient depend upon their own water resources at the time? These are important questions concerning the insects' biology and are not difficult to investigate. Similar as well as different questions arise about most other desert arthropods, and exploration of the field will be well worthwhile.

VIII. Conclusion

In this chapter we have considered insects such as domestic cockroaches, blowflies, tsetse flies, and locusts, as well as other more strictly desert forms. The reason is clear; although there has been a developing interest in desert arthropods during recent years there is still a great dearth of information about their comparative physiology, behavior, and ecology. Fortunately, many of the physiological processes involved are probably common to most insects, so that the use of information derived from non-desert species is not likely to lead to error. On the other hand, several behavioral and phenological aspects of the biology of desert forms can only be studied in deserts, making use of the species that live there, and much remains to be done in this regard. What seem to be some of the main opportunities and needs for further inquiry have been mentioned in the body of this chapter. They include comparative work on integumental structure in relation to permeability; on almost any aspect of the heat and water relationships of noninsectan arthropods; on the relationship between O_2 uptake, metabolic substrates, and water balance; on the factors which determine body temperature in natural conditions; and, by no means least, on orientation mechanisms in relation to distribution and movement within the habitat.

Deserts have been called extremely terrestrial environments, and indeed they are by definition drier than elsewhere and are often exceedingly hot. For some aspects of comparative physiology, therefore, desert species provide admirable material, and if we are interested in the adaptations of animals to terrestrial life it may well be that the best place to look is where terrestrialness is greatest. In this way the potentialities of various kinds of animal organization are displayed for the investigator to the best advantage. Desert arthropods, for example, include species with the most efficiently waterproofed cuticles, lending themselves to the analysis of a physiological mechanism which is of general significance. Others have the power of water vapor absorption well developed and may prove to be valuable in attempts to understand the mechanism of that process.

On the other hand, there is great structural and physiological diversity among different groups of arthropods—the result of very different evolutionary histories—so that adaptations to desert living open to one are not open to all, and we should not expect to find the maximum possible development of adaptive features in an arthropod simply because it occurs in areas marked as deserts on maps. Rather we should expect a *relatedness* between one adaptation and another and between these and the basic structure and physiology of the groups concerned. Most adult insects fly, but other arthropods do not, and their adaptations to desert life will differ correspondingly. Desert beetles have very impermeable integuments and tolerate high body temperatures, while desert cockroaches live below the sand, have more permeable integuments, and absorb water vapor. In fact, there is probably no single aspect in which all desert arthropods differ from all others.

Certainly the arthropod organization, in some of its forms at least, is capable of producing highly efficient desert species, and investigation of the adaptations involved is an absorbing field of research. At the same time, it may be well to recognize another side to the picture which is of general biological interest; this concerns the question as to whether the evolution of adaptations to desert environments necessarily involves loss of adaptation to more mesic habitats. If indeed deserts are just extremely "harsh" environments, and if our animals have solved the problems of living there, should they not be much better at living in "easier" environments? Why, for example, are such hardy insects as *Glossina morsitans* not found in tropical forests? Sometimes there are obvious answers—sand roaches need sand dunes to live in—but more often there are not.

IX. Summary

Most classes of arthropods, including terrestrial crustaceans, are represented in the desert fauna, although insects predominate. Their small size and large relative surface forbids the use of evaporative cooling as a long-term measure and necessitates an impermeable integument. The insect organization, which is already very suitable for terrestrial existence, lends itself to further quantitative changes in adaptation to desert environments.

There is a broad correlation in arthropods between cuticle permeability and habitat. Impermeability of the cuticle is conferred largely by lipid material in the epicuticle, and this reduces transpiration into dry air from tsetse fly pupae to as little as 0.3 μg/cm^2/mm Hg/hour (0.9×10^{-4} cm/second). Loss of water from the respiratory membranes is inevitable but is controlled by spiracular mechanisms so that in resting tsetse flies and desert locusts this amounts only to about one-third of the total water loss. When these insects are active, spiracular water loss increases owing to the need for greater O_2 uptake, but not necessarily proportionately. In some insects total transpiration is regulated according to water needs by spiracular control and by controlling the water content of fecal material.

In locusts, dry air seems to decrease cuticle permeability, and water loss is further controlled by reducing ventilatory movements. Oxidation (metabolic) water is but one component of water balance, although an important one, for desert arthropods. Its significance during the prolonged migratory flight of locusts has been shown by Weis-Fogh (1967).

Excretion of waste nitrogen as uric acid involves little water loss, and the Malpighian tubule–rectal gland complex regulates osmotic and ionic concentrations. Water may be absorbed from the rectum against an overall water activity gradient when necessary, and there is mounting evidence that in such cases water follows the active transport and recycling of K^+ or other ions.

Uptake of water occurs with feeding and drinking, but it is doubtful whether feeding or metabolism increase under water stress. Active uptake of water vapor is known in a few arachnids and insects including the desert cockroach, *Arenivaga investigata,* which, after partial dehydration, absorbs water vapor from humidities down to 82.5% until its normal water content is restored. The mechanism is not fully understood, but the energy involved is relatively small. This insect also regulates its hemolymph osmotic pressure against changes in overall water content.

There is no convincing evidence that desert arthropods tolerate greater water depletion than others—they probably rely on more efficient conservation. There is some evidence that they tolerate higher temperatures than mesic forms do. Thus the camel spider survives for 24 hours at an air temperature of 50°C, the tenebrionid beetle, *Adesmia,* tolerates a similar soil temperature, but measurements of body temperature are scanty. Body temperature may be reduced for short periods by evaporative cooling, and depressions of 3°C have been measured in the desert isopod, *Hemilepistus.* In tsetse flies, a small temperature depression at near lethal temperature is achieved by opening the spiracles.

The significance of surface coloration is not clear, but other morphological adaptations are evident. Thus sand swimmers such as *Arenivaga* are flat with short, spiny legs, while surface runners such as *Onymacris* have long, spindly legs. Behavioral mechanisms are important in enabling arthropods to avoid intolerable conditions. Many are nocturnal and some are strongly seasonal in appearance. The appropriate relation of development to seasonal changes is exemplified by locusts, which achieve sexual maturity only after feeding on fresh vegetation and which are carried, as swarms, to areas where rain is likely.

Among tenebrionids in the Namib Desert, beetles that are active in full sunlight have higher lethal temperatures and lower water loss rates than those that come out by night.

The evolutionary history of different groups of arthropods restricts the range of possible adaptations of each group to desert conditions and hence partly determines their mode of life. Adaptations shown by a particular species are related to each other as well as to the habitat. The question is raised as to whether the acquisition of adaptations to deserts implies loss of adaptation to mesic environments, and if so, why.

ACKNOWLEDGMENTS

I owe a special debt to the late Dr. C. Koch, who until his death in 1970 was Director of the Namib Desert Research Station. His work and very wide knowledge of the desert, particularly of the tenebrionid fauna, has been an inspiration to many, including myself.

I am grateful to Dr. W. C. Sloan, Dr. W. J. Hamilton, Erik Holm, Dr. Evert Schlinger, Dr. R. D. Farley and Dr. Paul Rauch for permission to refer to unpublished data, and to the authors and publishers of certain figures and material used in this chapter for permission to do so. Al Bennet, David Gibo, Stuart Haynes, Joan McFarlane, and others have collaborated with me in much of the work on *Arenivaga*.

Some of the work referred to above was supported by grants to the author from the National Science Foundation and the Guggenheim Foundation. These are gratefully acknowledged.

REFERENCES

Abushama, F. T. (1968). Rhythmic activity of the grasshopper *Poecilocerus hieroglyphicus* (Acrididae: Pyrgomorphinae). *Entomol. Exp. Appl.* **11,** 341–347.

Abushama, F. T. (1970). Loss of water from the grasshopper *Poecilocerus hieroglyphicus* (Klug.) compared with the tree locust *Anacridium melanorhodon melanorhodon* (Walker). *Z. angew. Entomol.* **66,** 160–166.

Adams, P. A., and Heath, J. E. (1964a). Temperature regulation in the sphinx moth, *Celerio lineata. Nature (London)* **201,** 20–22.

Adams, P. A., and Heath, J. E. (1964b). An evaporative cooling mechanism in *Pholus achemon* (Sphingidae). *J. Res. Lepidoptera* **3,** 69–72.

Ahearn, G. A. (1969). Components of transpiratory water loss in desert tenebrionid beetles. *Amer. Zool.* **9,** 219.

Ahearn, G. A. (1970a). Changes in hemolymph properties accompanying heat death in the desert tenebrionid beetle *Centrioptera muricata. Comp. Biochem. Physiol.* **33,** 845–857.

Ahearn, G. A. (1970b). The control of water loss in desert tenebrionid beetles. *J. Exp. Biol.* **53,** 573–595.

Ahearn, G. A. (1970c). Water balance in the whipscorpion, *Mastigoproctus giganteus* (Lucas) (Arachnida, Uropygi). *Comp. Biochem. Physiol.* **35,** 339–353.

Ahearn, G. A., and Hadley, N. F. (1969). The effects of temperature and humidity on water loss in two desert tenebrionid beetles, *Eleodes armata* and *Cryptoglossa verrucosa. Comp. Biochem. Physiol.* **30,** 739–749.

Altmann, G. (1956). Die Regulation des Wasserhaushaltes der Honigbiene. *Insectes Soc.* **3**, 33–40.

Baker, D. N., and Lloyd, E. P. (1970). Effect of age on respiration and transpiration in the boll weevil, *Anthonomus grandis. Ann. Entomol. Soc. Amer.* **63**, 100–104.

Barton-Browne, L. (1964). Thirst in the blowfly, *Lucilia cuprina. Nature (London)* **202**, 1137–1138.

Beament, J. W. L. (1945). The cuticular lipoids of insects. *J. Exp. Biol.* **21**, 115–131.

Beament, J. W. L. (1958). The effect of temperature on the waterproofing mechanism of an insect. *J. Exp. Biol.* **35**, 494–519.

Beament, J. W. L. (1961). The water relations of the insect cuticle. *Biol. Rev. Cambridge Phil. Soc.* **36**, 281–320.

Beament, J. W. L. (1964). The active transport and passive movement of water in insects. *Advan. Insect Physiol.* **2**, 67–129.

Beament, J. W. L. (1965). The active transport of water : Evidence, models and mechanisms. *Symp. Soc. Exp. Biol.* **19**, 273–298.

Beament, J. W. L., Noble-Nesbitt, J., and Watson, J. A. L. (1964). The waterproofing mechanisms of arthropods. III. Cuticular permeability in the firebrat, *Thermobia domestica* (Packard). *J. Exp. Biol.* **41**, 323–330.

Berridge, M. J. (1965). The physiology of excretion in the cotton stainer, *Dysdercus fasciatus* Signoret. I. Anatomy, water excretion and osmoregulation. *J. Exp. Biol.* **43**, 511–521.

Berridge, M. J. (1966). The physiology of excretion in the cotton stainer *Dysdercus fasciatus* Signoret. IV. Hormonal control of excretion. *J. Exp. Biol.* **44**, 553–566.

Berridge, M. J. (1967). Ion and water transport across epithelia. *In* "Insects and Physiology" J. W. L. Beament and J. E. Treherne, ed,.), pp. 329–347. Amer. Elsevier, New York.

Berridge, M. J. (1968). Urine formation by Malpighian tubules of *Calliphora.* I. Cations. *J. Exp. Biol.* **48**, 159–174.

Berridge, M. J. (1969). Urine formation by the Malpighian tubules of *Calliphora.* II. Anions. *J. Exp. Biol.* **50**, 15–28.

Berridge, M. J. (1970). Osmoregulation in terrestrial arthropods. *In* "Chemical Zoology." (M. Florkin and B. T. Scheer, eds.), Vol. 5, Part A, pp. 287–320. Academic Press, New York.

Berridge, M. J., and Gupta, B. L. (1967). Fine structural changes in relation to ion and water transport in the rectal papillae of the blowfly, *Calliphora. J. Cell Sci.* **2**, 89–112.

Berridge, M. J., and Gupta, B. L. (1968). Fine structural localization of adenosine triphosphate in the rectum of *Calliphora. J. Cell Sci.* **3**, 17–32.

Berridge, M. J., and Oschman, J. L. (1969). A structural basis for fluid secretion by Malpighian tubules. *Tissue Cell* **1**, 247–272.

Berry, L., and Cloudsley-Thompson, J. L. (1960). Autumn temperatures in the Red Sea hills. *Nature (London)* **188**, 843.

Bodenheimer, F. S. (1953). Problems of animal ecology and physiology in deserts. *Desert Res., Proc., Int. Symp., 1952* Spec. Publ. No. 2, pp. 205–229.

Bolwig, N. (1957). Experiments on the regulation of the body temperature of certain tenebrionid beetles. *J. Entomol. Soc. S. Afr.* **20**, 454–458.

Browning, T. O. (1954). Water balance in the tick *Ornithodoros moubata* Murray with particular reference to the influence of carbon dioxide on the uptake and loss of water. *J. Exp. Biol.* **31**, 331–340.

Browning, T. O. (1969a). Permeability to water of the shell of the egg of *Locusta migratoria migratorioides*, with observations on the egg of *Teleogryllus commodus*. *J. Exp. Biol.* **51**, 99–105.

Browning, T. O. (1969b). The permeability of the shell of the egg of *Teleogryllus commodus* measured with the aid of tritiated water. *J. Exp. Biol.* **51**, 397–405.

Buck, J. (1958). Cyclic CO_2 release in insects. IV. A theory of mechanism. *Biol. Bull.* **114**, 118–140.

Buck, J. (1962). Some physical aspects of insect respiration. *Annu. Rev. Entomol.* **7**, 27–56.

Buck, J., and Keister, M. (1955). Cyclic CO_2 release in diapausing *Agapema* pupae. *Biol. Bull.* **109**, 144–163.

Bursell, E. (1957a). Spiracular control of water loss in the tsetse fly. *Proc. Roy. Entomol. Soc. London* **32**, 21–29.

Bursell, E. (1957b). The effect of humidity on the activity of tsetse flies. *J. Exp. Biol.* **34**, 42–51.

Bursell, E. (1958). The water balance of tsetse pupae. *Phil. Trans. Roy. Soc. London* **241**, 179–210.

Bursell, E. (1959a). The water balance of tsetse flies. *Trans. Roy. Entomol. Soc. London* **111**, 205–235.

Bursell, E. (1959b). Physiological studies on *Glossina*. *Annu. Rep. East Afr. Tsetse Trypanosomiasis Res. Organ., Nairobi, 1958* pp. 32–35.

Bursell, E. (1960). Loss of water by excretion and defaecation in the tsetse fly. *J. Exp. Biol.* **37**, 689–697.

Bursell, E. (1964a). Environmental aspects: Humidity. *In* "The Physiology of Insecta" (M. Rockstein, ed.), Vol. 1, pp. 323–361. Academic Press, New York.

Bursell, E. (1964b). Environmental aspects: Temperature. *In* "The Physiology of Insecta" (M. Rockstein, ed.), Vol. 1, pp. 283–321. Academic Press, New York.

Bursell, E. (1970). "An Introduction to Insect Physiology." Academic Press, New York.

Buxton, P. A. (1923). "Animal Life in Deserts: A Study of the Fauna in Relation to the Environment." Arnold, London.

Buxton, P. A. (1922). Heat, moisture and animal life in deserts. *Proc. Roy. Soc., Ser. B* **96**, 123–131.

Buxton, P. A. (1930). Evaporation from the mealworm (*Tenebrio,* Coleoptera) and atmospheric humidity. *Proc. Roy. Soc., Ser. B* **106**, 560–577.

Buxton, P. A. (1931). The measurement and control of atmospheric humidity in relation to entomological problems. *Bull. Entomol. Res.* **22**, 431–447.

Buxton, P. A., and Lewis, D. J. (1934). Climate and tsetse flies: Laboratory studies upon *Glossina submorsitans* and *tachinoides*. *Phil. Trans. Roy. Soc. London, Ser. B* **224**, 175–240.

Church, N. S. (1960). Heat loss and the body temperature of flying insects. I. Heat loss by evaporation of water from the body. II. Heat conduction within the body and its loss by radiation and convection. *J. Exp. Biol.* **37**, 171–212.

Cloudsley-Thompson, J. L. (1956). Studies in diurnal rhythms. VI. Bioclimatic observations in Tunisia and their significance in relation to the physiology of the fauna, especially woodlice, centipedes, scorpions and beetles. *Ann. Mag. Natur. Hist.* **9**, 305–329.

Cloudsley-Thompson, J. L. (1959). Studies in diurnal rhythms. IX. The water relations of some nocturnal tropical arthropods. *Entomol. Exp. Appl.* **2**, 249–256.

Cloudsley-Thompson, J. L. (1961a). Observations on the biology of the scorpion, *Leiurus quinquestriatus* (H. & E.) in the Sudan. *Entomol. Mon. Mag.* **97,** 153–155.

Cloudsley-Thompson, J. L. (1961b). Some aspects of the physiology and behavior of *Galeodes arabs. Entomol. Exp. Appl.* **4,** 257–263.

Cloudsley-Thompson, J. L. (1962a). Lethal temperatures of some desert arthropods and the mechanism of heat death. *Entomol. Exp. Appl.* **5,** 270–280.

Cloudsley-Thompson, J. L. (1962b). Some aspects of the physiology and behaviour of *Dinothrombium* (Acari). *Entomol. Exp. Appl.* **5,** 69–73.

Cloudsley-Thompson, J. L. (1964a). On the function of the subelytral cavity in desert Tenebrionidae (Col.). *Entomol. Mon. Mag.* **100,** 148–151.

Cloudsley-Thompson, J. L. (1964b). Terrestrial animals in dry heat: Arthropods. *In* "Handbook of Physiology" (Amer. Physiol. Soc., J. Field, ed.), Sect. 4, pp. 451–465. Williams & Wilkins. Baltimore, Maryland.

Cloudsley-Thompson, J. L. (1967). The water relations of scorpions and tarantulas from the Sonoran desert. *Entomol. Mon. Mag.* **103,** 217–220.

Cloudsley-Thompson, J. L. (1969). "The Zoology of Tropical Africa." Norton, New York.

Cloudsley-Thompson, J. L. (1970). Terrestrial invertebrates. *In* "Comparative Physiology of Thermoregulation" (G. C. Whittow, ed.), Vol. 1, pp. 15–77. Academic Press, New York.

Cloudsley-Thompson, J. L., and Chadwick, M. J. (1964). "Life in Deserts." Dufour, Philadelphia, Pennsylvania.

de Bessé, N., and Cazal, M. (1968). Action des extraits d'organes périsympathiques et de corpora cardiaca sur la diurèse de quelques insectes. *C. R. Acad. Sci.* **226,** 615–618.

Délye, G. (1969). Perméabilité du tegument et resistance aux temperatures élevées de quelques arthropodes sahariennes. *Bull. Soc. Entomol. France* **74,** 51–55.

Dethier, V. G., and Evans, D. R. (1961). The physiological control of water ingestion in the blowfly. *Biol. Bull.* **121,** 108–116.

Diamond, J. M., and Tormey, J. Mc D. (1966). Studies on the structural basis of water transport across epithelial membranes. *Fed. Proc., Fed. Amer. Soc. Exp. Biol.* **25,** 1458–1463.

Digby, P. S. B. (1955). Factors affecting the temperature excess of insects in sunshine. *J. Exp. Biol.* **32,** 279–298.

Dizer, Y. B. (1955). On the physiological role of the elytra and the sub-elytral cavity in the steppe and desert black beetles (Tenebrionidae). *Zool. Zh.* **34,** 319–322.

Djajakusumah, T., and Miles, P. W. (1966). Changes in the relative amounts of soluble protein and amino acids in the haemolymph of the locust *Chortoicetes terminifera* Walker (Orthoptera, Acridiae) in relation to dehydration and subsequent rehydration. *Aust. J. Biol. Sci.* **19,** 1081–1094.

Edney, E. B. (1947). Laboratory studies on the bionomics of the rat fleas *Xenopsylla brasiliensis* Baker and *X. cheopsis* Roths. II. Water relations during the cocoon period. *Bull. Entomol. Res.* **38,** 263–280.

Edney, E. B. (1951). The evaporation of water from woodlice and the millipede *Glomeris. J. Exp. Biol.* **28,** 91–115.

Edney, E. B. (1953). The temperature of woodlice in the sun. *J. Exp. Biol.* **30,** 331–349.

Edney, E. B. (1957). "The Water Relations of Terrestrial Arthropods," Monogr. Exp. Biol. No. 5. Cambridge Univ. Press, London and New York.

Edney, E. B. (1958). The microclimate in which woodlice live. *Proc. Int. Congr. Entomol., 10th, 1956* Vol. 2, pp. 709–712.

Edney, E. B. (1960). The survival of animals in hot deserts. *Smithson. Inst., Annu. Rep.* pp. 407–425.

Edney, E. B. (1966a). Absorption of water vapour from unsaturated air by *Arenivaga* sp. (Polyphagidae, Dictyoptera). *Comp. Biochem. Physiol.* **19,** 387–408.

Edney, E. B. (1966b). Animals of the desert. *In* "Arid Lands" (E. S. Hills, ed.), pp. 181–218. UNESCO, London.

Edney, E. B. (1968). The effect of water loss on the haemolymph of *Arenivaga* sp. and *Periplaneta americana. Comp. Biochem. Physiol.* **25,** 149–158.

Edney, E. B. (1971a). Some aspects of water balance in tenebrionid beetles and a thysanuran in the Namib desert of Southern Africa. *Physiol. Zool.* 44: 61–76.

Edney, E. B. (1971b). The body temperature of tenebrionid beetles in the Namib desert of southern Africa. *J. Exp. Biol.* 55:253–272.

Edney, E. B., and Barrass, R. (1962). The body temperature of the tsetse fly, *Glossina morsitans* Westwood (Diptera, Muscidae). *J. Insect Physiol.* **8,** 469–481.

Edney, E. B., and McFarlane, J. (1973). The effect of temperatures on transpiration in the desert cockroach *Arenivaga investigata* and in *Periplaneta americana. Physiol. Zool.* (in press).

Edney, E. B., and Spencer, J. O. (1955). Cutaneous respiration in woodlice. *J. Exp. Biol.* **32,** 256–269.

Edney, E. B., Haynes, S. S., and Gibo, D. (1973). Activity and distribution of the desert cockroach *Arenivaga investigata* in relation to microclimate. *Ecology* (in press).

Edwards, G. A., and Nutting, W. L. (1950). The influence of temperature upon the respiration and the heart activity of *Thermobia* and *Gryllolblatta. Psyche* **57,** 33–44.

Ellis, P. E., and Carlisle, D. B. (1965). Desert locusts: Sexual maturation delayed by feeding on senescent vegetation. *Science* **149,** 546–547.

Fraenkel, G. (1929). Untersuchungen über Lebensgewohnheiten, Sinnes Physiologie und Socialpsychologei der wandernden Larven der Afrikanischer Wanderheuschrecke *Schistocerca gregaria* (Försk). *Biol. Zentralbl.* **49,** 657–680.

Fraenkel, G., and Blewett, M. (1944). The utilisation of metabolic water in insects. *Bull. Entomol. Res.* **35,** 127–139.

Friauf, J. J., and Edney, E. B. (1969). A new species of *Arenivaga* from desert sand dunes in southern California (Dictyoptera, Polyphagidae). *Proc. Entomol. Soc. Wash.* **71,** 1–7.

Gates, D. M. (1962). "Energy Exchange in the Biosphere." Harper, New York.

Gilby, A. R. (1965). Lipids and their metabolism in insects. *Ann. Rev. Entomol.* **10,** 141–160.

Grimstone, A. V., Mullinger, A. M., and Ramsay, J. A. (1968). Further studies on the rectal complex of the mealworm, *Tenebrio molitor,* L. (Coleoptera, tenebrionidae). *Phil. Trans. Roy. Soc. London Ser. B* **253,** 343–382.

Gunn, D. L. (1942). Body temperature in poikilothermal animals. *Biol. Rev. Cambridg. Phil. Soc.* **17,** 293–314.

Gupta, B. L., and Berridge, M. J. (1966). A coat of repeating subunits on the cytoplasmic surface of the plasma membrane in the rectal papillae of the blowfly, *Calliphora erythrocephala* (Meig.), studied *in situ* by electron microscopy. *J. Cell Biol.* **29**, 376–382.

Hackman, R. H. (1971). The integument of arthropods. *In* "Chemical Zoology," Vol. 6, Part B. (M. Florkin and B. T. Scheer, eds.), p. 1–6. Academic Press, New York.

Hadley, N. F. (1970a). Water relations of the desert scorpion, *Hadrurus arizonensis*. *J. Exp. Biol.* **53**, 547–558.

Hadley, N. F. (1970b). Micrometerorology and energy exchange in two desert arthropods. *Ecology* **51**, 434–444.

Hadley, N. F., and Williams, S. C. (1968). Surface activities of some North American scorpions in relation to feeding. *Ecology* **49**, 726–734.

Hafez, M., and Makky, A. M. M. (1959). Studies on Desert Insects in Egypt. III. On the bionomics of *Adesmia bicarinata* Klug (Coleoptera: Tenebrionidae). *Bull. Soc. Entomol. Egypt* **43**, 89–113.

Hawke, D. D., and Farley, R. D. (1973). Ecology and behavior of the desert burrowing cockroach, *Arenivaga* sp. (Dictyoptera, Polyphagidae). *Oecologia* **11**, 263–279.

Heath, J. E., and Wilkin, P. J. (1970). Temperature responses of the desert cicada, *Diceroprocta apache* (Homoptera, Cicadidae). *Physiol. Zool.* **43**, 145–154.

Heeg, J. (1967). Studies on Thysanura. I. The water economy of *Machiloides delanyi* Wygodzinsky and *Ctenolepisma longicaudata* Escherich. *Zool. Afr.* **3**, 21–41.

Heinrich, B. (1970). Thoracic temperature stabilization by blood circulation in a free-flying moth. *Science* **168**, 580–582.

Heinrich, B. (1971). Temperature regulation of the Sphinx Moth, *Manduca sexta*. II. Regulation of heat loss by control of blood circulation. *J. Exp. Biol.* **54**, 153–166.

Heinrich, B., and Bartholomew, G. A. (1971). An analysis of pre-flight warm up in the sphinx moth, *Manduca sexta*. *J. Exp. Biol.* **55**, 223–239.

Hinton, H. E. (1960). A fly larva that tolerates dehydration and temperatures of $-270°$ to $+102°C$. *Nature (London)* **188**, 336–337.

Holdgate, M. W., and Seal, M. (1956). The epicuticular wax layers of the pupa of *Tenebrio molitor* L. *J. Exp. Biol.* **33**, 82–106.

Holm, E., and Edney, E. B. (1973). Daily activity of Namib Desert arthropods in relation to climate. *Ecology* **54**, 45–56.

Irvine, H. B., and Phillips, J. E. (1971). Effect of respiratory inhibition and ouabain on water transport by isolated locust rectum. *J. Insect Physiol.* **17**, 381–383.

Kanungo, K. (1965). Oxygen uptake in relation to water balance of a mite (*Echinolaelaps echidninus*) in unsaturated air. *J. Insect Physiol.* **11**, 557–568.

Kennedy, J. S. (1939). The behaviour of a desert locust (*Schistocerca gregaria* Försk. Orthoptera) in an outbreak centre. *Trans. Roy. Entomol. Soc. London* **89**, 385–542.

Knulle, W. (1965). Die Sorption und Transpiration des Wasserdampfes bei der Mehlmilbe (*Acarus siro* L.) *Z. Vergl. Physiol.* **49**, 586–604.

Knulle, W. (1967). Physiological properties and biological implications of the water vapour sorption mechanism in larvae of the oriental rat flea, *Xenopsylla cheopis* (Roths). *J. Insect Physiol.* **13**, 333–357.

Knulle, W. and Devine, T. L. (1972). Evidence for active and passive components of sorption of atmospheric water vapour by larvae of the tick *Dermacentor variabilis*. *J. Insect Physiol.* **18**, 1653–1664.

Knulle, W., and Spadafora, R. R. (1969). Water vapor sorption and humidity relationships in *Liposcelis* (Insecta: Psocoptera). *J. Stored Prod. Res.* **5**, 49–55.

Knulle, W., and Wharton, G. W. (1964). Equilibrium humidites in arthropods and their ecological significance. *Acarologia* **6**, 299–306.

Koch, C. (1961). Some aspects of abundant life in the vegetationless sand of the Namib desert dunes. Positive psammotropism in tenebrionid beetles. *J. S. W. Afr. Sci. Soc.* **15**, 8–34 and 77–92.

Lawrence, R. F. (1959). The sand-dune fauna of the Namib Desert. *S. Afr. J. Sci.* **55**, 233–239.

Lee, R. M. (1961). The variation of blood volume with age in the desert locust (*Schistocerca gregaria* Försk.). *J. Insect Physiol.* **6**, 36–51.

Lees, A. D. (1946). The water balance in *Ixodes ricinus* L. and certain other species of ticks. *Parasitology* **37**, 1–20.

Lees, A. D. (1947). Transpiration and the structure of the epicuticle in ticks. *J. Exp. Biol.* **23**, 379–410.

Lees, A. D. (1948). Passive and active water exchange through the cuticle of ticks. *Discuss. Faraday Soc.* **3**, 187–192.

Locke, M. (1961). Pore canals and related structures in insect cuticle. *J. Biophys. Biochem. Cytol.* **10**, 589–618.

Locke, M. (1964). The structure and formation of the integument in insects. *In* "The Physiology of Insecta" (M. Rockstein, ed.), Vol. 3, pp. 379–470. Academic Press, New York.

Locke, M. (1965). Permeability of insect cuticle to water and lipids. *Science* **147**, 295–298.

Loveridge, J. P. (1968a). The control of water loss in *Locusta migratoria migratoriodes* R. & F. I. Cuticular water loss. *J. Exp. Biol.* **49**, 1–13.

Loveridge, J. P. (1968b). The control of water loss in *Locusta migratoria migratoriodes* R. & F. II. Water loss through the spiracles. *J. Exp. Biol.* **49**, 15–29.

Lowe, C. H. (1968). Appraisal of research on fauna of desert environments. *In* "Deserts of the World" (W. G. McGinnies, B. J. Goldman, and P. Paylore, eds.), pp. xxviii and 788. Univ. of Arizona Press, Tucson.

McFarlane, J. E. (1970). The permeability of the cricket egg shell. *Comp. Biochem. Physiol.* **37**, 133–141.

Maddrell, S. H. P. (1962). A diuretic hormone in *Rhodnius prolixus* Stal. *Nature (London)* **194**, 605–606.

Maddrell, S. H. P. (1964). Excretion in the blood-sucking bug *Rhodnius prolixus* Stal. III. The control of the release of the diuretic hormone. *J. Exp. Biol.* **41**, 459–472.

Maddrell, S. H. P. (1966). The site of release of the diuretic hormone in *Rhodnius*. A new neurohaemal system in insects. *J. Exp. Biol.* **45**, 499–508.

Maddrell, S. H. P. (1967). Neurosecretion in insects. *In* "Insects and Physiology" (J. W. L. Beament and J. E. Treherne, eds.), pp. 103–118. Amer. Elsivier, New York.

Maddrell, S. H. P. (1969). Secretion by the Malphigian tubules of *Rhodnius*. The movements of ions and water. *J. Exp. Biol.* **51**, 71–97.

Maddrell, S. H. P. (1970). Neurosecretory control systems in insects. *Symp. Roy. Entomol. Soc. London* **5**, 101–116.

Maddrell, S. H. P. (1971). The mechanisms of insect excretory systems. *Advan. Insect Physiol.* **8**, 199–331.

Makings, P. (1968). Transpiration through Slifer's patches of Acrididae (Orthoptera). *J. Exp. Biol.* **48**, 247–263.

Markl, H., and Lindauer, M. (1965). Physiology of insect behavior. *In* "The Physiology of Insecta" (M. Rockstein, ed.), Vol. II, pp. 3–122. Academic Press, New York.

Matthée, J. J. (1951). The structure and physiology of the egg of *Locustana paradalina* (Walk). *S. Afr., Dep. Agr. Sci. Bull.* **316**, 1–83.

Mead-Briggs, A. R. (1956). The effect of temperature upon the permeability to water of arthropod cuticles. *J. Exp. Biol.* **33**, 737–749.

Mellanby, K. (1932a). The effect of atmospheric humidity on the metabolism of the fasting mealworm (*Tenebrio molitor* L., Coleoptera). *Proc. Roy. Soc., Ser. B* **111**, 376–390.

Mellanby, K. (1932b). Effects of temperature and humidity on the metabolism of the fasting bedbug (*Cimex lectularis*), Hemiptera. *Parasitology* **24**, 419–428.

Mellanby, K. (1934). Effects of temperature and humidity on the clothes moth larva, *Tineola biselliella* Hum. (Lepidoptera). *Ann. Appl. Biol.* **21**, 476–482.

Mellanby, K. (1942). Metabolic water and desiccation. *Nature* (*London*) **150**, 21.

Mellanby, K. (1958). Water content and insect metabolism. *Nature* (*London*) **181**, 1403.

Miller, P. L. (1964). Respiration—aerial gas transport. *In* "The Physiology of Insecta" (M. Rockstein, ed.), Vol. 3, pp. 557–615. Academic Press, New York.

Mills, R. R. (1967). Hormonal control of excretion in the American cockroach. I. Release of a diuretic hormone from the terminal abdominal ganglion. *J. Exp. Biol.* **46**, 35–41.

Mills, R. R., and Whitehead, D. L. (1970). Hormonal control of tanning in the American cockroach: Changes in blood cell permeability during ecdysis. *J. Insect Physiol.* **16**, 331–340.

Mordue, W. (1969). Hormonal control of Malpighian tube and rectal function in the desert locust *Schistocerca gregaria*. *J. Insect Physiol.* **15**, 273–285.

Moriarty, F. (1969). Egg diapause and water absorption in the grasshopper *Chorthippus brunneus*. *J. Insect Physiol.* **15**, 2069–2074.

Munson, S. C., and Yeager, J. F. (1949). Blood volume and chloride normality in roaches [*Periplaneta americana* (L.)] injected with sodium chloride solutions. *Ann. Entomol. Soc. Amer.* **42**, 165–173.

Neville, A. C. (1970). Cuticle ultrastructure in relation to the whole insect. *Symp. Roy. Entomol. Soc. London* **5**, 17–39.

Neville, A. C., and Luke, B. M. (1969a). A two-system model for chitinprotein complexes in insect cuticles. *Tissue Cell* **1**, 689–707.

Neville, A. C., and Luke, B. M. (1969b). Molecular architecture of adult locust cuticle at the electron microscope level. *Tissue Cell* **1**, 355–366.

Neville, A. C., Thomas, M. G., and Zelazny, B. (1969). Pore canal shape related to molecular architecture of arthropod cuticle. *Tissue Cell* **1**, 183–200.

Noble-Nesbitt, J. (1969). Water balance in the firebrat, *Thermobia domestica* Packard. Exchanges of water with the atmosphere. *J. Exp. Biol.* **50**, 745–769.

Noble-Nesbitt, J. (1970a). Water uptake from sub-saturated atmospheres: Its site in insects. *Nature* (*London*) **225**, 753–754.

Noble-Nesbitt, J. (1970b). Water balance in the firebrat, *Thermobia domestica* (Packard). *J. Exp. Biol.* **52**, 193–200.

Nunez, J. A. (1956). Uber die Regelung des Wasserhaushaltes bei *Anisotarsus cupripennis* Germ. *Z. Vergl. Physiol.* **38**, 341–344.

Okasha, A. Y. K. (1971). Water relations of an insect, *Thermobia domestica*. I. Water uptake from sub-saturated atmospheres as a means of volume regulation. *J. Exp. Biol.* **55**, 435–448.

Okasha, A. Y. K. (1972). Water regulations in an insect, *Thermobia domestica*. II. Relationships between water content, water uptake from sub-saturated atmospheres and water loss. *J. Exp. Biol.* **57**, 285–296.

Oschman, J. L., and Wall, B. J. (1969). The structure of the rectal pads of *Periplaneta americana* L. *J. Morphol.* **127**, 475–510.

Parry, D. A. (1951). Factors determining the temperature of terrestrial arthropods in sunlight. *J. Exp. Biol.* **28**, 445–462.

Parry, D. A. (1954). On the drinking of soil capillary water by spiders. *J. Exp. Biol.* **31**, 218–227.

Pepper, J. H., and Hastings, E. (1952). The effects of solar radiation on grasshopper temperature and activities. *Ecology* **33**, 96–103.

Phillips, J. E. (1964). Rectal absorption in the desert locust, *Schistocerca gregaria* Forskal. I. Water. II. Sodium, potassium and chloride. III. The nature of the excretory process. *J. Exp. Biol.* **41**, 15–80.

Phillips, J. E. (1970). Apparent transport of water by insect excretory systems. *Amer. Zool.* **10**, 413–436.

Pierre, F. (1958). "Écologie et peuplement entomologique des sable vifs du Sahara Nord-Occidental," Ser. Biol., Central National de la Recherche Scientific, Vol. I. Paris.

Pilcher, D. F. M. (1970a). Hormonal control of the Malpighian tubules of the stick insect, *Carausius morosus*. *J. Exp. Biol.* **52**, 653–665.

Pilcher, D. F. M. (1970b). The influence of the diuretic hormone on the process of urine formation by the Malpighian tubules of *Carausius morosus*. *J. Exp. Biol.* **53**, 465–484.

Popov, G. B. (1958). Ecological studies on oviposition by swarms of the desert locust (*Schistocerca gregaria* Forskal) in Eastern Africa. *Anti-Locust Bull.* **31**, 1–70.

Porter, W. P. and Gates, D. M. (1969). Thermodynamic equilibria of animals with environment. *Ecol. Monogr.* **39**, 227–244.

Rainey, R. C. (1951). Weather and the movements of locust swarms: A new hypothesis. *Nature (London)* **168**, 1057–1060.

Rainey, R. C., Waloff, A., and Burnett, G. F. (1957). The behavior of the red locust (*Nomadacris septemfasciatia* Serville) in relation to the topography, meteorology and vegetation of the Rukwa Rift Valley, Tanganyika. *Anti-Locust Bull.* **26**, 1–96.

Ramsay, J. A. (1935). The evaporation of water from the cockroach. *J. Exp. Biol.* **12**, 373–383.

Ramsay, J. A. (1964). The rectal complex of the mealworm *Tenebrio molitor* L. (Coleoptera, Tenebrionidae). *Phil. Trans Roy. Soc. London, Ser. B* **248**, 279–314.

Riegel, J. A. (1971). Excretion–Arthropoda. *In* "Chemical Zoology" (M. Florkin and B. T. Scheer, Eds.), Vol. 6, Part B, pp. 249–277. Academic Press, New York.

Roffey, J., and Popov, G. (1968). Environmental and behavioral processes in a desert locust outbreak. *Nature (London)* **219**, 446–450.

Rucker, F. (1939). Über die Ultra-rot-reflexion tierischer Körperoberflachen. Z. Vergl. Physiol. **21**, 275–280.

Sauer, J. R., Levy, J. J., Smith, D. W., and Mills, R. R. (1970). Effect of rectal lumen concentration on the reabsorption of ions and water by the American cockroach. Comp. Biochem. Physiol. **32**, 601–614.

Schmidt-Nielsen, K. (1954). Heat regulation in small and large desert mammals. In "Biology of Deserts" (J. Cloudsley-Thompson, ed.), pp. 182–187. Institute of Biology, London.

Schmidt-Nielsen, K. (1964). "Desert Animals." Oxford Univ. Press, London and New York.

Schneiderman, H. A., and Williams, C. M. (1955). An experimental analysis of the discontinuous respiration of the Cecropia silkworm. Biol. Bull. **109**, 123–143.

Schultz, F. N. (1930). Zur Biologie des Mehlwurms (Tenebrio molitor L.). I. Der Wasserhaushalt. Biochem. Z. **127**, 112–119.

Schulze, L. (1969). The Tenebrionidae of southern Africa. Part XLII. Description of the early stages of Carchares macer Pascoe and Herpiscius sommeri Solier with a discussion of some phylogenetic aspects arising from the incongruities of adult and larval systematics. Sci. Pap. Namib Desert Res. Sta., Dr. Fitzsimons commemorative Vol. No. 53, pp. 139–149.

Shulov, A. (1956). The role of water in the eggs of Acrididae. Proc. Int. Congr. Zool., 14th, 1953 pp. 395–401.

Shulov, A., and Pener, M. P. (1963). Studies on the development of eggs of the desert locust (Schistocerca gregaria Forskal) and its interruption under particular conditions of humidity. Anti-Locust Bull. **41**, 1–58.

Slifer, E. H. (1938). The formation and structure of a special water absorbing area in the membrane covering the grasshopper egg. Quart. J. Microsc. Sci. **80**, 437–457.

Solomon, M. E. (1966). Moisture gains, losses and equilibria of flour mites, Acarus siro L., in comparison with larger arthropods. Entomol. Exp. Appl. **9**, 25–41.

Speeg, K. V., and Campbell, J. W. (1968). Formation and volatilization of ammonia gas by terrestrial snails. Amer. J. Physiol. **214**, 1392–1402.

Spencer, J. O., and Edney, E. B. (1954). The absorption of water by woodlice. J. Exp. Biol. **31**, 491–496.

Stobbart, R. H. (1968). Ion movements and water transport in the rectum of the locust Schistocerca gregaria. J. Insect Physiol. **14**, 269–275.

Stobbart, R. H., and Shaw, J. (1964). Salt and water balance: Excretion. In "The Physiology of Insecta" (M. Rockstein, ed.), Vol. 3, pp. 189–258. Academic Press, New York.

Stower, W. J., and Griffiths, J. E. (1966). The body temperature of the desert locust (Schistocerca gregaria). Entomol. Exp. Appl. **9**, 127–178.

Taylor, C. R. (1968). Hygroscopic food: A source of water for desert antelopes? Nature (London) **219**, 181–182.

Tevis, L., and Newell, I. M. (1962). Studies on the biology and seasonal cycle of the giant red velvet mite, Dinothrombium pandorae (Acari, Trombidiidae). Ecology **43**, 497–505.

Tinkham, E. R. (1965). Studies in Nearctic desert sand dune Orthoptera. Part X. A new genus and species of stenopelmatine crickets from the Kelso dunes, with notes on its multi-annual life history and key. Great Basin Natur. **25**, 63–72.

Tinkham, E. R. (1968). Studies in Nearctic desert sand dune Orthoptera. Part

XI. A new arenicolous species of *Stenopalmatus* from Coachella Valley with key and biological notes. *Great Basin Natur.* **28**, 124–131.

Wall, B. J. (1967). Evidence for antidiuretic control of rectal water absorption in the cockroach *Periplaneta americana* L. *J. Insect Physiol.* **13**, 565–578.

Wall, B. J. (1970). Effects of dehydration and rehydration on *Periplaneta americana*. *J. Insect Physiol.* **16**, 1027–1042.

Wall, B. J., and Ralph, C. L. (1964). Evidence for hormonal regulation of Malpighian tubule excretion in the insect *Periplaneta americana* L. *Gen. Comp. Endocrinol.* **4**, 452–456.

Warburg, M. R. (1965a). The microclimate in the habitats of two isopod species in Southern Arizona. *Amer. Mid. Natur.* **73**, 363–375.

Warburg, M. R. (1965b). Water relations and internal body temperature of isopods from mesic and xeric habitats. *Physiol. Zool.* **38**, 99–109.

Warburg, M. R. (1965c). The evaporative water loss of three isopods from semi-arid habitats in South Australia. *Crustaceana* **9**, 302–308.

Weis-Fogh, T. (1967). Respiration and tracheal ventilation in locusts and other flying insects. *J. Exp. Biol.* **47**, 561–587.

Wharton, D. R. A., Wharton, M. L., and Lola, J. (1965). Blood volume and water content of the male American cockroach *Periplaneta americana* L. Methods and the influence of age and starvation. *J. Insect Physiol.* **11**, 391–404.

Wharton, G. W., and Devine, T. L. (1968). Exchange of water between a mite, *Laelaps echidnina,* and the surrounding air under equilibrium conditions. *J. Insect Physiol.* **14**, 1303–1318.

Wieser, W., and Schweizer, G. (1970). A re-examination of the excretion of nitrogen by terrestrial isopods. *J. Exp. Biol.* **52**, 267–274.

Wigglesworth, V. B. (1931). The physiology of excretion in a bloodsucking insect, *Rhodnius prolixus* (Hemiptera, Reduviidae). I. Composition of the urine. *J. Exp. Biol.* **8**, 411–451.

Wigglesworth, V. B. (1945). Transpiration through the cuticle of insects. *J. Exp. Biol.* **21**, 97–114.

Wigglesworth, V. B. (1965). "The Principles of Insect Physiology." Dutton, New York.

Williams, C. B. (1924). Bioclimatic observations in the Egyptian desert in March 1923. *Min. Agr. Egypt. Tech. Sci., Serv. Bull.* **37**, 1–18.

Williams, C. B. (1954). Some bioclimatic observations in the Egyptian desert. *In* "Biology of Deserts" (J. L. Cloudsley-Thompson, ed.), pp. 18–27. Institute of Biology, London.

Woodrow, D. F. (1965a). Laboratory analysis of oviposition behavior in the red locust, *Nomadacris septemfasciata* (Serv.). *Bull. Entomol. Res.* **55**, 733–45.

Woodrow, D. F. (1965b). Observations on the Red Locust (*Nomadacris septemfasciata* Serv.) in the Rukwa Valley, Tanganyika, during its breeding season. *J. Anim. Ecol.* **34**, 187–200.

Yeager, J. F., and Munson, S. C. (1950). Blood volume of the roach *Periplaneta americana* determined by several methods. *Arthropoda* **1**, 255–265.

CHAPTER VII

DESERT FISHES

James E. Deacon and W. L. Minckley

> . . . *hear these springs*
> *That spurt out everywhere with a chuckle*
> *Each filling a private pool for its fish* . . .
> W. H. Auden. In Praise of Limestone

I. Introduction

Climatic deserts include many aquatic habitats where fishes and other organisms persist and often thrive. Such habitats may be special in some of their characteristics, or they may resemble lakes, streams, or springs of temperate or tropical zones. Fishes in deserts are similarly heterogenous. Some species are unique and isolated, while others range widely in complex patterns dictated by past and present drainage connections and environmental conditions, and have highly variable morphologies and bodily functions. With the recent invasions of deserts by modern man, whole habitats have disappeared as new ones arose. Some fish species have been dispersed widely, by accident or design. Other, native ones, have been extirpated, or their stocks were greatly depleted forcing them back into the most inaccessible parts of their ranges. In this chapter we stress, insofar as possible, the inland, indigenous fishes of deserts; their habitats in the pristine state; and their behavioral, morphological, and physiological adaptations for life.

Fishes as a group are remarkably diversified, reflecting in considerable detail the rigorous environmental forces under which they operate. Special environmental features require special adaptations, "adjustments . . . to diverse niches in the environment" (Hubbs, 1941a). Thus, some perpetually torrential streams support highly specialized fishes and other animals that have evolved sucking discs or hooks. Modifications of their mouths, fins, or other body parts hold against the constant turbulence and thrust of current (Hora, 1922). At the other extreme, downstream parts of rivers, lakes, or quiet springs are lentic in nature, and deep-bodied, slowly moving fishes may predominate. In open water of quieter places, small, slim, silvery species occupy pelagic space. Some moderately heavy-bodied forms live on or near the bottoms. In rocky areas or dense beds of aquatic vegetation, laterally compressed, deep-bodied, or elongated, snake-like forms may occur (Nikolsky, 1961, 1963; Lagler *et al.,* 1962).

In habitats between extremes, creeks of intermediate gradient, for example, a major proportion of the fishes are typically small, with rounded bodies and moderately expansive fins. A limbo of variability in such environments, from torrent in flood to pool in drought, dictates a highly adaptable body form and function. With a few notable exceptions, fishes successful in desert waters display generalized shapes. A few minor adjustments in form and function allow their successful exploitation of the sometimes harsh environments.

Coverage in this chapter emphasizes hotter deserts of southwestern United States and northern Mexico, which are the geographic focus of our researches. Information on fishes and aquatic habitats of those regions not specifically attributed to other sources is compiled from our unpublished data. We follow Cole (1968) in embracing a broader definition of desert than might a terrestrial ecologist, since many waters discussed here transcend a number of biomes. With the exception of springs fed by subterranean waters, aquatic habitats of arid lands depend upon surface flow or subsurface infiltration of water from adjacent, more mesic zones (Smith, 1968). Special adaptations of fishes to aquatic circumstances in nondesert regions, which parallel those of desert species, are also drawn upon. However, discussion of fish species alien to deserts, but now present there, is limited generally to effects they have had upon systems into which they were introduced. We have attempted conservation of space by emphasizing reviews of literature when possible.

II. Aquatic Environments of Deserts

A. DESERT RIVERS

Stream habitats are open-ended systems characterized by net, unidirectional movement of water, and by great spatial and temporal variability. Lotic habitats in deserts are exemplified at one extreme by large, through-flowing rivers such as the Nile River of Africa, and the smaller Colorado River of western North America, and at the other extreme by small, almost dry creeks (Figs. 1a–d and 4).

Major streams that flow through deserts usually have their origins in distant places of higher elevation that receive comparatively high, persistent or seasonal, precipitation. Their regimes of discharge are therefore dictated in large part by temporality of rains or melting snows. Large, through-flowing streams have major tributaries that also rise in uplands, but subside into the sands or evaporate, reaching to the mainstream on the surface only in times of flood. Lesser watercourses, lying for the most part on the desert floor, contribute water only during local storms, unless directly spring-fed. Large rivers are more predictable than smaller ones, since the latter are greatly influenced by cyclonic storms so characteristic of many arid regions. The Nile River, prior to its stabilization by Aswan High Dam, was doubtless the epitome of predictability. The spring floods occurred so regularly as to have provided a principal basis for development of the Egyptian civilization.

However, gross variability of desert rivers seems the rule, with most of them subject to long periods of reduced flow, then scoured by major flooding. For instance, the Colorado River at Yuma, Arizona, prior to upstream dams, varied from a peak discharge of near 4.25×10^5 m^3 of water per minute in 1916, to a mere 20.5 m^3/minute in 1934 (Dill, 1944). The Murray–Darling River system of eastern Australia has a drainage area comparable in size, but greater in aridity, than the Colorado, and is even more prone to drought, often becoming a series of isolated pools for hundreds of kilometers of its lower channel (C.S.I.R.O., Australia, 1960; Weatherley, 1967). This is not only a function of low precipitation, but also of high evapotranspiration rates in deserts, which typically exceed precipitation by a substantial percentage (Logan, 1968; McGinnes et al., 1968).

Under natural conditions, water temperatures in large desert rivers are higher in winter than in streams of temperate zones. For example, water

Fig. 1a. Sycamore Creek at Sheep Crossing, Maricopa County, Arizona July, 1972 at a flow of about 0.33 m³/minute. Discharge at this point is typically less than 0.4 m³/minute. Photograph by Robert L. Smith.

temperatures in the Colorado or Murray–Darling systems rarely drop below 10° or 12°C in the winter. Temperatures in the main channel also are moderate in the summer, rarely exceeding 30°C, despite intense radiation which produces air temperatures that average near 40°C, and often range to more than 50°C. This maximum water temperature is scarcely greater than that achieved in large, temperate rivers of Europe and the United States, and is presumably maintained through evaporation from the flowing water into exceedingly dry air (Weatherley, 1963a). Backwaters and more lentic areas often exceed 35°C at the surface in summer.

Highest temperatures in small, flowing Arizona creeks have been recorded in July and August; maxima range from 24° to 40.3°C. Higher temperatures often are present in backwaters (33°–42.7°C). Pronounced variability occurs linearly in some creeks, with cold spots where subsurface water rises at a dike and hot spots after longer flow on the surface and (possible) sinking of cooler waters into interstices. This also may occur in larger rivers where coarse bottom materials allow slow percolation of night-cooled water into warm water of the day (Campbell, 1962). Inflow from springs may also ameliorate temperatures, as may shading by stream-

Fig. 1b. Same locality as in (a), 2 days before, at a discharge of about 35 m³/minute. This was a rapid, high-intensity discharge, derived from a lateral wash which was a normally dry tributary; no rainfall was recorded at weather stations in the vicinity. Photograph by Robert L. Smith.

side vegetation (Macan, 1958) or canyon walls. Orientation of a channel may effect completely different regimes of insolation, and therefore heating. On a single day, the time that maximum temperature is achieved may be successively later at each station downstream, and minimum temperatures that are achieved may be elevated in streams of mesic zones, as volume of water increases and variation in summer air temperatures decreases at lower elevations (Schmitz, 1954). This is generally reversed at the lower ends of desert streams. In those with diminutions of discharge at both up- and downstream ends, the least variation may occur in middle reaches. Streams that receive melt water from montane snows have a later summer maximum in temperature than those receiving water from other sources. Interesting reversals of almost all factors may occur in streams fed by large thermal springs, and all these variations amount to a formidable array of environmental problems for the low desert fish.

Most fishes of desert streams live in main rivers or in the high-elevation parts of tributary networks. Some smaller washes and "dry creeks" support

Fig. 1c. Río los Positos, Cuatro Ciénegas basin, Coahuila, Mexico. This stream, fed by a number of small springs, is about 1.5 meters across in the immediate foreground. Deposition of travertine and other salts along its channel precludes development of woody, riparian vegetation. Photograph by Charles Stone, August 1960.

aquatic animals in places far downstream from upstream segments of perennial flow, but this occurs only when water percolating through coarsegrained sediments of the channel is forced to the surface by transverse deposits of impervious stone. Reaches such as this persist year-round, especially in canyons where shaded from direct, intense insolation, and they have long been important to the desert traveler—be it man, beast, fish, or fowl.

Desert watercourses are plagued by extremes, and one of the most spectacular is the flash flood produced when local runoff concentrates into a relatively narrow channel. Conditions in a smaller creek, or even in a river,

Fig. 1d. Colorado River in Grand Canyon. While much of the native fish fauna persists here, introduced species predominate.

may change from essentially clear water to highly turbid in a matter of seconds. Water temperatures may drop more than 15°C, and current and turbulence may change radically. Even stable bottoms may be scoured and mobilized (Ives, 1936; Jahns, 1949; Kesseli and Beaty, 1959; Thomson and Schumann, 1968), only to be redeposited in about the same configuration as waters recede (Leopold and Maddock, 1955; Leopold, 1962). On the other hand, periods of drought may be accompanied by water temperatures exceeding 40°C, by overgrowth of pools and channels by algae, by evaporative concentration of salts, and, finally, by total desiccation.

Climatic oscillations over past millenia (Martin and Mehringer, 1965), and prior to that the processes of mountain building and elevational adjustments, quite obviously influenced the sizes, positions, and permanences of desert waters. Great valley systems exist within the Sahara Desert

(Gautier, 1935) which certainly are inconsistent with present climatic regimes, and fossil assemblages of vertebrates along these watercourses attest to big river habitats across the presently arid lands (Joleaud, 1935). Similar situations of ancient, now dry valleys, or remnants of terraces produced by streams larger than those now present, occur in many other desert regions (Leopold and Miller, 1954; Wright, 1956; Alimen, 1965).

In some instances, remaining waters of such extinct systems support remnant fish populations, reconfirming drainage connections long since disrupted and obscured (Pellegrin, 1914, 1931, 1934; Braestrup, 1940; Miller, 1946a, 1949a; Hubbs and Miller, 1948a).

Man's activities over the past few decades in North America—and far longer in some other deserts—have accelerated desiccation of streams, especially larger ones. These have almost all been beheaded by impoundment and their waters spread over lowlands to irrigate domesticated crops.

At the time of settlement, large rivers such as the Colorado and Gila of the Sonoran Desert had complex marshes, lakes, and sloughs along their lower courses, as did their major tributaries (Sykes, 1937; Leopold, 1953; Miller, 1961a). Desert creeks also were far more permanent in their lower parts. Smaller streams in southern Arizona flowed through broad, marshy floodplains in multiple channels, or moved by seepage (Hastings, 1959a,b; Miller, 1961a; Hastings and Turner, 1965; Minckley, 1969a). Dark, organic soils form parts of the walls of now dry washes. These soils are remnants of marsh, or *ciénega* deposits (Martin and Mehringer, 1965). Riparian galleries of cottonwood (*Populus*), and other, broad-leafed, deciduous trees, so conspicuous at present along some desert waterways (Lowe, 1967), may well have been restricted to places of relatively good drainage in the recent past. Areas of entrenched channel doubtless were present (Hastings, 1959a,b), bordered by mesquite (*Prosopis*) and forming *bosques* on terraces. Under such conditions stream bottoms are typically of mud and organic debris, except in places of channel degradation or the presence of stony dikes. Currents are slow, impeded by debris and the tortuous nature of channels, and flooding effects are minimized (Miller, 1961a; Minckley, 1969a). The present aspect of many streams in southwestern United States, with broad, sandy, braided channels, may therefore be a disclimatic phenomenon.

A trend toward erosion of channels originated in the 1880's with a cycle of arroyo cutting that may be continuing today (Miller, 1961a; Hastings and Turner, 1965). Similar erosive events were recorded, at about the same time, over a large geographic area, and the relative uniformity "makes it difficult to link settlement . . . with arroyo cutting, the uniform onset . . . on the other hand, points toward operation of a broad regional factor like climate" (Hastings and Turner, 1965). However, in southern

Arizona, at least, severe overgrazing by domestic cattle in the period 1870–1890 resulted in death of about 75% of the herd when protracted drought grasped the region in 1891–1894. Effects of this catastrophe on water and vegetation are vividly documented by paired photographs published by Hastings and Turner, which contrast the late 1800's with the present. There is little doubt that aquatic habitats, and fishes, especially those of streams, were also severely affected. The largest streams have, in addition, been subjected to channelization and stabilization of flow through impoundment (Beland, 1953; Miller, 1961a), which has essentially eliminated the indigenous fauna (Minckley and Deacon, 1968; Minckley, 1971), and appears to have substantially altered and decreased the value of the introduced sport fishes as well (Beland, 1953).

B. Springs and Marshes

Desert springs (Fig. 2a,b) range from swift-flowing origins of creeks (*rheocrenes*), to quiet, limpid pools (*limnocrenes*) in caves, in travertine cones, or at ground level (the last perhaps best fitting the classical concept of the oasis), and through mere trickles along canyon walls to extensive seepages into raised marshes. Larger, permanent springs in arid lands are most often positioned at points of discharge of meteoric waters along fracture zones, in regions of intensive, relatively recent geologic activity such as folding and faulting. Many emit thermal, magmatic waters, or meteoric water heated by contact with volcanics or by passage through the normal geothermal gradient, which in regions of relatively undisturbed, uniform rocks means a temperature increase with depth of 1°C for each 15–30 meters (Waring, 1965). Confined aquifers rising as springs along faults are perhaps most common. Less frequent are those flowing in the lower parts of basins just above the seal created by impervious lake beds, or at the toes of bajadas leading from montane catchments. Large, limestone springs, such as those of humid, karsted regions of many continents (Swinnerton, 1942; Easterbrook, 1969) are rare in deserts, but a few important ones exist in arid parts of New Mexico, Texas, northern Mexico, and elsewhere. These often are represented by deep sinkholes, in the bottoms of which water and aquatic organisms persist.

Desert springs often are supplied from catchments located as many as a few hundred kilometers away, with water moving by interbasin transport to the discharge point (Maxey, 1968). These types of recharge areas, or origins from deep, magmatic sources, favor relative independence of discharge from local patterns of precipitation. Climatic shifts do, however, result in changes in discharge of springs of meteoric origin (Haynes,

Fig. 2a. Posos de la Becerra, Cuatro Ciénegas basin, Coahuila, Mexico. Prior to essential drainage in 1964; a large limnocrene which harbored about 15 species of fishes and fed marshes and streams estimated to have covered more than 200 hectares. From Minckley (1969b); photograph by Charles Stone, August 1970. Note two persons standing to the far left to provide some perspective.

1967), and minor regional changes in climate of a major catchment might even tend to be magnified at the point of water discharge. Interdiction of flows of meteoric water by man-made wells quite obviously effects changes downslope, resulting in decline of discharges (Fiero and Maxey, 1970), and in many cases their total failure (Miller, 1961a; Haynes, 1967; Minckley and Deacon, 1968).

Despite considerable evidence for the antiquity of such spring systems, or major desert springs, orogenic disturbances in geologically active areas may greatly influence their temporal and spatial relations. For example, an indication of northward tilting of the floor of Death Valley, California, since the time of pluvial Lake Manley (Hunt and Mabey, 1966), strongly suggests that many springs may have been shut off, and others created. These changes, sometimes occurring only recently, offer one explanation for the absence of fishes in some apparently suitable habitats of Death Valley (LaBounty and Deacon, 1971), and perhaps elsewhere, and their presence in others. Numerous fossil springs, marked by deposits of travertines, sinter, or peat mounds, mutely attest to gradual, overall reductions in surface flow in southwestern United States, and in most other desert areas,

Fig. 2b. Posos de la Becerra, Cuatro Ciénegas basin, Coahuila, Mexico, 3 days after opening of the drainage canal to the right; all marshes, center and to the right, and flowing streams, now are dry, and the surface area of the spring is less than one hectare. From Minckley, 1969; photograph by William S. Brown, December 1964.

over the past few thousands of years. (Brues, 1928; Hubbs and Miller, 1948a; Waring, 1965; Mehringer, 1967).

Variations because of climatic shifts and orogenic disturbances contrast with the relative thermal, chemical, and volumetric constancy of desert springs. Thermal springs, those which maintain water temperatures somewhat above that of the mean annual air temperature of the area in which they emerge, are sometimes remarkable in their constancy (Waring, 1965). Arago (1838) even suggested that hot springs near Bône, Algeria, could not have varied more than 4°C over a period of 2000 years! Springs issuing from shallower aquifers may be constant at a temperature approximating that of prevailing annual means for air, or may fluctuate with season, sometimes in a delayed manner that reflects winter precipitation by issuance of cooler water in summer, and vice versa. Certain areas have complex patterns of warm and cool springs interspersed together (Meinzer, 1917; Brues, 1928; Minckley, 1969b), which indicate totally different sources of water for the two types. In some regions, cool springs are far

Fig. 2c. Cottonball marsh, Death Valley National Monument, California. Type locality of *Cyprindon n.* sp. at 80 m below mean sea level. (Photo by Dwight Warren, U.S. National Park Service.)

more fluctuant than warmer ones (Minckley, 1969b), further suggesting a shallower origin and greater influence of contemporaneous climatic phenomena. Temperature conditions, usually hot but sometimes cool, limit the occurrence of some fishes in desert areas.

Chemical constancy of desert spring waters also is a general rule. Dissolved substances are typically a function of sediments through which flow percolates before reaching the surface. Series of springs that discharge in progressively lower parts of a groundwater system show increasingly greater content of dissolved solids near their termini, due to longer passage through various deposits (Maxey and Mifflin, 1966), or perhaps through reinfiltration of evaporatively concentrated water. Spring sources range from very fresh water, to highly mineralized, but high total dissolved solids usually predominate. Springs carrying large amounts of dissolved materials, especially bicarbonates, often deposit extensive formations of travertine, building cones or terraces downflow (Graf, 1960a,b; Cole and Batchelder, 1969). This generally comprises part of a remarkable sequence of changes that occurs as spring waters move onto the desert floor. Chemical features of some springs also include extremely low dissolved oxygen,

Fig. 2d. Topock Marsh and the adjacent Colorado River, Arizona–California, one of the last great desert marshes in North America. Note that the stream flows turbid, a result of a local cyclonic storm, and a condition that historically must have been a general rule. (Photograph by Robert D. Ohmart, November, 1972.)

high dissolved solids, or the presence of toxic materials such as free carbon dioxide, which may preclude occupation by fishes.

Marshes (Fig. 2c,d), usually densely vegetated by sedges (*Scirpus*) are integral parts of spring systems, and also occur in association with most other aquatic habitats in deserts (Bradley, 1970). Many differ radically from their immediate sources of water, tending to be highly fluctuant in temperature and other features. The normally high organic content is productive of marked variations in oxygen, carbon dioxide, and other gaseous compounds, under differing conditions of respiration by their biotas. Desert marshes are highly saline in times of low water, but fresh at other times. As one passes away from the immediate water supply, variability in marshes, or in channels flowing through a marsh, become so extreme that only salt grasses (*Distichlis*) and chenopods may exist, or higher plants and most animal life are entirely excluded. In many respects, desert marshes resemble those of estuarine and other coastal environments (Chapman, 1960), in which variations limit the biota to those organisms with a large potential for physicochemical stress compensation (Kinne, 1963, 1964, 1966). Variations that are associated with riverine environments, or larger, strongly flowing springs, are, however, typically less extreme.

C. Lakes

In some arid regions, water from rivers or springs may accumulate in closed basins to form major lacustrine habitats (Fig. 3). Such basins are termed endorheic, and the lakes produced therein depend upon fine balances of inflow, evaporation, and seepage, to maintain their transitory existence (Cole, 1963, 1968; Williams, 1967a). In the not too distant past, tremendous lakes occupied large expanses of western North America and northern Mexico (Hubbs and Miller, 1948a; Snyder *et al.,* 1964; Weidie and Murray, 1967), fluctuating with changes in climate to ultimately evaporate and form the broad expanses of saline flats, termed playas, that we see today. Hubbs (1941b) provided a lucid, verbal picture of these massive, extinct habitats, as follows:

> Through examination of physiographic features we learn that large streams once flowed permanently through now dry washes . . . either to reach the main rivers that continue to the sea, or to feed the clear lakes and great in-

Fig. 3. Pyramid Lake, Nevada, a remnant of pluvial Lake Lahonton. Water level has declined about 27 m since 1867 largely because of a diversion dam for irrigation constructed in 1905. Reduced flows below the dam which resulted in a very shallow delta at the lake, in combination with the barrier imposed by the dam, resulted in destruction of spawning runs of Lahonton cutthroat trout by 1929. (Photograph by Thomas J. Trelease, January, 1948.)

land seas which, in place of alkali flats, once floored the many basins in the area of interior drainage. Across the larger of the bare and level lake beds we may drive in any direction, foot down on the pedal and hands off the wheel if we wish, ever chasing the mirage of water which the heat waves cause to rise before us. Glancing back the mirage is seen to follow us, as though the ghost of the waters that once filled the basin were rushing to engulf us. As the coolness of the evening dispels these unreal waters, the mountains come forth in the ruggedness of their naked rock, in clearness that belies their distance. Across their bases, yet to a height of many hundreds of feet are seen clear-cut terraces and great sea cliffs . . . which were cut by the very obviously real waters of former times. By reason of the dry climate, the terraces have been preserved through centuries with such fidelity that geological skill is not needed to interpret their significance. Great bars of wave-washed gravel, now bone-dry, also tell convincingly of former shore lines and strong currents . . . . The great Quaternary seas of the west—some comparable in area and depth with the Great Lakes—may have persisted long enough to have been gazed upon by desert Indians, who had legends of great waters. These seas, however, had evaporated into the dry desert air long before civilized man arrived to paint their glory in colors and words, to cover their surfaces with great ships of commerce, and to pollute their waters with the waste products of the great cities which would surely have arisen along their now dry and unpeopled shores.

Few natural lakes presently exist in deserts, and many of those that do are too saline or astatic to support fishes. Many remnant lakes have only recently become extinct or uninhabitable by fishes because of salinity, as a result of beheading of tributary streams by dams (Minckley and Cole, 1968), actual drainage (Williams, 1967b), pumpage from their basins, or other man-induced catastrophes. It is notable that the reverse situation also has rarely occurred, such as the inadvertent formation of the Salton Sea in the basin of pluvial Lake LeConte (Hubbs and Miller, 1948a) beginning when the Colorado River broke through irrigation works in the flood of 1905 and produced a lake 25 meters deep and 1334 km² in surface area (MacDougal, 1914; Walker, 1961).

With few exceptions, environments of closed-basin lakes include shallow waters subject to severe wind action and thermal variations, at least local conditions of high turbidity and salinity, and a pronounced monotony of bottoms, shorelines, and other features. On occasion, diverse deposits of travertines are formed (Dunn, 1953). Dome-shaped formations, the algal biostromes of Carozzi (1962), grow through accretion of salts and debris, physicochemically and by algae, in places generally protected from violent waves. As with marshes, some desert lacustrine habitats resemble in many respects lagoons along desert sea coasts.

Only a few deep, relatively ancient lakes persist in arid lands, such as Pyramid Lake, Nevada (Fig. 3). Lakes associated with riverine environments, and large limnocrenes, are discussed relative to their origins.

III. General Ecology

A. PHYSICAL FACTORS

1. Current and Turbulence

Flashflooding, one of the more frequently dicussed features of deserts, seldom annihilates fishes from a habitat despite its impressive violence. As is typical in nature, desert fishes avoid the problem if possible, moving behind boulders, or along the banks at the onset of flooding, then into backwaters as water overrides the banks. In narrow, high-gradient streams, no refuge may be available. John (1964) recorded possible extirpation of a population of speckled dace (*Rhinichthys osculus*) from a small mountain creek in the Chiricahua Mountains, Arizona. Hubbs and Miller (1943) wrote of depletion and changes in population structure of the minnows *Siphateles* (= *Gila*) *mohavensis, Gila orcutti,* and their hybrids, after severe flooding in the Mohave River, southern California, and in a later paper (Hubbs and Miller, 1948a) they hypothesized that a number of tributaries to pluvial Lake LeConte (Salton Sink) were fishless as a result of past flooding. One population of the Gila chub (*Gila intermedia*) was severely decimated, if not destroyed, in the narrow gorge of Fish Creek, Maricopa County, Arizona, by flooding in winter of 1965–1966. That canyon ranges from 6 to 20 meters wide, and Fish Creek typically consists of a series of deep pools connected by trickles of water. Marks on the walls were 12 meters above normal water levels in narrower places.

A tremendous flood in September, 1970 in Sycamore Creek, Maricopa County, Arizona, completely scoured the stream channel, destroyed all gauging devices, caused unestimated damage to property and streamside habitat, and took a number of human lives. Only a few longfin dace (*Agosia chrysogaster*) lived through the catastrophe, but within 1 week young of that species were hatching, and by 1 month, young fish virtually filled the creek. Adults were exceedingly rare, occurring in only the largest, most permanent and protected pools, but their populations seemed to increase in those places through the days following flooding, perhaps through migration of fish back into their home areas after displacement downstream.

A similar, but somewhat less severe flood was observed in 1960 in Río Cañon, north of Cuatro Ciénegas, Coahuila, Mexico. Rain exceeded 5 cm overnight, and the creek that normally flowed about 12 m³/minute rose 3 meters, filling its canyon wall to wall as it concentrated in narrow places. Severe flooding occurred in the village which lies near the canyon mouth, and numerous cichlid fishes (*Cichlasoma* spp.) were stranded in the streets when water receded. These presumably washed from the pond at a winery, since they were not known to occur in the creek itself (Minckley, 1969b). Riparian vegetation was sorely damaged by the flood, and the bottom of the stream was scoured deeply. No data were obtained on the fishes, but adults and young of all native species were common the following April.

In August, 1964, a smaller flood was observed in the same area, and the fishes either moved laterally into vegetation inundated along the banks (a poeciliid, *Gambusia marshi*), or seemingly remained in the channel, despite pronounced increases in current (a catfish, *Ictalurus lupus* [?], and the Mexican tetra, *Astyanax fasciatus mexicanus*). The catfish and tetra are found frequently in swifter waters of the Cuatro Ciénegas area, at least for part of the time (Minckley, 1969b). The only mortality seen was of *Gambusia* trapped in shallow backwaters, which soon dried.

Effects of additional flooding were observed in August, 1964 in narrow canyons east of Cuatro Ciénegas where headwaters of the Río Salado de los Nadadores pass out of the Sacramento basin toward the Río Grande. At this point the canyon is perhaps 100 meters wide and was almost totally choked with a luxuriant stand of reeds (*Phragmites communis*) that grew to more than 5 meters high. The entire stand was flattened to the ground, and marks on canyon walls indicated that at least 4 meters of water raced through the area, coming mostly from mountains to the north. No flooding occurred through the canyon connecting the Cuatro Ciénegas and Sacramento basins; water from the Río Cañon simply sank into an extensive alluvial fan. There was no evidence for significant damage to the fishes of the Río Salado de los Nadadores, and in April, 1965, few traces of the spate remained; even the reeds had totally recovered.

An incident in India, quite different from those already discussed, involved failure of a dam that produced a flood said to have destroyed an entire downstream fish fauna (Nikolsky, 1963). A similar happening in central Arizona followed heavy rains of 1965–1966 that prematurely melted a montane snow-pack. Accumulation of runoff exceeded storage capacity of reservoirs, and when flood gates were opened, flow in the channel of the Salt River rose from a few tens of m^3/minute to more than 1.2×10^5 m^3/minute in a few hours. High discharge was maintained for some days, and when water receded a remarkable number of fishes were dead in the few trees that remained on terraces. Most were introduced species, such as threadfin shad (*Dorosoma petenense*) and sunfishes (*Lepomis* spp.) from upstream lakes. Fishes still living in abundance in the channel were almost exclusively native suckers (*Catostomus* and *Pantosteus*), while introduced forms common there prior to the massive discharge were destroyed. A number of alien kinds, abundant in downstream areas of waste-water ponds, have not again been found (Minckley and Deacon, 1968; Minckley, 1971).

Broad, shallow, braided stream channels without well-defined (or confining) banks do not typically experience severe scour and modification of habitat during floods. Changes in species composition or of abundances of certain kinds frequently occur, but extirpation of the fauna is again almost never indicated. In the Death Valley system, for example (Miller, 1948), both the Salt Creek pupfish (*Cyprinodon salinus*) and the Nevada pupfish (*C. nevadensis amargosae*) of the Amargosa River mainstream must have survived innumerable floods, and they even persist in the relatively narrow canyons of those streams (Miller, 1943, 1948; LaBounty, 1968). Morphological variability is pronounced in the Amargosa River subspecies of Nevada pupfish, especially in downstream populations, and this was attributed most likely to flood transport of slightly differentiated upstream fish into the lower area (Miller, 1948).

Floods in the Amargosa have had little discernible effect on populations of fish, but many individuals were displaced downstream where they died as pools evaporated (Wauer, 1962; unpublished data). The Red River pupfish (*Cyprinodon rubrofluviatilis*) is another species of this group that lives in broad, sandy-bottomed rivers, and apparently copes successfully with major flooding so characteristic of Plains streams. The desert pupfish (*Cyprinodon macularius*) must also have had such capabilities in streams of southern Arizona. It now is extirpated in most of that area through interactions with alien fish species (Minckley and Deacon, 1968).

High waters, in addition to sorting out different species on the bases of their resistances or avoidance reactions, may also affect young fishes more severely than adults. John (1964) noted that young speckled dace were carried farther in flood than were adults, and we have similar information on that species, and on longfin dace and suckers (*Pantosteus clarki* and *Catostomus insignis*) in Arizona creeks. In other instances, no sorting by sizes was evident after spates (Barber *et al.*, 1970). Fishes may also sort themselves actively in relation to current, with larger (stronger) ones moving into rapids and young remaining in quieter waters, or more downstream.

Shifting of bedload in a stream is of major importance during flood. Not only does it produce tremendous molar action that may physically damage animals, but also fills pools with sand and rock (Fig. 4), especially when a spate is of high intensity and short duration. Fajen (1963) found marked population instability resulting from wandering of fishes in such a shifting stream. There was a general lack of homing since pools and well-marked riffles were periodically destroyed or displaced. We know of no similar studies of desert streams but there is a strong tendency for larger individuals of most desert fishes in Arizona creeks to remain in a given, permanent place, if such is available. In streams with sand bottoms, con-

Fig. 4. Sycamore Creek at Sheep Crossing, Maricopa County, Arizona June, 1971, at a rate of discharge of about 0.3 m³/minute. Note extensive aggradation of channel in comparison to Figs. 1(a) and 1(b). (Photograph by J. Jerry Landye.)

figuration of canyon walls or boulders often create permanency by inducing currents that consistently deepen some parts of the stream.

In some creeks, man-created diversion dams provide almost the only deep water available to large fishes, and in this instance some benefits may accrue from man's activities. Many major changes in the ichthyofauna of the American Southwest have, however, been attributed to increased bed-load and filling of pools after the 1800's period of arroyo cutting (Miller, 1961a).

Springs that are subject to flooding rarely harbor distinctive fish or invertebrate faunas, and in rivers that originate in larger springs, unique animals found at the sources are often totally restricted there (Hubbs *et al.*, 1953; Hubbs and Springer, 1957; Hubbs, 1957a,b; Minckley, 1969b). These facts presumably result, in part, from periodic scouring and filling with debris during spates, and other variations. This situation is illustrated particularly well in the Pecos River system, southern New Mexico and northwestern Texas. Springs adjacent to, but protected from, the river support cyprinodontoid fishes and other animals of similar habitat requirements (Koster, 1957). Those in the channel of the river or on its immediate floodplain contain only typical riverine species. Some isolated desert springs may receive influx of water and debris after periods of unusually heavy runoff, but such events must be rare since endemic fishes and other organisms have persisted in them for millenia. Devil's Hole, Nevada (James, 1969), and some spring pools immediately adjacent to mountains surrounding the Cuatro Ciénegas basin, Coahuila, were influenced in this manner in July, 1968, with little discernible result other than temporary turbidities.

Emphasis on floods and their direct and indirect effects may detract the reader from the far greater importance of constant, specific influences of everyday, or normal, current (a term used by us to embrace both net, unidirectional flow and the turbulence within that flow). Repeated reference to this in past (and future) sections therefore will be summarized and expanded later, emphasizing modal conditions as more important than the extremes. The latter seem invariably stressed in works such as this since they catch the human interest, and of course provide insight into the ways of life of the animals under discussion.

2. Suspended Solids and Sedimentation

In rivers or lakes situated in areas of finely divided soils, under conditions of drainage from denuded basins, or sometimes persistently in shallow windswept lakes or highly degrading streams, turbidity and sedimentation of silts have great impact on aquatic habitats and fishes. Exceedingly high concentrations of suspended solids may physically suffocate fishes by accumulation in the branchial chamber and on the gill filaments (Wallen, 1951; Buck, 1956). Kills of small-mouthed, riffle-inhabiting catostomids have been recorded in nature in the United States (Black, 1949; Trautman, 1957; Minckley, 1971), and similarly of species of cyprinoids and other groups in montane regions of India and Afghanistan (Nikolsky, 1963). Mass mortalities in the last areas were related to greatly increased suspension of solids produced by runoff from monsoon rains, and even a sisorid catfish, *Glyptosternum reticulatum,* highly adapted for life in swift, turbid waters, died under conditions that prevailed.

Some fishes, notably a lungfish (*Lepidosiren*) and an eel (*Pisodonophis boro*), possess body mucus that precipitates or coagulates finely divided sediments (principally clays). Precipitation is effected as a result of neutralization of negative charges on colloidal clays, by a rapid change from circum-neutral to acidic in the mucus. This change occurs when the mucus contacts water (van Oosten, 1957), and the fish moves in a cell of clear water through fine muds that often comprise its habitat. In addition, mucus has a lubricating effect on suspended particles, tending to move them away from the skin or surfaces of the gills.

High turbidity tends to shade aquatic habitats and suppress development of algae and other plants, but on the other hand, input from land is obviously necessary in the overall trophic economy of natural waters. Sedimentation of suspended solids, however, may have a detrimental effect on bottom-dwelling fish-food organisms, or may physically smother fish eggs or larvae (Starrett, 1950a, 1951).

Other adaptations to, or against, suspended solids in natural waters include development of barbels and other types of cutaneous sense organs for increase in the proportion of nonvisual sensory input (Moore, 1950; Branson, 1966), sometimes a considerable reduction in the exposed surface of the eye (Moore, 1950), development of special surfaces within the eye for concentration of light (Moore, 1944a), and reductions in squamation, or development of a leathery skin with minute, embedded scales, the last two presumably in response to the abrasive nature of certain highly turbid waters (Hubbs, 1940, 1941a).

Morphology of the brain in fishes also varies according to their mode of feeding (Miller and Evans, 1965; Davis and Miller, 1967), which is related to the level of light in their environment that is, in turn, a partial function of turbidity. It is interesting in this respect that the morphology of brains of fishes from relatively constant habitats, whether they are perennially turbid or typically clear, tends to be far less variable than that from fishes living in markedly variable habitats (Davis and Miller, 1967). This tendency was found within the species level when subspecies of wide-ranging forms were compared, and among species.

As with flooding, tremendous increases in turbidity pose severe, immediate problems for fishes, and they similarly tend to avoid it or to move to areas where current assists in minimizing its physical effects (Trautman, 1957).

3. Drought and Desiccation

Downstream displacement of fishes by flood, recorded in some large rivers of more mesic zones (Viosca, in Trautman, 1957), may have fatal results under desert conditions. Fish populations from streams tributary to closed-basin lakes or playas, or to now dry channels of formerly large rivers, may be left on dry flats or injected into salinities of lethal concentrations.

In the Namib and Kalahari Deserts of southern Africa, rare flows of water in ancient river beds carry fishes from the southwest African Plateau and western Transvaal Highveld into arid zones, where they typically perish as the rivers again desiccate (Jubb, 1969). Included in these pioneering species are three cyprinids, genus *Barbus,* a clariid catfish, and two cichlids. None of these have special adaptations for survival, other than their broad, ecological tolerances, but the clariid has epibranchial organs that allow it to persist under "most austere conditions" (Jubb, 1969). Only the catfish and the cichlids maintain small, relatively permanent, stunted populations on the desert floor (Jubb, cited in Cole, 1968).

In deserts of the American Southwest, the longfin dace and some species of *Cyprinodon* are the only native fishes that presently penetrate far into temporary waters at times of high precipitation and runoff (Minckley and Barber, 1971; unpublished data), but a number of introduced forms, the red shiner (*Notropis lutrensis*), fathead minnow (*Pimephales promelas*), Río Grande killifish (*Fundulus zebrinus*), mosquitofish (*Gambusia affinis*), and green sunfish (*Lepomis cyanellus*), spread into temporary streams at any opportunity. All the last species are considered highly resistant to extremes, and/or as colonizers, within their native ranges (Koster, 1957; Cross, 1967).

In periods of almost-terminal drying of desert watercourses, the processes of evapotranspiration may demand essentially all the surface water of a small stream during the day (Campbell and Green, 1968). Mass mortalities of fishes occur. Longfin dace, however, persist alive beneath saturated mats of algae and debris, and at night when flow is resumed under reduced temperatures, incident radiation, and photosynthesis, the fish swim about and feed in a few millimeters of water. For a 14-day period in 1965, an ever-declining population of longfin dace persisted in this manner in Sycamore Creek, under alternating, wet and dry, diel cycles. A small rain in August rejuvenated the stream (Minckley and Barber, 1971). Kilby (1955) found sheepshead pupfish (*Cyprinodon variegatus*) on the Florida coast remaining beneath algal mats between tides, a roughly analogous situation.

In years past, prior to introduction of mosquitofish, the Gila topminnow (*Poeciliopsis o. occidentalis*) was also characteristic of such desert habitats, "appearing from the sands" of dry washes after surface flows commenced. The fish doubtless spread to repopulate such streams from more permanent habitats upstream, or from local, isolated refugia (Hubbs and Miller, 1941; Minckley, 1969c). This species, and the desert pupfish of Arizona streams (which also must have lived under intermittent conditions), now are essentially eliminated. Pupfish continue to exhibit their remarkable colonizing ability in Death Valley and Cuatro Ciénegas streams and marshes and in a few other places.

An interesting hazard for longfin dace in Arizona streams is the water-net alga, *Hydrodictyon,* which sometimes chokes backwaters and smaller channels of drying creeks. This alga effectively gill-nets small fishes; they become entangled in its meshes and ultimately die. Lewis (1961) recorded this in Illinois ponds and noted an apparent avoidance of the thalli by survivors after an initial period of mortality.

On occasion, fishes transported into ephemeral waters may persist for a time, even for a number of years, until evaporation, salinization, or temperatures exceed their tolerances. Populations of temporary lakes or streams also may be cyclical, oscillating with vagaries of inflow from springs or tributary streams (Kosswig, 1961; Minckley, 1969b; Minckley and Barber, 1971).

Information on specific effects of drought on fishes of deserts in western North America and elsewhere is largely general and widely scattered. However, a number of workers have dealt with effects of low water on fishes of eastern United States: James (1934), Stehr and Branson (1938), Paloumpis (1957, 1958), Larimore et al. (1959), Deacon (1961), and Deacon and Metcalf (1961), to name but a few. Their results generally correspond with data we have accumulated in low-elevation, desert streams. Survival of fishes in remnant pools is similar in all kinds of climate. Crowding is extreme and diseases may decimate them, as may starvation and heavy predation by a broad spectrum of other animals, ranging from mammals to dytiscid coleopterans and decapod crustaceans (James, 1934; Minckley and Barber, 1971). Cannibalism by larger fish also seems to occur, or young succumb to environmental extremes in a differential manner.

The presence of a single, large, predatory fish in a drying pool may spell doom for all other fishes similarly trapped. Accumulation of organic matter such as leaves in intermittent pools (Larimore et al., 1959), a rare event in sparsely vegetated deserts, death and decomposition of part of the biota, or the simple presence of a large number of fishes (Lowe et al., 1967) may deplete dissolved oxygen, and only those species capable of using atmospheric oxygen or oxygen from the thin surface film may survive.

Numerous groups of fishes have species adapted for survival in foul water, or in essentially dry habitats. Auxillary respiratory surfaces are developed in the bucco-pharyngeal region as invaginations, pouches, or special epibrachial organs, in the digestive tract, and even in external skin (Black, 1951; Todd and Ebeling, 1966; Teal and Carey, 1967). The lungfishes (Dipnoi) have gas bladders that are respiratory, as in the lungs of higher vertebrates, and many physostomus fishes are facultative air-breathers, utilizing vascularized tissues associated with their gas bladders. Even in physoclistous species, a considerable respiratory advantage is imparted to those forms having a dorsally oriented mouth (Poeciliidae and Cyprinodontidae, among others), since they have far greater access to the air–water interface (Lowe et al., 1967; Lewis, 1970). Physiological mechanisms also exist that allow greater tolerances to low levels of dissolved oxygen and to other parameters in fishes frequenting harsh environments (Lowe et al., 1967).

Highly developed capabilities for land locomotion, ranging from refined "walking" in some species to a mere flipping from pool to pool, are developed in certain estuarine and marine fishes (Stebbins and Kalk, 1961; Todd, 1968). Similar capabilities are present in marine-derived or obligate fresh water fishes of many mesic zones (Graham, 1911; Laird, 1956). We know of no such adaptations in desert fishes.

In places with extremely porous bottom materials, such as coarse gravels of creek beds, fishes may escape desiccation by moving into water flowing through interstices (Stegman and Minckley, 1959). Neel (1951) suggested that they might survive drought by moving into burrows of crayfish, much as some coastal, marine fishes use mud burrows of invertebrates (Barlow, 1961a), or construct burrows of their own (Stebbins and Kalk, 1961). The notorious burrowing and aestivating capabilities of some lungfishes are so well publicized that reiteration here seems unnecessary.

In Australian deserts, gobiomorids and the native "minnows" (family Galaxiidae, *Galaxias* spp.) may survive drought by burrowing in muds or moist soils, much in the manner of lungfishes (Whitley, 1959). A great number of species of diverse groups utilize this same type of avoidance behavior in drying pools of tropical zones, especially those fishes having accessory respiratory devices. American pupfishes may live as long as 10 days in moist muds or organic debris. The mosquitofish has been known to survive 4 days in the bottoms of almost dry reservoirs, if temperatures did not exceed 18°C, humidity remained higher than 85%, and the fish were not exposed to direct sunlight (Afanasev, 1944). Many cyprinodont fishes bury in the substrate under severe conditions, especially in colder weather, or as a means of escape (Cowles, 1934; Minckley and Itzkowitz, 1967; Deacon, 1968a; Minckley and Klaassen, 1969a). The longfin dace may also bury, but this has been infrequently and unsatisfactorily observed (Minckley and Barber, 1971).

It must be reemphasized that only a few of the fish species discussed above live under desert conditions, and morphological and behavioral adaptations of these types are found primarily in forms living in tropical areas that enjoy high, but seasonal, rainfall. Overriding forces of desiccation under low humidities, high incident light, and usually high temperatures (plus, perhaps, accumulation of salts), appear too extreme for fish life to persist in most instances of drought in deserts.

4. Direct Effects of Light

The broad importance of light and light-related factors in activity of fishes, reproductive cycles, and so on, will be discussed in Section IV. However, some direct effects of incident radiation may best be discussed here. Intense solar radiation coupled with clear, shallow water may damage fishes, although the results of desiccation of epidermis exposed to air may confuse the issue somewhat. We have found longfin dace and pupfishes with whitened, sloughing tissue on their dorsolateral surfaces, and with severely damaged caudal and dorsal fins, presumably as a result of sunburn, drying, or both (Minckley and Barber, 1971, and subsequent observations). Pupfishes, afflicted with gaseous distension of their digestive tracts which forced them to the surface (Minckley and Itzkowitz, 1967), were similarly injured. Sunburn has been demonstrated in hatchery-maintained salmonid fishes at various latitudes (DeLong et al., 1958; Allison, 1960; Corson and Brezosky, 1961), and cataracts of the eyes in salmonids also have been related to sun exposure (Allison, 1962). Direct damage usually is followed by secondary infection by bacteria or fungi, and death often ensues in desert fishes we have studied.

Certain wavelengths of light (ultraviolet) are lethal to the embryos of killifish (*Fundulus*) exposed at early stages of development (Hinrichs, 1925); exposure of older embryos resulted in delayed hatching. Haempel and Lechler (1931) theorized that summer levels of ultraviolet in nature would be lethal at midday to exposed salmonid embryos and larvae. Most wavelengths of radiation that contact fishes, however, are in the visible spectrum, since water allows only poor transmission of ultraviolet or infrared. Inhibition of hatching of eggs or growth of larvae by visible light has been widely reported (Perlmutter, 1961; Breder, 1962), and some pelagic ova of marine species rise at night and sink in the day, possibly as an adaptation toward limiting exposure to radiations (Breder, 1962).

On the other hand, the total absence of light may also inhibit hatching of eggs of fishes of epigean habit (Rasquin and Rosenbloom, 1954; Breder, 1962). Breder proposed that the transparency of eggs and larvae of some fishes were adaptations allowing radiations to pass through (i.e., not to be absorbed), and therefore not to influence sensitive tissues or enzyme systems. Pigments, colored oils or fat globules, or physical placement of ova in sheltered places away from light, are other presumed means of avoiding radiation exposures. Almost all the shallow-water fishes with which we are familiar in deserts deposit their eggs beneath the surface of the substrate, on or within aquatic vegetation, or on debris.

Most cyprinodontids have pigmented larvae, with melanophores heavily investing the dorsum of the head and visceral cavity, at least. Cyprinoids, on the other hand, are essentially transparent and have darkened areas on the midline of the back and over the cranial vault. In general, fishes with permanently exposed pineal areas of the brain usually produce transparent eggs and larvae, and those which produce heavily pigmented eggs have thick skulls or heavy pigmentation over the pineal region. Many intermediate groups can control pineal exposure to light. Unexpectedly, they expose the region in light and tend to cover it in darkness (Breder, 1962). Therefore, the protective nature of some of these features, along with an often-stated correlation between darkened meninges of the brain, darker dorsal surfaces of the head, or blackened peritonea of adult fishes, with incident radiation [the "protective adaptations against the light" of Nikolsky (1963)] seems problematical. Darkened peritonea also appear to correlate with a long digestive tract and an herbivorous diet (Hubbs and Black, 1947; Smith, 1966).

5. Temperature

Conditions of constant high temperature in springs and of widely fluctuating temperatures in other desert waters may introduce stresses to which only a few fish species have successfully adapted. Problems of thermal adaptations and acclimation in aquatic poikilotherms have been discussed by many authors, and reviews by Fry (1947, 1957), Brett (1956), Prosser (1958), Prosser and Brown (1961), and Kinne (1963) summarize much of the information available and establish terminology and general concepts. All fishes have a range of temperature within which they are capable of survival, and they usually have a somewhat narrower range where maximum respiratory efficiency is maintained. The optima for a species may change with seasonal trends, through gradual acclimation. Prior acclimation determines in part the upper and lower limits of tolerance, and the full range of acclimation temperatures, along with consequent shifts in maximum and minimum lethal temperatures, defines the zone of thermal tolerance. Such zones have been determined for relatively few fishes, but they provide a most convenient method for comparing thermal labilities.

In general, Brett (1956) showed that among North American fishes, Salmonidae have the narrowest and Ictaluridae the broadest zones of thermal tolerance of groups studied to that date. Poeciliids exhibited a tolerance nearly equal to that of ictalurids, while cyprinids, with the exception of the Asiatic goldfish (*Carassius auratus*), which had the broadest zone of all species tested (see also Fry *et al.,* 1942), were generally intermediate.

Another measure of thermal capabilities is the incipient lethal temperature, defined as the temperature that 50% of a population can withstand for an infinite period of time. Levels above or below these upper and lower limits may be tolerated for short periods, and such resistance time is exceedingly important in deserts since it permits fishes to enter (or temporarily persist in) temperatures that eventually would be lethal.

Some workers, notably Heath (1962, 1967) and Lowe and Heath (1969), have used the critical thermal maximum as a measure of temperature tolerance in fishes. This technique subjects experimental populations that have been acclimated at a constant temperature to a gradual increase or decrease until death ensues.

Some of the higher temperatures tolerated by poikilothermous vertebrates have been recorded for desert fishes, and most field maxima
correspond well to those recorded by various techniques under laboratory
conditions. Numerous records of high temperatures in nature are doubtful
(Miller, 1949b), and it seems likely that any tolerance higher than about
45°C should be seriously questioned and carefully examined. However,
variations in resistance times of fishes are great and maximum recorded
temperatures are generally highest for the most eurythermal species or
populations (Table I). Maximum constant temperatures occupied by reproducing populations of fishes, presumably comparable to the incipient
lethal temperatures of laboratory studies, rarely exceed 35°C.

A number of pitfalls exist for the unwary investigator of high temperature tolerances of fishes in nature, and description of some of these serves
also to define the ecology of extreme habitats. Vast differences exist in
densities of water of differing temperatures, and stratified flows often may
be detected in springs or their outlets. Miller (1949b), for example, found
a molly (*Mollinesia* [= *Poecilia*] *sphenops*) at Lake Amatitlán, Guate-
mala, living in waters of 33.3°–35.6°C. Temperatures as hot as 49°C
were recorded in water flowing over them at the surface, and local people
were convinced that the fish were living at "boiling" water temperatures.

In outflows of hot springs, temperatures are typically warmest in the
main current and noticably cooler along the banks. Fishes will move upstream along the shoreline, and temperatures in that area will often be
1°–3°C or more cooler than in the channel. The reverse situation also
often occurs with springhead fishes that move downstream in the channel
of larger outflows. Temperatures along the shorelines in these situations may
be substantially lower than any recorded before for the species. This is
especially true in larger *ríos* of the Cuatro Ciénegas basin, where *Cyprinodon bifasciatus* moves long distances from the springs in summer, but dies
or moves back into the immediate area of thermal water in winter. It is
interesting that a similar dispersion relative to minor temperature differences is demonstrated by thermophilic algae and other microorganisms in
hot springs (Brock, 1967).

Shading may also create microdifferences in water temperatures (Young
and Zimmerman, 1956) that are used to advantage by fishes. Barlow
(1958a) found one shaded area of less than 100 cm² in an isolated pool
along the Salton Sea, California, that remained a full 2°C cooler than water
in full sunlight. An undescribed *Cyprinodon* from Cottonball Marsh in
Death Valley seems to retreat beneath shelves of encrusting salts, where
water temperatures may be a few degrees cooler than in the open water
of their severe habitat. Air temperatures in that area range as high as
55°C, and the species may consistently inhabit the most severe habitat

TABLE I
SELECTED RECORDS OF TEMPERATURE AND OXYGEN TOLERANCE IN FISHES[a]

Fishes	Minimum O_2 (mg/liter)	Temp. max. (°C)	Temp. min. (°C)	Reference[b]
Clupeiformes				
Clupeidae				
Dorosoma cepedianum		35.9	10.8	Brett, 1956
Dorosoma petenense			13	Brett, 1956
Salmonidae				
Oncorhynchus kisutch		25	0.2	Brett, 1956
Oncorhynchus nerka		24.8	0	Brett, 1956
Cypriniformes				
Cyprinidae				
Cyprinus carpio	0.6			Brett, 1956
Carassius auratus	0.5	38.6	2	Fry *et al*, 1942; Brett, 1956
Notemigonus crysoleucus	0.2	34.7	1.5	Brett, 1956
Gila robusta		30.5	0	
Ptychocheilus lucius		27	0	
Moapa coriacea		36	18	Hubbs and Miller, 1948a,b; Deacon and Bradley, 1971
Eremichthys acros	2	40.5	2	Nyquist, 1963; Hubbs and Miller, 1948a,b
Rhinichthys atratulus		29.3	2.2	Brett, 1956
Rhinichthys osculus		33–35		John, 1964
Agosia chrysogaster		36.8		Minckley and Barber, 1971[c]
Tiaroga cobitis		30.5[d]		
Gila robusta		30.5[d]		
Notropis lutrensis		39.5	1	Brues, 1928
Lepidomeda mollispinis	0.9		0	
Ictaluridae				
Ictalurus nebulosus	0.2	36.5	−1	Brett, 1956
Plotosidae				
Tandanus tandanus		38	3	Lake, 1967
Cyprinodontiformes				
Cyprinodontidae				
Aphanius dispar		31.7		Fox, 1926
Aphanius fasciatus		35–40	9	Pellegrin, 1931; Beadle, 1943
Tellia apoda		23		Beadle, 1943
Crenichthys baileyi	0.7	38	19.4	Hubbs and Hettler, 1964; Hubbs *et al.*, 1967; Deacon and Wilson, 1967
Crenichthys nevadae	0.5	38	20	Hubbs and Hettler, 1964; Hubbs *et. al.*, 1967; Deacon and Wilson, 1967

TABLE I (*Continued*)

Fishes	Mini- mum O_2 (mg/liter)	Temp. max. (°C)	Temp. min. (°C)	Reference[b]
Cyprinodon variegatus		43	0	Fries, 1952; Harrington and Harrington, 1961
Cyprinodon macularius	0.13	44.6	7	Barlow, 1958a,b, 1961a,b,c, Lowe and Heath, 1969
Cyprinodon nevadensis nevadensis	2.4	44	1.7	Deacon, 1968a,b
C. n. amaragosae		31	10	Miller, 1948
C. n. calidae		40	32.5	Miller, 1948
C. n. mionectes		34	2	Miller, 1948
C. n. pectoralis		33	20	Miller, 1948
Cyprinodon radiosus		20.8	18.5	Miller, 1948
Cyprinodon diabolis		38	8	James, 1968
Cyprinodon atrorus		47.2	2	
Lucania interioris		41.5[d]	2[b]	
Poeciliidae				
Gambusia affinis		37.3	1.5	Brett, 1956
Gambusia marshi		44[d]	2[b]	
Gambusia longispinis		40.3	2[b]	
Poeciliopsis o. occidentalis		34.8	1.5	Heath, 1962
Poecilia sphenops		35.6		Miller, 1946a,b
Perciformes				
Serranidae				
Plectroplites ambiguus		37	3	Lake, 1967
Theraponidae				
Bidyanus bidyanus		38	2	Lake, 1967
Terapontodae				
Hephaestus fuliginosus		39	"cold"	Whitley, 1959
Cichlidae				
Cichlasoma cyanoguttatum			14	Hubbs, 1951
Cichlasoma spp. (3 unde- scribed from Cuatro Ciénegas)		37.7[c]	9–11[d]	

[a] Many records result from field data, and special attention has been given to desert species. Other fishes are included primarily for comparative purposes. Maximum temperatures may result from either laboratory or field data and, therefore, may be considerably modified by further careful analysis.

[b] See also data in the text, some of which is not repeated here.

[c] W. L. Minckley, unpublished data.

[d] Present work, see text.

known for the genus (LaBounty, 1968; LaBounty and Deacon, 1971). *Cyprinodon atrorus* in the Cuatro Ciénegas basin behaves similarly in small pools where gypsum crystals form outward from the sides, but they more frequently remain near or within dense clumps of *Chara* that persist in the center of desiccating pools. Temperatures within such clumps are as much as 5°C lower than surface temperatures at midday in spring and winter; unfortunately, no summer temperatures have been recorded. Fox (1926) similarly reported close association of *Cyprinodon* (= *Aphanius*) *dispar* with beds of algae in salt pools at Kabret.

Great differentials in temperature may also occur in flowing creeks. In tributaries of the Red River in northern Texas, *Cyprinodon rubrofluviatilis* was concentrated in shade of a bridge at 11 A.M. in April, 1964, water temperature in the channel was 34.8°C, and in their immediate vicinity 30°C; *Gambusia affinis* and *Fundulus kansae* both remained in the channel or along banks near debris. In Sycamore Creek, Arizona, temperature variations commonly exceed 12°C in different habitats at a given moment in summer, at depths ranging from 0.5 cm to slightly more than 5.0 cm. Deep pools stratify strongly in Fish Creek, Arizona, with surface temperatures of 29°C contrasting with 18°C at depths of only 1 meter; downstream, 0.5 km below the canyon, surface temperatures in riffles were as high as 31.5°C in August 1965.

Chemical stratifications may also occur when saline water fails to mix with fresh water that flows over it. The saline lens may then accumulate heat retained because of the overlying stratum that inhibits evaporative cooling. Beadle (1943) recorded this phenomenon in Algerian pools, Cole *et al.* (1967) in Arizona, and Cole and Minckley (1968) in Coahuila, Mexico. To encounter such circumstances is a remarkable experience. In the Mexican instance, surface water was 24°C and numerous fishes were evident. Minckley stepped into the first of two pools, then quickly retreated when bottom water (about 48 cm deep) of 45°C was encountered by his sneaker-clad feet. Temperature in a second, undisturbed pool was 24°C at the surface (total dissolved solids 14.63 gm/liter; specific gravity at environmental conditions, 1.01) and 47°C at the bottom (total dissolved solids 111.26 gm/liter; specific gravity 1.075) (Cole and Minckley, 1968). Fishes conspicuously avoided the warm stratum, hiding along the banks when disturbed.

One of the warmer records for fishes in North America is that of the spring from which *Lucania browni* (= *Cyprinodon macularius*) was described from northeastern Baja California (Jordan and Richardson, 1907). The temperature of 48.9°C was taken with a standardized instrument by highly trained personnel (Miller, 1948, 1949b), and has not, to our knowledge, again been checked, unless the spring visited by Kniffin (1932) was the same (temperature range of 44.5°–48.9°C; Miller, 1948). Also, Norman's (1931) record of a *Cyprinodon* (= *Aphanias*) from Arabia in water "hot to the hand," and a cichlid (*Tilapia*) in springs on the eastern shore of Lake Magadi, Kenya, Africa, at temperatures ranging from 26.7° to 48.9°C, have not yet been confirmed. Perhaps density currents or similar phenomena explain these records.

Seasonal maxima in shallow, sometimes ephemeral desert waters may approach the dubious records just discussed (Table I). A maximum of 47.2°C for *Cyprinodon atrorus* was confirmed by use of two thermometers in August 1968, near Cuatro Ciénegas, Coahuila. Some spring-fed marshes in that basin have water levels that fluctuate seasonally (Minckley, 1969b), and the fish were found in a remnant pool of such a marsh. The pool less than 1 meter in diameter was in full sunlight. The pool averaged about 1 cm deep except for a 3 cm strip, ∼4 cm deep, produced by passage of a burro cart. About 25 adults and many hundred young, ranging from yolk-sac fry to 20 mm in length, were present, hyperactive, but not otherwise evidently in distress. Activity of the adults was confined principally to the deeper water, and the movements had mixed the water adequately to create uniform temperatures. Young were in the shallowest, 1 to 5 mm, areas. A gallon of water was removed, 20 adults were placed in it, and carried in a truck for about 3 hours. After arriving at camp the temperature of water in the gallon jar remained at 44°C. The adult fish were later transported to Arizona, where they reproduced to establish a stock still in existence. On the following afternoon the place was visited again; the remnant pool had dried, and no living fish were found.

Also in August, 1968, Cole and Minckley studied a number of small pools adjacent to Laguna de San Pablo, Cuatro Ciénegas basin, where tremendous populations of *C. atrorus,* plus a few *Gambusia marshi,* persisted at temperatures of 43°–44°C. The pools were shallow and elongate, no more than 20 cm at the deepest and 3–5 meters wide by 8–12 meters long, with numbers of small bays, and shorelines densely vegetated by sedges and salt grass. The riparian plants afforded no shading to the water, which had receded to expose narrow, saline flats. Fish were concentrated in shallows, several males were defending territories, and young were very abundant. Only large, brightly colored males were dead; other fish seemed to behave normally.

Cyprinodon n. nevadensis in a marsh associated with Saratoga Spring, Death Valley, has been found swimming voluntarily at 43°C (Deacon, 1968a). They could be chased into 44°C water. Under experimental confinement in the field this form was killed at 43°–44°C in July and survived exposure to 43.5°C in early September. Miller (1948) reported short-term tolerance of 35°–37.8°C for pupfishes in creeks of the Death Valley system, and a maximum tolerance in nature of 40°C for *C. nevadensis calidae*. One form of the Nevada pupfish now is known to move voluntarily into waters of 42°C (Soltz and Brown, 1970). Desert pupfish from the Salton Sea, California, (Barlow, 1958a) had thermal preferences similar to those of *C. n. calidae* and were found holding territories at a maximum of 38.3°C (Barlow, 1961b). A population of *Cyprinodon* at the Steinhart aquarium was almost entirely killed when malfunction of an aquarium heater raised the temperature to 43.3°C (Seale, in Miller, 1949b). It was subsequently determined that *C. macularius* lived at 38.9°C, but would exhibit marked discomfort and death at 40.6°C. Lowe and Heath (1969) reported an experimental critical thermal maximum of 44.6°C for *C. macularius* from Quitobaquito, Arizona, and found that form living in nature at about 41°C.

The principal data on poeciliid fishes have been compiled for *Gambusia affinis,* and its critical thermal maximum is near 40°C (Brett, 1956). At Ojo Caliente, near Hermanas, Coahuila, México, *Gambusia marshi* avoided water at 41.5°C, occurred rarely along the banks at temperatures of 40.5°C, seemed very hesitant to cross the channel (41°C), but spread to inhabit the entire flow at 40° ± 0.5°C. In the Cuatro Ciénegas basin that species maintains a small population in Escobeda (36.7° ± 1°C), but is very common in other springs that range from 17° to 35°C. The Escobeda population exhibits a high percentage of vertebral anomalies similar to those reported by Hubbs (1959) for *G. affinis* in hot springs (34.5°–35.5°C) of Big Bend National Park, Texas. In fluctuating habitats, *Gambusia marshi* has been found highly emaciated and in small numbers at temperatures of 43° to 44°C on one occasion. Otherwise the maximum temperatures recorded in this type of habitat where *G. marshi* was present are near 39.5°C; this is the same maximum temperature at which Hubbs (1959) found *G. affinis*.

Tolerances of some cyprinid species to high temperature may approach those for cyprinodontoids. Some of the higher records are 39.5°C for red shiner in New Mexico hot springs (Brues, 1928), 38°–40.5°C for *Eremichthys acros* (desert dace) in Soldier Meadows, Nevada (Nyquist, 1963; Hubbs and Miller 1948b), 34°–36°C for *Moapa coriacea* in Moapa Valley, Nevada (Hubbs and Miller, 1948b) and 36.8°C for adult longfin dace in Arizona. Most minnow species have lower tolerances, in the range of 30°–34°C, and these maxima seem typical for most other groups that have been studied (Table I).

Acclimation to warm waters occurs much more rapidly than to cold (Brett, 1956; Doudoroff, 1957), and thus it follows that heating is likely to have less effect on survival than does rapid cooling. Few cases of natural heat death of fishes have been recorded (Bailey, 1955; Norris, 1963; Lowe and Heath, 1969). However, in the more severe habitats we have studied, thermal (or thermal-related) deaths are not uncommon, especially at lower ends of streams such as Salt Creek and the Amargosa River, channels in Cottonball Marsh, all in Death Valley, and in cut-off pools of lagunas and streams in Cuatro Ciénegas, México. Fishes of intermediate elevations in Arizona often move downstream in spring or in years of abundant runoff and die there as low discharges of summer ensue, presumably as a result of high temperatures. Numerous loach minnows (*Tiaroga cobitis*) have been found dead and dying at 30.5°C in lower Aravaipa Creek, Arizona. Colorado chubs (*Gila robusta*) in side pools of the Salt River also succumbed at 30.5°C.

John (1964) studied temperature tolerances of *Rhinichthys osculus*, a species with a longitudinal distribution in streams that often resembled that of *Gila* and *Tiaroga. Rhinichthys* ranges to higher elevation, however. In the Chiricahua Mountains, where his study was performed, the highest summer water temperature recorded in a flowing stream was 31°C. In standing pools the maxima were 36°C at the surface and 33°C at the bottom (8 cm deep). Minimum in the study periods was 16°C. In laboratory tests the ultimate incipient upper lethal temperatures for young fish (20 mm standard length) was about 33°C, and for older fish (more than 35 mm standard length) it was ~32°C. In addition, older fish died after less exposure to increasing temperature. Incipient upper lethal temperatures of fish subjected to abrupt changes from 31°C (temperature of acclimatization) to 33°–35°C showed no correlation with size, but time to death for 50% of the population decreased rapidly and total mortality increased as temperature was increased.

In view of environmental temperatures, John (1964) attributed little significance to a 2°C greater tolerance to high temperature by young of speckled dace when compared to that of adults. However, he noted that in cut-off pools, adult fish would realize lethal temperatures while juveniles might not, a fact of considerable potential importance to a species. Many other fish species show the same type of response to extremes (Gunter, 1945).

Deaths from cold have been frequently reported (Norris, 1963). In most instances it appears that rapidity of onset of cold temperatures, and the fact that cold water mixes rapidly to the bottom of aquatic habitats, linked with an inherently slow rate of gain of cold tolerance, results in mortality. This is despite the fact that low temperatures often remain within the biokinetic range. By contrast, layering of warmed water at the surface provides opportunity for behavioral avoidance of change during thermal adjustment to rapid warming (discussed later). In the very shallow desert waters, however, such layering may be minimal.

Most eurythermal fishes of deserts can survive water temperatures below 2°C (Table I), and a number of kinds successfully live beneath ice cover for brief periods, which occur even in Death Valley on occasion (Wauer, 1962). More stenothermal species, such as those of tropical derivation living at the limits of their ranges, or occupants of large, permanent springs, may die at much higher temperatures. *Herichthys* (= *Cichlosoma*) *cyanogutattus,* the only cichlid native to the United States, suffers severe mortality when temperatures drop to 14°C (Hubbs, 1951). All three undescribed cichlid species from the Cuatro Ciénegas basin die at temperatures ranging from 10° to 15°C, with young living longer than adults. Marine fishes are, in general, far more stenothermous than freshwater species, and catastrophic mortalities have been recorded in shallow, coastal waters when rapid cooling occurs (Gunter, 1952). The freshwater *Cyprinodon bifasciatus* has a similarly high lower temperature tolerance in warm-spring populations, but some stocks in tiny creeks are considerably broader in their low-temperature capabilities (Arnold, 1970). *Moapa coriacea, Crenichthys baileyi, C. nevadae,* and *Eremichthys acros* occur only in temperatures above 18°C or so, even though considerable habitats having lower temperatures is available to them (Hubbs and Miller, 1948b; Wilson *et al.,* 1966; unpublished data).

Some desert species now essentially restricted to constant temperature springs are far more eurythermal than might be expected. The desert dace has not been taken at temperatures lower than 18°C in nature (Hubbs and Miller, 1948b; Nyquist, 1963), but it can withstand short-term cooling to 2°C under laboratory conditions. Many forms of *Cyprinodon* from constant-temperature habitats have over-wintered, even under short periods of ice cover, in experimental ponds in Arizona (*C. elegans* from Phantom Spring, Texas, *C. n. nevadensis* from Saratoga Springs, California and other subspecies of *nevadensis* from the Death Valley system, and *C. macularius* from the source of Quitobaquito Spring, Arizona). All these have adjacent populations that live in marshes, pools, or canals subject to seasonal variations. Even the Devil's Hole pupfish (*Cyprinodon diabolis*), which has lived in Devil's Hole, Nevada, for millenia at a presumably constant temperature near 33°C, can tolerate a range of 8° to 38°C (James, 1969), at least for short periods. This eurythermality coupled with depositional evidence for variations in water level suggests, however, that habitat temperatures may well have been considerably more variable than previously assumed.

Seasonal changes in temperature to which desert fishes are subjected are preceded by gradual, natural acclimation, and probably are less critical than diurnal ranges which occur. A major feature of warm deserts is the vast fluctuation in air temperatures during a day. Below 1000 meters in

Arizona, air temperature may change as much as 30°C from day to night in spring and autumn, especially where drain of colder, montane air flows down canyons at night. In summer, variation is of a lesser magnitude, perhaps 15°–20°C, overall, and this also is true in winter ranging from 4° to 10°C at night to 25°C in the day (Green and Sellers, 1964). Water temperatures tend to change more slowly but nevertheless fluctuate over a similar range.

Maximum diel variations recorded in small pools of Cuatro Ciénegas basin have been 13°–31°C in April, 24°–44°C in August, and 1.3°–18.5°C in December. Cooler temperatures are achieved, as witnessed by formation of ice that will hold the weight of a man (Minckley, 1969b), and water as hot as 53°C has been found in almost azoic, salt-encrusted pools in summer. Comparable data in Death Valley waters include maximum diel variations of 27°–42°C in the marsh at Saratoga Springs in July, 13.9°–25°C in March, and 4°–20°C in December. Since these temperatures were taken in open water, greater daily ranges are to be expected in the shallower parts of the marsh. The most extreme thermal variations in fish habitats of Death Valley probably occur in Cottonball Marsh where temperature data unfortunately have not been taken. Barlow (1958a) reported diel temperature ranges of as much as 20°C in shore pools of the Salton Sea, quite comparable to those in Death Valley and Cuatro Ciénegas, but ranging only to a maximum of 38.7°C. Lowe and Heath (1969) report diel ranges of 22°–26°C in shallow waters of Quitobaquito Spring, Arizona, to a maximum of 41°C.

Intermittent pools in creeks have similar ranges in temperature, but flowing waters are typically less extreme. Maximum diel ranges of 20°C occur in Sycamore Creek, Arizona, to a maximum of about 40.3°C; however, adult fishes have not been recorded at temperatures higher than 36.8°C. Temperature relations in small streams are highly complex, as detailed earlier (Section II,A). Volume of flow in large rivers, plus other factors, tends to reduce variability.

Under conditions of summer extremes the period of potential recovery and repair during cooler times may be highly significant to desert fishes. Some insight into biochemical mechanisms involved in such repair periods is provided by Baslow (1967). Biochemical changes occur first in the brain, and then elsewhere, in fishes subjected to thermal stress. Biochemical equilibrium to new thermal environments is attained only after several days or weeks, and involves changes in levels of amino acids and enzymes to accomplish acclimation. A cyclical daily regime apparently permits more gradual, and therefore biochemically more satisfactory, adjustment than is possible under sudden exposure to markedly different thermal conditions. Initial reactions in the central nervous system appear a few hours after application of stress. The relatively brief exposure to thermal stress at mid-day doubtless results in similar phenomena that are rectified at times of more hospitable conditions.

Probably significantly related to the above mechanism is the observation by Schlieper *et al.* (1952) that brown trout and *Planaria alpina* survive longer at lethal temperatures and show a reduction in the rate of increase of respiration as temperature increases when much Ca^{2+} is added to the medium. As temperatures of desert pools increase in the summer, evaporation usually results in increasing the concentrations of salts.

Some desert fishes seem to have remarkable resistance to thermal shock. *Eremichthys acros* has been subjected experimentally to reciprocal transfers between waters of 2° and 23°C (Nyquist, 1963) without apparent adverse reaction. *Cyprinodon n. nevadensis* withstood changes from 2.8° to 23.9°C in December, 9.2° to 38.4°C in March, and 26° to 43.5°C in September over a 9- to 15-hour period under experimentally confined conditions in the field. *Cyprinodon baconi* from the Bahamas, where water temperatures may vary from 10° to 37°C (Krumholz, 1963), but rarely do so, is capable of withstanding cold shock down to 6°C. It quickly revives, if not held at that low level (Fries, 1952). By contrast, acute temperature changes (of about 15°C) are lethal to both golden shiners (*Notemigonus crysoleucus*) and Virgin River spinedace (*Lepidomeda mollispinis*) (Espinosa and Espinosa, 1970), and changes of about 15°C or more kill salmonids (Black, 1953; Brett, 1941). Desert fishes often move abruptly from shallow, hot waters, to cold, deeper waters, or vice versa, when startled or to feed, and this may involve changes of 10°C or more in a deep, stratified pool.

Restriction of a species to relatively narrow thermal ranges may be imposed at some level of development other than the adult. This has been suggested for some marine species whose eggs have precise temperature requirements (Norris, 1963). Kinne and Kinne (1962a) demonstrated developmental arrest of embryos of desert pupfish at a constant temperature of 36°C. Different developmental stages also had different thermal optima. An actual need for variation may also exist in development of gametes or for completion of various other stages in diverse life cycles. This has been discussed in reference to aquatic invertebrates in springs (Ide, 1935), and almost certainly applies as well to fishes.

B. Chemical Conditions

1. Hydrogen-Ion Concentration

Hydrogen-ion concentration, expressed as pH, is of little consequence to fishes except at its upper and lower ranges (>9.5 or<4.0; Jones,

1964). Most desert waters we have studied are slightly to strongly alkaline and have pH values between 7.2 and 9.0, or so. Values above 8.6 are associated with high salinities or with high photosynthetic rates of plants that are capable of utilizing half-bound carbon dioxide. Spring waters are typically circumneutral, buffered by interactions of free carbon dioxide and various ions (principally bicarbonates), but they may sometimes be somewhat acidic. Downflow changes in such waters, principally the loss of free carbon dioxide from the water surface and through photosynthetic activities, may result in deposition of carbonates (travertines) in the channels, and this may be quickly detected by pH determination (Cole and Batchelder, 1969). Ranges of pH at which desert fishes have been found are given in Table II.

2. Salinity

Desert fish habitats are not only characterized by impressive thermal extremes, but equally by their high content of dissolved solids. This of course is a natural consequence of surface water standing in a desiccating environment. Flushing action which maintains the fresh character of waters in exorheic zones is an infrequent occurrence in endorheic situations. The hypersaline commonality of desert waters was stressed by Cole (1968), who also noted the numerous, relatively unique exceptions. In light of these facts, it is not surprising that some of the most striking adaptations to hypersaline conditions are among desert fishes and their relatives. Unfortunately, opportunities for elucidation of such adaptations have yet to be exploited in any major way. Much of our discussion of the life of desert fishes in hypersaline conditions is speculative, fragmentary, and largely dependent upon data from fishes living in less extreme environments.

Terminology to be used in reference to waters of high dissolved solid content may become complex (Hedgpeth, 1959; Macan, 1963; Bayly, 1967). We use the term salinity in the sense of Hutchinson (1957) "as the concentration of all ionic constituents present." But we are in complete sympathy with the need for more precise designation of chemical features of aquatic habitats and thus provide in Table II a resume of chemical features of some of the more extreme desert waters in which fishes have been found. Differences in the ways of reporting salinities in the literature, ranging from specific gravities to diverse gravimetric units per volume, also complicate the issue, and some comparisons may be rather crude. We present the approximate relationships of various types of measurements in Fig. 5.

As with temperature, chemical stratification and other microdifferences may confuse field measurements of salinities, and a few percentage points may be exceedingly important to fishes distributing themselves relative to

TABLE II

CHEMICAL FEATURES (IN mEq/LITER) OF REPRESENTATIVE WATERS IN WHICH DESERT FISHES ARE FOUND[a]

Locality	Species present	TDS (gm/liter)	Ca^{2+}	Mg^{2+}	Na$^+$	K$^+$	SO$_4^{2-}$	CO$_3^{2-}$	HCO$_3^-$	Cl$^-$	pH	Reference
Duckwater T13-12N, R56E	Crenichthys nevadae	3.08	3.03	1.62	1.24	0.18	1.24	0.19	2.62	0.25	8.4	b
Lockes	Crenichthys nevadae	4.57	3.29	1.73	2.26	0.26	1.23	0.00	6.16	0.28	7.9	b
Preston Big Spring	Crenichthys baileyi,	2.40	1.57	1.60	0.56	0.08	0.85	0.09	2.07	0.33		b
	Pantosteus intermedius,	2.40	1.57	1.60	0.56	0.08	0.85	0.09	2.07	0.33		b
	Lepidomeda albivallis,	2.40	1.57	1.60	0.56	0.08	0.85	0.09	2.07	0.33		b
	Rhinichthys osculus	2.40	1.57	1.60	0.56	0.08	0.85	0.09	2.07	0.33		b
Mormon Spring	Crenichthys baileyi	2.96	3.17	1.81	1.00	0.00	0.96	0.00	4.77	0.25	8.3	b
Iverson's Warm Spring	Crenichthys baileyi,	6.3	3.49	2.14	4.39	0.28	3.73	0.00	4.49	1.71	7.5	Eakin, 1964
	Moapa coriacea	3.08	1.65	2.80	42.19	0.77	21.66		5.86		8.1	
Saratoga Spring, Death Valley, Calif., spring marsh	Cyprinodon nevadensis	7.94	3.14	4.11	126.63		55.20	3.67		56.42	9.0	Deacon, 1968a,b
Salt Creek, Death Valley, Calif.	Cyprinodon salinus	23.59	5.68	30.39	341.45	12.83	77.28	4.00	8.85	290.50	8.6	Miller, 1943
Cottonball Marsh, Death Valley, Calif.	Cyprinodon sp.	70^c 160	20.96	40.88	1062.62	49.63	201.22			592.41		LaBounty and Deacon, 1971; Hunt et al., 1966
Salton Sea, Calif.	Cyprinodon macularius	40.42	40.12	81.60	514.34	4.91	157.27	0.70	2.80	197.19	8.4	Walker, 1961

Locality	Species									pH	Reference
Laguna Grande, Cuatro Ciénegas Basin Coahuila, Mexico	*Cyprinodon atrorus, Gambusia marshi, Gambusia longispinis*	4.64	31.14	15.23	18.41	5.17	56.24	4.03		8.21	Minckley and Cole, 1968
Lake Robe, Australia	*Taeniomembras* sp.	134	43.19	431.04	1452.9	37.59	129.15	10.33	1825.19	7.4	Bayly and Williams, 1966; Lee, 1969; Lee and Williams, 1970
Small lake near Lake Eliza, Australia (12)	*Taeniomembras* sp.	56	28.44	148.07	665.55	17.64	93.74	8.19	758.85	7.9	Bayly and Williams, 1966; Lee, 1969; Lee and Williams, 1970
Small lake near Lake Eliza, Australia (13)	*Taeniomembras* sp.	69	32.93	187.55	813.45	19.94	152.06	7.21	894.26	7.7	Bayly and Williams, 1966; Lee, 1969; Lee and Williams, 1970
Lake Ain-ez-Zauia, Cyrenaica	*Aphanius dispar, Aphanius fasciatus*	25.25	58.88	27.56	330.16	8.49	38.43	4.73	380.84	7.4	J. L. B. Smith, 1952
Lac Merdjadja, 5 km south of Touggouert, Algeria	*Aphanius fasciatus*	38[d]	75.85	159.58	375.41	20.87	242.04		447.60	8.3	Beadle, 1943
Ourlana, 35 km north of Touggouert, Algeria	*Aphanius fasciatus*	12[d]	43.91	60.87	82.21	2.40	83.94		121.30	8.3	Beadle, 1943
Sea water		34.48	20.61	1744.0	458.92	9.72	55.18	0.23	540.22		

[a] Desert waters are often highly variable. Thus more concentrated situations are emphasized here, where we also restrict data to those waters for which relatively complete analyses are available. There is some question about whether fish actually inhabited water in Cottonball Marsh of 160 gm/liter TDS.

[b] Univ. of Nevada, DRI, Reno, unpublished data.

[c] Estimated by extrapolation from total cations/TDS relationship of other localities in the table.

[d] Estimated by use of Fig. 5.

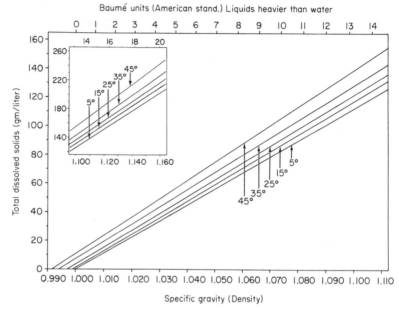

Fig. 5. Relationships of measurements of total solids in water at different environmental temperatures. Note that this is intended only as a generalized figure, since various ionic compositions create different densities (Agnihotri and Tewari, 1968), etc. Data on densities and total dissolved solids were extracted and/or extrapolated from information provided by Schureman (1941), and for Baumé units from the Merck Index (Strecher, 1968).

almost-lethal osmotic stress. For example, *Cyprinodon* (= *Aphanius*) *dispar* was taken from a brine pool near Kabret, northeastern Africa, which had densities of 1.176 throughout most of the pool, but 1.040 near the margins (Fox, 1926). The fish were most abundant near the edges where filamentous algae grew, but a few were in areas of maximum concentrations of dissolved solids. All ions except calcium increased with increasing density. The similarly vast chemical (and thermal) differences in stratified pools of Cuatro Ciénegas basin (Cole and Minckley, 1968) have already been discussed (Section III,A,5). Association of fishes with aquatic plants such as filamentous algae (Fox, 1926) or *Chara* in saline ponds may indicate slight chemical changes in the vicinity of the plants due to photosynthetic activities, but this has not been specifically studied. The plants may of course also be surviving only in the least toxic part of such a pool.

In general, fishes of diverse groups have demonstrated the capability of persisting in salinities up to 2 or 3 times the concentration of sea water

($\sim$35 gm/liter), and a few records imply survival at considerably greater concentrations. An early, questionable record by Coleman (1926) suggests tolerance of *Cyprinodon macularius* of 200 gm/liter. Barlow (1958b), on the other hand, found 90 gm/liter to be about the maximum tolerated by that fish at relatively high temperatures in shore pools of the Salton Sea. Simpson and Gunter (1956) documented survival of a substantial population of *Cyprinodon variegatus* at 142.4 gm/liter, and a total mortality of that species at 147 gm/liter. The fish occurred at 63 of 84 stations they sampled along the south Texas coast, 26 of which were more saline than seawater, and three higher than 70 gm/liter.

The *Cyprinodon* from Cottonball Marsh, Death Valley, can survive in salinity of 78 gm/liter (LaBounty and Deacon, 1971), and data of Hunt *et al.* (1966) imply that concentrations of 160 gm/liter may sometimes occur in parts of their habitat. *Cyprinodon atrorus* successfully tolerates up to 95 gm/liter in the Cuatro Ciénegas basin. Recently dead fish (not yet decomposed, a possible result of brine preservation) were found in August 1968 at 240 gm/liter (Arnold, 1970).

An Australian atherinid, *Taeniomembras* sp., has an implied range of salinity tolerance from 20–130 gm/liter, and suffered no mortality under laboratory conditions between salinities of 10 and 100 gm/liter (Bayly and Williams, 1966; Lee, 1969; Lee and Williams, 1970). Acclimation seemed to have a remarkably small influence on upper or lower tolerances in this fish (Lee, 1969).

Numerous other records of high salinity tolerances in fishes are available, principally in cyprinodonts (Kosswig, 1961; Steinitz, 1951a), in a cichlid (Steinitz, 1951b), and in innumerable marine species (Gunter, 1956, 1961, 1967), but specific data on concentrations present are lacking, or pertain to fishes that do not occur naturally under inland desert conditions.

A fish kill in the lower Colorado River, downstream from Yuma, Arizona, was attributed (Sykes, 1937) to a small flood on the Gila River in the late 1800's. The Gila was considerably more saline than the Colorado, and at the time was exceedingly low because of protracted drought (the Gila now is dry throughout its lower course as a result of upstream modifications). The alkali water of the Gila was retained by a dam to avoid contamination of irrigation supplies, and a small rise passing down the channel overrode the dam and emptied the toxic water into the Colorado. Fishes were reportedly destroyed in a matter of a few days from Yuma, Arizona, to the Gulf of California, México, a distance of more than 125 km.

Euryhalinity of some desert fishes seems based upon highly specialized physiological and biochemical mechanisms. Insight into some of the probable systems may be gleaned from reviews by Kinne (1963) and Love (1970) and from those presented in volumes edited by Brown (1957) and Hoar and Randall (1969). Nearly all fishes investigated show initial tendencies to desiccate when exposed to hypersaline waters. Adjustment is accomplished by drinking water, about 70–80% of which is absorbed through the gut wall along with the monovalent ions of sodium, potassium, and chloride. The divalent ions, calcium, magnesium, and sulfate, except for small amounts that are absorbed, form insoluble oxides and hydroxides in the alkaline intestinal environment and are largely eliminated via mucus tubes and with the feces. Insoluble mixed carbonate salts also left in the intestinal lumen are eventually voided. The fraction of divalent ions absorbed are finally excreted by the kidney. Monovalent ions are eliminated through specialized secretory cells of the gills and sometimes in the oral epithelium, as has been demonstrated in *Fundulus heteroclitus*.

It is of particular interest that almost all species for which data are available continue to produce a urine hypotonic to their blood, even in the most hypertonic environments to which they have been experimentally subjected. Total urine volume, however, is greatly diminished. The one documented exception is the Plains killifish (*Fundulus kansae*) which not only produces greatly reduced quantities of urine, but also a hypertonic urine when first introduced into hypertonic environments Temperature may greatly influence survival, since *Fundulus parvipinnis* desiccates in its natural medium, seawater, when environmental temperatures are low (Doudoroff, 1945). As with virtually all other mechanisms discussed here, there are practically no data from fishes able to withstand the most extreme salinities and abrupt salinity changes of desert waters.

The absence of parathyroid glands, and presumably therefore of parathormone, appears to explain the well-known dependence of fishes on calcium in the environment. Since parathormone mobilizes calcium reserves from bones of terrestrial vertebrates, its absence in bony fishes suggests that such a mechanism does not exist. They therefore appear dependent upon environmental reserves to maintain desirable levels of the element. Marine fishes live in an environment rich in calcium, and when transferred to fresh water they may suffer numerous complications or even death due to a complex of responses centering around a calcium deficiency caused by a general increase in membrane permeability. The antagonistic mechanism, i.e., control of hypercalcemia, involves production of calcitonin by the unusually well-developed ultimobranchial bodies of gnathostome fishes. The probable function of calcitonin is control of calcium transport across cell membranes, especially in the gut, kidney, and/or gill surfaces. Additional evidence has been presented to suggest that calcitonin may function in suppressing calcium resorption from bone in fishes with cellular bones (*Anguilla anguilla, Ictalurus melas*). This effect was not demonstrated in *Fundulus heteroclitus,* a species with acellular bone.

These mechanisms are called into play immediately when there is a change in the osmotic composition of the environment. In *Fundulus kansae* complete adaptation to seawater after direct transfer from fresh water occurs in 20 days. Hypertonic environments become lethal to fishes when the capacity of the secretory cells of the gills (and oral epithelium) and kidney is exceeded and salt begins to accumulate in the tissues.

Salinity tolerances of different stages in a life cycle may vary radically. Kinne (1960) and Kinne and Kinne (1962a,b) demonstrated that eggs of *Cyprinodon macularius* will develop in salinities up to 70 gm/liter (with varying rates and structural consequences), whereas adults live in salinities up to 80 to 85 gm/liter. Barlow (1958b) indicates that juveniles of *C. macularius* are capable of surviving in salinities up to 90 gm/liter, but that most adults die sooner. Renfro (1960) reported survival of yolk-sac larvae of sheepshead pupfish at 110 gm/liter. Our observations of other species of pupfishes in drying pools indicate a greater tolerance of subadults than of either tiny young, or larger old individuals.

Minimum salinity tolerances have been infrequently reported. LaBounty and Deacon (1971) maintained adult *Cyprinodon salinus* and *Cyprinodon* sp. from Death Valley in distilled water. Kinne and Kinne (1962a) found that some eggs of *C. macularius* developed in glass-distilled water, although mortality was quite high. They documented normal development over a wide range of temperature in water made up of half tap water and half distilled water. Simpson and Gunter (1956) caught *C. variegatus* at 1.8 gm/liter, and Gunter (1950) recorded it at 0.4 gm/liter. Kilby (1955) recorded a minimum for that species of 0.0 gm/liter, a highly unlikely total dissolved solids determination from natural water. The Australian *Taeniomembras* studied by Lee (1969) lived for a week after direct transfer from 70 gm/liter to 2.0 gm/liter salinity, but mortality was about 50%. Such changes in nature, in an almost instantaneous manner, certainly occur when marginal pools are rapidly flooded by rising streams or lakes, or during heavy, seasonal rainfall, or when waves suddenly fill shore pools along margins of desert lakes.

3. Dissolved Gases

Dissolved gases have been far less studied relative to desert fishes than have physical and more easily analyzed chemical features. Incidental analyses have been generally omitted here, unless directly pertaining to a species or group of fishes; references to broad limnological works dealing in part with dissolved gases are given earlier. Flowing waters, other than those issuing from springs, generally have high to moderate amounts of gases (unless polluted) due to mixing by turbulence, and they also are generally ignored in this section. Natural desert waters are typically rather clear of pollutants, but interfering substances may nonetheless be high and earlier dissolved oxygen analyses, for example, may be subject to considerable doubt. Also, the high total dissolved solids in many desert pools may influence analysis of gases to a greater or lesser degree; this aspect often has been neglected as a variable by field investigators. As with salinity then, some data may be valid only in a general way, and the reader should refer to the original work prior to generalizing from this review.

a. *Oxygen*. The oxygen supply of natural waters is probably the most frequent single factor influencing the life of desert fishes, or for that matter, of freshwater fishes in general. Adequate supplies of this gas may be defined by survival of fishes at a given level, but quite often low levels that may be tolerated in nature are, in fact, detrimental, causing losses of weight, impaired swimming abilities, malformed or weakened larvae, and so on (Doudoroff and Warren, 1965). The voluminous literature on relations of fishes and dissolved oxygen has been recently reviewed by Fry (1957, 1960), Jones (1964), Bemish and Dickie (1967), and Phillips (1969). Trout, salmon, and goldfish have been most intensively investigated.

Metabolic demands for oxygen increase as activity increases. However, below a certain level in the environment, activity and therefore oxygen utilization become oxygen dependent (and oxygen limited) (Fry, 1957). This incipient limiting point marks the level at which additional uptake by the fish is limited by its ability for absorbing oxygen from the environment, rather than by the ambient availability of the gas. The level that forces a fish to reduce maximum activity is distinctive for each species, and in many oxyphilic forms corresponds to 100% saturation, or at high temperatures, to a supersaturation (Fry, 1957; Macan, 1963). As Macan has pointed out, theoretically, the most important parameter from the ecological standpoint is not the amount of oxygen consumed by an organism, but rather the concentration at which consumption is reduced by oxygen availability (i.e., the incipient limiting point). This information is specifically available for only a few fishes (Jones, 1964), none of which live naturally under desert conditions.

In general, fishes respond to oxygen depletion by increasing the frequency, regularity, and amplitude of respiratory movements (Jones, 1964). Different species demonstrate various characteristic avoidance reactions to water of low dissolved oxygen. Nervous, erratic responses that increase activity (and therefore oxygen demand) may well allow species, living in habitats where escape from local oxygen depletion is possible, to do so. However, in confined desert pools, a response that reduces activity would be more appropriate. Such is suggested by data presented by Lowe *et al.* (1967) for the desert pupfish. In addition to its remarkable ability to survive low dissolved oxygen, that species apparently moved less than any other used in an experiment in catastrophic selection. Three other species, two minnows and a sucker, shared the experimental tank. The sucker had physiological tolerance to low oxygen second only to the pupfish. Because of its heavy body that required considerable effort to move, its increased movements under stress, and its inferior mouth utilization of atmospheric oxygen was hampered. Hence the sucker was the least capable of surviving of all species tested.

Minimum tolerances and LD_{50} have been determined for several fish species, some of which live in deserts. The lowest minima known, 0.13 mg/liter and 0.22 mg/liter oxygen, respectively, are for the desert pupfish (Lowe *et al.,* 1967). Many other species of *Cyprinodon* most likely survive similarly low concentrations, but they are yet to be studied. These species dive into the reducing, odoriferous mud bottoms of their habitats, as has been mentioned before. Since hydrogen sulfide is readily oxidized, but occurs in considerable volume in the malodorous sediments, such substrates must be essentially devoid of oxygen. The fish frequently bury themselves completely, but sometimes remain with their mouths or entire heads exposed. Fish in the last position may obtain oxygen through normal respiratory movements, or abnormally when the opercles are blocked. Some individuals, however, have been found 2 cm below the mud–water interface and certainly could not obtain water from above the mud surface. Blazka (1958) and Eckberg (1962) reported an ability of crucian carp (*Carassius carassius*) to survive for long periods during winter under anaerobic conditions. It seems likely that *Cyprinodon* may share such an ability.

Minimum levels of environmental oxygen, along with ambient temperatures when available, in which desert fishes are known to have survived are summarized in Tables I and II. These data obviously provide no indication of survival (or resistance) times at the recorded levels, and such may be an important consideration that allows survival through a period of temporary environmental stress that would prove lethal if it were sustained.

Diel changes in oxygen content of open spring waters rarely involve decreases below critical levels (Deacon and Wilson, 1967; Arnold, 1970), although they may sometimes be of a magnitude sufficient to elicit behavioral adjustments in fishes (Section IV,A,5). However, in smaller pools, changes from below 10% saturation to more than 150% may obtain; oxygen depletion most likely occurs at the mud–water interface or beneath beds of aquatic plants, at least at night. In the latter habitat, bottoms often indicate reducing conditions at the mud–water interface throughout the day, and such substrates are generally avoided by other than certain invertebrates (chironomid dipterans, some oligochaetes) capable of essentially anaerobic existence. The ova of cyprinodontids that are deposited within such bottom sediments must be capable of resisting considerable periods of anoxia.

In clear desert pools and in springs, gas production by algae and other photosynthetic organisms in or on bottom sediments may be very high (Minckley and Itzkowitz, 1967; Arnold, 1970). However, this may not contribute oxygen to the water, and may actually tend to reduce supersaturations by creating vertical turbulence, or by modifying other gases through phenomena of partial pressure adjustments in the rising bubbles. Accumulation of gases in sediments have been known to be an indirect cause of mortality of pupfishes. Ingested bubbles caused the fish to float, where they were exposed to sunburn and to predators (Minckley and Itzkowitz, 1967). Algal flotation in periods of high insolation may "raft" food organisms (including algae) into areas where they are more available to fishes as food, or may provide cover and additional substrate for certain isolated populations, such as the Devil's Hole pupfish (James, 1969).

The springfishes, *Crenichthys baileyi* and *C. nevadae,* have been examined more thoroughly than other desert fishes with regard to their oxygen relations. Minimum environmental oxygen levels to which these species are exposed range from 0.5 mg/liter upward (Table II). Extended exposure of *C. nevadae* to oxygen levels below 0.7 mg/liter at 32°C is lethal, and normal activity at that temperature appears to be suppressed by oxygen levels below about 2 mg/liter (Hubbs *et al.*, 1967). Such amounts therefore approximate the level of no excess activity and the incipient limiting point, respectively, for *C. nevadae* at about 32°C. Similar levels are suggested for *C. baileyi* by Hubbs and Hettler (1964), Hubbs *et al.* (1967), and Deacon and Wilson (1967). Data presented by Sumner and Sargent (1940), Sumner and Lanham (1942), and Brues (1928, 1932) on environmental conditions show that *C. baileyi* has been living under the conditions of low oxygen and high temperature for a long period of time (and probably for millenia). The fish move relative to dissolved oxygen content of the waters, and therefore remain in relatively amenable conditions through behavioral regulations (Section IV,A,5).

Crenichthys appears to have a markedly enlarged head, which is broad in the opercular region, and this is especially noticeable in larger specimens. Such enlargement accommodates exceptionally well-developed and proportionately large gills, an apparent advantage to a fish living in a low-oxygen environment. Measurements of gill surface area in *C. baileyi* range from about 200 to 850 mm^2/gm body weight. By comparison, the stream-dwelling minnow *Lepidomeda mollispinis* has a gill surface area ranging from about 50 to 200 mm^2/gm body weight. Comparisons of individuals of the two species having the same weight indicate that *C. baileyi* consistently has 50–200% more gill surface area than does the minnow. Small individuals of both species have proportionately more gill surface area than larger individuals.

This last relationship probably exists in most fishes and may partially explain the general trend that juvenile to subadult fish may survive adversity longer than large, mature individuals. Comparisons of survival in nature have not been made. However, preliminary laboratory data suggest that the range of 0.9–1.2 mg/liter dissolved oxygen at 15–20°C approximates the level of no excess activity for *Lepidomeda*. Survival, in fact swimming activity, of *C. nevadae* in 0.8 mg/liter dissolved oxygen at 32.3°C (Hubbs *et al.,* 1967), and the indication that *C. baileyi* lives in Mormon Spring, Nevada, at very low levels of oxygen concentration ($< \sim 1.0$ mg/liter; Deacon and Wilson, 1967), suggests that *Crenichthys* would undergo little stress under a combination of oxygen and temperature that is fatal to *Lepidomeda*. A situation such as this appears to obtain in some Nevada springs now infested with introduced poeciliids. *Crenichthys* lives essentially undisturbed in the low-oxygen, high-temperature springheads, and the poeciliids occur only downflow, in less severe conditions (Hubbs and Hettler, 1964).

b. Carbon Dioxide. Hutchinson (1957) discussed the complex chemical relations of carbon dioxide in water, and in 1967 he reviewed its role in the phytoplankton. After several workers established that free carbon dioxide in water was of primary significance to fishes, data were reviewed and evaluated by Doudoroff and Katz (1950), Doudoroff (1957), and Jones (1964). Desert habitats, as with most open waters, rarely contain concentrations of free carbon dioxide sufficiently high to create problems for fishes. The highest contents usually are in springs, where in most instances high dissolved solids (especially carbonates) tends to buffer any direct effects of the gas. Cole (1968), however, reported presence of free carbon dioxide in amounts up to 600 mg/liter in Montezuma Well, Arizona, a large limnocrene, and suggested that the absence of fishes might relate to the high concentrations present. According to local testimony, fishes introduced into the well die quickly. Doudoroff (1957) considered ~ 200 mg/liter as the approximate upper lethal concentration for moderately susceptible freshwater fishes.

An inverse relationship exists between oxygen and carbon dioxide tolerance in fishes (Jones, 1964); the ability of a fish to utilize oxygen seems to decrease as concentration of carbon dioxide increases. Levels of free carbon dioxide necessary to cause a marked change in oxygen utilization range widely, from a partial pressure of ~ 10 mm Hg in trout to more than 100 mm Hg in more resistant forms (ictalurids, cyprinids, and others; Fry, 1957). No typical desert species have been studied, but changes in pH, dissolved oxygen, temperature, and so on, in desert habitats, indicate comparable changes in other gases and ions and vast tolerances to carbon dioxide in some species.

Schaut (1939) observed no adverse reaction by unspecified minnow species exposed to carbon dioxide-free water for 2 hours.

c. Hydrogen Sulfide. Hydrogen sulfide is commonly present within the bottoms of desert aquatic habitats, but few actual measurements of its concentration are available. The most extreme example we have found is by Smith (1952) in a small, sulphur-depositing marsh in Cyrenaica which contained a range of 12–200 mg/liter. *Cyprinodon* (= *Aphanius*) *dispar* and *C.* (= *A.*) *fasciatus* were living in that habitat, being taken only in the areas of lower concentration (but no search was made for them elsewhere); other features of this extreme habitat are given in Table II. Kosswig (1961) illustrated cyprinodontids in some waters of the Anatolian basin, Turkey, with their bodies covered by (elemental?) sulfur, and noted production of sulfur compounds in shallow waters, presumably as a result of oxidation of hydrogen sulfide.

Jones (1964) indicates a decreasing toxicity of hydrogen sulfide to fishes with increases in pH. This occurs because un-ionized hydrogen sulfide penetrates living tissue more readily than its disassociated ions do, as also is true of cyanide, and the proportion of undisassociated gas increases with decreases in pH. This has been demonstrated for numerous teleosts of a number of families (Jones, 1964; Bonn and Follis, 1967). The toxicity of hydrogen sulfide seems based on the sulfide, which creates a tissue anoxia resulting from inactivation of respiratory carriers. If concentrations are not too great, sulfide may be oxidized within the body to relatively innocuous sulfate; thus recovery from sublethal dosage may be expected.

General levels of tolerance for hydrogen sulfide range from about 1 mg/liter for trout, to 8–12 mg/liter for carp (*Cyprinus carpio*) and tench (*Tinca tinca*). Schaut (1939) found unspecified minnows to be killed after a short exposure to water containing 6 mg/liter hydrogen sulfide, but to survive with no apparent adverse reaction during 24 hours of exposure to 4 mg/liter. An initial concentration of 5 mg/liter hydrogen sulfide was reduced to 1.4 mg/liter during a 24-hour period. This test condition produced a 50% fish mortality.

Mechanisms utilized by *Aphanius* in surviving >12 mg/liter hydrogen sulfide are unknown and were not investigated by Smith (1952). The pH was 7.4, which might have aided in reducing the unionized component of the concentration. In shallower, desert waters the presence of hydrogen sulfide in daytime may be essentially prevented by oxidizing effectiveness of intense sunlight coupled with high primary productivity. At night, however, conditions may be otherwise.

Bottom muds of many desert habitats have relatively high concentrations of hydrogen sulfide, as based on olfaction after they are disturbed. Pupfishes, and apparently some other cyprinodontids, spend relatively long periods of time, especially in winter, within such sediments. Toxicity sometimes must be near-lethal. Martin (1968) suggested possible damage to sheepshead pupfish exposed to hydrogen sulfide from a bottom agitated by collecting activities. Minckley (in Hubbs and Miller, 1965) reported a total kill of fish (*Cyprinodon atrorus*) resulting from agitation of a deep silt bottom in a hot (41.5°C), drying pool. However, factors other than hydrogen sulfide certainly could have been involved under such severe conditions. It seems entirely probable, however, that *Cyprinodon* and its relatives may have evolved a physiological means of coping with hydrogen sulfide in their severe habitats.

IV. Biological Responses to Desert Water Conditions

A. Dispersion Relative to Environment

Fishes native to deserts, almost without exception, have their distributions limited either by geographic barriers, or by a need (or tolerance) for some special environmental feature. Only one of the 200 or so native fishes in western North America, the speckled dace, may be considered widespread (Miller, 1959), and it consists of a myriad of local, variously differentiated forms that may well represent a species-flock rather than a polymorphic, single entity. The relatively depauperate nature of this western fauna, resulting from long years of vast geologic and climatic change, makes it particularly instructive. The relationships of morphology and environment are perhaps more clearly seen here than in places where speciose faunas saturate the habitat, and biotic factors obscure biologic–environmental interrelations.

1. Stream-Dwelling Fishes

Under relatively stable conditions of discharge, or as an average over a period of time, fishes and other organisms in the linear system provided by a stream tend to distribute themselves into different sections according to their requirements or preferences. Many factors other than current, temperature, substrate, competition from other organisms, and so on, may be involved, especially in situations such as streams fed by springs. But the physical gradient, to which current is intimately related, is the factor against which distributions of fishes are usually compared (Minckley,

1963), and in the main seems the most important single variable. This understanding resulted in large part from early studies by Shelford (1911a,b) on ecological succession, in which he emphasized the physiographic influences in streams as being far more important than biotic factors (Allee *et al.*, 1949). Geologic maturation of streams was considered as a successional phenomenon, followed by succession of the fish fauna at a given point from those of swift headwater situations to species with proclivities and morphologies more adapted to downstream or lentic situations. Such relationships have been demonstrated throughout the world where fishes inhabit streams.

Figure 6 outlines the actual or generalized distributions of fishes in a number of regions or stream systems and illustrates correlations between fish morphology and habitat features of different stream segments. This correlation cuts across taxonomic groupings, in most part, and serves to illustrate the close ties between body shape in fishes and the environments in which they live. That the correlative factor in such situations is current (or gradient) may easily be demonstrated by examining unusual streams which flow through flat lands in their headwaters, then enter a section of higher gradient in their lower reaches; the longitudinal distribution of fishes is similarly reversed (Larimore *et al.*, 1952). In Aravaipa Creek, Arizona, a high-gradient area is sandwiched between two low gradient sections. Headwater fishes occur mostly in the middle reach of that stream (Barber and Minckley, 1966). In fact, the simple presence of an area of swift water between pools—a riffle—provides living space for headwater fishes in the midst of lakelike conditions.

Careful examination of shorelines of larger rivers, as opposed to eddies along the current of the main channel, or the swift, central part, reveal similar current-related habitat preferences. In well-watered zones, or in large, persistently flowing desert rivers, a tremendous diversity of species may exist within this complex type of environment. In other places, a group may diversify into a number of niches or habitats.

Segregation of a group into differing regimes of current (or current-related habitats) is remarkably developed in cyprinoid fishes of the Colorado River basin of western North America. The swift-water minnows and suckers of that system display some of the most bizarre morphological adaptations to the constant stress of current (and likely suspended solids) that are known in any river in the world (Hubbs, 1940, 1941a).

> In more obvious adaptation . . . the fish tend to be larger and much more stream-lined . . . , with more terete bodies, sharper entering wedges and, particularly, with much slenderer caudal peduncles and longer and more falcate fins; and often with more rays in one or more fins or with smaller scales (which provide a smoother surface) (Hubbs, 1941a).

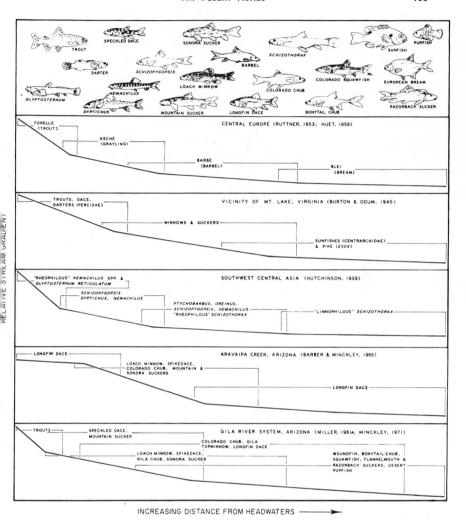

Fig. 6. Linear dispersion of fishes in streams of various parts of the world, and sketches of body forms of representative species found in various segments of streams or stream systems. Note that factors other than stream gradient, such as sizes, turbidity, or water chemistry, were correlated with these distributions by some authors, and that this figure oversimplifies some patterns originally described.

Chubs of the genus *Gila* are most impressive, ranging from the thick-bodied *G. intermedia* that lives in smaller, quieter habitats of the Gila River basin, through *G. robusta* of intermediate-sized rivers and moderate currents, to the exceedingly specialized *G. elegans* and *G. cypha* of the mainstream Colorado River (Miller, 1946b; Cole, 1968; Rinne and

Minckley, 1970). These fishes have been variously interpreted, over the years, as ecological types of one species or as different genera, but have recently been defined as full species (Rinne, 1969; Holden and Stalnaker, 1970). *Gila cypha* still is in doubt (Holden and Stalnaker, 1970), principally because of collection of numbers of putative hybrids between it and other species from a disturbed part of the river basin (the Lake Powell area). *Gila cypha* is rare in collections, and its ecology may only be inferred.

Vanicek *et al.* (1970) found *G. elegans* and the less streamlined *G. robusta* living sympatrically in pools and eddies of the Green River, Utah, sometimes adjacent to, but never in, swift currents. Swift-water forms of the bluehead mountain-sucker (*Pantosteus discobolus*), a species with morphotypes differentiated similar to those of *G. elegans* and *G. robusta* (in the mainstream and in smaller tributaries, respectively), were consistently in current, and usually in the swiftest parts. The highly variable *Rhinichthys osculus* also has numerous morphotypes that similarly reflect the impact of current on its body form within the Colorado River system. The extreme body shape of the bonytail chub (*G. elegans*) perhaps correlates most closely with their potential for movement through swift waters in periods of low or modal flow, and within current in times of flood.

The general lack of development of organs of attachment in Colorado River fishes must reflect the instability of bottoms and channels in that remarkably erosive stream. Instead, a highly modified body shape permits the fish to be held against the bottom under conditions of turbulence (through pressure of water on the curved dorsal surfaces and expanded fins). Shape thus substitutes for holdfast organs. It is notable that bonytail chub maintaining reproducing populations in larger impoundments of the Colorado system retain their streamlined body shapes, apparently moving about in an active, limnetic manner (Minckley, 1971) as do some oceanic fishes of similar morphology.

Basic modifications of body shape seem to have occurred in parallel in many groups of fishes, and these modifications may relate to sediment loads and to river currents which carry them. The woundfin (*Plagopterus argentissimus*) is a species characteristic of the mainstream of the relatively swift and silt-laden Virgin River, Utah–Arizona–Nevada (Deacon *et al.*, 1971). Many of its traits are similar to features of some bottom-dwelling, swift-water, silty-stream minnows of eastern United States, and elsewhere.

Barbels are present on the eastern fishes now referred to the genus *Hybopsis* (Moore, 1968) and also are well developed on *Plagopterus*. Dermal keels similar to those of the woundfin are present on the antero-dorsal scales of *Hybopsis gelida* (Cross, 1967). Coarse, close-set papillae on the intermandibular (gular) region of the woundfin (Snyder, 1915) are superficially quite like those on *H. gelida* (Branson, 1966). General shape of *Plagopterus* (depressed, ventrally flattened head, dorso-lateral and relatively small eyes; large fins; etc.) all strongly resemble the shapes of a number of riverine *Hybopsis,* and even of diverse other fishes: river sturgeons of the genus *Scaphirhynchus* (Bailey and Cross, 1954); diverse catfishes (Hora, 1930) and cyprinids (Nikolsky, 1961) of Eurasia and elsewhere; loaches (Cobitidae; Hutchinson, 1939); North American catfishes (Taylor, 1969); and other groups of similar habit and habitat from other parts of the world.

Barbels of those silty-water fishes that have been studied, and in general of fishes from any dimly lit environment, are profusely invested with chemoreceptors, the numbers and sizes of which often increase with growth of the fish (Davis and Miller, 1967). Similar organs may also be distributed over the lower surface of the head and body, lips, and sometimes even on the interradial membranes of fins. These organs greatly increase the surface area that may provide information on the immediate environment.

Two forms of the minnow *Hybopsis aestivalis* from turbid streams of the southern Great Plains swim slowly just above the bottom with their pectoral fins spread widely and barbels in contact with the sand (Davis and Miller, 1967). There was no evidence of visual selection of food by these fishes, despite artificially clear water in aquaria, but they quickly detected dried and live foods that sank to the bottom, searching with exaggerated movements and even greater spreading of the fins. No change toward sight feeding was evident after three months in clear-water aquaria. The woundfin has almost identical behavior in captivity, but it will occasionally rise to take floating objects or live foods at a considerable distance from the bottom, or at the surface.

Internal morphological features also correlate with habitats and habits of fishes. Relative sizes and degrees of development of the brain seem to reflect with some accuracy the expanded sensory equipment of some other parts of the body (Miller and Evans, 1965). Fishes with hypertrophy of the facial lobes of the brain usually have reduced optic lobes, reflecting less sensory input from vision and more from organs arranged in the skin. Those fishes that sort food from debris taken into the mouth have vast numbers of bucco-pharyngeal receptors and correspondingly enlarged vagal portions of the brain. Skin tasters and mouth tasters obviously predominate in silty waters, and included with the former is the razorback sucker (*Xyrauchen texanus*) endemic to the Colorado River (Miller and Evans, 1965).

As discussed before, fishes of the mainstream of the Colorado River demonstrate an unusual parallelism in morphology, and this includes not only their body shapes, but also the presence of thick, leathery skins, with scales reduced, absent, or deeply embedded (see Section III,A,1). This is especially pronounced on surfaces that first contact onrushing water, such as the leading edges of fins, dorsum of head, nape, and antero-dorsal surfaces of the sides. All the species have relatively small eyes, set in small, bony orbits, but none is as extreme as a chub from the highly turbid Missouri River (*Hybopsis meeki*) which often has an overgrowth of leathery skin almost covering the eye surface (Moore, 1950; Davis and Miller, 1967).

2. Fishes in Gradients of Springs

Gradients of dispersion created by gradual changes in habitat downflow from a spring are somewhat more fixed, and considerably more evident, than those in streams fed by surface runoff. One, or perhaps two or three, factors present overriding forces in such a gradient. Thus the Moapa dace appears as a thermal endemic (Hubbs and Miller, 1948b), as do *Crenich-thys* spp. (Hubbs, 1932). *Cyprinodon bifasciatus* (Miller, 1968) and others discussed before are capable of completing their life cycles in thermal and chemical constancy, but are incapable of doing so downstream, either because of physiological constraints or because of competitive interactions with other fish species.

Springheads are notoriously depauperate in species, and this holds, gen-erally, for most animal groups (Minckley, 1963). However, in large, com-plex limnocrenes, such as in the Cuatro Ciénegas basin, heterogeneity may allow a substantial fauna to co-inhabit.

When the springs are arranged by size (Fig. 7), faunal diversity may, however, be demonstrated to increase with decreasing constancy. At the terminus of the spectrum, the sumps of springs in desiccating lakes and pools, variability is so great that it acts as an overriding force, again limit-ing the fauna to one species, or a few species, capable of resisting, or per-sisting under, the prevailing regime.

The patterns of dispersion in a spring-fed environment therefore may theoretically result from the same basic factors producing longitudinal suc-cession of fishes in streams of classical physiographic gradient (Fig. 6). Small faunas of headwater creeks correspond to those in sumps of desert systems—only colonizers capable of resisting great extremes can live in either place. Springheads correspond to the relatively greater constancy of large, lowland rivers of temperate zones. When the springs are large enough they may support a comparably large and diversified fauna. Intermediate habitats, by nature both diversified and relatively permanent, support the greater variety of fishes.

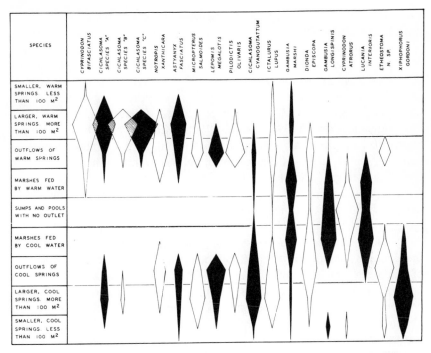

Fig. 7. Habitat preferences and general abundances of fishes of the Cuatro Ciénegas basin, central Coahuila, northern Mexico; compiled from Minckley (1969b) and unpublished data. No comparison between species, other than from the aspect of differing habitat preferences, is intended. The area within the blackened or outlined area is the same for each species, and the greater or lesser width at a given point (or habitat type) indicates an estimate of its abundance in that environment.

3. Population Responses to Changes in Habitat

Despite the capability of some silty-water, current-adapted, or spring-head fishes to persist under altered conditions, it is evident that distributions of such highly specialized forms are restricted by availability and continuity of their special habitat. Gradual but continuing depletion and reductions in range of Colorado River fishes, Colorado River squawfish (*Ptychochilus lucius*), chubs (*Gila* spp.), razorback sucker, flannelmouth sucker (*Catostomus latipinnis*), and woundfin, all characteristic of the mainstream, have occurred with increasing modifications of the system by man. Most of these are large fishes. They simply appear to cease reproducing in periods of stress, depending upon their long life expectancy to ultimately perpetuate their kind. They cannot, however, outlive conditions imposed by continued, intensive impoundment even though it is transitory when viewed in perspective of geologic time through which many of the forms have lived. Their extinction within a few years therefore seems inevitable.

Conditions which are severe for one fish species may of course enhance another. Tolerant forms have an advantage in severe conditions and become common. Intolerant forms may shift their ranges, compensating for severe events, and become locally extinct only to return or even to extend their ranges when suitable habitat is created (Trautman, 1942, 1957; Minckley and Cross, 1959; Starrett, 1950b; Minckley and Deacon, 1968). Short-lived species may almost, or in fact, disappear. Intermittency of tributaries in a large system results in retreat of the fauna to havens in rivers or springs (Paloumpis, 1956; Deacon, 1961; Deacon and Metcalf, 1961). However, in desert regimes, the lower, larger parts of a basin may dry first, and major extinction can occur in disjunct areas of the drainage system.

The longfin dace is the most adaptable and widespread fish native to the Sonoran Desert. In years of abundant precipitation, large populations of dace may build, many kilometers from annually reliable, permanent flow. In 1965, more than 45 km of surface water persisted in the desert portion of the Sycamore Creek system, Maricopa County, Arizona, below about 1000 meters elevation, throughout most of the year (Minckley and Barber, 1971). Young of 1965 *Agosia,* displaced in part downstream from higher elevations, matured and reproduced to densely populate the entire reach. In the years 1963–1965, and again in 1967–1969, only three 30 to 100 meter segments of surface flow were known in that reach of creek, and each supported remnant populations of dace. Similar situations of colonization and extirpation are known for a great number of species in almost all deserts that have been studied. Some of the most spectacular examples are the cyprinodontids, especially *Cyprinodon* and *Aphanius.*

More subtle changes also occur in stream-fish populations, and sometimes in a remarkably short period of years. Barber and Minckley (1966) found only one individual of *Rhinichthys osculus* in Aravaipa Creek, Arizona, in 1963–1964; longfin dace were exceedingly common. After substantial precipitation and increasingly persistent flow in 1965–1966, speckled dace became more abundant and *Agosia* relatively less so. In 1968, *Rhinichthys* was again almost absent, and *Agosia* was swarming throughout the area. But in 1970 after good flow in 1969, *Agosia* was again rare. In Sonoita Creek, southern Arizona, an identical response occurred over the much longer period from 1904–1965. The fauna of that stream slowly declined (with unknown fluctuations year to year) as stream flow deteriorated, until in 1959 only *Agosia* was found by Miller (1961a). In 1963, it took 4 hours and a detailed search for suitable habitat to obtain two specimens each of speckled dace and Gila mountain-sucker (*Pan-*

tosteus clarki); millions of *Agosia* were present. In 1964, no *Rhinichthys* and three *Pantosteus* were found; no collection was made in 1965. In 1966 after an increase of flow the preceding winter and spring, both the formerly rare species had realized a profuse spawn, and by 1967 *Pantosteus* made up almost 30% of the fauna, and *Rhinichthys* was frequent in collections (Minckley, 1969a).

Similar fluctuations in fish populations occurred throughout Arizona in the period 1965–1967. Some rare and restricted fishes, such as the Little Colorado River spinedace (*Lepidomeda vittata*), spread to reoccupy most of their former ranges (Minckley and Carufel, 1967). It is notable that in the almost-constant environment of the spring-fed Moapa River, southern Nevada, based on collections made over the same time period (1963–1969), native fish populations remained essentially stable (Deacon and Bradley, 1971).

Relative stability of some stream-fish populations, usually of larger species, contrasts with variations just outlined. Spatial relations of stream-fish populations have been studied in eastern United States (Gerking, 1950, 1953, 1959; Larimore, 1952; Fajen, 1963), but to our knowledge have not been defined in desert streams. By inference from observational data, restricted movements by desert stream fishes are highly characteristic of adults, whereas young seem to disperse more widely. In the Chiricahua Mountains, Arizona, John (1963, 1964) found that adult speckled dace remained in permanent pools in flood (see also Section III,A,1) and in drought. Yet flooding moved smaller fishes downstream rapidly and sometimes almost completely decimated the young of the year. In southern Arizona, the Sonoran chub (*Gila ditaenia*) lives in a small, intermittent stream near the International Boundary. A major pool that has been studied sporadically since 1963 has always supported a few adult chubs. In times of persistently high discharge the adults do not move from the pool, even though many hundreds of meters of habitat is then available (Minckley and Deacon, 1968). This also is evident in some populations of *Agosia,* in more or less temporary streams. If displacement occurs, the fish appear capable of returning to the permanent pools. Gunning (1959) demonstrated the olfactory capabilities of the longear sunfish (*Lepomis megalotis*) in identification of its home pools. Perhaps some desert species also have such a capability.

Short-term stability of populations of some other stream-dwelling species is indicated by the month to month similarity of population structure, such as in the spikedace (*Meda fulgida*) in Aravaipa Creek (Barber *et al.,* 1970). This is even more strongly indicated by a lack of morphological variability in some populations over a long period of time. If much gene flow occurred throughout systems studied by Rinne (1969), through transport of fishes by flood or by movements of the fish up- or downstream, such uniformity could scarcely persist. In one instance, however, when an entire indigenous morphotype was destroyed by chemical eradication, re-invasion by a dowstream population was evidenced by changes in the morphology easily detectable by character analysis. Many such examples of indicated stability are available in desert fishes, despite variations of environment that would seem directly opposed to such a phenomenon on a long-term basis.

4. Broader Distributional Relations

Distributional patterns of fishes that range widely often appear to correlate with climate, chemical factors, relief, or a combination of these and other environmental parameters (Hubbs, 1957b). This often involves species interactions at the margins of their ranges, such as in the speckled and longfin daces in Arizona (Fig. 8). Boundaries, as discussed above, may move up- and downstream with changes in runoff. Isolated populations may be severely limited in range, such as the cold-water trouts on desert mountains surrounded by hot or dry lower rivers which are totally inhospitable to them (Miller, 1950a, 1971; Needham and Gard, 1964). It is perhaps noteworthy that such trout now are as (or more) effectively isolated as are pupfish in a spring; in actuality they are desert fishes too, and as such serve to illustrate one of the difficulties involved in our selection of species to discuss here.

Excluding local isolates and some fishes so highly specialized, such as Gila cypha, or thermal endemics such as Moapa, Crenichthys, and others, as to be restricted to the biotope in which they presumably evolved, more subtle patterns relative to environment are discernible. Pupfishes exploit their remarkable tenacity for life by successfully occupying places unavailable to other fish species because of environmental extremes. With a few exceptions, they never become abundant except in places too severe for, or isolated from, a substantial, competing or predatory fish fauna. This results in an apparently discontinuous distribution, even in integrated river basins. The Pecos River of south-central United States flows through an area of salt domes and strata from which solution occurs, and salinities may approach that of seawater. Cyprinodontoids, some with affinities to Atlantic and Gulf of Mexico coastal forms, dominate the local fauna (Koster, 1957; Hubbs and Miller, 1965). Aquatic crustaceans of similar affinity have also been found (Cole and Bousfield, 1970). In the dilute headwaters of the Pecos, and in the Río Grande above and below the mouth of the Pecos, these fishes are rare, absent, or restricted to creek mouths, backwaters, or other protected habitats. The Plains killifish seems

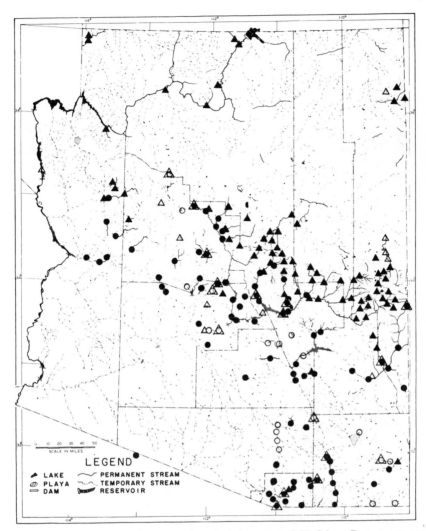

Fig. 8. Distributions of two species of Arizona cyprinid fishes. Dots represent collection sites for longfin dace since 1960; open circles denote former localities of occurrence. Closed triangles are for collections of speckled dace since 1960; open triangles indicate now-extirpated populations. Of 17 sites at which both species occurred at some time, 5 now support neither species, and 12 support longfin dace alone, an indication of stream deterioration and upstream invasion of the latter, a low desert species, to higher elevation as stream temperatures ameliorate and speckled dace are forced upstream.

limited in its eastern distribution by the less saline waters (or by the more saturated fauna of more well-watered zones). It often comprises the only fish in seasonally hot, silty, far-western Kansas rivers (Metcalf, 1966; Cross, 1967). Only a few have been taken after flooding in the eastern side, but its proclivity for severe environments is nicely demonstrated by the most eastern, reproducing population that occurs in a salt spring of Missouri (Miller, 1955).

Salinities may also strongly limit the distribution of species. Rivers flowing parallel and in close approximation, then entering the sea, may have quite different components in their obligate, freshwater fish fauna. Springs and streams entering closed-basin, saline lakes, may be even more isolated. Great Salt Lake, for example, has freshwater fishes in tributary streams and on their deltas (Sigler and Miller, 1963). Yet the open waters support no aquatic vertebrate life. In the Anatolian basin of central Turkey, Kosswig (1961) and his associates have studied populations of cyprinodonts (*Aphanius, Anatolichthys,* and *Kosswigichthys*). These have undergone complex differentiation, then anastomosis through hybridization for thousands of years, alternating isolation by saline lake waters with periods of intermingling when lake conditions permitted (Kosswig, 1956, 1961, 1963; Villwock, 1958, 1966). The same type of situation may have prevailed in some fishes of the Cuatro Ciénegas basin, Mexico, before canalization destroyed most of the large, *barrial* lakes (Minckley, 1969b). LaBounty and Deacon (1971) have drawn parallels with the apparently more desiccated aquatic habitats in Death Valley.

Temperature may strongly influence the northern limits of ranges for warm-adapted fishes such as the cyprinodontoids, cichlids, and characids. In some instances, the northern limit of a fish's range may be extended by selection of cold-hardy stocks, as in the case of mosquitofish (Krumholz, 1944, 1948), or through man-made structures or conditions that allow them to overwinter. Damming of streams produces amelioration of winter temperatures in some instances. This may have allowed the Mexican tetra to establish in Oklahoma (Moore, 1968), and the threadfin shad to move up the Ohio River (Minckley and Krumholz, 1960).

Hot waters from steam plants now allow some warm-water fishes to live at northern latitudes (Dryer and Benson, 1957), and introductions of tropical fishes into warm springs of cold climates have often succeeded (McAllister, 1969; Lachner *et al.*, 1970). The reciprocal also is true. Witness the relict populations of trout far south of the major regions of cool or temperate climate, on high mountains of arid regions, such as Arizona, Baja California, Mexico, and the northwestern part of the Mexican Plateau (Miller, 1950a, 1971; Needham and Gard, 1959, 1964), as well as the success of stocking salmonids at high elevations far south of their natural ranges.

5. Activity Cycles

Study of normal, daily activities of some desert fish has received attention in recent years. Harker (1958) reviewed diurnal rhythms in animals, and defined two types, as follows: (1) endogenous systems which continue to operate when environmental conditions are held constant and (2) exogenous rhythms occurring as responses to regular environmental cycles. Endogenous rhythms of metabolic rates in largemouth bass (*Micropterus salmoides*) (Clausen, 1936), *Fundulus paravipinnis* (Wells, 1935), and many other fish species (Harker, 1958) have not been demonstrated for desert fishes, but doubtless exist. Numerous cyprinodontids and poeciliids from southwestern United States and Mexico, for example, demonstrate typical spring surges in reproduction (although breeding throughout the year) under laboratory conditions of constant light and temperature.

Field studies cannot distinguish between the two types of rhythms, but frequently do permit definition of environmental components affecting rhythmicity. Exogenous rhythms based on light as the dominant factor seem a general rule for fishes that are considered diurnal, nocturnal, crepuscular, or even arrhythmatic (Spencer, 1939; Spoor and Schloemer, 1939; Hasler and Villemonte, 1953; Hobson, 1965). Most desert fishes, particularly those living in springs, seem visually oriented, and are therefore diurnal. The springfishes, *Crenichthys baileyi* and *C. nevadae,* have activity cycles that are light-initiated and dark-inhibited (Deacon and Wilson, 1967; Hubbs *et al.*, 1967), with some inferred modifying influences by temperature and dissolved oxygen content. Populations of this genus reduce normal activities in response to oxygen levels below 2 mg/liter, temperatures above 35°C, or cloud cover. Changes in the normal activity pattern (generally compression of activity into a relatively short period of the day) also resulted from apparent stress induced by establishment of exotic species and/or an increased incidence of parasitism. Similar light-initiated, dark-inhibited activities have been documented for a number of species of pupfishes (Barlow, 1958a; Deacon, 1967; James, 1969; Arnold, 1970) and for cichlids of the Cuatro Ciénegas area.

Midday depression of activity seems a rule in many desert fish species, as has been observed for *Crenichthys* (Deacon and Wilson, 1967), *Cyprinodon* (Deacon, 1967; James, 1969), and *Empetrichthys. Cyprinodon diabolis,* on one hand, seems to actively avoid direct sunlight (James, 1969). *C. n. nevadensis* in Zzyzx pond, California (LaBounty, 1968), and a number of other species (Barlow, 1958a; Itzkowitz and Minckley,

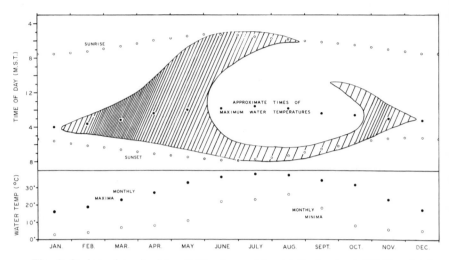

Fig. 9. Period of territorial activities in pupfish at latitude about 33° N, related to some environmental variables. Maximum activity is indicated by lesser distance between oblique lines. Generalized data based principally on behavior of *Cyprinodon atrorus* in seminatural, outdoor pools, but also upon observations of other species in nature.

1969), appear to seek direct sunlight (until temperature becomes limiting). Suppression of activity at midday in pupfishes (excepting *C. diabolis,* perhaps) therefore does not seem light related and must reflect some other factor(s). *Gila mohavensis* at Zzyzx avoided direct sun at all times (LaBounty, 1968), and other species of *Gila* seem also to remain in shade, or cover at least, during the day. Wynne-Edwards (1962) suggested that synchronized activity such as this may have considerable importance in organizing the population to impart sensory information for control of its size or dispersion. Midsummer suppression of territorial behavior by male pupfish (Fig. 9), although perhaps a thermal response, might also be pertinent to this hypothesis.

Hubbs *et al.* (1967) also demonstrated a direct relationship of activity, as indicated by trap catches, with sound production in *Crenichthys.* Diurnal and seasonal variation in sound production also were demonstrated by Knudson *et al.* (1948) in an exhaustive study of the phenomenon in a croaker (*Micropogon undulatus*) and more recently in a number of other fish species (Tavolga, 1960).

Comparisons of activity patterns of populations living in constant conditions with those of the same species in variable habitats indicate that basic patterns may be obscured by stresses imposed by a myriad of factors —physical, chemical, and biological. Avoidance reactions of fishes toward acute environmental conditions are now recognized, in part at least, as regulatory in function, activities which place the animal under the most optimal conditions available within a given environmental spectrum. This represents a selection of the most favorable habitat available along an environmental gradient in which the biotic elements assume a somewhat dominant position. Refinement of such behavior varies considerably, as does the detail and quality of its observation.

Behavioral selection of favorable conditions permits a population to continue its normal activities. Alterations of normal behavior, i.e., changes in activity patterns and changes in the population dispersion in the habitat, apparently enhance survival of those forms possessing a sufficiently labile behavioral repertoire. Behavioral thermoregulation in fishes, for example, has only recently been described, and Norris (1963) reviewed available evidence for the phenomenon. The responses seem relatively widespread in fishes as a group and are extremely well developed and important in desert species. Lowe and Heath (1969), for instance, showed that desert pupfish at Quitobaquito Spring, Arizona, commonly (and preferentially) occupied water at 40°–41°C, which is within 2° or 3°C of the level for thermal death. Barlow (1958a) also noted *C. macularius* in shore pools of the Salton Sea moving to occupy waters just cooler than 36°C and avoiding waters above or below that level, if possible. In temperature gradients of streams fed by hot springs near Tecopa, California, *C. n. calidae* occurred most abundantly at 36°C (Miller, 1948). Maximum activity of *C. n. nevadensis* in the marsh at Saratoga Springs, Death Valley, California, occurred between 30° and 34°C, and was severely restricted above 38°C.

More recently, observations of another population of *Cyprinodon* occupying outflows of newly constructed artesian wells a few miles north of Tecopa indicate a somewhat higher voluntary tolerance, causing the population to follow the seasonally changing 42°C isotherm as it moves up or down the stream channel (Soltz and Brown, 1970). Male *Crenichthys baileyi* from Crystal and Mormon springs, Nevada, oriented evenly between a minimum available temperature of 32°C and 36°C, in Mimbres Hot Spring, New Mexico, and could be chased into 38°C water (Hubbs and Hettler, 1964). *Gambusia marshi* was most abundant at 39.5°–40.5°C in Ojo Caliente, Coahuila (Section III,A,5).

Thermal conditions need not be extreme for behavioral responses to occur. LaBounty (1968) presented data on activity of *C. n. nevadensis* from Zzyzx Pond, California, on four different occasions during the year. Temperature ranges were 10.9°–21.8°C on February 27 and 26.3°–32.2°C on August 31; thus, lethal temperatures were never approached. The fish consistently selected the warmest temperatures in the pond and were most active during the warmest time of day. They avoided cooler waters and were inactive at night. Selection of the warmest available water was clearly occurring in this instance since population movement of about 40 meters was required for them to remain in the warmest water and to avoid the coolest. *Gila mohavensis* in the same pool usually exhibited an opposite response to temperature, always occupying the coolest water available.

Longfin dace also perform movements in response to environmental temperatures, and the complexity of stream environments provides a fertile area for investigation of such behavior. When flowing water approximately 1 cm deep was 36.8°C in the center of Sycamore Creek, Arizona, temperatures in slightly deeper places adjacent to algal mats were 33.1°–34.2°C, and in a quiet place near an overhanging tree, 30.4°C was recorded. Adult dace all were concentrated in shade of the tree. Juveniles were generally distributed along the banks, darting occasionally across the warmer channel. At water temperatures between 30° and 33°C, most dace were active throughout the creek (and at those temperatures in Aravaipa and Sonita creeks on other dates as well).

Low temperatures may also elicit behavioral responses in desert fishes. Thermal preferentia of *Cyprinodon macularius* in the Salton Sea in winter ranged from a low of about 8°C in early morning to about 20°C in mid-afternoon (Barlow, 1958a). Winter activity of Nevada pupfish in the marsh associated with Saratoga Springs occurs only when temperatures exceed 10° to 12°C. In Cuatro Ciénegas, *C. atrorus* becomes active between 7° and 9°C. Individuals of *C. n. nevadensis* lose equilibrium at 5°–6°C, and can move only in violent, erratic paths. Only weak, uncoordinated, swimming movements were possible in the last species at experimental temperatures of about 2.8°C. Temperatures lower than about 7°C completely preclude activity in undisturbed pupfishes studied by us in nature. All typically burrow in the substrate or seek cover beneath debris, and remain inactive there until temperatures increase. The report by Cox (1966) of total dormancy of pupfish at Quitobaquito from October to April at temperatures varying up to 19.8°C is in error, according to our data recorded for that population over a number of years.

Burrowing by *Cyprinodon* occurs at any time, often in response to disturbance, but it may also be a means of avoiding temperature extremes from which other forms of escape are impossible. At low temperatures the fish must burrow actively (as has frequently been observed) into the soft bottom prior to becoming immobilized. The mud doubtless provides both thermal insulation and protective cover, and potential metabolic advantages of residence in anaerobic muds may be quite high (Blazka, 1958; Eckberg, 1962). Some pupfish confined in cages at Saratoga Marsh, Death Valley, burrowed without artificial disturbance. Water temperatures ranged from

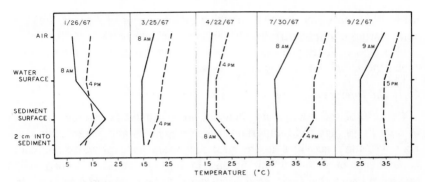

Fig. 10. Temperature relationships among air, water, and bottom sediment in Big Lake, Saratoga Springs, Death Valley National Monument, California at various times of the year (from Deacon, 1968a).

25° to 35°C, and warmest sediment immediately adjacent to a buried fish was 33.5°C. Duration of occupancy of sediment was variable, but often lasted more than 1 hour. Stimulus for burrowing was problematical since temperatures of the upper 2 cm of sediment within the cages remained identical to, or slightly higher than, water temperature. However, extensive measurements of temperature profiles through water and into the undisturbed sediment at Saratoga Marsh (Fig. 10) showed that burrowing could impart a considerable thermal advantage to the population.

Different sizes of fish of a given species may have vastly different preferentia and cycles of activity. Young or smaller pupfish notoriously frequent warmer temperatures than adults (Lowe et al., 1967; LaBounty, 1968; and our observation), as do young of longfin dace, speckled dace, Mohave club, and a myriad of other cyprinoids in streams of the warmer deserts. Larval catostomids, for example, move to the shallowest, warmest parts of streams, where current is essentially absent—usually behind sand bars, beds of algae, or other obstructions. Recorded temperatures in these places are the highest for any stream habitat in the Sonoran Desert (Section II, A). As the larvae grow, they progressively move into cooler, less extreme environments. It is notable that larval mortality from obvious thermal extremes seems rare, despite temperatures that may approach 40°C in late spring and early summer.

Effects of alien species on activity patterns of native desert fishes have scarcely been studied, but are inferred to occur. We have noted interruption of breeding activity by native fishes when disturbed by other species (see also Liu, 1969). Shifts in apparent habitat preference were recorded in Ash Meadows, Nevada, where *C. n. mionectes* was originally concentrated near the surface, then moved to a more uniform distribution throughout the water column following establishment of *Poecilia latipinna* and *Gambusia affinis* in Jackrabbit Spring. A similarly uniform distribution is also evident in Big Spring, Nevada, but data prior to establishment of exotic species at that locality are lacking.

6. Biotic Interactions, Man-Induced and Otherwise

Because of the relative simplicity of aquatic habitats in deserts, studies of their fishes may yield important insight into inter- and intraspecific interactions. Man's activities in the past few years have provided numerous experiments in nature which pertain to such problems. Competition of one form or another is generally considered to be of importance in control of population sizes in freshwater fishes (Larkin, 1956), but other factors may sometimes become more critical. There appear three distinct schools of thought: (1) competition is of primary importance (Nicholson, 1933, 1954); (2) predation and parasitism are more important than competition (Utida, 1953; Larkin, 1956); and (3) climatic factors far outweigh biotic factors in influencing population sizes (Bodenheimer, 1938; Andrewartha and Birch, 1954).

We have examined the above views with reference to fishes of desert waters, with special emphasis on the influences of man-induced changes which have occurred and are occurring. The last view, that of climatic control of population sizes, has been repeatedly discussed in earlier sections [assuming that an aquatic "climate," the averages and range of "under-water weather" (Minckley, 1963), is acceptable to the reader], and is not again covered.

Larkin (1956) defined competition as ". . .the demand, typically at the same time, of more than one organism, for the same resources of the environment . . ." This was offered in a discussion of interspecific competition, but seems to apply equally well to intraspecific interactions, and would imply that competition for food between individuals of a single species would be most intense. Such does not seem to be the case, according to Ivlev (1961). The apparent reduction in competitive intensity within a species seems due to a diversity of behavioral responses (Wynne-Edwards, 1962). Different-sized individuals of various fish species notoriously inhabit different habitats, displaying an ontogenic change by moving from place to place with increases in size; food habits may change radically with size, season, and so on, and territoriality also is highly developed in some groups, and is sometimes of a complex nature (reviewed in part by Liu, 1969). Segregation by sex also is highly developed in some desert fishes (Minckley and Carufel, 1967; Arnold, 1970; Barber *et al.,* 1970; Rinne, 1970).

Intraspecific competition obviously does exist, however, such as in the prolific threadfin shad where older year classes suppress growth of younger ones and are reciprocally influenced (Johnson, 1970). Similar effects may well occur in desert fishes, but their protracted spawning, and other factors, make the patterns less easily discernible. Species capable of survival under a wide spectrum of environments are furthermore less likely to exhibit clear-cut competitive relationships than more specialized kinds, and further complication arises since flexibility in growth rates tends to dampen out effects of competition.

Numerous experimental examples exist of one fish species causing sharp reductions in abundance of another (Ivlev, 1961). It is notable that many such examples involve closely related forms, or in the cases of transfers of alien animals to new areas, the interacting species quite often are ecologically similar although taxonomically distant in relationships. A few instances of apparent breakdown of the Gaussian hypothesis (Ross, 1957; Fryer, 1959; Weatherley, 1963b) have been attributed in part to a superabundance of food, but even under more typical circumstances, demonstration of actual competition between species in nature is very difficult and has rarely been accomplished (Larkin, 1956; Ivlev, 1961). Larkin attributes this to the fact that freshwater habitats are geologically short-lived (see, however, Minckley, 1963 relative to streams), highly diversified, and subject to very rapid ecological succession. All of these tend to favor generalization rather than specialization, in fishes at least. It seems reasonable, and concordant with our observations, that behavioral interactions (= competition) at the interspecific level may induce adjustments allowing coexistence of species where a single kind of environment exists over a sufficient period of time. Similar reinforcement of isolating mechanisms between closely related species was proposed by Dobzhansky (1940) (see, however, Dobzhansky et al., 1968). When such systems are disrupted either at the physicochemical or biological environment levels, substantial changes accrue.

Predators presumably are limited in their population sizes by food supply (prey), and at the same time impose limitations on their prey through cropping. In some instances this fails, as indicated by the lack of ability of largemouth bass to control some prey species in artificial ponds (Bennett, 1962).

On the other hand, at least two instances of extinction of desert fish populations are known certainly to have resulted from introduction and establishment of largemouth bass (Deacon, 1968b; Deacon and Bunnell, 1970). Other such occurrences involving the centrarchid, other fishes, or even bullfrogs (*Rana catesbiaena*) (Miller and Hubbs, 1960) have resulted in declines or extinction also. In the two instances studied by us in Nevada, extinction of the native fish populations (*Crenichthys baileyi* and *Cyprinodon nevadensis mionectes*) was followed by a marked decline in condition of the predators. The scanty fauna of such special habitats appears insufficient to maintain their populations at any but a minimal level, and the lack of evolutionary experience by the native fish obviously negated their capability for maintaining populations under the stress of predation. Parasitism, like predation, is self-limiting as soon as host populations decline.

Johnson and Soong (1965) presented evidence suggesting that exotic species find it difficult or impossible to successfully invade and establish populations in Malaya where a large and diversified fauna holds forth. In habitats simplified or modified by man, exotic species may, and do, become established. Elton (1958) emphasized this same principle in his "Ecology of Invasions." Generally, the species that do succeed when introduced into a faunally saturated area are those with amazingly wide spectra of tolerances, such as the carp or mosquitofish. On the other hand, when one or a few fish species occupy a given habitat, such as in most desert waters, exotic species may establish readily, and with various results.

In relatively pristine desert habitats, those uncontaminated by alien fishes, there is a marked segregation of species into different niches. In addition, only three families comprise the bulk of the fish fauna of western North America, yet in only a few instances are two species of the same genus sympatric (in the geographic sense), and when this occurs they are typically ecologically allopatric.

An excellent example of the last situation occurred in the minnow genus *Gila* (Section IV,A,1) prior to suppression of diversity in the Colorado River system by man's activities. In Aravaipa Creek, Arizona, seven native species coexist, five minnows and two suckers. In addition to having markedly different ranges within the stream (Fig. 6), their local habitats, behavior, periods of reproduction, and food habits scarcely overlap (Barber and Minckley, 1966; Barber *et al.*, 1970; unpublished data). This type of order also seems to exist in larger, diversified springs. For example, in the Cuatro Ciénegas area, 10–14 kinds of fishes coexist in large springheads (*lagunas*), and they also seem segregated quite highly in various aspects of their life histories. In that area, a local race of largemouth bass is naturally sympatric with *Cyprinodon bifaciatus,* and both exist in reasonably stable, viable populations. Fewer species exist in Nevada and California springs, but where more than a single kind is present, niche segregation or different spatial habitats are evident. Single-species populations typically exploit all of their available habitats.

Changes with time, in climate, geology, and so on, obviously effected decimation of the desert fishes—there are fewer kinds in all of western North America, for example, than in many states (or single rivers) of the more mesic eastern United States. However, a substantial number persisted. In Arizona (and most of the other desert regions), there was little evident extinction or marked changes in population sizes indicated through the period of arroyo cutting at the turn of the century (Section II,A)—or even with the early habitat alterations such as damming and diversion of streams (Minckley, 1971).

In about the 1930's, however, introduced species began to form a substantial proportion of the fauna, and populations of native forms began to decline, in some instances to extinction. The Gila topminnow and desert pupfish are essentially gone, presumably through interactions with mosquitofish. More recently, the red shiner appears to have essentially replaced the spikedace and loach minnow throughout substantial parts of their ranges (Minckley and Deacon, 1968; Minckley, 1971). The recent (1970) collection of spikedace in the Verde River, where it was thought extirpated, may indicate a resurgence of its population after a period of adjustment.

In Nevada habitats, several instances of reduction of native fishes have been closely studied following establishment of alien species. Population decline of the Pahrump killifish following establishment of goldfish at Manse Spring was discussed by Deacon et al. (1964) and by Minckley and Deacon (1968). Subsequent data also indicate a reduction in the average sizes of individuals in the native population, and in the median number of eggs per female. Following an initial reduction in numbers, the killifish population recovered to a somewhat lower than original level, but lengths of individual fish and numbers of ova remained low. Since rather drastic alterations of the habitat occurred almost simultaneously with introduction of goldfish, it is impossible to segregate the influence of competitive interactions from those of habitat alteration.

Deacon et al. (1964) and Hubbs and Deacon (1964) presented corroborative information on other cyprinodontids from several Nevada springs. General reductions in size of individual native fishes occurred in apparent response to establishment of exotics; additional data collected since that time confirm this trend. However, in most instances a variable amount of physical change in addition to introduction of alien fishes also was associated with depletion of natives.

In most of these situations, if extinction of the native population does not occur, the interactions result in rapid, apparent, niche segregation. For example, mosquitofish, shortfin mollies (*Poecilia mexicana*), and sailfin mollies (*P. latipinna*) tend to frequent surface and marginal habitats, forcing the native *Crenichthys baileyi* and *Cyprinodon nevadensis* subspp. into deeper areas. In springs with extreme gradients of temperature or dissolved oxygen, native fishes utilize their unique physiological tolerances and segregate spatially from the introduced forms by moving up-gradient into areas inhospitable for the aliens.

It is notable that mosquitofish have been implicated in the decline of many fish species, in North America and elsewhere (Myers, 1965). In light of its essentially world-wide dissemination by man for use in mosquito control (Gerberich and Laird, 1965), it is likely that an untold amount of damage has been done by this species, especially in faunally depauperate areas. Mosquitofish may actively prey upon other fishes, however, rather than compete with them for food or space.

Most desert fish populations were relatively devoid of parasites prior to 1930 or so (Wilson *et al.*, 1966; James, 1968); and a general correlation between introduction of alien fish species and an increase in incidence of parasitic crustaceans on natives has been demonstrated. This may have resulted from an initial introduction of the parasite along with stocked fishes, and a high susceptibility of indigenous forms to its depredations, or to a weakening of native fishes under competitive stress of exotics, or both.

B. MODES OF REPRODUCTION AND DEVELOPMENT

Reproductive habits of fishes are receiving ever-increasing study by physiologists, ethologists, and others, and a vast amount of information, too voluminous to be reviewed here, is currently available. Breder and Rosen (1966) include many references plus a broad synthesis of reproductive behavior in a systematic treatment. Carlander (1969) provided an overall view of many life-history data for North American species, including information on fecundity, spawning times, etc. Physiological aspects of reproductive cycles and sexuality have been covered in volumes edited by Brown (1957), Hoar and Randall (1969), and others cited therein.

1. Sexual Cycles and Behavior

In temperate zones, reproductive activities of fishes may be closely attuned to changes in photoperiod and temperature. As one moves toward the tropics, other factors, such as seasonal rains, may provide triggering reproductive stimuli. And, where conditions warrant year-round reproduction, energy demands for gamete production may dictate cyclical phenomena, at the individual level at least (Hoar, 1969). Fishes may also develop unique reproductive cycles geared to their special habitats.

For example, some species, notably those of perennially turbid streams, appear to spawn at whatever time in spring or summer the rivers reach flood stage. Eggs and larvae of the Arkansas River shiner (*Notropis girardi*) drift free near the water surface, and development is so rapid that swimming initiates 3 or 4 days after hatching. Eggs deposited in the shifting, sandy bottom would be buried, and in backwaters they would be covered by sedimenting muds (Moore, 1944b). A number of large cyprinid fishes in rivers of Eurasia spawn similarly, and it is suggested that this type of behavior also makes the pelagic eggs less conspicuous to predators (Nikolsky, 1963). In Australian rivers, silver perch (*Bidyanus bidyanus;* family Theraponidae) and golden perch (*Plectroplites ambiguus;* family Serranidae) spawn with the same kind of timing to floods (Lake, 1967).

The stimulus of water-level changes, or related factors, in the reproduction of many large-river fishes is well documented. North American buffalofishes (genus *Ictiobus*) are notorious for this feature (Yeager, 1936). Van Ihering (1935) reports it for several South American species, Boulenger (1907) for numerous fishes of the Nile, and Hora (1945) related water-level changes and phases of the moon as stimuli for certain Indian cyprinids. Some fishes of desert lakes, such as the cui-ui (*Chasmistes cujus*) of Pyramid Lake, Nevada, move into influent streams to spawn in spring. Changes in river level strand many eggs, young, and even adults, to die on gravel bars (Snyder, 1917; LaRivers, 1962).

Fishes characteristic of the lower ends of large desert rivers, as elsewhere, may depend upon periodic flooding of marginal habitats for their reproductive activities or for feeding by themselves or by their young. The nutrients on fertile floodplains stimulate rapid development of plankton, not to mention the provision of a vast volume of terrestrial organic material (Evans-Prichard, 1940; Stubbs, 1949; Hickling, 1961; Nikolsky, 1963). Beheading of many desert streams by dams has had a profound effect on these and other lower-river fishes.

Some forms such as the massive Colorado River squawfish seem to have performed upstream "runs" prior to damming (Dill, 1944; Miller, 1961a), and the physical barriers may have blocked a critical stage in that species' life cycle (as it does in salmonids, such as *Oncorhynchus* spp., and other fishes that run into rivers from the sea to spawn).

On the other hand, changes in a myriad of other factors has been evidenced by alterations of the entire fauna of the Colorado system. Vanicek *et al.* (1970) have impressively documented the absence of reproduction by indigenous fishes in a 105-km reach of the Green River, Utah, below Flaming Gorge Dam. This was attributed to lowered water temperatures in summer periods of high discharge of water from the lake's hypolimnion. Below the mouth of the Yampa River, a major tributary of the Green, conditions resembled those existing prior to the dam, and native fishes reproduced successfully. Sexual activities of all the larger cyprinids (Squawfish and *Gila* spp.) seemed closely related to peak water temperatures and a decline in volume of flow (Vanicek and Kramer, 1969). Reproduction of these fishes at inception of low discharge and by the sand shiner (*Notropis stramineus*) in the western part of the Great Plains (Summerfelt and Minckley, 1969), may well be an attunement to avoid high turbidities and shifting stream beds by taking advantage of low, clear, summer flow.

In smaller habitats low waters appear to inhibit reproduction, despite the stimuli of increasing day length and temperatures in spring. This may, of course, result from nutritional deficiencies, or other factors related to crowding in intermittent habitats. John (1963) found that speckled dace in the Chiricahua Mountains, Arizona, spawned after spring runoff and again after late summer rains had produced freshets. He related day length, temperature, and flooding to spawning activity, but without the last, no summer spawning occurred.

Similar habits are implied by Koster (1957) for longfin dace and Río Grande mountain-sucker (*Pantosteus plebeius*) in New Mexico. However, in Aravaipa Creek, Arizona, no correlation of spawning activity with flooding by any of the seven native species of fishes has been detected. Longfin dace and the Gila mountain-sucker produced young continuously from December through June 1967 (and perhaps through July), despite fluctuations in water levels, and no late summer spawn was detected that related to flooding (in part, Barber *et al.*, 1970). Rinne (1970) also has noted protracted spawning in a mountain-sucker of the Virgin River system in Utah.

A pattern largely emerging from unpublished studies of stream minnows of the Sonoran and Mohave Deserts indicates a predominance of reproduction in spring, first by older females and later by younger ones. Old females may then develop additional complements of eggs, in some instances throughout the summer. Males follow similar patterns, with a surge of spawning in spring and with a few reripening at later times of the summer period. In some instances, small fish of both sexes, spawned late in the preceding summer, may achieve mature sizes in midsummer and develop gametes then (Minckley and Carufel, 1967; Barber *et al.*, 1970; Rinne, 1970; Minckley and Barber, 1971). This produces a complex pattern of recruitment in some species, which resembles a temperate cycle in spring and for younger fish, and a tropical cycle (periodic, protracted spawning) through the summer by older fish in the population.

Such a system certainly seems adaptive since at least a few reproductive adults are available to capitalize on suitable conditions, almost throughout the year. Catostomid fishes seem more fixed in habit, spawning principally in late winter and early spring. The reason for the long season of reproduction by Gila mountain-suckers in Aravaipa Creek is unknown. Another native catostomid of that stream, the Sonora sucker (*Catostomus insignis*), totally failed to produce young in 1967. This also is unexplained.

Despite the volume of information on pupfishes (reviewed by Liu, 1969), only a general pattern of reproduction may yet be described. Variability is quite high among species and apparently among populations of a given species. In many cyprinodontids, including pupfishes, a few eggs are spawned each day over a period of days, and then a period of ovarian repair and ovum production ensues, followed by subsequent spawning throughout the breeding season (whenever that might be). A certain percentage of fish in many populations seem capable, on the basis of sizes and morphology of their gonads, of producing gametes essentially throughout the year. In fact, some species and populations seem to have a pattern perhaps far more refined and complex than that described before for minnows.

In fluctuating environments, between 27° N latitude (Cuatro Ciénegas basin) and 36°–37° N (Death Valley system), there seems to be about a month's difference in timing of the overall sexual cycle of pupfishes. Some Nevada pupfishes initiate breeding activities in marshes and shallower pools in February, utilizing warm, marginal waters in midafternoon. Some breeding activity continues throughout the seasons through mid-October. Barlow (1961b) noted that males of the desert pupfish also "come into nuptial colors and take up territories" in winter, as he observed on February 11, in pools along the Salton Sea, California (latitude 33° N); their last observed spawn was also in October.

Cyprinodon atrorus begins sexual activities in late January in experimental ponds in Arizona (latitude 33° N), and in early January (in small numbers) in its natural habitats of the Cuatro Ciénegas basin. That species spawns as late as November, but no reproduction or breeding behavior has been noted from early December through early January. Young of *C. atrorus* are, however, produced every month of the year in experimental ponds, and they also appear in some natural waters in midwinter. Sac-fry in experimental ponds in December and early January may well have resulted from delayed hatching of ova (Kinne and Kinne, 1962a) spawned in October or November and/or retarded growth rates of the young themselves (Kinne, 1960).

Temperatures available to these fishes are similar in all areas discussed above, according to our field data, with latitudinal effects being moderated by higher altitudes at more southern localities. Day length therefore seems to be a major factor in timing of their annual surges of reproduction.

Thermal springs provide a test of sorts for temperature versus day length as primary stimuli for reproduction in fishes, since the constancy of the former may suppress effects of the latter and allow year-round sexual activity. Miller (1948, 1950b, 1961b) and LaRivers (1962) suggested that this was the case in some Death Valley cyprinodonts. Liu (1969), however, considered day-length control as a prevailing factor for reproduction by stenothermous pupfishes and suggested that year-round reproduction by species of that group seemed unlikely above 11° or 12° N latitude. Variability in interpretation of scattered studies is again the rule, and no broad pattern seems to exist.

Production of young throughout the year is, however, known from fishes in some thermal springs at higher latitudes. Arnold (1970) found patterns of gonadal development in *Cyprinodon bifasciatus* that included no pronounced differences, at the population level, between winter and summer in thermal waters of the Cuatro Ciénegas basin. Individual fish appeared to have cyclical development of gonads throughout the year. Young of that species are present, in variable numbers, at all times, and studies of length frequency distributions of various populations indicate relatively constant recruitment. More reproductive activity is, however, evident in summer than in winter, as based on relative numbers of territorial males on breeding grounds. Espinosa (1968) found a similar asynchrony in development among females of the White River springfish (*Crenichthys baileyi*) from warm springs in southern Nevada. Despite some seasonality in reproduction by the population as a whole, some females spawned in each month of the year. Espinosa summarized the spawning habits of this springfish as follows:

> . . . asynchronous, individual spawning periodicity, two spawning periods per individual [per year], long spawning periods, and a protracted spawning season . . ."

A most complex pattern(s) certainly not under control of a single feature such as day length.

Poeciliids living in constant temperature springs of Arizona (Gila topminnow; Schoenherr, 1970), Texas (Pecos gambusia, *Gambusia nobilis*), and northern Mexico (*Gambusia marshi, G. longispinis,* and northern platyfish, *Xiphophorus gordoni*), seem to reproduce year-round in constant springs, but they demonstrate spring–summer surges in reproductive success in a pattern similar to those of cyprinodontids. In the Cuatro Ciénegas basin, fishes of tropical derivation (Mexican tetra and cichlids) rarely reproduce in autumn, but seem to do so in all other seasons, and fishes of northern affinities (sunfishes, catfishes, and minnows) appear to have more typical spring–summer spawning periods.

Some fishes living in constant springs exhibit marked seasonality in reproduction that closely resembles that of species of streams and lakes of temperate zones, but the direct relationship of such cycles to physical factors in the environment remains somewhat in doubt. *Cyprinodon diabolis,* for example, lives at an almost constant 33°C, but has marked seasonality of recruitment (James, 1969). Populations increase radically in March, and small fish are present to October, but are in greatly reduced numbers after July. Some adults, however, were ripe in other periods (including winter), and presumably could have reproduced. James indicated that mortalities and reduced condition factors resulting from diminution of food supplies in winter, and possible predation by planarian flatworms, among other things, collectively resulted in a cycle that resembled the reproductive patterns that might occur under direct control of seasonal change in daylength. The fish live in Devil's Hole, a shaft with water >15 meters below the ground surface. Sunlight contacts the water directly in summer, but not in autumn, winter, or spring, so that algal production, and secondary production including that of fish, are intimately linked to incoming energy. Light effects therefore may be only indirectly responsible for the spawning cycle in this fish, operating principally through nutritional or other biotic pathways.

Cyprinodon n. nevadensis in Saratoga Spring also is strongly cyclical. Ovarian sizes increase in January–February to a peak in June or July, then slowly decline to a low in November. Variation from fish to fish was high, however, and some females appeared capable of reproducing through midsummer and into autumn at least, but little recruitment occurred after June. The same pattern was unexpectedly evident in Saratoga Marsh, a fluctuating habitat connected directly to the spring.

Cessation of recruitment similar to that observed in *C. n. nevadensis* has been repeatedly duplicated in small experimental ponds with a number of pupfish species from both stenothermal and eurythermal habitats. We are tempted to attribute this to food limitations and/or population density in smaller habitats, and this certainly appears the case in Saratoga Spring (although perhaps not so in the marsh). Hubbs and Strawn (1957) similarly negated the importance of day length in breeding of greenthroat darters (*Etheostoma lepidum*) from central Texas, stressing that nutritional condition of the fish and suitable temperatures were far more important.

Termination of reproductive success in midsummer does not appear to result from high water temperatures, since pupfish continue to exhibit reproductive behavior and to spawn apparently at temperatures approaching their upper lethal limits. However, a myriad of other factors may come into play. The barraging effect of inter- and intraspecific encounters involving territorial males may suppress successful spawning, and population sizes most often are largest at about the time reproductive success declines in pupfish populations. Cannibalism, either of young or ova, may be a factor in some species, as may be the simple presence of a large population which creates a stress syndrome. Additional research on these problems is obviously called for. It is our impression that density-dependent factors may be more important in creating seasonal spawning cycles in desert fishes we have studied (see also Liu, 1969) than are physical or chemical features of the environment.

In addition to seasonal cycles, diel patterns of reproductive activity may be complex and quite precise. Hermaphroditic rivulus (*Rivulus marmoratus*) self-fertilizes at dawn and oviposits at noon, and there is a seasonal change in the pattern that appears controlled by light. Sexuality of the fish is also under some environmental control (Harrington, 1961, 1963, 1967). Ovulation in the rice fish (*Oryzias latipes*) is under light and temperature control, and it occurs between 0100 and 0500 hours. Oviposition occurs between 0400 and 0700 hours, and only follows the stimulation of mating contacts between the sexes (Egami, 1959a,b; Egami and Nambu, 1961). Visual stimuli, physical contact, and a diversity of environmental cues are used by other cyprinodontids in their diel pattern of sexual activities (Breder and Rosen, 1966), but precise studies are again needed prior to generalizing too far.

No such detailed work has been done on desert cyprinodontids of North America. Such fish do display complex sequences of behavior relative to diel changes in environment (Itzkowitz, 1968; Itzkowitz and Minckley, 1969; Liu, 1969; Arnold, 1970). Pupfishes move about only in the day, resting at night within or upon the substrate. Breeding males are highly territorial, and conspicuous, generally defending areas along shallow shorelines.

Territorial males may remain in their areas at night, as in *C. macularius* (Barlow, 1961b), or they may move elsewhere. At first light, schooling and feeding behavior prevail for a time (Liu, 1969) under most circumstances. Territories are established or reoccupied shortly before (in midsummer) or within a seasonally variable period after sunlight strikes the water surface. In some species a territory is occupied continuously by a given male for a period of days or perhaps weeks. Males are highly active in defense of territories at the peak of breeding, but there are marked seasonal and diurnal variations in fluctuating environments that appear to be related principally to thermal changes. Figure 9 was constructed as a conceptual model of territorial activity in a pupfish. It is based on obervation of numerous species, but principally upon qualitative observations of *Cyprinodon atrorus* in nature and in outdoor experimental ponds.

2. Ovum and Larval Ecology

Parental care of ova and young in desert fishes is as diverse as the species present, ranging from none, where eggs are broadcast over the bottom and young fend for themselves; through indirect, where ova are laid and hatch within the territories of male pupfish, and therefore receive protection; to extreme in livebearers and in some cichlids. Specific information on ecology of these critical life-history stages scarcely exists, except as scattered bits in works dealing with other aspects of biology of various species. We have included such data in other sections, where appropriate, and include this brief statement to emphasize the need for research. Other than for salmonids, pelagic marine clupeoids, and a few other groups mostly of commercial importance, this field remains essentially untapped.

3. Environmental Influences on Morphology

Influence of environment on morphology of fishes has long been of interest to ichthyologists. Jordan (1891) established the general principle that numbers of vertebrae, and therefore body segments, increase as average temperature decreases. This principle has been further examined and expanded to include other meristic features and body proportions relative to temperature and other environmental factors (Hubbs, 1922, Tåning, 1952; Itazawa, 1959; Barlow, 1961c; Sweet and Kinne, 1964). Variability of some desert fish habitats markedly contrasts with constancy of others. Superimposed on this is the isolation in some, versus lack of isolation in other, habitats. These factors, of major importance in the biology of desert fishes, are especially well illustrated in a consideration of the influence of environment on morphology.

Miller (1948) found no consistent correlation between environmental temperatures and meristics among several subspecies of *Cyprinodon nevadensis*. In general, populations living in warmer waters collectively averaged lower numbers of meristic features than those living in cooler waters. These populations were, however, isolated from each other, and considerable variation occurred from spring to spring. Comparisons within the various isolated stocks indicated headspring fish of each subspecies examined had lower numbers of segmental features than did fish from the outflows (which averaged cooler). The various populations of pupfishes also maintained considerable stability in meristic phenotype through time, regardless of whether they lived under constant or variable habitat conditions.

Morphology of each pupfish population presumably responded to environmental influences within the limits of genetic plasticity of the stock, and local environment comprised a complex of factors to which the genetic materials available responded in an average manner. Similar data have been compiled for various populations of *Cyprinodon bifasciatus* in the Cuatro Ciénegas basin (Minckley *et al.*, 1971). It is notable here that remarkable stability in morphology has also been detected in stream-fish populations that have been subjected to marked environmental change in the past few years (Rinne, 1969), and even in subpopulations of a hybrid swarm of pupfishes (Minckley, 1969b, and unpublished data).

A lack of expected correlation between meristics and temperature in isolated populations of desert fishes may result from independent differentiation of the stocks. The general reality of such correlation in fishes of more continuous distribution, i.e., in freshwaters of more mesic zones or in the sea, suggests the requisite of gene flow if such a pattern is to be maintained. More broadly stated, genetic continuity permits expression of environmental influences while isolation may obscure such effects.

Notwithstanding such complications, there appears a direct tendency for greater numbers of scales in western American pupfishes inhabiting more saline waters. In most instances there seems an inverse relationship between number of fin rays and salinity (Miller, 1948, 1950b; LaBounty, 1968; LaBounty and Deacon, 1971). A direct relationship between salinity and number of rays on the second dorsal fin and anal fin was recently demonstrated for two populations of an Australian atherinid (*Taeniomembras* sp.) (Lee and Williams, 1970). Other features appear in warm-spring fishes, viz., the dorsal fin seems to be farther back on the body; the head, eye, and anterior part of the body is greater in size (perhaps relating in part to greater gill area (Section III,B,3); the fins are often more expansive and the body sizes tend to be smaller (Hubbs and Kuehne, 1937; Miller, 1948, 1950b). In many respects these features indicate neoteny, and the last characteristics to appear during ontogeny are most labile (Barlow, 1961c).

Sweet and Kinne (1964) have done some of the most thorough studies presently available on fish body shape as influenced by temperature, salinity, and a combination of those factors. At 35 gm/liter salinity, the level at which all eggs were laid, relative body shape of desert pupfish at hatching remained isometric under all experimental incubation temperatures. However, eggs transferred either to higher or lower salinities after deposition showed thermal responses in body shape. Body depth and width at hatching were greater at lower salinities (which produced a rounder fish with a smaller surface area to volume ratio), and all body dimensions were smaller when development proceeded at higher salinities. Body lengths at hatching in fresh water were greatest at 32°–33°C, and decreased when development was at either higher or lower temperatures. In water of 35 gm/liter salinity, body length was less at hatching at each successively higher temperature (tests were not made at lower than 28°C). Blaxter (1969) suggested that the preceding data probably reflect existence of temperature (and salinity?) optima for yolk utilization by the embryos. It should be noted that while length at hatching of desert pupfish at 31.8°C was maximal in fresh water, and decreased with increasing salinities (Kinne and Kinne, 1962a), final sizes in the salinity ranges from fresh to 35 gm/liter were not significantly different, at least at the moderate temperature of about 25°C (Kinne, 1965).

Vertebral numbers, and some other features of fishes, plotted as a function of temperature or other environmental factor, seem often to produce a V-shaped curve. The number of rays, vertebrae, or body lengths, as noted by Sweet and Kinne (1964), are minimal at some intermediate temperature or salinity. This, and other related phenomena have been discussed by Barlow (1961c) and more recently by Blaxter (1969). Developmental rates and sequences, along with differing sensitivities to environmental influences by diverse structures and processes, combine to create an exceedingly complex situation when fishes are considered as a group. Generalizations exist, but the many exceptions in these instances often weaken the rules.

Although salinities and temperatures have been emphasized as influencing body form, other environmental factors can also come into play. Low oxygen tensions may induce morphological variations (Kinne and Kinne, 1962a). Increased light intensity (McHugh, 1954) and increasing duration of light (Lindsey, 1958) have been shown to effect changes in vertebral numbers. Lindsey suggested that some clines in meristic features may be induced more by day length than by temperature, mostly because of the marked regularity of change in day length with latitude.

4. Delayed Hatching

The annual fishes, cyprinodontids of Africa and South America that produce delayed-hatching eggs capable of withstanding desiccation (Myers, 1952), mostly occur in tropical zones with pronounced seasonality of rainfall. But some are distributed in semiarid regions, especially in eastern Africa (Turner, 1964). They are a diversified group, still poorly known taxonomically (Weitzman and Wourms, 1967). Much of the interest generated in them comes from aquarists (Myers, 1952; Sterba, 1967), and more recently, from their possibilities for use as larvivores in mosquito control (Haas, 1965; Bay, 1966).

These annual fishes are characteristic of more or less ephemeral habitats, although some species appear to live equally well in more permanent waters (Hildemann and Walford, 1963). Fertilized eggs may persist in moist sediments below crusted muds of dried pools for many months (Foersch, 1961), and even when in permanent waters they appear to go through a period of quiescence prior to hatching (Haas, 1965). The embryos pass into a latent phase, and hatching is triggered in response to a decline in dissolved oxygen that typically occurs soon after such a pond is filled with water (Peters, 1963). Each species appears to have a particular threshold of oxygen (or something else) that stimulates its final development, and within a given species not all eggs develop and hatch at the same time.

In *Cynolebias ladigesi* some eggs were hatchable at 3–7 months, and others developed only after 8–15 months (Foersch, 1961); thus the entire population of embryos would not be subject to catastrophe that might result from periodic or unreliable filling of their waterholes. Although the temperature ranges tolerated by eggs and adults of these fishes appear similar to those to be expected under hot, or fluctuating, desert climates, the tolerances to total dissolved solids indicated in the literature available to us seems too low for survival (a maximum of about 325 mg/liter in *Nothobranchius brieni;* or "water salty to the taste," Myers, 1952). We have not, however, reviewed salinity tolerances for this group and have maintained a number of kinds in aquaria at total dissolved solids of more than 1200 mg/liter. It must also be noted that some aquarists feel that addition of a small quantity of seawater stimulates final development of eggs in some species (Breder and Rosen, 1966). As might be expected, young of the annual fishes develop rapidly, and sexual maturity may be attained in fewer than 6 weeks after hatching (Turner, 1964; Bay, 1966). The ease with which they may be maintained, and the unique life cycles, now have attracted experimental biologists (Walford and Liu, 1965), so that much additional information may soon be expected.

Delayed hatching of eggs of the marsh killifish (*Fundulus confluentus*) and the gulf killifish (*Fundulus grandis*) stranded in air on grassy swales in Florida salt marshes was reported by Harrington and Haeger (1958) and by Harrington (1959). They suggested that other species of that large genus might also have such capabilities.

Species of *Fundulus* inhabiting the western, semiarid Plains region of North America (Koster, 1948; Minckley and Klaassen, 1969b) are not known to have delayed-hatching ova, although stranding in wet sands of the streams they inhabit is a distinct possibility in periods of fluctuating levels. Habits of the *Fundulus* species of California and Baja California, to our knowledge, have yet to be described or are not known to include delayed hatching of eggs (Hubbs, 1965).

Hatching of stranded eggs of marsh killifish is unique since they are left exposed among plant litter rather than buried in moist soils as in the annual fishes (Harrington, 1959). But it seems likely that some eggs of the latter develop similarly (Sterba, 1967). As in the annuals, *Fundulus* embryos hatch rapidly when flooded, usually within 15–30 minutes.

Delayed hatching is also known in another cyprinodontoid, *Oryzias melastigma*, in the vicinity of Madras, India (Jones, 1944). The eggs typically hatch in 8–10 days, but if water is not changed in summer, hatching may be delayed for up to 42 days. Addition of fresh water, such as would occur with natural rainfall, stimulated hatching immediately. As pointed out by Harrington, however, work by Ishida (1944a,b) on *Oryzias latipes* indicated that termination of latency of embryos occurred at the onset of opercular movements, and that this could be stimulated by change in any number of variables—oxygen, carbon dioxide, various ions, pH, or even physical disturbance.

Of the fishes discussed, only *Oryzias melastigma* might be found under desert conditions in India. One record of spawning in temporary waters by *Aphanius iberus,* a cyprinodont in Spain, is intriguing but is not accompanied by other salient facts (Schreitmuller, 1921). That genus is ecologically quite similar to the American pupfishes, many of which live in deserts (as do some *Aphanius*). Pupfish eggs have been known to hatch within a few hours from muds of dried experimental ponds in Arizona after resting there for about 1 week.

Kinne and Kinne (1962a) studied the effects of temperature, salinity, and dissolved oxygen content on development of embryos of desert pupfish and found that arrested development could be induced by various combinations of these variables; temperature-influenced developmental rates alone created a variation in hatching time from 3.8 to 53 days (Kinne and Kinne, 1962a). In Arizona ponds, all these factors might have come into play. In another incident, eggs of *Cyprinodon atrorus* hatched from mats of filamentous algae that had laid on the ground surface in full summer sun for 2 days. Again, the only result was contamination of a stock of another pupfish, when the slightly moist (on the lower surface only) mats were placed in a pool to provide cover for adults of *Cyprinodon elegans.*

Eggs of longfin dace stranded in moist sand by fluctuating water levels in Arizona creeks hatched normally when flooded (Minckley and Barber, 1971), but this did not obviously involve delayed hatching of the type discussed above. Such must be a common occurrence in smaller streams of arid areas, such as those inhabited by *Fundulus kansae* and *F. zebrinus.* Eggs of longfin dace also can survive application of Derris (rotenone), however, as attested to by a massive hatch closely following a fish eradication operation in Cave Creek, Arizona, in the spring of 1970. Percolation of water through the sands most likely maintained the eggs on surficially desiccated bars. Such percolation may also filter noxious substances.

C. FOODS AND FEEDING

Desert fishes are opportunistic in their feeding, as are most fish species. Sources of food in desert springs, marshes, and intermittent streams typically consist of algae, aquatic invertebrates, and detrital material, the first two of which, at least, may undergo marked diel and seasonal changes in abundance or availability. Species in larger, more diversified habitats, such as permanent lakes, larger creeks, and rivers, usually have a greater diversity of foods available as a more stable resource. More kinds of fishes typically are present in larger habitats, and feeding niches often are arranged so as to partition the food supplies. Partitioning of niches in smaller habitats is both impossible because of food limitations and is unnecessary because of a lack of diversity in the fishes themselves. Feeding periodicity usually corresponds with the most active periods of the diel activity cycle either in mono- or polyspecific populations (Darnell and Meierotto, 1965; Leser and Deacon, 1968).

Many fish species, especially those achieving large sizes, show marked changes in foods ingested during different periods of their lives. For example, Vanicek and Kramer (1969) found diets of the Colorado squawfish to change from microcrustaceans and chironomid dipterans at total body lengths of less than 50 mm, to mostly insects between 50 and 100 mm, and to primarily and then exclusively fishes at lengths greater than 100 and 200 mm, respectively. Bonytail and roundtail chubs shorter than about 200 mm ate chironomid dipteran larvae and Plecoptera nymphs; individuals longer than 200 mm mostly ingested terrestrial insects—beetles, ants, and grasshoppers—plus plant debris taken mostly from the surface.

Dietary changes determined by stomach analysis often may be accompanied by (or occur as a function of) changes in morphology. A critical stage in the life history of the white sucker (*Catostomus commersoni*) occurs when the antero-dorsal mouth of the larva migrates to become ventral, as it is in the adult (Stewart, 1926). This also occurs in other catostomids of western North America, and is marked by a distinct shift in feeding from surface and mid-water debris and invertebrates, to benthic organisms (plant and animal), plus detritus. At a more advanced level, Arnold (1970) demonstrated a correlation in *Cyprinodon bifasciatus* between lengthening of the alimentary tract and a shift from primarily animal foods (up to a total length of about 29 mm) to mostly bottom ooze rich in diatoms (at larger sizes). Leser and Deacon (1968) detected no such diet-related morphological changes in *C. n. nevadensis*.

Seasonal changes in diets of Nevada pupfish were, however, quite evident (Leser and Deacon, 1968). Frequency of occurrence of the various food items indicated dominance of algae and amphipod crustaceans in the spring months, algae in the summer, gastropod molluscs in the autumn, and gastropods plus coleopteran larvae in the winter. Organic and inorganic debris were important throughout the year, but significantly more so in the summer. Many of the ingested algae did not appear digested and may therefore have contributed little as a source of energy. Martin

(1970) found some algae eaten by sheepshead pupfish showed cytoplasmic streaming and were viable when removed from the hindgut. We have recovered living algae from the hindgut of threadfin shad and mosquitofish, as have Velasquez (1939), Kutkuhn (1958), and Fish (1951) from various other species. In *C. n. nevadensis* at least, relatively heavy use of indigestible algae in summer, when the population is most dense, may indicate a scarcity of other foods, or other interactions, that place the fish under nutritional stress. Apparent starvation of some individuals in summer, but not at other times, suggests that some population limitations may be imposed.

Many pupfishes appear to feed almost exclusively on bottom sediments, at least at certain sizes and at certain times of year. Some sediments of springs are copropelic and may be quite high in various organic nutrients. In Cuatro Ciénegas, copropel and included organisms in springs and other habitats appear to be a major food material for pupfishes (Minckley and Itzkowitz, 1967; Arnold, 1970) and for some cichlids. In Lake Victoria, Africa, some bottom sediments are so high in organic materials that they are used as food for domestic cattle and fowl (Hickling, 1961). One of the most extreme, and unusual, feeding habits of a desert fish involves an endemic catfish, *Clarias cavernicola,* which lives in a deep, pitlike spring in the Kalahari Desert and appears to subsist mostly on the excrement of a local colony of baboons (Jubb, in Cole, 1968).

Food eaten by a fish depends largely upon its abundance or availability at the time of feeding and on the vulnerability of the prey species. The loach minnow in Aravaipa Creek feeds exclusively on blackfly larvae (Simuliidae) when they are abundant, but it rapidly shifts to mayfly nymphs after blackfly emergences. Food habits may also display delayed shifts to newly available food sources. Harrington and Harrington (1961), for example, traced the predation of a number of fishes upon a developing mosquito hatch. Mosquitofish fed voraciously from the beginning, but the typically herbivorous *Poecilia* only began to feed on the dipterans after the hatch was well along in its development.

The Gila topminnow feeds mostly on amphipod crustaceans and plant material (detritus) in Monkey Spring, Arizona (Schoenherr, 1970). Few mosquitos are found in the restricted habitats where the fish now persists, and their absence in stomachs must reflect intensive and almost complete cropping. Under other conditions, *P. occidentalis* feeds avidly on mosquito larvae. Aquatic plants, heterogenous bottoms, etc., may also protect prey species. Various specializations such as open cephalic lateral line systems in Poeciliidae (Rosen and Mendelson, 1960), a surface habit, and perhaps even the generally small adult sizes of larvivorous fishes have occurred to circumvent such problems.

Most fishes are less efficient at cropping food animals within dense vegetation. However, Danielson (1968) obtained data indicating a greater suppression of mosquito populations by *C. n. nevadensis* in areas with cover than in open waters.

Partitioning of foods, mentioned before, is marked in certain habitats. Fryer (1959) demonstrated extensive partitioning of food niches by cichlid fishes in Lake Nyassa, Africa. But he also found some species using essentially identical niches, the latter presumably because of the large habitat and a superabundance of foods (see also, Section IV,A,6). Predation in that lake may also have limited populations of potential herbivore competitors, at levels below those of interaction.

Three undescribed cichlids in the Cuatro Ciénegas basin appear to have differentiated at least in part through nutritional specialization (Taylor and Minckley, 1966; Minckley, 1969b). One has fine, delicate teeth on its fragile pharyngeal arches and feeds principally on bottom debris. A second has thick bones and molariform teeth used in crushing shells of its molluscan foods. A third has elongated teeth on the pharyngeal bones, and elongated head, jaws, and body, and appears mostly piscivorous. The assumed ancestor of this small species flock, *Cichlasoma cyanogutattum,* has modifications of its feeding apparatus that encompass almost all the three types, with sharp, elongated teeth on the pharyngeal bones grading medially to molariform ones. Its feeding is similarly generalized.

The fauna of Aravaipa Creek, discussed before (Section IV,A,6; Fig. 6), shows a marked partitioning of niche with respect to foods, space, and so on. The top carnivore is the Colorado chub. As an adult it feeds upon young of all larger species and even upon adults of smaller species, plus larger invertebrates. Adults of all carnivorous forms feed on larvae of all other fishes, but this depredation has not been adequately assessed. A midwater species of pools, the spikedace, feeds on terrestrial and aquatic drift (principally invertebrates). Speckled dace, semi-midwater in slightly swifter places and on deeper riffles, also eats drift, but it principally feeds from the bottoms. Loach minnows, discussed before, are almost monophagus on Simuliidae and baetid mayflies. The other minnow, *Agosia chrysogaster,* lives on broad, slow, sandy areas, and feeds upon finely divided organic materials, algae, and micro-invertebrates. Two catostomids partition even more markedly, with *Pantosteus clarki* exclusively using encrusting algae (and associated materials) scraped from bottoms in riffles, while *Catostomus insignis* lives on bottom invertebrates extracted from sand and gravel substrates. It is notable that the feeding activities of both suckers stir bottoms severely, and this causes a dislodgment of a large proportion of the foods used by midwater fishes of the brook.

In summary, foods used by desert fishes provide a pattern of increasing restriction in variety in the diet as ichthyofaunal diversity increases. Tolerant forms living alone usually are ubiquitous in feeding. Kinds living in faunistically more saturated habitats exhibit increased specialization of feeding niches.

One marked difference in foods available in low desert streams is the general absence of allochthonous detritus. Input of vegetative debris is obviously far more important in more mesic zones, and may provide a major food base in aquatic habitats of such regions (Hynes, 1961; Minckley, 1963; Darnell, 1967; Minshall, 1968). Allochthonous animals, however, may provide a major part of the food base.

High water temperatures in deserts may create exceptional nutritional problems for fishes. Metabolic demands at high ambient temperatures must be intense, and a number of authors have noted a maximum in feeding activities at higher environmental temperatures (Barlow, 1961b; Deacon, 1968a; Lowe and Heath, 1969), so long as the temperatures do not rise high enough to suppress activity (Deacon, 1968a) or to initiate an avoidance reaction (Barlow, 1958a).

Barlow (1961b) suggested that high temperatures demand almost continuous feeding because of the elevated metabolic activity, and Kinne (1960) documented more than a 24-fold increase in food intake of desert pupfish as temperature was increased from 15° to 30°C. However, conversion efficiency declined markedly as temperatures were increased above 20°C. Foods passed through the digestive tract in a nearly undigested state. Leser and Deacon (1968) obtained similar results at even cooler temperatures and also under conditions when fish were supplied an excess of food. The situation when desert fish cannot digest and assimilate adequate food may be aggravated in a territorial male pupfish, for example, to such a degree that its incipient lethal tolerance may be lowered. This may explain the deaths of only larger, mature, brightly colored males, under certain conditions of hyperthermia.

Lowe and Heath (1969) suggested that high food intake at high midday temperatures might be adaptive, in that lower temperatures at evening would allow conversion to proceed at a more efficient level. Studies of *C. n. nevadensis* (Leser and Deacon, 1968, and subsequent information) have shown complete assimilation of food to occur in about 16 hours at 22°C. Thus, even at higher thermal levels, food would likely remain in the gut long enough for the normal diel temperature cycles to permit its efficient use by the fish. It seems probable that, especially for young, maximum conversion efficiency is less important than maximum rate of growth. The latter is achieved in *C. macularius* at 30°C with unrestricted food intake. Maximum conversion efficiency in that species was at 20°C and maximum food intake was at 35°C. It therefore appears that the system is attuned to a cyclical daily pattern of temperature, combining maximum intake at high temperature with greater conversion efficiencies at lower thermal levels.

It is pertinent to recall that cyclic rather than constant conditions also appear to enhance tolerances to various environmental extremes, through acclimation. This seems an appropriate theme on which to end a discussion of fishes in deserts.

V. Addendum

Since completion of this chapter there has been considerable new information published that should be examined by the serious student. For example, the six-volume series on "Fish Physiology," only partially published during the writing phase of this effort, has now been completed. In addition, some excellent reference books, as well as much recent information pertinent to desert fishes, have been published in such places as *Copeia, Transactions of the American Fisheries Society, Evolution, Scientific American, Southwestern Naturalist, California Fish and Game, Occasional Papers San Diego Natural History Society, Australian Journal of Marine and Freshwater Research,* and *Journal Arizona Academy of Science.*

REFERENCES

Afanasev, S. F. (1944). Some facts on *Gambusia* viability and other phenomena observed during its dissemination in the reservoirs of the Checkeno-Ingushetian Republic. *Med. Parazitol. Parazit. Bolez.* **13,** 71–73.

Agnihotri, S. K., and Tewari, D. N. (1968). TDS and specific gravity in ground waters. *J. Amer. Water Works Ass.* **60,** 733–737.

Alimen, H. (1965). The Quaternary era in the northwest Sahara. *Geol. Soc. Amer., Spec. Pap.* **84,** 273–289.

Allee, A. E., Emerson, E., Park, O., Park, T., and Schmidt, K. (1949). "Principles of Animal Ecology." Saunders, Philadelphia, Pennsylvania.

Allison, L. N. (1960). "Sunburning" fingerling lake trout with ultraviolet light and the effect of a niacin-fortified diet. *Prog. Fish Cult.* **22,** 114–116.

Allison, L. N. (1962). Cataract among hatchery-reared lake trout. *Prog. Fish Cult.* **24,** 155.

Andrewartha, H. G., and Birch, L. C. (1954). "The Distribution and Abundance of Animals." Univ. of Chicago Press, Chicago, Illinois.

Arago, D. F. J. (1838). Instructions concernant la météorologie et la physique du globe. *C.R. Acad. Sci.* **7,** 206–224.

Arnold, E. T. (1970). Behavioral ecology of pupfishes (genus *Cyprinodon*) from the Cuatro Ciénegas basin, Coahuila, Mexico. Ph.D. Dissertation, Arizona State University, Tempe.

Bailey, R. M. (1955). Differential mortality from high temperature in a mixed population of fishes in southern Michigan. *Ecology* **36,** 226–228.

Bailey, R. M., and Cross, F. B. (1954). River sturgeons of the American genus *Scaphirhynchus*: characters, distribution, and synonymy. *Pap. Mich. Acad. Sci., Arts Lett.* **39**, 169–208.

Barber, W. E., and Minckley, W. L. (1966). Fishes of Aravaipa Creek, Graham and Pinal counties, Arizona. *Southwest. Natur.* **11**, 313–324.

Barber, W. E., Williams, D. C., and Minckley, W. L. (1970). Biology of the Gila spikedace, *Meda fulgida*, in Arizona. *Copeia* pp. 9–18.

Barlow, G. W. (1958a). Daily movements of desert pupfish, *Cyprinodon macularius*, in shore pools of the Salton Sea, California. *Ecology* **39**, 580–587.

Barlow, G. W. (1958b). High salinity mortality of desert pupfish, *Cyprinodon macularius*. *Copeia* pp. 231–232.

Barlow, G. W. (1961a). Intra-and interspecific differences in rate of oxygen consumption in gobiid fishes of the genus *Gillichthys*. *Biol. Bull.* **121**, 209–229.

Barlow, G. W. (1961b). Social behavior of the desert pupfish, *Cyprinodon macularius*, in the field and in the laboratory. *Amer. Mid. Natur.* **65**, 339–359.

Barlow, G. W. (1961c). Causes and significance of morphological variation in fishes. *Syst. Zool.* **10**, 105–117.

Baslow, M. H. (1967). Temperature adaptation and the central nervous system of fish. *In* "Molecular Mechanisms of Temperature Adaptation," Publ. No. 84, pp. 205–226. Amer. Ass. Advan. Sci., Washington, D.C.

Bay, E. C. (1966). Adaptation studies with the Argentine pearl fish, *Cynolebias bellottii*, for its introduction into California. *Copeia* pp. 839–846.

Bayly, I. A. E. (1967). The general biological classification of aquatic environments, with special reference to those of Australia. *In* "Australian Inland Waters and their Fauna, Eleven Studies" (A. H. Weatherley, ed.), pp. 78–104. Australian National Univ. Press, Canberra.

Bayly, I. A. E., and Williams, W. D. (1966). Chemical and biological studies on some saline lakes of southeast Australia. *Aust. J. Mar. Freshwater Res.* **17**, 177–228.

Beadle, L. C. (1943). An ecological survey of some inland saline waters of Algeria. *J. Linn. Soc. London, Zool.* **41**, 218–242.

Beamish, F. W. H., and Dickie, L. M. (1967). Metabolism and biological production in fish. *In* "The Biological Basis of Freshwater Fish Production" (S. D. Gerking, ed.), pp. 215–242. Wiley, New York.

Beland, R. D. (1953). The effect of channelization on the fishery of the lower Colorado River. *Calif. Fish Game* **39**, 137–139.

Bennett, G. W. (1962). "Management of Artificial Lakes and Ponds." Van Nostrand-Reinhold, Princeton, New Jersey.

Black, E. C. (1951). Respiration in fishes. *Univ. Toronto Stud., Biol. Ser.* **59**, 1–91.

Black, E. C. (1953). Upper lethal temperatures of some British Columbia fresh water fishes. *J. Fish Res. Bd. Can.* **10**, 196–210.

Black, J. D. (1949). Changing fish populations as an index to pollution and soil erosion. *Trans. Ill. State Acad. Sci.* **42**, 145–148.

Blaxter, J. H. S. (1969). Development: Eggs and larvae. *In* "Fish Physiology" (W. S. Hoar and D. J. Randall, eds.), Vol. 3, pp. 177–252. Academic Press, New York.

Blazka, P. (1958). The anaerobic metabolism of fish. *Physiol. Zool.* **31**, 117–128.

Bodenheimer, F. S. (1938). "Problems of Animal Ecology." Oxford Univ. Press, London and New York.

Bonn, E. W., and Follis, G. J. (1967). Effects of hydrogen sulfide on channel catfish, *Ictalurus punctatus*. *Trans. Amer. Fish. Soc.* **96**, 31–36.

Boulenger, G. A. (1907). "The Fishes of the Nile." Hughs Rees, Ltd., London.

Bradley, W. G. (1970). The vegetation of Saratoga Springs, Death Valley National Monument, California. *Southwest. Natur.* **15**, 111–129.

Braestrup, F. W. (1940). Remarks on faunal exchange through the Sahara. *Vidensk. Medd. Dan. Naturh. Foren.* **110**, 1–15.

Branson, B. A. (1966). Histological observations on the sturgeon chub, *Hybopsis gelida* (Cyprinidae). *Copeia* pp. 872–876.

Breder, C. M., Jr. (1962). On the significance of transparency in osteichthid fish eggs and larvae. *Copeia* pp. 561–567.

Breder, C. M., Jr., and Rosen, D. E. (1966). "Modes of Reproduction in Fishes." Natural History Press, Garden City, New York.

Brett, J. R. (1941). Tempering versus acclimation in the planting of speckled trout. *Trans. Amer. Fish. Soc.* **70**, 397.

Brett, J. R. (1956). Some principles in the thermal requirements of fishes. *Quart. Rev. Biol.* **31**, 75–87.

Brock, T. D. (1967). Life at high temperatures. *Science* **158**, 1012–1019.

Brown, M. E., ed. (1957). "The Physiology of Fishes," Vols. 1 and 2. Academic Press, New York.

Brues, C. T. (1928). Studies on the fauna of hot springs in the western United States and the biology of thermophilous animals. *Proc. Amer. Acad. Arts Sci.* **63**, 139–228.

Brues, C. T. (1932). Further studies on the fauna of North American hot springs. *Proc. Amer. Acad. Arts. Sci.* **67**, 183–303.

Buck, D. H. (1956). Effects of turbidity on fish and fishing. *Okla. Fish. Res. Lab. Rep.* **56**, 1–62.

Burton, G. W., and Odum, G. P. (1945). The distribution of stream fish in the vicinity of Mountain Lake, Virginia. *Ecology* **26**, 182–194.

Campbell, C. J., and Green, W. (1968). Perpetual succession of streamchannel vegetation in a semiarid region. *J. Ariz. Acad. Sci.* **5**, 86–98.

Campbell, L. S. (1962). "Basic Survey and Inventory of Species in the Rio Grande River of Texas of Region 3-B," Job Compl. Rep. F-5-R-8, pp. 1–57. Fed. Aid Fish. Restor.

Carlander, K. D. (1969). "Handbook of Freshwater Fishery Biology." Iowa State Univ. Press, Ames.

Carozzi, A. V. (1962). Observations on algal biostromes in the Great Salt Lake, Utah. *J. Geol.* **70**, 246–252.

Chapman, V. G. (1960). "Salt Marshes and Salt Deserts of the World." Wiley (Interscience), New York.

Clausen, R. G. (1936). Oxygen consumption in fresh water fishes. *Ecology* **17**, 216–266.

Cole, G. A. (1963). The American Southwest and Middle America. *In* "Limnology in North America (D. G. Frey, ed.), pp. 393–434. Univ. of Wisconsin Press, Madison.

Cole, G. A. (1968). Desert limnology. *In* "Desert Biology" (G. W. Brown, Jr., ed.), Vol. 1, pp. 423–486. Academic Press, New York.

Cole, G. A., and Batchelder, G. L. (1969). Dynamics of an Arizona travertine-forming stream. *J. Ariz. Acad. Sci.* **5**, 271–283.

Cole, G. A., and Bousfield, E. L. (1970). A new freshwater *Gammarus* (Crustacea: Amphipoda) from western Texas. *Amer. Midl. Natur.* **83,** 89–95.

Cole, G. A., and Minckley, W. L. (1968). "Anomalous" thermal conditions in a hypersaline inland pond. *J. Ariz. Acad. Sci.* **5,** 105–107.

Cole, G. A., Whiteside, M. C., and Brown, R J. (1967). Unusual monomixis in two saline Arizona ponds. *Limnol. Oceanogr.* **12,** 584–591.

Coleman, G. A. (1926). A biological survey of the Salton Sea. *Calif. Fish Game* **15,** 218–227.

Corson, B. W., and Brezosky, P. E. (1961). Hatchery production experiment designed to prevent sunburn in landlocked salmon. *Progr. Fish Cult.* **23,** 175–178.

Cowles, R. B. (1934). Notes on the ecology and breeding habits of the desert minnow, *Cyprinodon macularius* Baird and Girard. *Copeia* pp. 40–42.

Cox, T. J. (1966). A behavioral and ecological study of the desert pupfish (*Cyprinodon macularius*) in Quitobaquito Springs, Organ Pipe Cactus National Monument, Arizona, Ph.D. Dissertation, University of Arizona, Tucson.

Cross, F. B. (1967). Handbook of fishes of Kansas. *Misc. Publ. Mus. Natur. Hist. Univ. Kans.* **45,** 1–357.

C.S.I.R.O., Australia. (1960). "The Australian Environment." Melbourne Univ. Press, Melbourne.

Danielson, T. L. (1968). Differential predation on *Culex pipiens* and *Anopheles albimanus* mosquito larvae by two species of fish (*Gambusia affinis* and *Cyprinodon nevadensis*), and the effects of simulated reeds on predation. Ph.D. Dissertation, University of California, Riverside.

Dannevig, A., and Hansen, S. (1952). Faktover av betydning for fiskeeggenes og fiskeyngelens oppkekst. *Rep. Norw. Fish. Mar. Invest., Rep. Technol. Res.* **10,** 1–36.

Darnell, R. M. (1967). The organic detritus problem (estuaries). *In* "Estuaries," Publ. No. 83. pp. 374–375. Amer. Ass. Advan. Sci., Washington, D.C.

Darnell, R. M., and Meierotto, R. R. (1965). Diurnal periodicity in the black bullhead, *Ictalurus melas* (Rafinesque). *Trans. Amer. Fish. Soc.* **94,** 1–8.

Davis, B. J., and Miller, R. J. (1967). Brain patterns in minnows of the genus *Hybopsis* in relation to feeding habits and habitat. *Copeia* pp. 1–39.

Deacon, J. E. (1961). Fish populations, following drought, in the Neosho and Marais des Cygnes rivers of Kansas. *Publ. Mus. Natur. Hist. Univ. Kans.* **13,** 359–427.

Deacon, J. E., ed. (1967). "The Ecology of Saratoga Springs, Death Valley National Monument," Mimeo. Rep. to National Park Service.

Deacon, J. E., ed. (1968a). "Ecological Studies of Aquatic Habitats in Death Valley National Monument, with Special Reference to Saratoga Springs," Mimeo. Rep. to National Park Service.

Deacon, J. E. (1968b). Endangered non-game fishes of the west: Causes, prospects, and importance. *Proc. 48th Annu. Conf. West. Ass. Game Fish Comm.* pp. 534–549.

Deacon, J. E., and Bradley, W. G. (1971). Fishes of the Moapa River, Nevada. Unpublished manuscript.

Deacon, J. E., and Bunnell, S. (1970). Man and pupfish. *Cry Calif.* **5,** 14–21.

Deacon, J. E., and Metcalf, A. L. (1961). Fishes of the Wakarusa River in Kansas. *Publ. Mus. Natur. Hist. Univ. Kans.* **13,** 311–322.

Deacon, J. E., and Wilson, B. L. (1967). Daily activity cycles of *Crenichthys baileyi,* a fish endemic to Nevada. *Southwest. Natur.* **12,** 31–44.

Deacon, J. E., Hubbs, C., and Zahuranec, B. J. (1964). Some effects of introduced fishes on the native fish fauna of southern Nevada. *Copeia* pp. 384–388.

Deacon, J. E., LaBounty, J. F. and Bradley, W. G. (1971). Fishes of the Virgin River, a tributary of the Colorado River. Unpublished manuscript.

DeLong, D. C., Halver, J. E., and Mertz, E. T. (1958). Nutrition of salmonoid fishes. VI. Protein requirements of chinook salmon at two water temperatures. *J. Nutr.* **65,** 589–599.

Dill, W. A. (1944). The fishery of the lower Colorado River. *Calif. Fish Game* **30,** 109–211.

Dobzhansky, T. (1940). Speciation as a stage in evolutionary sequence. *Amer. Natur.* **74,** 312–321.

Dobzhansky, T., Ehrman, L., and Kastritsis, P. A. (1968). Ethological isolation between sympatric and allopatric species of the *obscura* group of *Drosophila. Anim. Behav.* **16,** 79–87.

Doudoroff, P. (1945). The resistance and acclimatization of marine fishes to temperature changes. II. Experiments with *Fundulus* and *Atherinops. Biol. Bull.* **88,** 194–206.

Doudoroff, P. (1957). Water quality requirements of fishes and effects of toxic substances. *In* "The Physiology of Fishes" (M. E. Brown, ed.), Vol. 2, pp. 403–430. Academic Press, New York.

Doudoroff, P., and Katz, M. (1950). Critical review of literature on the toxicity of industrial wastes and their components to fish. I. Alkalines, acids, and inorganic gases. *Sewage Ind. Wastes* **22,** 1432–1458.

Doudoroff, P., and Warren, C. E. (1965). Dissolved oxygen requirements of fishes. *U.S., Pub. Health Serv., Publ.* **999-WP-25,** 145–155.

Dryer, W., and Benson, N. G. (1957). Observations on the influence of the new Johnsonville steam plant on fish and plankton populations. *Proc. 10th Annu. Conf. Southeast. Ass. Game Fish Comm.* pp. 85–91.

Dunn, J. R. (1953). The origin of the deposits of tufa in Mono Lake. *J. Sediment. Petrol.* **23,** 18–23.

Eakin, T. E. (1964). Ground-water Reconnaissance Series Report 25. U.S. Geol. Sur., pp. 1–40.

Easterbrook, D. J. (1969). "Principles of Geomorphology." McGraw-Hill, New York.

Eckberg, D. R. (1962). Anaerobic and aerobic metabolism in gills of the crucian carp adapted to high and low temperatures. *Comp. Biochem. Physiol.* **5,** 123–128.

Egami, N. (1959a). Effects of exposure to low temperature on the time of oviposition and the growth of the oocytes in the fish, *Oryzias latipes. J. Fac. Sci., Univ. Tokyo* **8,** 539–548.

Egami, N. (1959b). Effect of removal of eyes on oviposition of the fish *Oryzias latipes. Dobutsugaku Zasshi* **68,** 374–385.

Egami, N., and Nambu, M. (1961). Factors initiating mating behavior and oviposition in the fish, *Oryzias latipes. J. Fac. Sci., Univ. Tokyo* **9,** 263–278.

Elton, C. S. (1958). "The Ecology of Invasions by Animals and Plants." Methuen, London.

Espinosa, F. A. (1968). Spawning periodicity and fecundity of *Crenichthys baileyi,* a fish endemic to Nevada. M.S. Thesis, University of Nevada, Las Vegas.

Espinosa, S., and Espinosa, A. (1970). Personal communication.

Evans-Prichard, E. (1940). "The Nuer." Oxford Univ. Press (Clarendon), London and New York.

Fajen, O. F. (1963). The influence of stream stability on homing behavior of two smallmouth bass populations. *Trans. Amer. Fish. Soc.* **91,** 346–349.

Fiero, G. W., and Maxey, G. B. (1970). "Hydrogeology of the Devil's Hole Area, Ash Meadows, Nevada," pp. 1–26. Cent. Water Resour. Res., Desert Res. Inst., Univ. of Nevada System, Reno.

Fish, G. R. (1951). Digestion in *Tilapia esculenta*. *Nature (London)* **167**, 900–901.

Foersch, W. (1961). *Trop. Fish Hobbyist* **9**, 33.

Fox, H. M. (1926). Cambridge expedition to the Suez Canal, 1924. *Trans. Zool. Soc. London* **22**, 1–64.

Fries, E. F. B. (1952). Observations on chill tolerance and applied chill coma in sub-tropical American marine fishes, especially *Bathygobius*. *Copeia* pp. 147–152.

Fry, F. E. J. (1947). Effects of the environment on animal activity. *Univ. Toronto Stud., Biol. Ser.* **55**, 5–62.

Fry, F. E. J. (1957). The aquatic respiration of fish. *In* "The Physiology of Fishes" (M. E. Brown, ed.), Vol. 1 pp. 1–63. Academic Press, New York.

Fry, F. E. J. (1960). The oxygen requirements of fish. *In* "Biological Problems in Water Pollution" (C. M. Tarzwell, ed.), Pub. Health Serv., Tech. Rep. **W60–3**, 106–109. U.S. Pub. Health Serv., Washington, D.C.

Fry, F. E. J., Brett, J. R., and Clawson, G. H. (1942). Lethal limits of temperature for young goldfish. *Rev. Can. Biol.* **1**, 50–56.

Fryer, G. (1959). The trophic interrelationships and ecology of some littoral communities of Lake Nyassa with especial reference to the fishes, and a discussion of the evolution of a group of rock-frequenting Cichlidae. *Proc. Zool. Soc. London* **132**, 153–281.

Gautier, E. F. (1935). "Sahara, the Great Desert" (translated by D. F. Mayhew). Columbia Univ. Press, New York.

Gerberich, J. B., and Laird, M. (1965). An annotated bibliography of papers relating to the control of mosquitos by the use of fish. *World Health Organ.* **WHO/EBL/66.71**, 1–107.

Gerking, S. D. (1950). Stability of a stream fish population. *J. Wildl. Manage.* **14**, 193–202.

Gerking, S. D. (1953). Evidence for the concepts of home range and territory in stream fishes. *Ecology* **34**, 347–365.

Gerking, S. D. (1959). The restricted movements of fish populations. *Biol. Rev. Cambridge Phil. Soc.* **34**, 221–242.

Graf, D. L. (1960a). Geochemistry of carbonate sediments and sedimentary carbonate rocks. I. Carbonate minerology, carbonate sediments. *Ill. State Geol. Surv., Circ.* **297**, 1–39.

Graf, D. L. (1960b). Geochemistry of carbonate sediments and sedimentary carbonate rocks. II. Sedimentary carbonate rocks. *Ill. State Geol. Surv., Circ.* **298**, 1–43.

Graham, W. M. (1911). A fish that preys on mosquito larvae in southern Nigeria. *Bull. Entomol. Res.* **2**, 137–139.

Green, C. R., and Sellers, W. D. (1964). "Arizona Climate." Univ. of Arizona Press, Tucson.

Gunning, G. E. (1959). The sensory basis for homing in the longear sunfish, *Lepomis megalotis megalotis* (Rafinesque). *Invest. Ind. Lakes Streams* **5**, 103–130.

Gunter, G. (1945). Studies on marine fishes of Texas. *Publ. Inst. Mar. Sci., Univ. Tex.* **1**, 1–90.

Gunter, G. (1950). Distributions and abundance of fishes on the Arkansas National Wildlife Refuge. *Publ. Inst. Mar. Sci. Univ. Tex.* **1**,89–101.

Gunter, G. (1952). The import of catastrophic mortalities for marine fisheries along the Texas coast. *J. Wildl. Manage.* **16**, 63–69.

Gunter, G. (1956). A revised list of euryhaline fishes of North and Middle America. *Amer. Midl. Natur.* **56**, 345–354.

Gunter, G. (1961). Some relations of estuarine organisms to salinity. *Limnol. Oceanogr.* **6**, 182–190.

Gunter, G. (1967). Vertebrates in hypersaline waters. *Contrib. Mar. Sci.* **12**, 230–241.

Haas, R. (1965). Preliminary report on experimental introductions of *Nothobranchius guentheri* (Pfeffer), an annual cyprinodont fish, as a potential mosquito larvivore. *World Health Organ.* WHO/EBL/**65.39**, 1–9.

Haempel, O., and Lechler, H. (1931). Über die Wirkung von ultravioletter Bestrahlung auf Fischeier und Fischbrut. *Z. Vergl. Physiol.* **14**, 365–372.

Harker, J. E. (1958). Diurnal rhythms in the animal kingdom. *Biol. Rev. Cambridge Phil. Soc.* **33**, 1–52.

Harrington, R. W., Jr. (1959). Delayed hatching in stranded eggs of marsh killifish, *Fundulus confluentus. Ecology* **40**, 430–437.

Harrington, R. W., Jr. (1961). Oviparous hermaphroditic fish with internal self-fertilization. *Science* **134**, 1749–1750.

Harrington, R. W., Jr. (1963). Twenty-four-hour rhythms of internal self-fertilization and of oviposition by hermaphrodites of *Rivulus marmoratus. Physiol. Zool.* **36**, 325–341.

Harrington, R. W., Jr. (1967). Environmentally controlled induction of primary male gonochorists from eggs of the self-fertilizing hermaphrodite fish, *Rivulus marmoratus* Poey. *Biol. Bull.* **132**, 174–199.

Harrington, R. W., Jr., and Haeger, J. S. (1958). Prolonged natural deferment of hatching in killifish. *Science* **128**, 1511.

Harrington, R. W., Jr., and Harrington, E. S. (1961). Food selection among fishes invading a high subtropical salt marsh: From onset of flooding through the progress of a mosquito brood. *Ecology* **42**, 646–666.

Hasler, A. D., and Villemonte, J. R. (1953). Observations on the daily movements of fishes. *Science* **118**, 321–322.

Hastings, J. R. (1959a). Vegetation change and arroyo cutting in southeastern Arizona during the past century: An historical review. *In* "Arid Lands Colloquia" (A. R. Kassander, ed.), pp. 24–40. Univ. of Arizona Press, Tucson.

Hastings, J. R. (1959b). Vegetation changes and arroyo cutting in southeastern Arizona. *J. Ariz. Acad. Sci.* **1**, 60–67.

Hastings, J. R., and Turner, R. (1965). "The Changing Mile." Univ. of Arizona Press, Tucson.

Haynes, C. V. (1967). Quaternary geology of the Tule Springs area, Clark county, Nevada. *In* "Pleistocene Studies in Southern Nevada" (H. M. Wormington and D. Ellis, eds.), Anthropol. Pap. No. 13, pp. 15–105. Nevada State Mus., Carson City.

Heath, W. G. (1962). Maximum temperature tolerance as a function of constant temperature acclimation in the Gila topminnow (*Poeciliopsis occidentalis*). Ph.D. Dissertation, University of Arizona, Tucson.

Heath, W. G. (1967). Ecological significance of temperature tolerance in Gulf of California shore fishes. *J. Ariz. Acad. Sci.* **4**, 172–178.

Hedgpeth, J. W. (1959). Some preliminary considerations of the biology of inland mineral waters. *Arch. Oceanogr. Limnol.* **11,** Suppl., 111–141.

Hickling, C. F. (1961). "Tropical Inland Fisheries." Wiley, New York.

Hildeman, W. H., and Walford, R. L. (1963). Annual fishes—promising species as biological control agents. *World Health Organ.* **WHO/EBL/7,** 1–6.

Hinrichs, A. M. (1925). Modification of development on the basis of a differential susceptibility to radiation. I. *Fundulus* and U. V. radiations. *J. Morphol.* **41,** 239–265.

Hoar, W. S. (1969). Reproduction. *In* "Fish Physiology" (W. S. Hoar and D. J. Randall, eds.), Vol. 3, pp. 1–72. Academic Press, New York.

Hoar, W. S., and Randall, D. J., eds. (1969). "Fish Physiology," Vols. 1, 2, and 3. Academic Press, New York.

Hobson, E. S. (1965). Diurnal-nocturnal activity of some inshore fishes in the Gulf of California. *Copeia* pp. 291–302.

Holden, P. B., and Stalnaker, C. B. (1970). Systematic studies of the cyprinid genus *Gila,* in the upper Colorado River basin. *Copeia* pp. 409–419.

Hora, S. L. (1922). Structural modifications in the fish of mountain torrents. *Rec. Indian Mus.* **24,** 31–61.

Hora, S. L. (1930). Ecology, bionomics, and evolution of the torrential fauna, with special reference to the organs of attachment. *Phil. Trans. Roy. Soc. London* **218,** 171–282.

Hora, S. L. (1945). Analysis of the factors influencing the spawning of carps. *Proc. Nat. Inst. Sci. India* **11,** 3–39.

Hubbs, C. (1951). Minimum temperature tolerances for fishes of the genera *Signalosa* and *Herichthys* in Texas. *Copeia* p. 297.

Hubbs, C. (1957a). *Gambusia heterochir,* a new peociliid fish from Texas, with an account of its hybridization with *G. affinis. Tulane Stud. Zool.* **5,** 1–16.

Hubbs, C. (1957b). Distributional patterns of Texas freshwater fishes. *Southwest. Natur.* **2,** 89–104.

Hubbs, C. (1959). High incidence of vertebral deformities in two natural populations of fishes inhabiting warm springs. *Ecology* **40,** 154–155.

Hubbs, C. (1965). Developmental temperature tolerance and rates of four southern California fishes, *Fundulus parvipinnis, Atherinops affinis, Leuresthes tenuis,* and *Hypsoblennius* sp. *Calif. Fish Game* **51,** 113–122.

Hubbs, C., and Deacon, J. E. (1964). Additional introductions of tropical fishes into southern Nevada. *Southwest. Natur.* **9,** 249–251.

Hubbs, C., and Hettler, W. F. (1964). Observations on the toleration of high temperatures and low dissolved oxygen in natural waters by *Crenichthys baileyi. Southwest. Natur.* **9,** 245–248.

Hubbs, C., and Springer, V. G. (1957). A revision of the *Gambusia nobilis* species group, with descriptions of three new species, and notes on their variation, ecology, and evolution. *Tex. J. Sci.* **9,** 279–326.

Hubbs, C., and Strawn, K. (1957). Survival of F_1 hybrids between fishes of the subfamily Etheostominae. *J. Exp. Zool.* **134,** 33–62.

Hubbs, C., Kuehne, R. A., and Ball, J. C. (1953). The fishes of the upper Guadalupe River, Texas. *Tex. J. Sci.* **5,** 216–244.

Hubbs, C., Baird, R. C., and Gerald, J. W. (1967). Effects of dissolved oxygen concentration and light intensity on activity cycles of fishes inhabiting warm springs. *Amer. Midl. Natur.* **77,** 104 –115.

Hubbs, C. L. (1922). Variations in the number of vertebrae and other meristic characters of fishes correlated with the temperature of water during development. *Amer. Natur.* **56**, 360–372.

Hubbs, C. L. (1932). Studies of the fishes of the order Cyprinodontes. XII. A new genus related to *Empetrichthys*. *Occas. Pap. Mus. Zool. Univ. Mich.* **252**, 1–5.

Hubbs, C. L. (1940). Speciation of fishes. *Amer. Natur.* **74**, 198–211.

Hubbs, C. L. (1941a). The relation of hydrological conditions to speciation in fishes. *In* "A Symposium on Hydrobiology" (J. G. Needham, ed.), pp. 182–195. Univ. of Wisconsin Press, Madison.

Hubbs, C. L. (1941b). Fishes of the desert. *Biologist* **22**, 61–69.

Hubbs, C. L., and Black, J. D. (1947). Revision of *Ceratichthys*, a genus of American cyprinid fishes. *Misc. Publ. Mus. Zool. Univ. Mich.* **66**, 1–56.

Hubbs, C. L., and Kuehne, E. (1937). A new fish of the genus *Apocope* from a Wyoming warm spring. *Occas. Pap. Mus. Zool. Univ. Mich.* **343**, 1–21.

Hubbs, C. L., and Miller, R. R. (1941). Studies of the fishes of the order Cyprinodontes. XVII. Genera and species of the Colorado River system. *Occas. Pap. Mus. Zool. Univ. Mich.* **433**, 1–9.

Hubbs, C. L., and Miller, R. R. (1943). Mass hybridization between two genera of cyprinid fishes in the Mohave desert, California. *Pap. Mich. Acad. Sci., Art. Lett.* **28**, 343–378.

Hubbs, C. L., and Miller, R. R. (1948a). Correlation between fish distribution and hydrographic history in the desert basins of the western United States. *Bull. Univ. Utah, Biol. Ser.* **38**, 17–166.

Hubbs, C. L., and Miller, R. R. (1948b). Two new, relict genera of cyprinid fishes from Nevada. *Occas. Pap. Mus. Zool. Univ. Mich.* **507**, 1–30.

Hubbs, C. L., and Miller, R. R. (1965). Studies of Cyprinodont fishes. XXII. Variation in *Lucania parva*, its establishment in western United States, and description of a new species from an interior basin in Coahuila, Mexico. *Misc. Publ. Mus. Zool. Univ. Mich.* **127**, 1–111.

Huet, M. (1959). Profiles and biology of western European streams as related to fish management. *Trans. Amer. Fish. Soc.* **88**, 155–163.

Hunt, C. B., and Mabey, D. R. (1966). Stratigraphy and structure, Death Valley, California. *U.S., Geol. Surv., Prof. Pap.* No. 494-A, pp. 1–138.

Hunt, C. B., Robinson, T. W., Bowles, W. A., and Washburn, A. L. (1966). Hydrologic basin, Death Valley, California. *U.S., Geol. Surv., Prof. Pap.* No. 494-A, pp. 1–162.

Hutchinson, G. E. (1939). Ecological observations on the fishes of Kashmir and Indian Tibet. *Ecol. Monogr.* **9**, 145–182.

Hutchinson, G. E. (1957). "A Treatise on Limnology," Vol. I. Wiley, New York.

Hutchinson, G. E. (1967). "A Treatise on Limnology," Vol. II. Wiley, New York.

Hynes, H. B. N. (1961). The invertebrate fauna of a Welsh mountain stream. *Arch. Hydrobiol.* **57**, 344–388.

Ide, F. P. (1935). The effect of temperature on the distribution of the mayfly fauna of a stream. *Univ. Toronto Stud., Biol. Ser.* **39**, 9–76.

Ishida, J. (1944a). Hatching enzyme in the fresh-water fish, *Oryzias latipes*. *Annot. Zool. Jap.* **22**, 137–154.

Ishida, J. (1944b). Further studies of the hatching enzyme of the fresh-water fish, *Oryzias latipes*. *Annot. Zool. Jap.* **22**, 255–264.

Itazawa, Y. (1959). Influence of temperature on the number of vertebrae in fish. *Nature (London)* **183**, 1408–1409.

Itzkowitz, M. (1968). Courtship and spawning in a pupfish (genus *Cyprinodon*) from Coahuila, Mexico. M.S. Thesis, Arizona State University, Tempe.

Itzkowitz, M., and Minckley, W. L. (1969). Qualitative behavior of a pupfish (*Cyprinodon atrorus*) in differing environments. *Gt. Basin Natur.* **29**, 169–180.

Ives, R. L. (1936). Desert floods in the Sonoyta Valley. *Amer. J. Sci.* **32**, 349–360.

Ivlev, V. S. (1961). "Experimental Ecology of the Feeding of Fishes." Yale Univ. Press, New Haven, Connecticut.

Jahns, R. H. (1949). Desert floods. *Eng. Sci.* **12**, 10–14.

James, A. E. (1968). *Learnea* (copepod) infection of three native fishes from the Salt River basin, Arizona. M.S. Thesis, Arizona State University, Tempe.

James, C. J. (1969). Aspects of the ecology of the Devil's Hole pupfish, *Cyprinodon diabolis*. M.S. Thesis, University of Nevada, Las Vegas.

James, M. C. (1934). Effect of 1934 drought on fish life. *Trans Amer. Fish. Soc.* **64**, 57–62.

John, K. R. (1963). The effect of torrential rains on the reproductive cycle of *Rhinichthys osculus* in the Chiricahua Mountains, Arizona. *Copeia* pp. 286–291.

John, K. R. (1964). Survival of fish in intermittent streams of the Chiricahua Mountains, Arizona. *Ecology* **45**,112–119.

Johnson, D. S., and Soong, M. H. H. (1965). The fate of introduced freshwater fish in Malaya. *Proc. Int. Congr. Zool., 16th, 1963* Vol. 1, p. 246.

Johnson, J. E. (1970). Age, growth, and population dynamics of threadfin shad, *Dorosoma petenense* (Günther), in central Arizona reservoirs. *Trans. Amer. Fish. Soc.* **99**, 739–753.

Joleaud, L. (1935). Gissements de vertebrés quaternaires du Sahara. *Bull. Soc. Hist. Natur. Algeria* **26**, 23–29.

Jones, J. R. (1964). "Fish and River Pollution." Butterworth, London.

Jones, S. (1944). On the occurrence of diapause in the eggs of Indian cyprindonts. *Curr. Sci.* **13**, 107–108.

Jordan, D. S. (1891). Report of explorations in Colorado and Utah during the summer of 1889, with an account of the fishes found in each of the river basins examined. *Bull. U.S. Fish Comm.* **9**, 1–40.

Jordan, D. S., and Richardson, R. E. (1907). Description of a new species of killifish, *Lucania browni,* from a hot spring in lower California. *Proc. U.S. Nat. Mus.* **33**, 319–321.

Jubb, R. A. (1969). Personal communication.

Kesseli, J. E., and Beaty, C. B. (1959). "Desert Flood Conditions in the White Mountains of California and Nevada," Tech. Rep. **EP-198**. U.S. Army Quartermaster Res. Eng. Cent., Nantick, Massachusetts.

Kilby, J. D. (1955). The fishes of two gulf coastal marsh areas of Florida. *Tulane Stud. Zool.* **2**, 173–247.

Kinne, O. (1960). Growth, food intake and food conversion in a euryplastic fish exposed to different temperatues and salinities. *Physiol. Zool.* **33**, 288–317.

Kinne, O. (1963). The effects of temperature and salinity on marine and brackish water animals. I. Temperature. In "Oceanography and Marine Biology" (H. Barnes, ed.), Vol. I, pp. 301–340.

Kinne, O. (1964). The effect of temperature and salinity on marine and brackish water animals. II. Salinity and temperature-salinity relations, *In* "Oceanography and Marine Biology" (H. Barnes, ed.). Vol. II, pp. 281–339.

Kinne, O. (1965). Salinity requirements of the fish, *Cyprinodon macularius*. *U.S. Pub. Health Serv., Publ.* **999**-WP-**25**, 187–192.

Kinne, O. (1966). Physiological aspects of animal life in estuaries with special reference to salinity. *Neth. J. Sea Res.* **3**, 222–244.

Kinne, O., and Kinne, E. M. (1962a). Rates of development in embryos of a cyprinodont fish exposed to different temperature-salinity-oxygen combinations. *Can. J. Zool.* **40**, 231–253.

Kinne, O., and Kinne, E. M. (1962b). Effects of salinity and oxygen on developmental rates in a cyprinodont fish. *Nature (London)* **193**, 1097–1098.

Kniffin, F. B. (1932). Lower California studies. IV. The natural landscape of the Colorado delta. *Univ. Calif., Berkeley, Publ. Geog.* **5**,149–244.

Knudsen, V. O., Alford, R. S., and Emling, J. W. (1948). Underwater ambient noise. *J. Mar. Res.* **7**, 410–429.

Kosswig, C. (1956). Über Makro- und Mikro-populationen des Zahnkarpfen. *Anatolichthys. Zool. Anz.* **1956**, 75–90.

Kosswig, C. (1961). Speciation in the earlier central Anatolian Lake basin. *In* "Vertebrate Speciation" (W. F. Blair, ed.), pp. 561–593. Univ. of Texas Press, Austin.

Kosswig, C. (1963). Ways of speciation of fishes. *Copeia* pp. 238–244.

Koster, W. J. (1948). Notes on the spawning activities and the young stages of *Plancterus kansae* (Garman). *Copeia* pp. 25–33.

Koster, W. J. (1957). "Guide to the Fishes of New Mexico." Univ. of New Mexico Press, Albuquerque.

Krumholz, L. A. (1944). Northward acclimatization of the western mosquitofish, *Gambusia affinis affinis. Copeia* pp. 82–85.

Krumholz, L. A. (1948). Reproduction in the western mosquitofish, *Gambusia affinis affinis* (Baird and Girard), and its use in mosquito control. *Ecol. Monogr.* **18**, 1–43.

Krumholz, L. A. (1963). Relationships between fertility, sex ratio, and exposure to predation in populations of the mosquitofish, *Gambusia manni* Hubbs, at Bimini, Bahamas. *Int. Rev. Ges. Hydrobiol.* **48**, 201–256.

Kutkuhn, J. H. (1958). Utilization of plankton by juvenile gizzard shad in a shallow prairie lake. *Trans. Amer. Fish. Soc.* **87**, 80–103.

LaBounty, J. F. (1968). Some ecological and taxonomic considerations of Death Valley cyprinodonts. M.S. Thesis, University of Nevada, Las Vegas.

LaBounty, J. F., and Deacon, J. E. (1971). A new species of cyprinodont fish from Death Valley, California (genus *Cyprinodon*). Unpublished manuscript.

Lachner, E. A., Robins, C. R., and Courtenay, W. R., Jr. (1970). Exotic fishes and other aquatic organisms introduced into North America. *Smithson. Contrib. Zool.* **59** 1–29.

Lagler, K. F., Bardach, J. E., and Miller, R. R. (1962). "Ichthyology." Wiley, New York.

Laird, M. (1956). Studies of mosquitoes and freshwater ecology in the South Pacific. *Roy. Soc. N. Z., Bull.* **6**, 1–213.

Lake, J. S. (1967). Principal fishes of the Murray-Darling River system. *In* "Australian Inland Waters and their Fauna, Eleven Studies" (A. H. Weatherley, ed.), pp. 192–213. Australian National Univ. Press, Canberra.

Larimore, R. W. (1952). Home pools and homing behavior of smallmouth black bass in Jordan Creek. *Ill. Natur. Hist. Surv., Biol. Notes* **28**, 1–12.

Larimore, R. W., Pickering, Q. H., and Durham, L. (1952). An inventory of the fishes of Jordan Creek, Vermillion county, Illinois, *Ill. Natur. Hist. Surv., Biol. Notes* **29**, 1–26.

Larimore, R. W., Childers, W. F., and Hekcrotte, C. (1959). Destruction and reestablishment of stream fish and invertebrates affected by drought. *Trans. Amer. Fish. Soc.* **88**, 261–285.

LaRivers, I. (1962). "Fishes and Fisheries of Nevada." State Printing Off., Carson City, Nevada.

Larkin, P. A. (1956). Interspecific competition and population control in freshwater fish. *J. Fish. Res. Bd. Can.* **13**, 327–342.

Lee, C. L. (1969). Salinity tolerance and osmoregulation of *Taeniomembras microstomus* (Günther, 1861). (Pisces: Mugiliformes: Atherinidae) from Australian salt lakes. *Aust. J. Mar. Freshwater Res.* **20**, 157–162.

Lee, C. L., and Williams, W. D. (1970). Meristic differences between two conspecific fish populations in Australian salt lakes. *J. Fish. Biol.* **2**, 55–56.

Leopold, L. B. (ed.) (1953). "Round River." Oxford Univ. Press, New York.

Leopold, L. B. (1962). Rivers. *Amer. Sci.* **50**, 511–537.

Leopold, L. B., and Maddock, T. (1955). The hydraulic geometry of stream channels and some physiographic implications. *U.S., Geol. Surv., Prof. Pap.* **252**, 1–57.

Leopold, L. B., and Miller, J. P. (1954). A postglacial chronology for some alluvial valleys in Wyoming. *U.S., Geol. Surv., Water-Supply Pap.* **1261**, 1–90.

Leser, J. F., and Deacon, J. E. (1968). Food utilization of *Cyprinodon n. nevadensis* in the main spring pool at Saratoga Springs, Death Valley National Monument. *In* "Ecological Studies of Aquatic Habitats in Death Valley National Monument, with Special Reference to Saratoga Springs" (J. E. Deacon, ed.), Mimeo. Rep., pp. 15–33. Report to National Park Service.

Lewis, W. M. (1961). Mortality of fingerling shiners resulting from becoming entangled in the alga *Hydrodictyon*. *Ecology* **42**, 835–836.

Lewis, W. M. (1970). Morphological adaptations of cyprinodontoids for inhabiting oxygen deficient waters. *Copeia* pp. 319–326.

Lindsey, C. C. (1958). Modification of meristic characters by light duration in kokanee, *Oncorhynchus nerka*. *Copeia* pp. 134–136.

Liu, R. K. (1969). The comparative behavior of allopatric species (Teleostei-Cyprinodontidae: *Cyprinodon*). Ph.D. Dissertation, University of California, Los Angeles.

Logan, R. F. (1968). Causes, climates and distribution of deserts. *In* "Desert Biology" (G. W. Brown, Jr., ed.), Vol. 1, pp. 21–51. Academic Press, New York.

Love, R. M. (1970). "The Chemical Biology of Fishes." Academic Press, New York.

Lowe, C. H. (1967). "The Vertebrates of Arizona." Univ. of Arizona Press, Tucson.

Lowe, C. H., and Heath, W. G. (1969). Behavioral and physiological responses to temperature in the desert pupfish, *Cyprinodon macularius*. *Physiol. Zool.* **42**, 53–59.

Lowe, C. H., Hinds, D. S., and Halpern, E. A. (1967). Experimental catastrophic selection and tolerances to low oxygen concentration in native Arizona freshwater fishes. *Ecology* **48**, 1013–1017.

McAllister, D. E. (1969). Introduction of tropical fishes into a hotspring near Banff, Alberta. *Can. Field Natur.* **83**, 31–35.

Macan, T. T. (1958). The temperature of a small stony stream. *Hydrobiologia* **12**, 89–106.

Macan, T. T. (1963). "Freshwater Ecology." Wiley, New York.

MacDougal, D. T. (1914). The Salton Sea. *Carnegie Inst. Wash. Publ.* **193**, 1–182.

McGinnes, W. G., Goldman, B. J., and Paylore, P. (eds) (1968). "Deserts of the World, an Appraisal of Research into their Physical and Biological Environments." Univ. of Arizona Press, Tucson.

McHugh, J. L. (1954). The influence of light on the number of vertebrae in the grunion, *Leuresthes tenuis. Copeia* pp. 23–25.

Martin, F. D. (1968). Feeding habits of *Cyprinodon variegatus* (Cyprinodontidae) *variegatus* Lacépède. *Ecology* **49**, 1186–1188.

Martin, F. D. (1970). Feeding habits of *Cyprindon variegatus* (Cyprinodontidae) from the Texas coast. *Southwest. Natur.* **14**, 368–369.

Martin, P. S., and Mehringer, P. J. (1965). Pleistocene pollen anaysis and biogeography of the southwest. *In* "The Quaternary of the United States" (H. E. Wright and D. G. Frey, eds.), pp. 433–451. Princeton Univ. Press, Princeton, New Jersey.

Maxey, G. B. (1968). Hydrogeology of desert basins. *Ground Water* **6**, 10–22.

Maxey, G. B., and Mifflin, M. D. (1966). Occurrence and movement of ground water in carbonated rocks of Nevada. *Nat. Speleol. Soc., Bull.* **28**, 141–157.

Mehringer, P. J. (1967). Pollen analysis of the Tule Springs site, Nevada. *In* "Pleistocene Studies in Southern Nevada" (H. M. Wormington and D. Ellis, eds.), Anthropol. Pap. No. 13 pp. 130–200. Nevada State Mus., Carson City.

Meinzer, O. E. (1917). Geology and water resources of Big Smoky, Clayton, and Alkali Spring valleys, Nevada *U.S., Geol. Surv., Water-Supply Pap.* **423**, 1–167.

Metcalf, A. L. (1966). Fishes of the Kansas River system in relation to zoogeography of the Great Plains. *Publ. Mus. Natur. Hist. Univ. Kansas* **17**, 23–189.

Miller, R. J., and Evans, H. E. (1965). External morphology of the brain and lips in catostomid fishes. *Copeia* pp. 467–487.

Miller, R. R. (1943). *Cyprinodon salinus,* a new species of fish from Death Valley, California. *Copeia* pp. 69–78.

Miller, R. R. (1946a). Correlation between fish distribution and Pleistocene hydrography in eastern California and southwestern Nevada, with a map of the Pleistocene waters. *J. Geol.* **54**, 43–53.

Miller, R. R. (1946b). *Gila cypha,* a remarkable new species of cyprinid fish from the Colorado River in Grand Canyon, Arizona. *J. Wash. Acad. Sci.* **36**, 409–415.

Miller, R. R. (1948). The cyprinodont fishes of the Death Valley System of eastern California and southwestern Nevada. *Misc. Publ. Mus. Zool. Univ. Mich.* **68**, 1–155.

Miller, R. R. (1949a). Desert fishes—clues to vanished lakes and streams *Natur. Hist., N.Y.* **58**, 447–451 and 475–476.

Miller, R. R. (1949b). Hot springs and fish life. *Aquarium J.* **20**, 286–288.

Miller, R. R. (1950a). Notes on the cutthroat and rainbow trouts, with the description of a new species from the Gila River, New Mexico. *Occas. Pap. Mus. Zool. Univ. Mich.* **529**, 1–42.

Miller, R. R. (1950b). Speciation in fishes of the genera *Cyprinodon* and *Empetrichthys,* inhabiting the Death Valley region. *Evolution* **4**, 155–163.

Miller, R. R. (1955). An annotated list of the American cyprinodontid fishes of the genus *Fundulus,* with the description of *Fundulus persimilis* from Yucatan. *Occas. Pap. Mus. Zool. Univ. Mich.* **568**, 1–27.

Miller, R. R. (1959). Origin and affinities of the freshwater fish fauna of western North America. *In* "Zoogeography," (C. L. Hubbs, ed.) Publ. No. 51, pp. 187–222. Amer. Ass. Advan. Sci., Washington, D.C.

Miller, R. R. (1961a). Man and the changing fish fauna of the American Southwest. *Pap. Mich. Acad. Sci., Arts Lett.* **46**, 365–404.

Miller, R. R. (1961b). Speciation rates in some freshwater fishes of western North America. *In* "Vertebrate Speciation" (W. F. Blair, ed.), pp. 537–560. Univ. of Texas Press, Austin.

Miller, R. R. (1968). Two new fishes of the genus *Cyprinodon* from the Cuatro Ciénegas basin, Coahuila, México. *Occas. Pap. Mus. Zool. Univ. Mich.* **659**, 1–15.

Miller, R. R. (1971). Classification of the native trouts of Arizona. Unpublished manuscript.

Miller, R. R., and Hubbs, C. L. (1960). The spiny-rayed cyprinid fishes (Plagopterini) of the Colorado River system. *Misc. Publ. Mus. Zool. Univ. Mich.* **115**, 1–34.

Minckley, C. O., and Klaassen, H. E. (1969a). Burying behavior of the Plains killifish, *Fundulus kansae. Copeia* pp. 200–201.

Minckley, C. O., and Klaassen, H. E. (1969b). Life history of the Plains killifish, *Fundulus kansae* (Garman), in the Smoky Hill River, Kansas. *Trans. Amer. Fish. Soc.* **98**, 460–465.

Minckley, W. L. (1963). The ecology of a spring stream, Doe Run, Meade County, Kentucky. *Wildl. Monogr.* **11**, 1–124.

Minckley, W. L. (1969a). Aquatic biota of the Sonoita Creek basin, Santa Cruz County, Arizona. *Ecol. Stud. Leafl.* **15**, 1–8.

Minckley, W. L. (1969b). Environments of the Bolsón of Cuatro Ciénegas, Coahuila, México, with special reference to the aquatic biota. *Tex. West. Press, Univ. Tex. El Paso Sci. Ser.* **2**, 1–65.

Minckley, W. L. (1969c). Native Arizona fishes. Part I. Livebearers. *Wildl. Views* **16**, 6–8.

Minckley, W. L. (1971). Fishes of Arizona. Unpublished manuscript.

Minckley, W. L., and Barber, W. E. (1971). Some aspects of the biology of the longfin dace, a cyprinid fish characteristic of streams in the Sonoran Desert. *Southwest. Natur.* **15**.

Minckley, W. L., and Carufel, L. (1967). The Little Colorado River spinedace, *Lepidomeda vittata,* in Arizona. *Southwest. Natur.* **12**, 291–302.

Minckley, W. L., and Cole, G. A. (1968). Preliminary limnologic information on waters of the Cuatro Ciénegas basin, Coahuila, México. *Southwest. Natur.* **13**, 421–433.

Minckley, W. L., and Cross, F. B. (1959). Distribution, habitat, and abundance of the Topeka shiner, *Notropis topeka* (Gilbert), in Kansas. *Amer. Midl. Natur.* **61**, 210–217.

Minckley, W. L., and Deacon, J. E. (1968). Southwestern fishes and the enigma of "endangered species." *Science* **159**, 1424–1432.

Minckley, W. L., and Itzkowitz, M. (1967). Ecology and effects of intestinal gas accumulation in a pupfish (genus *Cyprinodon*). *Trans. Amer. Fish. Soc.* **96**, 216–218.

Minckley, W. L., and Krumholz, L. A. (1960). Natural hybridization between the clupeid genera *Dorosoma* and *Signalosa,* with a report on the distribution of *S. petenensis. Zoologica* **44**, 171–180.

Minckley, W. L., Lysne, J. L., and Arnold, E. T. (1971). Distribution and variation in a thermophilous pupfish (*Cyprinodon bifasciatus*) from northern Coahuila, México. Unpublished manuscript.

Minshall, G. W. (1968). Community dynamics of the benthic fauna in a woodland springbrook. *Hydrobiologia* **32**, 305–339.

Moore, G. A. (1944a). The retinae of two North American teleosts, with special reference to their tapaeta lucida. *J. Comp. Neurol.* **80**, 369–379.

Moore, G. A. (1944b). Notes on the early life history of *Notropis girardi. Copeia* pp. 209–213.

Moore, G. A. (1950). The cutaneous sense organs of barbeled minnows adapted to life in the muddy waters of the Great Plains Region. *Trans. Amer. Microsc. Soc.* **69**, 69–95.

Moore, G. A. (1968). Fishes. *In* "Vertebrates of the United States" (by W. F. Blair, A. P. Blair, P. Brodkorb, F. R. Cagle, and G. A. Moore), pp. 21–165. McGraw-Hill, New York.

Myers, G. S. (1952). Annual fishes. *Aquarium J.* **23**, 125–141.

Myers, G. S. (1965). *Gambusia,* the fish destroyer. *Trop. Fish Hobbyist* **13**, 31–32 and 53–54.

Needham, P. R., and Gard, R. (1959). Rainbow trout in Mexico and California, with notes on the cutthroat series. *Univ. Calif., Berkeley, Publ. Zool.* **67**, 1–124.

Needham, P. R., and Gard, R. (1964). A new trout from central Mexico: *Salmo chrysogaster,* the Mexican golden trout. *Copeia* pp. 169–173.

Neel, J. K. (1951). Interrelations of certain physical and chemical features of a headwater limestone stream. *Ecology* **32**, 368–391.

Nicholson, A. J. (1933). The balance of animal populations. *J. Anim. Ecol.* **2**, 132, 178.

Nicholson, A. J. (1954). An outline of the dynamics of animal populations. *Aust. J. Zool.* **2**, 9–65.

Nikolsky, G. V. (1961). "Special Ichthyology." (translated by J. I. Lengy and Z. Krauthamer). Israel Program for Scientific Translations, Jerusalem.

Nikolsky, G. V. (1963). "Ecology of Fishes." Academic Press, New York.

Norman, J. R. (1931). "A History of Fishes." A. A. Wyn, New York (reprint edition).

Norris, K. S. (1963). The functions of temperature in the ecology of the percoid fish *Girella nigricans* (Ayres). *Ecol. Monogr.* **33**, 23–62.

Nyquist, D. (1963). The ecology of *Eremichthys acros,* an endemic thermal species of cyprinid fish from northwestern Nevada. M.S. Thesis, University of Nevada, Reno.

Paloumpis, A. A. (1956). Stream havens save fish. *Iowa Conserv.* **15**, 60.

Paloumpis, A. A. (1957). The effects of drought conditions on the fish and bottom organisms of two small oxbow ponds. *Trans. Ill. State Acad. Sci.* **50**, 60–64.

Paloumpis, A. A. (1958). Responses of some minnows to flood and drought conditions in an intermittent stream. *Iowa State Coll. J. Sci.* **32**, 547–561.

Pellegrin, J. (1914). Fresh water vertebrates of the Sahara. *Ass. Fr. Avan. Sci., Tunis* pp. 346–352.

Pellegrin, J. (1931). Reptiles, batrachians and fish of the central Sahara collected by Pr. Seurat. *Bull. Mus. Hist. Natur., Paris* [2] **3**, 216–218.

Pellegrin, J. (1934). Reptiles, batrachians and fish of the central Sahara. *Mem. Soc. Hist. Natur. Afr. Nord* **4**, 50–57.

Perlmutter, A. (1961). Possible effect of lethal visible light on year-class fluctuations of aquatic animals. *Science* **133**, 1081–1082.

Peters, N., Jr. (1963). Embryonale Anpassungen oviparer Zahnkarpfen aus periodisch austrocknenden Gewassern. *Int. Rev. Hydrobiol.* **48**, 257–313.

Phillips, A. M., Jr. (1969). Nutrition, digestion, and energy utilization. *In* "Fish Physiology" (W. S. Hoar and D. J. Randall, eds.), Vol. 1, pp. 391–432. Academic Press, New York.

Prosser, C. L., ed. (1958). "Physiological Adaptation." Amer. Physiol. Soc., Washington, D.C.

Prosser, C. L., and Brown, F. A., Jr. (1961). "Comparative Animal Physiology," 2nd ed. Saunders, Philadelphia, Pennsylvania.

Rasquin, P., and Rosenbloom, L. (1954). Endocrine imbalance and tissue hyperplasia in teleosts maintained in darkness. *Bull. Amer. Mus. Natur. Hist.* **104**, 359–426.

Renfro, W. C. (1960). Salinity relations of some fishes in the Aransas River, Texas. *Tulane Stud. Zool.* **8**, 83–91.

Rinne, J. N. (1969). Cyprinid fishes of the genus *Gila* from the lower Colorado River basin. M.S. Thesis, Arizona State University, Tempe.

Rinne, J. N., and Minckley, W. L. (1970). Native Arizona fishes. Part IV. "Chubs." *Wildl. Views* **17**, 2–19.

Rinne, W. (1970). Personal communication.

Rosen, D. E., and Mendelson, J. R. (1960). The sensory canals of the head in poeciliid fishes (Cyprinodontiformes), with reference to dentitional types. *Copeia* pp. 203–210.

Ross, H. (1957). Principles of natural coexistence indicated by leafhopper populations. *Evolution* **11**, 113 –129.

Ruttner, F. (1953). "Fundamentals of Limnology" (translated by D. G. Frey and F. E. J. Fry). Univ. of Toronto Press, Toronto.

Schaut, G. G. (1939). Fish catastrophes during droughts. *J. Amer. Waterworks Ass.* **31**, 771–822.

Schlieper, C., Blasing, J., and Halsband, E. (1952). Experimentelle Veranderungen der Temperaturtoleranz bei stenothermen und eurythermen Wassertieren. *Zool. Anz.* 149, 163–169.

Schmitz, W. (1954). Grundlagen der Untersuchung der Temperaturverhaltnisse in den Fliessgewassern. *Berlin. Limnol. Flusstation Freudenthal.* **6**, 29–250.

Schreitmuller, W. (1921). *Lebia iberus* C. u.V., seine Zucht und Pflege. *Bl. Aquar.-Terrarienk.* **30**, 313–316.

Schoenherr, A. (1970). Personal communication.

Schureman, P. (1941). Manual of tide observations. *U.S., Geol. Surv., Spec. Publ.* **196.**

Shelford, V. E. (1911a). Ecological succession. I. Stream fishes and the method of physiographic analysis. *Biol. Bull.* **21**, 9–34.

Shelford, V. E. (1911b). Ecological succession. II. Pond fishes. *Biol. Bull.* **22**, 1–38.

Sigler, W. F., and Miller, R. R. (1963). "Fishes of Utah." Utah State Dept. of Fish and Game, Salt Lake City.

Simpson, D. G., and Gunter, G. (1956). Notes on habitats, systematic characters, and life histories of Texas salt water Cyprinodontes. *Tulane Stud. Zool.* **4**, 115–134.

Smith, G. R. (1966). Distribution and evolution of the North American catostomid fishes of the subgenus *Pantosteus,* genus *Catostomus. Misc. Publ. Mus. Zool. Univ. Mich.* **129**, 1–132.

Smith, H. T. U. (1968). Geologic and geomorphic aspects of deserts. In "Desert Biology" (G. W. Brown, Jr., ed.), Vol. 1, pp. 51–100. Academic Press, New York.

Smith, J. L. B. (1952). Cyprinodont fishes from a suphur-producing lake in Cyrenaica. Ann. Mag. Natur. Hist. 12, 888–892.

Snyder, C. T., Hardman, G., and Zdenek, F. F. (1964). Pleistocene lakes in the Great Basin. U.S., Geol. Surv., Misc. Geol. Invest. Maps I-416.

Snyder, J. O. (1915). Notes on a collection of fishes made by Dr. Edgar A. Mearns from rivers tributary to the Gulf of California. Proc. U.S. Nat. Mus. 49, 573–586.

Snyder, J. O. (1917). An account of some fishes from Owens River, California. Proc. U.S. Nat. Mus. 54, 201–205.

Soltz, D., and Brown, J. (1970). Personal communication.

Spencer, W. P. (1939). Diurnal activity rhythms in freshwater fishes. Ohio J. Sci. 39, 119–132.

Spoor, W. A., and Schloemer, C. L. (1939). Diurnal activity of the common sucker, Catostomus commersonii (Lacépède), and the rock bass, Ambloplites rupestris (Rafinesque), in Muskellunge Lake. Trans. Amer. Fish. Soc. 68, 211–220.

Starrett, W. C. (1950a). Food relationships of the minnows of the Des Moines River, Iowa. Ecology 31, 216–233.

Starrett, W. C. (1950b). Distribution of the fishes of Boone County, Iowa, with special reference to the minnows and darters. Amer. Midl. Natur. 43, 112–127.

Starrett, W. C. (1951). Some factors affecting the abundance of minnows in the Des Moines River, Iowa. Ecology 32, 13–27.

Stebbins, R. C., and Kalk, M. (1961). Observations on the natural history of the mud-skipper, Periopthalmus sabrinus. Copeia pp. 18–27.

Stegman, J. L., and Minckley, W. L. (1959). Occurrence of three species of fishes in interstices of gravel in an area of subsurface flow. Copeia p. 341.

Strecher, P. G., ed. (1968). "The Merck Index: An Encyclopedia of Chemicals and Drugs." Merck and Company, Inc., Rahway, New Jersey.

Stehr, W. C., and Branson, J. W. (1938). An ecological study of an intermittent stream. Ecology 19, 294–310.

Steinitz, H. (1951a). The fishes of Ein Feshkha, Palestine. Nature (London) 167, 531–532.

Steinitz, H. (1951b). A new subspecies of Tilapia nilotica (L.) from Palestine. Ann. Mag. Natur. Hist. 4, 513–518.

Sterba, G. (1967). "Freshwater Fishes of the World." Pet Library, Ltd., New York.

Stewart, N. H. (1926). Development, growth, and food habits of the white sucker, Catostomus commersonii LeSueur. Bull. U.S. Fish. Bur. 42, 147–183.

Stubbs, J. M. (1949). Fresh water fisheries in the northern Bahr el Ghazal. Sudan Notes 30, 216–284.

Summerfelt, R. C., and Minckley, C. O. (1969). Aspects of the life history of the sand shiner, Notropis stramineus (Cope), in the Smoky Hill River, Kansas. Trans. Amer. Fish. Soc. 98, 444–453.

Sumner, F. B., and Lanham, V. N. (1942). Studies of the respiratory metabolism of warm and cool spring fishes. Biol. Bull. 88, 313–327.

Sumner, F. B., and Sargent, M. C. (1940). Some observations on the physiology of warm spring fishes. Ecology 21, 45–54.

Sweet, J. G., and Kinne, O. (1964). The effects of various temperature-salinity combinations on the body form of newly hatched *Cyprinodon macularius* (Teleostei). *Helgolaender Wiss. Meeresunters.* **11,** 49–69.

Swinnerton, A. C. (1942). Hydrology of limestone terranes. *In* "Hydrology, Physics of the Earth" (O. E. Meinzer, ed.), Vol. IX, pp. 656–677. McGraw-Hill, New York.

Sykes, G. (1937). The Colorado Delta. *Carnegie Inst. Wash., Publ.* **460.**

Tåning, A. V. (1952). Experimental study of meristic characters of fishes. *Biol. Rev. Cambridge Phil. Soc.* **27,** 69–193.

Tavolga, W. N. (1960). Sound production and underwater communication in fishes. *In* "Animal Sounds and Communications" (W. E. Layon and W. N. Tavolga, eds.), pp. 93–136. Amer. Inst. Biol. Sci., Washington, D.C.

Taylor, D. W., and Minckley, W. L. (1966). New world for biologists. *Pac. Discovery* **19,** 18–22.

Taylor, W. R. (1969). A revision of the catfish genus *Noturus* Rafinesque, with an analysis of higher groups in the Ictluridae. *U.S., Nat. Mus., Bull.* **282,** 1–315.

Teal, J. M., and Carey, F. G. (1967). Skin respiration and oxygen debt in mudskipper, *Periopthalmus sabrinus. Copeia* pp. 677–679.

Thomson, B. W., and Schumann, H. H. (1968). Water resources of the Sycamore Creek watershed, Maricopa County, Arizona. *U.S., Geol. Surv., Water Supply Pap.* **1861,** 1–53.

Todd, E. S. (1968). Terrestrial sojourns of the long-jaw mudsucker, *Gillichthys mirabilis. Copeia* pp. 192–194.

Todd, E. S., and Ebeling, A. W. (1966). Aerial respiration in the longjaw mudsucker, *Gillichthys mirabilis* (Teleostei: Gobiidae). *Biol. Bull.* **130,** 265–288.

Trautman, M. B. (1942). Fish distribution and abundance correlated with stream gradients as a consideration in stocking programs. *Trans. N. Amer. Wildl. Conf.,* **7,** 211–223.

Trautman, M. B. (1957). "The Fishes of Ohio." Ohio State Univ. Press, Columbus.

Turner, B. J. (1964). An introduction to the fishes of the genus *Nothobranchius. Afr. Wild Life* **18,** 117–124.

Utida, S. (1953). Interspecific competition between two species of bean weevil. *Ecology* **34,** 301–307.

Vanicek, C. D., and Kramer, R. H. (1969). Life history of the Colorado squawfish, *Ptychocheilus lucius,* and the Colorado chub, *Gila robusta,* in the Green River in Dinosaur National Monument, 1964–1966. *Trans. Amer. Fish. Soc.* **98,** 193–208.

Vanicek, C. D., Kramer, R. H., and Franklin, D. R. (1970). Distribution of Green River fishes in Utah and Colorado following closure of Flaming Gorge Dam. *Southwest. Natur.* **14,** 297–315.

Van Ihering, R. (1935). Die Wirkung von Hypophyseninjektion auf den Laichakt von Fischen. Kannibalismus bei Diplopoden. *Zool. Anz.* **111,** 273–279.

van Oosten, J. (1957). The skin and scales. *In* "The Physiology of Fishes" (M. E. Brown, ed.), Vol. 1, pp. 207–243. Academic Press, New York.

Velasquez, G. T. (1939). On the viability of algae obtained from the digestive tract of the gizzard shad, *Dorosoma cepedianum* (LeSueur). *Amer. Midland Natur.* **22,** 376–412.

Villwock, W. (1958). Weitere genetische Untersuchungen zur Frage der Verwandtschaftsbeziehungen anatolischer Lahnkarpfen. *Mitt. Hamburg. Zool. Mus. Inst.* **56,** 81–152.

Villwock, W. (1966). Isolations Mechanismen und Artbildung bei Fischen, unter besonder Berücksichtigung geographischer Isolationsfaktoren. *Zool. Anz.* **177,** 84–104.

Walford, R. L., and Liu, R. K. (1965). Husbandry, life span, and growth rate of the annual fish, *Cynolebias adolffi* E. Ahl. *Exp. Gerontol.* **1,** 161–171.

Walker, B. W., ed. (1961). The ecology of the Salton Sea, California, in relation to the sport fishery. *Calif. Dep. Fish. Game, Fish. Bull.* **113,** 1–204.

Wallen, I. E. (1951). The direct effect of turbidity on fishes. *Bull. Okla. Agr. Mech. Coll.* **48,** 1–27.

Waring, G. A. (1965). Thermal springs of the United States and other countries of the world: A summary. *U.S., Geol. Surv., Prof. Pap.* **492,** 1–383.

Wauer, R. H. (1962). "Collecting of *C. n. amargosae* from Drying Pools in Amargosa River," File Rep. Death Valley National Monument, California.

Weatherley, A. H. (1963a). Zoogeography of *Perca fluviatilis* (Linnaeus) and *Perca flavescens* (Mitchill), with special reference to the effects of high temperature. *Proc. Zool. Soc. London* **141,** 557–576.

Weatherley, A. H. (1963b). Notions of niche and competition among animals with special reference to freshwater fish. *Nature (London)* **197,** 14–17.

Weatherley, A. H., ed. (1967). "Australian Inland Waters and their Faunas, Eleven Studies." Australian National Univ. Press, Canberra.

Weidie, A. E., and Murray, G. E. (1967). Geology of the Parras basin and adjacent areas of northeastern Mexico. *Amer. Ass. Petrol. Geol., Bull.* **51,** 678–695.

Weitzman, S. H., and Wourms, J. P. (1967). South American cyprinodont fishes allied to *Cynolebias,* with the description of a new species of *Austrogundulus* from Venezuela. *Copeia* pp. 89–100.

Wells, N. A. (1935). Variation in the respiratory metabolism of the Pacific killifish, *Fundulus parvipinnis,* due to size, season, and continued constant temperature. *Physiol. Zoo.* **8,** 318–335.

Whitley, G. P. (1959). The freshwater fishes of Australia. *In* "Biogeography and Ecology in Australia" (A. Keast, R. L. Crocker, and C. S. Christian, eds.), Monogr. Biol., pp. 136–149. Junk, The Hague.

Williams, W. D. (1967a). The chemical characteristics of lentic surface waters: A review. *In* "Australian Inland Waters and their Faunas, Eleven Studies" (A. H. Weatherley, ed.), pp. 18–77. Australian National Univ. Press, Canberra.

Williams, W. D. (1967b). The changing limnological scene in Victoria. In "Australian Inland Waters and their Faunas, Eleven Studies" (A. H. Weatherley, ed.), pp. 240–251. Australian National Univ. Press, Canberra.

Wilson, B. L., Deacon, J. E., and Bradley, W. G. (1966). Parasitism in the fishes of the Moapa River, Clark County, Nevada. *Trans. Calif.-Nev. Sec. Wildl. Soc.* pp. 12–23.

Wright, H. E. (1956). An extinct wadi system in the Syrian desert. *Bull. Res. Counc. Isr., Sect. G* **7,** 53–57.

Wynne-Edwards, V. C. (1962). "Animal Dispersion in Relation to Social Behavior." Hafner, New York.

Yeager, L. E. (1936). An observation on spawning buffalofish in Mississippi. *Copeia* pp. 238–239.

Young, F. N., and Zimmerman, J. R. (1956). Variations in temperature in small aquatic situations. *Ecology* **37,** 609–611.

CHAPTER VIII

MAN IN ARID LANDS: THE PIMAN INDIANS OF THE SONORAN DESERT

Bernard L. Fontana

When studied narrowly in himself by anthropologists or jurists, man is a tiny, even a shrinking, creature. His over-pronounced individuality conceals from our eyes the whole to which he belongs; as we look at him our minds incline to break nature up into pieces and to forget both its deep inter-relations and its measureless horizons: we incline to all that is bad in anthropocentrism. And it is this that leads scientists to refuse to consider man as an object of scientific scrutiny except through his body. . . . The true physics is that which will, one day, achieve the inclusion of man in his wholeness in a coherent picture of the world. Pierre Teilhard de Chardin (1961)

I. Man in the Desert

To strive toward an understanding of man in the desert is to take a faltering step toward the "true physics" of which Père Teilhard de Chardin

speaks. The true desert man, moreover, is one who was born in it, whose
cultural roots are desert-bound, and, above all, whose whole way of life,
including his material possessions and technology, are desert-derived. Such
are the men with whom we are primarily concerned in this study.

A. World-Wide Studies

Since the publication in 1962 by UNESCO of the proceedings of the
Paris Symposium relating to problems of the arid zone, there has been
a near deluge of such reports about the arid regions of the world (see,
for example, the lists of references and bibliographies appearing in Brown,
1968; Hodge, 1963; McGinnies and Goldman, 1969; McGinnies *et al.*,
1968). The seed which gave birth to this modern upsurge in interest, at
least in the United States, was probably planted in the soil of studies carried out during World War II designed to enable Allied soldiers to survive
and to become efficient warriors in the dry battleground of North Africa
(Lee, 1963, pp. 341–350).

In the years following the end of the war there has arisen a global real-
ization that about 14% of the earth's surface is "desert" [see McGinnies
(1969, pp. 280–282) for a discussion of the problems in defining the
"desert" concept]; that approximately half the nations of the world have
significant reaches of arid lands within their boundaries; and that given
the earth's rapid growth in human population and simultaneous depletion
of natural resources, more should be learned about this one-seventh of
the total land surface which annually receives 25 cm of rainfall or less.
It was the delegation from India which in 1948 proposed at the UNESCO
General Conference in Lebanon that studies of arid zones be undertaken
and coordinated on an international scale. The result was the UNESCO
Arid Zone Programme which lasted until 1964. Today there are more than
250 institutions in the world involved in arid-lands activities of one kind
or another, and the list is doubtless growing (Paylore, 1967).

Considering that what presumably spawned this plethora of desert research was a regard for man and his relationship to dry climes, the comparative scarcity of publications which address themselves directly to the
subject is noteworthy. Information abounds concerning saline and alkali
soils, the growth of desert shrubs, invertebrate fauna, Pleistocene volcanic
activity, the physics of wind erosion, and the hydrology of desert littoral
zones. The emphasis in arid-land studies clearly has been in physical
geography and natural history rather than in cultural geography and the
social sciences.

There are, as a matter of fact, abundant data bearing on man in the desert. Except for studies of the effects of aridity on man's physiological system, however, most such efforts address themselves to the interrelationship between man and desert in only a secondary way. There are ethnohistoric and ethnographic accounts of virtually every extant culture in the world, including those of desert-dwelling pastoralists, hunting and gathering nomads, gardeners, dry farmers, and irrigation agriculturalists [see Murdock (1967) for a list of the world's cultures and their salient ethnographic features]. For more than six decades archaeologists have been plumbing the depths of desert sands from the *tells* of Egypt to the trash mounds of southern Arizona. Yet, this work has been done by students and scholars in the same way, and for the same reasons thought has been directed toward the study of man throughout the world in all environments. The focus of ethnologists has been on man; it has been secondarily on the desert if the men under consideration happened to live in one. Studies of the aboriginal cultures of Australia, for example, would have been carried out even were all of Australia's climate a tropical one.

At the moment, there is no single source, nor is there any convenient group of sources, to which one may turn to obtain a world-wide overview of the variability of human cultures whose native locus is the desert. Nor is there even a simple listing of the world's deserts naming the peoples native to those deserts. If there is, at least, I have been unable to find it. This provides a thought-provoking picture of the status of our knowledge of man in arid lands.

B. Sonoran Desert Studies

The Sonoran Desert is an area of about 250,000 km² lying in southwestern Arizona, southeastern California, western Sonora, and northeastern Baja California (Dunbier, 1968). Some investigators would add the whole of central Baja California and another 50,000 km² to this figure (Shreve and Wiggins, 1964, p. 12).

Most research efforts involving the Sonoran Desert have been carried out at the University of Arizona in Tucson. The university is situated within this desert near its eastern boundary.

A recently published bibliography of arid-lands research conducted at the University of Arizona between 1891 and 1965 contains 1609 references arranged under 17 topical subheadings. One of these, "Ancient and Modern Peoples and Land Use," has a mere 47 entries, and the criterion for their selection was clearly man's use of land rather than his total involvement with it (Paylore, 1966).

To cite another example, man is not listed in the Check List of the Recent Mammals in "The Vertebrates of Arizona" (Lowe, 1964, pp. 249–259). In spite of the fact that man is a vertebrate, and in spite of the fact that he is an Arizona "native," having been on the scene for at least 12,000 years, he is mentioned only once in the entire text: "With regard to the vertebrates, however, a single bird, the water pipit (*Anthus spinoletta alticola*) nests in the alpine tundra (meadow) of San Francisco Mountain, and there are no mammals or other kinds of vertebrate animals represented (reproductively) there; man (*Homo sapiens*) is an occasional intruder" (Lowe, 1964, p. 81).

By eliminating *Homo sapiens* from such accounts, whatever the motives may be, men have somehow reserved for man an isolated niche in the overall scheme of things—or the total biota, should you prefer—to which he clearly is not entitled. He is, in fact, a mammal; he lives within biotic communities, however disruptive to them he may sometimes be; and he is restricted in certain ways, as all other living things, by his habitat.

Major studies of the Sonoran Desert, to cite a few of them, have been in the realms of botany (Bell and Castetter, 1937; Benson, 1950; Benson and Darrow, 1944; Brand, 1936; Shreve, 1951; Shreve and Wiggins, 1964), ecology (Dice, 1939; Hastings and Turner, 1965; Kniffen, 1931; Lowe, 1959, 1964, pp. 24–31 and 94–98; McGee, 1895; Turnage and Hinckley, 1938), meteorology (Hastings, 1964a,b; Hastings and Humphrey, 1969a,b; Ives, 1949; Turnage and Mallery, 1941), and geology (Bryan, 1922, 1925; Galbraith, 1959; Halpenny, 1952; Heindl and Cosner, 1961; Ives, 1964b; Simmons, 1965; Wilson, 1933; see Moore and Wilson, 1965, for an extensive bibliography).

Among these writers, Hastings and Turner (1965) are concerned with *Homo sapiens* insofar as he may or may not have effected vegetation changes within his Sonoran Desert habitat; and McGee (1895), looking broadly at the relationship between man and his surrounding flora and fauna in southern Arizona and northern Sonora, speculated in the 19th century—and probably correctly so—that there was something in this relationship which gave rise to the beginnings of agriculture. Bryan (1925) takes Indian and non-Indian systems of water control and use into full account, even though his basic interest is in physical geology.

There are, of course, studies of modern, postindustrial man in the Sonoran Desert. This is the major thrust of Dunbier's (1968) outstanding geography, and there are problem-oriented reports on Tucson (Wilson, 1963), the Salt River Valley (Smith and Padfield, 1969), and Puerto Peñasco (Hodges, 1969), for example, which concern themselves with water and its distribution for man's use. There are, moreover, hundreds of articles written about agriculture and its related fields as they are presently practiced in the Sonoran Desert (see Paylore, 1966).

In aboriginal times the human fauna included people whose cultures have been labeled Piman (including Pimas, Papagos, Sobaipuris, Sobas, and Lower Pimas); Cahitan (Yaquis and Mayos); Yuman [Cocopas, Quechans (Yumas), Cocomaricopas, and Halchidhomas]; Seris; and taking southern California and Baja California into account, Kamia, Diegueño, and Cochimi.

The ethnographic and ethnohistorical literature concerning these people is abundant (see Murdock, 1960, pp. 99–106 and 297–354), but few authors indicate a primary interest in the mutual adaptations evolved in the desert among man, other animals, flora, and such resources as salt, soil, and water. The works of Aschmann (1959), Castetter and Bell (1942, 1951), Castetter and Underhill (1935), Fontana (1964), Hackenberg (1962, 1964a,b), Hoover (1929, 1935a,b, 1938), Mark (1960), and Woodbury and Woodbury (1964), perhaps more than others, recognize the importance of the total Sonoran Desert setting in their discussions of the Indians who live here. But they are exceptions which prove the rule.

The prehistorians have fared better than ethnographers in paying due respect to the total environment. Excavators in the Sonoran Desert, as well as those other scientists involved in examining long-term change—the dendrochronologists, paleontologists, palynologists, and geologists—have looked intensively and extensively at the evidences for alterations in vegetation, climate, and nonhuman fauna that they might better understand how man's cultures situated here have evolved over a 12,000-year period (summaries and bibliographies can be found in Martin, 1963; el-Zur, 1965).

Finally, and with the emphasis on human physiology, there have been studies in the Sonoran Desert on the ability of man to withstand its heat and dryness (see, for example, Adolph, 1947; McGee, 1906).

II. The Sonoran Desert Setting

Based on its types of vegetation, the Sonoran Desert has been classified into subdivisions. These are the Lower Colorado Valley, Arizona Upland, Plains of Sonora, Foothills of Sonora, Central Gulf Coast, Vizcaino Region, and the Magdalena Region (Shreve and Wiggins, 1964, Map 1). Characterized as ". . . far and away the most varied of North American deserts," the Sonoran Desert is the lowest and the hottest of these. It is comprised of innumerable microclimates and scores of habitats. "The end result . . . is a multitude of little worlds, fragmented and varied, all existing within the larger framework of a 'desert'" (Hastings and Turner, 1965, pp. 7, 8, and 11).

THE PIMERÍA ALTA

When New Spain first extended its religious and secular conquests into the northern reaches of the Sonoran Desert in the late 17th century, its clerical, military, and civil representatives found the region inhabited by several groups of Indians, all of whom spoke mutually intelligible dialects of the same language and who came by Europeans to be called "Piman" Indians. Linguistic brethern of these same people had already been encountered to the south, the Pima Bajo, so by extension, the northern Pimans were called "Pimas Altos" and their vast domain, Pimería Alta, the northern lands of the Piman Indians.

Although Pimería Alta lies almost wholly within the Sonoran Desert, its native inhabitants were spread over two major subdivisions of it, the Lower Colorado Valley and the Arizona Upland. The aboriginal boundaries of the Upper Piman Indians seem in the late 17th century to have been the Colorado River on the west, the Gila River on the north, the San Pedro River and Río San Miguel on the east, the Río Magdalena and Río Concepción in the south, and the Gulf of California in the southwest (Bolton, 1948). There was a single Pima village on the headwaters of the Río Sonora, east of the Río San Miguel, but the Spaniards removed these people in the 1690's (Spicer, 1962, pp. 118–119) (see Fig. 1, showing mountains and valleys).

The parts of Pimería Alta beyond the desert pale were those portions of the upper and central San Pedro River Valley, the Upper Santa Cruz River Valley, adjacent mountains and tributaries, and the Baboquivari Mountains, which get into desert–grassland and evergreen–woodland (oak–piñon–juniper) country. The numbers of Pimans living here was always a small proportion of the total, however, and they were dislodged from the San Pedro Valley and surrounding mountains by Apache Indians early in the 18th century never to return.

It is convenient to subdivide the Pimería Alta into three major districts based on the availability of water. These are the extremely arid western portion (0–13 cm of annual rainfall), the seasonally more moist central portion (13–25 cm of annual rainfall), and the northern–eastern–southern perimeter which is comprised of river systems that once had permanently flowing water in them and which in places received about 25–38 cm of rainfall a year. Local variability is of course enormous, and yearly averages conceal the fact that many years of virtually no rain might be interspersed with a 1 day downpour that dumps more water than the locale

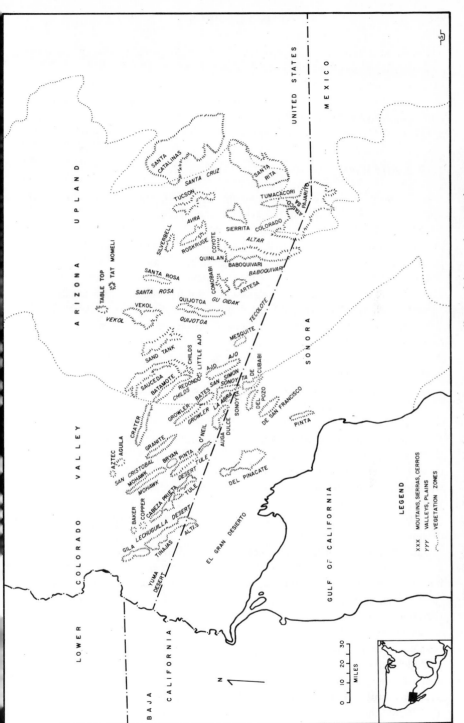

Fig. 1. Map showing mountains, sierras, cerros, valleys, plains, and vegetation zones.

has seen in a half a decade [see Shreve and Wiggins (1964, p. 21) for a rainfall map and Hastings and Turner (1965, p. 11) for a detailed and up-to-date discussion of the problem].

In spite of the variability, however, the threefold division of Pimería Alta based on the areal distribution of water, western, central, and riverine, holds up extremely well (see Fig. 2, showing rainfall lines and villages).

1. The Arid West

a. Climate. The southwestern corner of Arizona and the northwestern corner of Sonora are among the driest, hottest places in America. San Luis, situated at the northwestern point of Sonora, received only 0.01 cm of rain in 1956, and its mean annual rainfall for the years 1963–1967 was a parched 2.3 cm, or 0.9 inches (Hastings, 1964b, Hastings and Humphrey, 1969b, p. 68). In Arizona, and moving from west to east across western Pimería Alta, Yuma gets about 8.84 cm annual rainfall; the Lechuguilla Desert, 10.9 cm; Tinajas Altas, 12.9 cm; Tule Tank, 10.5 cm; Agua Dulce, 17.5 cm; and Growler Pass, 17.5 cm (Turnage and Mallery, 1941, pp. 4–5). In the Pinacate Plateau in Sonora the annual rainfall is 14.2 cm. At Quitovac and Sonoita, both also in northwestern Sonora, the mean annual rainfall for the years between 1963–1967 was 28.6 cm and 19.6 cm, respectively (Hastings and Humphrey, 1969b, pp. 29 and 33).

The rain which falls in the Sonoran Desert tends to come during two seasons: summer and winter. The periods of greatest precipitation are July–August and December–January. The summer "monsoons" are convective storms, often no more than 1 mile in diameter, and the rain from these is widely scattered. Even so, the summer rains, which move in from the Gulf of Mexico heading west, provide dependable sources of water year in and year out. The winter rains, which are widespread and cyclonic in nature, come to the Sonoran Desert from the Pacific (Hastings and Turner, 1965, pp. 11–12).

This biseasonal nature of precipitation is crucial with regard to plant growth. In western Pimería Alta, about half the rain falls in winter and half in summer, with winter slightly favored. The percentage of summer rainfall increases moving from west to east and from south to north over the region (Hastings and Turner, 1965, pp. 13–15.).

Just as aridity is greater in the west, so is the temperature. At Yuma, temperatures ranging from −5.5° to 49°C over a 65-year period have provided a yearly average temperature of 23.9°C. At Ajo, Arizona, at the eastern edge of this western zone of Pimería Alta, it is cooler, 21.9°C average annual temperature, with 44-year extremes of −8.3° to 46.1°C. The highs and lows are almost consistently reached in July and January,

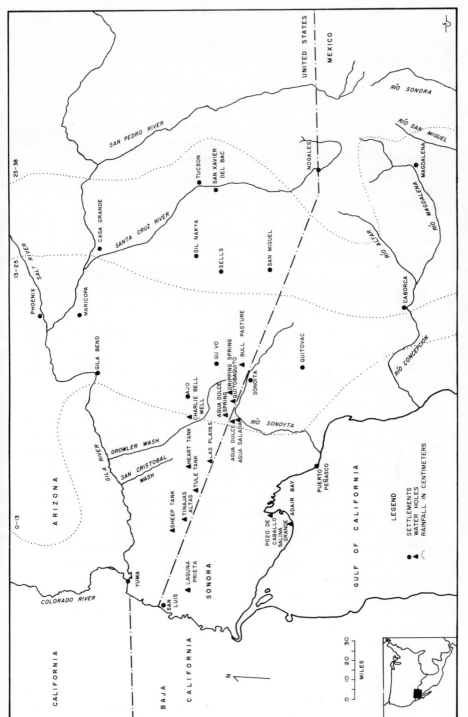

Fig. 2. Map showing settlements, water holes, rivers, and rainfall.

respectively (Hastings and Turner, 1965, p. 16; Simmons, 1965, p. 10). Although western Pimería Alta is nearly frost-free, as the above figures for Yuma and Ajo indicate, temperatures below the freezing point have occasionally been recorded.

The amounts, regional variations, and seasons of precipitation and temperature fluctuations determine in large part the efficient use of rainfall which can be made by native vegetation. Ecologists have defined "effective precipitation" as that which "penetrates the soil surface far enough to become available to plants, without percolating on through" (Hastings and Turner, 1965, p. 15). Furthermore, it is clear that the amount of water thus becoming available to plants also depends on the nature of the soil, the gradient of slopes, and on the amount of runoff as contrasted to the amount of penetration. The physical geology and topography of the region, therefore, are also important considerations.

b. Physiography. Virtually all of Pimería Alta, physiographically speaking, lies within the so-called Desert Region of the Basin and Range Province (Wilson, 1962, Fig. 13). This is comprised of a series of alternating mountain ranges and valleys, both generally lying diagonally in a southeast to northwest direction and both generally increasing in altitude above sea level moving from west to east.

The arid west of Pimería Alta is made up of rows of mountain ranges and hills rising sharply out of their intermontane valleys. In Arizona, these "rows" include the Gila–Tinajas Altas mountains (960 meters maximum elevation), Baker Peaks–Copper–Cabeza Prieta–Tule mountains (890 meters), Sierra Pinta–O'Neil–Davidson Hills (850 meters), Mohawk–Bryan–Agua Dulce mountains (890 meters), Aztec Hills–Aguila–Granite mountains (533 meters), Growler–Bates–Puerto Blanco–Sonoyta mountains (1013 meters), Crater–Childs-Little Ajo mountains (710 meters), and the Batamote–Redondo-Ajo mountains (1403 meters). Adjacent to these lines of mountains and hills lie the Yuma Desert (150 meters), Lechuguilla Desert (215 meters), Mohawk Valley–Tule Desert (250–275 meters), San Cristobal Valley–Growler Valley–La Abra Plain (350 meters), and Childs Valley–Valley of the Ajo–Sonoyta Valley (460 meters). The "valleys" and "plains" are deserts in every sense of the word, and even the highest of these peaks never rise above the lower Sonoran life zone (see Fig. 1).

The topography of northwesternmost Sonora is relatively simple. Immediately east of the Colorado River is the low-lying Sonoran Mesa, bounded on its east by the Great Sand Dunes. To the east of these dunes, sometimes called "El Gran Desierto" (Powell, 1964, 1966), lie the crater-pocked Sierra del Pinacate, a few isolated mountain clusters [Sierra Pinta, Sierra de San Francisco, Sierra del Pozo (Sierra de los Tanques), Sierra del

Cubabi], and the Desierto de Altar. The Sierra del Pinacate, rising to 1291 meters above sea level, dominates all (Ives, 1964b). The soil in these mountains and valleys, like that throughout the Sonoran Desert, is probably formed chiefly by the disintegrating action of 16°–21°C rainwater falling on basaltic rocks heated to 66°–71°C by the sun's rays. Low-lying hills and rocks are also ground to soil by the effects of sand and wind erosion (Shreve and Wiggins, 1964, p. 22). According to Shreve and Wiggins (1964, p. 22):

> The general features of the relation of land forms and physiographic processes to soil history are the same in arid and humid climates. A series of soils ranging from mountainside or talus slope through outwash slope and bajada to playa or flood plain will exhibit a decreasing number of large stones and an increasingly finer texture. Because of torrential rains and the lack of continuous cover of vegetation, there is a more ready downgrade movement of coarse material in the arid climate, and a consequent coarser texture in the soils of such relatively mature surfaces as the lower bajadas.

Where the gradients of upper mountain slopes are steeper, as they are in western Pimería Alta, the bajadas are shorter and, because of sheetflood erosion, more likely to be devoid of soils capable of supporting much plant life. Humus in these desert soils is normally less than 1%, and such organic matter as it may contain is quickly oxidized and decomposed. The intermontane basins, which are flat, receive insufficient rainfall and runoff to allow their stream beds to carry the water to the sea, with the result that the valleys are like land-locked basins. Furthermore, this means that the soluble salts found in desert soils that are flushed out by rainfall are ultimately deposited in these basins where they become a detriment to the growth of most plants (Shreve and Wiggins, 1964, pp. 24–25).

  c. Plant Life. Because nearly all of western Pimería Alta lies within Shreve's Lower Colorado Valley vegetational subdivision, what Shreve says concerning this province is apropos here (Shreve and Wiggins, 1964, pp. 49–50 and 57–68). He points out that about 85% of the area, excluding the delta of the Colorado River, is made up of plains and bajadas of low gradient and that these, in turn, have a plant population which is comprised of 90–95% *Larrea tridentata* (creosote bush) and *Franseria dumosa* (white bursage; burro weed). It is this *Larrea–Franseria* combination which earns the label "microphyllus desert" for the Lower Colorado Valley.

  The remaining microenvironments within the subdivision—the margins of drainageways in plains and lower bajadas, upper bajadas, sandy plains and dunes, malpais fields and volcanic hills, older volcanics, and granitic mountains and hills—support a richer vegetation. Mesquite (*Prosopis*

Fig. 3. The arid western portion of Pimería Alta is exemplified in the Tule Desert. Drainageways are easily seen, marked by lines of plant growth. View is from the western bajada of the Sierra Pinta looking west toward the Cabeza Prieta Mountains.

juliflora), blue palo verde (*Cercidium floridium*), foothill palo verde (*C. microphyllum*), and ironwood (*Olneya tesota*) are among the more common trees. The elephant tree (*Bursera microphylla*) and catclaw (*Acacia greggii*) also occur (see Fig. 3).

There are several perennial cacti and shrubs, including several species of chollas (*Opuntia* spp.), prickly pears (*Opuntia* spp.), organ pipe cactus (*Lemaireocereus thurberi*), saguaro (*Carnegiea gigantea*), smoke tree (*Dalea spinosa*), desert broom (*Baccharis sarothroides*), burro brush (*Hymenoclea monogyra*), ocotillo (*Fouquieria splendens*), brittle bush (*Encelia farinosa*), desert agave (*Agave desertii*), and sotol (*Dasylirian Wheeleri*).

What the Lower Colorado Valley lacks by way of perennial plants is sometimes compensated for in ephemerals, especially in herbaceous species. West of longitude 114°, in the extreme western Pimería Alta, these are likely to emerge in sandy soils after the late winter rains. Because summer rains are less dependable in this region, summer ephemerals are less likely to appear each year. East of longitude 114°, however, there is also a good possibility of summer ephemerals putting in their appearance. A list of these plants, many of them important food sources for *Homo sapiens*, is given by Shreve (Shreve and Wiggins, 1964, pp. 136–42). Lists of the remainder of the plants, including data on their distributions, can be found in Shreve and Wiggins (1964), Benson (1950), Benson and Darrow (1944), Kearney and Peebles (1960), and Simmons (1966).

d. Water. More or less permanent sources of water in western Pimería Alta are few and far between. The only "permanently flowing" stream in the entire region, excluding the boundary-defining Lower Gila and Colorado rivers, is the Sonoyta River in northwestern Sonora. To be more precise, the Colorado River is the sole permanent stream; both the Lower Gila and Sonoyta rivers are intermittent, flowing after rains, and interrupted, flowing over short lengths of their courses all year long.

The Sonoyta's water is provided by drainage from the Baboquivari and Quijotoa valleys coming across the Great Plain in ephemeral streams to join with similar ephemeral streams in Sonora, all emptying into the Sonoyta bed. Earlier in this century, the channel was dry except after floods and in the immediate neighborhood of Sonoita, Sonora, where a clear stream $\frac{1}{3}$ meter deep and 4 meters wide managed to flow (Bryan, 1925, pp. 119–120). Downstream from Sonoita, at Agua Salada, Agua Dulce, and El Carrizal, water could easily be found by digging in the channel. El Carrizal, in fact, had surface water in the early 18th century (Ives, 1964a, pp. 60–62). Even today much of the Sonoyta River Valley is a green, irrigated belt across an otherwise brown and forbidding-looking desert floor.

Besides ephemeral streams, the most important of which are San Cristobal Wash and Growler Wash, surface water in western Pimería Alta, discounting modern wells and represos made possible by industrial technology, is found in the form of springs, lakes and ponds, charcos, and rock tanks. There is a pond about 150 meters in diameter at Susuta, Sonora, 3 km south of the international boundary and at the eastern edge of western Pimería. There is another at Laguna Prieta in the Gran Desierto. A pond occasionally forms at Las Playas, a normally dry lake bed in the southern portion of the Cabeza Prieta Game Range. All these water sources depend on immediate rainfall (Bryan, 1925, pp. 121 and 335; Lumholtz, 1912, p. 246; Powell, 1966, pp. 67–69).

Charcos, which are defined here as natural water holes in adobe (clay) flats and washes, also depend on rainfall and ephemeral streamflow for their water. They occur sporadically in this dry western region.

Both fracture and fault springs give rise to the most reliable, year round water sources in Pimería. In the west, these include Agua Dulce Spring, a fracture spring on the southern slope of the Agua Dulce Mountains in Arizona; Quitobaquito, a fault spring in Organ Pipe National Monument in Arizona; Dripping Spring, a fracture spring also in Organ Pipe National Monument; Bullpasture, a small but permanent spring just beneath the Ajo Mountains on their west; Quitovac, Sonora, a series of small springs which emanate from the edge of a mesa-like deposit of calcareous matter; Dripping Springs at the north end of the Tinajas Altas Mountains; and the few springs at the head of the Gulf of California along the shores of Adair Bay, as at Pozo de Caballo and Salina Grande (Bryan, 1925, pp. 161–66; Ives, 1964a, p. 62; Lumholtz, 1912, p. 170; Simmons, 1965, pp. 37 and 40). Oral tradition indicates that there was until recently a fracture spring at Charlie Bell Well in the Growler Mountains, and the abundant evidence of former Indian occupation tend to bear this out.

The source of surface water most characteristic of this arid western zone, and that on which fauna relied perhaps more than any other, is the rock tank. According to Bryan (1925, p. 123): "A rock tank is a watering place consisting of a cavity or depression in rock which fills periodically with rain or flood water. Most Mexicans and many Americans use the Spanish word *tinaja,* meaning a bowl or jar, in speaking of a rock tank."

Although there are doubtless rock tanks in western Pimería Alta away from stream channels which hold water for a few hours or a few days after rains, even as there are "kiss" tanks—very shallow rock depressions in shaded places which collect dew condensation—the most important tinajas are found in stream channels (Bryan, 1925, pp. 123–35; Ives, 1962). Some of these natural catchments hold many hundreds of liters of water.

The largest rock tanks in this region, and therefore those most likely to have water in them most of the time, include the nine tinajas at the southern end of the Tinajas Altas Mountains, five tinajas in the Cabeza Prieta Mountains, Tule Tank in the Tule Mountains, Heart Tank in Arizona's Sierra Pinta, and Sheep Tank in the northern end of the Growler Mountains (Bryan, 1925, pp. 132–34; Simmons, 1965, pp. 39–43). Virtually the only sources of "permanent" water in the Sierra Pinacate, where there are no springs reported and whose waterways are strictly ephemeral, are the dozen or more rock tanks such as Tinajas de los Papagos, Tinaja del Tule, Tinajas de Emilia, Tinaja las Figuras, and Tinaja de Cuervo (Hayden, 1967, Fig. 1; Ives, 1964b, pp. 31–34). There are possible rock tanks elsewhere in northwestern Sonora, as in the Sierra del Cubabi and Sierra de San Francisco, but if so, they have not been reported in the literature (see Fig. 4).

e. Animal Life. The fauna of the region are ultimately limited in their potential ranges by the distribution of vegetation and surface water sources. The paucity of both in western Pimería Alta also presumably exercises a limiting factor on sizes of faunal populations. The area cannot

Fig. 4. A man stands next to the Heart Tank in the Sierra Pinta. Such *tinajas* are crucial water sources in western Pimería Alta. (Photograph by N. Simmons.)

be said to teem with wildlife, and at least one ecologist has argued "that the apparently rugged landscape of this arid area is by nature more delicately balanced between stability and deterioration than that of most such areas. The desert plants and animals are more highly specialized and easily destroyed" (Simmons, 1967, p. 133).

Although their ranges are to a certain extent related to immediate sources of food and water, the desert bighorn sheep (*Ovis canadensis*) and the kit fox (*Vulpes macrotis*), and the gray fox (*Urocyon cinereoargenteus*) show a decided preference for the bare rock slopes. They are by no means confined to this habitat, however, and desert bighorn sheep, capable of going without drinking water for more than 1 week, have been known to travel over successive valleys and ranges of mountains for more than 70 km (Simmons, 1965, p. 46; Simmons, 1967, pp. 131–32). The sheep, as well as bats (Chiroptera) and pack rats (*Neotoma* spp.), also like the shade and shelter provided by the many caves and rock shelters among the barren peaks.

The javelina, or wild pig (*Peccari tajacu*), roams the upper bajadas and shrub-lined washes, while the mule deer (*Odocoileus hemionus*), white-tailed deer (*Odocoileus virginianus*), and Sonoran pronghorn antelope

(*Antilocarpa americana sonorensis*) prefer the lower bajadas and inter-montane plains. They share this preference with the coyote (*Canis latrans*), antelope jackrabbit (*Lepus alleni*), blacktail jackrabbit (*Lepus californicus*), and bobcat (*Lynx rufus*). The spotted skunk (*Spilogale putorius*), badger (*Taxidea taxus*), various small rodents (Rodentia), in-cluding the kangaroo rat (*Dipodomys* spp.), the ringtail (*Bassariscus astutus yumanensis*), and most of the lizards and snakes (Reptilia), avoid the intense heat via their nocturnal habits or burrowing, or both (Simmons, 1965, p. 46). The desert cottontail (*Sylvilagus auduboni*), less common than the hares (*Lepus* spp.), shares this life pattern. There are dozens of other species of small mammals in western Pimería Alta, and their names and distributions are given by Cockrum (1960).

Bird life is reigned over by the golden eagle (*Aquila chrysaetos*). It is known to nest high in the Sierra Pinta in southern Arizona (Phillips *et al.*, 1964, p. 24), and I have seen one soaring above the Growler Moun-tains near Charlie Bell Well. Various ducks and geese (Anatidae) are seasonal migrants through the area, and a fair number of hawks (Ac-cipitrinae) and the white-necked raven (*Corvus cryptoleucus*) are regular residents. There are dozens of smaller species of birds which variously breed in, migrate through, reside in, or occasionally visit the Arizona por-tion of western Pimería Alta. Complete data are furnished by Phillips *et al.* (1964).

The bird story for northwestern Sonora is virtually the same except that Sonoran Pimería, unlike the Arizona portion, has a saltwater seacoast on the head of the Gulf of California. Here there are innumerable shore and sea birds, not to mention, of course, a rich fauna of fish, shellfish, sea turtles, and ocean-going mammals. There are also gray wolves (*Canis lupus*) in northwestern Sonora, and the mountain lion (*Felis concolor*) is an occasional visitor here as he is also in southwestern Arizona.

f. Summary. In a very general way, what can be said of the arid west of Pimería Alta is that its eastern and southern portions are wetter and cooler. Their valleys and mountains are higher and the bajadas are wider and less steep. The vegetation and fauna are more varied and more dense, and the possibilities of sustained life are greater than they are in the west and north. Even so, the region taken as a whole is still among the driest and hottest in North America.

2. Central Pimería Alta

The central portion of Pimería Alta is infinitely more hospitable to all forms of life than the arid west. It lies almost entirely within the Arizona Upland vegetational province of the Sonoran Desert; annual rainfall over the whole region is generally between 13 and 25 cm; the intermontane valleys and mountain ranges are higher; and, unlike western Pimería, parts of the central area climb into the Upper Sonoran life zone. Its boundaries are the Sauceda–Batamote–Redondo–Ajo mountains on the west; the Tucson–Sierrita–Cerro Colorado-Tumacacori–Atascosa–Pajarito mountains on the east; the Gila River on the north, excluding the river and flood plain; and the Río Magdalena and Río Concepción on the south, also excluding the rivers proper and their valleys (see Figs. 1 and 2).

  a. Climate. Rainfall throughout the region, like that in the west, is biseasonal, but here most of it falls during the summer monsoons. At Gu Vo, a Papago Indian village just east of the Ajo Mountains, the average annual rainfall is 22.4 cm, with 12.6 cm falling in the summer and 9.75 cm in the winter. At Sells, in the very heart of this more than 1,200,000 ha domain, the average annual rainfall is 25.2 cm, with 16.1 cm in summer and 9.16 cm during the comparatively more dry winter. At San Miguel, at the southern end of the Baboquivari Valley in Arizona, the annual average is 31.0 cm, two-thirds of it falling in summer and one-third in winter (Bryan, 1925, p. 38; Hackenberg, 1964a, p. 65). The Baboquivari Mountains are topped by the 2360-meter Baboquivari Peak, and in the upper reaches of such mountain ranges (including the Coyote and Quinlan mountains) the rainfall figure is more than 38 cm/year. Throughout the entire region the mean annual temperatures range from about 18° to 22°C (Hastings and Turner, 1965, p. 185). Disregarding extremes related to vertical heights of mountain ranges, the climate trends found in the Lower Colorado Valley continue in the Arizona Upland: from east to west it becomes more warm, less wet, and less likely to rain more in summer than in winter.

  b. Physiography. The physiography is still characteristic of the Desert Region of the Basin and Range Province, with its alternating mountain ranges and valleys, both increasing in altitude above sea level moving from west to east. Less that half the area is comprised of bajadas of low gradient or of intermontane plains, a marked contrast to the 85% of the Lower Colorado Valley typified by such topography. Moving from west to east, the major rows of mountains are the Sauceda–Batamote Redondo–Ajo ranges, the Sand Tank–Mesquite mountains, Table Top–Vekol–Quijotoa mountains, Tat Momoli–Santa Rosa–Comobabi–Artesa mountains, Silverbell–Roskruge–Coyote–Quinlan–Baboquivari mountains, and the eastern boundary cited above. Major intervening valleys are the Rainbow–Vekol and San Simon valleys, Santa Rosa–Gu Oidak–Tecolote valleys, Baboquivari Valley, and the Altar (Avra) Valley (see Fig. 2).

  Mountain slopes are less steep, pediments are wider, and the floors of valleys are less flat and more sloping, with the drainages in their centers more clearly demarked. Greater erosion of mountains, brought on by heavier rains, has done more to enrich the soil of bajadas and valleys, and rich alluvial fans have built up at the mouths of washes. Central Pimería Alta is devoid of dry lake beds and land-locked basins, and the greater rainfall and sloping plains ensure that the washes carry the water away rather than allowing it to settle, thus avoiding large accumulations of salts at the earth's surface. This is in spite of the fact that central Pimería also lacks perennial streams, and that all surface water flow tends to be interrupted, intermittent, and ephemeral. Drainage is into the Gila, Sonoyta, Altar, Magdalena, and San Miguel rivers.

c. Plant Life. Although most of the vegetation is characteristic of Shreve's Arizona Upland province, the Baboquivari Mountains and the area to the southeast of them actually lie beyond the Sonoran Desert altogether. The mountains here are within the Upper Sonoran life zone and have an evergreen–woodland vegetation (oak–juniper–piñon) and the valleys have an Upper Sonoran desert–grassland vegetation. Neither of these vegetation types is characteristic of a "true" desert (Lowe, 1964, pp. 36, 40–43, and 50–56).

The outstanding feature of Arizona Upland vegetation is that the foothill palo verde, chollas, and prickly pears tend to dominate the scene in place of creosote bush and bursage. This is also the heartland of the saguaro cactus; there are more, and larger, ironwoods, mesquites, and acacias; and other succulents, such as the barrel cactus (especially *Ferocactus wislizenii*), occur in comparative profusion. It is thus that the microphyllus desert (*Larrea–Franseria* region) of the Lower Colorado Valley becomes the crassicaulescent (stem succulent) desert (*Cercidium–Opuntia* region) in the Arizona Upland.

In the plains and lower bajadas of the Arizona Upland, the creosote bush continues to dominate, providing from 10 to 20% of the cover. Acacias, mesquites, and chollas are also found here, as are occasional isolated plants of ocotillo, saguaro, and barrel cactus. In the upper bajadas, which comprise half the intermontane plain area of this central region, is the largest number of perennials per unit area outside of Sonoran Desert flood plains. Creosote bush, palo verde, chollas, ocotillo, *Lycium,* gray thorn (*Condalia lycioides*), netleaf hackberry (*Celtis pallida*), and mesquite are the dominant plants, with jojoba (*Simmondsia chinensis*), saguaro, ironwood, barrel cactus, and Mexican crucillo (*Condalia spathulata*) playing a conspicuous role. Smaller perennials include bursage, brittlebush, fairy duster (*Calliandra eriophylla*), zinnia (*Z. grandiflora*), and bush muhly (*Muhlenbergia porteri*). Also not to be discounted are the Thornber, or banana yucca (*Yucca baccata*), mountain yucca (*Y. schottii*), small-flowered agave (*Agave parviflora*), desert agave (*A.*

desertii), Huachuca agave (*A. parryi* var. *huachucensis*), and mescal (*A. palmeri*). The last two species grow beyond the desert in the Upper Sonoran life zone (Shreve and Wiggins, 1964, pp. 68–77; Benson and Darrow, 1944, pp. 78 and 94). Other important plants in central Pimería Alta include the juniper (*Juniperus* spp.), oak (*Quercus* spp.), Mexican piñon (*Pinus cembroides*), Mexican tea (*Ephedra trifurca*), boundary ephedra (*E. nevadensis* var. *aspera*), beargrass (*Nolina microcarpa*), and the organ pipe cactus (*Lemaireocereus thurberi*) (see Fig. 1).

d. Water. The number of charcos and springs as sources of surface water is much larger in central Pimería Alta then it is in the west. Because of greater rainfall, increased runoff, and cooler temperatures, moreover, the charcos, the important water holes in the intermontane plains, are likely to retain water for longer periods of time. Rock tanks, although they occur here, are insignificant sources of water.

It can be stated, in general, that every major valley in this central region has its charcos, and that all of them are capable of holding water for periods of 1–3 months or more after the seasonal rains. Permanent springs, on the other hand, are confined to the foothills and mountains, with the flow in most of them increasing after rains. Not all these springs are plotted on maps; it is likely that every mountain range in central Pimería Alta has one or more springs. Important and better-known springs are in the Sand Tank Mountains at Mesquite Tank; at Sauceda; at Poso Verde in the Poso Verde Mountains in Sonora; in the Coyote Mountains, with two springs on the west slope and one on the east slope in Mendoza Canyon; at the village of Sil Nakya at the northeast end of the North Comobabi Mountains; in at least a dozen places on both slopes of the Baboquivari Mountains; and in at least a dozen additional places beyond the desert in the Tumacacori and adjacent mountains. Hackenberg (1964a, pp. 66–67) lists 44 "aboriginal" watering places for the Arizona portion of central Pimería Alta, and nearly all of these are springs or places dependent on spring water.

e. Animal Life. Except that western Pimería Alta has varieties of certain species of fauna that are peculiar to it and that the central region has no seacoast, the animal inventory for·both areas is essentially the same. The crucial difference between them lies in population sizes: central Pimería has more wildlife. Mule and white-tailed deer which are infrequent in the western desert are found commonly scattered in the region to its east. Desert bighorn sheep are today rare in the central area, presumably having been decimated by firearms-using *Homo sapiens,* but there is no reason to believe that they were formerly less abundant here than elsewhere. The same situation prevails with respect to the Sonoran pronghorn antelope.

f. Summary. In summary, central Pimería Alta witnesses a continuation of climatic and topographic trends already described for the arid west. It has a greater variety of vegetation and there is more of it. Water is more readily available both in springs and as a result of rainfall and lower evaporation rates, and the fauna, except for that characteristic of ocean and seashore, is more abundant. Even so, there are no perennial streams, and running water, except in the immediate vicinity of springs, is wholly dependent on the biseasonal rains.

3. The Riverine Perimeters

The southern, eastern, and northern boundaries of Pimería Alta are marked by perennial streams. About 1700, these were the Middle and Lower Gila River on the north, the parallel-running San Pedro and Santa Cruz rivers on the east in Arizona, the Río San Miguel on the east in Sonora, and the Río Magdalena and Río Concepción—which would be regarded as a single stream in the United States—on the south in Sonora. There may have been a few Upper Piman settlements between the Río Magdalena–Concepción and Río Sonora, but these are not well documented for this early, "aboriginal" period. A fifth river of considerable importance, and one which marks the approximate western limit of riverine-dwelling Pimans, should the Río Sonoyta be momentarily excluded from consideration, is the Río Altar in northern Sonora.

Of these rivers, the Middle and Lower Gila, the Altar, the Magdalena–Concepción, the San Miguel, and more than two-thirds the length of the Santa Cruz lie within the Sonoran Desert. All are in Arizona Upland except the Middle and Lower Gila and the Concepción, which are in the Lower Colorado Valley vegetation province. The only part of the San Pedro inhabited by Pimans, the middle portion, lies wholly within desert–grassland habitat beyond the Sonoran Desert. A small part of the Santa Cruz is in oak woodland in the vicinity of the international boundary.

According to Shreve, "The alluvial flood plains of the Arizona Upland are one of the most favorable desert environments with respect to water supply and depth and texture of soil" (Shreve and Wiggens, 1964, p. 79). This remark may be extended to include parts of the Middle Gila as well.

The water in these rivers comes largely from drainage off the surrounding mountains through which they pass. This is particularly the case with the Gila, which is ultimately the drainage for much of central and southern Arizona. Both the San Pedro and Santa Cruz empty into it, while the Altar runs into the Gulf of California-bound Río Concepción. The San Miguel, on the other hand, empties into the Río Sonora, even as the Gila empties into the Colorado River. The water which remains after transpiration, irrigation, absorption, and evaporation have taken their toll eventually arrives to lose its potability in the Gulf of California.

a. Climate. Rainfall at various points on or near these rivers is generally greater than elsewhere in Pimería Alta, especially in the east. Tucson, which is on the Santa Cruz River at an elevation of 721 meters, gets a mean summer rainfall of 16.2 cm and a winter rain of 12.5 cm, for an average annual total of 28.7 cm. Magadalena, Sonora, which is on the Río Magdalena, gets 42.1 cm of rain per year, while Nogales, midway between Magdalena and Tucson, has an annual mean of 41.1 cm. Caborca, Sonora, in the Lower Colorado Valley vegetation zone and downstream from Magdalena below the junction of the Río Altar and Río Magdalena, gets a fairly scant 18.5 cm/year, a situation comparable to that of Phoenix, Arizona, a short distance north of the Gila and which gets 19.1 cm/year. Farther down the Gila, at Gila Bend, the annual rainfall figure drops to 15.3 cm. At Casa Grande and Maricopa, both somewhat south of the Middle Gila, the annual totals are 16.7 and 17.2 cm, respectively (Bryan, 1925, pp. 34–40; Hackenberg, 1964a, p. 135; Hastings and Humphrey, 1969b, pp. 8 and 19). Temperature trends are the same, with some of the riverine sections of Pimería Alta, even discounting adjacent mountains, being the coolest in the entire region.

b. Physiography. Riverine Pimería Alta, like the rest of it, lies within the Basin and Range physiographic province, but the San Pedro and parts of the Santa Cruz and San Miguel Rivers lie in the Mountain Region rather than in the Desert Region. The highest point of the Catalina Mountains, which rise between the Santa Cruz and San Pedro, is the 2790-meter Mount Lemmon. And Mount Wrightson (Old Baldy) in the Santa Rita Mountains, also between these two rivers, looms to 2880 meters above sea level. The transition life-zone (pine forest) and the Canadian life-zone (Douglas fir forest) are represented in the upper reaches of several of these ranges (Lowe, 1964, pp. 63–73). The river valleys themselves are higher above sea level in their upper reaches than intermontane plains elsewhere in Pimería Alta. The Santa Cruz and San Pedro are inclined from south to north; the San Miguel from northeast to southwest; and the Gila and Magdalena–Concepción generally from east to west.

c. Plant Life. The vegetation along the banks and margins of streamways, as well as in their surrounding flood plains, is the most dense and supports the largest specimens of species common to the Sonoran Desert and its immediate surrounds. Mesquite, ironwood, palo verde, and acacias are larger in these river valleys than elsewhere in Pimería Alta, and it is in the canyons of the neighboring mountains, except those of the Middle and Lower Gila, that at least four species of oak trees are common as well as cottonwood (*Populus fremontii*), Goodding willow (*Salix gooddingii*), velvet ash (*Fraxinus velutina* var. *toumeyi*), walnut (*Juglans major*), Arizona sycamore (*Platanus wrightii*), and Mexican elder (*Sambucus mexicana*). Other trees, shrubs, and perennials characteristic of these river valleys are listed by Shreve (Shreve and Wiggins, 1964, pp. 77–80). Nor are these valleys without their cacti, including both prickly pears and chollas (*Opuntia* spp.) as well as the saguaro (chiefly in Arizona) and organ pipe (chiefly in Sonora).

d. Water. With respect to availability of surface water, all these rivers have more water in them during and after the summer and winter precipitation seasons. At certain seasons all also have dry stretches in them, more so today, in fact, than 250 years ago. Changes in climate, changes brought about by *Homo sapiens,* and changes effected by the introduction of cattle have in the past 70 or 80 years brought about channel cutting and erosion and a depletion, by diversion or otherwise, in the amount of water running throughout the entire courses of these streams. In 1700, they were more shallow—even surface-flowing in many places—and less intermittent and interrupted than they are today [see Hastings and Turner (1965) for an analysis of the entire problem].

Because the rivers themselves supply—or, at least, formerly supplied—surface water, ephemeral tributaries, rock tanks, springs, and charcos were of correspondingly less importance to the maintenance of life.

e. Animal Life. The river valleys and surrounding mountains also were the habitats for heavy concentrations of wildlife (see Cockrum, 1960). The word "were" has to be used because these same valleys are today those which support the densest populations of *Homo sapiens,* a mammal not presently noted for living in a harmonious ecological balance with other fauna. The wildlife in these valleys and mountains about 1700 was essentially the same as that found in the central area, except that black bear (*Euarctos americanus*), coati (*Nasua narica*), porcupine (*Erethizon dorsatum*), raccoon (*Procyon lotor*), and possibly the American bison (*Bison bison*) should be added to the list. The mountain lion and white-tailed deer are also more common to these regions, with the exception of the Lower and Middle Gila again. This is also the case with the gray wolf. The muskrat (*Ondatra zibethicus*) and beaver (*Castor canadensis*) are native to both the San Pedro and Middle Gila rivers.

As even a cursory glance at the distribution maps in Phillips *et al.* (1964) will indicate, bird life along the streamways is infinitely richer and more diverse here than elsewhere in Pimería Alta. The presence of water and protective vegetation in these valleys and their tributaries, not to mention increased sources of food from vegetation and insects, make the riverine systems of this region the most attractive of its areas insofar as birds are concerned.

Not surprisingly, the riverine perimeters of Pimería Alta were also the home of several species of freshwater fishes. These included Colorado chub (*Gila robusta*), Sonora chub (*Gila ditaenia*), Colorado squawfish (*Ptychocheilus lucius*), speckled dace (*Rhinichthys osculus*), longfin dace (*Agosia chrysogaster*), loach minnow (*Tiaroga cobitis*), Mexican stoneroller (*Campostoma ornatum*), spikedace (*Meda fulgida*), Sonora sucker (*Catostomus insignis*), Yaqui sucker (*Catostomus bernardini*), Gila sucker (*Pantosteus clarki*), humpback sucker (*Xyrauchen texanus*), desert pupfish (*Cyprinodon macularius*) which is also found at Quitobaquito in western Pimería Alta, and the Gila topminnow (*Poeciliopsis occidentalis*). The checklist of fishes is provided by Miller and Lowe (Lowe, 1964, pp. 133–151; see also Chapter VII of this volume).

Finally, a great many amphibians and reptiles are also common to these riverine areas, as they are elsewhere in Pimería Alta (see Lowe, 1964, pp. 153–174; Mayhew, 1968, Chapter VI, Volume I of this treatise).

f. Summary. The most important environmental consideration to be made concerning the riverine perimeter of Pimería Alta is water itself. It is the comparative permanence of flowing surface water and the greater precipitation in higher mountain slopes which contribute to the greater abundance of animal and plant life in this generally arid region, only a small part of which is beyond the Sonoran Desert.

III. Piman Indians

The Piman Indians of northern Sonora and southern Arizona are today divided into two groups: the Pima Indians, whose homes are on the Gila River and Salt River reservations near Phoenix, Arizona; and the Papago Indians, who live on the San Xavier, Gila Bend, Ak Chin, and Papago reservations in southern Arizona, as well as in a few scattered settlements in northern Sonora. This is to say nothing, of course, of the many Pimas and Papagos who live off-reservation in non-Indian society, especially in the metropolitan centers of Phoenix and Tucson.

When first seen by Europeans in the late 17th and early 18th centuries, these Pimans, or groups of them, were variously referred to as Pimas, Sobaipuris, Sobas, Papabotes, Papagos, or Gileños, the last being a term restricted to Piman Indians who lived in the Gila River Valley. None of these terms were used by Pimans to refer to themselves or to one another. Their universal appellation for themselves was, and is, *o-otam,* which translated means something like, "we, the people."

The literature concerning Piman Indians is extensive, but as noted above, very little of it bears directly upon the relationships between these particular groups of *Homo sapiens* and the rest of their environment. Unpublished claims case reports by Hackenberg (1964a) and Fontana (1964), written solely in connection with the Papago Indians of southern Arizona, provide the most notable exceptions.

To arrive at an understanding of the aboriginal, or pre-European circumstance of Piman Indian culture, it has been necessary to draw upon accounts of these Indians written by non-Indians who saw them in the late 1600's and throughout the 1700's, years during which their native culture was presumably less affected by European contact than it came to be in the following century and a half. It has further been necessary to rely on ethnographic data collected almost entirely during the present century and by analogy and extrapolation to turn the culture clock backward, as it were, to surmise what the Piman "native" state of existence may have been. Such a procedure assumes that in the last half of the 1800's and almost until now there have been certain features, at least, of Piman culture which have survived—in memory and in oral tradition if not in living reality—since aboriginal times. This is clearly a bold assumption to make, but within bounds and in combination with other kinds of data, I believe it can be a correct one. And finally, there is a limited amount of information from archaeological sources upon which to draw.

Although the primary historical sources describing Piman Indians at the time of European contact and for 100 years afterward number in the many dozens, only a few of them are absolutely basic and continue to be those relied upon by scholars interested in the ethnohistory of these peoples. These are the works by Bolton (1930, 1948, 1960), Coues (1900), Garcés (1965), Manje (1954), Nentvig (1951), Pfefferkorn (1949), Treutlein (1945), and Wyllys (1931). All these sources are either by or about Jesuit and Franciscan missionaries with the exception of the accounts of Manje (1954) and Juan Bautista de Anza (cited in Bolton, 1930), both of whom were soldiers.

Similarly, there are dozens of ethnographic reports—as well as modern economic, demographic, linguistic, medical, and physiological studies—concerning Pimans, but only a handful are basic to an attempted reconstruction of aboriginal Piman life. These are the works by Castetter and Bell (1942), Castetter and Underhill (1935), Childs (1954), Ezell (1961), Hackenberg (1964b), Hoover (1935b), Jones (1962), Joseph *et al.* (1949), Lumholtz (1912), Nolasco A. (1965), Underhill (1936, 1938, 1939, 1946), and Russell (1908).

The only major archaeological work in Piman sites—and one of these may well not be Piman at all—has been done by Di Peso (1953, 1956).

The putative picture of native Piman culture drawn below is based on these sources, on my own ethnographic and archaeological field studies, and on other references as cited.

A. Western Nomads

On February 15, 1694, the Jesuit priests Eusebio Francisco Kino and Marcos Antonio Kappus, with a military escort commanded by Ensign Juan Mateo Manje, were traveling in northwestern Sonora very close to the Gulf of California. They ". . . came upon some squaws who were filling some *tinajas* [earthenware jars] with water from a small water hole. . . . The Indians went about naked, covering their bodies only with small pieces of hare furs. . . . We gave them a supply of food since they were poor and hungry, living on roots, locusts and shell fish." And later, on March 20, 1694, we learn of Indians in the same vicinity who were ". . . poor people who lived by eating roots of wild sweet potatoes, honey, mesquite beans and other fruits. They traveled about naked; only the women had their bodies half covered with hare furs" (Manje, 1954, pp. 14, 17, and 30).

In these words, Manje gives the first written description available of Indians whom the Spaniards called "Sobas," and who came in later times to be known more commonly as "Sand Papagos." These Piman-speaking Indians, who probably never numbered more than 500 men, women, and children, wrested a livelihood from the arid west of Pimería Alta by hunting wild game, collecting plants and insects, gathering shellfish and other seafoods from the Gulf of California, and by trading ceremonies and salt gathered from salt deposits at the head of the Gulf for food and earthenware pottery with the Yuman-speaking Cocopas who lived adjacent to the Lower Colorado River and its delta.

These Pimans were true nomads. They had no fixed village locations; "home" was much of the Lower Colorado Valley. Divided into an undetermined number of bands comprised of members of extended families, the band size was probably never much larger than 80 or 90 people at most, and then only under optimum conditions, as when people could congregate at a ripe food source. One band, the so-called Pinacateños, had its principal "headquarters" near rock tanks in the Sierra del Pinacate where in 1701 the Spaniards ". . . counted 50 persons, poor and naked people, who sustain themselves by roots, locusts and lizards, which they call iguanas [Iguanidae, probably *Dipsosaurus dorsalis*], and some fish" (Manje, 1954, p. 160; Hayden, 1967, p. 341).

The sparseness of vegetation and other fauna made it necessary for

Homo sapiens to range throughout western Pimería Alta in a continual search for foods on which they depended. They wandered from place to place in seasonal cycles, but always within the limits of the same huge area, one bounded by the Lower Gila River, the Lower Colorado River, the Ajo Mountains, and the Río Concepción.

1. Food and Drink

Probably the mainstays in the diet of Sand Papagos were sea foods, reptiles, insects, and small mammals, especially jackrabbits (*Lepus* spp.). When the full moon changed to a new moon and the tides of the Gulf of California were consequently at their highest, the Indians waited with spears in hand for the tide to roar in. Onrushing waters brought with them large fish chasing smaller ones, and when the tide broke and receded, these fish were left stranded in shallow pools of water on the beach. Sometimes they were stranded in low stone enclosures built as traps. Papagos speared the big fish with the tail bone of a barbed stingaree (*Dasyatis* spp.) hafted to a small willow branch. The prey were strung on a rope until the fisherman had all he could carry. These were taken to camp to be distributed and eaten, the camp usually being situated immediately next to the line of high tide.

Shellfish, especially the easy-to-catch clams, were eaten in abundance, and occasionally, if the tides were low enough, the Indians could make their way to coral reefs to catch oysters. Because they built no boats or rafts, they had to wade to the oyster beds.

Sea foods, which included sea turtle in addition to fish, shrimps, clams, and oysters, were eaten both fresh and dried. Dried fish and shrimp were put up in little cakes, in which form the food lasted longer and could be easily carried.

Land animals hunted in addition to rabbits were the mountain sheep, deer, antelope, small rodents, and various lizards. Papagos also ate various insects, including the larva of the white-lined sphinx moth (*Celerio lineata*). Buzzards, hawks, and eagles were tabooed for food, but the latter were prized for their feathers. Quail, and probably doves, were eaten, and the former were trapped in a simple saguaro rib box propped up by a stick, taken live when the waiting Indian pulled a string attached to the prop.

Hunting was usually done with a bow and arrow and by stealth. A hunter would sit quietly at some mountain spot until eventually a curious mountain sheep would approach within easy shooting range. Once killed, the sheep's horns were removed and added to a pile of horns taken in a similar fashion. This resulted in several shrine-like piles of horns of desert bighorn sheep scattered throughout western Pimería Alta.

Antelope and deer were tracked for many kilometers, and when an animal lay down, the tracker, too, would drop from view to the ground. This was kept up until the hunter was able to walk up on the lying prey and shoot it. In a similar way, Papagos stalked rabbits in the sand until the latter became exhausted. Pack rats and other rodents were caught by burning them out of their nests where they were hidden in rock crevices surrounded by spines of cholla cactus.

The list of plant foods gathered by these western nomads is long, but chief among them were the beans of ironwood, mesquite, palo verde, and acacias; buds of certain chollas; the fruit of saguaro, organ pipe, desert-thorn (*Lycium* spp.), and prickly pears; the caudex and stem of the desert agave; the stem of the sand root (*Ammobroma sonorae*) and the stalks and seeds of careless weed (*Amaranthus palmeri*); and various parts of other plants, including the blue bell (*Brodiaea capitata*), lambsquarter (*Chenopodium murale*), patata (*Monolepsis nuttalia*), sundrop (*Oenothera trichocalyx*), barrel cactus, sage (*Salvia columbariae*), and desert lavender (*Hyptis emoryi*).

These foods were prepared in various ways: roasting, drying, boiling, powdering, and mixing in water. Some were eaten raw. Wine was made from fermented saguaro fruit syrup; fruits of organ pipe were converted to jam.

Lacking the technology and kinds of tools which would enable them to drill deep wells or to convert salt water to potable water, western Papagos had to develop an intensive knowledge of the kinds and locations of natural surface water sources in this exceptionally arid land. That they succeeded is attested to in the many kilometers of desert footpaths which link the springs and rock tanks together and which can be seen even today. It is near these water sources, moreover, that the material evidence of Piman wanderers remains: bits of broken pottery, worked stone, and ground seashells.

2. Clothing, Tools, and Shelter

Although the Sand Papagos may have appeared "naked" to an over-dressed Spaniard in the late 17th century, these Indians did, in fact, wear clothes. The men wore breech cloth, sandals, and very often a shirt. The women wore hide skirts which reached to their knees in addition to sandals. They were otherwise bare from the waist up.

Sandals were made from hide, at times from the hides of sea lions killed where they rested on shoreline rocks along the Gulf of California. Women's skirts, and probably men's breech cloths, were tanned hides of rabbit, antelope, deer, or mountain sheep. Hair was scraped from the hide either with bone from the animal's foreleg or with whale rib found lying on the beach. The skin was smeared with animals brains, trained in the root of torote (*Jatropha canascens*) which had been crushed and left in water, and softened finally by rubbing with a smooth stone. The skirts were made of fringes hanging down from buckskin waist straps, and occasionally they were painted red or orange with mineral or vegetal dyes. The men plaited badger's hair to make twine to hold up their breech cloths and to make ribbons for their own hair.

Tools of these nomads included bows fashioned from desert willow growing along stream beds; arrows of arrowweed (*Pluchea sericea*) plumed with hawk feathers; carrying nets of twined string; earthenware pottery, virtually all of which was obtained in trade with Yuman Indians; gourd water containers; baskets made of torote, willow, and other plants; the harpooned fishing spear; stone grinding tools, including slab grinder, handstone, and mortar and pestle; and stone projectile points. The far-reaching western Papagos were not overburdened during their lengthy foot travels by too much material culture. Much of what they had, moreover, could be safely cached near where it was needed and left until the owners returned.

The "houses" of these nomads were merely crude stone corrals or stone sleeping circles. They were rings of medium-sized rocks, the cobbles being stacked one or two courses high. Openings, when there were any, were away from the prevailing wind. The Indians placed uprooted clumps of grass against the rocks of these unroofed shelters for additional protection against the wind. Much of the time, indeed, people simply slept on leveled ground in the open, retreating to shelters only in cold or windy emergencies.

3. Relations with Other Homo sapiens

Judging from all accounts, the western Papagos were a tough and quarrelsome lot. As early as the 1680's they had fought with, and killed, riverine-dwelling Piman Indians who apparently had invaded their territory (Bolton, 1948, Vol. 1, pp. 123–124), and in about 1850 Papagos from the desert to the east were given an unfriendly reception by them (Hayden, 1967, p. 341). One traveler early in the 20th century said these sand people were ". . . rapacious and probably merciless to strangers, whether Indian or Mexican" (Lumholtz, 1912, p. 329).

What good relations they had with other *Homo sapiens* seem to have been with the Cocopas living on the Lower Colorado River. In return for pottery and agricultural products, the Sand Papagos danced and sang for the Cocopas, and they brought them salt and seashells.

The western nomads, unlike the remaining Pimans, have today disappeared as cultural entities. Many of them died of yellow fever about 1851;

others were killed by Mexicans and Anglo-American visitors to their territory; and the remainder wandered off to become assimilated with other Indians or to lose themselves in non-Indian towns and mining camps during the second half of the 19th century. One Pinacateño hermit, Juan Caravajales, survived in the Sierra del Pinacate until the second decade of the present century, and it is possible that Piman-speaking Indians living at Dome, Arizona, today are Sand Papago descendants (Hayden, 1967, pp. 341–342; Vivian, 1965, pp. 125–126). In point of fact, however, with the passing of these hardy people the North American Continent had seen the last of its truly nomadic *Homo sapiens*.

B. ARENEÑOS

Although frequently grouped with the Sand Papagos in various historical and ethnographic accounts, the term *Areneños* should most probably be preserved for those Piman Indians in southwestern Arizona and northwestern Sonora who lived part of the year and farmed along the Sonoyta River or next to the few large springs in the region capable of supporting agriculture. Their habitations were less permanently fixed than those of Pimans living in Pimería Alta's major riverine valleys, and at the very best their farming supplemented in only a small way food garnered by hunting, gathering, and collecting. The major settlements of these people, those at Quitobaquito and Sonoita, were along the Lower Colorado Valley–Arizona Upland vegetation province boundary, just inside the latter on its west. Areneños, besides practicing a small amount of irrigation along the Sonoyta River and at Quitobaquito, also carried on *temporale* farming, dependent on flood waters in usually dry arroyos, somewhere west of the Sierra del Pinacate, along San Cristóbal Wash, on the western fringe of what is now Organ Pipe National Monument, in the valley just east of the Growler Mountains, and probably at other locations lost to history. And if their modern-day presence means anything, beans (*Phaseolus wrightii*) and teparies (*Phaseolus acutifolius*) at Agua Dulce Spring (Simmons, 1966, p. 101) may formerly have been planted there by these Indians.

Except that they farmed, raising cucurbits (gourds, pumpkins, squash, and melons), beans (*Phaseolis* spp.), and corn (*Zea mays*); made their own earthenware pottery and were only seasonally nomadic in a more restricted area, the Areneños were very much like the Sand Papagos in other respects. Both groups utilized much the same wild plant and animal resources; both apparently availed themselves of the Gulf of California and its marine fauna. Trade, on the other hand, seems to have been with other Piman Indians rather than with the Yumans.

Fig. 5. Sil Nakya village in the heart of central Pimería Alta is a typical winter or "well" village of Papago indians, a living survivor of the old two-village system of Arizona upland adaptation.

Data concerning the Areneño are best summarized in Childs (1954), Hayden (1967), and Thomas (1953).

C. TWO-VILLAGE PEOPLE

When the early Spaniard or the modern geographer says "Papago Indian," he is most likely referring to a member of any of a number of extended family–village groups whose aboriginal range was in that portion of the Arizona Upland vegetation province devoid of perennial streams. They were "two-village" people in that they maintained winter habitations in the mountain foothills next to permanent springs of water as well as summer habitations in the intermontane plains where they farmed after the June–July–August rains had enriched their fields. This seasonal migration pattern, from summer-field to winter-mountain spring and back again, is one called transhumance, and it was at the core of the way of life of more than 4000 Piman-speaking Indians at the onset of the historic period (see Fig. 5).

1. Food and Drink

Before the coming of white man to their country, these two-village peoples, or central Papagos, probably raised about one-fifth of their total food supply on 0.1–1 ha family-sized farm plots. Hunting, gathering, and trading provided the rest of their subsistence.

The planting of native crops, corn (maize), beans, and cucurbits, was done by the men just after the onset of summer rains. There was but a single planting period and a single crop each year.

As soon as it rained hard enough to put water in valley charcos and to flood the ground plain at the mouths of arroyos, Papago men and older children went to the fields. Seeds were dropped in holes made with digging sticks and dirt was then scraped over the hole with the feet. During the rainy season Papagos attempted to control the distribution of water in the valley fields by judicious placing of low embankments, brush dikes, and short and shallow ditches. The idea was to keep crops well watered until they began to set fruit.

The harvest usually got underway in October and November. This was women's work. Crops were variously eaten or stored, and the families remained in the valleys either until the water had dried in the charcos or until the food supply became exhausted.

As for hunting and gathering, the inventory is the same as that for western Papagos, except that more plants and animals were at hand—more individual specimens and more species. These included a few nondesert foods, such as acorns from the oak forests. Relatively full descriptions of the variety of plants and animals taken by Papagos and the many uses to which they were put are found in Castetter and Underhill (1935). Interestingly enough, the central Papagos, like all Upper Pimans, seem to have eschewed high mountain summits and slopes except for ceremonial purposes. Their world was that of the Lower Sonoran and Upper Sonoran life zones in the lower altitudes. They were truly a desert people.

2. Tools, Shelter, and Village Organization

The list of material possessions of the central Papagos was not unlike that of the Piman-speaking natives to the west. The differences were generally in quantity rather than in kind. Clothing, ornaments, hair style, body painting, and tattooing of all Papagos were essentially the same. Central Papagos had more tools, especially those associated with farming and food preparation and storage. They made a wide variety of earthenware vessels for specific purposes even as they made many styles of baskets.

The most noteworthy addition of material culture was the brush house, a dome-shaped structure made with mesquite supports and covered with branches or grass, especially with sacaton (*Sporobolus* spp.). These houses, moreover, were arranged in village clusters. Although the houses were often widely separated from one another, they nonetheless formed villages called "rancherías" by the Spaniards. Village members were con-

nected either by blood or marriage, and when a village became too large
to be supported by its local resources, a group of its residents would leave
to found a related village in another location. The result was that throughout central Pimería Alta there were groups of geographically separated,
but related winter villages whose members would usually farm the same
valley drainages during the summer. There were about a dozen such related
village groups in aboriginal times, and their members spoke about a half-
dozen different dialects of the Piman language. Each major or parent village had its recognized headman and its council of village elders. Govern-
ing was strictly by consent of all the governed; no one had autocratic
powers. Above all, there was no central or binding authority among members of all these village clusters, no "chief" of all the Papagos. Kinsmen
attended their own affairs.

3. Relations with Neighbors

The two-village people seem to have gotten along with one another
rather well. People from unrelated villages often met on ceremonial occasions, as at great intervillage games and contests whose sanctions were
chiefly religious. During those times of year when farming was not being
done or when hunting and gathering might be slack, the central Papagos
traveled far and wide, especially visiting among riverine-dwelling Pimans.
It appears, in fact, that in some years Papagos forsook their own fields
to labor for Pimans living on the Gila and Santa Cruz. They got along
well with Areneños, but seem to have had little intercourse with Yumans
or Sand Papagos. Their most deadly enemies were the nomadic and
marauding Apaches.

D. RIVERINE PIMANS

The largest villages of Piman Indians were situated in the fertile valleys
of the riverine system forming three-fourths of the perimeter of Pimería
Alta. The people living here were called "Pimas" and "Sobaipuris" by the
early Spaniards. The villages were fairly permanently fixed in their locations—discounting the fact that people might move from one side of a
river to the other should a flood or death of an important person occasion
it—and village residents were permanent. Sometimes people would sleep
next to their fields for convenience, but the fields of a village were seldom
much more than 1 km from one's house. It was, in short, along the perennial streams that Piman life assumed its most anchored form.

Crops, except for the addition of cotton (*Gossypium* spp.), were the
same as those grown in central Pimería Alta. The planting and cultivation
of crops, relying more on ditches and irrigated fields than the flash-flood

Fig. 6. Aerial view of the Santa Cruz Valley village of Bac. This Piman riverine settlement continues to rely in part on irrigation agriculture for its economy. In 1690, it was the largest settlement in southern Arizona. (Photograph by R. Sense.)

farming to the west, required a fairly complex organization of manpower and division of labor. This seems to have reached its zenith among the Pimas of the Middle Gila River.

San Xavier del Bac, a Sobaipuri settlement and the largest village in Pimería Alta at the opening of the historic period, had over 800 inhabitants. Other villages along the San Pedro, Santa Cruz, Middle Gila, San Miguel, Magdalena, Concepión, and Altar rivers varied in size from 20 to 50 houses and from 100 to 600 men, women, and children. The houses, oval and made of mesquite and brush, were often covered with plaited mats (see Fig. 6).

Generally, these riverine Pimans also had to supplement farming with hunting and gathering—and with fishing—but to a lesser degree than other Indians of Pimería. The hunting and gathering resources were the richest in the desert. The clothing, ornaments, baskets, pottery, and tools of these Pimans; their religious beliefs and ceremonies; their social organization; and their music and oral traditions were in all likelihood so much like those of other Pimans that they could not easily be distinguished in kind. On the other hand, greater supplies of food and larger and permanent villages suggest that political and economic organization within the settlements was more detailed. There was more leisure time among these Pimas and Sobaipuris with a consequently greater number of part-time specialists at certain trades and a greater production of goods. Permanent streams also afforded the main routes of travel through the Sonoran Desert, and villages along the way were more likely to be centers of trade and commerce than villages elsewhere. Greater wealth resulting from all this was reflected in more and fancier clothing—including that of locally grown cotton—and in turquoise and shell ornaments.

The riverine peoples were decidedly the aristocrats among the Pimans. "The character of these Indians," wrote a Spanish missionary ". . . is haughty and proud, a fact which can be recognized in the manner in which they talk—with little esteem—about those Indians of the west. These western Indians [Papagos], either because of being less haughty or because of some other motive, consider them superior and look up to them with special respect" (Manje, 1954, p. 242).

IV. Conclusions

The important lesson to be learned from glimpsing the role of aboriginal Piman Indians in the Sonoran Desert is not a new one. It is, however, one that needs ever to be reiterated. It is simply that man is part of the living fauna, and as such he interacts with other fauna, with plants, with climate, and with physiography in ways that are indispensable to his life. So interconnected are *Homo sapiens* and his environment, indeed, that whether one begins with rainfall, rabbits, or mountain gradient to tell the story, the choice is purely arbitrary.

Nor is the Piman case a study in environmental determinism. There were food taboos imposed by cultural traditions rather than by edibility of certain plants and animals; resources available in life zones above the Upper Sonoran were not exploited; and there is nothing in the riverine and central Pimería habitat which indicates that *Homo sapiens* has to farm. Indeed, the riverine peoples could just as well have been comparatively wealthy hunters and gatherers had they chosen.

The fact is, however, that the pre-Hispanic period Piman Indians of the Sonoran Desert, using tools which could be fashioned from regional subenvironments within the desert, worked their habitat to the limits of the technology thus provided. For example, once given the tradition of living in the Lower Colorado Valley—whatever the first reasons may have been—Pimans utilizing this ecological niche were of necessity nomadic wanderers. The lack of surface water made farming and fixed habitations an impossibility.

Similarly, the two-village people practiced what agriculture was possible within the limits of their technology and with the lack of perennial streams within their domain. And the riverine peoples, who were able to plant the biggest crops, were also able to plant the biggest and most permanent villages. Added to this was the successively greater abundance in wild plant and animal resources moving from west toward east and into the river vally perimeters.

There is perhaps another lesson to be learned here, one that is still vague and considerably more abstract. This stems from observations made as early as the mid-1890's (McGee, 1895) to very recent times that: "In arid regions there has been much less competition [among plants]. The greatest 'struggle' of the plants has not been with one another, but with the environment. Therefore the conditions tending toward the elimination of certain types and the survival and dominance of a relatively uniform one have not been operative" (Shreve and Wiggins, 1964, p. 27). This view has been echoed recently by another botanist, who writes, ". . . thus far all information reported indicates that there is among individual plants no competition which regulates the composition of the desert flora, but that it rather is the growth regulation independent of the neighboring plants of different species" (Went, 1969, p. 230).

In short, cooperation rather than competition seems to be a key word in the understanding of desert plant communities, and if my reading of Piman history and ethnography is correct, the Pimans, as another part of the desert fauna, seem to have understood this well. They used their environment but never usurped it.

The Spaniards, and ultimately other non-Indians of European extraction, introduced innumerable changes among Pimans. Cattle, horses, goats, and sheep were brought in; wheat became an important crop; and money supplanted salt and ceremonial songs as a medium of exchange. A whole new technology based in the final analysis on coal and iron, neither of which is native to the Sonoran Desert, made it possible to tap deep supplies of underground fossil water, to build all-weather roads, and to make gasoline-powered transportation on them the mode of the day.

But Piman origins are not altogether lost in this great desert. Tucson, Phoenix, Caborca, and Magdalena—the largest urban centers in southern Arizona and northern Sonora—are riverine settlements which, save for Phoenix, were once Piman villages. Tucson and Caborca, indeed, are Piman-derived words, as is "Arizona." The railroads and superhighways which link these cities follow the river-paralleling routes used for many millenia.

The central area of Pimería today belongs to Papago and Mexican cattlemen, and in spite of deep wells and a cash economy, the region remains strangely dependent on rainfall for the well-being of many of its human citizens. As for western Pimería Alta, vast reaches once walked over by Pimans are today totally uninhabited save for an occasional hunter or rock collector or desert sightseer bounding along in his four-wheel drive vehicle. Only Ajo, because of a copper mine, and Puerto Peñasco, because of commercial fishing and the attraction of the Gulf of California to Arizona residents, now stand where no permanent settlements stood before.

The final lesson of which we need be reminded is that modern *Homo sapiens* has neither conquered nor cooperated with his desert environment. He has "adapted" to it, unlike his Piman forebears, only by importing a whole economy and technology based on material goods that are native to environments elsewhere in the world. This is a fact whose implications need to be better understood if we are to cope with man's present and future in arid lands.

REFERENCES

Adolph, E. F. (1947). "Physiology of Man in the Desert." Wiley (Interscience), New York.

Aschmann, H. (1959). The central desert of Baja California. *Ibero-Americana* **42.**

Bell, W. H., and Castetter, E. F. (1937). The aboriginal utilization of tall cacti in the American Southwest. *Univ. N. Mex. Bull.,* **307,** Biol. Ser. Vol. 5, No. 1; *Ethnobiol. Stud. Amer. S.W.* **4.**

Benson, L. (1950). "The Cacti of Arizona." Univ. of New Mexico Press, Albuquerque.

Benson, L., and Darrow, R. A. (1944). A manual of southwestern desert trees and shrubs. *Univ. Ariz. Bull.* **15,** 2; *Biol. Sci. Bull.* **6.**

Bolton, H. E., transl. and ed. (1930). "Anza's California Expeditions," 5 vols. Univ. of California Press, Berkeley.

Bolton, H. E., transl. and ed. (1948). "Kino's Historical Memoir of Pimería Alta," 2 vols. in 1. Univ. of California Press, Berkeley and Los Angeles.

Bolton, H. E. (1960). "Rim of Christendom." Russell & Russell, New York.

Brand, D. D. (1936). Notes to accompany a vegetation map of Northwest Mexico. *Univ. N. Mex. Bull.* **280,** Biol. Ser. Vol. 4, No. 4.

Brown, G. W., Jr., ed. (1968). "Desert Biology." Academic Press, New York.

Bryan, K. (1922). Erosion and sedimentation in the Papago country, Arizona. *U.S., Geol. Surv., Bull.* **730,** 19–90.

Bryan, K. (1925). The Papago country, Arizona. *U.S., Geol. Surv., Water-Supply Pap.* **499.**

Castetter, E. F., and Bell, W. H. (1942). "Pima and Papago Indian Agriculture." Univ. of New Mexico Press, Albuquerque.

Castetter, E. F., and Bell, W. H. (1951). "Yuman Indian Agriculture." Univ. of New Mexico Press, Albuquerque.

Castetter, E. F., and Underhill, R. M. (1935). The ethnobiology of the Papago Indians. *U. N. Mex. Bull.* **275,** Biol. Ser. Vol. 4, No. 3; *Ethnobiol. Stud. Amer. S.W.* **2.**

Childs, T. (1954). Sketch of the "Sand Indians." *Kiva* **19** (2–4), 27–39.

Cockrum, E. L. (1960). "The Recent Mammals of Arizona." Univ. of Arizona Press, Tucson.

Coues, E., transl. and ed. (1900). "On the Trail of a Spanish Pioneer." Harper, New York.

Dice, L. R. (1939). The Sonoran biotic province. *Ecology* **20**, 118–119.

Di Peso, C. C. (1953). "The Sobaipuri Indians of the Upper San Pedro River Valley, Southeastern Arizona," 6. Amerind Found., Inc.

Di Peso, C. C. (1956). "The Upper Pima of San Cayetano del Tumacacori," 7. Amerind Found., Inc.

Dunbier, R. (1968). "The Sonoran Desert." Univ. of Arizona Press, Tucson.

el-Zur, A. (1965). Soil, water, and man in the desert habitat of the Hohokam culture. Ph.D. Dissertation, University of Arizona, Tucson.

Ezell, P. (1961). The Hispanic acculturation of the Gila River Pimas. *Mem. Amer. Anthropol. Ass.* **90.**

Fontana, B. L. (1964). Report before the Indian Claims Commission. Docket No. 345. The Papago Tribe of Arizona v. United States of America. Ms., copy on file in Arizona State Museum Library, University of Arizona, Tucson.

Galbraith, F. W. (1959). Craters of the Pinacates. *S. Ariz. Guideb.* **2**, 160–64.

Garcés, F. (1965). "A Record of Travels in Arizona and California" (J. Galvin, transl. and ed.). Howell, San Francisco, California.

Hackenberg, R. A. (1962). Economic alternatives in arid lands. *Ethnology* **1,** 186–196.

Hackenberg, R. A. (1964a). "Aboriginal Land Use and Occupancy of the Papago Indians," mimeogr. Copy on file in Arizona State Museum Library, University of Arizona, Tucson.

Hackenberg, R. A. (1964b). Changing patterns of Pima Indian land use. *Contrib. Commun. Desert Arid Zone Res. S.W. Rocky Mt. Div. A.A.A.S.* **7**, 6–15.

Halpenny, L. C. (1952). Groundwater in the Gila River Basin and adjacent areas, Arizona. *U.S., Geol. Surv., Open-File Rep.*

Hastings, J. R. (1964a). Climatological data for Baja California. *Tech. Rep. Meteorol. and Climate Arid Reg.* **14.**

Hastings, J. R. (1964b). Climatological data for Sonora and northern Sinaloa. *Tech. Rep. Meteorol. and Climate Arid Reg.* **15.**

Hastings, J. R., and Humphrey, R. R. (1969a). Climatological data and statistics for Baja California. *Tech. Rep. Meteorol. Climate Arid Reg.* **18.**

Hastings, J. R., and Humphrey, R. R. (1969b). Climatological data and statistics for Sonora and Northern Sinaloa. *Tech. Rep. Meteorol. Climate Arid Reg.* **19.**

Hastings, J. R., and Turner, R. R. (1965). "The Changing Mile." Univ. of Arizona Press, Tucson.

Hayden, J. D. (1967). A summary prehistory and history of the Sierra Pinacate, Sonora. *Amer. Antiquity* **45**, 127–133.

Heindl, L. A., and Cosner, O. J. (1961). Hydrologic data and drillers' logs, Papago Indian Reservation, Arizona. *Ariz. State Land Dep., Water Resourc. Rep.* **9.**

Hodge, C., ed. (1963). "Aridity and Man—The Challenge of the Arid Lands in the United States," Publ. No. 74 Amer. Ass. Advan. Sci., Washington, D.C.

Hodges, C. (1969). A desert seacoast and its future. *In* "Arid Lands in Perspective" (W. G. McGinnies and B. Goldman, eds.), pp. 119–126. Univ. of Arizona Press, Tucson.

Hoover, J. W. (1929). The Indian country of Southern Arizona. *Geogr. Rev.* **19**, 38–60.

Hoover, J. W. (1935a). Development and sites of the Papago villages of Arizona and Sonora. *Yearb. Ass. Pac. Coast Geogr.* **1**, p. 23.

Hoover, J. W. (1935b). Generic descent of the Papago villages. *Amer. Anthropol.* **37**, 257–264.

Hoover, J. W. (1938). The Papago villages of Arizona and Sonora. *Yearb. Ass. Pac. Coast Geogr.* **4**, 28–29.

Ives, R. L. (1949). Climate of the Sonoran Desert. *Annu. Ass. Amer. Geogr.* **39**, 143–187.

Ives, R. L. (1962). Kiss tanks. *Weather* **17**, 194–196.

Ives, R. L. (1964a). Geography and history in the arid West. *Amer. West* **1**, 54–63.

Ives, R. L. (1964b). The Pinacate region, Sonora, Mexico. *Occas. Pap. Calif. Acad. Sci.* **47.**

Jones, D. J. (1962). A description of settlement pattern and population movement on the Papago Reservation. *Kiva* **27**(4), 1–9.

Joseph, A., Spicer, R. B., and Chesky, J. (1949). "The Desert People." Univ. of Chicago Press, Chicago, Illinois.

Kearney, T. H., and Peebles, R. H. (1960). "Arizona Flora," 2nd ed. Univ. of California Press, Berkeley.

Kniffen, F. B. (1931). The primitive cultural landscape of the Colorado delta. *Univ. Calif., Berkeley, Publ. Geogr.* **5**, 2; *Lower Calif. Stud.* **3.**

Lee, D. H. K. (1963). Human factors in desert development. *In* "Aridity and Man—The Challenge of The Arid Lands in The United States," Publ. No. 74, pp. 339–367. Amer. Ass. Advan. Sci., Washington, D.C.

Lowe, C. H. (1959). Contemporary biota of the Sonoran Desert. *Univ. Ariz. Arid Lands Colloq.* pp. 54–74.

Lowe, C. H., ed. (1964). "The Vertebrates of Arizona." Univ. of Arizona Press, Tucson.

Lumholtz, C. (1912). "New Trails in Mexico." Allen & Unwin, London.

McGee, W. J. (1895). The beginnings of agriculture. *Amer. Anthropol.* **8**, 350–375.

McGee, W. J. (1906). Desert thirst as a disease. *Interstate Med. J.* **13**, 279–300.

McGinnies, W. G. (1969). Arid-lands knowledge gaps and research needs. *In* "Arid Lands in Perspective" (W. G. McGinnies and B. Goldman, eds.), pp. 277–287. Amer. Ass. Advan. Sci., Washington, D.C. and Univ. of Arizona Press, Tucson.

McGinnies, W. G., and Goldman, B., eds. (1969). "Arid Lands in Perspective." Univ. of Arizona Press, Tucson.

McGinnies, W. G., Goldman, B. J., and Paylore, P., eds. (1968). "Deserts of the World." Univ. of Arizona Press, Tucson.

Manje, J. M. (1954). "Unknown Mexico and Sonora" (H. Karns, transl. and ed.). Arizona Silhouettes, Tucson.

Mark, A. K. (1960). Description of and variables relating to ecological change in the history of the Papago population. Master's Thesis, University of Arizona, Tucson.

Martin, P. S. (1963). "The Last 10,000 Years." Univ. of Arizona Press, Tucson.

Moore, R. T., and Wilson, E. D. (1965). Bibliography of the geology and mineral resources of Arizona, 1848–1964. *Ariz., Bur. Mines, Bull.* **173.**

Murdock, G. P. (1960). "Ethnographic Bibliography of North America," 3rd ed. Human Relations Area Files, New Haven, Connecticut.

Murdock, G. P. (1967). "Ethnographic Atlas." Univ. of Pittsburgh Press, Pittsburgh, Pennsylvania.

Nentvig, J. (1951). "Rudo Ensayo." Arizona Silhouettes, Tucson.

Nolasco A., M. (1965). Los pápagos, habitantes del desierto. Anales, 1964 17, 375–448.

Paylore, P. (1966). "Seventy-Five Years of Arid-Lands Research at the University of Arizona." Office of Arid Lands Research, University of Arizona, Tucson.

Paylore, P. (1967). "Arid-lands Research Institutions." Univ. of Arizona Press, Tucson.

Pfefferkorn, I. (1949). "Sonora. A Description of the Province" (T. E. Treutlein, transl. and ed.), Coronado Cuarto Centennial Publ., 1540–1940, No. 12.

Phillips, A., Marshall, J., and Monson, G. (1964). "The Birds of Arizona." Univ. of Arizona Press, Tucson.

Powell, J. (1964). Nothing is as lonely as the Gran Desierto. Desert 27(12), 19–21 and 34.

Powell, J. (1966). In the Gran Desierto. Explorers' J. 44, 66–70.

Russell, F. (1908). The Pima Indians. Annu. Rep. Bur. Amer. Ethnol. 26, 1–389.

Shreve, F. (1951). Vegetation of the Sonoran Desert. Carnegie Inst. Wash. Publ. 591.

Shreve, F., and Wiggins, I. L. (1964). "Vegetation and Flora of the Sonoran Desert," 2 vols. Stanford Univ. Press, Stanford, California.

Simmons, H. L. (1965). "The Geology of the Cabeza Prieta Game Range," Mimeogr., Ajo, Arizona. Copy in the University of Arizona Library, Tucson.

Simmons, N. M. (1966). Flora of the Cabeza Prieta Game Range. J. Ariz. Acad. Sci. 4, 93–104.

Simmons, N. M. (1967). Refuge in a wilderness. Explorers' J. 45, 127–133.

Smith, C. L., and Padfield, H. I. (1969). Land, water, and social institutions. In "Arid Lands in Perspective" (W. G. McGinnies and B. Goldman, eds.), pp. 325–336. Amer. Ass. Advan. Sci., Washington, D.C. and Univ. of Arizona Press, Tucson.

Spicer, E. H. (1962). "Cycles of Conquest." Univ. of Arizona Press, Tucson.

Teilhard de Chardin, P. (1961). "The Phenomenon of Man." Harper (Torchbooks), New York.

Thomas, R. K. (1953). "Papago Land Use West of the Papago Indian Reservation South of the Gila River and the Problem of Sand Papago Identity," Dittoed, Ithaca, New York. Copy on file in the Arizona State Museum Library, University of Arizona, Tucson.

Treutlein, T. E., transl. and ed. (1945). The relation of Philipp Seggesser. Mid-America 27, 139–187 and 257–260.

Turnage, W. V., and Hinckley, A. L. (1938). Freezing weather in relation to plant distribution in the Sonoran Desert. Ecol. Monogr. 8, 529–550.

Turnage, W. V., and Mallery, T. D. (1941). An analysis of rainfall in the Sonoran Desert and adjacent territory. Carnegie Inst. Wash. Publ. 529.

Underhill, R. M. (1936). The autobiography of a Papago woman. Mem. Amer. Anthropol. Ass. 46.

Underhill, R. M. (1938). A Papago calendar record. Univ. N. Mex. Bull. 322,

Anthropol. Ser. Vol. 2, No. 5.

Underhill, R. M. (1939). Social organization of the Papago Indians. *Columbia Univ. Contrib. Anthropol.* **30.**

Underhill, R. M. (1946). Papago Indian religion. *Columbia Univ. Contrib. Anthropol.* **33.**

UNESCO (1962). The problems of the arid zone. *Arid Zone Res.* **22.**

Vivian, R. G. (1965). An archaeological survey of the Lower Gila River, Arizona. *Kiva* **30,** 95–146.

Went, F. W. (1969). Challenges and opportunities for desert plant physiologists. *In* "Physiological Systems in Semiarid Environments" (C. C. Hoff and M. L. Riedesel, eds.), pp. 219–230. Univ. of New Mexico Press, Albuquerque.

Wilson, A. W. (1963). Tucson: A problem in uses of water. *In* "Aridity and Man—The Challenge of the Arid Lands in the United States," Publ. No. 74, pp. 483–489. Amer. Ass. Advan. Sci., Washington, D.C.

Wilson, E. D. (1933). Geology and mineral deposits of southern Yuma County, Arizona. *Ariz., Bur. Mines, Bull.* **134.**

Wilson, E. D. (1962). A résumé of the geology of Arizona. *Ariz., Bur. Mines, Bull.* **171.**

Woodbury, R. B., and Woodbury, N. F. S. (1964). The changing patterns of Papago land use. *Actas Mem. Congr. Int. Amer., 35th, 1962* pp. 181–186.

Wyllys, R. K. (1931). Padre Luis Velarde's relacion of Pimeria Alta, 1716. *N. Mex. Hist. Rev.* **6,** 111–157.

CHAPTER IX

MAN IN ARID LANDS: NORTH FROM JIDDAH

Paul F. Hoye

Years ago in America the lonely grandeur of plain and sky and mountain inspired a hymn that sang of a vast and lovely land stretching away to the majesty of purple mountains towering up toward blue and spacious skies. The hymn was called America the Beautiful.

Recently, beneath the spacious skies of another much older land, the lyrics of that hymn came, almost unconsciously, to the lips of a small party of Americans traveling through the north-western corner of Saudi Arabia. For there, in a valley of golden sandstone, they found Arabia the Beautiful.

The valley is called Mada'in Salih—the "City of Salih"—and it lies on an ancient caravan route 500 miles north of Jiddah deep in the region called the Hijaz. Around it are other valleys dotted with high spines of eroded sandstone marching off in rows toward the west where, legends say, lie even larger valleys, rich in formations of unimaginable beauty.

It is a strange country, almost entirely unknown to the West. The Hijaz Railway once served the region, but that was in an era when few travelers ventured into Saudi Arabia. Until very recently, in fact, visitors were numbered in the dozens, but by 1965 fewer than 200 Westerners had ever been there. Here is an account of travel in this beautiful and awesome region. A map of the region appears in Fig. 1.

Jiddah

MARCH 1

The trucks are ready and so are we and at dawn, *Inshallah,* we head north—north from Jiddah to Medina, to the ruins of the Hijaz Railway, to what I hear are areas of scenic grandeur unmatched this side of the American Southwest, and to Mada'in Salih, with its tombs, legends, and its ancient curse.

The trucks are preposterous—huge red Ford 800's big enough to bowl in and fitted with 12-ply tires, special sand gears, and belly tanks that can hold 150 gallons of gasoline. However, with a thousand miles of what I'm told is pretty rugged driving ahead, I assume they're necessary.

We loaded our gear aboard this afternoon and Moody seems to have touched all the bases. There's food enough for a battalion—everything from Maine lobster to peanut butter—two tents I think they got from Ringling Brothers, compact two-burner Primus stoves, lamps, cots, sleeping bags, and—since it's supposed to get very chilly there—a pair of rather elegant, if incongruous, *après ski* boots.

There are also six barrels of drinking water and the photographic equipment—cameras for both Moody and Sa'id and two large leather cases crammed with light meters, lenses, filters in all the colors of the spectrum, a tripod, and enough film to make Mathew Brady go green. And, of course, there's my equipment too: one spiral notepad, one pencil, and two felt-tipped pens. Pity they already found Livingstone; we would have found him faster, and covered it more thoroughly.

In jotting down the above notes, I was thinking that this seemed like an excessive amount of gear to take along for two weeks no matter how rugged the country up there is supposed to be. Tonight, however, during a visit with a man who has been there I discovered that I may have been

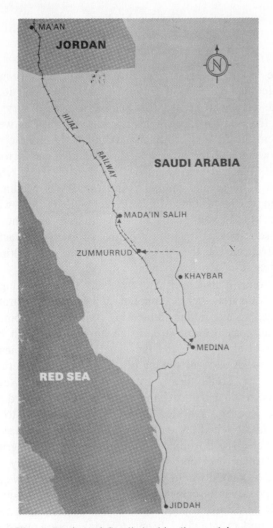

Fig. 1. Region of Saudi Arabia discussed in text.

hasty. "You're not going for a drive in Central Park," he said. "You're going to Mada'in Salih and that's 500 tough miles from here. If you forget anything, forget it for good." Since he's one of the few Westerners who have been up there, he ought to know. . .

Anyway we're ready and in the morning we go. If even half of what we have heard is true this ought to be quite a trip. We'll soon see.

Outside Medina

MARCH 2

Somewhere in the darkness over this hill, where we've made our first camp, lies Medina, the Second City of Islam. They call it the "Radiant City" and the man who coined that phrase was as observant as he was poetic. I wouldn't be surprised if he first saw the city as we did today— through a break in the low brown mountains at the precise moment when the hot brassy glare of the afternoon sun was giving way to the soft red-gold of sunset. We had just rounded a bend in the road when the driver silently raised a finger and pointed. And there was Medina, a dramatic flash of white in the distance, a long rectangle of low walls and high mosques, the thin needle points of the minarets and the dome of the Prophet's Mosque poking up from a jumble of low whitewashed buildings. We stared entranced and then it was gone and we were jolting west across the sands in search of a place to camp.

Until that point, it had been a drowsy day. This morning, late, and in that state of confusion that no amount of advance preparation can ever quite allow for, we left Jiddah, lumbering past the handsome palaces that look across the coastal boulevard to the harbor, and then heading north up the coast. At first there was the usual lift of excitement, but as we droned along, roadside signs ticking off the kilometers, there was less and less of note to see. Traffic, heavy around Jiddah, dwindled and soon there was only an occasional bus carrying pilgrims north to Medina. Off to the left, west, the Red Sea sparkled in the hot sun and off to the right the flat gravel plains stretched off to shadowy hills in the distance. By the roadside, at intervals, stood simple accommodations for pilgrims and rude stands where soft drinks and food are sold. Occasionally a man would wave his hand or a child would yell and once, just before we swung inland, we swept by a caravan of camels—there were exactly 73—marching along in that steady awkward rhythm that is the camel's own. But still time passed slowly and eventually I began to think about our destination and to review what I'd read about it.

Mada'in Salih, I recalled, is a valley some 500 miles north of Jiddah where an ancient people called the Nabateans carved a series of tombs into the rock, and where, according to tradition, a prophet named Salih later called down a curse upon the inhabitants when they killed a miraculous camel brought forth from the rocks by God. From that time on, naturally, the Bedouins and most travelers generally avoided the place, which accounts, I suppose, for the relative isolation of Mada'in Salih despite its location on a major caravan route and the old Hijaz Railway. Few dared defy the curse and so, for more than twelve centuries, the tombs, and whatever else was there, have mouldered in the sun, untouched, unexplored, unexplained. . . .

In Camp

MARCH 3

Out of the darkness this evening, silently and without preamble, strode an old Bedouin. *"Assalumu 'alaykum,"* he said, the traditional "Peace be unto you," and crouched down to try Muhammad's tea. He liked it and I can understand why. Muhammad—he's the No. 2 driver—makes superb tea. He makes it in a small, smoke-blackened kettle over a twig fire. *Only* over a twig fire, in fact. We offered him the use of a camp stove and his scorn was scathing. "The flavor," he said, "is in the smoke."

Today was tiring. We had heard that there are two ways to circle Medina, one that takes almost 2 hours and another that takes 40 minutes. We found the short route, a meandering track that cuts west and wanders northward through a long valley commanded by a circular mud-brick fort on a ridge 300 feet above. The valley is spotted with small deserted villages of brown mud-brick, the bricks melded one into the other so that the surfaces have become sagging lumpy masses of crumbling sand. With the boles of palm trees poking out of the walls at roof level they could be adobe huts in Mexico or Arizona.

Even though we took the short route, however, we didn't save much time. Halfway around, Muhammad's truck bogged down in soft sand. One minute we were racing along confidently on what looked to be a firm, packed-gravel surface. The next we were roaring like mired elephants as the big 12-plys bit fruitlessly into deep loose powder. Misfir, the head driver, sensed the trap the very second that the surface changed, swiftly shifted down, engaged the big sand gear and tramped hard on the gas. He almost escaped completely and was close enough to firm ground to coax it out. Muhammad wasn't so fortunate. He sank to the hubcaps. To get him out we had to lay track of thick planks and metal treads, wrench the planks and treads out of the sand as fast as the truck drove over them and ram them down in front of the tires again while the wheels were still moving. It took sweat, swearing, hard work, and all the power those big Fords could muster. Preposterous, did I call them?

With Medina behind us, the land, almost imperceptibly, began to change. Yesterday, only the arid brownness of the low mountains—or perhaps they should be called *jabals*—broke the flat monotony of the coastal plains. But this afternoon the land began to roll in gentle swells and there appeared great stretches covered with a layer of round black stones that look as if someone had painstakingly sorted them for size and then carefully leveled them with a rake. Geologists, I believe, call them igneous rock and say they were flung out of the earth centuries, or maybe even eons ago, by the belching fury of volcanic action.

As the afternoon wore on the changes became more pronounced. The smooth black stones gave way to larger jagged fragments heaped up in huge mounds and looking as if they had been soaked in tar and set out to dry. For contrast, occasional dunes of soft beach sand sloped off from lee ridges, improbably golden against the black sheen of the rock. There were also salt flats, blindingly white, like snow on an Alpine slope, and, rarely, from patches of alfalfa, flashes of bright green like English grass in the spring. Finally, impossibly, there was a lake—a big lake, cool and blue in the shadow of a great brown *jabal*. I felt an overpowering urge to stop and swim in the cool waters and looked tentatively at the driver only to see him dissolve into laughter. My lake was a mirage, nothing but a mirage. . .

In Camp

MARCH 4

Before we get underway this morning and I get distracted again, I must jot down a few notes about our head driver Misfir. We didn't realize it until yesterday, but Misfir is a remarkably able and resourceful individual. That was when he rescued two drivers, one of whom had been stranded for four days.

The first rescue took place not far from a town called Khaybar. An unusually heavy rain had washed out nearly a hundred yards of roadway and since repairs hadn't yet been made it was necessary to make a wide swing through the sand to get by. Just before we regained the road, a driver flagged us down and pointed to a half-ton Dodge truck hub-down in a wadi. It turned out that the Dodge was not only stuck, but that the motor wouldn't start. It looked like a lost cause, but Misfir nonchalantly ordered the driver to jack the truck up until the wheels were free, bent and began to spin the wheel. It struck me then what he was doing—changing the position of the fly wheel so the starter could be released. Something clicked and Misfir climbed in, thumbed the motor to life and began to jockey the vehicle backward out of the sand with indifferent ease. Twenty minutes later the driver waved his thanks and was gone.

The second rescue took place on the barren track that wanders off to the west from the paved road. A truck was parked up ahead surrounded by half a dozen Bedouins. The driver signaled for help, and told us he had been stranded there for four days, depending on the Bedouins to sup-

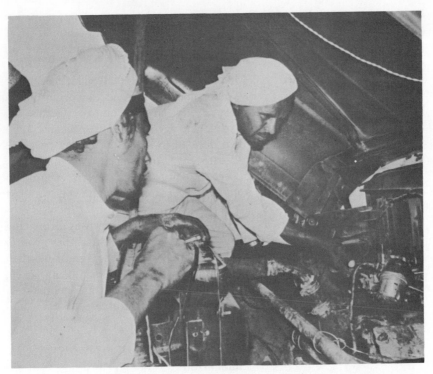

Fig. 2. Working on the plugged gas line.

ply him with food and water. Misfir took about five minutes to give his diagnosis: the gas line was plugged (see Fig. 2). He detached the line, blew air through it and tried the starter. The truck coughed and caught. Misfir explained to the man what he must do if the line continued to fill up and in a few minutes that driver too went roaring down the road.

As we got back in the cab and started off again, I inspected him more closely. He's a big man with the barest trace of a beard, and a hearty laugh. He's also very strong. Just the day before, I recalled, Muhammad had stalled and to get him started Misfir had to "crank" the truck, by spinning simultaneously the wheels, drive shaft, and fanbelt. He's also un-usually alert. Shortly after we left the paved road he looked sharply at our other truck and suddenly reached up and yanked the cord to the horn and sent a two-note bellow echoing over to Muhammad. When Muham-mad stopped, Misfir pointed to a trickle of precious water coming from the spigot in one of the hiptanks. I could barely see the trickle even then. And shortly after that he saw a movement by the side of the road and before I could even guess what it was, he had stopped and begun to fill the goatskin water bag of a Bedouin woman who was walking with two children to a distant encampment. He had ignored dozens of similar pleas prior to that point but somehow knew that in that case it was an emergency.

From Sa'id we learned that Misfir came from a small village near the Yemen border, that as a very young man he crossed the peninsula to Dhahran, got a job with the Arabian American Oil Company (Aramco), and began to go to school. He spent six years studying mechanics and working in Aramco shops and then decided to strike out on his own. He bought a truck and began to haul cargo over the rugged road to Yemen. Later, he bought a second truck and has just added a service station to his holdings. I would risk a small wager that it won't be the last addition. . . .

I should add one more note. The other night Moody was explaining that the reason we slept in the truck was that we'd been told that *agharib* (scorpions) abounded in the region. Misfir looked surprised and then laughed. *"Agharib,"* he said contemptuously and pantomimed being bitten, sucking out the venom and spitting it on the ground. He then deliberately stretched out on the sand, wiggled deep into a comfortable position, and closed his eyes. We did not join him.

Zummurrud

MARCH 4

Over the horizon about 2 hours ago there appeared an exciting sight. It was a building—Zummurrud, a station on the old Hijaz Railway.

Somehow it was a surprise to find Zummurrud. We'd been jolting along for hours on the faint rugged track that twisted through hills as black and high as slag heaps by Pennsylvania coal mines, past stretches of flat sand touched with tones of pink and green, and, at one point, by the whitened bones of a camel. Then, unexpectedly, there was the station, a square strong shadow standing in solitude on the empty plains. Moody nearly impaled himself on his tripod as he scrambled to the platform over the cab to get distance shots of the structure. I can't say I blame him. For some reason, reaching Zummurrud was an exciting moment—possibly because it meant we had reached the Hijaz Railway with its inevitable suggestions of the valor, the dangers, the battles of a bygone era (see Figs. 3 and 4).

We stopped to explore the station, of course, and afterward sat in the shade for lunch and looked out at the empty plains and savored the silence and began, inevitably I guess, to wonder what it was like 50 years ago when the crews of workers and soldiers swarmed southward, mile by dusty

Fig. 3. Freight car on some remaining rail of the old Hijaz Railway.

mile, spiking the rails to the desert floor, fighting off hostile Bedouins and wondering when their hot hard labors would ever end. Then, no doubt, Turkish sentries paced the parapets above each station, and looked down the tracks to the south where a great purple mountain looms large against the sky, or north across the empty prairie, waiting, perhaps, for the sight of smoke signaling another train carrying pilgrims south to Medina. Later, probably, as war came, the sentries crouched nervously behind the heavy doors set deep in stone casements, rifles loaded and cocked, and peered out through narrow slits wondering when the nearby hills would yield up a line of mounted raiders behind the robed figure of Colonel Lawrence. Over there, for example, behind that jabal. The riders could assemble quietly there, form a rough line of battle and then move out at a trot,

Fig. 4. Zummurrud, a station on the old Hijaz Railway.

swinging wide to encircle the station, breaking finally into a galloping charge, their rifles winking fire and the staccato reports of gunfire exploding into the silence and rolling off in echoes across the great empty plains. . .

Mada'in Salih

MARCH 5

The first truck, its tires spewing a high arch of yellow dust into the air, careened around a high formation of sandstone and suddenly halted. Misfir braked too and Moody leaned out motioning urgently behind him. We looked, Misfir and I, and there, carved into the face of the cliff, etched deeply into the rough pinkish rock, was what seemed to be the entrance to a great temple, but was, of course, a tomb. We had arrived at Mada'in Salih.

In a word the first impact of Mada'in Salih is wonder, although by then the sheer grandeur of the land had already begun to exhaust our quota

Fig. 5. Al 'Ula oasis.

of wonderment. Last night we camped near an oasis (see Fig. 5) called Al 'Ula—which has, we noticed, its own tombs carved into a great red cliff high above the scented gardens of the oasis. This morning we left early, following the railbed as usual, squirmed under a great overhang, and swung west. After a wild dash through a field of fine but treacherous white sand we entered a valley and paused in amazement. Suddenly, unbelievably, we were no longer in Saudi Arabia, but in the American Southwest—Utah, perhaps, with its Monument Valley, or Arizona with its

Painted Desert. Before us stretched the country of Mada'in Salih, a country
best described by Parker T. Hart, former U.S. Ambassador to Saudi
Arabia, after he saw it from the air 2 years ago:

> For about forty miles the valley stretched north–south like a sea of yellow
> sand from which rose innumerable great islands of tawny pink sandstone, of-
> ten sheer walled and several hundred feet in height, sculptured by wind and
> sand into columns, pinnacles, spires, saw teeth, natural bridges, profiles and
> every oddment of erosion conceivable to man's imagination. At the base of
> many, the tomb entrances were clearly visible. The width of the great valley
> varies from perhaps ten to twenty-five miles, larger than the Grand Canyon
> and far more impressive than Bryce Canyon or Cedar Breaks, sandstone clas-
> sics of the American Southwest. . .

To which I can add little, except perhaps the sense of surprise at finding
such unlikely country in Saudi Arabia. We got out of the trucks and just
stood there for a little while trying to take it in. Moody and Sa'id set up
their cameras and I wandered off and sat down in a circle of shade under
an acacia tree. By my foot a colony of black ants with golden dots on
their tails scurried about on industrious errands. Overhead, two large, jet-
black ravens wheeled and swooped and then, borne by an updraught of
warm air, shot upward and out of sight. One of the drivers pointed east
and there, outlined in perfect profile against the morning sun, was the un-
mistakable silhouette of a great stone eagle, its wings partially extended,
its beak curved sharply toward the ground. To the north, poised upon a
towering ridge, was still another eagle, this one facing us, his wings spread
wide for flight. "The Valley of the Eagles," someone murmured. Indeed,
indeed.

MARCH 6

This morning, just a few minutes ago, Mada'in Salih welcomed us.

It was barely dawn. The sky was touched with pink and white and the
breeze was cool, and a bird I couldn't see was chirping with what I must
say was understandable enthusiasm. Some distance from camp, Moody,
sweatered and hooded against the chill, was squinting through his long
telephoto lens waiting for the clean fresh rays of morning sunlight to filter
through the valley and bring the rich muted color of rocks and sand to
glowing life. Over the sands behind him, walking swiftly, came an old man
(Fig. 6). He was a Bedouin wearing a black cape and hood and a white
robe. He was barefoot and smiling and in his hand he held a brass coffee
pot with a sharp curved spout.

"*Assalumu 'alaykum,*" he said and dashed thin, tart Arab coffee into a
cup. Three times he poured and three times I drank. "*Shukran,*" I said

Fig. 6. Bedouin making coffee rounds.

finally and he moved on to Saʻid and the drivers. When everyone had been served he bowed slightly, smiled again, and trotted back off across the desert. We don't know where he lives but there's no habitation visible for nearly a mile so he must have walked at least that far and must have gotten up in the dark to pound the coffee and brew it. A memorable beginning to our stay and a pointed reminder that the tales of Bedouin hospitality are founded not on myth but on heart-warming fact. . .

From up here, the summit of a twisted crag in this weird jumble of rock called Jabal Ethlieb, the valley of Madaʼin Salih has a harsh but compelling beauty. It's just past noon and in the heat of the sun the valley is creeping into the shade to await the coolness of the afternoon. Here and there, to be sure, there are small flutters of motion. A Bedouin woman, small and shapeless in black, walks from one low tent to another. A white kid prances stiff-legged away from the herd. A camel nibbles cautiously at the top of a thorn bush. A lizard, almost invisible, skitters up a dune and darts into a hole, his tail leaving a thin, shivery line traced in the sand. But over most of the valley the stillness of the afternoon is descending, a stillness as tangible and as heavy as the heat itself.

Actually it's hard to decide which is more impressive—the natural wonders carved by the hot abrasive touch of the wind or the tombs carved by the Nabateans. I incline toward nature. Just south of here, for example, a few hundred yards away, is a globe of sandstone shaped like the crown of an English bowler. Across the valley there's a formation that looks like a Greek amphora (see Fig. 7), another that resembles a coyote, his howling nose pointed at the sky, and a third that is surely the stern of a Spanish galleon. All around are the pitted cliffs, battlements, turrets, and steeples.

Yet to decide in favor of nature at this point wouldn't be fair, since we've only just begun to really look at the tombs. We started out yesterday, Moody, Sa'id, and I, hiking and climbing throughout the valley, Moody to capture it on film, I on paper, and actually the only valid observation I can make so far is that the Nabateans certainly moved a hell of a lot of rock.

That observation, I know, is not exactly remarkable but neither is it entirely facetious. Some rough measurements I made today suggest that the construction of these tombs required prodigious labor. One tomb, for example, is set back into the cliff 10 feet, measures some 30 feet across and possibly 60 feet high. This means that just to get into the cliff deep enough to start cutting out the facade, the Nabateans had to first excavate some 18,000 cubic feet of sandstone. Then they had to carve the facade itself before burrowing in to excavate the chamber and the burial niches. Not far from this summit where I'm making notes is located what has been called *Diwan* or "Council Chamber." It's no more than a huge cubic space cut into the sandstone, but if my paced measurements are anywhere near accurate, some 47,000 cubic feet of stone had to be excavated to create it. Considering the rude instruments available at the time, and that the 29 tombs counted so far are a long way from the total number here, it seems logical to assume that carving the tombs must have kept a lot of men busy for a long time. (Which suggests, in turn, I imagine, that this valley must have once supported a large and vigorous population. I suspect that the archeologists will have a great time when they come.)

Fig. 7. Sandstone formations of Mada'in Salih.

I'm beginning to see what Lady Crowe meant.

Lady Crowe is the wife of the former British Ambassador to Saudi Arabia. She came here 2 years ago in the same diplomatic party that included Ambassador Hart and Dana Adams Schmidt of *The New York Times*. She later wrote an excellent account of the trip in which she said that the tombs of Mada'in Salih have a "provincial" look to them and suggested that the artisans who worked on the tombs merely copied or adopted certain simple Roman and Greek designs. I agree. Once the first excitement of seeing them has subsided it's clear that the tombs gain much of their attraction from their inaccessibility and the magnificence of their settings; as works of art the imposing facades promise much more than they contain.

After visiting the rest of the tombs on the east side—there are 64 in all, 22 of them in the *Kasr al-Bint* butte—I made a rough map of all the sites and then examined it carefully to see if they formed some pattern that might indicate which were done first or explain why one rock face was chosen over another, or why one decoration was applied to Tomb A and an entirely different decoration to Tomb B. But I found nothing.

Moody, incidentally, climbed to the "bower" itself, a tomb carved on a ledge some 300 feet up in the air. There, goes a legend, a girl's lover was killed by the girl's father for the usual reasons. Moody, looking for a good spot from which to photograph the tombs on the west side of the valley, found an easy way up at the south end—the same one apparently that Charles M. Doughty mentions in his "Travels in Arabia Deserta." He says it leads across the face to just above the Maiden's Bower. He also says there are some burial niches cut into the rock right out in the open.

MARCH 7

We began checking the tombs on the west side this morning. There are more than I thought, many tucked away in little *culs-de-sac* or cut into small isolated formations. These over here are apparently exposed to the wind; they're badly eroded and in several places are almost obliterated.

Unless there are any tombs I haven't seen—and since I made a rather wide sweep in all directions, I doubt it—there are 111 tombs in Mada'in Salih. The total is probably higher, but I eliminated five that were so badly eroded they might have been natural caves.

MARCH 8

The only trouble with Mada'in Śalih is that there's too much to see and time is running out.

Moody, for example, has just been told by a Bedouin that there is a large formation near here literally covered with inscriptions. Obviously, we'll have to go see it. Also we want to inspect the ancient wells, especially those dug out recently by Bedouins in search of more water for crops. And, of course, there's still the Mountain of the Camel.

The Mountain of the Camel—it's actually an enormous butte, not a mountain—is a towering ridge at the western edge of the valley. It stands in a brooding purple haze like a great Gothic cathedral, distant, intriguing and somehow mysterious. We've been calling it the Mountain of the Camel because we thought it was the mountain from which Salih called forth the miraculous she-camel. We're not as sure of that now, but we do know that it is the mountain into which the she-camel's calf is supposed to have vanished when the aroused residents of the valley sought to kill it. It is also the scene of a new and fascinating postscript just related to us by a Bedouin from Yemen.

"On certain moonlit nights, when the cool winds blow across the sand," he said, "the Bedouins of the valley have heard a strange sound in the distance, from high up and far away—the sound, they say, of a frightened baby camel crying for its mother."

I had planned to hike over there anyway, but since hearing that story and noting that a full moon is at hand, I've given it first priority. . . .

Well, I have seen the Mountain of the Camel.

This morning, from here, I thought it imposing. Tonight "imposing" just won't do. I left camp early, expecting to reach it in less than an hour, and even though I detoured through the clusters of *jabals* west of camp (on the off-chance that there might be unrecorded tombs tucked away in there) I still thought I'd reach it quickly. But after crossing a flat clay plain and climbing a high dune I discovered that the butte still seemed to be a good distance away. It certainly was. It took another 2 hours to get there and only then, as I trudged down the far side of another dune, did I realize just how large it is. Large? It is stupendous! From the base, where great hills of black shale slope down several hundred feet more and fragments of broken rock as big as cottages form jagged pyramids, the sheer cliff, streaked with tawny stripes of rust as wide as highways, rises up and up and up. A thousand feet? Twelve hundred feet? I couldn't begin to estimate. Moody will have to get it on film.

MARCH 9

In the moonlight, as in the sunlight, Mada'in Salih has an unforgettable beauty. Off there to the east the weird shapes of Jabal Ethlieb lean at drunken angles against the dark sky. In the west, the bulking shadow of the Mountain of the Camel looms large and mysterious. Above, the heavens are alive with glittering pinpoints of brilliant light; you could hang your coat on the Big Dipper and almost read by the North Star. The wind is cool and the moon is rising higher. Since this is our last night, it is a good time for summing up. . .

Today, in high spirits at the prospect of leaving, Muhammad and Misfir treated us to a hair-raising drive through the valley, a bruising, full-gallop run between and over the hummocks that dot the valley floor. I will say that we got around the valley in a hurry, and could at least take a look at and photograph some of the things we had missed: the inscriptions, characters about 3 inches high cut into the face of a large stone about 12 feet across and 16 feet high; a series of mounds laid out at roughly regular intervals, along what could easily have been a street; ancient wells recently re-excavated; a particular tomb we hadn't inspected; and, again, the Mountain of the Camel.

As we visited these places and speculated about them, it occurred to me that all we had come up with in our 5 days of exploration of Mada'in Salih were questions. Who, for instance, cut those inscriptions we saw this morning? When? And why in this particular place, not even close to a tomb? Above the inscriptions a triangular hole pierces the stone. Was it cut through with the iron tools of the Nabateans or by the silent abrasion of wind? And is it an accident that this hole throws a triangle of light almost exactly on top of a mound at sunrise? Or could this be an altar where some unknown rite came to its climax as the sun climbed over the twisted rocks of the Jabal Ethlieb?

And the mounds? Are they the houses of an ancient village, or merely the remnants of some post-Nabatean settlers? Or just mounds? And when were the wells first dug? By prehistoric man? By the Nabateans?

The questions actually are limitless. I noticed, for example, that in almost all the tombs are the dry, gray shells of old wasp's nests, hundreds of nests which must have housed hundreds of thousands of wasps. Since wasps must have great quantities of water and vegetation—sophisticated vegetation at that—doesn't that imply that there must have been a tremendous amount of cultivated vegetation in the valley at one time? And doesn't that, in turn, imply agriculture? And people? And homes?

Looking out at the valley tonight, a desert valley, lonely, incredibly silent under the stars, it's hard to even imagine Mada'in Salih as it might have been then, lush with growth, perhaps dotted with small homes from which people bustled forth to greet caravans plodding into the valley with cargoes of incense or myrrh from South Arabia. But it could have been and if so—the central question of Mada'in Salih—what happened?

No one knows, of course, but it probably won't be long before the answers begin to emerge. The Hijaz Railway is being rebuilt and in a few years travel to Mada'in Salih will be relatively easy. Then the archeologists will come and will put their shovels into the great dunes near Jabal Ethlieb and the Mountain of the Camel and into the dirt in the tombs in the rock. and soon the valley will give up its secrets.

In a sense this is very sad. There are not many regions like this left in the world—isolated, peaceful, undisturbed by the probings of the scientist and the browsings of the tourist, and retaining that certain aura of mystery and legend that the modern world so rarely has room for any more.

That, however, is in the future. Tonight Mada'in Salih is still inviolate, still shrouded in legend and touched with romance. Which is why, a few minutes from now, I think I shall take a final look around. From the west there is a cool wind blowing across the sands and in the sky the moon is getting brighter. I think I'll just walk and listen in the stillness. You never know what you might hear—the cry of a lamed camel for instance, or the deep ominous thunder of an ancient earthquake or—who knows— maybe even a baby camel on a dark ridge crying faintly for a mother who will never come. . .

Notes on the Nabateans

Thomas C. Barger

In 312 B.C., about 10 years after the death of Alexander the Great, a Greek general who had served with Alexander led an expedition against a city called Petra in what is now Jordan. He captured the main fortress, looted it, and retired with the city's treasure. As he retreated, however, the defenders of the city counterattacked in an unexpected night raid, massacred the Greeks, and recaptured the treasure. The defenders were called Nabateans, and this was their first appearance in recorded history.

Who were the Nabateans? To give an exact answer is difficult; reliable information about them is sketchy. After their initial appearance, for example, they dropped out of historical sight until about 169 B.C., nearly a century and a half later. And even then there is only an unexplained reference to their capture of a certain high priest. Again there is a period of silence until about 100 B.C. when they began to appear with more frequency—in their own inscriptions as well as in Roman, Greek, and Jewish sources. Their period of prominence was so short, however, that much of what is believed today has been pieced together as much from conjecture as from evidence.

Apparently the Nabateans were of Arab origin, probably Bedouins out of the Arabian desert, who settled, at least for a time, in a wild, mountainous land south of the Dead Sea and clustered around what is famous today as the "rose-red city" of Petra, a city carved from sandstone and guarded on its eastern approach by a narrow, easily defended defile and a fortress on an immense rock that could be reached only by a single, hand-cut ascent. All around the city were rose-red sandstone formations and the Nabateans expended a great deal of time and effort carving tombs into the cliffs. These tombs had facades representing elaborate temples—Greek-inspired, probably—with small, plain, unadorned chambers cut in behind the "doors" to serve as crypts.

With the well-guarded Petra as a base of power the Nabateans were able to control the important roads to the coast south of the Dead Sea and all the desert country lying to the east of the towns in what is today Jordan and western Syria. In other words, they controlled all the lands east of the settled country ruled by the Jews and Romans and other sedentary peoples. (Including, probably, Damascus, so that it is likely that at the time St. Paul was making his escape by being let down the city wall in a basket, the governor of the city was a Nabatean.) They also maintained access to the Mediterranean through an area due west of Petra that is today known as the Gaza Strip, and extended their control south into what is today Mada'in Salih in Saudi Arabia.

To the Nabateans, control of this territory was probably no less than a matter of survival. Through it ran the ancient caravan routes over which came the main source of the Nabateans' wealth and importance: incense.* In that era the Roman Empire and the Greek states used incredible quantities of incense for their civil and religious ceremonies, and nearly all the incense seems to have come from South Arabia—from what is today Southern Yemen and Hadhramaut. Incense comes from the sap of a certain tree found then and to this day in the highlands of those regions.

Because their prosperity depended almost exclusively on incense, however, the Nabateans were bound to suffer if their Roman customers could find a cheaper way of getting it. And the Romans did find a cheaper way. They shipped it on their galleys up the Red Sea to ports closer to Egypt and the Mediterranean. Since the caravans plodding overland could not compete with the swift galleys, it was virtually the end of Nabatean wealth and influence. Toward the end of the first century A.D. they began to decline and a century later had disappeared altogether as a separate state and people, and their magnificent capital in Petra was left, deserted and empty, to the wind and sun and an occasional Bedouin, for 1600 years.

Up to this point most of the information is reasonably well documented. But there are other aspects of Nabatean history and culture which are still open to speculation and dispute. One of the most important questions has to do with Mada'in Salih.

There is no doubt that Mada'in Salih was a Nabatean settlement—

---

* Frankincense: the gum resin of *Boswellia* sp., here probably *B. carterii* of Somali and the opposite coast of Saudi Arabia. Myrrh: the gum resin of *Balsamea* (= *Balsamodendron*) *myrrha* of the same region (Ed.).

Charles Doughty's sketches of the stone inscriptions proved that beyond any doubt—but there is disagreement as to whether it was merely an outpost of the Nabateans from which the Nabateans picked up the incense and transshipped it to Petra, or a large thriving settlement strong and self-sufficient enough to dictate terms to the tribes to the south.

The first view stems from the basic belief that the Nabateans were not only of nomadic origin, but were still nomads in the era of Nabatean eminence. It is based on what so far is a failure to find ruins which might indicate a settlement. This theory is helped along by the writings of a Roman called Diodorus, whose sources are unknown but who wrote that the Nabateans were completely nomadic and that they abstained from planting and sowing under threat of death as well as from drinking wine and building permanent homes.

In the absence of data to refute it, this view, of course, must be considered. But other findings suggest quite another story. First of all there have been no excavations in Mada'in Salih and it is entirely possible that there are ruins there—beneath certain dunes and mounds that are certainly not natural. More importantly, ruins in and around Jordan show that the Nabateans were most ingenious in conserving and using water for agriculture and probably had more land in crops than there is now. In Mada'in Salih itself the Bedouins today are cleaning out wells which in size and number suggest that at one time there might have been several square miles of gardens in the vicinity—enough to have supported a sizable population. Furthermore, the Nabateans produced a distinctive pottery of excellent quality and workmanship—all of which means that if the Nabateans were nomads they were most unusual nomads since nomadic people rarely develop water conservation systems or fine pottery.

The other view—that Mada'in Salih was a large, strong settlement—seems more reasonable if only because it is unlikely that the South Arabian tribes would have simply halted their northern advance at a given point because the Nabateans asked them to. It is much more likely that they stopped because the settlement at Mada'in Salih was big enough and strong enough to bar them from going further.

Supporting this view is the interesting fact that the tombs to be found on the sandstone cliffs above the oasis of Al 'Ula—just a few miles south of Mada'in Salih—are not Nabatean tombs. They are similar, but key differences in the pattern and inscriptions found there indicate that the people who carved those tombs were probably South Arabians, not Nabateans. Thus it seems that between Mada'in Salih and Al 'Ula there existed a definite frontier marking the southernmost extension of the Nabatean Kingdom and the northernmost penetration of the South Arabian traders.

If that were the case, however, it would leave the major question about Mada'in Salih unanswered: What happened to it?

It is logical that with the decline of the incense trade—after the Romans conquered the Nabateans—Petra would have declined. It also seems reasonable that if Mada'in Salih were a small outpost of nomads, it, too, would have vanished with the end of the incense trade. But if there were a large agricultural settlement there, why would it disappear? The fortunes of Al 'Ula were also dependent on incense, but because of its agriculture it survives to this day: So what happened?

No one can answer that question with any dependable degree of certainty, but there might be a clue in the Koranic story of the prophet Salih in which an "earthquake" shook the valley to punish the villagers for rejecting God's prophet. Geologists see no evidence of an earthquake in Mada'in Salih. But the Koranic word translated "earthquake" can also mean "a calamity from God." Couldn't it have been, for example, a plague that drove the Nabateans away forever?

The only honest answer, of course, is: No one knows. This is why Mada'in Salih is perhaps the most fascinating part of the story of the Nabateans.

ACKNOWLEDGMENTS

The material of this chapter appeared in a special issue (Arabia the Beautiful) of *Aramco World,* Vol. 16 (No. 5) September–October, 1965. The editor is indebted to the Arabian American Oil Company, Inc. for the use of this material. Some minor changes in text have been made by the editor, for which he is solely responsible. All photographs in this chapter are by Burnett H. Moody, Chief Photographer of the Arabian American Oil Company, Inc.

AUTHOR INDEX

Numbers in italics refer to the pages on which complete references are listed.

A

Abdel-Malek, Y., 73, *94*
Abd El Rahman, A. A., 219, 253, *302, 306*
Abdulaziz, A. I., 147, *157*
Abu Fahkr, M. S. S., 57, 80, *94*
Abushama, F. T., 348, 374
Adams, P. A., 350, 355, *374*
Adolph, E. F., 493, *524*
Afanasev, S. F., 408, *470*
Agnihotri, S. K., 424, *470*
Ahearn, G. A., 320, 321, 322, 323, 326, 327, 348, 363, 368, *374*
Akzhigitova, N. I., 70, *94*
Al-Ani, H., 76, *94*
Al-Ani, T. A., 147, *157*
Al-Doory, Y., 76, *94*
Alexander, L. T., 71, *94, 98*
Alexander, M., 76, *94*
Alford, R. S., 446, *480*
Alia Medina, F., 107, 149, *160*
Alimen, H., 109, 110, 124, *157,* 392, *470*
Allee, A. E., 434, *470*
Allen, J. S., 71, *98*
Allison, L. N., 409, *470*
Altmann, G., 336, *375*
Andrewartha, H. G., 450, *470*
Arago, D. F. J., 395, *470*
Arnold, E. T., 418, 425, 429, 430, 445, 450, 458, 460, 461, 466, 467, *470, 484*
Aschmann, H., 493, *524*
Aubert, G., 79, *95*
Audry, P., 76, *94*

B

Bagnouls, F., 122, *157*
Bailey, R. M., 416, 437, *470, 471*
Baird, R. C., 412, 445, 446, *477*
Baker, D. N., 325, *375*
Ball, J. C., 403, 430, 431, *477*
Balout, L., 109, *157*
Barber, W. E., 402, 406, 407, 408, 409, 412, 434, 440, 441, 450, 452, 456, 465, *471, 483*
Bardach, J. E., 386, *480*
Barlow, G. W., 408, 411, 413, 416, 419, 425, 427, 445, 447, 448, 457, 460, 461, 462, 463, 469, *471*
Barrass, R., 355, *378*
Barrs, H. D., 243, *302*
Barry, J. P., 110, 150, *157*
Bartholomew, G. A., 352, *379*
Barton-Browne, L., 336, *375*
Bazilevič, N. I., 218, *307*
Baslow, M. H., 419, *471*
Batalin, A., 297, *302*
Batanouny, K. H., 219, 253, *302*
Batchelder, G. L., 396, 421, *472*
Bauer, G., 264, *309*
Bauman, L., 245, 246, 254, *302*
Baumgärtner, H., 196, *210*
Bay, E. C., 463, 464, *471*
Bayly, I. A. E., 421, 423, 425, *471*
Bazilevic, N. I., 218, *307*
Beadle, L. C., 412, 414, 423, *471*
Beadle, N. C. W., 175, 183, *211,* 264, *308*
Beament, J. W. L., 319, 320, 322, 340, 347, *375*
Beamish, F. W. H., 428, *471*

SUBJECT INDEX

See also the Systematic Index

A

Abdominal ganglion, 331
Absorption, by plants, 140–142
Acacia tree, 80, 506, 509, 515, 540
Acheb, 128, 139
Acorns, 519
Actinomycetes, 75
Activity cycles
  in fishes, 445–450
  in insects, 365–371
Adaptation, *see also* Phenology
  in fishes, 386, 404–405, 407–408,
    409–410, 456, 463–464
  in insects, 356–363, 371–372
  in man, 524
  of vegetation, 137–138, 139–149, 217,
    247
Adrar of Iforas, 139
Aestivation, 408
Afghanistan, desert pavements of, 50
Africa, *see also* North African deserts;
    South Africa; South African deserts
  desert soils of, 49, 57, 79–80
  halophytes of, 287
Agave, desert, 515
Aggregation, 52–53
Agriculture
  aquifer depletion and, 27
  among Piman Indians, 517, 518–519,
    520–521, 523
Aguelmane, 129
Air temperature, in Sahara Desert, 114,
    117–118, 119
Aizoaceae, 177
Ala-Chan Desert, 85

Ala Shan Desert, 85
  climate, 224
Alberta, vegetation of, 253
Alfalfa, 534
  osmotic potential of, 246
Algae, 73–74, 166, 264
  desert varnish and, 58, 186–187
  distribution, 167–168
  ecology, 203
  edaphic, 168–177
  fishes and, 406, 424, 466–467, 468
  gas production by, 430
  hydrature of, 229
  insolation of, 183
  interrelation with lichens, 194–196
  lithophytic, 178–179
  nitrogen fixation and, 183–184, 186
  rock weathering and, 186
  of Sahara Desert, 134
  soil and, 156
  taxonomy, 166–167, 202–203
  water sources for, 179, 181
Alluvial deposits, 36, 37, 47
  stratification of, 44, 46
Altar River, 508
Alumina, 57
American bison, 510
American Southwest, *see also* specific
    deserts
  algae of, 74, 169, 172–173, 175, 178,
    202–203
  aquatic environments of, 392, 393, 398
  desert winds of, 34
  fungi of, 76, 202
  halophytes of, 293
  legumes of, 63

lichen growth and, 192–193
reproduction in fishes and, 457–459, 460
Lime, *see* Carbonates
Limestone
  algal weathering of, 186
  springs in, 393
  streams in, 3
Lithium, 70
Lithosols, 33, 37, 47
Little Colorado River spinedace, 441
Lizards, 504, 513, 514, 542
Loach, 437
Loach minnow, 416, 453, 467, 468, 511
Locust
  body temperature, 350–351, 352
  morphological adaptations, 359
  multiplication of, 364, 365
  phenology, 364–365
  water balance, 320, 325–326, 327, 331, 332–333, 334, 338–339, 345–346
Loess, 52
Loma Desert, 89
Longear sunfish, 441
Longfin dace, 400, 402, 406, 408, 416, 440, 442, 448, 449, 456, 465, 511
Lower Cambrian, Saharan, 107
Lower Pimas, *see* Piman Indians
Luminosity, in Sahara Desert, 122
Lungfish, 404, 407, 408

M

Macromycetes, 202
Mada'in Salih, Saudi Arabia, 532, 538, 541–547
Magnesium, 60, 70
  in Argids, 40
  in groundwater, 18, 20
Magnesium hydroxide, 57
Mali
  clay plains in, 44
  locust outbreak in, 364
  piping in, 51
Malpighian tubules, 316, 328–330, 331, 334
Man, *see also* Piman Indians
  decimation of desert bighorn sheep by, 507
  effects of wind on, 119
  effects on fish distribution, 444–445

influence on desert rivers, 392–393
salt tolerance, 18
study of, in deserts, 490–493
tolerance of dehydration, 348
Manchuria, saline soils in, 277
Manganese
  deficiency, 67
  in desert varnish, 186–187
Manganese oxides, 48
Manna, 190
Mannitol, effect on halophytes, 279–280
Mantids, microclimate and, 156
Marshes, 397
Marsh killifish, 464
Matric potential, salt uptake and, 280–281
Mauritania
  clay plains in, 44
  fungi of, 76
Mayos, 493
Mealworm, water balance, 320, 321, 326, 334–335, 336, 340, 346
Medina, Saudi Arabia, 532
Mediterranean region
  osmotic potential in, 237
  soil aggregation in, 52
  xerophytes of, 266–267, 269
Mescal, 507
Mesothoracic ganglia, 331
Mesozoic
  Nubian Aquifer deposition during, 21
  Saharan, 107, 109
  sandstone of, 23
Mesquite, 16, 90, 392, 499, 506, 509, 515, 519, 521
Metabolic heat, 350
Metabolism
  in fishes, temperature and, 469–470
  water balance and, 337, 338–339
Mexican crucillo, 506
Mexican elder, 510
Mexican piñon, 507
Mexican stoneroller, 511
Mexican tea, 507
Mexican tetra, 401, 444, 458
Mexico, *see also* Sonoran Desert
  desert algae of, 170, 178
  desert soils of, 41, 90
Mica, 47
Microclimates, 122, 318

SYSTEMATIC INDEX

A

Abies concolor, 235
Acacia, 136, 142, 144, 153–154, 263, 540
Acacia greggii (catclaw), 230, 232, 500
Acacia laeta, 154
Acacia mellifera, 222
Acacia paucispina, 230, 232
Acacia raddiana (talha), 136, 156
Acacia seyal, 154
Acacia tortilis, 222
Acalypha virginica, 236
Acarosphora, 188–189
Acarospora bella, 188
Acarospora bullata, 193
Acarospora carnegiei, 193
Acarospora chilensis, 188
Acarospora chlorophana, 194
Acarospora cf. intermixa, 188
Acarospora cf. veronensis, 188
Acarospora cf. versicolor, 188
Acarospora fuscata, 193
Acarospora gallica, 193
Acarospora pitardi, 188
Acarospora reagens, 189
Acarospora schleicheri, 194
Acarospora strigata, 188
Acarospora sulphurata, 188
Acarospora tucsonensis, 193
Acarosporaceae, 188–189, 192, see also individual organisms
Acarus siro (mite), 342
Achillea santolina, 81
Acipipitrinae (hawks), 504
Acrostichum aureum, 293
Actinochloris, 170
Actinomyceteae, 200, see also individual organisms
Adesmia (tenebrionid beetle), 348, 373
Adiantum capillus veneris, 230, 232

Agave americana, 230–231
Agave desertii (desert agave), 500, 506–507
Agave palmeri (mescal), 230–231, 507
Agave parryi var. huachucensis (huachuca agave), 507
Agave parviflora (small-flowered agave), 506
Agave schottii, 230–231
Agosia, 440–441
Agosia chrysogaster (longfin dace), 400, 412, 468, 511
Agriotes, 322
Agropyron spp. (wheatgrass), 91
Aizoaceae, 177, see also individual organisms
Allenrolfea occidentalis (pickleweed), 16
Allionia incarnata, 230, 231
Allium cernuum, 235
Aloe dichotoma, 271
Alternaria, 76, 181, 200, 201
Alyssum maritimum, 289–290
Amaranthus palmeri (careless weed), 230–231, 515
Ambrosia psilostachya, 230–231
Ammobroma sonorae (sand root), 515
Ammosperma cinereum, 154
Amorpha fruticosa, 236
Amorphonostoc, 170, 171
Ampelopsis quinquefolia, 236
Amphibia, 451, 511
Anabaena, 170
Anabaena salicola, 171
Anabaena variablis, 171
Anabasis, 136
Anabasis aphylla, 300
Anabasis aretioides (desert cauliflower), 138, 145–146, 154
Anabasis articulata, 81

586

Z

A 4
B 5
C 6
D 7
E 8
F 9
G 0
H 1
I 2
J 3